D0205282

# AMERICAN
# LITERARY
# MAGAZINES

# AMERICAN LITERARY MAGAZINES

## The Eighteenth and Nineteenth Centuries

*Edited by*

## Edward E. Chielens

Historical Guides to the World's Periodicals and Newspapers

Greenwood Press

New York • Westport, Connecticut • London

**Library of Congress Cataloging-in-Publication Data**

Main entry under title:
American literary magazines.

 (Historical guides to the world's periodicals and
newspapers, ISSN 0742–5538)
  Includes index.
  1. American literature—19th century—Periodicals—
Bibliography.  2. American literature—Colonial period,
ca. 1600–1775—Periodicals—Bibliography.  3. American
literature—1783–1850—Periodicals—Bibliography.
4. American periodicals—Bibliography.  I. Chielens,
Edward E.  II. Series.
Z1231.P45A43  1986  [PS201]   810'.9'003   85–24793
ISBN 0–313–23985–1 (lib. bdg. : alk. paper)

Library of Congress Catalog Card Number: 85–24793
ISBN: 0–313–23985–1
ISSN: 0742–5538

First published in 1986

Greenwood Press, Inc.
88 Post Road West, Westport, Connecticut 06881

Printed in the United States of America

The paper used in this book complies with the
Permanent Paper Standard issued by the National
Information Standards Organization (Z39.48–1984).

10 9 8 7 6 5 4 3 2 1

# Contents

# Acknowledgments

I would like to thank the scholars who contributed to this book, not only for their essays but also for their very helpful advice. I would also like to thank my wife, Carole, for her help in the completion of this project.

# Introduction

*American Literary Magazines: The Eighteenth and Nineteenth Centuries* is the first half of a two-part reference guide. A companion book will cover twentieth-century magazines founded after 1900. These two books are intended as comprehensive sources of information on a relatively neglected aspect of literary history, the magazines, many now forgotten, that were the medium through which much important literature reached the reading public. Ninety-two of the most important are profiled in this book, and less important titles are covered in an accompanying appendix.

The names of important eighteenth- and nineteenth-century writers appear here at times in contexts that may surprise the student of American literature. For instance, a number of literary figures now remembered solely for their writing were important editors of magazines as well. Noah Webster, whose pioneering *American Dictionary* was published in 1828, was one of the first of many writers and scholars to found and edit a magazine that would reflect and promote his views on language, literature, and culture. In 1787, at the age of twenty-nine, Webster, a Federalist, started the *American Magazine*\* in New York, intending to foster American culture and investigate and record its founding and development. His magazine lasted only one year, ending with a serious financial loss for the young editor, but its twelve issues established Webster as a leading essayist of his day, and it contains valuable linguistic and political reflections of its editor and others. Ralph Waldo Emerson was already well established when he assumed the editorship of the Boston *Dial*\* from Margaret Fuller in 1842. Emerson had been involved in the founding of the *Dial* in 1840, and he struggled to keep it alive, promoting the work of Henry David Thoreau and other transcendentalists. He even allowed Thoreau to edit the April 1843 issue while he was on a lecture tour. But the struggle ended in 1844, with Emerson out $300 and unsold copies of the *Dial* going to his attic and finally to the ragman. The *Dial* is a storehouse of the best writing of the transcendentalists, but Emerson's disillusionment caused him to refuse the editorship of the *Massachusetts Quarterly Review*.* Even more disappointing was James Russell Lowell's *Pioneer*,* started in 1842 with Robert Carter. Its three issues were of remarkably high quality, including works such as Edgar Allan Poe's "The Tell-Tale Heart" and "Lenore" and Nathaniel Hawthorne's "The Hall of Fantasy" and "The Birth-Mark." But disappointing sales and a very severe publishing contract brought the *Pioneer* to a premature end, with a thousand-dollar loss for the editors, a financial liability from which it took Lowell three years to recover. Edgar Allan Poe's editorial experience was more extensive and successful than any of these. He edited the *Southern Literary Messenger*,* *Burton's Gentleman's Magazine*,* *Graham's Magazine*,* and the *Broadway Journal*.* But Poe's intention to publish important literature and criticism was incompatible with the aims of the magazines' owners and publishers. He dreamed of having his own magazine, tentatively named the *Penn* or *Stylus*, which would contain the highest quality literature as well as criticism free of bias. Although Poe went so far as to write a prospectus and gather material for inclusion, his dream was never realized.

Other writers, however, found editing compatible with their personalities and talents, and their work on magazines gave them valuable and satisfying experience. At thirty-four, William Dean Howells was promoted by James T. Fields from assistant to editor of the distinguished *Atlantic Monthly*.* Howells's ten-year stay on the *Atlantic* changed the focus of the Boston publication from regional to national. He published work of the realists, including Hamlin Garland, Mark Twain, and Henry James, Jr., and he added more articles on current affairs, thus increasing the magazine's popularity. Howells's own awareness of contemporary problems grew with his editorial experience. In later years he looked back fondly to his stay on the *Atlantic*, even dreaming at times of returning.

The careers of two notable Western writers benefited from their work as editors. Most successful was Bret Harte, whose editorship of the San Francisco *Overland Monthly** from 1868 to 1870 brought national recognition to himself and the magazine. His own "The Luck of Roaring Camp" appeared in the second issue, but only after he overcame the objections of a shocked proofreader, backed by Anton Roman, the *Overland*'s owner (their concern being the language of the miners and the inclusion of a prostitute as the main character). Harte promoted local-color regional writers, but he resisted the tendency toward boosterism and wrote critiques of Eastern writers in his fiercely independent editorial column "Etc." Harte's own "The Outcasts of Poker Flat," "Miggles," and "Tennessee's Partner" were published in the *Overland*, and in 1872 he left for the East Coast with a secure reputation and promising career with the *Atlantic*. The same general development was followed later by Frank Norris, who served as an assistant editor of the weekly *Wave** in San Francisco from 1896 to 1898. During this formative period in his career, he contributed fiction, reviews, and news items to the *Wave*, meeting the pressure of weekly journalism by contributing, in 1897, an average of one story per week, this during the time he was writing

*McTeague*. It was in the *Wave* that S. S. McClure, founder of *McClure's Magazine* in New York, saw an installment of Norris's novel *Moran of the "Lady Letty"* and offered him an editorial position. Thus Norris's work for the *Wave* provided him with valuable training and opportunity, while at the same time the magazine benefited from his interests, outlook, and style.

Of course, magazines played important parts in the careers of other writers as well, supporting them and exposing them to readers unfamiliar with their work. The support of Walt Whitman by Henry Clapp's *Saturday Press\** and later the *Galaxy,\** both New York publications, is a good example. Clapp, the "King of Bohemia" and associate of the writers and artists who gathered at Pfaff's Beer Cellar, opposed and ridiculed the narrow puritanical morality of American culture. He met Whitman at Pfaff's while the poet was working on *Leaves of Grass*, and as a result Clapp published "A Child's Reminiscence," later entitled "Out of the Cradle," accompanying the poem with editorial praise. Whitman was grateful for the support, stating years later that Clapp befriended him at an important time in his life when the rest of the American press was indifferent or hostile. After the Civil War, when Whitman had gained a modest reputation, much of it in England, he still faced a hostile press at home. But in 1866 the *Galaxy*'s editors, Colonel William Church and Frank Church, agreed to publish John Burroughs's "Walt Whitman and His 'Drum Taps.' " From then until 1871, they published six of Whitman's works, including two parts of what would later become *Democratic Vistas*, as well as a number of other pieces by his disciple Burroughs. The Churches paid Whitman well and gave him access to a major monthly at a time when their rivals the *Atlantic, Harper's,\** and *Scribner's\** were hostile. But the *Galaxy*, in spite of its open-mindedness, failed in 1878, while its rivals went on successfully for years.

The failure of the *Galaxy* is indicative of the conflict between popular taste, which tended toward the trite and sentimental, and the high ideals of some editors and publishers. Some financially successful and long-lived magazines did manage to bridge that gap, however. One remarkable example was *Godey's Lady's Book,\** published by Louis Godey from 1830 to 1898 and edited by Sarah Josepha Hale from 1837 to 1877. Their formula for success included sentimental fiction and poetry, articles on clothing and hair styles, and ornate engravings. And yet Godey and Hale also published original contributions from Oliver Wendell Holmes, Henry Wadsworth Longfellow, Hawthorne, and Poe, including Poe's sensational "The Literati of New York." A different but equally successful formula was followed by *Harper's Monthly Magazine*, founded in 1853 by the Harper brothers, who reprinted English novels in the periodical and then published them in book form. Because of the lack of an international copyright, the works cost them little or nothing, and this caused the resentment of editors of other magazines who were attempting, at great expense, to support American authors. *Harper's Monthly* did support American authors after the Civil War, but its financial success had been assured by supplying its readers with the works of well-known English authors at little expense to itself.

The criticism levelled at *Harper's Monthly* was one part of the campaign in support of American literature that began with the earliest magazines and continued beyond the first half of the nineteenth century. Noah Webster's interest in American culture and language has been mentioned. The *Columbian Magazine*,* a Philadelphia contemporary of Webster's *American Magazine*,* was the first to pay its contributors, to actively seek out and promote American writers, and to avoid the usual policy of reprinting the works of English writers. Although the *Columbian* achieved a higher circulation than any of its contemporaries, it was never able to cover its costs, and it died in 1792 after a six-year struggle. A similar but more summary fate awaited the *Portico*,* published in Baltimore from 1816 to 1818. Editor John Neal worked diligently and without pay to support American writers. Perhaps the most remarkable of these magazines was *Putnam's Monthly*,* founded in 1853 with Charles Briggs as editor. *Putnam's* declared its literary nationalism at the outset, and its roster included Thoreau, Herman Melville, James Fenimore Cooper, William Cullen Bryant, and Lowell, among others. Melville received crucial financial support from *Putnam's*, which published installments of *Israel Potter*, and "Bartleby, the Scrivener," "Benito Cereno," and "I and My Chimney." But circulation steadily dropped after 1855, and Putnam sold the magazine. It finally merged with *Emerson's United States Magazine* in 1857. A brief revival occurred from 1868 to 1870, but the magazine never achieved its earlier quality. And this was while *Harper's* was pursuing its successful policy of reprinting English authors.

A second source of conflict among magazines of this period was regional loyalty, as the titles of many of these publications suggest. Magazines in New England, the South, and the West reflected and helped to develop regional consciousness that fostered distinct and separate literary traditions and attitudes. The New England tradition can be traced from the *Monthly Anthology and Boston Review*\* through the *North American Review*,* the *Dial* and other transcendental journals, to the *Atlantic Monthly* under its first editor James Russell Lowell. The *Atlantic* was founded in 1857 specifically as an outlet for writers in the area of Boston, Cambridge, and Concord, intending to be a cultural guide for the nation. Under Lowell and James T. Fields, before William Dean Howells assumed the editorship in 1871, over two-thirds of the contributors to the *Atlantic* were from New England. When the *Galaxy* was founded by the Churches in New York in 1866, writers in that city and other areas of the country, including even John Esten Cooke in Virginia, welcomed the new publication as an alternative to the *Atlantic*, which they perceived as a powerful but parochial magazine closed to their work. The *Atlantic*, which with *Harper's Monthly* and *Scribner's Monthly*\* was a custodian of the genteel culture in the last half of the nineteenth century, finally proved too powerful a rival for the *Galaxy*, which lacked through most of its career the financial backing of a big publishing house. Ironically, in 1878 the *Galaxy*'s subscription list was sold to the owners of the *Atlantic*.

The number of Southern magazines included in this volume, published both before and after the Civil War, indicates the strong feeling among writers and editors from the South that their literature and culture were distinct from those of the North and, in addition, that Northern publications neglected or were biased against Southern writers. Almost all of these magazines failed to achieve financial stability or to compete successfully against their Northern rivals. The career of William Gilmore Simms, the leading literary figure in the antebellum South, exemplifies the frustration of magazine publishing and editing even in Charleston, the literary center of the region. Upon resigning his editorship of the *Magnolia\** in 1843 after one year, Simms declared the experience "irksome," "disagreeable," and "fatiguing," only to take up the same responsibilities on his own short-lived *Southern and Western Monthly Magazine and Review\** in 1845 and the *Southern Quarterly Review\** from 1849 to 1854. He also was a leading contributor to other publications, including *Russell's Magazine,\** also of Charleston. These experiences led Simms to conclude that Southerners were not a "reading people," and he thought of moving North because of the lack of support for a literary culture. Similarly, Hugh Swinton Legaré was so disappointed with the reception given his excellent *Southern Review\** that he refused even to contribute to the *Southern Quarterly Review* ten years later, and Paul Hamilton Hayne, reacting to the lack of support for *Russell's,* declared that he was being driven even to consider "turning Yankee." The remarkable exception, however, was the *Southern Literary Messenger.\** Its thirty-year career was ended in 1864 by the war. The *Messenger* was exceptional in that it was founded as a Southern magazine with a national focus. It published Northern writers, muted sectional differences, and sought Northern readers, unlike other Southern magazines, which were stridently sectional. Through most of its career the *Messenger* avoided the volatile issue of slavery, although by 1854, responding to the political climate, it also became decidedly more sectional. A number of magazines appeared in the South after the war, their purpose to preserve the culture of their region, to relate the Southern view of the conflict, and to promote the work of Southern writers. Except for Albert Taylor Bledsoe's *Southern Review,\** these also were short lived. In 1887 the *Southern Bivouac,\** founded in 1882 in Louisville to give a fair accounting of the "lost cause," was absorbed by the *Century* (see *Scribner's Monthly\**), one indication of the growing power of the Northeastern literary establishment and the decline, for the time being, of regional, especially Southern, magazines.

A number of successful magazines appeared in the West, however, especially in the San Francisco area in the last half of the century. These publications fostered a growing local literary culture, and they promoted the work of local writers, offering important outlets for their work during an era dominated by the East. Harte's association with the *Overland Monthly* and Norris' with the *Wave* have been mentioned. The first such publication was the *Golden Era,\** founded in 1852 by two unsuccessful miners, Rollin M. Daggett and J. Macdonough Foard. Written for the miners of the Gold Rush, this popular weekly included poetry, short stories, and reports of the mining communities written by the miners themselves. Ambrose Bierce was an editor of first the *Argonaut,\** from 1877 to

1879, and then the *Wasp*,* from 1881 to 1886. The latter continued under its original title until 1928, but its best years were when it reflected the caustic personality of Bierce, whose *Devil's Dictionary* first appeared in its pages. At the end of the century a group of iconoclastic sophisticates who called themselves Les Jeunes founded the *Lark*,* edited by Gelett Burgess and Bruce Porter. Fastidiously edited and illustrated, the *Lark* was a response to the *Yellow Book* and the *Chap-Book*,* both of which Les Jeunes felt were too serious about themselves. An important part of the early development of the little-magazine revolt that became so important after 1900, the *Lark* is indicative of the sophisticated literary culture that had developed in San Francisco.

All of the magazines profiled in this study were founded before 1900. However, this is not an arbitrary cutoff point. The literary-magazine field changed radically at this time, just as it had in the 1850s when *Harper's* and the *Atlantic*, followed by *Scribner's*, began their domination of the field. At the turn of the century these old, established "qualities" were successfully challenged by cheaper publications, *Munsey's, McClure's*, and *Cosmopolitan*, which used sophisticated advertising and circulation techniques. These were the first truly modern, national, mass-circulation magazines. In addition, the little magazines, including the *Chap-Book*, the *Lark*, the *Philistine*, and *M'lle New York*,* began to appear in the 1890s. These publications, usually consciously iconoclastic and antiestablishment, are the beginning of an important literary-magazine tradition in the twentieth century.

While the cutoff date was easy to decide, the decision as to which magazines of the thousands published deserved coverage in full profiles was more difficult. First of all, there were very few purely "literary" magazines until the twentieth century. In the eighteenth and early nineteenth centuries, they usually made no restrictions at all on contents, as this subtitle of the *Massachusetts Magazine** indicates: *Containing, Poetry, Musick, Biography, History, Physick, Geography, Morality, Criticism, Philosophy, Mathematicks, Agriculture, Architecture, Chymistry, Novels, Tales, Romances, Translations, News, Marriages, Deaths, Meteorological Observations, &c. &c.* In the nineteenth century, literature was usually only one element in magazines that included articles on clothing fashions, politics, current events, and sociology. I have therefore defined as "literary" those magazines that included literature (fiction, poetry, and critical, philosophical, or familiar essays) as a significant, but not necessarily the only significant, element. Others, such as the *American (Whig) Review*,* are included for the parts they played in literary history. I also tried to use longevity as a criterion for inclusion, although it became clear early on that this would be a secondary consideration. Many high-quality magazines in America were of short duration; in fact, publications of high quality often failed precisely because of their refusal to appeal to the prevailing taste of the day. At the extreme, I have included a profile of Elizabeth Peabody's single-issue *Aesthetic Papers*,* a transcendental journal, but not, for example, *Peterson's*, a long-lived lady's magazine with an undistinguished history, one of the type represented here by the more interesting *Godey's Lady's Book.**

There are other reasons for including or excluding certain information and titles. These profiles emphasize the literary aspects and importance of the magazines. Details of their editorial and publishing histories, including circulation figures and finances, are covered only when these have a direct bearing on literary developments. This is a different emphasis from Frank Luther Mott's in his seminal *A History of American Magazines*, 4 vols. (Cambridge, Mass.: Belknap Press of Harvard University Press, 1957), which examines in detail the journalistic aspects of many of these publications. I have excluded a number of titles, such as *Vanity Fair, Puck,* and the *Philistine,* because they are being included in another book in this series on humor magazines, edited by David Sloane. There are also a few magazines that were founded before 1900 but which I have decided to include in my companion book. These publications are best known for their careers in the twentieth century, and I felt it appropriate to make them exceptions to the 1900 cutoff point. They include the Chicago and New York *Dial, Scribner's Magazine,* and *Reedy's Mirror.* On the other hand, I have included magazines which, though their contributions to literary history are not as important as others', are examples of important or interesting types that should be represented. Two of these are the *Boston Notion,** one of the "mammoth weeklies," and *Beadle's Monthly,** a venture into the field by Beadle and Adams, the successful publishers of dime novels. In coming to these decisions I have been fortunate to receive the expert advice of a number of scholars of eighteenth- and nineteenth-century American literature, including those who contributed to this volume.

Two appendices follow the profiles, one listing and annotating magazines that made relatively minor contributions to literary history. The word "relatively" is important here, as again some of these magazines are more significant than others. Also, this list is as selective as the list of magazines fully profiled. For instance, in her thorough *Annotated Bibliography of American Literary Periodicals, 1741–1850* (Boston: G. K. Hall, 1977), Jayne Kribbs includes 940 titles. In making my selections, I have also listed some publications that were predominantly nonliterary but with some important literary content. The second appendix presents a chronological perspective of literary-magazine history not readily seen in the alphabetically listed profiles.

The bibliographical material following each profile is intended to lead interested readers to further, perhaps more detailed, information on the magazine. The bibliographies are selective. Indexes are included only if they list authors, titles, and perhaps subjects for the entire magazine, whether for certain years or the full run. These may be separate publications or the internal indexes that were often included within bound volumes. We have attempted to list all reprint, including microform, editions, relying on the *Guide to Microforms in Reprint, Guide to Reprints,* and *University Microforms International, Serials in Microform.* Many of these magazines have now been made available to scholars in the American Periodical Series of University Microfilms. If so, series and reel numbers have been provided.

The locations of original complete and partial runs of each magazine are also provided. However, if ten or more libraries hold a title, it is listed as "widely available," with no indication of locations. In these cases scholars should consult first the *Union List of Serials* and second the *National Union Catalog* for individual locations. The *British Union Catalogue of Periodicals* lists holdings in British Libraries.

The following explanation may also prove helpful to users of this book.

Throughout this volume an asterisk after the title of a magazine indicates that the magazine is covered by a full profile. In each entry a magazine has an asterisk only the first time it is mentioned.

When the magazine being profiled is cited, volume and page or number and page in parentheses are given in the text.

When a magazine underwent a change in title, entries are included referring the reader to the title under which the magazine is profiled. For example: *Our Continent*. See *The Continent*.

Also, when a magazine was founded near the end of the nineteenth century but is profiled in the companion book on twentieth-century magazines, such as *Scribner's Magazine* or *Reedy's Mirror*, as mentioned earlier, an entry is included in this volume to direct the reader to the companion volume.

Edward Chielens

# PROFILES OF AMERICAN LITERARY MAGAZINES, 1774–1900

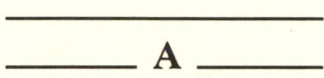

## AESTHETIC PAPERS

Although only one issue of *Aesthetic Papers* was ever published, in 1849, it merits more than just a passing note in the history of American periodicals. Its impressive and wide-ranging collection of writings, revealing astute editorial judgment, in many ways accurately mirrors the social and intellectual life of antebellum New England. Among other notable articles included in the volume are Ralph Waldo Emerson's lecture on "War"; Nathaniel Hawthorne's "Main-Street"; John Sullivan Dwight's analysis of the universality of "Music"; Sampson Reed's oration on "Genius"; and Henry David Thoreau's "Resistance to Civil Government," the first appearance in print of the essay now canonized as "Civil Disobedience."

The guiding force behind this promising but unfortunately stillborn project was Elizabeth Palmer Peabody, its editor and publisher. Sister-in-law of Hawthorne and of the educator Horace Mann, Peabody was, with Margaret Fuller, one of the most talented and accomplished women associated with the transcendental circle. A lecturer, publisher, and reformer, as well as an innovative educator in her own right, Peabody had worked closely with and numbered among her friends many of the illuminati of the era. She had studied Greek under Emerson; had served as amanuensis for the Reverend William Ellery Channing, leading spokesman for Unitarianism; and had assisted Bronson Alcott in his progressive Temple School. Her keen mind, energetic constitution, and humanitarian spirit earned her the respect and admiration of all those who came to know her. Commenting about Peabody in his journal after a visit in 1865, Alcott expressed the opinion shared by all: "The good purposes that she has furthered and brought to consummation during the last thirty years, who shall find out and properly celebrate? I think her one of the most generous souls that I have ever known, and a part of the life of New England."[1]

*Aesthetic Papers* was launched at the end of two decades of intense social and intellectual ferment in New England. William Lloyd Garrison and other abolitionists were crusading to end slavery; Orestes Brownson had created a ministry to the working classes; Peabody and Fuller had conducted "conversations" to help educate women; Alcott, at Fruitlands, and George Ripley, at Brook Farm, had experimented with communitarianism; and Emerson and Frederic Henry Hedge, joined by other "infidels" who were also dissatisfied with the prevailing state of religion and literature, had formed the Transcendental Club to shape the ideas of the "New School." And to provide public forums for their radical views, which were invariably excluded from mainstream, orthodox journals, the transcendentalists established a number of periodicals, among them the *Western Messenger*,* the *Boston Quartely Review*,* the *Dial*,* (Boston) and the *Harbinger*.*

It was in this context, then, that Peabody decided to add yet another title to the growing list of Transcendental periodicals. She was well aware of the difficulties that so often beset such ventures and was not without firsthand experience in the practical side of the publishing trade. Throughout the 1840s she operated a bookstore at 13 West Street in Boston where she sold periodicals as well as foreign and domestic books and, in 1842–1843, published the *Dial*. "Always an enthusiast [who] undertook nothing to which she did not give the most devoted service,"[2] Peabody modeled the "form, size, and type" of *Aesthetic Papers* on the prestigious *British and Foreign Review*. Each number was to appear "whenever a sufficient quantity of valuable matter shall have accumulated to fill 256 pages," between once and three times a year as she calculated ("Prospectus," iv).

In the spring of 1849 Peabody gathered enough material to release the first, and what turned out to be the only, number of *Aesthetic Papers*. As an introduction to the volume, following her "Prospectus," Peabody wrote a short article on "The Word 'Aesthetic.' " Arguing for a less restrictive conception of aesthetics—one that would not only recognize the "aesthetic element" as an "indivisible part in all human creations which are not mere works of necessity" (1) but also replace the popular meaning of personal likes and dislikes—Peabody explained the term as "that phase in human progress which subordinates the individual to the general, that he may re-appear on a higher plane of individuality" (4). To elucidate her point and to show that all art is essentially national in origin and character, she contrasted the subjectivity of the French school of "taste" with what she (and other transcendentalists) regarded as the superior objectivity of German criticism.[3]

Of the twelve articles that follow Peabody's prefatory essay, five focus on questions of art, creativity, and related philosophical matters. In "Criticism" Samuel Gray Ward, a Boston merchant and disciple of Emerson, also extolled the virtues of the analytical techniques used by the Germans; also, sensing the possibility for "a conscious greatness" in the United States, he saw the practice of "higher culture" (24) as a salutary counterforce to the growing materialism of the age. John Sullivan Dwight, former teacher at Brook Farm and later the editor of the country's first musicological journal, contributed an insightful discourse on "Music," his "most important statement" on the subject.[4] In another article, "Language," Peabody advocated the necessity of linguistic study, especially as formulated by the Hungarian educator Dr. Charles Kraitsir.[5] The centrality of Swedenborgianism to transcendentalist philosophy is evident in "Correspondence" by J. J. Garth Wilkinson, an English physician and a transatlantic contributor to the *Harbinger*. Originally delivered in 1821 as his M.A. oration at Harvard, Sampson Reed's "Genius" reveals the transcendentalists' interest in the organic nature of the mind. The theories of Reed, a Boston druggist who was also a prominent Swedenborgian, profoundly influenced the development of Emerson's thought.

Perhaps to illustrate the "aesthetic element" in the creative mode, Peabody also incorporated six poems into the volume. Though not of the same high quality as the prose pieces, the poems are fairly typical of the verse of the American romantic movement. Only one is signed, "Crawford's Orpheus" by Peabody herself. "The Twofold Being" has been attributed to Thomas Wentworth Higginson, "The Favorite" to his sister Louisa, and "Hymn to a Spirit Shrouded" to the recently deceased Ellen Sturgis Hooper, whose first published poetry appeared in the *Dial*. "A Spirit's Reply" and "Meditations of a Widow" were probably written by Peabody's sisters, Sophia Peabody Hawthorne and Mary Peabody Mann.[6]

Five of the remaining seven essays are concerned with history, society, and government. In "War," initially read in 1838 as part of a lecture series sponsored by the American Peace Society, Emerson depicted war and peace as "a mercury of the state of civilization" (45). He felt that as nations became more advanced and pursued higher principles they would become less bellicose. "Abuse of Representative Government" by Stephen Higginson Perkins, a Boston businessman, recommended an improved and expanded educational system as the best hope for producing an enlightened populace that would not elect or countenance the kind of self-serving politicians who were violating the premises of the Constitution by enacting such immoral measures as proslavery legislation. Fourierist Parke Godwin, another Brook Farmer and an editor of the *Harbinger*, contended in "Organization" that the "perfection" of any society depends on the willingness of individual members to "act harmoniously towards one end" (51). A quite different view of the individual's relationship with society was struck by Thoreau in "Resistance to Civil Government," which he first offered to the public in 1848 as a lecture before the Concord Lyceum. Peabody's "Dorian Measure, with a Modern Application" looked to the example of the early Greeks to find a model of a society that achieved a high standard of art and successfully balanced the opposing claims of social order and individual liberty. Peabody was not altogether sanguine, however, about the possibility of fashioning in this country "a social organization which does as much justice to the Christian religion and philosophy, as the Dorian state did to Apollo" (86).[7]

In addition to these polemical writings Peabody also included two interesting and eminently readable essays on Salem, one a scientific report, the other a literary sketch. The former, "Vegetation about Salem, Mass." by "An English Resident," was probably written by Thomas Spencer of London, who had made Salem his home from 1815 to 1839.[8] The latter, Hawthorne's "Main-Street," proved to be, among the small audience who read *Aesthetic Papers*, a very popular contribution by an author whose most celebrated works of fiction similarly exploit native subject matter.

Despite its judiciously chosen, engaging selections and its not unreasonable price—one dollar for subscribers, $1.25 at the bookstores—*Aesthetic Papers* failed to find a sufficient readership to warrant its continuance. Only fifty subscriptions were secured, with no encouraging signs that more would be forthcoming, and the bookstore copies sold poorly. In a broader context, however, its fate was no different from that of philosophically kindred periodicals. All of them were relatively shortlived, and nearly all were defunct by 1849. Indeed, as one historian has rightly pointed out, virtually all of the Transcendentalists' reform activities had ceased by 1850 when, during the advent of American Victorianism, the entire country experienced "a mood of acquiescence to the ills of industrial capitalism, mixed with pride in its visible achievements."[9] For whatever practical and theoretical reasons *Aesthetic Papers* did not succeed, we must finally agree that "It is a bitter indictment of American taste during the forties that a journal containing important works by three of the outstanding figures in our literary history should have failed as soon as it made its first appearance."[10]

## Notes

1. *The Journals of Bronson Alcott*, ed. Odell Shepard (Boston: Little, Brown, 1938), p. 376.

2. George Willis Cooke, *An Historical and Biographical Introduction to Accompany The Dial*, 2 vols. (Cleveland: The Rowfant Club, 1902), 1:151.

3. For a detailed discussion of the subject, see John B. Wilson, "The Aesthetics of Transcendentalism," *Emerson Society Quarterly* no. 57 (4 Qtr. 1969):27–34.

4. Irving Lowens, "Writings about Music in the Periodicals of American Transcendentalism (1835–50)," *Journal of the American Musicological Society* 10 (Summer 1957):74.

5. For Peabody's interest in language see Philip F. Gura, "Elizabeth Palmer Peabody and the Philosophy of Language," *ESQ: A Journal of the American Renaissance* 23 (3 Qtr. 1977):154–63.

6. For attributions see Cooke, 1:194; Clarence L. F. Gohdes, *The Periodicals of American Transcendentalism* (Durham: Duke University Press, 1931), p. 155; and Joseph Jones, "Introduction" to *Aesthetic Papers* (1849; rpt. Gainesville: Scholars' Facsimiles & Reprints, 1957), pp. viii-ix.

7. For further analysis see John B. Wilson, "Elizabeth Peabody and Other Transcendentalists on History and Historians," *Historian* 30 (November 1967):72–86.

8. Jones, p. viii.

9. Anne C. Rose, *Transcendentalism as a Social Movement, 1830–1850* (New Haven: Yale University Press, 1981), p. xi.

10. Gohdes, pp. 155–56.

## Information Sources

BIBLIOGRAPHY:

Cooke, George Willis. *An Historical and Biographical Introduction to Accompany the Dial.* 2 vols. Cleveland: The Rowfant Club, 1902.

Gallant, Barbara Gans. "The New England Transcendentalists and the European Revolutions of 1848." M.A. thesis, University of Florida, 1966.

Gohdes, Clarence L. F. *The Periodicals of American Transcendentalism.* Durham: Duke University Press, 1931.

Gura, Philip F. "Elizabeth Palmer Peabody and the Philosophy of Language." *ESQ: A Journal of the American Renaissance* 23 (3 Qtr. 1977):154–63.

Jones, Joseph. "Introduction." *Aesthetic Papers.* Ed. Elizabeth P. Peabody. 1849; rpt. Gainesville: Scholars' Facsimiles & Reprints, 1957, Pp. v–xii.

———. "Villages as Universities: *Aesthetic Papers* and a Passage in *Walden.*" *Emerson Society Quarterly* 7 (2 Qtr. 1957):40–42.

*The Journals of Bronson Alcott.* Ed. Odell Shepard. Boston: Little, Brown, 1938.

Lowens, Irving. "Writings about Music in the Periodicals of American Transcendentalism (1835–50)." *Journal of the American Musicological Society* 10 (Summer 1957):71–85.

Neussendorfer, Margaret. "Elizabeth Palmer Peabody." In *The Transcendentalists: A Review of Research and Criticism.* Ed. Joel Myerson. New York: Modern Language Association, 1984. Pp. 233–41.

Rose, Anne C. *Transcendentalism as a Social Movement, 1830–1850.* New Haven: Yale University Press, 1981.

Tharp, Louise Hall. *The Peabody Sisters of Salem.* Boston: Little, Brown, 1950.

Warders, Donald F. "Transcendentalist Periodicals." In *The Transcendentalists: A Review of Research and Criticism.* Ed. Joel Myerson. New York: Modern Language Association, 1984. Pp. 69–83.

Wilson, John B. "Activities of the New England Transcendentalists in the Dissemination of Culture." Ph.D. diss., University of North Carolina, 1941.

———. "The Aesthetics of Transcendentalism." *Emerson Society Quarterly* 57 (4 Qtr. 1969):27–34.

———. "Elizabeth Peabody and Other Transcendentalists on History and Historians." *Historian* 30 (November 1967):72–86.

INDEXES: None

REPRINT EDITIONS: Scholars' Facsimiles & Reprints. Gainesville, 1957. AMS Press, New York, 1967. Microform: Xerox University Microfilms (American Culture Series).

LOCATION SOURCES: Widely available.

## Publication History

MAGAZINE TITLE AND TITLE CHANGES: *Aesthetic Papers.*

VOLUME AND ISSUE DATA: The only issue of *Aesthetic Papers* was published in 1849 without volume or issue number.

FREQUENCY OF PUBLICATION: "The plan of publication for this Work is like that
of the 'British and Foreign Review,' which has been the model of its form, size,
and type; namely, that a number should appear whenever a sufficient quantity of
valuable matter shall have accumulated to fill 256 pages. This will in no case
happen more than three times a year; perhaps not oftener than once a year"
(Peabody's "Prospectus," p. iv).
PUBLISHERS: Elizabeth P. Peabody, Boston. G. P. Putnam, New York.
EDITOR: Elizabeth P. Peabody.

*Larry A. Carlson*

# THE ALBUM

When the premier issue of the *Album* appeared in Charleston, South Carolina,
on Saturday, 2 July 1825, it made literary history as the first Southern periodical
devoted exclusively to literature. Although the *South-Carolina Weekly Museum*
(1797–1798) and the Charleston *Monthly Register and Literary Miscellany* (1805–
1807) had come close to preceding it for this honor, these periodicals also stressed
historical accounts, news of European events, and "Foreign and Domestic Intelligence." With the *Album*, however, the editors' single aim was to further
"the Literary character of our state" through "cultivating *Native talent*." Their
"Weekly Literary Miscellany," as the editors described it, would not depend
on translations or excerpts from foreign authors to fill its pages but would rely
on the original works of local writers.

The eight pages of a typical issue of the *Album* contained an installment of a
long story (like "The Robber" or "Moonshine") or short novel ("The Ruins
of St. Oswald"); several sketches, notes, brief essays on literary matters, anecdotes, essays advising the ladies, or book reviews; five or six poems; and occasionally a complete short story. The great majority of these were original, and
sometimes all were. Because the contributions were published under pseudonyms
or initials, it has been difficult to identify many of the authors. The editors
resisted in every issue the great temptation to publish material on politics. In
this respect, writes the *Album*'s first student, it is truly "a rarity among early
Southern periodicals."[1]

The *Album* was influenced by, if not indeed modelled after, yet another early
American literary periodical, the *New-York Mirror, and Ladies' Literary Gazette,** founded two years before in 1823. Both were eight-page weekly miscellanies stressing originality, scorning politics, and catering to a female audience.
Whereas, however, the *Mirror* accepted for publication everything sent it by
contributors in its early years, the *Album* was selective and at times less than
diplomatically harsh in describing the faults of a composition it rejected. "Or-
lando" is told, for example, that his work "is too trite"; and "M. G. A." does
not exercise proper judgment (1:16). When "Vernon" angrily protests his rejection, the editors invite him to a second opinion elsewhere, for his work "shall

not disgrace ours'' (1:62). For those who wish to publish poetry in the *Album*, the editors advise, ''Never be content with the bare symphony of sweet sound'' as are some of the contributors, who are ''particularly averse as well to reason as rule, and are satisfied by merely stringing rhymes together'' (1:40). The *Album*, then, at the outset, established rather high critical standards, which made its works, on the whole, of a higher quality than the *Mirror*'s in its early years.

A direct possible tie to the New York magazine may have come through James Wright Simmons (1790–1858), a Charlestonian, who, after travelling widely in Europe and living in London, where he knew Leigh Hunt and his literary circle, worked on the *Mirror* under George Pope Morris and returned to Charleston by February 1825.[2] Here, he was a friend of the *Album*'s editorial staff and, with one of them, became coeditor of the *Album*'s literary successor, the *Southern Literary Gazette*, in 1828. Although it can only be speculation at this point, Simmons may have been in some way a force in the founding of the *Album* and the shaping of its format. He may likewise have been the ''A.B.C.'' of the Charleston *Courier* (15 June 1825) who appealed to the Charleston public to support this literary endeavor and who stated that it would be modelled after the *Mirror*.[3]

Such speculation is necessitated by the strict anonymity of the *Album*'s editors. The closest they come to announcing their identity is to call themselves ''young Charlestonians'' and a ''Society of Young Gentlemen,'' likely accurate descriptions. Only two of their number can as yet be positively identified: William Gilmore Simms and William Allen, both of whom contributed heavily to the periodical's pages. Simms, who was but nineteen years old at the time, was to become known as a major literary figure of his day; but little information exists on Allen. Simms, in 1870, described him as ''another of those promising lads of literature in our city . . . a ready and indefatigable writer in prose and verse . . . a thin, nervous person, of spasmodic eagerness and impulse'' who ''dabbled in chemistry as well as literature'' and who died young, ''having swallowed a solution of phosphorus in mistake for water.''[4] Under the initials ''W.A.'' and the pseudonyms ''Juan,'' ''I.A.O.,'' and ''St. Pierre,'' he published many poems and stories in the *Album*. Just how many other editors were also a part of this literary ''Society of Young Gentlemen'' is not known.

The *Album* also made literary history in 1825 as Simms's first editorial venture, his initial periodical in a long series of editorships that would include the *Southern Literary Gazette, Charleston City Gazette, Cosmopolitan, Southern and Western Monthly Magazine and Review,* \* *Magnolia,* \* *Orion,* \* *Southern Quarterly Review,* \* and *Columbia Phoenix*. Here in his first periodical, at the age of nineteen, he would publish some of his earliest fiction and verse and his first-known letters, which detail an 1826 journey to the Southwest, a series which is of great significance. One of the stories, ''Moonshine,'' is the forerunner of his first revolutionary romance, *The Partisan* (1835). Through the pages of the *Album*, then, one is able to trace the beginnings of a significant career in American literary history. In all, there are more than seventy items in the extant issues that can be proved to be by Simms. These include sixty-one poems, eight works of fiction, several reviews, and the series of letters.[5] It is through Simms's close involvement with the *Album*, coupled with the fact that it is the first exclusively literary journal in the South, that the periodical becomes of some major importance.

Just how long the *Album* lasted is a matter of conjecture. Its first weekly number appeared 2 July 1825, and the last extant issue bears the date 24 June 1826. With the issue of 7 January 1826, the subtitle *"Or, Charleston Literary Gazette"* was added, thus suggesting the chance that the periodical continued in some form for the rest of 1826 and into 1827 as a bridge to Simmons's and Simms's next editorial endeavor, the *Southern Literary Gazette* of 1828–1829. The fact that the very existence of the *Album*'s 1826 numbers first came to light only in 1983 should discourage a too easy rejection of the possibility. Thus, though the *Album* is proved to have existed for a minimum of a year, it may possibly have lasted unbroken for four years until 1829 in the new form of the *Southern Literary Gazette*.

In its minimum of fifty-one octavo issues, the *Album*, for its modest size, made a rather spectacular mark on American literary history. Still, nothing is known of its contemporary reception. Many of its readers were likely ladies (as the title the *Album* would suggest, as well as the essays of advice to them on such topics as flattery and marriage), but just who and how many were its subscribers cannot be surmised. The fact that the contributions were original and competent points toward its connection with an intelligent circle of readers. As for its influence on Simms, John Guilds summarizes that his *Album* contributions show "the spade work for some of his best poems and for at least one of his major novels." In addition, his editorial experience here gave him an opportunity to formulate his future editorial policies in that, already, "he had learned to strike out boldly and fearlessly as a critic; and already he had hit what was to be the keynote of his career as a magazine editor: the advancement of Southern literature."[6] In the *Album* can be seen the first serious stirrings of that movement to cultivate native genius in a distinctively Southern literature, a call that Simms restated in almost identical language a few years later in the *Southern Literary Gazette*. With more intensive study of the *Album* and its Southern milieu and hopefully with the discovery of more of its missing issues, future scholars should be better able to document the impact and significance of this first Southern literary magazine.

## Notes

1. John C. Guilds, Jr., "Simms's First Magazine: *The Album*," *Studies in Bibliography* 8 (1956):174.

2. Simmons published a work in the Charleston *Courier*, 18 February 1825. For mention of his involvement with the *Mirror*, see William L. King, *The Newspaper Press of Charleston* (Charleston, S.C.: Lucas & Richardson, 1882).

3. Interestingly, two prose works, "Green-Mountain Life" and "Marriage," also appeared in the *Mirror* signed "A. B. C.," 15 January 1825. Many items with South

Carolina ties are in the magazine from 1824 to 1825: "To the Poets and Poetesses of the *New-York Mirror*" (16 October 1824) by "Sobieski," who describes himself as a "wanderer" and "stranger" from the South; "Sullivan's Island" (20 November 1824) by "Sobieski;" "Sergeant Jasper" (30 October 1824), "Emily Geiger" (4 September 1824), "Isole" (26 February 1825), and "Francis Marion" (21 May 1825), unsigned; and "To Isabel" (5 February 1825) by "S. of Charleston."

4. William Gilmore Simms, "Reminiscences of South Carolina," *The XIX Century* 2 (May 1870):50–51.

5. For a description of these works, see Guilds, and James E. Kibler, "*The Album* (1826): The Significance of the Recently Discovered Second Volume," *Studies in Bibliography* 39 (1986). For proof of the pseudonyms under which Simms published them see James Kibler, *The Pseudonymous Publications of William Gilmore Simms* (Athens: University of Georgia Press, 1976).

6. Guilds, p. 181.

## Information Sources

BIBLIOGRAPHY:
Guilds, John C., Jr. "Simms's First Magazine: *The Album*." *Studies in Bibliography* 8 (1956):169–83.
Kibler, James E. "*The Album* (1826): The Significance of the Recently Discovered Second Volume." *Studies in Bibliography* 39 (1986).
————. *The Pseudonymous Publications of William Gilmore Simms.* Athens: University of Georgia Press, 1976.
King, William L. *The Newspaper Press of Charleston.* Charleston, S.C.: Lucas & Richardson, 1882.
INDEXES: None
REPRINT EDITIONS: None.
LOCATION SOURCES: Volume 1: South Caroliniana Library, University of South Carolina; volume 2, issues 4, 5, 9, 10, 13, 17, 20, 25 only extant: collection of James Kibler.

## Publication History

MAGAZINE TITLE AND TITLE CHANGES: *The Album*, 2 July–24 December 1825. *The Album. Or, Charleston Literary Gazette*, 7 January–24 June 1826.
VOLUME AND ISSUE DATA: Volumes 1–2, 2 July 1825–24 June 1826.
FREQUENCY OF PUBLICATION: Weekly.
PUBLISHERS: Gray & Ellis, No. 9 Broad-Street, Charleston, South Carolina. Cost of 25 cents per month, 3 dollars per year to country subscribers.
EDITORS: "A Society of Young Gentlemen" of Charleston, only two members of which can be positively identified: William Allen and William Gilmore Simms.

*James Everett Kibler*

## THE AMERICAN LITERARY GAZETTE AND NEW YORK WEEKLY MIRROR. See THE NEW-YORK MIRROR, AND LADIES' LITERARY GAZETTE

## THE AMERICAN MAGAZINE

In December 1787, the first issue of Noah Webster's monthly *American Magazine* was published in New York. At twenty-nine Webster had already published his *A Grammatical Institute of the English Language* and enjoyed a modest success. Dr. Benjamin Rush had urged him to stay in Philadelphia and publish his magazine there, and to call it the *Monthly Asylum*.[1] But Philadelphia already had a firmly established monthly, the *Columbian Magazine*.* New York promised to be the commercial hub of America, an appropriate location since Webster intended his publication to transcend regionalism and be national in scope. His ambitions for the *American Magazine* and his optimism are revealed in a letter written to Jeremy Belknap in February 1788 in which he explains his plans "to enlarge [his magazine] so as to make it a federal publication."[2] He writes that "The smallest number of subscribers to be expected is 3,000; the probability is there would be 5,000." In reality, his subscription list probably never had reached five hundred when, eleven months later, he abandoned the enterprise. However, in October 1787 Webster left Philadelphia for New York, secured Samuel Loudon as his printer, at no financial risk to Loudon, and in November travelled throughout Connecticut securing subscriptions from friends.[3]

In his first issue Webster emphasized his determination to publish "as many original Essays as possible; and particularly such as relate to this country" (1:3). He proposed to publish a miscellany, the scope of which is indicated by "the Editor's wish to gratify every class of readers—the Divine, the Philosopher, the Historian, the Statesman, the Moralist, the Poet, the Merchant and the Laborer— and his *fair readers* may be assured that no inconsiderable pains will be taken to furnish *them* with entertainment" (1:3). Webster published much of his varied material in series form, installments often running no more than three pages, not an unusual format for the time. Although he asserts in the March issue that his magazine "contains more original matter than any other periodical publication in America" (1:193), Webster did borrow heavily, especially from English publications. This is ironic, considering that throughout the magazine's run he emphasizes the importance of fostering and developing a distinctively American culture. Frank Luther Mott notes, however, that this heavy borrowing was conventional magazine policy and that the *American Magazine* "did strive for originality."[4]

As part of his program to foster an American culture and help to establish the new democracy on a solid philosophical basis, Webster published much historical and political material. The first issue begins a series of excerpts from John Smith's *History of Virginia* (1:19–22), and the second includes excerpts from Thomas Jefferson's *Notes on the State of Virginia* (1:106–116). Indicative of Webster's belief in progress through rational thought is his reprinting of old, repressive colonial laws. After printing one such example from early Connecticut, he concludes that it serves "to contrast the narrow views and bigoted zeal of the last century, with the catholic temper, and mild condescension of sentiment, which distinguish the present age. Yet the triumph of reason over fanaticism is still incomplete'' (1:52). In a series of essays under the pseudonym Giles Hickory, Webster defends the new Constitution and debates the momentous political issues of the day. He defends representative as opposed to direct democracy (1:75–80), and, consistent with his belief that rational men can live harmoniously in a democracy, he argues against a Bill of Rights as an unnecessary limitation of the citizens' right to govern themselves (1:137–45). Harry Warfel notes that ''Beside the monumental *Federalist* Webster's essays fade into unimportance, but the good effect of their barbed shafts of ridicule was frequently commented upon.''[5] Beginning in the March issue in the regular department called ''Review of New Publications,'' he began reviewing the *Federalist Papers* of James Madison, Alexander Hamilton, and John Jay, explaining and supporting their argumentation (1:260–61). In the June issue he concludes by saying, ''They will be useful in diffusing political knowledge in the American republics, and will probably be republished and read with pleasure and approbation'' (1:507).

Webster's lifelong interests in American education and language are also reflected in the *American Magazine*. In a series of essays he argued vehemently for his theories of education, presenting the opposing views in letters signed by ''Beelzebub.'' For example, he called for school readers to be ''A selection of essays, respecting the settlement and geography of America—the history of the late revolution and of the most remarkable characters and events that distinguish it'' (1:216). Textbooks dominated by English authors were not appropriate for the children of the new Republic. In a series of ''Original Letters from a Gentleman to His Friend,'' Webster reflects upon American culture for an Englishman unfamiliar with it. A number of these observations reveal his interest in language, as in this comment from Letter IV on the idiomatic expression to be married ''upon'' someone: ''Marriage is designed for mutual assistance, and not for *burden*. Marriage is a perpetual knot or yoke . . . surely it is not desirable to be tied forever *upon*'' (1:479). In Letter VI he complains of the irregularities of American English and asks, ''Is not the proposal once made by Swift to the Earl of Oxford for correcting, improving and ascertaining the English Tongue practicable, and could not something of this kind be done in America?'' (1:692) Years later, of course, Webster's greatest work was to take up this proposal.

The strictly literary content of the *American Magazine* is of less importance. Most of it, including fictitious letters involving marriage and romance, Oriental tales, and the three or so pages of poetry published in each issue, was the typical sentimental and moralistic fare of the times. Timothy Dwight's poetry appeared occasionally. Webster defended Dwight's *Conquest of Canaan* from an attack in the *London Review* that called it a weak allegory of the Revolution: ''Is it impossible that an English Critic should view the smallest literary production in America, thro any medium but that of *national prejudice*?'' (1:564) However, after Webster accused Dwight of illiberality and plagiarism in his *Triumph of Infidelity* and then defended his criticism in the *Daily Advertiser*, Dwight contributed no more to the magazine.[6] John Trumbull's *The Progress of Dulness*

("The Rare Adventures of Tom Brainless") was reprinted (1:59–61, 117–20), as were extracts from Joel Barlow's *The Vision of Columbus* (1:263–65).

But disappointments dogged Webster's enterprise from the beginning. The need for a national copyright law became more apparent to him than ever when, as he complained in the February issue, "Several trespasses upon the property of the Editor, in different parts of the country, have already been committed" (1:130). When promised material failed to be submitted, he devised a plan whereby leading literary figures throughout the country would become proprietors in the magazine, thus making it a cooperative enterprise.[7] However, jealousies and animosities, to at least some extent caused by Webster's own imperiousness and contentiousness, caused the plan to fail. Facing a financial loss of £250, a disappointing subscription list, and frustrated marital prospects because of his financial situation, Webster abandoned the magazine. In the last issue he wrote that "A beginning has been made by an individual under every possible disadvantage, and the experiment will warrant a continuation of the work, by persons whose business, citizenship and connections shall command more general patronage. It is not consistent with the proprietor's interest and views in life to devote his whole time to a work of this kind" (1:756). A tentative agreement made with Jeremy Belknap and Ebenezer Hazard to publish a combined magazine and register of historical documents failed, and the *American Magazine* ceased publication. Nevertheless, Warfel concludes that "the superiority of the *American Magazine*, so much of it being from [Webster's] pen, gave him the position of America's leading essayist."[8] The magazine remains today a valuable reflection of Webster's views and character as well as of early American thought.

## Notes

1. John S. Morgan, *Noah Webster* (New York: Mason/Charter, 1975), p. 113.
2. *Letters of Noah Webster*, ed. Harry R. Warfel (New York: Library Publishers, 1953), p. 74.
3. Harry R. Warfel, *Noah Webster: Schoolmaster to America* (New York: Macmillan, 1936), p. 172.
4. Frank Luther Mott, "*The American Magazine*," A History of American Magazines, 4 vols. (Cambridge, Mass.: Belknap Press of Harvard University Press, 1957), 1:105.
5. Warfel, p. 178.
6. Warfel, p. 174.
7. Warfel, pp. 187–88.
8. Warfel, p. 188.

## Information Sources

BIBLIOGRAPHY:

Morgan, John S. *Noah Webster*. New York: Mason/Charter, 1975.
Mott, Frank Luther. "*The American Magazine*." A History of American Magazines, 4 vols. (Cambridge, Mass.: Belknap Press of Harvard University Press, 1957), 1:104–7.

Richardson, Lyon N. *A History of Early American Magazines, 1741–1789*. New York: Thomas Nelson and Sons, 1931.

Warfel, Harry R. *Noah Webster: Schoolmaster to America*. New York: Macmillan, 1936.

INDEXES: "Contents of the First Volume of the American Magazine," pp. 878–82, lists titles in order of appearance, but not authors or pseudonyms.

REPRINT EDITIONS: American Periodicals: Series I, 1741–1800. University Microfilms, Ann Arbor. Reel 2.

LOCATION SOURCES: Widely Available.

## Publication History

MAGAZINE TITLE AND TITLE CHANGES: *The American Magazine. Containing a Miscellaneous Collection of Original and Other Valuable Essays, in Prose and Verse, and Calculated Both for Instruction and Amusement.*

VOLUME AND ISSUE DATA: Volume 1, December 1787-November 1788.

FREQUENCY OF PUBLICATION: Monthly.

PUBLISHERS: December 1787-February 1788: Samuel Loudon, New York. March-November 1788: S. & J. Loudon, New York.

EDITOR: Noah Webster.

*Edward Chielens*


# THE AMERICAN MONTHLY KNICKERBOCKER. See
## THE KNICKERBOCKER


# THE AMERICAN MONTHLY MAGAZINE

The *American Monthly Magazine* took on the literary personalities of its three primary editors, Henry William Herbert, Charles Fenno Hoffman, and Park Benjamin. The magazine nurtured the talents and ambitions that carried each of the three to later successes. It established Herbert as a professional writer, solidified Hoffman's reputation, and drew Benjamin into the world of New York periodicals.

Born into England's landed gentry and educated at Eton and Cambridge, Herbert immigrated to New York in 1831. While teaching Greek at one of the city's better schools, he met Scotsman Andrew D. Patterson, and they initiated the *American Monthly* in August 1833. An introductory essay, "On the Utility of Periodical Literature" (1:1–12), outlines their intention to make high learning and literature available to the reading public through moral essays, poetry, biography, travel sketches, reviews, translations, scientific reports, fiction, and discussion of the fine arts.

Herbert's classical education and inherited interest in history, art, and drama dictated editorial policy. Long series of articles deal with Greek and Roman dramatists. Translations of obscure passages from classical writers provide page fillers. Most travel and historical pieces deal with European subjects. Fiction ranges from moral fables by James Kirke Paulding to historical, often medieval, romances. Poetry is politely romantic. Herbert contributed translations, fiction, verse, and reviews, but the sports writing for which he would gain fame as Frank Forester appears in only two sketches of "Wild Sports in Many Lands" (4:136–39, 413–16). The most notable features of the early issues are the perceptive, detailed accounts of New York art exhibits and theatrical productions in the "Miscellaneous Notices."[1]

Patterson retired during the magazine's first year, and Hoffman was named coeditor in February 1835 (4:423). Son of a distinguished New York jurist, the new editor united experience on the *New-York American* and the *Knickerbocker*\* with some celebrity as author of *A Winter in the West* (1835). Asserting his control in a March notice,[2] Hoffman probably assumed responsibility for the "Miscellaneous Notices" as early as April 1835.[3] Under Hoffman the *American Monthly* served a slightly altered version of the menu defined by Herbert. Translations are more often from German than Greek or Italian, and the classical fillers gradually disappear. Travel writing concentrates on America rather than Europe. Hoffman's fascination with American Indians displaces much of Herbert's interest in the Middle Ages. The moralism of earlier fiction and poetry diminishes. The "Miscellaneous Notices" emphasize books above art and theater, on occasion becoming exclusively "Literary Notices."

The "Editorial Address" introducing Hoffman also formalizes an intention to make the *American Monthly* "the national periodical of our almost boundless country" (4:424). Early issues had drawn contributions from such non–New Yorkers as William Gilmore Simms, but Hoffman resolved to publish nationally. A note in February 1836 announces merger with the *New England Magazine*,\* editorial partnership with Benjamin, and simultaneous publication in New York and Boston (6:478–79). Two issues of the new *American Monthly* had appeared in January and February 1836 to resolve the discrepancy between fiscal years. Philadelphia joined the coalition in March 1837, when Robert Montgomery Bird accepted an editorial role (n.s. 3:305–6) and a Philadelphia firm was added to the publishers. Bird, however, resigned in October (n.s. 4:501), and Benjamin moved to New York. Though Robert M. Walsh of Philadelphia became "associated in the Editorship" in January 1838 (n.s. 5:viii), publication reverted solely to New York.

Merle M. Hoover describes the new series as "more scholarly, more restrained in tone than the *New-England Magazine* and . . . at the same time, livelier, especially in its critical material, than the preceding numbers of the *American Monthly*."[4] While pure classicism retreats, articles on Shakespeare, Sir Thomas Browne, and Cervantes, as well as frequent German and French translations, retain a belletristic flavor. Current books oust art and theater from the "Critical Notices," but the fine arts appear in American Lyceum addresses by Thomas Cole and William Dunlap, essays on Horatio Greenough and Washington Allston, and Benjamin's experiments with verse drama. New England writers, including Nathaniel Hawthorne and Oliver Wendell Holmes, appear prominently, and reviews, including one identifying the authorship of many of Hawthorne's early tales and sketches (n.s. 2:405–7), spotlight Boston publications. Contributions from Robert Montgomery Bird, Poe, and many New Yorkers, along with travel sketches of the South and West, maintain a truly national scope. A frontispiece is added to each issue.

Three significant changes took place in the new series. Herbert and Hoffman had insisted on anonymity to let works speak for themselves and, perhaps, to disguise the number of contributions from the editors. As he had done in the *New England Magazine*, Benjamin allowed poetry, fiction, and travel sketches to be signed, initialed revealingly, or identified in editorial comments. Herbert and Hoffman had written cogent but generally restrained reviews. Though far from uncritical, they stressed the positive, particularly when doing so would encourage new authors. Benjamin brought out his barbed pen, voicing objections sarcastically and intensifying the venom with backhanded praise. Herbert's own *Cromwell* (1838) is dubbed "a decided failure" filled with "heavy, dull, ill-constructed and inharmonious sentences" advancing a "rather meagre" plot (n.s. 6:289).

"The Times," the lead article for September 1837, announces the largest departure from the magazine's origins. Aside from a series of essays on copyright laws beginning in February 1837 (n.s. 3:153–58), Herbert and Hoffman had shielded themselves from party affiliation and political debate. "The Times," however, openly aligns the *American Monthly* with the Whigs and institutes political commentary as a standard feature. Claiming that the magazine has adhered to Whig principles, though "pressing them always, so far as we could, without embroiling ourselves in the mere party struggles of the day," the author asserts that "the time has now arrived when the views of the AMERICAN PARTY, and the doctrines of Free Trade and States' Rights are no longer matters to be touched upon after this desultory fashion" (n.s. 4:210). In January 1838, consequently, the *American Monthly* became a review focusing on foreign as well as domestic works and combining political and literary discourse (n.s. 4:600; n.s. 5:iii–v). Though contents and contributors change less radically than format, the break with the past is symbolized on the title page of the new volume, where the motto "True Liberty" replaces a quotation from Persius.

Neither a new format nor political affiliation could salvage the *American Monthly* when its editors drifted toward other pursuits. Hoffman shifted his attention to the *New-York Mirror, and Ladies' Literary Gazette*,* though he contributed to the *American Monthly* as late as September 1838. Influenced by Horace Greeley, who may have inspired changes in the *American Monthly*, Benjamin embraced the aggressively commercial editing prospects that would mature into the *New World*. A decline in subscribers and the publisher's failure ended publication with the October 1838 issue.[5]

The *American Monthly*'s sixty-five issues printed original pieces by several important authors as well as work by such writers as Albert Pike, Alfred B. Street, Grace Grafton, and Mrs. E. F. Ellet. It reviewed the significant American books issued during its life span. It fostered three literary careers. Like Herbert,

Hoffman, and Benjamin, the *American Monthly* was a star of moderate intensity in the periodical galaxy of the 1830s. While indexing the period's popular taste, it retains more historical value as a record of the New York art scene. Herbert's "Miscellaneous Notices" and articles by or about important artists provide insight into the fine arts of the United States during a decade when they, like the nation's literature, were struggling for recognition.

## Notes

1. Identifying authorship in the *American Monthly* is often complicated by official anonymity, by lack of precise dating of changes in editors, and by Herbert and Hoffman's simultaneous use of the initial "H" as a signature. Like reviews, the "Miscellaneous Notices" are unsigned, but they are almost certainly the work of the controlling editor, in this case Herbert. See William Mitchell Van Winkle and David A. Randall, *Henry William Herbert (Frank Forester) A Bibliography of His Writings, 1832–1858* (Portland, Maine: The Southworth-Anthaensen Press, 1936), p. 126.

2. The notice, signed by Hoffman, appears on the inside back cover of the March 1835 issue and is quoted in full by Homer F. Barnes, *Charles Fenno Hoffman* (1930; rpt. New York: AMS Press, 1966), pp. 68–69.

3. Van Winkle and Randall, p. 134.

4. *Park Benjamin, Poet and Editor* (New York: Columbia University Press, 1948), p. 70.

5. Benjamin announces the discontinuation of the *American Monthly* in the *New-Yorker* of 3 November 1838 (6:109), where he attributes failure to the impossibility of combining literature with politics. Subscribers would receive the *New-Yorker* in November and December.

## Information Sources

BIBLIOGRAPHY

Barnes, Homer F. *Charles Fenno Hoffman*. 1930; rpt., New York: AMS Press, 1966.

Hoover, Merle M. *Park Benjamin, Poet and Editor*. New York: Columbia University Press, 1948.

Hunt, William Southworth. *Frank Forester (Henry William Herbert) A Tragedy in Exile*. Newark, N.J.: The Carteret Book Club, 1933.

Mott, Frank Luther. "*The American Monthly Magazine* (Benjamin's)." *A History of American Magazines*. 4 vols. Cambridge, Mass.: Belknap Press of Harvard University Press, 1957, 1:618–21.

Van Winkle, William Mitchell, and David A. Randall. *Henry William Herbert (Frank Forester) A Bibliography of His Writings 1832–1858*. Portland, Maine: The Southworth-Anthaensen Press, 1936. Pp. 126–37.

White, Luke M., Jr. *Henry William Herbert and the American Publishing Scene, 1831–1858*. Newark, N.J.: The Carteret Book Club, 1943.

INDEXES: None

REPRINT EDITIONS: American Periodicals: Series II, 1800–1850. University Microfilms, Ann Arbor. Reels 376–377.

LOCATION SOURCES: Complete runs: Grosvenor Reference Division, Buffalo and Erie County Public Library; Newberry Library; New York Public Library; University of Virginia. Incomplete runs: Boston Public Library; Brown University; University of Michigan; University of North Carolina; Free Library of Philadelphia; Library Company of Philadelphia.

### Publication History

MAGAZINE TITLE AND TITLE CHANGES: *The American Monthly Magazine.*

VOLUME AND ISSUE DATA: Volumes 1–6, March 1833-February 1836; new series volumes 1–6, January 1836-October 1838.

FREQUENCY OF PUBLICATION: Monthly. [No issue published in October 1834; two issues each in February 1835 and January and February 1836.]

PUBLISHERS: March 1833-February 1834: Monson Bancroft, New York, J. Wiley, New York, Peter Hill, New York, and G. and C. and H. Carvill, New York. March 1834–February 1835: Monson Bancroft, New York, Peter Hill, New York, and G. and C. and H. Carvill, New York. March 1835-August 1835: D. K. Minor and T. and C. Wood, New York. September 1835-February 1836: George Dearborn, New York. January 1836-February 1837: George Dearborn, New York, and Otis, Broaders, and Co., Boston. March 1837-October 1837: George Dearborn, New York, Otis, Broaders, and Co., Boston and T. Cotrell Clarke, Philadelphia. November 1837-December 1837: George Dearborn, New York, Otis, Broaders, and Co., Boston, and J. R. Pollock, Philadelphia. January 1838-October 1838: George Dearborn, New York.

EDITORS: Henry William Herbert and Andrew D. Patterson, March 1833-February 1834; Henry William Herbert, March 1834-February 1835; Charles Fenno Hoffman and Henry William Herbert, March 1835-February 1836; Charles Fenno Hoffman and Park Benjamin, January 1836-February 1837; Park Benjamin, Charles Fenno Hoffman, and Robert Montgomery Bird, March 1837-October 1837; Park Benjamin and Charles Fenno Hoffman, November 1837-December 1837; Park Benjamin and Robert M. Walsh, January 1838-October 1838.

*Kennedy Williams, Jr.*

# THE AMERICAN MUSEUM

On 21 February 1787 the *Pennsylvania Gazette* announced, "This day is published, by Matthew Carey, In Front-street [Philadelphia] . . . The American Museum." In after years Mathew Carey remembered: "In January, 1787, I issued the first number of the American Museum . . . which I continued for six years, ending December, 1792. . . . Never was more labor bestowed on a work with less reward. During the whole six years I was in a state of intense penury. . . . That it had considerable merit is universally acknowledged. . . . The American Museum met with the most unqualified approbation of some of the most distinguished citizens of the United States."[1] A leading authority on early American magazines asserts, "Carey was the greatest of eighteenth century magazine editors; he had the qualities necessary for editorial success—versatility and wide interests, personal magnetism, industry, and optimism."[2] He also "possessed a solid inclination toward decency, morality, and high seriousness" and "was apparently unappreciative of light verse and wit for their own sake."[3]

In the Preface to the July 1788 issue Carey informs his readers: "This work lays little or no claim to originality. . . . To *preserve* for posterity—as well as to *disseminate* among the present generation—valuable fugitive publications, hastening to oblivion—are its primary objects." While it does reprint much of the best in eighteenth-century American literature, the *Museum* can in fact lay claim to originality, especially after January 1789, when it changed its subtitle; "in the latter half of the magazine's file about one-third of the contents are original."[4] Whereas the *Columbian Magazine** "avoided the serious political and social problems of the day to devote much of its space to agricultural concerns and the beginnings of manufactures, the *Museum* reflected faithfully and fully the internal situation of the newly independent nation."[5] The political complexion of the *Museum*, which reveals a Federalist bias, is manifest in its reprinting of Paine's *Common Sense* (January-March 1787), John Trumbull's *M'Fingal* (April 1787), *The Federalist* Nos. I-IV (November-December 1787), Paine's *Crisis* Nos. I-II (May, September 1788), John Dickinson's *Letters from a Farmer in Pennsylvania* (September-December 1788), and Francis Hopkinson's *A Pretty Story* (July-December 1791). It is works like these that prompted George Washington to write Carey on 25 June 1788: "I believe the American Museum has met with . . . universal approbation from competent judges: . . . the work is not only eminently calculated to disseminate political, agricultural, philosophical, and other valuable information—but . . . has been uniformly conducted with taste, attention, and propriety. . . . I consider such easy vehicles of knowledge, more happily calculated than any other, to preserve the liberty, stimulate the industry, and meliorate the morals of an enlightened and free people" (July 1788).

Much of the prose in the *Museum* takes the form of essays. Benjamin Rush contributed many essays to it just as he did to the *Columbian*, only here the emphasis tends to be medical. Thus he writes on tetanus (November 1787; July 1788), "Hipocondriasis" (July 1788), pulmonary consumption (March-April 1789), "the relation of tastes and ailments to each other" (June 1789), "the benefits of exercise, in preference to medicine, in chronic diseases" (July 1789), and, most important of all, "the influence of physical causes upon the moral faculty" (February 1789), which had been delivered before the American Philosophical Society on 27 February 1786.

Francis Hopkinson is a more literary essayist than Rush. No fewer than fourteen of his essays are printed or reprinted in the *Museum*. His essay "on annual white-washings" (January 1787), reprinted from the *Pennsylvania Packet* for 18 June 1785 and the one to which Nitidia replies in the *Columbian* for April 1787 (q.v.), declares:

> When a young couple are about to enter on the matrimonial state, a never failing article in the marriage treaty is, that the lady shall have and enjoy the free and unmolested exercise of the rights of *white-washing*. . . . If, when the husband rises in the morning, he should observe in the yard a wheel-barrow with a quantity of lime in it, or should see certain buckets

with lime dissolved in water, there is no time to be lost—he immediately locks up the apartment or closet where his papers or his private property are kept, and putting the key in his pocket, betakes himself to flight (1:49–50).

The husband having fled and the house being evacuated, "the next operation is to smear the walls and ceilings of every room and closet with brushes, dipped in a solution of lime, called *white-wash*" (1:50). This done, the furniture is replaced; "the sole object is to *make things clean*: it matters not how many useful, ornamental, or valuable articles are mutilated or *suffer death under the operation*" (1:51). "A principal part of the gratification consists in the ladies having an uncontrouled right to torment her husband at least once in a year, and to turn him out of doors, and take the reins of government into her own hands" (1:51–52).

In "On the Establishment of a high Court of Honour" (May 1787), reprinted from the *Pennsylvania Packet* for 23 December 1780, F. H., in order to make the newspapers once again "the vehicles of intelligence, not the common sewers of scandal," proposes that there be established a "high court of honour" which "shall have jurisdiction in all matters of controversy between man and man" (1:433–34). When A. B. brings an accusation against C. D., they shall plead their case at a hearing, after which "the court shall give their final sentence" (1:435), from which there can be no appeal. In "Some thoughts on the diseases of the mind" (October 1788), reprinted from the *Pennsylvania Gazette* for 17 September 1788, Hopkinson says, granted that "there is an intimate connexion between the soul and the body . . . it seems more natural, that mental remedies should be prescribed for mental disorders, and corporeal physic for bodily diseases" (4:327–28). "*Cacoethes maledictionis . . .* is best managed by allowing a free emission to the peccant humours" (4:328–29) through actions or words, preferably words. "The art of printing has been a great blessing to mankind. . . . Before this invention, murders, assassinations, rebellions, and revolutions were much more frequent than since" (4:329). My proposal "is a scheme by which envy and revenge may be gratified without danger, and without cost; and abuse, slander, and invective spend themselves, like rockets, in harmless explosions" (4:330).

Essay serials abound in the *Museum*, notably *The Visitant* (August 1788-October 1789), *The American Spectator* (December 1789-July 1790), *The Columbian Observer* (February-December 1791), *Letters to a Young Lady* (second series) (January-June 1792), and, what is our concern here, Hopkinson and Paine's *The Old Bachelor* (November-December 1787; January-March, June, August, December 1788), which was reprinted from the *Pennsylvania Magazine* (1775–1776). Hopkinson's Old Bachelor—for the character is largely his creation—when asked why he doesn't get married, replies: "A fine affair I should make of it, at sixty-five. . . . I ought to be *hanged* for not being married *before*—but I ought to be *hung* in chains, if I get married *now*" (2:499). Being reformed these two years, he repents the consequences of his fornications: "To beget them was a *natural* crime; to disown them, a *proud* one; and to neglect them, a *cruel* one" (2:499–500). "As badly off as I am," declares the Old Bachelor, "I had rather be a solitary bachelor, than a miserable married man. No wife is better than a bad one, and the same of a husband" (3:89–90). The Old Bachelor says that the Philadelphia tradesman who was bullied by his wife into journeying to New York and then was hurried home again on short notice is hen-pecked, "and hens never triumph over any other than a dunghill cock; the want of dignity in the one, begets insult in the other. . . . A governing woman is never truly happy, nor a submitting husband perfectly reconciled . . . when a woman acts the man, the man acts the fool. . . . Were I young, and had a wife, you should see other doings" (3:267). "Upon the whole," he concludes, "I find so many reasons to wish I was a married man, and see so many reasons to rejoice I am not, that I am like the pendulum of a clock, hanging in suspence, and perpetually vibrating between two opinions" (3:567). Conventionally the old bachelor, a character long associated with the periodical essay in England and America, was good natured, old fashioned, a member of the gentry in easy circumstances, and, especially from the time of Sterne, eccentric. Hopkinson's Old Bachelor stands near the head of a succession of American bachelors and is as memorable as any in this gallery—an erstwhile fornicator now experiencing the inconveniences of keeping bachelor's hall but too chauvinistic to take the plunge into matrimony.

While the poetry in the *Museum* is on the whole didactic and sentimental, reflecting Carey's taste, he had the discrimination to publish the work of important American poets: Richard Lewis's "Journey from Patapsco to Annapolis" (June 1791); four poems by Hopkinson, including "The Battle of the Kegs" (January 1787); seventeen by Philip Freneau, including "An Indian Burying Ground" (November 1787); twelve by David Humphreys, including "An Elegy on the Burning of Fairfield" (March 1787); five by Timothy Dwight, including "Address of the Genius of Columbia to the Members of the Continental Convention" (June 1787); six by John Trumbull, including *M'Fingal*; and thirty-four by Dr. Joseph Brown Ladd, a still obscure poet who died at the age of twenty-four from wounds incurred in a duel. While many of Ladd's poems are short love lyrics from himself (as Arouet) to an orphan heiress (as Amanda) whose guardians would not consent to her marrying him, his longest and most ambitious work is "The Prospect of America" (May 1787), dedicated to Washington and celebrating congressional and military heroes of the Revolution.

The most significant poem published in the *Museum* is *M'Fingal*, the work that secured Trumbull a permanent if secondary place in American literary history. Undertaken in 1775 as a satirical attack on Thomas Gage, military governor of Massachusetts, this poem, when finally completed seven years later, became "probably the most popular American poem of its length before Longfellow's *Evangeline*."[6] Squire M'Fingal, a New England Tory double-dyed, is twice bested by the Whigs, first in extended debate with Honorius in town meeting and then in armed combat before the Liberty Pole. Like his literary ancestor

Hudibras, M'Fingal is quarrelsome, boastful, stubborn, one who would bully his opponent into submission in meeting or on the field of battle but never quite succeeds in doing either. *M'Fingal* towers above all other Hudibrastic poems written in America as to largeness of design, artistic control, and invention.

The Postal Act of 1792, which operated to the disadvantage of magazines, forced the *Museum*, like the *Columbian*, (q.v.), to discontinue publication with the December issue. On the last day of the year Carey deplored "the late post-office law, by which the postmaster here [at Philadelphia] has absolutely refused to receive the Museum into the post-office an any terms" (December 1792). But he could draw satisfaction from the fact that during its six-year existence the *Museum* had grown into a respectable anthology of American literature.

## Notes

1. "Autobiography of Mathew Carey," *The New-England Magazine* 6 (January 1834):65, 66.
2. Frank Luther Mott, *A History of American Magazines, 1741–1850* (New York and London: D. Appleton and Company, 1930), p. 30.
3. Lyon N. Richardson, *A History of Early American Magazines, 1741–1789* (1931; rpt. New York: Octagon, 1966), p. 316.
4. Mott, p. 103.
5. Howard Eugene Sylvester, "*The American Museum*, a Study of Prevailing Ideas in Late Eighteenth-Century America" (Ph.D. diss., University of Washington, 1954), p. 351.
6. Alexander Cowie, *John Trumbull: Connecticut Wit* (Chapel Hill: The University of North Carolina Press, 1936), p. 181.

## Information Sources

BIBLIOGRAPHY:
"Autobiography of Mathew Carey," *The New-England Magazine* 5 (November-December 1833): 404–12, 489–96; 6 (January-May 1834), 60–67, 93–106, 227–34, 306–14, 400–408; 7 (July-December 1834), 61–70, 145–48, 239–44, 320–29, 401–6, 481–85.
Mott, Frank Luther. *A History of American Magazines, 1741–1850.* New York and London: D. Appleton and Company, 1930. Pp. 100–103.
Richardson, Lyon N. *A History of Early American Magazines, 1741–1789.* 1931; rpt., New York: Octagon, 1966. Pp.314–34.
Smyth, Albert H. *The Philadelphia Magazines and Their Contributors, 1741–1850.* 1892; rpt. Detroit: Gale, 1970. Pp. 67–73.
Sylvester, Howard Eugene. "*The American Museum*, A Study of Prevailing Ideas in Late Eighteenth-Century America." Ph.D. diss. University of Washington, 1954.
INDEXES: None.
REPRINT EDITIONS: Microfilm edition in *American Periodicals: 18th Century—1800–1850.* Ann Arbor: University Microfilms, 1956. Reels 4–5.
LOCATION SOURCES: Complete runs are widely available, as are partial runs.

## Publication History

MAGAZINE TITLE AND TITLE CHANGES: *The American Museum; or Repository of Ancient and Modern Fugitive Pieces &c. Prose and Poetical.* In January 1789 the title became *The American Museum, or, Universal Magazine: Containing, Essays on Agriculture—Commerce—Manufactures—Politics—Morals—and Manners. Sketches of National Characters—Natural and Civil History—and Biography. Law Information—Public Papers—Intelligence. Moral Tales—Ancient and Modern Poetry, &c. &c.*

VOLUME AND ISSUE DATA: Volumes 1–12, January 1787-December 1792.
FREQUENCY OF PUBLICATION: Monthly.
PUBLISHERS: January 1787-December 1788: Mathew Carey, Philadelphia. January 1789-December 1791: Carey, Stewart and Co., Philadelphia. January-December 1792: Mathew Carey, Philadelphia.
EDITOR: Mathew Carey.

*Bruce Granger*

# THE AMERICAN QUARTERLY REVIEW

In March 1827 in his native city of Philadelphia, Robert Walsh established the *American Quarterly Review*, which, according to Frank Mott, was a "resuscitation" of the *American Review of History and Politics*, edited by Walsh in 1811 and 1812.[1] In the years between the two ventures, Walsh had gained much publishing experience as editor of the *American Register*, the *Museum of Foreign Literature*, and the *National Gazette and Literary Register*, the last a newspaper that he continued to operate along with the new *Review*. He had also expanded his knowledge of literature and the literary world and could boast of the new *Review*'s coverage of literature and its many distinguished reviewers, among them George Ticknor, James Kirke Paulding, and George Bancroft.[2]

Walsh's prospectus made it clear that the *American Quarterly Review* was to be for Philadelphia and its environs what the *North American Review** was for Boston and the Northeast. Philadelphia's talent, according to the prospectus, was rarely employed by *North American Review* proprietors; moreover, there was a need for a journal "established in a central position, more conversant with the productions of the middle, southern, and western parts of the Union, more diversified in its topics and texture, and enriched from domestic sources which are not open to a distant enterprise."[3] The new publication, which would cost five dollars per year, would seek readership in all states and in Europe, would pay its contributors "liberally" (usually at two dollars per page), and would be "truly American in spirit and drift."[4] "Rigorously excluded," vowed the prospectus, would be expressions of "mere party or local politics, polemical theology . . . and whatever tends to disturb essential morals, fundamental Christian faith, or republican theory."[5]

Walsh modeled the quarterly on his favorite English review journals, the *Edinburgh Review* and the *London Quarterly*. Each number of his quarterly contained about 250 octavo pages of essay-reviews, usually ten essays per number, on a wide range of topics. Generally, from one to three articles in a number were devoted to reviewing literature, not only American but English, European, biblical, and classical as well. Often the reviewer would point out what American writers could learn from the literature of older countries, for Walsh and his contributors believed that American literary excellence could be attained by following the best literary models. The "best" for the quarterly's reviewers meant European literature through the neoclassical age, that is, the literature of Dante, Shakespeare, Milton, Pope, Johnson, Addison, and Burns. Throughout most of the *Review*'s run, its reviewers expressed little regard for the new English romantic literature of Wordsworth, Coleridge, and Shelley and were adamant in insisting that good American poetry should not follow this false model.

Several articles stressed the urgent need for an American national literature, presumably based on sound English models but using American subject matter. In the September 1837 number, for example, a review of *York Town, A Historical Romance* complained that American history as subject matter had not been fully depicted. A review of Richard Henry Dana in the March 1828 number insisted that the American continent provided an opportunity and "a vast mass of material" for a truly great literature. And another piece in the December 1827 number exclaimed that "the spirit of poetry is among us" and that we have only to await a truly national poet, an American Homer or Milton.

In addition to its review-essays on literature, the publication included pieces on such topics as politics, science, math, logic, travel, history, biography, music, law, and education. Reviewers were anonymous, although the identity of some, such as Walsh himself and James McHenry, became known almost immediately because of controversy, while the identity of others became known through modern scholarship. Some contributors, however, are still unidentified.[6] The tone of the publication was learned, sure, authoritative. Much background information was provided, and arguments for or against a work were usually presented with many quotations and examples. Critics sometimes called the publication dull—perhaps because of its lengthy articles and sentences—but, as Mott points out, it was probably no more dull than the *North American Review* or the *Edinburgh Review*, and a certain amount of dullness in a serious review was even considered a virtue.[7]

Early in its eleven-year run the publication and its contributors became embroiled in extended controversies. One of these involved criticism of America from abroad. When the *London Quarterly Review* printed articles attacking American political and court systems, American social customs, and the American press, Walsh's *Review*, in June 1828, presented a passionate defense of America. Although admitting that some of the *London Review*'s criticism was fair, it charged that Englishmen have in general "manifested no disposition to engender or reciprocate friendly feeling with us"—this despite the fact that we have a "common ancestry" with them and harbor "no ungenerous hostility" toward them (3:473). Later, in September 1832, the *Review* took issue with Mrs. Trollop's *Domestic Manners of the Americans*, charging that she was scarcely in this country long enough to form her negative opinion and that she neglected the very real accomplishments, such as the comparatively few professional beggars in America. The reviewer's prejudice and bias toward an eighteenth-century idea of order are apparent when he displays pique at the favorable attention Mrs. Trollop gave to an American woman's plan to educate black and white children equally. Mrs. Trollop does not understand, wrote the reviewer, that such a plan goes against "the order of established things" (12:111).

The controversy that gave the *Review* most notoriety, that jeopardized its reputation, and that set Walsh at odds with much of the New York literati involved the publication's assessments of the "new" poetry in America, particularly that of William Cullen Bryant.[8] Although two poetry reviews (by Joseph Hopkinson and George Bancroft) in 1827 caused little stir, one written by Walsh for the September 1829 number established sides in what was to become a protracted battle of periodicals. Reviewing Samuel Kettell's *Specimens of American Poetry*, a vast collection of material printed in America, Walsh found most of it dross, fit neither for publication nor praise.[9] While we ought not to undervalue American writers, Walsh wrote, we ought not to overestimate them either. Walsh's comments were aimed at the New York presses, which, he felt, were blindly chauvinistic in glorifying literature if it was American and especially if its writers were from New York or the Northeast.

Walsh's sentiments were repeated and augmented by his reviewer James McHenry in a March 1832 article entitled "American Lake Poetry." McHenry lamented that just when American poetry was reaching for excellence, poets such as Bryant and N. P. Willis were mistakenly following the "false style" of the English romantics. Our poets, according to the review, "have filled their compositions with epithets without meaning, and sentiment without pathos. They are careless without ease, and laborious without showing polish. Their decorations are tawdry, and impart no elegance to their diction. Their versification is in general sluggish, and often intolerably rugged." And the reviewer adds, "the injudicious praise which these poets have received from pretended friends and sciolous editors of newspapers, has been their great misfortune" (11:154–55).

The review set off a three-year literary war. The *American Quarterly Review*, McHenry, and Walsh were severely criticized in many New York publications (the *New-York Mirror and Ladies' Literary Gazette*,* the *American Monthly Magazine*,* the *Knickerbocker**) for "ruthless" and "indiscriminate" remarks, and especially for their unflattering opinions of Bryant.[10] Walsh retaliated in several articles in the *National Gazette and Literary Register* as well as in further reviews in the *American Quarterly Review*. In June 1834 he published another McHenry review that bemoaned the poor quality of recent American poetry and that again chided New York publishers for damaging the cause of poetry by "indiscriminate eulogy."[11]

Sectional rivalry was in good part responsible for the controversy. On the one side, the New York presses were notorious for their puffery of writers from New York and New England; on the other side, McHenry's March 1832 piece was cold not only to Bryant but to all of New England, which he declared was not the most hospitable area for the production of poetry. The controversy, however, was also about poetic taste and editorial responsibility—that is, about how to encourage a truly American literature, a literature of quality. Throughout Walsh's nine-year reign as editor, the *Review* followed his conservative literary taste, his regard for the old school, and his dislike of "Lake Poetry." Only after Walsh's illness forced him to relinquish control (on 1 January 1836) did the publication, under the editorship of Walsh's son, Robert Moylan Walsh, modify its stance.

A review entitled "American Lyric Poetry" in the March 1836 number and another on "Bryant's Poems" in December 1836 acknowledged Bryant's fame in the United States and abroad, bestowed muted praise on his work, and urged him to reach for grander themes. A more obvious change in stance was adopted in a September 1836 review of Wordsworth. Whereas Wordsworth and the entire Lake School of poetry had been disparaged in earlier numbers, this reviewer, describing an "awakening to the truth," judged Wordsworth's poetry to be of the highest order—truthful, moving, elegant, and highly polished. In other numbers published during the final two years, reviewers softened the publication's earlier criticism of Shelley and Coleridge and even praised much of their philosophy and poetics.

Not all of the *Review*'s literary articles were controversial, of course. Under Walsh's editorship, the *Review* assessed, seriously and intelligently, such writers as Charles Brockden Brown, R. H. Dana, Cooper, Irving, James Gates Percival, and William Dunlap. It reviewed works in many literary genres: the essay, novel, romance, and drama. And throughout it offered suggestions for the establishment of a national literature. Were it not for the controversies that for three years surrounded its poetry reviews, according to Frank Mott, the *American Quarterly Review* would have had a reputation and an importance equal to that of the *North American Review*.[12]

## Notes

1. Frank Luther Mott, "*The American Review* and *The American Quarterly Review*," *A History of American Magazines, 1741–1850* (New York and London: D. Appleton & Co., 1930), pp. 271–72.

2. Although all reviewers were anonymous, Walsh named many of them, without indicating which articles they authored, in the 28 January 1835 issue of the *National Gazette and Literary Register*, and Mott, p. 276, reports that he used a file of authors' names housed in the Cadmus Book Shop, New York.

3. Prospectus of the *American Quarterly Review*, separately printed. (Philadelphia: Carey and Lea, 1827?), p. 1. Copy held at the American Antiquarian Society, Worcester, Mass.

4. Prospectus, p. 2.

5. Prospectus, p. 2.

6. See Ralph M. Aderman, "Contributors to the *American Quarterly Review*, 1827–1833," *Studies in Bibliography* 14 (1961):163–76, and Guy R. Woodall, "More on the Contributors to the *American Quarterly Review* (1827–1837)," *Studies in Bibliography* 23 (1970):199–207.

7. Mott, p. 273.

8. See Guy R. Woodall, "Robert Walsh's War with the New York Literati: 1827–1836," *Tennessee Studies in Literature* 15 (1970):25–47.

9. Walsh's own poetry was not included in Kettell's anthology, which Walsh's review mentioned in passing and which led William Snelling (in *Truth; a New Year's Gift for Scribblers*, Boston, 1831, pp. 48–50) to assume was the primary reason for Walsh's severe criticism. Woodall (in "Robert Walsh's War," p. 45), however, states that "not too much importance should be attached to Snelling's opinion."

10. See Woodall, "Robert Walsh's War," pp. 27–44, for an account of all combatants.

11. Mott, p. 274, notes that McHenry, in charting the decline of American literature, failed to acknowledge the publication of Poe's *Poems* of 1831, as well as works by Bryant, Whittier, Irving, Paulding, Bancroft, David Crockett, James Hall, and Albert Pike.

12. Mott, p. 273.

## Information Sources

BIBLIOGRAPHY:

Aderman, Ralph M. "Contributors to the *American Quarterly Review* 1827–1833." *Studies in Bibliography* 14 (1961):163–76.

Mott, Frank Luther. "The *American Review* and the *American Quarterly Review*." A *History of American Magazines, 1741–1850*. New York and London: D. Appleton & Co., 1930. Pp. 271–76.

Woodall, Guy R. "More on the Contributors to the *American Quarterly Review* (1827–1837)." *Studies in Bibliography* 23 (1970):199–207.

————. "Robert Walsh's War with the New York Literati: 1827–1836." *Tennessee Studies in Literature* 15 (1970):25–47.

INDEXES: None

REPRINT EDITIONS: American Periodicals: Series II, 1800–1850. University Microfilms, Ann Arbor. Reels 298–301.

LOCATION SOURCES: Widely available.

## Publication History

MAGAZINE TITLE AND TITLE CHANGES: *The American Quarterly Review*.

VOLUME AND ISSUE DATA: Volumes 1–22, 1827–1837. Semiannual volumes.

FREQUENCY OF PUBLICATION: Quarterly.

PUBLISHERS: March 1827-June 1829: Carey, Lea, & Carey, Philadelphia. September 1829-December 1832: Carey & Lea, Philadelphia. March-June 1833: Carey, Lea & Blanchard, Philadelphia. September-December 1833: Carey & Lea, Philadelphia. March-December 1834: Key & Biddle, Philadelphia. March-December 1835: Lydia R. Bailey, Printer, Philadelphia. March 1836-December 1837: Adam Waldie, Philadelphia.

EDITORS: Robert Walsh, 1827–1836; Robert Moylan Walsh, 1836–1837.

*Laura Jehn Menides*

# THE AMERICAN REVIEW AND LITERARY JOURNAL.
See THE MONTHLY MAGAZINE, AND AMERICAN REVIEW

**THE AMERICAN REVIEW: A WHIG JOURNAL OF
POLITICS, LITERATURE, ART, AND SCIENCE.** See
THE AMERICAN (WHIG) REVIEW


## THE AMERICAN (WHIG) REVIEW

The *American Review: A Whig Journal of Politics, Literature, Art, and Science*,
later called the *American Whig Review*, was founded, according to its prospectus,
in order to advocate "the permanent maintenance of Whig principles and improvement of American literature."[1] The first number, dated January 1845, was
issued early—at the end of October 1844—as an electioneering device for Henry
Clay, the Whig party's candidate for president against the Democrats' James K.
Polk. Editor of the journal was George H. Colton, who had authored *Tecumseh,
or the West Thirty Years Since*, a narrative poem commemorating Whig hero
William Henry Harrison, and who, according to Frank Mott, wanted again in
the Whig *Review* "to marry politics with literature profitably."[2]

The journal's prospectus declared that it would oppose "pernicious" and "dangerous" policies of the Jacksonian Democrats: usurpation of executive power, refusal to
protect American industry by tariffs, and other "Jacobinical opinions, from which, if
suffered to gain ground, we can look for nothing but the corruption of our morals, the
degradation of our liberties, and the ultimate ruin of the Commonwealth."[3] Fifty-three
Whig members of Congress put their names to the prospectus and applauded its goals,
and of these, sixteen agreed to contribute "communications" for its pages. Among
the latter were Daniel Webster, D. D. Barnard, Robert Winthrop, Hamilton Fish, J. P.
Kennedy, J. R. Ingersoll, and Rufus Choate.

The prospectus made it plain that politics was the journal's first but not its
only concern: "Each number, containing from one hundred and twelve to one
hundred and twenty-eight pages, printed in double columns, on fine paper, will
consist of a leading political article, with a variety of literary miscellany, in
history, biography, criticism, fiction, poetry, statistics, science and the arts."[4]

The second number of the journal, dated February 1845, lamented the defeat of
Henry Clay but insisted that the Whig party was "beaten, not vanquished." The editors asserted that American Whigs more than ever needed an "organ of opinion" to
counter their adversaries' publication, the *Democratic Review* (see *United States
Magazine* and *Democratic Review**). According to the February 1845 note to subscribers, the Whig *Review* would speak for "people in different sections who are alike
opposed to radicalism, corruption and misrule." Under Colton's leadership and with
the political contributions of D. D. Barnard, the journal's stance was conservative,
profoundly nationalistic, and conciliatory between North and South, much in line with
the principles of Henry Clay, the Whigs' great pacificator. In the March 1845 issue
the *Review* opposed the immediate annexation of Texas because it would upset the
balance between slave and nonslave states; in the January 1846 issue it bemoaned

European interference on the American continent; and in several numbers it advocated tariffs for the protection of the American economy.

The journal's literature and literary criticism also reflected Colton's conservatism and nationalism. But Perry Miller notes that in the Whig *Review* conservatism in literature meant "not so much devotion to Clay's American System as a stylistic sanity," or a "stabilization of public taste against anarchical shifts of fashion," for the journal published work not only by Whigs but also by Democrats and radicals who "conformed to its stylistic code."[5] Thus, although the writings of Emerson and of most other transcendentalists offended Colton's taste and sense of truth and propriety, he did publish Edgar Allan Poe, Walt Whitman, and James Russell Lowell, writers whose works appeared in Democratic journals, including the *Democratic Review*, at the same time.

Colton published "The Raven" in the February 1845 number (with the byline "___ Quarles") and prefaced it with glowing words about "one of the most felicitous specimens of unique rhyming which has for some time met our eye." The poem also appeared on 29 January, a few days before the *Review*'s publication, in the *Evening Mirror*, which did attribute it to Poe. Colton's *Review* published several other Poe pieces, including criticism, fiction, and poetry: Poe's review of American drama in August 1845, "Some Words with A Mummy" and two poems in April 1845, and "Ulalume" in 1847. Colton and Poe were "antagonistic," according to some reports, which Mott suggests were exaggerated.[6] Certainly the two had ample opportunity to assess each other's work. Colton did so in selecting which of Poe's submissions would be published and reviewed in his journal, and Poe did so as well in an 1846 essay, which declared, "I cannot conscientiously call Mr. Colton a good editor, although I think that he will finally be so." According to Poe, Colton was a bit too timid, too lacking in "fire," and too much impressed by Puritan literature. And, Poe continued, although *Tecumseh* suffered from being too long, some of Colton's "shorter compositions . . . have afforded indications even of genius."[7]

Among Colton's selections for publication in the *Review* were Lowell's "Orpheus" (1:1845) and some of Whitman's early fiction. "The Boy-Lover" and "The Death of Wind-Foot," highly romantic tales of young love and of Indian intertribal vengeance, were published anonymously in the May and June 1845 issues, although the index to volume 1 acknowledged their author to be "Walter Whitman." These contributions to a Whig publication brought Whitman some criticism later in the *Brooklyn Daily Advertiser* (3 and 5 April 1847), which asked whether "the editor of the *Eagle* was a Whig some few seasons before he was hired to write locofoco editorials for the *Eagle*." Other writers who contributed to the Whig *Review* included Frances Osgood, Alfred B. Street, Mrs. E. F. Ellet, Colton himself, and James D. Whelpley, the last two sometimes using the pseudonyms Earlden and Cyonides.

Under Colton's leadership (1845–1847), the journal's literary criticism was, as Frank Mott puts it, "vigorous, and rather belligerent." Aside from Colton and Poe, George W. Peck wrote many long reviews. In February 1848 Peck criticized Longfellow's "Evangeline" as lacking in "consonance between the form and the substance." He quotes Longfellow's passage about stars being "the thoughts of God in the heaven," calls it "naughty," and states, "we fear we will never meet Mr. Longfellow in the place he mentions, if he allows himself to use such expressions" (n.s.1:164). In the April 1846 number Melville's *Typee* was judged "plain and unpretending, but racy and pointed." R. H. Dana, William Beckford, John Greenleaf Whittier, and Nathaniel Hawthorne were reviewed, as were American visual artists, actors, and performances. Collections and editions, such as Rufus Griswold's *Prose and Poetry in America*, were scrutinized as well.

In several long and thoughtful articles on the state of American literature and culture, the Whig *Review* took stock of American authors and asked probing questions about what makes American literature unique. Frequently, as in a February 1845 piece, the *Review* called for a national literature and for a fellowship of American writers.

Although the journal sought to promote and to promulgate American literature and to protect American authors by international copyright, it was not patronizing but rather demanded high quality and originality in American writing. Nor did the journal ignore classical, British, and Continental writers. In its pages, readers could find critical pieces on such authors as Horace, Shakespeare, Goethe, Wordsworth, Coleridge, George Sand, and Elizabeth and Robert Browning.

Under Colton's editorship, the Whig *Review* was particularly critical of Emerson, Carlyle, German mysticism, and American transcendentalism. A March 1845 article quoted and disparaged passages from the *Dial** (Boston) magazine and called transcendentalism "partial" and "inadequate," a philosophy that "sinks God and Nature in Man." Another piece, in volume 3, 1846, offered several further debunking definitions of the term: "metaphysical bombast," "pseudo-poetry," and "any absurd or incomprehensible notion that pretends to an unusual refinement or spirituality."

Throughout its eight-year run, the Whig *Review* earned notice and respect for its practice of paying its writers, usually at the rate of one or two dollars per page. It also became well known for its biographies and its fine engraved portraits of national leaders such as John Quincy Adams and Benjamin West. Its drama and fiction were usually well received at the time but today seem less than exceptional.[8] An important feature of nearly every issue was "Critical Notices," that is, short reviews of books on a wide variety of subjects by American and non-American authors. The January 1846 number, for example, reviewed J. Fenimore Cooper's *Lives of Distinguished Naval Officers*, Percy Shelley's *Poetical Works*, and Bunyan's treatises, as well as books about mineral springs, game shooting, German criminal trials, and the French Reformation. And despite the publication's chauvinistic attitude toward America, it did not hesitate to criticize bad writing. An example is one work that it called "very patriotic and very poor."

In December 1847 the *Review* was well established and growing in reputation and circulation[9] when Colton, only thirty years old, died of typhus. The January

1848 number came out as a new series with a new title, a new typeface, and new editor and publisher. James D. Whelpley, contributor of poetry and criticism under Colton, took over as editor, and I. C. Colton and J. Priestly became "administrators" of the newly named *American Review: A Whig Journal Devoted to Politics and Literature*. Barnard continued to write political articles and Peck to supply reviews and publication continued at 118 Nassau Street.[10]

The journal had a change of name again during 1850 (to the *American Whig Review*) and a change of editor in 1851 when Whelpley left to pursue projects in Honduras. Although the new editor is never named, Mott gives good evidence for his being George W. Peck during the journal's final two years, 1851–1852." These and other changes (Barnard left in 1850 to become minister to Prussia, and during 1852 several contributors resigned over questions of quality and policy) signaled a loss in the publication's initial singlemindedness and direction.

Other factors, however, contributed to the journal's demise. First was the competition it received from *Harper's Monthly Magazine*,* which prospered by pirating and reprinting, without payment, literature by European writers. In contrast, the Whig *Review* sought out and paid native writers. A July 1852 Whig *Review* article openly criticized *Harper's* for practices that kept American writers in poverty and jeopardized American periodicals. Plainly, the economic competition from *Harper's* was severe not only for the Whig journal, but also, ironically, for its rival *Democratic Review*. In its final year the Whig *Review* attempted to increase revenues. It accepted more advertising in its pages, and it tried to increase subscriptions by lowering its price from $5 to $3 per year. Neither measure was able to forestall the end.

The second important reason for the *Review*'s demise was that its fortunes were linked to those of the Whig party, which tried, against all odds, to keep the question of slavery from dividing the country. The Whig *Review* never took a firm stand on the slavery issue, but instead prided itself on presenting articles giving both Northern and Southern points of view (only to be criticized by both). Shortly after the Whig party was defeated in 1852, the *Review* ceased publication. Its subscription list was sold to *Putnam's Monthly Magazine*.*[12]

## Notes

1. "Prospectus of The American Review: A Whig Journal of Politics, Literature, Art and Science," separately printed. (New York: July 1844), p. 1. Copy held at the American Antiquarian Society, Worcester, Mass.

2. Frank Luther Mott, *"The American Whig Review," A History of American Magazines, 1741–1850* (New York and London: D. Appleton & Co., 1930), p. 751.

3. "Prospectus," pp. 1–2.

4. "Prospectus," p. 2.

5. Perry Miller, *The Raven and the Whale* (Westport, Conn.: Greenwood Press, 1973), pp. 122–23.

6. Mott, p. 751, n. 4.

7. From *Edgar Allan Poe: Essays and Reviews* (New York: Library of America, 1984), pp. 1122–23.

8. See, for example, a review in the *New York Rover* 5 (31 May 1845):176. See also the October 1852 number of the *American Whig Review* for an article that reprints several favorable reviews of the publication.

9. See Mott, p. 753, and n. 8 and 9.

10. During 1848 and 1849, no publisher's name was listed in the journal or on the cover sheet. Mott assumes that the publisher was D. W. Holly, but that name did not appear until 1850. Starting in April 1852 Champion Bissell was listed as publisher.

11. Mott, p. 753 and n. 7. Mott is mistaken in saying that Whelpley was "nowhere named." Although not listed in the journal, his name did appear prominently on the sheets of the separate numbers. Peck, however was not named in the numbers or on the cover sheets.

12. Mott, p. 420.

## Information Sources

BIBLIOGRAPHY:

Hart, James D. "The American Whig Review." *The Oxford Companion to American Literature*. New York: Oxford University Press, 1983. P. 29.

Mott, Frank Luther. "*The American Whig Review*." *A History of American Magazines, 1741–1850*. New York and London: D. Appleton & Co., 1930. Pp. 750–54.

Perkins, H. C. "The Defense of Slavery in the Northern Press on the Eve of the Civil War." *Journal of Southern History* 9 (November 1943):501–31.

Robinson, E. B. "The Dynamics of American Journalism from 1787 to 1865." *Pennsylvania Magazine of History and Biography* 61 (October 1937):435–45.

INDEXES: None

REPRINT EDITIONS: American Periodicals: Series II, 1800–1850. University Microfilms, Ann Arbor. Reels 302–4.

LOCATION SOURCES: Widely available.

## Publication History

MAGAZINE TITLE AND TITLE CHANGES: *The American Review: A Whig Journal of Politics, Literature, Art, and Science*, January 1845-December 1847. *The American Review: A Whig Journal Devoted to Politics and Literature*, January 1848-April 1850. *The American Whig Review*, May 1850-December 1852.

VOLUME AND ISSUE DATA: First series, volumes 1–6, 1845–1847; second series, volumes 1–10 (whole numbers 7–16), 1848–1852. Semiannual volumes.

FREQUENCY OF PUBLICATION: Monthly.

PUBLISHERS: January-July 1845: Wiley and Putnam, New York. July 1845-December 1847: George H. Colton, New York. January 1848-April 1950: Published at 118 Nassau Street, New York, D. W. Holly(?), New York. May 1850-December 1851: D. W. Holly, New York. January-March 1852: Published at 120 Nassau Street, New York. April-December 1852: Champion Bissell, New York.

EDITORS: George H. Colton, 1845–1847; James D. Whelpley, 1848–1850; George W. Peck (?), 1851–1852.

*Laura Jehn Menides*

# THE ANALECTIC MAGAZINE

From January 1809 to December 1812 the *Select Reviews, and Spirit of the Foreign Magazines* (whose title changed to *Select Reviews of Literature, and Spirit of Foreign Magazines* in July 1811) was edited in Philadelphia by Enos Bronson and his successor Samuel Ewing. Late in 1812, Moses Thomas, a Philadelphia bookseller, bought the magazine and changed both title and editor.

According to Thomas's plans, the *Analectic Magazine* appeared in January 1813 under the editorship of Washington Irving. "I mentioned in former letters," wrote Irving to his brother Peter on 30 December 1812, "that I had undertaken to conduct the Select Reviews at a salary of 1,500 dollars."[1] Much like the *Select Reviews*, the *Analectic* depended heavily on reprinted articles and reviews from leading British periodicals, and so Irving's task could initially seem to him "an amusing occupation, without any mental responsibility of consequence. I felt very much the want of some such task in my idle hours; there is nothing so irksome as having nothing to do."[2]

The *Analectic*'s masthead suggested the extent and nature of Irving's duties. The subtitle indicated the contents: *Containing Selections from Foreign Reviews and Magazines, of such Articles as are Most Valuable Curious or Entertaining*. The epigraph stated the guiding principle: "The wheat from these publications should, from time to time, be winnowed, and the chaff throw away." Thus, the magazine included poetry selections by Lord Byron, Sir Walter Scott, and Robert Southey and prose selections by David Hume, Oliver Goldsmith, and David Garrick. It also featured reprinted travel and familiar essays, as well as numerous reprinted reviews and criticism.[3]

Nonetheless, in his two years as editor, Irving did contribute a good deal of original material. He reviewed the works of Robert Treat Paine; a collection of odes, naval songs, and poems by Edwin C. Holland; James Kirke Paulding's *Lay of the Scottish Fiddle*; and a collection of Byron's poetry. Irving likewise wrote two short pieces ("Traits of Indian Characters" and "Philip of Pokanoket"), which he later incorporated into his *Sketch Book*, and he contributed a series of biographies of naval heroes of the War of 1812—James Lawrence, William Burrows, Oliver Perry, and David Porter. The *Analectic* was not alone in this celebration of national military figures, and Irving especially delighted in his sketches "of that choice band of gallant spirits who had borne up the drowning honor of their country by the very locks."[4] In addition to his own work, Irving solicited contributions from Gulian Verplanck and Paulding.

Irving, however, soon grew weary of his editorial duties. As he admitted in one article, "I do not profess the art and mystery of reviewing, and am not ambitious of being wise or facetious at the expense of others."[5] On 21 October 1814, Irving wrote to Moses Thomas that "as I have not been able to attend to the work of late, I shall not insist of full pay for the subsequent months; and am afraid that I shall have to give up all formal agency in the work after the close of the year."[6]

Shortly after Irving's decision, the *Analectic* encountered serious financial difficulties. On 15 January 1815, Irving wrote to his brother William that "on arriving in Philadelphia I find that Bradford and Inskeep have failed and ruined poor Moses Thomas, the bookseller who publishes the Analectic."[7] An advertisement appeared in the 7 January 1815 issue of the *New York Evening Post* stating that "owning to untoward circumstances, the Magazine for January will not be ready for delivery."[8] Although he had relinquished his editorial position, Irving felt the magazine should not be allowed to fail. As he wrote to Gulian Verplanck, Irving believed that Thomas "is considered an industrious, obliging meritorious man," and the *Analectic*'s "circulation is so extensive & the Subscription list so valuable that it is worth while to maintain such a channel of literary information."[9] With Irving and Verplanck's assistance, Thomas was able to continue the magazine, but under a new editor.

In January 1815, Irving wrote that he had suggested Verplanck as a replacement: "I at the same time told him [Thomas] that I thought it probable you [Verplanck] would be willing to continue the Editor provided you were secured in a proper compensation for the irksome labor of the business."[10] Although Verplanck may have previously assisted Irving, he never did assume the editorship, and Thomas turned to Thomas Isaac Wharton.

Wharton, a native Philadelphian and graduate of the University of Pennsylvania, had practiced law and served in the Washington Guards during the War of 1812 prior to assuming the editor's chair. He was among Joseph Dennie's circle of friends and had contributed to both the *Port Folio** and the *Analectic*. It is not entirely clear when (or if) Wharton left the *Analectic*, but after the magazine's demise in 1821, Wharton continued his flourishing law practice and legal writing and was a member of the American Philosophical Society, the Library and Atheneum companies, and the Historical Society of Pennsylvania.

Under Wharton's industrious leadership the *Analectic* increased the number of original contributions, maintained its series of literary reviews and survey articles, and continued its distinctive monthly illustrations—including copper and wood engravings and lithography. In September 1815, Wharton began a history of the United States Navy and beginning with the January 1816 issue added *Naval Chronicle* to the magazine's title.

The *Analectic* maintained its character (and apparently its subscription list) through 1819. In January 1820, however, the *Analectic* added a new subtitle (*Comprising Original Reviews, Biography, Analytical Abstracts of new publications, Translations from the French journals, and Selections from the most esteemed British periodicals works, &c*) and began a new series (monthly issues, gathered in semiannual volumes). In February the publisher announced an "improved style of exterior appearance and embellishment," with two engravings in each issue and paper and typography "more elegant than has heretofore been exhibited in periodical publications."[11] The publisher likewise requested "the patronage of the American people to remunerate the expense of this, now, very elegant publication." The engravings in the first volume (January-June 1820) included illustrations of the lighthouse at Cape Henlopen, Jefferson's natural bridge in Virginia, a view of the capital, a bird's eye view of Congress Hall, the president's house, a portrait of Henry Clay, and six others. The articles continued to include travel essays (e.g., a voyage to South America, Yellow Stone expedition, Dodwell's tour in Greece) and literary reviews and criticism ("British Notices of American Literature," Croatian literature, "Mrs. Heman's Poems") with additional material drawn from American agriculture and business, British society and manners, and French customs and letters.

In the December 1820 issue, however, a prospectus appeared for a new magazine: *The Literary Gazette; or, Journal of Criticism, Science, and the Arts, being a Third Series of the Analectic Magazine.* "Experience has demonstrated to the editors of various magazines which have at different times appeared in the United States," began the prospectus, "that monthly journals are not popular with our reading public" (n.s. 2:509). "For many purposes," the prospectus continues, "a monthly journal is too brief, for many others its periods of return are too remote" (n.s. 2:510). James Maxwell, the publisher who would continue this third series of the *Analectic*, promised a weekly quarto journal of sixteen pages, by which "the editors will be enabled to give more than twice as much matter during the year." (n.s. 2:510). Wharton remained as editor, and he cited as his aim to provide "some account of the most promising new publications immediately after, and sometimes before their appearance in public, interesting extracts from others, abridgements of the most valuable articles in foreign and domestic journals, proceedings of learned or useful societies, discoveries in science, improvements or inventions in the arts, essays on men and manners" (n.s. 2:510). Wharton also promised abstracts of congressional and state legislative acts, an analytical account of the chief articles in leading British, French, and American periodicals, and selections from fifteen British journals (including the *Edinburgh Review, Blackwood's, Constable's,* and the *London Literary Gazette*) regularly received by the publishers. Thus, at the end of 1820 the *Analectic* yielded to the *Literary Gazette*, whose first issue appeared in January 1821.

The *Literary Gazette* was in fact a weekly (or "weakly," as A. H. Smythe noted)[12] continuation of the *Analectic*, explicitly modeled on the *London Literary Gazette.* It included sections of original and selected poetry, biography, travel, book reviews, essays, and miscellaneous extracts, anecdotes, and literary notices. As the year wore on, the number of reprinted selections increased. The subscription list never did approximate that of the *Analectic* in its earlier versions, and the last issue was dated 29 December 1821.

## Notes

1. Washington Irving, *Letters*, vol. 1, *1802–1823*, ed. Ralph Aderman et al. (Boston: Twayne, 1978), p. 350.

2. Irving, *Letters*, pp. 350–51.

3. For more detailed list of contents, see entry for the *Analectic* in Jayne Kribbs, *An Annotated Bibliography of American Literary Periodicals, 1741–1850* (Boston: G. K. Hall, 1977), p. 15.

4. Pierre Irving, *The Life and Letters of Washington Irving* (1863; rpt., Detroit: Gale, 1967), p. 300.

5. Irving, *Life*, pp. 299–300.

6. Irving, *Letters*, p. 382.

7. Irving, *Letters*, p. 385.

8. Irving, *Letters*, p. 385.

9. Irving, *Letters*, p. 385.

10. Irving, *Letters*, p. 386.

11. This announcement appeared in an unpaginated insert in the February 1820 issue. It is bound as the first page, unnumbered, of volume 1 second series, 1820.

12. Quoted in Frank L. Mott, *A History of American Magazines, 1741–1850* (New York: D. Appleton and Company, 1930), pp. 282–83.

## Information Sources

BIBLIOGRAPHY:

Hedges, William L. *Washington Irving: An American Study, 1802–1832*. Baltimore: Johns Hopkins University Press, 1965.

Irving, Pierre. *The Life and Letters of Washington Irving*. New York: G. P. Putnam, 1863; rpt., Detroit: Gale, 1967.

Irving, Washington. *Letters*, volume 1, *1802–1823*. Ed. Ralph Aderman et al. Boston: Twayne, 1978.

McCloskey, John C. "The Campaign of Periodicals After the War of 1812 for National American Literature." *PMLA* 50 (1935): 262–73.

Mott, Frank Luther. *A History of American Magazines, 1741–1850*. New York: D. Appleton and Company, 1930, Pp. 179–283.

Williams, Stanley T. *The Life of Washington Irving*. 2 vols. 1935; rpt., New York: Octagon Books, 1971.

INDEXES: No complete index available, although the *Analectic* is indexed in Poole's and is included in Kribbs' *Annotated Bibliography*.

REPRINT EDITIONS: American Periodicals: Series II, 1800–1850. University Microfilms, Ann Arbor. Reels 61–64.

LOCATION SOURCES: Widely available.

## Publication History

MAGAZINE TITLE AND TITLE CHANGES: *The Analectic Magazine, Containing Selections from Foreign Reviews and Magazines, of Such Articles as Are Most Valuable, Curious, or Entertaining*. January 1813 to December 1814; *The Analectic Magazine, Containing Selections from Foreign Reviews and Magazines, Together with Original Miscellaneous Compositions*, January 1815 to December

1815; *The Analectic Magazine and Naval Chronicle*, January 1816-December
1819; *The Analectic Magazine, Comprising Original Reviews, Biography, Analytical Abstracts of New Publications, Translations from French Journals, and Selections from the Most Esteemed British Reviews*, January 1820 to December 1820;
*The Literary Gazette: or, Journal of Criticism, Science, and the Arts. Being a Col-
lection of Original and Selected Essays*, 6 January 1821 to 29 December 1821.
VOLUME AND ISSUE DATA: First Series, volumes 1–14, January 1813-December
     1819; second series, volumes 1–2, January-December 1820; third series, volume
     1, January-December 1821.
FREQUENCY OF PUBLICATION: Monthly (*Analectic*); weekly (*Literary Gazette*).
PUBLISHERS: January 1813-December 1819, Moses Thomas, Philadelphia. January
     1820-December 1821, James Maxwell, Philadelphia.
EDITORS: Washington Irving, January 1813-December 1814; Thomas Isaac Wharton,
     January 1815-December 1821(?).

*Timothy K. Conley*


# APPLETONS' JOURNAL


In the immediate post-Civil War years, the publishing firm of D. Appleton &
Co. was one of the country's most prosperous, known particularly for its great
*New American Cyclopedia* and extensive line of scientific publications and school
and college texts.[1] But wishing to broaden and extend its reputation as a general
publisher, Appleton & Co. considered establishing "a weekly paper of a literary
and artistic character" to bring it the same "business value" as "*Harper's
Weekly*, or as *Every Saturday*, then published by Ticknor & Fields," brought
to their respective firms. At the same time, Edward Livingston Youmans, the
Appletons' editorial advisor on scientific subjects, was urging that the company
establish a "magazine which should deal with scientific subjects in such a way
as to educate the people."[2] The resulting magazine, *Appletons' Journal of Popular Literature, Science and Art*, was a compromise, an attempt to combine the
usual features of a literary periodical aimed at a large audience—fiction and
poetry, generous illustrations, familiar essays and reviews—with a new emphasis
on "valuable information," particularly in science. *Appletons' Journal* would
both entertain and instruct.

The Appletons installed Youmans as editor. The leading American expositor
of scientific ideas and champion of the cause of scientific education, he welcomed
the position as a means not only of informing the people of the latest discoveries
and theories but also of introducing them to a new way of thinking. In "What
We Mean By Science," published in the first number, 3 April 1869, he explained
that science means "to know *accurately*. . . . In the course of time and experience,
knowledge slowly passes from the indefinite to the definite, from the vague to
the precise. . . . Science may be defined as the higher or more perfect stage of
developing knowledge." He claimed that the mental discipline of science is "the
best preparation for action in all circumstances of responsibility" (1:23).

Youman's biographer, John Fiske, has written that "in such a novel enterprise the publishers were haunted by a nervous dread of boring the general reader" by including too much science.[3] Apparently they had reason, for, as Youmans wrote to Herbert Spencer in England, the "bare announcement" that the new journal would include "science and valuable thought raised an almost universal condemnation of it in advance as a certain failure."[4] It appears that while Youmans was nominally in charge, the Appletons—either directly or through their literary manager, Oliver Bell Bunce—retained final authority and allowed precious little science to enter their popular journal. The focus of the opening number was Victor Hugo, whose novel *The Man Who Laughs* began a long serialized run in the *Journal*. An illustrated essay praised Hugo not for the scientific precision of his thought, but for being "figurative and imaginative to the utmost license of language" (1:12). The opening number also included poetry by William Cullen Bryant and R. H. Stoddard, an essay by Eugene Benson, a short story, such columns as "Literary Notes" and "Table-Talk," and an elaborate foldout "cartoon" showing expensive carriages and their fashionable occupants promenading in Central Park. In addition to "What We Mean By Science," the only articles dealing even remotely with science were "Why We Sleep" by W. A. Hammond and a piece by Youmans titled, appropriately enough, "Adulteration and Its Remedies." The pattern of giving limited attention to science while featuring serializations of foreign novels persisted, and Youmans resigned after the first year. In 1872 he would establish *Popular Science Monthly* and through it carry on in unadulterated form his "crusade for scientific autonomy and respectability."[5] The extraordinary popularity of this magazine surprised both Youmans and the Appletons, who published it.

Robert Carter succeeded Youmans, serving as editor for two years (1870–1872). He was followed by Bunce and Charles Henry Jones, who ran the magazine jointly until its demise in 1881. It became a monthly in 1876. Of all the editors it was Bunce who most influenced the personality of *Appletons' Journal*. Admittedly opinionated, Bunce had been involved with the magazine from the outset, and he seems to have written the greatest number of the editor's "Table-Talk" columns.[6]

While careful to avoid partisan politics and religious controversies, *Appletons'*, both through timely articles and the editor's "Table-Talk" column, managed to touch upon many of the important questions of the day. As Frank Luther Mott has observed, *Appletons'* "furnished a better picture of the varied life of the times" than almost any other magazine published after the Civil War.[7] But clearly it painted its "picture" of the contemporary world from the point of view of the conservative middle-class urbanites who were its primary audience. For instance, in July 1873, taking note of charges that America had entered a "Period of Greed," the editor defended greed as a "powerful motor in civilization. Selfish desires and the thirst for gain have led to the discovery of continents, have populated the wildernesses, have covered the sea with ships, and the land with roads, have led to innumerable discoveries and inventions, have made civilization what it is" (10:89–90). *Appletons'* employed just this concept

of "civilization" to justify the removal of the "savage" Indians from before
the westward march of "progress" as white America settled the West. Taking
note of the "wanton destruction of the buffalo" on the western plains, the editor
lamented the waste to the East of potentially valuable foodstuffs and then observed that the most important consequence would be to deprive the nomadic
and intractable Indian of his primary source of food. But since the "Indians
have shown no disposition to abandon their vagrant habits" and are "unwilling
to stoop to manual labor," *Appletons'* saw no reason to interfere with the slaugh-
ter of the buffalo: "Bison and savage are traveling rapidly the road to extinction
and the child is born to whom both will be almost as much an object of curiosity
in our country as the elephant is now" (9:26). "Notwithstanding logic, notwithstanding even fairness," the editor opposed female suffrage (10:217) and
opposed as well the proposed expenditure of municipal funds to develop a public
beach on Coney Island because to do so might encourage the poor to look to
the government for assistance and not depend on their own efforts. "The poor
can never be bettered by coddling," he affirmed (11:824–25). Apparently, few
readers of *Appletons'* were disposed to quarrel with such an assertion.

At the same time the editors sought to entice and flatter their prosperous
readers with images of the fashionable life. The editor could not imagine anything
more "stirring, more vivid or more brilliant" than the procession in Central
Park of the expensive carriages and their fashionable occupants, which it pictured
in the foldout cartoon in its opening number. He termed these carriages an apt
symbol of the "wealth, luxury and taste" of New York. *Appletons' Journal* was
edited to cater to that taste. To accompany Winslow Homer's sketch of young
women playing croquet entitled "Summer in the Country," Bunce wrote, "What
should we do without our vacations? How could we endure the monotony of
professional labors, or of city occupations, if the summer months every year did
not seduce us into the fields and mounts" (1:465). It was not necessary for
Bunce to provide an antecedent for "we."

For its readers the *Journal* developed a miscellaneous mixture of light fiction
and poetry; travel articles; sketches of notable figures; articles on science; discussions of books, music, and theatre; and the editor's "Table-Talk." In early
volumes its fiction was largely imported from England, with novels by Mrs.
Oliphant, Dickens (*Edwin Drood*), Trollope (*Ralph the Heir*), and others serialized concurrently with their publication in English monthlies (1:474). Over the
years, however, *Appletons'* came to publish more fiction by American writers,
including Constance Fenimore Woolson, Christian Reid, Julian Hawthorne, Horace Scudder, and Nora Perry. Other contributors included R. H. Stoddard, Paul
Hamilton Hayne, John Esten Cooke, J. Henry Browne, "M.E.W.S." (Mrs.
Sherwood), Joel Benton, George M. Towle, and John Burroughs. Essays were
kept short, and nothing was particularly demanding.

In 1870 *Appletons' Journal* began its "Picturesque America" series. It sent
the artist Harry Fenn on a tour of the Southern states, and his sketches of
picturesque views, accompanied by descriptive essays, met with such popularity

that the series was expanded to include other sections of the country. Before long the publishers determined to produce a full "Pictorial Delineation of the Mountains, Rivers, Lakes, Forests, Water-falls, Shores, Canyons, Valleys, Cities, and other Picturesque Features of our Country," and the project had to be taken from the magazine, which evidently could not generate the revenues necessary to support such an expensive undertaking.[8] The publisher claimed that the resulting two-volume set, *Picturesque America; or, The Land We Live In*, was nothing less than "the greatest work of the kind ever produced in the world," and it was sold in part by subscription. *Picturesque America* was an enormous success with sales, according to one source, of "nearly a million sets."[9] William Cullen Bryant's name appeared on the title page as editor, but *Picturesque America* was in fact under Bunce's editorial supervision. The work is an apt symbol of American nationalism in the post-Civil War years. Symbolically, it brought the South back into the Union and, in fact, unified the entire country by presenting it all from a single aesthetic perspective. But it was a perspective made possible by the railroad, that apt expression of the capitalist civilization of the East, which was transforming the virgin places of the continent and uprooting the aboriginal inhabitants, even while Appleton's artists and writers were focusing attention on its pretty features. Although the series outgrew the physical confines of *Appletons' Journal*, *Picturesque America* remains an expression of its cultural and political vision of America.

As might be expected, the publishers, at the conclusion of the first volume, announced "the complete success of *Appletons' Journal*." They promised that "no pains or expense will be spared to render *Appletons' Journal* in every way valuable and attractive." But it is clear that the "success" of the weekly was something less than "complete," and it would be necessary for the editors to spare some expenses. First, they reduced the number and quality of illustrations; after the first few years, the reader is unable to find reproductions of paintings by such notable American artists as J. F. Kensett, Homer, J. M. Hart, A. F. Bellows, and W. F. Haseltine, whose work appeared in the first volume. The editors eliminated the elaborate foldout cartoons that grace the early volumes. Evidently as a weekly *Appletons' Journal* was not able to make much headway in competing with *Harper's Weekly*, its major competitor. As a monthly it could not compete with *Harper's Monthly** or *Scribner's Monthly,** which dominated the field. The magazine's uncertain start contributed to its failure to build the sort of extensive subscription list that was necessary to support its ambitious plans. Further, despite its work in publicizing the picturesque in all of America, it remained, as Mott has well noted, "distinctively of New York," and so never developed the national appeal necessary to sustain a magazine with its ambitions.[10] As a monthly it became ever more miscellaneous and so had lost its identity well before its demise in December 1881.

### Notes

1. Anonymous, "Sketches of the Publishers: D. Appleton & Co.," *Round Table* 3 (13 January 1866):26–27.

2. John Fiske, *Edward Livingston Youmans: Interpreter of Science for the People* (New York: D. Appleton & Co., 1894), p. 255.

3. Fiske, p. 259.

4. Letter dated 27 April 1869, quoted in Fiske, p. 260.

5. For an analysis of Youmans's work as editor, see William Leverette, Jr., "E. Y. Youmans' Crusade for Scientific Autonomy and Respectability," *American Quarterly* 17 (1965):12–32.

6. Bunce writes in the preface to *Bachelor's Bluff*, a collection of informal essays on such subjects as poetry, realism in art, nudity in art, domestic bliss, and woman's rights, that "Habitual readers of *Appletons' Journal*, who may chance upon this volume, will find in it many things with which they are already familiar." Needless to say, Bunce adopted a conservative stance on all these issues, opposing realism, woman's rights, Walt Whitman, nudity in art, and the provision of governmental services to the poor.

7. Frank Luther Mott, "*Appletons' Journal*," *A History of American Magazines*, 4 vols. (Cambridge, Mass.: Belknap Press of Harvard University Press, 1957), 3:417.

8. Taken from an advertisement that appeared in *Appletons' Journal*, n.s., 2 (January 1877):11.

9. Frank E. Comparato, "D. Appleton & Company," *Publishers for Mass Entertainment in Nineteenth Century America*, ed. Madeleine B. Stern (Boston: G. K. Hall, 1980), p. 19.

10. Mott, 420.

## Information Sources

BIBLIOGRAPHY:

Comparato, John. "D. Appleton & Company." *Publishers for Mass Entertainment in Nineteenth Century America*. Ed. Madeleine B. Stern. Boston: G. K. Hall, 1980.

Fiske, John. *Edward Livingston Youmans: Interpreter of Science for the People*. New York: D. Appleton & Co., 1894.

Mott, Frank Luther. "*Appletons' Journal*." *A History of American Magazines*. 4 vols. Cambridge, Mass.: Belknap Press of Harvard University Press, 1957. 3:417–21.

INDEXES: None

REPRINT EDITIONS: American Periodicals: Series III, 1850–1900. University Microfilms, Ann Arbor. Reels 244–49. Bell & Howell, Micro Photo Division.

LOCATION SOURCES: Widely available.

## Publication History

MAGAZINE TITLE AND TITLE CHANGES: *Appletons' Journal of Literature, Science and Art*, 1869–June 1876. *Appletons' Journal: A Monthly Miscellany of Popular Literature*, July 1876–1878. *Appletons' Journal: A Magazine of General Literature*, 1878–1881.

VOLUME AND ISSUE DATA: Volume 1, 3 April 1869–14 August 1869; volume 2, 21 August 1869–25 December 1869; volumes 3–15, 1870–26 June 1876; new series, volumes 1–11, July 1876–1881.

FREQUENCY OF PUBLICATION: Weekly, 2 April 1869–26 June 1876; monthly, July 1876–1881.

PUBLISHER: D. Appleton & Company, New York.

EDITORS: Edward Livingston Youmans, 1869–1870; Robert Carter, 1870–1872; Oliver Bell Bunce and Charles Henry Jones, 1872–1881.

*Robert J. Scholnick*

# ARCTURUS, A JOURNAL OF BOOKS AND OPINION

Arcturus is the name assigned to the star of the constellation of Boötes that blazes brightest of the stars in the northern night sky.[1] Arcturus is also the name that Evert A. Duyckinck and Cornelius Mathews chose for the organ that would speak for Young America. The choice of the magazine's name was indicative of the editors' ambitions. Both men hoped that *Arcturus, A Journal of Books and Opinion* would not only be the "bright and particular star of New York culture,"[2] but that it would also provide a means of enlightening all of America. The Young Americans were, after all, spokesmen for American nationalism, and the overly zealous Mathews realized the power of the press to further their cause. As Perry Miller states in *The Raven and the Whale*, Mathews was a "vociferous, incessant, obnoxious preacher of literary nationalism."[3]

The nurturing of literary nationalism, however, was not the only purpose of *Arcturus*. Frank Luther Mott notes in his history of American magazines that the monthly was also intended for "the cultivation of good literature, honest mirth, and truth."[4] *Arcturus* attempted to realize its high aims by combining both review and popular magazine material. In an appeal for patronage to readers and subscribers, the editor claims *Arcturus* contains "no line in its pages that is not meant for the humblest reader as well as the highest" (1:160), but most of the work appears to be best suited for the "highest" reader. A "Fine Arts" section covered the theater and painting. "The Loiterer" reviewed new publications, and "The City Article" addressed such topics of concern to the city as crime and capital punishment. Fewer lines were given to features such as "Table Talk" and "American Landscape Gardening," which treated subjects somewhat less important.

The high ideals of the editors could not keep *Arcturus* in print. The first number of the short-lived magazine is dated December 1840 and the last May 1842, but during these few months, Duyckinck and Mathews procured from contributors of particular prominence works to be included in the pages of *Arcturus*.[5] Among these notable figures are William A. Jones, Nathaniel Hawthorne, James Russell Lowell, and Henry Wadsworth Longfellow. Jones's work appears frequently, and Mott credits it with being "one of the best features of *Arcturus*," despite Poe's unfavorable comments to the contrary in the *Broadway Journal*.*[6]

Lowell was a frequent contributor, and his involvement with the publication seems to have been especially significant for the poet. His interest in and dedication to *Arcturus* is evidenced by the facts that he was a "subscriber [to it] from its beginning" and simply "out of his abundance" he contributed poetry to it for publication.[7] The numerous references to the magazine in the letters of Lowell also support the argument that *Arcturus* played a substantial role in the writer's career. Lowell was of no less significance to the magazine itself. Not only did Lowell's poetry grace its pages, but his description of *Arcturus* brought attention to the work. In a letter to G. B. Lorring, Lowell deemed *Arcturus* "as transcendental as Gotham can be."[8] Consequently, Lowell's comment created a lasting impression of the publication. As an ironic twist of fate, this transcendental magazine would be absorbed into another publication, the original editor of which rejected the "mistiness" of transcendentalism.[9]

Hawthorne's contributions, as well as Longfellow's, were perhaps less momentous than those of Lowell. Hawthorne submitted to *Arcturus* "The Man of Adamant," "The Canterbury Pilgrims," and "The Old Maid in the Winding Sheet"; this last had been printed in the *New England Magazine** seven years earlier.[10]

Although *Arcturus* published numerous pieces from these authors, many articles were written by Duyckinck and Mathews. Assuming a particularly strong voice, the latter won acclaim by writing and publishing serially a political satire, *The Career of Puffer Hopkins*. This series boasts illustrations by "Phiz," Hablot Knight Browne, best known for his graphic depictions of Dickens's stories. According to Duyckinck, Mathews's work was a precursor of "many similar attempts in local fiction and description."[11] Mathews also used the magazine to voice his opinions on copyright laws. Duyckinck's writing was less fervent, supporting Spiller's description of him as a man of "sounder scholarship, finer taste, and broader human sympathies."[12]

Despite its efforts to appeal to a variety of readers, *Arcturus* reflected Duyckinck's "finer taste," and such a magazine could not survive, however influential it might be. In his article "*Arcturus* and Keats," Thomas Ollive Mabbott implies that *Arcturus* was a powerful force in the art world.[13] Regardless of the power of the publication, *Arcturus* had its weaknesses; perhaps its greatest was its price. *Arcturus* was expensive. Even with a subscription price of five dollars, *Arcturus* failed to generate enough funds to continue publication.[14] Duyckinck therefore negotiated with Nathan Hale,[15] and in June of 1842, the magazine that had been at the zenith of New York literary circles was absorbed by The *Boston Miscellany of Literature and Fashion*.*

## Notes

1. *Encyclopedia Britannica*, 15th ed. (1983), s.v. "Arcturus."

2. Algernon Tassin, *The Magazine in America* (New York: Dodd, Mead, and Company, 1916), p. 129.

3. Perry Miller, *The Raven and the Whale: The War of Words and Wits in the Era of Poe and Melville* (New York: Harcourt, Brace, and World, Inc., 1956), pp. 85–86.

4. Frank Luther Mott, *A History of American Magazines* 4 vols. (Cambridge, Mass.: Belknap Press of Harvard University Press, 1957), 1:711.

5. Robert E. Spiller et al., *Literary History of the United States: Bibliography*, 4th ed., revised (New York: Macmillan Publishing Company, Inc., 1974), p. 46.

6. Mott, 1:712.

7. Leon Howard, *Victorian Knight-Errant: A Study of The Early Literary Career of James Russell Lowell* (Berkeley and Los Angeles: University of California Press, 1952), pp. 116–17.

8. Charles Eliot Norton, ed., *Letters of James Russell Lowell*, 2 vols. (New York: Harper and Brothers Publishers, 1894), 1:62.

9. Howard, p. 109.

10. "The Old Maid in the Winding Sheet by the *Author of 'The Gray Champion*,' " *New England Magazine* 9 (July 1835), 8–16.

11. Evert A. Duyckinck and George L. Duyckinck, *Cyclopaedia of American Literature Embracing Personal and Critical Notices of Authors and Selections From Their Writings From the Earliest Period to the Present Day*, 2 vols. (New York: Charles Scribner, 1855), 2:645.

12. Spiller, p. 240.

13. Thomas Ollive Mabbott, "*Arcturus* and Keats," *American Literature* 2 (1931):430–32.

14. Mott, 1:712.

15. Edward Everett Hale, *James Russell Lowell and His Friends* (Boston and New York: Houghton, Mifflin and Company, 1899), p. 84.

## Information Sources

BIBLIOGRAPHY:

Duberman, Martin. *James Russell Lowell*. Boston: Houghton, Mifflin Company, 1966.

Duyckinck, E. A. and George L. Duyckinck. *Cyclopaedia of American Literature Embracing Personal and Critical Notices of Authors and Selections From Their Writings From the Earliest Period to the Present Day*. 2 vols. New York: Charles Scribner, 1855.

Hale, Edward Everett. *James Russell Lowell and His Friends*. Boston and New York: Houghton, Mifflin, and Company, 1899.

Howard, Leon. *Victorian Knight-Errant: A Study of the Early Literary Career of James Russell Lowell*. Berkeley and Los Angeles: University of California Press, 1952.

Mabbott, Thomas Ollive. "*Arcturus* and Keats." *American Literature* 2 (1931):430–32.

Miller, Perry. *The Raven and the Whale: The War of Words and Wits in the Era of Poe and Melville*. New York: Harcourt, Brace, and World, Inc., 1956.

Mott, Frank Luther. "*Arcturus*." *A History of American Magazines*. 4 vols. Cambridge, Mass.: The Belknap Press of Harvard University Press, 1957. 1:711–12.

Stafford, John. *The Literary Criticism of "Young America": A Study in the Relationship of Politics and Literature, 1837–1850*. Berkeley and Los Angeles: University of California Press, 1952.

INDEXES: None

REPRINT EDITIONS: American Periodicals: Series II, 1800–1850. University Microfilms, Ann Arbor. Reel 734.

LOCATION SOURCES: Widely available.

## Publication History

MAGAZINE TITLE AND TITLE CHANGES: *Arcturus, A Journal of Books and Opinion*.

VOLUME AND ISSUE DATA: Volume 1, December 1840-May 1841; volume 2, June-November 1841; volume 3, December 1841-May 1842.

FREQUENCY OF PUBLICATION: Monthly.
PUBLISHERS: 1840–1841: Benjamin G. Trevett, New York. 1841–1842: George L. Curry and Company, New York.
EDITORS: Evert A. Duyckinck and Cornelius Mathews.

*Debra Brown*

# THE ARGONAUT

The *Argonaut* represents a new generation of magazines and journals that appeared in California during the 1870s. California's frontier era had ended. Pioneering journalistic efforts, such as *Hutchings' California Magazine*, the *Hesperian*, the *Pioneer*, and, in 1875, the *Overland Monthly*,* had ceased to exist. The founding editors of the *Argonaut* thought San Francisco was now ready for a weekly periodical that would help fill the void created by the demise of the *Overland Monthly* and would combine the best features of a newspaper, particularly its editorials, with those of a literary magazine.

Frank Pixley and Frederick Somers, the cofounders and editors, were determined to make the *Argonaut* an outspoken yet unsensationalizing journal intended not for the mass public but rather for satisfying the intellectual wants of cultivated minds. The first issue announced the intention to produce a political, satirical, literary, and society journal that would be "useful, amusing, instructive, and entertaining" (1:1). That the *Argonaut* successfully met these expectations is suggested by its life of more than eighty years.

Pixley, the moving force behind the editorial department of the *Argonaut* for its first eighteen years, has been characterized as complex, fearless, arrogant, irascible, profane to an extreme, merciless to his enemies, yet deeply committed to public affairs. All of these character traits and more are evidenced by editorials and other pieces he contributed to his journal. Although he had retired from his active role in political life (Pixley had been Governor Leland Stanford's attorney and President Grant's choice for attorney general), he used the *Argonaut*, beginning with its first issue on 25 March 1877, as a channel for influencing the course of political events in both the city and state. "America for Americans" perhaps best summarizes his firm stance in favor of white Anglo-Saxon Protestants. The Irish were singled out for greatest persecution, primarily because of their "bondage to papal authority." Other issues addressed by Pixley included the monopolistic plans of the Southern Pacific Railroad, San Francisco's water supply (a defense of the Spring Valley Water Company's right to a fair profit), the twin evils of whiskey and the saloon, and the wisdom of demolishing Chinatown and moving the Chinese out of the San Francisco Bay Area. Regardless of their inherent prejudices, however, Pixley's editorials rank among the best that American journalism produced at that time, and he has been favorably compared to the likes of Horace Greeley and Charles A. Dana.

Apart from its editorials, the reputation that the *Argonaut* acquired rested upon its original verse, articles, special features, and stories. In this arena, Pixley longed to perpetuate the romance of the West. Using personal recollections, memoirs, anecdotes, letters, diaries, and local histories, he wanted to make the *Argonaut* the "omnium gatherum" of this kind of information Readers came to regard the *Argonaut* as the *Atlantic Monthly*\* of the Pacific Coast. Pixley also wanted to provide a forum by which new Western writers could be heard.

Verse came largely from a group of relative amateurs and would have been inconsequential had not Bret Harte, Ina Coolbrith, Joaquin Miller, Gertrude Atherton, and other poets of some stature contributed pieces. Unknown writers also found a vehicle for expression in the pages of the *Argonaut*. Sam Davis of the Carson *Appeal* and Joseph Goodman of the *Territorial Enterprise* used mining as backdrops for their poetry as well as their stories. May Hawley, "the songstress of the Sierras," was, in Pixley's estimation, comparable to Harte and Mark Twain. Journalist Daniel O'Connell used his Irish heritage in creating verse that earned him an affectionate following. By the mid–1880s, however, the quality of original poetry had declined, and Pixley substituted reprints of classic verse and poetry that had appeared in other publications at other times.

The column "Olla Podrida," which was unsigned yet clearly written by Pixley, "was the irresponsible part of the *Argonaut*. . . . a galloping fanfaronade of words, with here and there an idea. It was a relaxation from thought" (8:1). Satire, gossip, and scandalmongering were regularly carried on in "Olla Podrida" with little thought about the consequences. Readers loved it. The church, both Catholic and Protestant (but especially the former); the rich and other pillars of the community; all politicians; and any other subject, organization, or group of people that Pixley deemed appropriate were regularly dissected, ridiculed, and found wanting. The column continued well into the 1880s and was revived occasionally for many years thereafter.

Ambrose Bierce, who was associate editor of the *Argonaut* for the first three years after its inception, propelled satire into the realm of poisonous attack. An enigmatic man whose lack of amiability earned him the title of "Bitter Bierce," he regularly attacked both public and private figures with caustic commentary. He even went so far as to reprint obituary verse, which had appeared in local newspapers, in order to ridicule it. Bierce's columns, "Prattle," "Little Johnny's Menagerie," and "Fables of Zambri the Parsee," were filled with lampoons, limericks, and doggerel, which seemed to delight *Argonaut* readers but embarrass its editors. When Bierce left in 1879 to partake in the Black Hills gold rush, he assumed his position at the *Argonaut* would be held open for him. Pixley refused his request for reinstatement, however, and Bierce amplified this slight into an extended grudge that was carried on through invective published in other journals for which Bierce later wrote, including the *Wasp*\* and the San Francisco *Examiner*.

The identity of most other *Argonaut* columnists has never been determined. Using pseudonyms such as "Parisina," "Flaneur," and "Cockaigne," the political, social, and economic life in Paris, New York, and London were examined by unknown "correspondents." Most columns of domestic news, however, bore the names of such writers as Gertrude Atherton, Isabel Strong, and Geraldine Bonner.

Perhaps the most remarkable column in the *Argonaut*, "Literary Notes," began as a modest commentary on new books and authors; it eventually grew to encompass several pages of short reviews, a couple dozen longer reviews, lists of publications recently received with one-line commentaries, and lists of forthcoming books. Summaries of the contents of other important magazines were also included as well as bookish news and gossip about authors, publishers, and book dealers. Those books that were seen as particularly important received special extended treatment.

Historical material dealing with California and the West and often published as extended series figured prominently in the *Argonaut* throughout its first decade. Based on original sources as well as verbal reminiscences of California's pioneers, the material was read avidly by subscribers and today forms an important and often unique source for historical research. But Western material was often supplemented, especially in the 1890s, by topics of national and international interest: the Dreyfus case, women's suffrage, and the controversy surrounding the construction of the Nicaragua and Panama canals, to name but three. Original travel literature submitted by regular contributors was often supplemented by reprinted articles from other notable magazines and newspapers, including *Lippincott's*, *Puck*, the *Atlantic Monthly*, the London *Fortnightly*, and the Edinburgh *Review*.

Jerome Hart, who had been associated with the *Argonaut* from its beginning, did not become an editor until Somers left the magazine. At first responsible for the mechanical side of the business, his literary talents soon came to the fore, and by the end of 1877 Hart was a regular contributor. Short stories, which Hart saw as one of literature's greatest forms, and translations of European authors (Zola, Balzac, de Maupassant) became his specialty, and upon Somer's departure Hart became Pixley's right-hand man and eventually his successor.

The list of other contributors to the *Argonaut* encompasses most of the important California writers of the period: E. H. Clough, Frank Bailey Millard, Flora Haines Loughhead, Margaret Collier Graham, Charles Lummis, Frank Norris, Will Irwin, and Jack London. Gertrude Atherton's first novel, *The Randolphs of Redwood*, appeared serially in the *Argonaut*; Emma Frances Dawson wrote tales of the supernatural, as did William C. Morrow and, of course, Ambrose Bierce. Robert Duncan Milne created highly imaginative science fiction stories, and Nathan Kouns incorporated mystic and psychological trends in his stories.

When Pixley died in 1895, Jerome Hart became principal stockholder and chief editor. He carried on Pixley's editorial policies, however. Hart's penchant for travel is reflected in the many sketches he sent for publication while abroad; these were later published in book form as *Argonaut Letters* (1900), *Two Argonauts in Spain* (1903), and *A Levantine Log Book* (1905). Hart managed to carry the *Argonaut* through the 1906 earthquake and fire in San Francisco; he was justifiably proud that the *Argonaut* never missed an issue, even though for several months it was actually printed in San Jose. The last issue of the *Argonaut* under Hart's editorship and ownership appeared on 19 January 1907, although a long series entitled "Seeking the Golden Fleece," his final contribution to the periodical, appeared in 1908 and 1909.

Hart's successor was Alfred Holman, whose major editorial change was to eliminate the fiction department after World War I; the *Argonaut* became strictly a journal of opinion. New editors carried on the old tradition, however, and wrote pieces that were essentially against labor, the eight-hour day, the closed shop, and prohibition.

Samuel Travers Clover tried to combine the *Argonaut* with the *Los Angeles Saturday Night* in the early twenties, but the journal was repurchased by several San Francisco businessmen who sought to restore the nineteenth-century tradition of excellence.

New editors appeared in the 1920s: Morton Todd, Bruce Ellis, Edward Morphy, and the brothers Joshua and Daniel Shanedling. In 1936 William Wallace Chapin became editor, and he managed to recapture at least a part of the brilliance the *Argonaut* had enjoyed under Pixley. Much of Chapin's success resulted from the staff with which he surrounded himself, including Joseph Henry Jackson, Ethel Shorb, Glen Wessels, Joyce Mayhew, and others. Under Chapin also the magazine was issued in covers, and illustrations (cartoons and excellent photographs) were used lavishly.

Chapin stayed at the helm of the *Argonaut* well into the 1950s, but by then his own physical difficulties combined with financial problems necessitated a sale of the magazine to Harry Huse Nasburg. Nasburg was apparently less interested in the *Argonaut*'s history and traditions and attempted rather to remake it into the Pacific Coast equivalent of the *New Yorker*. His lack of success brought insurmountable debt, and the last issue appeared in September 1958.

## Information Sources

BIBLIOGRAPHY:

Bepler, Doris West. "Descriptive Catalogue of Western Historical Materials in California Periodicals, 1854–1890, with Introduction on the History and Character of the Magazines." M.A. thesis, University of California, Berkeley, 1920.

Cummins, Ella Sterling. *The Story of the Files: A Review of Californian Writers and Literature*. [San Francisco]: World's Fair Commission of California, 1893.

Davenport, Robert. "San Francisco Journalism in the Time of Fremont Older." Ph.D. diss., University of California, Los Angeles, 1969.

"Death of Jerome A. Hart." *San Francisco Examiner*, 4 January 1937, p. 7.

"Death of Pixley." *San Francisco News Letter*, 17 August 1895, p. 1.

Hart, Jerome A. *Argonaut Letters*. San Francisco: Payot, Upham, 1901.

———. *In Our Second Century*. San Francisco: The Pioneer Press, 1931.

Wotherspoon, James R. "The San Francisco *Argonaut*, 1877–1897." Ph.D. diss. University of California, Berkeley, 1962.

INDEXES: None
REPRINT EDITIONS: None.
LOCATION SOURCES: Widely available.

### Publication History

MAGAZINE TITLE AND TITLE CHANGES: *The Argonaut.*
VOLUME AND ISSUE DATA: Volumes 1–137, 25 March 1877–6 September 1958.
FREQUENCY OF PUBLICATION: Weekly.
PUBLISHERS: 1877–1958: Argonaut Publishing Company.
EDITORS: Frank M. Pixley, 1877–1895; Jerome A. Hart, 1895–1907; Alfred Holman, 1907–1921; Samuel Travers Clover, 1921–1923; Edward Morphy, 1923–1928; Edward Morphy, Joshua & Daniel Shanedling, 1929–1930; A. H. Lyon, 1930–1935; Sprague Holden, 1935–1936; William Wallace Chapin, 1936–1957; Harry Huse Nasburg, 1957–1958.

*Bruce L. Johnson*


# THE ATLANTIC MONTHLY

The *Atlantic Monthly* was a child born to the advanced but still vigorous middle age of the New England literary renaissance. The magazine was originally conceived by Francis Underwood, an ardent member of the Free Soil party and an editorial assistant to the Boston publishing house of Phillips, Sampson and Company. By 1856, Underwood had organized a group of writers including James Russell Lowell, Oliver Wendell Holmes, Ralph Waldo Emerson, and E. P. Whipple, which met sporadically at the Parker House in Boston to discuss creating a Boston-based magazine that would promote good literature and speak out against slavery. Underwood's employer, Moses Phillips, aware that several Boston literary magazines like Joseph Tinker Buckingham's *New England Galaxy*, Lowell's *Pioneer*,* and the *Massachusetts Quarterly Review*\* had foundered financially, was reluctant to undertake the project. But he was finally persuaded by "the brilliant constellation of philosophical, poetical, and historical talent" Underwood had mustered.[1]

The *Atlantic* was partly born of a consciousness among a definable group of writers living in Boston, Cambridge, and Concord that they were producing a substantial body of literature and scholarship and had need, as Emerson wrote, of "a good vent for such wares as scholars have."[2] Beyond this utilitarian purpose, the *Atlantic* was born from a double sense of mission on the part of its founders. It was intended to enlist the power of literature and of several influential New England writers in the antislavery cause. It was also intended to fulfill a cultural mission, as Emerson noted in his journal, "to guide the age."[3] Thomas Wentworth Higginson later recalled that the writers of the *Atlantic* circle "were teachers, educators, and bringers of the light with a deep and affectionate feeling of obligation towards the young republic their fathers had brought into being. That New England was appointed to guide the nation, to civilize it, to humanize it, none of them doubted."[4] This sense of obligation to establish authoritative literary and intellectual standards and to promote high literate culture continued to influence the magazine's identity and its editorial policies in an increasingly democratic and pluralistic society.

The first issue of the *Atlantic*, published in November 1857, contained a general declaration of its editorial policies. In literature, the editors promised to balance "articles of an abstract and permanent value" with a "healthy appetite . . . for entertainment." They affirmed also that while they would solicit and publish foreign authors, "native writers will receive the most solid encouragement and will be mainly relied upon to fill the pages of the *Atlantic*."[5] This guarantee was fulfilled, although "native" meant mainly those living in close proximity to Boston. Mott estimates that during its first fifteen years fully two-thirds of the *Atlantic*'s contributors were New Englanders.[6]

From the beginning, the *Atlantic*'s format was visually spartan, expressing a disdain for alluring illustration and an unequivocal emphasis on the printed word. This refusal to sacrifice the printed word to visual display has been maintained by *Atlantic* editors in the face of increasing competition with such visually lavish magazines as *Harper's*,* later *Scribner's Monthly** and the *Century**, and more recently still the *New Yorker*.

During its early years somewhat more than half of the *Atlantic*'s 128 pages were given to essays, including many by Emerson and Holmes, on philosophy, literature, manners, art, and politics. Each issue contained between three and four stories and generally an installment of a serial novel. Typically, there were six or seven poems and at the end a seven-page department of "Literary Notices" reviewing diverse works published in English, French, and German.

The *Atlantic*'s first editor, James Russell Lowell, intended the editorship to share his time with his professorial duties at Harvard and his own writing. He had the conscientious Underwood as his "office assistant" to rough sort manuscripts, and he did not expect to have to solicit too arduously for contributors since so many were near at hand and had already pledged their support. Lowell was energetic but not systematic in his editing. Soon after publication of the first issue, he found himself inundated with three hundred manuscripts, and he seems never to have caught up again. He seldom blocked out issues a month in advance and often scribbled last-minute directions to the printers on the backs of envelopes. By his own account, manuscripts and correspondence languished in growing heaps. "I am afraid," he wrote apologetically to a contributor, "that at this moment there are at least one hundred and fifty unanswered letters in, on, and around my desk, whose blank [looks] seem to say 'how long?' "[7] Lowell's tendency to carelessness and expediency may have contributed as much as his brisk confidence in his own judgment to his alienating several writers including Henry David Thoreau, Parke Godwin, and Thomas Wentworth Higginson by taking editorial liberties with their manuscripts.

Lowell's *Atlantic* was mainly the vehicle of established New England writers including Emerson, Holmes, John Greenleaf Whittier, Henry Wadsworth Longfellow, Harriet Beecher Stowe, E. E. Hale, and Higginson. Lowell's failure to solicit beyond New England may have prevented the magazine from achieving diversity of view but did not keep it from being the best American literary magazine of its period. Nor can Lowell be accused of ignoring unestablished writers. Among the young writers he published frequently were Rose Terry, Louisa May Alcott, John T. Trowbridge, Harriet Prescott, and two young men who were to succeed him in editing the *Atlantic*, Thomas Bailey Aldrich and William Dean Howells.

The initial issue of the *Atlantic* sold 20,000 copies at 25 cents each. By 1860 the magazine had a regular readership of about 30,000 (compared to *Harper's** 200,000), many of them midwesterners who found the *Atlantic* a reassuring link with New England culture.[8]

In October 1859 the *Atlantic* was bought by the publishing house of Ticknor and Fields. While the new publishers recognized that Lowell had established the *Atlantic* as a source of cultural authority and intelligent entertainment, the younger partner, James T. Fields, was by 1861 chafing at Lowell's taste for scholarly articles and eager to take on the editorship himself.

Fields, who was largely self-educated and self-made, had succeeded in publishing by aggressively promoting good literature and by paying his authors relatively well. If the Brahmin Lowell had often selected manuscripts from a sense of cultural responsibility to educate his audience, Fields's selection was more often circumscribed by a shrewd sense of what would appeal to readers. By 1866, Fields had raised circulation to 50,000.

During his nearly ten years as editor, Fields promoted the *Atlantic* as the journal of the New England Olympians but also introduced some innovations. He managed, with increasing difficulty, to hold the *Atlantic*'s initial circle of authors intact, to regain the alienated Thoreau, and to add his friend Hawthorne. Fields also directed his assistant editors, first Higginson and then in 1866 Howells, to cultivate relationships with promising younger authors. This led to the publication of several early works by Rebecca Harding Davis (including *Life in the Iron Mills*), John W. DeForest, E. C. Stedman, Aldrich, and Henry James, Jr. As Higginson noted, "Fields is always casting about for good things, while Lowell is rather disposed to sit and let them come."[9] While Fields published some Emersonian essays, he also solicited essays by professional journalists like James Parton that reported contemporary social conditions rather than philosophical speculations. His encouragement of Mrs. Stowe and others to contribute essays on domestic subjects reflected his awareness that women constituted a large portion of his audience.

The *Atlantic* had from its birth vocally opposed compromise with the "slave powers," and during the war it fully backed Lincoln, while chafing that he was insufficiently aggressive in his prosecution of the war and his declaration of emancipation. Later Charles Sumner and others outlined the radical Republican program for reconstruction in the *Altantic*, and the magazine continued to consider the Republicans "the party of righteousness" until the 1890s when it became, and remained, genuinely nonpartisan.

Fields's choice of the thirty-four-year-old midwesterner Howells as his successor was farsighted. By 1871, the Olympians were receding into their twilight, the nation's literary center was shifting from Boston to New York, and the *Atlantic* faced increasing competition for authors and readers from several recently founded magazines, notably the *Nation* (1865), the *Galaxy\** (1866), *Putnam's\** (1868), and *Scribner's* (1870), as well as the thriving *Harper's*.

Howells was respectful of the Boston culture that had produced the *Atlantic*, but he knew that to maintain the magazine's literary quality and to promote literary realism he must cultivate a new generation of authors and readers from a broader geographical distribution. Accordingly, he solicited and published works by R. W. Gilder, Aldrich, H. H. Boyeson, T. S. Perry, G. W. Cable, "Charles Egbert Craddock," John DeForest, Sarah Orne Jewett, Edith Wharton, George Eggleston, Hamlin Garland, Mark Twain, and Henry James, Jr. As James later wrote, "The new American novel had . . . its first seeds . . . sewn very exactly in *Atlantic* soil."[10]

Howells recognized that the audience for literature was increasingly feminine while his male readers were increasingly concerned with current affairs. But he and his successors Aldrich and Horace Elisha Scudder were primarily literary men, and while they gradually increased the number of articles on politics, economics, and social problems, literature continued to be the *Atlantic*'s focus.

The witty, sociable, and languorous Aldrich was indifferent to current affairs and averse to the exertions of soliciting manuscripts, but he was highly fastidious in literary taste. He prized fiction that was, like himself, polished, entertaining, and facile. Literature, he felt, should contain nothing one could not discuss decorously with strangers in a drawing room.[11]

Displeased with Aldrich's lack of both zeal and editorial tact, the magazine's current publishers, Houghton, Mifflin and Company, replaced him in June 1890 with the industrious and high-minded Scudder, who assumed the *Atlantic* editorship in addition to maintaining full responsibilities as a senior editor in the firm's trade division, for which the magazine was supposed to draw authors. Scudder's aim was "to keep the magazine at the front of American liteature," but he felt that the *Atlantic* should also comment on current affairs from the perspective of enduring ethical principle.[12] Among the younger authors who found Scudder sympathetic to their work were Irving Babbitt, J. J. Chapman, Gamaliel Bradford, Charles T. Copeland, G. L. Kitteridge, W. V. Moody, George Santayana, Owen Wister, and Havelock Ellis.

In 1895, Scudder, with some misgivings, took on as assistant a brisk, ambitious, confident young Southerner named Walter Hines Page, who had recently proven himself a proficient journalist by resurrecting the *Forum*. Page, who became acting editor in 1896, considered literary criticism mere "talkee-talkee" and rejected a proffered story by Henry James with the comment that "people who have blood in their veins will yawn and throw it down."[13] Page was the first *Atlantic* editor whose primary interests were in current affairs, and although he left in July 1899 to help resuscitate the bankrupt house of Harper and eventually to found the *World's Work*, his editorial interests and policies foreshadowed the *Atlantic*'s course in the twentieth century.

Page's successor, Bliss Perry, recognized the need to address contemporary American issues. But Perry was by nature and training a literary scholar, not a journalist. He did solicit distinguished, largely theoretical commentaries on politics from Grover Cleveland, Theodore Roosevelt, J. J. Chapman, E. L. Godkin, W. A. White, and Woodrow Wilson. But fully half the space in a typical issue was given to literature or literary criticism. Perry was nonetheless uncomfortably aware that the blood ran thin and cold in the New England literary tradition. Dissatisfied with waiting for a Keats or Whitman who never materialized, Perry was glad to turn the burden over in 1909 to Ellery Sedgwick, whom he equivocally considered "a far better journalist," and return to teaching the great literature that he loved.

In 1908, Sedgwick formed a partnership that bought the *Atlantic* from Houghton Mifflin and formed the Atlantic Monthly Company. For the first time since Fields the magazine's editor was to be its owner. Sedgwick, a protégé and admirer of Page, had received vigorous journalistic training in the competitive world of New York magazine publishing during the muckraking era, where he had learned that active solicitation of contributors, engagement in the issues of the moment, and controversy give a magazine life and that a successful editor seeks out what will have immediate impact, not necessarily permanent literary value.

On the other hand, Sedgwick was personally sympathetic to the *Atlantic*'s cultural traditions and aware that too sudden a change would alienate its traditional constituency. Accordingly, he set about gradually shifting the balance from belles-lettres to current affairs and supplementing pallid fiction with nonfiction narratives of personal experience. As a result of Sedgwick's gradualist editorial policies and conservative literary tastes, the *Atlantic*—despite some adventures such as the early publication of Robert Frost, Amy Lowell, Randolph Bourne, and I. A. Richards—continued largely to represent the genteel tradition in literature that was the attenuated legacy of the vigorous old New England idealism.

In current affairs, by contrast, Sedgwick generated considerable innovation. He orchestrated articles on a broad variety of controversial topics and frequently arranged printed debates expressing opposing views. The coverage of World War I from every national, personal, and philosophical perspective contributed substantially to raising the *Atlantic*'s circulation from about 20,000 in 1908 to over 100,000 by 1920.[14]

Sedgwick's assistant and successor, Edward Weeks, spent sixty years at the *Atlantic*, twenty-eight as editor-in-chief. With the able assistance of Charles Morton, Weeks maintained Sedgwick's policy of diversification and the active solicitation of firsthand reports from those directly involved in the events about which they wrote. Circulation rose steadily during Weeks's editorship to 285,000 in 1966.[15]

Weeks also deserves credit for retrieving the *Atlantic* from its general literary backwater nearer to the mainstream of American literature by publishing such authors as Dylan Thomas, Somerset Maugham, Peter Ustinov, Albert Camus, Evelyn Waugh, Eudora Welty, and James Thurber. Frequently prevented from competing for established authors by the *Atlantic*'s traditionally parsimonious editorial budget, Weeks instituted the *Atlantic* novel prizes, the *Atlantic* "First" short story series, and the "Young Poets" pages to attract and publish younger writers.

In 1966, Weeks was succeeded by Robert Manning, who had been press secretary at the State Department as well as a correspondent for United Press and a senior editor at *Time*. Manning emphasized critical analysis of current events and made the *Atlantic* more visually appealing. Perceptive coverage of Vietnam, much of it highly critical of government policy, and later coverage of Watergate won Manning's *Atlantic* four National Magazine awards and raised circulation to 350,000. But by 1980, reduced public interest in current affairs, editorial drift, an editorial budget frozen since the mid-sixties, and astronomical increases in the cost of postage and paper resulted in an annual loss of about $495,000.[16]

In 1980, the Atlantic Monthly Co. was purchased by Boston real estate developer Mortimer Zuckerman, who rapidly quintupled the nonstaff editorial and art budget and lured William Whitworth from the *New Yorker* as editor. Whitworth, who can offer $1,500 to $5,000 for an article compared to Manning's $200 to $2,000, is considered a meticulous, decisive, cerebral, and highly capable editorial craftsman. Whitworth's issues have contained both incisive political journalism and good fiction, although critics note a high incidence of book excerpts. The current *Atlantic* also reflects an increased breadth of cultural criticism, much of it focused on nonverbal culture such as popular music and fashion.

Zuckerman's very liberal infusion of capital and Whitworth's considerable editorial capabilities make the *Atlantic* a good test of whether a "general interest" periodical, still graphically sparse, which offers the serious reader sophisticated fiction and intelligent critical reflection on culture and current affairs, can survive in the late twentieth century.

## Notes

1. Moses D. Phillips, Letter to his niece, May 1857, in Mark A. Dewolfe Howe, *The Atlantic Monthly and Its Makers* (Boston: Atlantic Monthly Press, 1919), pp. 14–15.

2. Ralph Waldo Emerson, *The Journals and Miscellaneous Notebooks of Ralph Waldo Emerson*, ed. Susan Smith and Harrison Hayward 16 vols. (Cambridge, Mass.: Harvard University Press, 1978), 14:167.

3. Emerson, *Journals*, 14:167.

4. Thomas Wentworth Higginson, *Cheerful Yesterdays* (Boston: Houghton Mifflin, 1898), p. 167.

5. "Publisher's Statement," *Atlantic Monthly*, November 1857, inside front cover.

6. Frank Luther Mott, *A History of American Magazines*, 4 vols. (Cambridge, Mass.: Harvard University Press, 1938), 2:495.

7. James Russell Lowell, Letter to R. G. White, 6 April 1859, quoted in Horace Scudder, *James Russell Lowell*, 2 vols. (Boston: Houghton Mifflin, 1901), 1:441–42.

8. Circulation figures for the *Atlantic* in Martin Duberman, *James Russell Lowell* (Boston: Houghton Mifflin, 1966), p. 179. Figures for *Harper's Monthly* in Mott 2:390–91.

9. Thomas Wentworth Higginson, *Letters and Journals of Thomas Wentworth Higginson: 1846–1906* (1921; rpt., New York: DaCapo Press, 1969), p. 111.

10. Quoted in Van Wyck Brooks, *William Dean Howells: His Life and World* (New York: E. P. Dutton, 1959), p. 56.

11. Ferris Greenslet, *Thomas Bailey Aldrich* (Boston: Houghton Mifflin, 1908), p. 148.

12. Horace Elisha Scudder, Diary, 17 June 1890, in Ellen Ballou, *The Building of the House: Houghton Mifflin's Formative Years* (Boston: Houghton Mifflin, 1970), P. 380.

13. Walter Hines Page, Manuscript Report 6743, in Ballou, p. 456.

14. Ballou, pp. 495–96.

15. John Felton, "Weeks Retires as Editor-in-Chief," *New York Times*, 24 January 1966, sec. 1, p. 22, col. 5.

16. Diane McWhorter, "The *Atlantic* in Search of a Role," *New York Times Magazine*, 14 February 1982, p. 52, col. 3.

## Information Sources

BIBLIOGRAPHY:
*Atlantic Monthly*. Fiftieth Anniversary number, vol. 100 (November 1907).
Austin, James C. *Fields of the Atlantic Monthly: Letters to an Editor, 1861–1870*. San Marino, Cal.: Huntington Library Press, 1953.
Ballou, Ellen. *The Building of the House: Houghton Mifflin's Formative Years*. Boston: Houghton Mifflin, 1970.
Duberman, Martin. *James Russell Lowell*. Boston: Houghton Mifflin, 1966.
Greenslet, Ferris. *The Life of Thomas Bailey Aldrich*. Boston: Houghton Mifflin, 1908.
Higginson, Thomas Wentworth. *Cheerful Yesterdays*. Boston: Houghton Mifflin, 1898.
Howe, Mark A. D. *The Atlantic Monthly and Its Makers*. Boston: Atlantic Monthly Press, 1919.
Lynn, Kenneth. *William Dean Howells: An American Life*. New York: Harcourt, Brace, Jovanovich, 1970.
Mott, Frank Luther. *"The Atlantic Monthly." A History of American Magazines*. 4 vols. Cambridge, Mass.: Harvard University Press, 1938. 2:493–515.
Perry, Bliss. *Park Street Papers*. Boston: Houghton Mifflin, 1908.
Sedgwick, Ellery. *The Happy Profession*. Boston: Atlantic-Little, Brown, 1947.
Weeks, Edward. *Writers and Friends*. Boston: Atlantic-Little, Brown, 1981.
INDEXES: Semiannual volumes are indexed. *Index to the Atlantic Monthly*. Volumes 1–38. Boston: 1877. *The Atlantic Index*. Volumes 39–62. Boston: Houghton Mifflin, 1889. *The Atlantic Index Supplement: 1889–1901*. Volumes 63–88. Boston: Houghton Mifflin, 1903.
REPRINT EDITIONS: Bell & Howell, Micro Photo Division. Microforms International Marketing Co. University Microfilms International.
LOCATION SOURCES: Widely available.

## Publication History

MAGAZINE TITLE AND TITLE CHANGES: *The Atlantic Monthly: A Magazine of Literature, Art and Politics*, November 1857-September 1865. *The Atlantic Monthly: A Magazine of Literature, Science, Art and Politics*, October 1865-June 1952. *The Atlantic*, July 1952-current.

VOLUME AND ISSUE DATA: Volumes 1–254, November 1857-current (semiannual volumes).

FREQUENCY OF PUBLICATION: Monthly.

PUBLISHERS: November 1857-October 1859: Phillips, Sampson and Company. November 1859-June 1868: Ticknor and Fields. July 1868–1870: Fields, Osgood and Company. 1871–1873: James Osgood and Company. 1874–1877: H. O. Houghton and Company. 1878–1879: Houghton, Osgood and Company. 1880-July 1908: Houghton Mifflin and Company. August 1908-current: Atlantic Monthly Company.

EDITORS: James Russell Lowell, November 1857-June 1861; James T. Fields, July 1861-July 1871; William Dean Howells, August 1871-January 1881; Thomas Bailey Aldrich, February 1881-March 1890; Horace Elisha Scudder, April 1890-July 1898; Walter Hines Page, August 1898-July 1899; Bliss Perry, August 1899-July 1909; Ellery Sedgwick, August 1909-June 1938; Edward A. Weeks Jr., July 1938-January 1966; Robert Manning, February 1966-December 1980; William Whitworth, April 1981-present.

*Ellery Sedgwick*

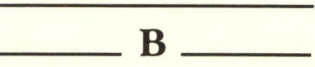

## BEADLE'S MONTHLY

*Beadle's Monthly, a Magazine of Today* even started in a halting, off-hand way. The *New York Tribune* for 21 November 1865 carried the announcement of its expected appearance on the twenty-fifth of that month. What appeared on that day, however, was merely another announcement postponing the first number (January 1866) until December 1.[1] This kind of uncertainty persisted more or less throughout its brief one and a half years of publication. *Beadle's* never identified its editor or printed the obligatory prospectus that subscribers expect as a matter of course from an outsetting periodical; it also never developed a firm editorial presence that might have given the magazine its character or an explicit purpose.

Mott assigns the editorship to Orville James Victor, but this is probably based on intelligent conjecture, because Victor edited various Beadle publications from 1861 to 1897.[2] Albert Johannsen, the undisputed authority on the publishing history of Beadle and Adams, proposes no candidate at all.

What its publishers felt made *Beadle's* unique is unclear. It had only one department, "Current Notes" (later changed to "Notes, Notices and Gossip"), but it lacked the quality and character of truly memorable ones in other first-class miscellanies. The *Atlantic Monthly*\* featured specialized departments on literature, politics, science, and music; *Harper's Monthly*\* offered the humor of its "Editor's Drawer," and there was Fanny Fern's tartly satirical column in Robert Bonner's *New York Ledger*. "Current Notes," instead, reads as a haphazard catchall for items that randomly passed across the editor's desk or caught his fancy, from recent discoveries in geology to speculations on the origins of cholera, publishing news and gossip, and statistics on wine consumption in France. Its tone was chatty, the materials faintly interesting, and its purpose, if any, obscure. It offered nary a clue as to the idea behind the founding of *Beadle's*.

In all likelihood, Beadle and Adams were making a bid to be counted among the great houses—Harper, Appleton, Putnam, Scribner, Wiley, and Carleton— each of which published its own literary periodical. After all, this firm had a fair claim in seeking entry into the circle of the publishing elite. Its business interests were as diverse as they were profitable. In the space of a mere ten years prior to the establishment of *Beadle's Monthly*, Beadle and Adams published two periodicals, the *Youth's Casket* (1852–1857) and the *Home* (1856–1860), some ten-cent songbooks, and a gaggle of handbooks on everything from needle-work and etiquette to billiards and baseball. They also published a whole spate of series: Dime Novel (including *Malaeska: The Indian Wife of the White Hunter* and *Seth Jones*), the Dime Biographical Library, Sixpenny Tale, American Li-brary Tales, Standard Library of Romance, Men of the Time, Sixpenny Biog-raphy, and Dime Classic. By opening a London branch in 1861, Beadle and Adams added the lustre of prestige to its already glittering coffers.[3] This was a firm that had to be reckoned with.

Some contemporary press comments, however, speculated that the firm in-tended *Beadle's Monthly* to compete with *Harper's Monthly*, a lead followed by both Mott and Johannsen. Mott declares that *Beadle's* "was clearly planned in imitation of *Harper's Magazine*, the great success of the day," while Johannsen similarly asserts "It was apparently planned to compete with *Har-per's Monthly*, and was of much the same character in size, illustration, and reading matter."[4]

In such a competition, *Beadle's* could only hope to finish second. And it did, soundly. While both periodicals were octavos, *Beadle's* length of 23.5 centi-meters was a full 2 centimeters less than *Harper's*; its length was the more customary 91 to 96 pages per issue against the unusual and packed 144 pages of *Harper's*. The average of thirty-five to fifty illustrations per issue in *Harper's* outstripped *Beadle's* by more than double. Because both were miscellanies, their reading matter was fairly similar though *Harper's* republished generous amounts of contemporary English fiction. By 1866 it had already published works by Edward Bulwer-Lytton, Thackeray, Charles Reade, Charles James Lever, Dick-ens, and Wilkie Collins. In comparison, *Beadle's* pirated no English works and even supported a literary nationalism though only perfunctorily so (1:100,292).

In taking the field against competitors such as the *Ledger, Leslie's*, and the *Atlantic, Beadle's* undertook at best a desperate venture, made well-nigh hopeless when it even disdainfully chose to ignore "the old idea of the potency of names" and scorned "professional contributors" (1:576). Perhaps this was but the des-perate bravado of a periodical struggling with limited financial support and encouragement. The consequences for *Beadle's* were only too predictable: writ-ing that was no different from that found in average periodicals and a lifespan lasting but a year and a half. Under the circumstances, *Beadle's* acquitted itself well enough. Its offerings were similar to those of other monthlies—serialized novels; short tales; poetry; general essays of scientific, historical, and cultural interest; and travel sketches. The writing, both for better or worse, was also of comparable quality.

The most prominent novelist to contribute to *Beadle's* was Metta V. Victor, who published two serialized novels, *Who Was He?* and *The Dead Letter*, the latter under the pseudonym Seeley Regester. Published elsewhere two years before it appeared in *Beadle's*, *The Dead Letter* eventually appeared in the Fifty Cent Novels series and had the distinction of being pirated by an English firm.[5] No doubt its popularity grew from a satisfying mix of murder unravelled (with locales ranging from Manhattan and Brooklyn to San Francisco and even Mexico), villainy unmasked, patient love rewarded, and, most sublimely, a beautiful woman's commemoration of her life to the memory of a dead fiancé. Its high effects and sentiments also more than satisfied any reader's desire for entertainment and good moral closure. *The Romance of the Green Seal*, another serialized novel, written by Catharine A. Warfield, is also governed by high effects and an edifying moral tag—the tragic consequences of pursuing a romantic conduct of life. William Wirt Sikes, another popular and well-published writer, serialized *Greenblow in Gotham*, a formulaic tale of the country-boy-who-debauches-in-the-big-city.

The short fiction that appeared in *Beadle's* is quite similar. In aiming at little more than providing readers with some diversion, it suffers from the same faults as the longer fiction did: simplistic divisions between good and evil, highly moralistic resolutions, melodramatic dialogue, and characters devoid of any interior lives. Most difficulties related to social position, money, and family are resolved in marriage; others are resolved by the satisfaction of eventual vindication, wisdom gained, or death's blessed release.

*Beadle's* published well-known writers: Charles D. Garnette, Caroline Cheseborough, Alfred B. Street, Nathan B. Urner, young Frank R. Stockton, Charles Dunning Clarke, and Harriet E. Prescott. They published in the likes of the *Galaxy*,* *Atlantic*, *Putnam's*,* *Aldine*, *Evening Post*, and *Harper's Weekly*; collectively they also published dime novels that can be counted in the hundreds. Less short stories than tales, the plots of their short fiction revolve around a single interesting or compelling incident and are formulaically resolved to accommodate an expected moral. Where the moral does not so facilely present itself, as occasionally happens, writers gamely contrive one: ''And here endeth my story. Moral to be invented hereafter'' (2:414) or ''The moral of all this is, that it is dangerous for a lion to like salt'' (2:135). Aside from the fact that these fail miserably as attempts at light-hearted wit, they convey the degree to which writers were concerned more with delivering some trite moralism than enlarging a reader's sympathies or awakening his knowledge.

The poetry too was a low average, though *Beadle's* contributors were widely published. Helen L. Bostwick's poetry had appeared in the *Atlantic*, *Arthur's*, the *National Era*, and the *Saturday Evening Post*; and the indefatigable Carey sisters, Alice and Phoebe, very nearly published in every mid-century magazine. *Beadle's* contributors also included Kate Putnam Osgood; Eben E. Rexford, author of over one thousand poems for the *Saturday Journal* and the *Banner Weekly* alone; and Edward Willet. The poems, many of them inspired by unrequited love, ruins, and any number of natural phenomena (especially disasters), are usually written in alternating rhyming lines and are as rhetorically extravagant as they are slight in thought. As with the short tales, a much larger number of contributors were complete unknowns, probably hopeful subscribers or outsetting amateurs.

The essays filled close to one-half of each issue. Devoted to travel both here and abroad, natural history, military matters (especially recent Civil War reminiscences), and literary and historical materials, they were well written and lively, often combining information with personal anecdotes. The most notable contributions included Albert D. Richardson's serialized sketches of Western travel entitled "Our New States and Territories," and Mrs. E. Oakes Smith's reminiscences of prominent literary figures. Other contributors included David Trowbridge, a prominent science writer; E. D. Sanborn; Kate Field; James Franklin Fitts and Col. A. J. H. Duganne, both of whom published Civil War sketches; Kate A. Sanborn; Henry Chadwick, America's earliest promoter of baseball; and William Wirt Sikes, who contributed a gory serial on "Assassins and Their Work."

*Beadle's* contributors are neither significant writers in American literary history nor personalities of great importance in this period. Rather, they belonged to that vast army of writers whose works swelled each issue of all contemporary periodicals. They are remembered, when at all, for writing works less of enduring literary merit than cultural documents that provide insights into the popular mind of this period. Such writers implicitly wrote from a view of literature that Orville Victor codified through a series of prohibitions for *Banner Weekly* writers. Literature was to exclude "all things offensive to good taste," characters who "carry an immoral taint," or anything that "cannot be read with satisfaction by every rightminded person—old and young alike."[6] The products of such guidelines account for the bulk of average writing during this period, an average that even editors lamented was woeful. This average overwhelmed each issue of *Beadle's*, making it "neither particularly fresh, vigorous, original nor piquant," a criticism "Current Notes" once levelled, ironically, at a new English miscellany, the *Argosy* (1:195).

Why *Beadle's* abruptly ceased publication is a matter of speculation. Johannsen believes it languished after the death of Robert Adams, the main inspiration behind its creation. Mott suggests that the public misunderstood *Beadle's* because it was not prepared to give attention to a serious periodical from a firm whose name was associated with cheap publications.[7] Perhaps, too, the real business of Beadle and Adams did not lie in periodical publication. For in the bright firmament of this publishing house, *Beadle's Monthly* figured as but the faintest star amid those veritable constellations—dime novels, libraries of cheap publications, and series—that grew exponentially in number and were to grow even brighter in the two decades after *Beadle's Monthly* faded.

## Notes

1. Albert Johannsen, *The House of Beadle and Adams*, 2 vols. (Norman: University of Oklahoma Press, 1950), 1:50.
2. Frank Luther Mott, *A History of American Magazines, 1850–1865* (Cambridge: Harvard University Press, 1938), p. 476; Johannsen, 2:286.
3. Johannsen, 1:19–51, passim.
4. Mott, p. 467; Johannsen, 1:421.
5. Johannsen, 1:421.
6. *Banner Weekly*, 17 December 1887, p. 4.
7. Johannsen, 1:54; Mott, p. 468.

### Information Sources

BIBLIOGRAPHY:

Johannsen, Albert. *The House of Beadle and Adams and its Dime and Nickel Novels: The Story of a Vanished Literature*. 2 vols. Norman: University of Oklahoma Press, 1950.

Mott, Frank Luther. *A History of American Magazines: 1850–1865*. Cambridge: Harvard University Press, 1938. Pp. 467–68.

INDEXES: None

REPRINT EDITIONS: American Periodicals: Series III, 1850–1900. University Microfilms, Ann Arbor. Reel 26.

LOCATION SOURCES: Widely available.

### Publication History

MAGAZINE TITLE AND TITLE CHANGES: *Beadle's Monthly, A Magazine of To-Day*.
VOLUME AND ISSUE DATA: Volumes 1–3, January 1866-June 1867.
FREQUENCY OF PUBLICATION: Monthly.
PUBLISHER: January 1866-June 1867: Beadle and Company, New York.
EDITOR: Unknown.

*Arthur Wrobel*

## THE BIBELOT

In the *Bibelot* Thomas Bird Mosher produced a miscellany of "exotics of Literature" for which the editor hoped to create a large audience. Frank Luther Mott suggests that Mosher's endeavor was one of the foremost earlier "little magazines," ranking with the *Chap-Book*\* and *Philistine*.[1] Although Mosher recognized that his was an avant-garde periodical, he emphasized that the *Bibelot* did not "profess to exploit the new forces and ferment of *fin de siècle* writers," but strove to provide its readers with "less accessible material." Since *Modern Art* and the *Chap-Book* enjoyed popularity, Mosher reasoned that his publishing venture would find a substantial readership and added that "such beautifully gotten up affairs have created a republic of their own." Regarded as an excellent anthologist, Mosher published poetry, drama, short fiction, and critical essays.

When the magazine ceased publication, William Marion Reedy commented that "the complete *Bibelot* . . . is an encyclopedia of the literature of rapture with the spirit of beauty." The *Bibelot* was truly an art-for-art's-sake periodical; Mott remarks that it had a "legitimate appeal to the self-culture motive of the nineties."[2] Its twenty-year run, however, far exceeds the life of its counterparts. Only because of the retirement of the sixty-two-year-old Mosher did the *Bibelot* cease publication in 1915.

Mosher began his little magazine in January of 1895. As both publisher and editor of the one-man operation, he alone determined the magazine's contents. Mott speculates that Mosher, whose first publishing venture was an edition of George Meredith's *Modern Love*, possessed a "predilection for verse and essay of a somber cast."[3] However, notwithstanding his early endeavor, he included a mixture of the serious and the jocular in the *Bibelot*. Mosher never altered the format. Each issue of the *Bibelot* was in duodecimo and contained twenty-four to forty-eight pages. For fifty cents a year a subscriber could generally expect twelve choice pieces of literature; occasionally a selection might be continued over two numbers. Even though the yearly rate later escalated to seventy-five cents, individual copies remained at five cents. Bound volumes or "testimonial editions" of the year's offerings could be purchased for $1.75. Seldom did the *Bibelot* carry illustrations. Each month Mosher introduced a work with an essay analyzing or presenting background on the text. Clearly intended for the national scene, the appeal of the *Bibelot* was limited to the literary elite who loved books.

The first issue included work by William Blake, Marcus Aurelius, James Thompson, D. G. Rossetti, Thomas Campion, and Percy Shelley. Subsequent tables of contents read like honor rolls of the greats of literature. Although he offered portions of such standard works as *Songs of Innocence, Songs of Experience*, and *The Cenci*, Mosher also included lesser known pieces—for example, the early works of William Morris. Mosher also chose compositions by "Fiona Macleod," Oscar Wilde, and Walt Whitman, and he even included a modern English translation of the medieval poem *Pearl* by S. Weir Mitchell. Further exemplifying his diversity, he included several critical essays on Aubrey Beardsley and Thackeray, among others. Two interesting entries in the *Bibelot* are a scene from the opera *La Vie de Bohême* and an essay on Handel's *Largo*.

Since it carried no advertisements and sold for a relatively small price, one wonders how the *Bibelot* could survive for two decades. Mosher managed to produce a high-quality publication cheaply by not paying contributors and by benignly violating copyright laws. But survive the *Bibelot* did, and it brought to its readers what its editor termed "specimens of the finer spirit."

## Notes

1. Frank Luther Mott, "*Bibelot*." *A History of American Magazines*. 4 vols. (Cambridge, Mass.: Belknap Press of Harvard University Press, 1957) 4:415–26.
2. Mott, 4:426.
3. Mott, 4:424.

## Information Sources

BIBLIOGRAPHY:

Hart, James D. *The Oxford Companion to American Literature*. 4th ed. New York: Oxford University Press, 1965. Pp. 484–85, 568–69.

Mott, Frank Luther. "*Bibelot*." *A History of American Magazines*. 4 vols. Cambridge, Mass.: Belknap Press of Harvard University Press, 1957. 4:424–27.

INDEXES: Index to volumes 1–12 in volume 12, compiled by Milton James Ferguson. Included as volume 21 in 1924 reprint edition.

REPRINT EDITIONS: Microform: University Microfilms International. W. H. Wise & Co., New York, 1924.

LOCATION SOURCES: Widely available.

## Publication History

MAGAZINE TITLE AND CHANGES: *The Bibelot: A Reprint of Poetry and Prose for Book Lovers Chosen in Part from Scarce Editions and Sources Not Generally Known.*

VOLUME AND ISSUE DATA: Volumes 1–20, January 1885-December 1915.

FREQUENCY OF PUBLICATION: Monthly.

PUBLISHER: Thomas Bird Mosher.

EDITOR: Thomas Bird Mosher.

*E. Kate Stewart*


**THE BIVOUAC.** See THE SOUTHERN BIVOUAC


**THE BOOK BUYER.** See *American Literary Magazines: The Twentieth Century*


# THE BOOKMAN

Although its tenor varied with its succession of owners and editors, the *Bookman* through its almost forty-year history consistently appealed to the literary and bibliographic interests of its readers. Indicative of this focus was the *Bookman*'s practice at its inception of listing those books most in demand in various cities in the United States, a policy adapted from the London *Bookman*. While it did not coin the term "best seller," the *Bookman* did much to popularize the concept and thus keep its readers informed of trends in the literary marketplace. Dubbed by Frank Luther Mott in his *A History of American Magazines* "a faithful historian of contemporary world literature,"[1] the *Bookman* earned this accolade not only by showcasing the works of prominent writers and by contributing to the development of literary criticism in America through its fine reviews but also by dealing with the business of literature—the publishing and selling of books.

Perhaps the periodical's dual emphasis on the art and on the business of literature stems from its founder and its early editors. Frank Howard Dodd, who was president of the Dodd, Mead Publishing Company, established the *Bookman*. He chose as its first editor Harry Thurston Peck, a scholarly, witty professor of language and literature at Columbia University. His junior editor was James MacArthur, an advisor to the Dodd, Mead firm. Thus, those involved with the periodical's foundation were well versed in both the aesthetic and the practical aspects of literature.

Harry Thurston Peck is often credited with the *Bookman*'s initial success—it reached a circulation of about 15,000 by the end of 1899. Earlier under his editorship *Acta Columbiana* had become the most famous undergraduate periodical in the United States.[2] The characteristics that made Peck a good editor—his brilliance, the scope of his knowledge of world literature, his wit, his perspicacity, and his lack of pretension—are amply illustrated by Thomas Beer in *The Mauve Decade*.[3] Peck wrote numerous articles and reviews for the *Bookman* and in 1896 initiated the "Bookman Letter Box," consisting of his commentary on selected letters. In appraising this feature of the *Bookman*, Mott finds Peck "dogmatic in regard to matters of English usage, manners, literary values, and public questions," comparing him to Richard Grant White of the *Galaxy*,* though Peck is "perhaps more a wit and less a savant than White."[4] Moreover, the Bohemian movement in America during this period, of which Peck was notably representative, can itself be seen as an impetus for the founding, the policy, and the success of the *Bookman*. A socio-literary movement whose adherents rejected the materialism of modern industrial society, Bohemianism was a dominant force in Western European literature. Though its influence in America was minor, its impact was nonetheless felt.[5] As the *Literary History of the United States* is clear to note, the movement spawned numerous magazines. American writers of the period, unlike their European counterparts, sought "rather to educate than to shock the middle class reader" and were desirous of spreading "a wide awareness of contemporary developments in taste and thought."[6] Given its contents through the Peck editorial years, such an end can be seen as the *Bookman*'s goal. The periodical was established at a time when there was a ready market for its wares.

From 1895 to 1899, the *Bookman* was subtitled "An Illustrated Literary Journal." It sought to illumine its audience about British, French, Italian, German, and Russian literature. In addition, it maintained a consistent focus on current American literature, reviewing, for example, Edith Wharton's first book as well as Edwin Arlington Robinson's. In the early years some articles were reprinted from the London *Bookman*, a practice soon abandoned. In addition to reviews, brief articles about writers, and the best-seller list, the *Bookman* also included serial stories and special serial articles dealing with literary, artistic, historical, and cultural topics. In these early years its pages were graced by critics George Saintsbury, Edmund Gosse, and Andrew Lang. Works by Rudyard Kipling, Thomas Hardy, George Meredith, and Arthur Conan Doyle often appeared.

The year 1899 brought about several changes for the *Bookman*. Its subtitle was revised to "A Review of Books and Life," and this was maintained until the journal's demise in 1933. Moreover, the junior editor, James MacArthur, who like Peck wrote numerous essays and reviews for each issue, left the *Bookman* and was succeeded by Arthur Bartlett Maurice. He injected his enthusiasm into his work and instituted a number of improvements in the periodical. Skillful and vibrant, he helped the *Bookman*'s circulation reach the forty thousand mark, the zenith in its publication history. With Peck's retirement from the editorship in 1907, Maurice assumed the position as editor, a role he ably maintained until 1917. Book reviews became less predominant during his tenure. Articles often reflected Maurice's concern for a sense of place in literature. The series "American Backgrounds for Fiction" clearly manifested this regionalistic approach as did Maurice's own publications—*New York in Fiction* (1901), *The New York of Novelists* (1916), and *The Paris of Novelists* (1919)—based on series he had done for the *Bookman*. Perhaps one of the most notable aspects of Maurice's editorship was the moratorium on fiction that lasted from 1910 until 1918. Critic and essayist Frank Colby Moore served as junior editor from 1907 to 1910.

After the *Bookman*'s founder, Frank Howard Dodd, died in 1916, Maurice resigned to assist Herbert Hoover with Belgian relief. Three editors who followed Maurice filled the position only briefly. Immediately after Maurice's departure, the *Bookman* was edited by G. G. Wyant for a year and continued the severe decline in circulation that had set in several years prior to his assumption of that role. In 1918 the periodical was bought by the George H. Doran Company, and a number of significant changes followed. Under the editorship of Robert Cortes Holliday, both illustrations and the best-seller list were abandoned in order to bring about a new look by breaking with some of the traditions of the past. Holliday edited the *Bookman* for two years and was succeeded by Henry Litchfield West, who served for only a year.

Then in 1921 John Chipman Farrar became the *Bookman*'s chief editor. During his six-year tenure, the *Bookman* soon became recognized as a "working guide to current literary movements."[7] The familiar best-seller list was resumed, essays were punctuated by humor and satire, book reviews were predominant as were serials. Noted writers whose work appeared in the *Bookman* in the 1920s were Joyce Kilmer, Arnold Bennett, Robert Benchley, Hugh Walpole, J. B. Priestley, Aldous Huxley, Louis Untermeyer, Heywood Broun, Henry Seidel Canby, Theodore Dreiser, Mary Austin, Katherine Mansfield, and Stephen Vincent Benet. While poetry had been regularly though not prolifically printed in past issues, it received an even more prominent place under Farrar's editorship, and poems by Conrad Aiken, H. D., Amy Lowell, Carl Sandburg, and Sara Teasdale appeared in the *Bookman*'s pages.

When the George H. Doran Company merged with Doubleday in 1927, Farrar took a position with the firm, and the *Bookman* was sold to Seward Collins. Although the periodical's circulation had improved somewhat, Collins, wanting to update the *Bookman* and inject new life into it, chose to renovate the magazine by combining the features of the literary review and the general magazine. He selected Burton Rascoe as his new editor. Formerly the literary critic for the

*Chicago Tribune* and the *New York Tribune* and an associate editor at *McCall's*, Rascoe had cultivated many important writers as friends. Thus, the pages of the *Bookman* were adorned with works by James Branch Cabell, E. E. Cummings, Theodore Dreiser, Dorothy Parker, and Upton Sinclair. In 1928 the *Bookman* featured the best newspaper stories published in America and serialized Sinclair's *Boston*, a novel about Sacco and Vanzetti.

In spite of a rather impressive beginning, Burton Rascoe did not remain long at the *Bookman*. He and Collins soon quarreled over the extent of editorial control the owner insisted on assuming. Collins desired more input into editorial matters than Rascoe cared to relinquish. In 1928 Rascoe left the *Bookman* and Collins assumed the editorship, continuing in that position until 1933 when he ceased publication of the periodical in favor of the less literary *American Review*. Under Collins's governance the *Bookman* became a more conservative but nonetheless still impressive review. Contributors included T. S. Eliot, John Gould Fletcher, Hamlin Garland, Aldous Huxley, and Rebecca West. Mott finds the most important aspect of Collins's years to be the *Bookman*'s role as "champion of the new and controversial humanist movement led by Irving Babbitt and Paul Elmer More."[8] And here probably lay the real difficulty between Rascoe and Collins. New Humanism, a critical and philosophical movement that flourished in the 1920s and 1930s in the United States, was a clear reaction to the realistic and naturalistic trends of the period as well as to the earlier romanticism. The Humanists sought to defend traditional and conservative values and stressed the dominance of man's reason and ethical sensibility over his animalism.[9] The *Literary History of the United States* cites a long list of modernist critics opposing the New Humanists, including Edmund Wilson, Malcolm Cowley, Kenneth Burke, Allen Tate, R. P. Blackmur, Lewis Mumford, and Burton Rascoe.[10] Rascoe's presence on this list points to the real difficulty in his relationship with Collins. For since Collins was an avid supporter of the New Humanists, a philosophical gulf would have divided him from Rascoe.

When the *Bookman* ended with its March 1933 issue, the literary world must have lamented its cessation. While longevity alone is scarcely sufficient to recommend any endeavor, the *Bookman* did serve its readers well for nearly forty years. In that time, it kept its readers fully informed of both the practical and the aesthetic aspects of literature. With the latest news about book buying and book sales, with special serial articles, with good fiction and poetry, with critical reviews and controversies, the *Bookman* consistently informed, entertained, and educated its audience.

## Notes

1. Frank Luther Mott, *A History of American Magazines, 1885–1905* (Cambridge: Harvard University Press, 1957), p. 441.

2. "Harry Thurston Peck," vol. 14, *Dictionary of American Biography* (1934), p. 377.

3. Thomas Beer, *The Mauve Decade: American Life at the End of the Nineteenth Century* (New York: Alfred A. Knopf, 1926), pp. 185–99.

4. Mott, p. 434.

5. For a useful survey of the Bohemian movement in America, see Albert Parry, *Garretts and Pretenders: A History of Bohemianism in America* (1933; rpt., New York: Dover, 1960).

6. Robert E. Spiller et al., *Literary History of the United States: History*, 4th edition (New York: Macmillan, 1974), p. 1067.

7. Mott, p. 438.

8. Mott, p. 441.

9. A good introduction to the New Humanism is *Humanism and America: Essays on the Outlook of Modern Civilisation*, ed. Norman Foerster (New York: Farrar and Rhinehart, 1930).

10. Spiller et al., p. 1360.

## Information Sources

BIBLIOGRAPHY:

Beer, Thomas. *The Mauve Decade: American Life at the End of the Nineteenth Century.* New York: Alfred A. Knopf, 1926.

Cleaton, Irene, and Allen Cleaton. *Books and Battles: American Literature, 1920–1930.* New York: Cooper Square Publishers, 1970.

Cook, George. "London's *Bookman* Letters." *Jack London Newsletter* 6 (May-August 1973):81–87.

Craven, Robert Kenton. "Seward Collins and the Traditionalists: A Study of the *Bookman* and the *American Review*, 1928–1937." Ph.D. diss., University of Kansas, 1967.

Doran, George H. *Chronicles of Barabbas, 1884–1934.* New York: Harcourt, Brace, 1935.

Maurice, Arthur Bartlett. "More Old Bookman Days." *The Bookman* 70 (1929):56–65.

———. "Old Bookman Days." *The Bookman* 66 (1927):20–26.

Mott, Frank Luther. "*The Bookman*." *A History of American Magazines, 1885–1905.* Cambridge: Harvard University Press, 1957. Pp. 432–41.

"The Bookman." *Hound & Horn* 1 (1927):175–77.

INDEXES: Eichelberger, Clayton L. *A Guide to Critical Reviews of United States Fiction, 1870–1910.* 2 volumes. Metuchen, New Jersey: Scarecrow Press, 1971.

REPRINT EDITIONS: American Periodicals: Series III, 1850–1900. University Microfilms, Ann Arbor. Reels 112–30. Bell and Howell Micro Photo Division. Microforms International.

LOCATION SOURCES: Widely available.

## Publication History

MAGAZINE TITLE AND TITLE CHANGES: *The Bookman: An Illustrated Literary Journal*, 1895–1899. *The Bookman: A Review of Books and Life*, 1899–1933.

VOLUME AND ISSUE DATA: Volume 1, February-July 1895; volume 2, September 1895-February 1896 (August-September combined); volumes 3–73, March 1896-August 1931; volume 74, September 1931-March 1932 (January-February combined); volume 75, April-December 1932; volume 76, January-March 1933.

FREQUENCY OF PUBLICATION: Volumes 1 and 2 monthly. Semiannually beginning
     March 1896.
PUBLISHERS: February 1895-August 1918: Dodd, Mead, and Company, New York.
     September 1918-August 1927: George H. Doran Company, New York. September
     1927-March 1933: Bookman Publishing Company, New York.
EDITORS: Harry Thurston Peck and James MacArthur, 1895–1899; Harry Thurston Peck
     and Arthur Bartlett Maurice, 1899–1907; Arthur Bartlett Maurice, 1907–1917
     (with Frank Moore Colby, 1907–1910); G. G. Wyant, 1917–1918; Robert Cortes
     Holliday, 1918–1920; Henry Litchfield West, 1920–1921; John Chipman Farrar,
     1921–1927; Burton Rascoe, 1927–1928; Seward Collins, 1928–1933.

*Frances M. Malpezzi*

# THE BOSTON MISCELLANY OF LITERATURE AND FASHION

Justifying his contribution to the *Boston Miscellany of Literature and Fashion*,
James Russell Lowell claimed that under the *Miscellany*'s "thin crust of fashion
and frivolity throb the undying fires of the great soul of man, which is the
fountain and centre of all poesy."[1] Lowell's comment is perhaps valid; the
*Miscellany* combined a wide variety of material that would appeal to a broad
range of tastes. This magazine of seemingly incongruous content resulted from
efforts by Bradbury, Soden and Company, who sought to publish a literary
magazine that would contain enough popular material to ensure financial success.
The publishers realized that "there was no class of readers who could sustain
creditably a purely literary magazine," but a number of "factory girls could be
relied upon to float" such, provided it included light reading and fashion news.[2]

Bradbury and Soden approached Nathan Hale, the editor of the *Daily Advertiser*, hoping that he could recommend a suitable editor for such an undertaking.
Hale led them to his eldest son, Nathan Hale, Jr., who accepted the editorship.[3]
He would be responsible only for the literature, which was to occupy forty-six
pages. Only two pages were to be devoted to fashion,[4] and each issue was to
contain sheet music.

In January of 1842, the first monthly issue of the *Boston Miscellany of Literature and Fashion* appeared. As Frank Luther Mott notes in *A History of
American Magazines*, Hale was a prominent member of the city's literary society
when "Boston was just beginning a literary dominance that was to continue for
some three decades."[5] Calling upon family alone, Hale could have produced a
respectable publication. In the first number of the *Miscellany* were Sarah Preston
Everett Hale's translations, Edward Everett Hale's story, and Edward Everett's
article—the editor's mother, brother, and uncle were directly involved in the new
enterprise. Hale also accepted for publication poems by James Russell Lowell and
W. W. Story; all three young men had been classmates at Harvard.[6] Clearly,
Bradbury and Soden had made the correct choice for editor.

Despite the *Miscellany*'s contributions from such reputable literary personages, the world of academe was appalled by a magazine that incorporated the gauche with the artistic.[7] Fashion plates paraded the latest styles from Paris while notable scholars reviewed and submitted works of literature. In the second volume of the *Miscellany* appeared Poe's review of Griswold's *Poets and Poetry of America*. Also included in the pages of the *Miscellany* was original work by Elizabeth Barrett (Browning). Lowell's work, including his series on English dramatists, appeared frequently; perhaps he often submitted his pieces to the magazine because he expected to be paid the healthy sum of fifteen dollars per poem.[8] Not yet known for *Uncle Tom's Cabin*, Harriet Beecher Stowe was less sure what to expect. When offered twenty dollars for each three-page article, she wrote to her husband to inquire whether the offer might be trusted.[9]

The magazine seems to have been willing to go to great lengths to please its patrons. The "Publisher's Notice" in the second volume promises that "every exertion will be made to make the *Miscellany* more and more acceptable to its readers" (2:281). Another notice entitled "Editor's Table" states the editor's desire to "make this monthly visiter [sic] a cheering guest in many dwellings, to breathe sweet counsel into the weary mind" (3:43).

Cornelius Mathews expressed a similar desire to be thus accepted. Mathews writes "A First Letter" dated 2 June 1842 in which he expresses hope that his contributions will be viewed favorably (2:31–32). Mathews, along with Evert A. Duyckinck, had been editor of *Arcturus** before the *Miscellany* absorbed it. Following this consolidation of the two magazines, both Mathews and Duyckinck wrote for the *Miscellany*.

By the end of the same year, Hale included his "Editor's Farewell" in the sixth number of volume two and surrendered his position to Henry Theodore Tuckerman, one of the few "thoroughbred men" in the world of tasteful literature.[10] Perhaps in an attempt to maintain the support of women, Tuckerman changed part of the title to "Lady's Monthly Magazine" in the third volume.[11] Unfortunately, Tuckerman's leadership proved fruitless; after assuming the editorship, he published only two numbers, thus ending the publication of the *Boston Miscellany*. The literary world could no longer reap the benefits of factory girls' desires to know the latest in fashion.

## Notes

1. Leon Howard, *Victorian Knight-Errant: A Study of the Early Literary Career of James Russell Lowell* (Berkeley and Los Angeles: University of California Press, 1952), p. 111.

2. Edward Everett Hale, *James Russell Lowell and His Friends* (Boston and New York: Houghton, Mifflin and Company, 1899), p. 83.

3. Frank Luther Mott, "*The Boston Miscellany*," *A History of American Magazines*, 4 vols. (Cambridge, Mass.: Belknap Press of Harvard University Press, 1957), 1:718.

4. Hale, pp. 82–83.

5. Mott, 1:718.

6. Mott, 1:718.

7. Algernon Tassin, *The Magazine in America* (New York: Dodd, Mead, and Company, 1916), p. 75.

8. Howard, pp. 108–9.

9. *Life and Letters of Harriet Beecher Stowe*, ed. Annie Fields (Boston and New York: Houghton, Mifflin and Company, 1897), p. 104.

10. Evert A. Duyckinck and George L. Duyckinck, *Cyclopaedia of American Literature Embracing Personal and Critical Notices of Authors and Selections From Their Writings From the Earliest Period to the Present Day*, 2 vols. (New York: Charles Scribner, 1855), 2:582–86.

11. Jean Hoornstra and Trudy Heath, eds., *American Periodicals, 1741–1900: An Index to the Microfilm Collections* (Ann Arbor, Michigan: University Microfilms International, 1979), p. 3.

## Information Sources

BIBLIOGRAPHY:

Duberman, Martin. *James Russell Lowell*. Boston: Houghton, Mifflin Company, 1966.

Duyckinck, Evert A., and George L. Duyckinck. *Cyclopaedia of American Literature Embracing Personal and Critical Notices of Authors and Selections From Their Writings From the Earliest Period to the Present Day*. 2 vols. New York: Charles Scribner, 1855.

Hale, Edward Everett. *James Russell Lowell and His Friends*. Boston and New York: Houghton, Mifflin and Company, 1899.

Howard, Leon. *Victorian Knight-Errant: A Study of the Early Literary Career of James Russell Lowell*. Berkeley and Los Angeles: University of California Press, 1952.

*Letters of James Russell Lowell*. Ed. Charles Eliot Norton. 2 vols. New York: Harper and Brothers, 1894.

Mott, Frank Luther. "*The Boston Miscellany.*" *A History of American Magazines*. 4 vols. Cambridge, Mass.: Belknap Press of Harvard University Press, 1957. 1:718–20.

*New Letters of James Russell Lowell*. Ed. M. A. Dewolfe Howe. New York: Harper and Brothers, 1932.

Reilly, Joseph J. *James Russell Lowell As a Critic*. New York: G. P. Putnam's Sons, 1915.

INDEXES: None

REPRINT EDITIONS: American Periodicals: Series II, 1800–1850. University Microfilms, Ann Arbor. Reel 310.

LOCATION SOURCES: Widely available.

## Publication History

MAGAZINE TITLE AND TITLE CHANGES: *The Boston Miscellany of Literature and Fashion*. Volume 3 titled *The Boston Miscellany and Lady's Monthly Magazine*.

VOLUME AND ISSUE DATA: Volume 1, January-June 1842; volume 2, July-December 1842; volume 3, January-February 1843.

FREQUENCY OF PUBLICATION: Monthly.

PUBLISHERS: Bradbury, Soden and Company, Boston.
EDITORS: Nathan Hale, Jr., 1842; Henry Theodore Tuckerman, 1843.

*Debra Brown*

## BOSTON NOTION

The *Boston Notion* was the second in a small group of historically important literary periodicals called "Mammoth Weeklies" that flourished between the late 1830s and the mid–1840s. During its eight-year run (1839–1847), the *Notion* was published by George Roberts from his State Street printing house in Boston. For all but four months of its lifetime, Roberts also edited the periodical. The appellation "Mammoth" was a reference to the extraordinary dimensions of the paper—37 inches by 52 inches in its folio edition of four pages. This size (which is about the width of two and a half modern newspapers and the length of two) made the paper one of the largest weekly publications ever printed. For nineteen months (October 1841 through April 1843), Roberts printed a smaller quarto edition of sixteen pages. For the first seven months of the *Quarto Notion*, Roberts continued to print the folio edition, but he stopped the folio on 23 April 1842 and did not resume it until 15 April 1843, when he closed the *Quarto Notion* at the end of its second volume. The *Quarto* was supposed to contain all the matter of the folio *Notion*, but, in the seven months that they ran concurrently, there were differences from the mastheads to the selections. In addition, the order of the duplicate material was seldom the same. The differences, however, were not critical enough to matter in the overall editorial policy. Further, just to improve on his claim to publishing the largest newspaper in the world, Roberts printed some bonus issues for subscribers. These irregularly appearing papers, called the *Double Notion* or *Quadruple Notion*, were typically 67 inches wide and 90 inches long and consisted of sixteen pages. These pages most often contained matter not in the other editions, although there was some overlapping. Only three of these gargantuan issues survive.

Roberts called his publication a newspaper (it was actually part book, part magazine, and part newspaper), but news was a minor consideration in its contents until late in its life. He published in newspaper format to take advantage of current postal regulations that allowed newspapers to be sent for one cent an issue for up to one hundred miles; over a hundred miles cost one and a half cents. Magazines of normal size cost four and a half to seven cents an issue to mail. Weight of newspapers was not really a consideration for the post office until 1852.[1] During this era the postal service considered newspapers to be necessary to the dissemination of knowledge to the general public, hence the cheap rates. It was further fortunate that weight was not a factor in mailing rates since the folio *Notion* typically weighed nearly a pound.[2]

Roberts was a hardheaded Yankee businessman who knew exactly what he was doing with the *Notion*. Most periodicals of the day accepted subscriptions without advance payments, and, as could be expected, many subscribers stayed in arrears. Roberts, however, demanded cash in advance. He sold subscriptions for three dollars yearly and extended no credit. Single issues of the folio and *Quarto Notion* were six cents; the *Quadruple Notion* was twenty-five cents to nonsubscribers but free to subscribers. These prices were remarkably low for the huge pages, each carrying nine or ten columns of closely printed matter (thirteen columns for the *Quadruple Notion*). Roberts calculated that his paper contained 3,888 square inches and 27 feet of type (nearly 900,000 pieces of type) and that one weekly issue contained the equivalent reading matter of an entire novel, which typically cost one or two dollars hardbound.

When Roberts started the *Notion*, his paper was the second "Mammoth Weekly." Park Benjamin and Rufus Wilmot Griswold had begun the *Brother Jonathan* in New York in July 1839. This pair soon left the *Jonathan* and founded the *New World*, a third "Mammoth," in June 1840. The *Notion* lasted longer than either of its two major competititors, probably because Roberts was not an amateur editor. He had been publishing the *Boston Daily Times* (1836–1857) for three years before he started the *Notion*, and his *Times* was already the best-selling penny daily in the North.

Roberts, ever one to make comparisons, pointed out with great frequency that his paper was the largest in the world, citing the number of square inches and brevier ems to prove his point. He even twitted his closest rivals with a woodcut masthead showing two giraffes holding up a single sheet (the front and back pages) of the *Notion*. A small crowd of people is gathered in front of this display. Two of the spectators are carrying large papers over their arms; one of the papers is the *New World*, the other the *Brother Jonathan*.

In his first issue, 28 September 1839, Roberts promised to supply "an immense quantity of reading matter, of such kinds as will be interesting or useful to all classes of people; but it [the *Notion*] will contain none of the slanderous persecution of politics" (p.2). He promised material not only from American writers but also from England as soon as "Mr. Cunard's line of steam packets come [*sic*] to Boston" (19 October 1839, p. 2). Roberts delivered on his promises, and, because there was no copyright law at the time, he and other editors could print what they wanted and pay what they wished. The *Notion*'s premier issue reprinted items from other literary periodicals of the day, most of which he received. Editors of literary magazines exchanged copies of their issues with other editors in hopes of favorable notice—which was considered good advertising. Roberts did "puff" many papers and then plunder the items he liked to fill his own huge sheets. The most important author represented in the first issue was the English writer G. P. R. James; there were some short stories, poetry, and criticism of new novels. Serial fiction soon became a mainstay; publishing several chapters a week of, for example, Charles Dickens's novel *Master Humphrey's Clock* (*The Old Curiosity Shop*) was not only popular but an intelligent marketing technique. The paper also printed biography, travel writing, history, theatrical criticism, and snippets of news from local and out of state newspapers. Advertising was confined to a quarter of the back page.

Nearly nine thousand copies of the first issue were sold, and by October 1839 Roberts was printing ten thousand. He distributed these copies through the paper carrier systems he had built with the *Times*, and he soon had agents not only in the Northern states but as far south as Augusta, Georgia, and as far west as Vicksburg, Mississippi. At its zenith in the early 1840s, the *Notion* sold nearly twenty-five thousand copies weekly, a remarkable figure when compared with other literary periodicals of the era and a testimony to the increasing appetite for reading matter by the increasingly literate masses. One of the lasting contributions made by the *Notion* is that it helped to whet the public's appetite for cheaper stories, novels, and poems. Publishing histories of the 1840s suggest that even major presses began to lower the price of their hardbound volumes as paperbound books and periodicals became more popular. By 1843, the prestigious Harper & Brothers firm had a line of novels in brown paper wrappers that sold for twenty-five cents each.

The *Notion* deserved its early popularity, for Roberts printed the most prominent authors of the day. Immediately recognizable writers included William Gilmore Simms (*Pelayo*), John Greenleaf Whittier ("The Opium Eater"), Edgar Allan Poe ("The Fall of the House of Usher," "Eleonora," "Morella"), and Nathaniel Hawthorne ("The Two Widows"). Along with these major writers were a large number of the lesser-known writers who toil in any age. The fiction of John Neal was published, as was that of Robert Montgomery Bird, Captain Marryat, Nathaniel P. Willis, Sam Slick (T. C. Haliburton), Eugène Sue, William Howitt, and George Sand (Madame Dudevant). Poets and poetasters alike helped to fill the *Notion*; Mary Howitt, Thomas Moore, Lydia Sigourney, Felicia Hemans, Willis Gaylord Clark, William Cullen Bryant, and Charles Fenno Hoffman were only a few of the scores of poets printed. Henry Wadsworth Longfellow's poetic drama "The Spanish Student" appeared. William Ellery Channing published several serious sermons, while "Reverend Caesar Lillywhite" wrote a series of "Nigger Sermons" in dialect. Theodore Parker penned a long series explaining transcendentalism. There was a biography of Poe and one of William Henry Harrison.

Judged by sales, the most popular tale printed in the *Notion* was Joseph Holt Ingraham's *The Dancing Feather*, a short novel that ran serially from 27 November 1841 until 5 March 1842. After its serial publication, Roberts reprinted the complete novel and eventually sold 47,000 paperback copies in five editions at twelve and a half cents a copy. Roberts and other publishers of the 1840s issued many tales between paper covers that can legitimately be considered forerunners of the Beadle and Adams "Dime Novels." It is ironically fitting that *Feather* was Roberts's most popular story. It is a tale of amateur pirates who plunder an occasional ship and live well until the money is spent. Roberts, a literary pirate who chose what he wanted to print from the material available to him, did pay for some work; Ingraham apparently received fifty dollars for *The Dancing Feather*'s original publication, although he did not share in the reprint royalties.

Since Roberts had strong opinions on what his paper should contain, it is no surprise that he edited as well as printed his *Notion* for nearly its entire existence. He made one exception. Louis Fitzgerald Tasistro edited the *Quarto Notion* for four months, from 19 November 1842 through 25 February 1843. Tasistro was a writer, translator, and editor of some repute when he came to work, but his influence on the *Quarto* was minimal. Tasistro did accomplish two things worthy of note. He wrote much more entertaining and literary editor's columns than did Roberts, and he adhered to a new policy of cutting down on the lengthy serials that ran for months at a time.

Roberts regained the editorship after Tasistro left and conducted business as usual for a while, but by late 1843 the *Notion* was beginning to falter. More and more literature came from British periodicals and less from American pens. More advertisements began to appear, and more news stories, particularly sensationally titled ones ("A Seducer Arrested," "Commencement of the Crusade for the Extermination of the Mormons"). There were more letters on political matters and more news of court proceedings; the paper no longer touted its own merits, and it printed less literature. In January 1844, the size of the paper shrunk by several inches with no explanation. Circulation was down to eighteen thousand copies a week. Roberts took a partner named Beach in 1845, but the *Notion* never recovered its energetic flamboyance. The last extant issue, 18 September 1847, returned to the full folio size, but the voyage of the *Notion* was over.

The verdict of history in ignoring the *Notion* is not completely justified but can be explained in part. The major problems include the size and quality of the paper. Few repositories can conveniently house such an enormous periodical, and the paper quality was so poor that even those libraries that today have copies find them disintegrating.[3] But its lack of availability cannot change the fact that the *Notion* was a remarkable creation for its time and place, one of the most popular periodicals and one that definitely added to the market for the literary magazinists in an age of magazines that catered to a growing reading public.

## Notes

1. Wayne E. Fuller, *The American Mail: Enlarger of the Common Life* (Chicago: University of Chicago Press, 1972), p. 122.

2. Fuller, p. 124.

3. Burton R. Pollin, "Poe and the *Boston Notion*," *English Language Notes* 8 (September 1970):23.

## Information Sources

BIBLIOGRAPHY:

Fuller, Wayne E. *The American Mail: Enlarger of the Common Life*. Chicago: University of Chicago Press, 1972.

Mott, Frank Luther. *A History of American Magazines*. 4 vols. Cambridge, Mass.: Belknap Press of Harvard University Press, 1957. 1:361–62; 2:45.

Pollin, Burton R. "Poe and the *Boston Notion.*" *English Language Notes* 8 (September 1970):23–28.

INDEXES: There is no modern index. The *Boston Quarto Notion* published its own partial index for its two volumes (9 October 1841–15 April 1843).

REPRINT EDITIONS: Microform: New England Micrographics, Inc.

LOCATION SOURCES: There are no complete runs extant. Partial runs: American Antiquarian Society. University of California at Los Angeles. Connecticut State Library. Library of Congress. Boston Public Library. University of Minnesota.

### Publication History

MAGAZINE TITLE AND TITLE CHANGES: *Boston Notion* [Folio]. *Boston Notion* [Quadruple or Double *Notion*]. *Boston Quarto Notion, or Roberts' Weekly Journal of American and Foreign Literature, Fine Arts, and General News, Containing New and Popular Novels, Tales and Romances, Original Sermons and Lectures, & C. & C.*

VOLUME AND ISSUE DATA: *Boston Notion* [Folio]: Volumes 1–8, 28 September 1839–23 April 1842; New Series, volumes 9–13, 22 April 1843–18 September 1847. [Not published 30 April 1842–15 April 1843; after 1844, there are missing issues]. *Boston Notion* [Quadruple or Double Notion]: 30 January 1841; 10 June 1841; 15 July 1841. [Only extant issues] *Boston Quarto Notion*: Volumes 1–2, 9 October 1841–15 April 1843.

FREQUENCY OF PUBLICATION: Weekly.

PUBLISHERS: 29 September 1839–10 May 1845: George Roberts, Boston. 21 June 1845–18 September 1847: [George] Roberts and Beach, Boston.

EDITORS: George Roberts, 29 September 1839–12 November 1842; Louis Fitzgerald Tasistro, 19 November 1842–25 February 1843; George Roberts, 4 March 1843–18 September 1847.

*Robert W. Weathersby II*

# THE BOSTON QUARTERLY REVIEW

The *Boston Quarterly Review* (1838–1842), the most comprehensive of Jacksonian journals, was founded, edited, and mostly written by Orestes Augustus Brownson (1803–1876). He was born in Vermont, but his early public career began in central New York state. Initially a Presbyterian, then a Universalist, next a no-church Independent preacher, he was all the while an editor and political spokesman for liberal causes, notably the Fanny Wright–Robert Dale Owen branch of the Workingman's party. He returned to New England in 1832 to become the Unitarian minister at Walpole, New Hampshire, bringing with him a reputation as a brilliant, outspoken, honest, but only partly reformed radical.

While in Walpole he studied French, began a lyceum program, and corresponded with William Ellery Channing, whose published sermons had brought Brownson to Unitarianism. He met other members of the New England circle on his numerous trips to Boston and, in 1834, became minister in Canton, south of Boston. He started another lyceum program, plus a library and reading program for young workmen, wrote for the religious journals of the area, and learned German along with Thoreau. At that time, Channing, George Ripley, and other ministers were concerned that Unitarianism (already a wealthy, elite sect) had lost its missionary zeal, so they encouraged Brownson in his wish to involve common people and workmen.

Accordingly, the Society of Christian Union and Progress was founded in Boston, with Brownson as its minister and spokesman. Out of this experience came *New Views of Christianity, Society, and the Church* (1836), an attempt to unite his heterodox political, social, and religious experiences. An early and active member of the Transcendental Club but impatient with intellectual conversation without action, he took over the editorship of a weekly journal, the *Boston Reformer*, to carry on his exciting (and, to many, radical) program.

Such a brilliant and energetic writer and speaker, advancing the Jacksonian cause in educated circles as well as with the workmen, soon attracted attention. George Bancroft, the historian, was also able to reward such activity. Just appointed collector of the Port of Boston, he had some federal appointments of his own to make and offered one to Brownson (another went to Hawthorne). The duties were slight, the pay adequate, and there was plenty of free time, so Brownson took the appointment, gave up the *Boston Reformer*, and started his own independent quarterly.[1]

He begins the first number (January 1838) with "Introductory Remarks" (1:1–8), explaining that although various periodicals in the region have "always been open to me" and "still would be," there was always the thought of "refusal," with its consequent inhibition. For his own journal, he welcomes contributions but plans to do most of the writing himself. His third article (1:21–33), the first major review of Whittier's abolition poems, praises Whittier's expression of the "American Idea" of freedom. The fourth (1:33–74) is a printing of his own "Address at the Democratic State Convention" on the previous September 20. The sixth, "Philosophy and Common Sense" (1:83–107), is a correction of a *Christian Examiner** article defining Locke's tabula rasa theory. From Locke's claim that people are molded by their environment, the Whigs, that is, the conservatives, relegate the masses to a subordinate role. Brownson is quick to correct this blunder: "They, the masses, are not so destitute as the Lockeites thought them, not so dependent on their betters, as *great* men have generally counted them" (1:102). Article seven is a review of Emerson's Phi Beta Kappa Oration. The address is praised, but Brownson, speaking from a basic conviction that the gaining of knowledge carries with it the duty of sharing that knowledge with others, asks, "When and how shall our Authors be found" (1:114).

In the second number for April 1838, article three expands on the observations of Francis Grund, a Viennese visiting America (1:161–92). Grund had "spoken of General Jackson in terms of respect" and had "even gone so far as to approve his administration," thus discomfiting his Whig hosts. Brownson then spoofs the Whig praise of such English literature as itself praises the glories of past regimes, such as Scott, but warns that "poor Shelley must not be mentioned, for he dreamed of social equality'' (1:165). For American literature the Whigs find it ''lawful to praise Washington Irving,'' for he writes nothing ''not acceptable to the *North American\** and the *London Quarterly*.'' James Fenimore Cooper was a Whig favorite when he ''took good care to show no sympathy for the democracy,'' but when he ''sought to infuse into his works some portion of American thought and feeling'' he came ''under the ban of all the Quarterlies in the world—except our own'' (1:165–66). And, indeed, in the next issue for July 1838, Brownson's review of Cooper's *American Democrat* (1:360–77) is the only distinctive Jacksonian analysis of that major work.[2]

In the April 1838 issue there is also a major statement of Brownson's progressive view of the course of history. He points out the great promise of the Peasant Rebellion, acknowledging his ''fellow-feeling with this same Walter the Tiler, who led on his sixty thousand peasants towards London, singing 'When Adam delved, and Eva span, / Where then was the gentleman?' '' (1:222) This background of progressive reform leads up to our own American Revolution, which now must be completed in the social revolution of the present Jacksonian time. Another major article is ''Alcott on *Human Culture*'' (1:417–32), the only significant defense of Bronson Alcott's educational philosophy and system as manifested in the much-derided ''Conversations with Children on the Gospels.'' There is also the first doctrinal difference with Emerson, although Brownson's correction of the ''Divinity School Address'' (1:500–14) is in no sense part of the conservative reaction of Andrews Norton and other religious reactionaries.

This liberal program continued through 1839, with further comments on Emerson (2:113–22), on Wordsworth's poetry from a Jacksonian and transcendental viewpoint (2:137–68), and a tribute to George Ripley for his translations of current French philosophy, with key implications for what we now call the New England Renaissance (2:187–205). Brownson also gives his corrected Jacksonian position of ''The Indians and Our Relation with Them'' (2:229–52). This is followed by a surprising defense of ''Bulwer's Novels'' (2:265–98) for their sociological value in revealing that criminals are often not so much enemies as victims of society. Later there is a Jacksonian analysis of Horace Mann's famous educational report (1:393–435), and still later an explanation of how churches, if they wish to survive, must work with the people's push for social reform (2:449–77).

For these first two years Brownson had all the contributor support he could handle. Although most of the articles were his, he did include work that tallied with the Jacksonian character of the journal. These were from such New England notables as Alcott, Bancroft, William Henry Channing, Alexander Everett, Margaret Fuller, Elizabeth Peabody, and George Ripley. But with the founding of the *Dial\** (Boston) in 1840, these changed their allegiance. Even without the *Dial* as an alternative, the *Review* would have become a one-man journal as Brownson became involved in the 1840 campaign. His Jacksonian rhetoric is even seen in ''American Literature'' (3:57–79), which would almost seem to be an invitation for a Walt Whitman poet.[3]

In July 1840, the first essay (3:265–322) relates to another program of the *Review*, the rejection of conservative orthodoxy as represented by Andrews Norton and the attack on Emerson. But in the excitement of the "Tippecanoe and Tyler Too" campaign, that important essay was overlooked in the notoriety of "The Laboring Classes" (3:358–96). This daring article, the first of two, had as its point of departure Carlyle's pamphlet *Chartism*, which points out that the laboring class is worse off in England than anywhere in Europe. The cause is not an oppressive aristocracy but a dominant middle class from which the manufacturing power springs, with the accompanying exploitation of the worker. Carlyle finds no remedy but universal education and emigration of the proletariat.

Brownson acknowledges that in America there is the further complication of slave labor, but he says again that both evils must be corrected by going far beyond Carlyle's desperate remedy. When he went on to explain that the best way to preserve equality of opportunity is for government to abolish the inheritance of property, the alarm was immediate. Brownson's fame, or rather, his notoriety, reached its peak as Whigs reprinted the article by the thousands and sent it throughout the country as dire warning of what a socialistic Jacksonian policy intended.

Van Buren reputedly blamed Brownson for his defeat, although no historian now would substantiate such a claim. But whatever the consequences to Van Buren, the electoral loss did not kill the *Review*—that is, immediately. It did, however, shock its editor out of his buoyant confidence in the wisdom of the common people. The notoriety of those bold articles still continues, leading to Brownson's title as the "American Marxist before Marx."[4] The label is true enough but a disservice to Brownson in thereby minimizing the broader aspects of his cultural analysis.

Through 1841 that analysis continued with only slight modification, but by 1842 the Jacksonian fervor had clearly diminished. Not only was circulation going down, but Brownson himself was now interested in exploring conservative approaches to American problems, for he was less than certain that social evils had a social remedy. He even began to correct his earlier judgments from his new conservative (he called it "realistic") outlook. The brilliant criticism continued but was clearly not what his subscribers wanted, so he transferred his list to the *Democratic Review* (see *United States Magazine and Democratic Review*\*), a monthly in New York. It was agreed that he would write a regular monthly article, which he did. But the necessity of modifying his blunt, combative, personal style to a new editor and group of readers became increasingly frustrating. So, in 1844, he started a new journal, now entitled *Brownson's Quarterly Review*,\* where he could speak from his now conservative mind with the freedom and force that his personality and character demanded.

## Notes

1. Thomas R. Ryan, *Orestes A. Brownson: A Definitive Biography* (Huntington, Ind.: Our Sunday Visitor Press, 1976), pp. 115–23. This extensive biography includes all available information about Brownson and his *Reviews*.

2. C. Carroll Hollis, "Orestes Brownson: Jacksonian Literary Critic," in *No Divided Allegiance: Essays in Brownson's Thought*, ed. Leonard Gilhooley (New York: Fordham University Press, 1980), pp. 51–83.

3. Edwin Fussell, *"Leaves of Grass* and Brownson," *American Literature* 31 (1959):77–78.

4. Arthur M. Schlesinger, Jr., "Orestes Brownson: An American Marxist Before Marx," *Sewanee Review* 47 (1939):317–23.

## Information Sources

BIBLIOGRAPHY:

Brownson, Henry F. *Orestes A. Brownson's Early Life: to 1844*. Detroit: H. F. Brownson, 1898.

Brownson, Orestes A. Brownson Papers: University of Notre Dame Archives (available on microfilm).

————. *The Convert: or Leaves from My Experience*. New York: D. & J. Sadlier, 1857.

————. *New Views of Christianity, Society, and the Church*. Boston: C. C. Little and J. Brown, 1836.

Caponigri, A. Robert. "Brownson and Emerson: Nature and History." *New England Quarterly* 18 (1945):368–90.

Gohdes, Clarence. *The Periodicals of American Transcendentalism*. Durham: Duke University Press, 1931.

Maynard, Theodore. *Orestes Brownson: Yankee, Radical, Catholic*. New York: Macmillan, 1943.

Mott, Frank Luther. *History of American Magazines, 1741–1850*. New York: D. Appleton, 1930. Pp. 685–91.

Ripley, George. "Brownson's Writings" *The Dial* 1 (1840):22–46.

Ryan, Thomas R. *Orestes A. Brownson: A Definitive Biography*. Huntington, Ind.: Our Sunday Visitor Press, 1976.

Schlesinger, Arthur M., Jr. *Orestes Brownson: A Pilgrim's Progress*. Boston: Little, Brown, 1939.

INDEXES: None

REPRINT EDITIONS: American Periodicals: Series II, 1800–1850. University Microfilms, Ann Arbor. Reel 380.

LOCATION SOURCES: Widely available.

## Publication History

MAGAZINE TITLE AND TITLE CHANGES: *The Boston Quarterly Review*.
VOLUME AND ISSUE DATA: Volumes 1–5, January 1838-October 1842.
FREQUENCY OF PUBLICATION: Quarterly (January, April, July, October).
PUBLISHER: Benjamin H. Greene, Boston.
EDITOR: Orestes A. Brownson.

*C. Carroll Hollis*


# THE BROADWAY JOURNAL

Although Edgar Allan Poe did not establish the *Broadway Journal*, a weekly paper in sixteen-page issues with the brief existence of one year, his name is the chief reason for that publication's remaining in memory. It was the last literary periodical he edited, it contained variant versions of many of his important writings, and he manipulated it to further his attempts at gaining recognition and fulfilling literary ambitions. The aims and the nature of the *Broadway Journal* have long been misunderstood among Poe scholars although in recent years new evidence has shed light on the genesis and altering courses of this publication. The founding editor, Charles F. Briggs, better known by his pseudonym, "Harry Franco," hoped to create a literary paper to further causes of a genuinely national American literature. During the 1840s and 1850s the North-South bifurcation in the United States increased, but Briggs wanted to reconcile some of those opposites in order to insure subscribers, contributors, and quality for his enterprise.

The *Broadway Journal* carried an "Introductory" that set forth intentions to maintain high standards in imaginative and critical writing, to promote a really national literature, and to work objectively toward those goals. Briggs, who was himself a Democrat in politics, calculated shrewdly in securing John Bisco, a former employee of the *Knickerbocker*,* a prestigious, conservative Whig monthly magazine in New York, as his publisher. Thus Briggs figured on appealing for support to the circle associated with that magazine and its editor, Lewis Gaylord Clark. Briggs was also a friend of James Russell Lowell and Maria Lowell, familiar Boston writers who were ardent supporters of abolitionist causes. The Lowells and other renowned authors assisted the *Broadway Journal*, among them Evert A. Duyckinck, Lydia Maria Child, William A. Jones, William Gilmore Simms, and Robert A. Carter. Henry C. Watson supplied much of the music criticism. Briggs wanted to notice not merely literature and literary matters, but to pay attention to music, the visual and plastic arts, and drama. He also hoped to use fine woodcut illustrations, but that hope never amounted to much as regards quantity of illustrations.

A typical issue of the *Broadway Journal* might include lengthy reviews, many of them quite substantial, a section on "The Fine Arts" (often containing solid criticism of painting and music), a piece on architecture, critiques of the drama, miscellaneous columns of filler as space permitted or required, ads, and occasional illustrations. The series "Sketches of American Prose Writers" opened auspiciously with Evert A. Duyckinck's article on William A. Jones. Four more, on Nathaniel Parker Willis, Henry Cary ("John Waters"), Richard Henry Dana, and Henry T. Tuckerman succeeded. Although such well-known subjects as these could have extended the series, it was dropped after the 22 February issue. Understandably, magazine writing and the magazine world received attention repeatedly. The criticism of music and drama supplies a need, because of its astuteness, that is matched in few other periodicals of the time. The American drama and theater, in particular, receive noteworthy commentary.

Failing to secure the continuing services of Nathaniel Parker Willis, whose reputation could have been beneficial, Briggs turned to Poe as a person who could give a needed boost to the security of the *Broadway Journal*. In lieu of regular payments, Poe was awarded an editorial title and was to share in the profits as they accrued. Two difficulties dogged the career of the paper. First, funds were insufficient from the start. Ultimately, financial failures caused the end of publication. Second, Briggs and Bisco originally agreed that neither could sell his interest in the *Broadway Journal* without consent of the other. By summer 1845 Briggs wished to take control wholly into his hands with services from another publisher. He had come to dislike Poe for several reasons. Not the least of these was Poe's altering the abolitionist stance of the paper. This manipulation lost the support of the Lowells and other Northeasterners who did not admire Southern attitudes. In consequence, many would-be contributors turned away. By this time, however, Poe and Bisco determined to continue on their own, and so Bisco demanded an exorbitant price from Briggs. The confusion resulted in no issue appearing for 5 July 1845. When Briggs failed to respond, Bisco and Poe shouldered ownership until October, when Bisco withdrew, leaving Poe as sole editor and owner. Poe's letters of these months and afterward reveal his financial straits; he finally sold the *Broadway Journal* to Thomas H. Lane, and Thomas Dunn English was left to edit the final issue for the press.

Briggs never forgot Poe's underhanded dealings, as he interpreted them, in relation to the *Broadway Journal*, and his early admiration for Poe turned to hostility. Poe later satirized him in a "Literati" paper; Briggs in turn lampooned Poe in a satirical novel, *The Trippings of Tom Pepper*, and he published a biased account of Poe the man and writer soon after Poe's death. Poe's own participation in the *Broadway Journal* was such that the original intention of using only fresh writings changed in order that his own published tales and poems could appear in revised versions. Many of these pieces constitute their creator's final revised texts, and therefore they increase the significance of the paper itself. To cite but one example, an early tale, "The Visionary," plotted around intrigue, passion, and suicide in suspense-filled Venetian surroundings, was retitled "The Assignation," doubtless to enhance the appeal and to diminish any overt comic surface that it might have had in Poe's abortive scheme for *Tales of the Folio Club*, a book-length collection of a literary club's frame-stories with humorous implications.

Poe probably used the *Broadway Journal* to promote another twofold purpose as well, namely, the drawing of sufficient attention to his literary stature to insure, first, publication of his fiction and poems in volume form by Wiley and Putnam—in their prestigious "Library of American Books" series—and, second, the continuance of his own scheme for a significant American literary journal. Consequently, Poe's conduct of the *Broadway Journal* may be regarded as one more among his many literary hoaxes. Poe had carried over to the *Broadway Journal* a charge of plagiarism against the famed American poet Henry Wadsworth Longfellow that he had begun in the New York *Evening Mirror* on 13 and 14 January 1845, which was reprinted in the New York *Weekly Mirror* on 25 January. Longfellow was defended in the *Evening Mirror* for 1 March by "Outis," who observed that such charges as Poe's only made their author seem contemptible. Poe used columns of the *Broadway Journal* during March and

April ostensibly to exonerate himself, but, because he prolonged his defense, one wonders if he wished primarily to keep his name in the public eye in order that he be deemed significant enough to be a good risk for a publisher. The columns of the paper subsequently contained notices of Poe's writings and his public appearances, like that at the Boston Lyceum (2:261–62, 309–11). Poe's high critical standards also suffered intermittent lapses when he wished to do well by certain writers or causes. Furthermore, although Briggs had had to resort to advertising for financial fluidity, Poe himself gave much space to publications from the established firms of Harper's and Wiley and Putnam. He may deliberately have acted thus to assist the causes of the Young America movement, counter to the conservatives in the *Knickerbocker* Whig circle, in furthering a national literature. Duyckinck, a prime mover in Young America, also was responsible for Poe's inclusion in the "Library of American Books." Poe had also wished for a publication connection with Harper's. He, therefore, did not hesitate to employ space in the *Broadway Journal* to attack the *Knickerbocker* and those associated with it, most notably the formidable editor, Lewis Gaylord Clark, and his twin, Willis Gaylord Clark.

Such tactics, however, brought no lasting success to the *Broadway Journal*, dogged as it was by insolvency and the alienation of many potential contributors. In the midst of other concerns, many contemporaneous American writers had sought or established periodicals sympathetic to their motives and needs. Poe's increasing lack of personal interest combined with these causes to end the project that began with exuberance and good will.

## Information Sources

BIBLIOGRAPHY:

Benton, Richard P. "Introduction: Some Remarks on Poe and His Critics." *The University of Mississippi Studies in English* 3 (1982):i-xii.

[Briggs, Charles F.] "Topics of the Month." *Holden's Dollar Magazine* 4 (December 1849):765–66.

Dunlap, Leslie W., ed. *The Letters of Willis Gaylord Clark and Lewis Gaylord Clark.* New York: The New York Public Library, 1940.

Ehrlich, Hayward. "*The Broadway Journal* (1): Briggs's Dilemma and Poe's Strategy." *Bulletin of the New York Public Library* 73 (February 1969):74–93.

Fisher, Benjamin Franklin, IV. "A Ten-Year Shelf of Poe Books." *The University of Mississippi Studies in English* 3 (1982):183–99.

———. *The Very Spirit of Cordiality: The Literary Uses of Alcohol and Alcoholism in The Tales of Edgar Allan Poe.* Baltimore: The Edgar Allan Poe Society, 1978.

Jacobs, Robert D. *Poe: Journalist & Critic.* Baton Rouge: Louisiana State University Press, 1969. Pp. 353, 375–78, 395.

Lowell, James Russell. *The Letters of James Russell Lowell.* Ed. Charles Eliot Norton. New York: Harper and Brothers, 1894. 2:83–102.

Mabbott, Thomas Ollive. "Annals." *The Collected Works of Edgar Allan Poe.* 3 vols. Ed. Thomas Ollive Mabbott with the assistance of Eleanor D. Kewer and Maureen C. Mabbott. Cambridge, Mass.: Belknap Press of Harvard University Press, 1969–1978. 1:527–72.

Miller, Perry. *The Raven and the Whale: The War of Words and Wits in the Era of Poe and Melville*. New York: Harcourt, Brace, and World, 1956.

Moss, Sidney P. *Poe's Literary Battles: The Critic in the Context of His Literary Milieu*. Durham, N.C.: Duke University Press, 1963; rpt., Carbondale & Edwardsville: Southern Illinois University Press, 1969; London and Amsterdam: Feffer & Simons, 1969, *passim*.

————. *Poe's Major Crisis: His Libel Suit and New York's Literary World*. Durham, N.C.: Duke University Press, 1970, *passim*.

Mott, Frank Luther. "*The Broadway Journal*." *A History of American Magazines 1741–1850*. New York and London: D. Appleton, 1930. Pp. 757–62.

Poe, Edgar Allan. *The Letters of Edgar Allan Poe*. Rev. ed. 2 vols. Ed. John Ward Ostrom. New York: Gordian Press, 1966.

Quinn, Arthur Hobson. *Edgar Allan Poe: A Critical Biography*. New York: Appleton Century Crofts, 1941; rpt., New York: Cooper Square Publishers, 1959. Pp. 452–94, 751–53.

Richard, Claude. "Poe and 'Young America.' " *Studies in Bibliography* 21 (1968):25–58.

Roche, Arthur John. "A Literary Gentleman in New York: Evert A. Duyckinck's Relationships with Nathaniel Hawthorne, Herman Melville, Edgar Allan Poe, and William Gilmore Simms." Ph.D. diss., Duke University 1973. Pp. 75–105.

Stafford, John. *The Literary Criticism of "Young America": A Study in the Relationships of Politics And Wit, 1837–1850*. Berkeley and Los Angeles: University of California Press, 1952. Pp. 29–35, 74–76.

Tebbel, John. *The American Magazine: A Compact History*. New York: Hawthorn Books, 1969. Pp. 49, 61–62, 70–80, 82, 87, 96.

Thompson, G. R. "Edgar Allan Poe." *Antebellum Writers in New York and the South*. Ed. Joel Myerson. [*Dictionary of Literary Biography*, vol. 3]. Detroit: Gale Research Co., 1979. Pp. 249–97.

Weidman, Bette S. "*The Broadway Journal* (2): A Casualty of Abolition Politics." *Bulletin of the New York Public Library* 73 (February 1969):94–113.

INDEXES: Within bound volumes.

REPRINT EDITIONS: American Periodicals: Series II, 1800–1850. University Microfilms, Ann Arbor. Reel 649. AMS Press Inc., New York, 1965.

LOCATION SOURCES: Widely available.

## Publication History

MAGAZINE TITLE AND TITLE CHANGES: *The Broadway Journal*.

VOLUME AND ISSUE DATA: Volumes 1–2, 4 January 1845–3 January 1846; no issue for 5 July 1845.

FREQUENCY OF PUBLICATION: Weekly.

PUBLISHERS: 4 January–18 October 1845: John Bisco, New York. 25 October–27 December 1845: Edgar Allan Poe, New York. 3 January 1846: Thomas H. Lane, New York.

EDITORS: Charles F. Briggs, 4 January–22 February 1845; Charles F. Briggs, Edgar Allan Poe, and Henry C. Watson, 1 March–28 June 1845; Edgar Allan Poe and

Henry C. Watson, 12 July–18 October 1845; Edgar Allan Poe, 25 October–27
December 1845; Thomas Dunn English, 3 January 1846.

*Benjamin Franklin Fisher IV*


# BROWNSON'S QUARTERLY REVIEW

In early-nineteenth-century America every major religion had one or more journals explaining or defending its doctrines. Of these, Catholicism was least represented. It was largely an immigrant church, predominantly Irish, and had little
attraction for most Americans. But in the 1840s the American counterpart of the
English Oxford movement led to a number of converts from old-line families.
This drew attention to the growing number of Catholic churches and schools,
with consequent curiosity among educated Americans. It was also apparent that
with increasing voter strength Catholics would assume a stronger role, with
consequent opposition from Native American and Know-Nothing movements.
One of the early converts, who became the best known Catholic editor and writer
of the period, was Orestes Brownson.[1]

He had made a brilliant, if somewhat mercurial, reputation as founder and editor of the *Boston Quarterly Review,** but when it merged with the *Democratic
Review* (see *United States Magazine and Democratic Review**) in 1842, Brownson was without a journal of his own. So, in 1844, he founded another journal,
gave it his own name, and set out to present and defend his new conservative outlook. That this course would soon bring him into the Catholic church he himself
could not know. But by October 1844, his readers were not surprised at his con-
version, although few believed he would remain a Catholic for long.

Brownson's temperament was such that he wrote at his best under the spur
of controversies. The plural is necessary, for he always seemed to have three
or four arguments going on at once in philosophy, religion, politics, or literature.
That was, indeed, the same four-part range of subject matter of the earlier journal,
and it is what he promises in the "Introduction" (1:1–28) to the first number
(January 1844) of *Brownson's Quarterly Review*.

Accordingly, the first article, "Berkeley and Idealism," translates the remarks
of the French philosopher Pierre Leroux on Bishop Berkeley and John Locke,
with paragraphs of Brownson's own as interveners. Later, "The Church Question" (1:55–84) starts off as a review of *Tracts for the Times* by John Henry
Newman and other Oxford Reformers but soon becomes the first indication of
that to which Brownson's religious investigations might lead. The next article,
"Demagogism" (1:84–104), opposes the party machinery and spoils system that
had led to Van Buren's 1840 defeat. Brownson does not mention his own
unintended contribution to that defeat, but he still supports (with a new conservative flavor) the party's democratic philosophy. However, the party now
needs new leadership, which Brownson then suggests ought to be John C.
Calhoun (1:105–31). To make sure there will be no misunderstanding, Brownson

concludes this first number of his new journal with a somewhat blunt editorial note stating that most of the articles will be his own: "This plan is adopted, because the views of its editor are so peculiar that it is impossible to open the pages to various contributors without destroying the necessary unity; and also because those who take it at all will take it for the writings of the editor" (1:136).

This range of treatment brought subscriptions and readers from a variety of disciplines both here and abroad. The *Review* was read in Paris and later Rome but had its largest European audience in England and Ireland, where it became perhaps the first American journal to have a London edition. The second or April number carries on this same spread of topics with the first of a series criticizing Immanuel Kant's *Critiques* (1:137–74). This was followed by a reminder to his friends at Brook Farm that the phalanx plan of the Fourierists would be fatal without the support and agency of a church (1:175–94). Then follows an attack on a baccalaureate address for its aristocratic implications (1:194–208), ending with this democratic mot juste: "You insist on an educated class. Certainly. But not on a class to be educated. The education determines the class, not the class the education."

There are too many controversies to treat chronologically, but the major ones can be seen selectively. On the notion of a "True Church," he had started with the review of *Tracts for the Times* already noted. That criticism occasioned a rejoinder from Anglicans in this country (notably Bishops Hopkins and Seabury) to which Brownson replied in two vigorous articles, ending the last one in October 1844 with this remark: "No man must think to frighten us by the cry of 'Popery.' Happy are we to acknowledge the authority of the Holy Father; more happy shall we be if we can so live as to secure his blessing" (1:514). Presumably, with his acceptance by the church later that month, he got that "blessing," although many in the church may later have wondered if it were of the "mixed" variety. He kept up his argument with the Tractarians, climaxing it with a stern and blunt rejection of Newman's well-known *Essay on the Development of Christian Doctrine*. That argument began in July 1846 and went on through six articles more, finally dying out eight years later, chiefly because Newman would not answer, and his friends and defenders, writing in the *Dublin Review*, ran out of refutations.[2]

An even more acrimonious controversy was that with the Irish in this country. The interchange began amicably enough in January 1845 with Brownson's major article "Native Americanism" (2:76–98). He demonstrated that Catholicism was fully compatible with republican government, and that fears that Catholics owe allegiance to a foreign power, the pope, are groundless, for the allegiance is to the head of a church, not to the head of a state. The article was just and well received, but in deference to even-handed justice he was aware that the Irish were, on their side, somewhat oversensitive. Accordingly, in the April number, he reminded the "Irish press in this country" that "native Americans have sensibilities as well as Irishmen" and it should cease the "offensive want of respect for American feelings" (2:267–68). That began a bitter debate (highlighted by his even stronger stand in "Native Americanism" of July 1854) that only ended after the Civil War. By then new waves of immigrants from Germany and other Continental countries made the sensitive Irish no longer the only significant national group in the church.

Within the Catholic church there had long been the doctrine *Extra Ecclesiam nulla Salus* (No Salvation outside the Church), but in a democratic country with many religions it was not strongly advocated nor stressed tendentiously—that is, not until Brownson. In strong language he insisted on a stringent and literal reading of the doctrine in a first article entitled "Recent Publications" (April 1847), followed in July by "The Great Question," and then, two years later, by "Civil and Religious Toleration." When he revived the *Review* many years later in 1873, he also revived this issue with four more articles. He insisted in all these trenchant articles, some objected to by the clergy themselves, that the doctrine was essential (otherwise why was he in the church?), but it is difficult to know how effective the whole bitter debate was in making converts.[3]

But the most important controversy that ultimately brought about the closing of the *Review* was related to the Civil War.[4] President Buchanan had lost Brownson's support with his inept handling of national problems, including Kansas and the question of slavery in the Territories. As a fervent patriot, once the war started Brownson supported Lincoln and pressured for an early emancipation act. But as the war went on, he convinced himself that Lincoln was too dilatory for the presidency in that time of national crisis. So Brownson closed the current series of the *Review* to start a new National Series to be devoted solely to national affairs. In so doing he made a crucial blunder by endorsing and supporting vigorously the candidacy of General Fremont in the spring and summer of 1864. The gamble was a risky one, but two of the Brownson's sons had been killed and another wounded in action and perhaps his impatience was understandable. In any case, dismayed by Fremont's September withdrawal, Brownson felt rightly that he had lost his audience and terminated the magazine.

Politics is the art of compromise, and Brownson's political journalism was the least successful avenue for his brilliant talents. The regrettable consequence of his political blunder was not that he had embarrassed himself nationally, for he was too straightforward for that. But when he closed the *Review* a number of controversies were dropped in mid-course: the mistaken role of the church in France in supporting Louis Napoleon; the equally mistaken role of the pope in maintaining the Papal States; the status of Vincenzo Gioberti, the Italian ontologist, in Catholic philosophy;[5] the ineptness of sentimental writing that claimed to be Catholic literature.[6]

In the ten-year interval before he revived the *Review*, he turned to writing for the *Catholic World*, founded by his protégé Isaac Hecker, and other religious magazines, but of course it was not the same. He also put together his major single book, *The American Republic*, considered by Lord Acton the best book on the subject. But he was at loose ends and needed money to support his family. Some Catholic admirers gathered sufficient funds for a small annuity, and he supplemented that income with many addresses and lectures. But his love was his *Review*, and in 1873 he revived it for what he called his "Last Series."

In that final three-year run, a major thrust was the pseudo-science of Darwin popularizers, but he also attacked Catholic scholars for complaining instead of getting into the laboratories themselves. He continued his critical analyses of philosophy and religion and of social and political thought, but without his being quite aware of it, the grounds had changed. Except for a brief exchange, when he attempted to renew the "No Salvation outside the Church" controversy, no one argued with him or against him. And without the spur of controversy the fire of his thinking and the brilliance of his style was dampened. He completed the final volume in 1875 and died the following year.

## Notes

1. Of the various biographies, the two that best deal with Brownson's so-called Catholic Period are Theodore Maynard, *Orestes Brownson: Yankee, Radical, Catholic* (New York: Macmillan, 1943) and Thomas R. Ryan, *Orestes A. Brownson: A Definitive Biography* (Huntington, Ind.: Our Sunday Visitor Press, 1976).

2. Ryan, pp. 366–80.

3. Maynard, pp. 152–91.

4. Brownson generally is wise and just in his social and political judgments, but in the excitement of war times there are some regrettable misjudgments. These are fairly treated by Leonard Gilhooley, "Brownson, the American Idea, and the Early Civil War," in *No Divided Allegiance*, ed. Leonard Gilhooley (New York: Fordham University Press, 1980), pp. 125–41.

5. A. Robert Caponigri, "European Influences on the Thought of Orestes Brownson: Pierre Leroux and Vincenzo Gioberti," in *No Divided Allegiance*, ed. Leonard Gilhooley (New York: Fordham University Press, 1980), pp. 100–125.

6. Americo Lapati, "The Literary Critic," *Orestes A. Brownson* (New York: Twayne, 1965), pp. 109–25.

## Information Sources

BIBLIOGRAPHY:

Brownson, Henry F. *Orestes A. Brownson's Middle Life: from 1845 to 1855*. Detroit: H. F. Brownson, 1899.

———. *Orestes A. Brownson's Latter Life: from 1855 to 1876*. Detroit: H. F. Brownson, 1900.

Brownson, Orestes A. Brownson Papers: University of Notre Dame Archives (available on microfilm).

———. *The Convert: or Leaves from My Experience*. New York: D. & J. Sadlier, 1857.

Caponigri, A. Robert. "European Influences on the Thought of Orestes Brownson." In *No Divided Allegiance: Essays in Brownson's Thought*. Ed. Leonard Gilhooley. New York: Fordham University Press, 1980. Pp. 100–125.

Gilhooley, Leonard. "Brownson, the American Idea, and the Early Civil War." In *No Divided Allegiance: Essays in Brownson's Thought*. Ed. Leonard Gilhooley. New York: Fordham University Press, 1980. Pp. 125–41.

Lapati, Americo D. *Orestes A. Brownson*. New York: Twayne Publishers, 1965.

Maynard, Theodore. *Orestes Brownson: Yankee, Radical, Catholic*. New York: Macmillan, 1943.

Ryan, Thomas R. *Orestes A. Brownson: A Definitive Biography*. Huntington, Ind.: Our Sunday Visitor Press, 1976.

INDEXES: None

REPRINT EDITIONS: American Literary Periodicals: Series II, 1800–1850. University Microfilms, Ann Arbor. Reels 507–8, 884–86.

LOCATION SOURCES: Widely available.

### Publication History

MAGAZINE TITLE AND TITLE CHANGES: *Brownson's Quarterly Review*.

VOLUME AND ISSUE DATA: First Series, volumes 1–3, January 1844-October 1846 (bound numbers 1–3); New Series, volumes 1–6, January 1847-October 1852 (bound numbers 4–9); Third Series, volumes 1–3, January 1853-October 1855 (bound numbers 10–12); New York Series, volumes 1–4, January 1856-October 1859 (bound numbers 13–16); Third New York Series, volumes 1–4, January 1860-October 1863 (bound numbers 17–20); National Series, volume 1, January 1864-October 1864 (bound number 21); Last Series, volumes 1–3, January 1873-October 1875 (bound numbers 22–24).

FREQUENCY OF PUBLICATION: Quarterly (January, April, July, October).

PUBLISHERS: 1844–1855: Benjamin H. Green, Boston. 1856–1859: E. Dunigan & Bro., New York. 1860–1864: D. & J. Sadlier, New York. 1873–1875: Fr. Pustet & Co., New York.

EDITOR: Orestes Brownson, January 1844-October 1875.

*C. Carroll Hollis*

# BURTON'S GENTLEMAN'S MAGAZINE

William Evans Burton (1804–1860), a British-born actor who gained fame on the American stage, established his *Gentleman's Magazine* in Philadelphia during July 1837. Burton conceived the magazine as a miscellany of art, literature, sports, and theater. With the exception of the one year that Edgar Allan Poe served as the magazine's primary editor, Burton himself screened submissions as well as contributed many of his own stories, essays, and book reviews. He was proud that many of the monthly's articles were pirated into English periodicals and subsequently appeared in other American magazines.[1] At the height of its popularity *Burton's Gentleman's Magazine* listed some 3,500 subscribers[2] and was known for its "raciness, humor, tact, and taste." Its numbers often contained beautiful plates; its leaves were large, its paper high quality, and its typography exceptional for magazines of the day.[3]

Burton carefully defined his audience on the title page of the first issue, quoting from Aubrey De Vere: "By a gentleman, we mean . . . whoever is open, just, and true; whoever is of a human and affable demeanor. Whoever is honorable in himself and in the judgment of others, and requires no law but his word to make him fulfill an engagement; such a man is a *gentleman*;—and such a man may be found among the tillers of the earth as well as the drawing rooms of the highborn and the rich.''

That Burton addressed a primarily male audience is clear from ''Experiences of a Modern Philosopher,'' a regular feature of the early numbers, consisting of practical advice for gentlemen on subjects from seduction to cigars. For example, seduction of female virtue is ''low, mean, and unworthy'' of a true gentleman—for virginity is a woman's ''richest treasure'' (1:32); only brandy should be drunk after eating oysters; and the finest cigars are rolled in Havana (1:397). The selection and training of a wife is a frequent topic: ''A dirty house is as bad as a foul tongue, and it is better to see your wife clean her teeth than play on the guitar'' (1:397). While the ''Modern Philosopher'' professes to have a high opinion of the female sex—''Woman is the flower of humanity . . . let us not debase her'' (1:32)—he advises gentlemen to keep a strong rein on their wives (1:173) and cautions against marriage with thin-lipped ladies (1:32).

Women are also the subject of the essay ''Pen and Ink Sketches of Various Members of the Young Lady Creation'' (3:25–27), which profiles several ''types'' of young ladies, romantic, matter-of-fact, evangelical, and lazy, so that, after a brief acquaintance, young gentlemen can easily spot each type. Other essays include discussions on religion, writers, actors, poets, and field sports. William Landor warns about the evils of mixing feeling with religion in ''Religion and Poetry'' (2:217–19), and Thomas Randolph deals with contemporary verse in ''Poets and Their Poetry'' (2:320). Some articles discuss outdoor recreation suitable for gentlemen. ''Field Sports and Manly Pastimes'' (4:110–11) takes up skating, archery, hunting, and more, while ''The Natural History of the Dog in All Its Varieties'' (4:113–17) tells sportsmen the relative advantages of various canines of the field, from foxhounds to pointers to Newfoundland dogs.

Many offerings in each issue derive from Burton's own pen. In ''A Day on Lake Erie'' (2:30–34), Burton observes life aboard a Great Lakes steamboat, in ''My First Performance'' (2:123–27), he recalls his debut on the stage, and in ''My First Cousin and My First Kiss'' (2:298–304), he reminisces about an early love. Burton also dabbles in musical composition in ''The Way the Money Goes'' (2:62), a comical song, and he delves into biography with his sketch of actor James W. Wallack (4:11–16). In addition, in volume two Burton introduces ''The Anniversary Register: or, Monthly Calendar of American Chronology,'' listing important dates of births and deaths of eminent men, sea and land battles, treaties and other matters connected with the history of America (2:59–61).

Book reviews under Burton's editorship lean toward the appreciative rather than critical. Typically, the reviewer offers a few introductory compliments and then quotes at length from the text. One exception is an attack on James Fenimore Cooper's *Gleanings of Europe* for its harsh rendering of British life and customs. Called an ''errant grumbler,'' Cooper is portrayed as a vagrant who ''wanders through the flower garden, and tramples down its finest buds, and defiles the beauty of its choicest flowers in an eager search after his favorite thistle'' (1:290).

But most books, such as Washington Irving's *The Rocky Mountains*—"a lively romance of real life"—(1:71) and Charles Dickens's *Pickwick Papers*—" 'Boz' is an unequalled painter of human life" (1:285), receive kinder treatment.

Sentimental verse, usually by little-known poets, fills gaps between reviews, narratives, and essays. The first few lines of "The Parted Lovers" by Charles West Thomson serve to illustrate the typical fare: "A maiden stood beside the moaning sea, / Her raven tresses o'er her neck were flung, / And wildest tones of nature's minstrelsy, / came forth in silver accents from her tongue" (1:398). The mournful tone of "The Parted Lovers" finds its opposite in saccharine poems like "To My Sleeping Boy on His First Birthday": "Thou hast had thy joyous frolic / On the fond maternal knee, / Thou has leapt and sported wildly / in thy young heart's ecstacy" (2:55). In addition to melancholy and sentimental verse, one finds such quasi-philosophical poems as "The Sum of Life," which sketches the cycle of birth and death from the wailing infant at his mother's breast to the "sightless" and "palsied" elder drawing his last breath, every stanza repeating the ponderous question, "Why are we here?" (2:61)

Noticeable changes occurred in the quality of verse and prose once Edgar Allan Poe became coeditor in July 1839. According to his own calculations, Poe contributed 132 pages of his writing to *Burton's Gentleman's Magazine*.[4] Although his relationship with Burton was "ill-starred" from its beginning,[5] Poe raised the quality of the magazine, as well as its number of subscribers.[6] Burton hired Poe at $10 per week for what, according to the actor, would amount to two hours of work per day. After only two weeks on the job, Poe abruptly quit when Burton insisted he tone down his criticism in book reviews.[7] Upon reconciliation, Poe returned but thereafter did not hold the magazine's founder in very high regard. Burton, for his part, lacked confidence in Poe's ability to remain a sober and, hence, reliable editor. According to Tassin, at least one number may have appeared late because of Poe's "besetting sin."[8]

Poe's contributions to the magazine were many and varied. He continued Burton's practice of using poetry to fill voids left at the end of prose articles, inserting some of his own verse beginning in the July 1939 number: "To Ianthe in Heaven" (5:49), extracted from his story "The Visionary," and a second poem, "Spirits of the Dead," which he printed anonymously. Although Poe wrote no new verse for the *Gentleman's Magazine*, he published several poems he had composed earlier: "Fairyland" [signed "P"] (5:70); "To———. [a Fair Maiden"] (5:75); "To a River" (5:99); "Silence" (5:144); and the fifteen-line "Silence. A Sonnet" (6:166).

Poe's tales and essays, in addition to his poems, added a new dimension to *Burton's Gentleman's Magazine*. Such ghastly Poe narratives as "The Man That Was Used Up" (5:66–70), with its theme of mutilation, represent a departure from the monthly's usual genteel flavor. Other Poe tales appearing during his coeditorship include "The Fall of the House of Usher" (5:145–52); "William Wilson" (5:205–12); "Morella" (5:264–66); "Peter Pendulum, the Businessman" (6:87–89); and "The Man of the Crowd" (published after the periodical became *Graham's Magazine*) (7:267–70). The first installment of Poe's serial narrative "The Journal of Julius Rodman, Being an Account of the First Passage Across the Rocky Mountains of North America Ever Achieved by Civilized Man" appeared in January 1840 (6:44–47) and then prematurely halted in June 1840 (6:255–59) when Poe left the magazine. As a result, the adventures of Rodman and his pioneers were abruptly cut off with his party stranded on the banks of the Missouri.[9] Poe's occasional essays include "The Philosophy of Furniture," in which he argues that an "aristocracy of dollars" determines taste in the United States and causes Americans to buy costly, rather than truly tasteful, furnishings. He also calls his contemporaries inept judges of carpet and criticizes them for lavishing their apartments with mirrors and gas lamps (6:243).

Book reviews during Poe's tenure became longer and more discerning, and more often they had poetry as their subject. Although all were unsigned, Poe wrote most of the reviews during his editorship. He takes Henry Wadsworth Longfellow to task for his "Voices of the Night" (6:100); he cudgels Cooper in a review of *The History of the Navy of the United States of America* (5:56); and in a feature article he praises the poet of "Thanatopsis," William Cullen Bryant (6:203–5). Poe's important review of Thomas Moore's "Alciphron, A Poem" (6:53) includes observations on Coleridge and other romantic poets and provides insights into Poe's own poetic theories. And, suggesting his own theory of aesthetics, Poe argues in his review of N. P. Willis's play "Tortesa, The Usurer" that the dramatist's skill is found "not in the imitation of Nature, but in the artistical adjustment and amplification of her features" (5:117).

Poe's many contributions to *Burton's Gentleman's Magazine* make clear that his and Burton's tastes were markedly different. It is no wonder, then, that their association was brief and sometimes acrimonious. When Poe departed in June 1840, Burton again became the magazine's sole editor. Anxious to invest more of his resources in a new Philadelphia theater, Burton soon sold his monthly to George R. Graham, editor and owner of the *Casket*.[10] In December Graham combined his publication with Burton's to establish *Graham's Lady's and Gentleman's Magazine,** which eventually became one of the most popular periodicals of its day.[11] Consequently, after three and a half years, the last issue to bear the title *Gentleman's Magazine* appeared in November 1840.

## Notes

1. Frank Luther Mott, *"Burton's Gentleman's Magazine," A History of American Magazines 1741–1850* (New York and London: D. Appleton and Co., 1930), p. 676.

2. Algernon Tassin, *The Magazine in America* (New York: Dodd, Mead, and Co., 1916), p. 91.

3. Mott, pp. 674–76.

4. Arthur Hobson Quinn, *Edgar Allan Poe: A Critical Biography* (New York: D. Appleton-Century, 1941), p. 299.

5. William L. Kease, *William E. Burton, Actor, Author, and Manager: A Sketch of his Career with Recollections of his Performances* (New York: G. P. Putnam's Sons, 1885), p. 19.

6. William Robert Bittner, *Poe, A Biography* (Boston: Little, Brown, 1962), p. 150.

7. Bittner, p. 146.

8. Tassin, p. 90.

9. Quinn, p. 293.

10. Mott, p. 676.

11. Tassin, p. 91.

## Information Sources

BIBLIOGRAPHY:

Bittner, William Robert. *Poe, a Biography*. Boston: Little, Brown, 1962.

Kease, William L. *William E. Burton, Actor, Author, and Manager: A Sketch of His Career with Recollections of His Performances*. New York: G. P. Putnam's Sons, 1885.

————. *William E. Burton, A Sketch of His Career Other Than That of Actor, With Glimpses of His Home Life, and Extracts From His Theatrical Journal*. 1891; rpt., New York: Burt Franklin, 1970.

Lauvriere, Emile. *The Strange Life and Strange Loves of Edgar Allan Poe*. Philadelphia: Lippincott, 1935. Pp. 149–57.

Mott, Frank Luther. *A History of American Magazines, 1741–1850*. New York and London: D. Appleton and Company, 1938. Pp. 673–76.

Tassin, Algernon. *The Magazine in America*. New York: Dodd, Mead, and Co., 1916. Pp. 89–91.

Quinn, Arthur Hobson. *Edgar Allan Poe: A Critical Biography*. New York: D. Appleton-Century, 1941. Pp. 278–304.

INDEXES: None

REPRINT EDITIONS: American Periodicals: Series II, 1800–1850. University Microfilms, Ann Arbor. Reel 311.

LOCATION SOURCES: Widely available.

## Publication History

MAGAZINE TITLE AND TITLE CHANGES: *The Gentleman's Magazine*, July 1837-December 1838. *The Gentleman's Magazine and Monthly American Review*, January-February 1839. *Burton's Gentleman's Magazine*, March-December 1839. *Burton's Gentleman's Magazine and Monthly American Review*, January-June 1840. *The Gentleman's Magazine*, July-November 1840.

VOLUME AND ISSUE DATA: Volumes 1–7, July 1837-November 1840.

FREQUENCY OF PUBLICATION: Monthly.

PUBLISHERS: July 1837-February 1839: Charles Alexander, Philadelphia. March 1839-November 1840: William E. Burton, Philadelphia.

EDITORS: William E. Burton, July 1837-June 1839; William E. Burton and Edgar Allan Poe, July 1839-June 1840; William E. Burton, July-November 1840.

*Robert S. Hughes, Jr.*

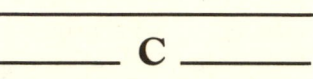

## C

## THE CARPET-BAG

On 1 May 1852 the *Carpet-Bag*, a weekly newspaper a little over a year old, hit the streets of Boston with an edition that would prove to be significant in the annals of American humor, for this particular issue brought together George Horatio Derby (age 29), Charles Farrar Browne (age 18), and Samuel L. Clemens (age 16). Through their personae, "John Phoenix," "Artemus Ward," and "Mark Twain," these men would eventually become three of the best-known "funny fellows" in America. Twain, of course, would achieve enduring greatness through his illustrious writing career, one beginning with this issue of the *Carpet-Bag* that contained his first known published work, a sketch set on the Mississippi River and entitled "The Dandy Frightening the Squatter."[1]

The *Carpet-Bag* was a comic weekly newspaper published in Boston, Massachusetts, from 29 March 1851 until 26 March 1853 for a total of 104 issues. Benjamin Penhallow Shillaber, creator of the popular Mrs. Partington character, was the editor-in-chief; assistant editors were S. W. Wilder, S. T. Pickard, S. D. Hancock, and C. Halpine. During its prime the *Carpet-Bag* was widely read and quoted in newspapers and journals throughout the North and Midwest. Distributors could be found in New York, Philadelphia, Cincinnati, St. Louis, and Louisville. One agent in Columbus, Ohio, sold fifty copies weekly. The *Hannibal Journal*, owned and edited by Orion Clemens and printed by Sam, clipped and quoted the paper on several occasions.[2]

Well printed and illustrated by woodcuts, the *Carpet-Bag* appeared in eight folio pages measuring about 13 by 18 inches. The handy size was chosen for the convenience of steamboat and train travellers, the primary audience for whom the paper was intended. This connection between the paper and travellers is underscored by the fact that the publisher of the *Carpet-Bag* was the Boston firm of Snow and Wilder, who also produced the widely read *Pathfinder Railway*

*Guide* and the *Boston Pathfinder*, annual guides to the transportation system of New England.[3] The publishers expected the newspaper and travel guides to complement one another, but this proved a fond hope and one that influenced significantly later editorial policy. When sales began to falter during the second year of publication, the editor announced that in forthcoming issues the last two pages would be devoted to items of primary interest to "traveling people" (no. 28:4). However, information on steamboats, locomotives, railway cars, and telegraphs did little to stimulate subscriptions, and the paper ceased publication six months later. Finally, at the collapse of the *Carpet-Bag*, Shillaber and Snow made a futile effort to capitalize on the travel trade by publishing two issues (April, May 1853) of a monthly periodical some ninety-six pages in length entitled the *Pocket Carpet-Bag*, one of the smallest paperback books (4 1/2 by 3 inches) printed in the nineteenth century.

The front page of the *Carpet-Bag* was headed by an eye-catching woodcut, designed by J. Wolcott and engraved by N. Brown, of a man's hand grasping the handle of a carpetbag of floral design. Along with the illustration the motto, "For the Amusement of the Reader," contributed to the genial tone of the paper—a tone possibly not evident to a later audience for whom the word "carpetbagger" would summon up negative connotations. Yet, in 1851 the term "carpetbag" held quite pleasant associations, a point made certain by an essay in the first issue entitled "Philosophy of a Little Carpet-Bag" (no. 1:3). The author of this piece states that a man carrying a carpetbag to a train station is "the most perfect type of independence extant," and, further, that the bag indicates "a short and pleasurable excursion" (no. 1:3). Thus, in antebellum America a carpetbag suggested much the same thing as an overnight kit does to a modern reader.

On the first editorial page Shillaber explores the metaphor of the carpetbag further by declaring that the name the *Carpet-Bag* was chosen to express "the miscellaneous character of a good paper, into which are crowded a variety of things, necessary for comfort and happiness while on the highway of life" (no. 1:5). And, while the overall aim of the paper was "to promote cheerfulness," the original design was not to publish only a humor publication but to print all types of literature, some to moralize and others to instruct (no. 1:5).

At first the *Carpet-Bag* did devote space to serious matters. Essays cover Daniel Webster (no. 6:3), Jenny Lind (no. 16:7), Louis Kossuth—"The Patriot of Hungary"—(no. 31:1), the Free-Soil movement (no. 34:3), and various historical events related to the growth of America. Lengthy book reviews inform readers about Nathaniel Hawthorne's *Twice-Told Tales* (no. 1:6) and *The House of Seven Gables* (no. 4:3), Longfellow's *The Golden Legend* (no. 40:2), Dumas's *Louise de la Valliere* (no. 1:6) and Goethe's *Wilhelm Meister* (no. 4:3). Extracts from Hawthorne's *The House of Seven Gables* (no. 5:2–3) and Dickens's *Household Words* (no. 39:1–3) run to two and three pages in length. Among the serious verse reprinted are Coleridge's "The Poet's Courtship" (no. 1:1), Byron's "The

Prisoner of Chillon'' (no. 46:5), Tennyson's "Mariana" (no. 2:2), and Poe's "Annabel Lee" (no. 9:2).

However, about midway through the first year's publication, it became apparent that the majority of readers were more interested in smiles than frowns, and so the *Carpet-Bag* quickly became a repository for quips, puns, jokes, and light anecdotes. With the humorous element now dominant, Shillaber conceded genially in an editorial marking the inauguration of the second volume that "our correspondents—jolly fellows—have had it their way, and we have become almost unwittingly, but agreeably, the dispensers of their heartiness" (no. 1:4).

A typical essay, "Management of Children," counsels parents to threaten a misbehaving child "with dismemberment, or everlasting annihilation, or any other trifling penalty, if he don't jump," and eventually the child may even come to believe the threat (no. 1:5). Wordplays appear by the hundreds, like a pun about John Milton who, although not a gambler, wrote a book about "a pair o'dice lost" (no. 1:7). A fake "Letter from Prince Albert" (no. 15:8) in which he complains about his wife's simplemindedness and a satiric review, "A Black Tragedy" (no. 20:3) , explaining *Othello* as an antislavery companion piece to Stowe's *Uncle Tom's Cabin*, display a sparkle and wit that a modern audience would find amusing.

The best and most characteristic writing satirized the foibles of middle-class America. Of the variety known as "crackerbox," the humor was, with the exception of a few ethnic slurs against first-generation Irish immigrants, gentle and relatively mild as it held up for ridicule people like eccentric housewives, penny-pinching husbands, and greedy merchants and lampooned subjects like spirit rapping and bloomers for women. To its credit, though, the *Carpet-Bag* never printed an intentionally mean-spirited article or cartoon.

While the *Carpet-Bag* could boast of many able writers, three of the best, Charles F. Browne, Charles Halpine, and B. P. Shillaber, worked on the paper. At age seventeen Charles F. Brown (1834–1867), later to add the final "e" to his name, joined the staff of the *Carpet-Bag* as a typesetter after having served as a printer's apprentice on five New England newspapers. His first contributions were anonymous, and like Benjamin Franklin, he had the pleasure of setting the type for his own work and secretly delighting in the editor's praise.[4] Soon, though, his submissions became known and were printed under several pseudonyms, the most widely admired being "Lieut. Chubb." After the demise of the *Carpet-Bag*, Browne wandered westward, eventually became a reporter for the Cleveland *Plain Dealer*, and in 1858 created the marvelous "Artemus Ward" persona.

Another contributor, one who became an assistant editor and part-owner of the paper, was Charles G. Halpine (1829–1868). The son of a Dublin clergyman, Halpine worked as a journalist in London and Boston before coming to the *Carpet-Bag*. More than anyone else, he was responsible for a noticeable change in the paper's humor during its second year, and, unfortunately, this new direction proved damaging to the subscription list. Since Halpine's humor was more sarcastic than that of his colleagues, the criticisms he wrote and sanctioned for publication began to alienate the prim and proper Bostonian readership. During Shillaber's absence, in an essay entitled "Literature of America," Halpine bemoans the vapid poetry and sentimental gush so prevalent in mid-century America and announces a campaign to lay "violent hands on this hydra-headed monster, with a view to the strangulation thereof" (no. 24:5). Seeing the popular sentimental poetry as silly and overly romantic, he set about to expose it in verse parodies that strongly resemble the later "Ode to Stephen Dowling Bots, Dec'd" in Twain's *Adventures of Huckleberry Finn* (1884). (Though somewhat dismayed by Halpine's approach, Shillaber supported his young assistant to the end). Later, Halpine became famous as the author of a collection of letters and dialect poems entitled *The Life and Adventures of Private Miles O'Reilly* (1864).

B. P. Shillaber (1814–1890), an outstanding editor, contributed dozens of clever sketches and poems to the *Carpet-Bag*, but the wittiest of these concerned the Yankee widow, Mrs. Ruth Partington, who could not speak a complete sentence without a malapropism, and her twelve-year-old nephew Ike—orphaned, high-spirited, borderline juvenile delinquent. Mrs. Partington is a good-hearted woman given to eccentric views on politics and the passing scene. As a stable but zany citizen she is perhaps the first middle-class American woman portrayed comically as a "dingbat." Significantly, the widow Partington and nephew Ike are highly suggestive of Twain's Aunt Polly and Tom Sawyer. Strangely enough, in what seems to be more than a coincidence, the frontispiece illustration in Shillaber's *Life and Sayings of Mrs. Partington* (1854) is the same print used to illustrate Aunt Polly at her knitting in *The Adventures of Tom Sawyer* (1876, p. 274).[5]

In addition, over one hundred talented contributors sent their original poems, sketches, stories, and letters to the *Carpet-Bag*. Among the best of these who deserve mention are John T. Trowbridge, creator of "Paul Creyton"; Sylvannus Cobb, Jr., who went by "Enoch Fitz-Whistler"; Benjamin Drew, who used the names "Doctor Digg" and "Erisme Gestus"; Fred T. Somerby, "Cymon"; and Matthew F. Whittier, brother of John Greenleaf and known as "Ethan Spike."[6] The best of the women writers are Elizabeth Akers Allen, or "Florence Perry"; Louise Chandler Moulton, known as "Ellen Louise"; and H. Marian Stephens.

Finally, though, the broad appeal and high quality of the humor were not enough to save the *Carpet-Bag*. And, while short runs of humor periodicals during the nineteenth century were common, the main problem with the decline of the *Carpet-Bag* was not a matter of burning out by burning too brightly, but rather one of a steadily eroding readership in an increasingly genteel East, especially in Boston. Without a solid base of support in a middle-class readership, it was fated to wilt away. Nevertheless, the *Carpet-Bag* achieved during its two-year run a permanent place in literary history as one of the best of America's early humor publications.

## Notes

1. Franklin J. Meine, *Mark Twain's First Story* (Chicago: Prairie Press, 1953), p. 3.

2. Walter Blair, *Native American Humor* (New York: Chandler Publishing Co., 1960), p. 151.

3. Frank Luther Mott, *A History of American Magazines*, 4 vols. (Cambridge: Harvard University Press, 1957), 2:181.

4. Jennette Tandy, *Crackerbox Philosophers in American Humor and Satire* (Port Washington, N.Y.: Kennikat Press, Inc., 1925), p. 133.

5. Meine, p. 6.

6. Franklin J. Meine, "American Comic Periodicals," *The Collector's Journal* 2 (1933):413.

## Information Sources

BIBLIOGRAPHY:

Blair, Walter. *Native American Humor*. New York: Chandler Publishing Co., 1960.

Meine, Franklin J. "American Comic Periodicals." *The Collector's Journal* 2 (1933):411–13.

————. *Mark Twain's First Story*. Chicago: Prairie Press, 1953.

Mott, Frank Luther. *A History of American Magazines*. 4 vols. Cambridge, Mass.: Harvard University Press, 1957. 2:180–81.

Spiller, Robert E., ed. *Literary History of the United States: A Bibliography*. 4th ed. rev. New York: Macmillan Publishing Co., Inc., 1974.

Tandy, Jennette. *Crackerbox Philosophers in American Humor and Satire* Port Washington, N.Y.: Kennikat Press, Inc., 1925.

INDEXES: None.

REPRINT EDITIONS: Bell & Howell Co., Micro Photo Division.

LOCATION SOURCES: Widely available.

## Publication History

MAGAZINE TITLE AND TITLE CHANGES: *The Carpet-Bag*, 29 March 1851–26 March 1853. *The Pocket Carpet-Bag*, April-May 1853.

VOLUME AND ISSUE DATA: Volumes 1–2, 29 March 1851–26 March 1853; new series, nos. 1–2, April-May 1853.

FREQUENCY OF PUBLICATION: Weekly, 29 March 1851–26 March 1853; monthly, April 1853-May 1853.

PUBLISHERS: 29 March 1851–13 September 1851: Snow & Wilder, Boston. 20 September 1851–26 June 1852: Wilder, Pickard, & Co., Boston. 3 July 1852–7 August 1852: Wilder, Halpine, & Co., Boston. 14 August 1852–2 October 1852: Randall, Halpine, & Co., Boston. 7 October 1852–26 March 1853: George K. Snow, Boston. April 1853-May 1853: George K. Snow, Boston.

EDITORS: B. P. Shillaber and S. W. Wilder, 29 March 1851–13 September 1851; B. P. Shillaber, S. W. Wilder, and S. T. Pickard, 20 September 1851–10 April 1852; B. P. Shillaber, S. W. Wilder, S. T. Pickard, and S. D. Hancock, 17 April 1852–

26 June 1852; B. P. Shillaber and C. Halpine, 3 July 1852–2 October 1852; B. P. Shillaber, 9 October 1852–26 March 1853; B. P. Shillaber, April 1853-May 1853.

*Harold Woodell*

## THE CENTURY. See SCRIBNER'S MONTHLY

## THE CENTURY ILLUSTRATED MONTHLY MAGAZINE. See SCRIBNER'S MONTHLY

## THE CHAP-BOOK

As a symbol of the ferment of American literary and intellectual life during the 1890s and the eventual progenitor of well over two hundred imitative competitors published within a decade of its own beginning, the *Chap-Book* occupied an important place in the rise of small American literary magazines. It began in the Cambridge coffeehouse environment of young literary writers and artists connected with Harvard University, when the undergraduate newspaper editor of the *Daily Crimson*, Herbert S. Stone, joined with fellow-student Hannibal Ingalls Kimball in 1893 to form the publishing firm of Stone & Kimball. Within one year the firm had successfully issued twenty finely printed and bound literary titles and sensed that a magazine of literary merit might provide both an appropriate forum for young, talented, and aspiring writers as well as a useful advertising medium for the firm's new books.

Issued at Cambridge in an innovative bibelot format on laid paper and with very attractive typographical layout, the first number of the *Chap-Book* (15 May 1894) inaugurated a series that appeared semimonthly for slightly over four years and totalled one hundred issues. Stone maintained editorial control throughout its lifetime. Bliss Carman, the Canadian-born vagabond poet, served as assistant editor for the first two months and later continued contributing critical literary essays, reviews, and poetry. Both men drew upon a substantial pool of young American literary and artistic talent that included Ralph Adams Cram, Richard Hovey, Louise Imogen Guiney, and Percival Pollard. English contributions (among them those of Aubrey Beardsley, William Sharp, H. G. Wells, Kenneth Grahame, and E. F. Benson) also found their place, as did the works of such French Symbolists as Stéphane Mallarmé and Paul Verlaine, with much of that latter attention due to the Francophile contacts of both Stone and his undergraduate colleague Harrison Garfield Rhodes, who assumed the assistant editorship in September 1894 and continued in that capacity for the life of the magazine.

During the summer of that year the *Chap-Book* moved to Chicago, where Stone's father, the journalist and founder of the *Chicago Daily News*, Melville E. Stone, provided substantial financial backing for the fledgling publishing firm.

As a city then flexing its economic muscle and capitalizing upon the great attention focused upon its art and culture during the highly touted World's Columbian Exposition of the previous year, Chicago offered the *Chap-Book* publishers expanding commercial connections as well as a local-color forum to which younger writers and artists excluded from the established Eastern literary magazines might be attracted. But well established figures from the literary schools of both romanticism and realism were also drawn in as contributors by the magazine's appeal. Among its better-known contributors were Hamlin Garland, Stephen Crane, W. B. Yeats, Gilbert Parker, Henry James, and Joel Chandler Harris. An open search for newer poets was undertaken with the third volume in May 1895, setting a precedent for literary magazines that found its later expression in Harriet Monroe's 1912 founding of *Poetry*.

Supplementing its significant literary contributions and the witty and critical editorial style of its essayists and reviewers, the *Chap-Book* presented a visual tour de force in magazine design brought about by Stone & Kimball's book production program, which stressed high artistic standards and quality printing. As house organ and advertising medium for the firm and its books, the magazine itself was prepared in both an innovative and visually stimulating style. Chicago printers for the *Chap-Book* included the Camelot Press under Frederic W. Goudy and the Lakeside Press of the Donnelley family. Uncut, laid paper and superior typography were employed, as were decorative cover designs in red and black. Woodcuts and line drawings by such noted artists as Beardsley, Max Beerbohm, Will Bradley, Frank Hazenplug, T. B. Meteyard, and Claude Bragdon were included, as were occasionally inserted supplements of colored plates and halftones. Stone & Kimball also contributed much to the development of the lithographic poster, with a series of *Chap-Book* posters advertising the firm's books or reproducing the journal's covers. The magazine's pamphlet format (7 1/2″ x 4 1/2″) and general eye-appealing design spawned a host of other American and European phantom periodicals of the 1890s, which, although most of them succumbed after only a few issues, did much to establish the little magazine as an important literary genre of the twentieth century.[1]

Like those imitators and competitors, the *Chap-Book* itself could not endure its own youthful enthusiasm and initial success. Circulation peaked at about 16,500 copies in early 1896. In April 1896, Kimball (who had been primarily entrusted with the business management of the partnership) broke with Stone, and the latter reorganized under the name of Herbert S. Stone & Company. In a vain attempt to increase badly needed general advertising revenue, Stone announced in the 1 January 1897 issue that the journal was about to take the "most significant step in its career"—the adaptation of an enlarged format (12″ x 8 1/2″) on smooth paper for the improved use of advertising halftones. That format change began in the following issue of 15 January 1897; the subtitle "A Miscellany and Review of Belles Lettres" was also added. However, few other publishers cared to place advertisements for their new books in a journal known for its rather critical reviewing style. Continued decreasing advertising and the

firm's bad business failure to maintain a comprehensive list of its annual subscribers (newsstand sales had been the primary marketing outlet) led to a financial crisis that even the addition of the book review supplement could not
halt.

The end came with the 15 July 1898 issue, which consisted rather of the
fortnightly issue of the Chicago-based, more conservative *Dial\** (which had
agreed to absorb the *Chap-Book* and its goodwill). A two-page printed apologia
of the same date revealed Stone's plan to continue book publishing only and his
conviction that it was no longer necessary to demonstrate that a quality literary
magazine could be published elsewhere than on the East Coast. Although some
national editorial opinion such as that of the *New York Times* for 23 July 1898
termed the *Chap-Book*'s demise long overdue because of its "want of destination," many others mourned the loss of its young energy, intellectual keenness,
and successful experimental design, which mirrored much of the changing cultural and intellectual life in America on the eve of the twentieth century.

## Note

1. Bibliographical information on those imitators is given by Frederick Winthrop
Faxon, "Ephemeral Bibelots: a Bibliography of the Modern Chap-Books and Their
Imitators, Including the Short-Story Magazines, From Their First Issue to April 1, 1903,"
*Bulletin of Bibliography*, 3 (1903): 72–74, 92, 106–7, 124–26.

## Information Sources

BIBLIOGRAPHY:
Manuscript materials: Substantial holdings in the Harvard University Archives and at the
        Newberry Library, Chicago.
Calkins, Ernest Elmo. "The Chap-Book Semimonthly." *The Colophon*, pt. 10 (April
        1932).
Duncan, Hugh Dalziel. *The Rise of Chicago as a Literary Center from 1885 to 1920; a
        Sociological Essay in American Culture*. Totowa, N.J.: The Bedminster Press,
        1964. Esp. pp. 60–65.
Faxon, Frederick Winthrop. "Ephemeral Bibelots; a Bibliography of the Modern Chap-
        Books and Their Imitators, Including the Short-Story Magazines, From Their First
        Issue to April 1, 1903." *Bulletin of Bibliography* 3 (1903): 72–74, 92, 106–7,
        124–26.
Fleming, Herbert E. *Magazines of a Market-Metropolis, Being a History of the Literary
        Periodicals and Literary Interests of Chicago*. Chicago: University of Chicago
        Press, 1906. A reprint of papers entitled "The Literary Interests of Chicago"
        from *The American Journal of Sociology*, vols. 11 and 12.
Kramer, Sidney. *A History of Stone & Kimball and Herbert S. Stone & Co., with a
        Bibliography of Their Publications 1893–1905*. Chicago: University of Chicago
        Press, 1940.
Mott, Frank Luther. *A History of American Magazines*. 4 vols. Cambridge, Mass.:
        Belknap Press of Harvard University Press, 1957. 4:450–52.
Schlereth, Wendy Clauson. *The Chap-Book, a Journal of American Intellectual Life in
        the 1890s*. Ann Arbor: UMI Research Press, 1982.

INDEXES: The publishers provided indexes to each of the eight completed volumes. Kramer, pp. 210–12, gives a complete list of literary and artistic contributors (without reference to the issues in which those contributions occur). Schlereth, pp. 123–30, has rectified that omission by listing all contributors along with the relevant volume and issue numbers.

REPRINT EDITIONS: Selected essays were reprinted by H. S. Stone & Co. under the titles: *Essays From the Chap-Book, Being a Miscellany of Curious and Interesting Tales, Histories, etc.* (1896) and *New Stories From the Chap-Book, Being a Miscellany of Curious and Interesting Tales, Histories, etc.* (1898). American Periodicals: Series III, 1850–1900. University Microfilms, Ann Arbor. Reel 61. AMS Film Service. Datamics, Inc. Kraus Microforms. Public Library Photographic Service.

LOCATION SOURCES: Widely available.

## Publication History

MAGAZINE TITLE AND TITLE CHANGES: *The Chap-Book Semimonthly*, 15 May 1894–1 January 1897. Subtitle "A Miscellany & Review of Belles Lettres" added with volume 6, number 5, 15 January 1897.

VOLUME AND ISSUE DATA: Volume 1, number 1–volume 9, number 4, 15 May 1894–1 July 1898. Volume 7, number 4, 1 July 1897, misnumbered volume 7, number 5. The next two issues also sequentially misnumbered as number 6 (July 15) and number 7 (August 1). That error in sequence corrected with the proper numbering of volume 7, number 7 (15 August 1897).

FREQUENCY OF PUBLICATION: Semi-monthly.

PUBLISHERS: 15 May 1894–15 April 1896: Stone & Kimball, Chicago and Cambridge (with the issue of 1 September 1894, Cambridge dropped from the imprint.) 1 May 1896–1 July 1898: H. (later Herbert) S. Stone & Company, Chicago.

EDITORS: Herbert Stuart Stone. Assistant editor for the first two months was Bliss Carman; Harrison Garfield Rhodes became assistant editor from 1 September 1894 until the demise of the magazine.

*Michael Hackenberg*

# THE CHRISTIAN EXAMINER

The founding of the *Christian Examiner* in January 1824 was essentially the continuation of the *Christian Disciple* under a new editor, John Gorham Palfrey. The *Disciple* had been established in 1813. Henry Ware, Jr., became editor in 1818, serving six years before turning editorial control over to Palfrey.[1] The motto used in the early years of the *Examiner*, "Speaking the truth in love," was inherited from the *Disciple*, and the *Examiner* carried the banner throughout its career, defending Unitarian doctrine and examining Unitarian history. The succession of editors is delineated by Frank Luther Mott, who notes that for all of these men work on the *Examiner* was an avocation, their primary interests being in other areas, "the pulpit, teaching, the writing of books."[2] The essentially religious purpose of the *Examiner* is noted in Joseph Henry Allen and Richard

Eddy's *A History of the Unitarians and the Universalists in the United States*: "The 'Christian Examiner' was founded in 1824 to take the place of the 'Christian Disciple,' whose tone was thought to be too smooth and vague."[3] However, the *Examiner*'s importance goes beyond its religious purpose. As Mott states, it also did "distinctive work in literary criticism, and its comment on social, philosophical, and educational problems" was of high quality.[4]

A strong feature throughout its history was its scholarly, thorough, and temperate reviews by leading liberal thinkers of the day. Articles were unsigned, although the authorship of almost all of them was ascertained by William Cushing in his index published in 1879. The *Examiner* was noted for its lack of vituperation. And yet the editors never lost sight of the basic religious focus of the magazine, no matter how willing to examine new books and ideas. A reviewer of Philip James Bailey's poetry in January 1856 concluded positive comments by saying, "Here we might end, but for remembering that this is a 'Christian Examiner,' and that therefore there is a further duty to be discharged towards the public,—a much more important duty than belongs to mere literary criticism" (60:136). The reviewer then criticizes Bailey's religious ideas. Typical is a review of Tennyson's *Poems, Chiefly Lyrical* in the January 1838 issue. The reviewer, John S. Dwight, praises Tennyson and defends his poem "The Miller's Daughter" from charges of frivolousness. And yet the review concludes, "But he seems a spirit pure as yet, only given too much to mere aesthetic enjoyment. What he has yet done is not worthy of himself. Let us hope for better things" (23:327). Even in May 1860, under the more liberal editorship of Frederick Hedge, a review and detailed analysis of Charles Darwin's *Origin of the Species* by John A. Lowell concludes: "Who indeed are we, to dare, in the imperfection of our knowledge, to assign the bounds, or explain the modes of action, of the great First Cause?" (68:469) The *Examiner* also remained conservative socially and politically in its reviews. Typically, an article on "Factory Life,—Its Novels and Its Facts," including discussion of Dickens's *Hard Times*, concludes that "The laws may remove hinderances—as they should—from the progress of the people, but that progress itself must result from the growth of moral convictions of truth and right and justice in the hearts and minds of the people, and that is beyond the reach of the law" (59:379).

In 1857, however, a general liberalization of policy occurred when the *Examiner* was purchased by Thomas B. Fox.[5] Hedge and Edward Everett Hale were appointed coeditors, although from the beginning Hedge controlled editorial policy. He had been associated with the Transcendentalists, and his appointment signalled a liberalization of the *Examiner*'s editorial policy. Indicative is the evolution of the editorial view of Ralph Waldo Emerson throughout the magazine's history. In November 1838, the *Examiner* says of Emerson's "Divinity School Address," "those notions, so far as they are intelligible, are utterly distasteful to the instructers of the School, and to Unitarian ministers generally, by whom they are esteemed to be neither good divinity nor good sense" (25:266). However, by 1856, in a review of *English Traits*, the *Examiner* takes a more moderate view of the wayward Emerson: "From the circumstance of its being more local and less abstract than most of his former writings, it will probably enlarge the circle of his readers" (61:309). In November 1856, in a negative review of Whitman's second edition of *Leaves of Grass*, the *Examiner* notes that "Mr. Emerson had written a letter of greeting to the author on the perusal of the first edition, the warmth and eulogium of which amazes us. . . . Thus the honored name of Emerson, which has never before been associated with anything save refinement and delicacy in speech and writing, is made to endorse a work that teems with abominations" (61:473). And by 1861 Hedge himself praises Emerson in a review of *The Conduct of Life*: "However we may mourn his loss to the Church and to Christian traditions, we cannot deny, but gratefully rejoice in, his prophetic mission. . . . And though his voice is no longer heard in Christian pulpits, yet what preaching can be more practical and evangelical than this?" (70:150)

Hedge also devoted more space to the consideration of literature than had previous editors, and reviewers discussed literary works without the obligatory religious or moralistic criteria of judgment found earlier. The *Examiner*'s earlier conservative attitude toward literature can be seen in this statement made in May 1829 under the editorship of Francis Jenks, Palfrey's successor: "Doubtless the habit of novel reading is injurious, for in its ordinary acceptation, it means an exclusive reading of works of mere amusement without judgment or selection" (6:173). By January 1860, however, a more liberal attitude is expressed: "Novel-reading may be misused, but argument for or against it is quite out-worn and superfluous" (68:113). The difference in outlook can be seen in the contrasting literary taste of the *Examiner* under Jenks compared to its taste under Hedge. The earlier *Examiner* champions the work of Felicia Hemans because of its highly moralistic and religious nature. Reviews of her work praise her on this basis as among the greatest of poets. The later *Examiner*, however, frequently praises Elizabeth Barrett Browning, calling her "the great woman-poet of our time" (72:88) and "the almost perfect artist, because she was a perfect woman" (75:43).

Before the Civil War, the *Examiner* stood against slavery but at times expressed a conservative fear of extremism and disorder. These feelings seem to result at times in waffling, as when Harriet Beecher Stowe's *Dred; a Tale of the Great Dismal Swamp* is reviewed in November 1856: "The impression which we ourselves derived from its perusal is so confused and interfered with by the multitude of discordant opinions that have been expressed concerning it, that we can hardly pronounce our own flat judgment upon it" (61:474). The review attacks the character of Dred as "a nightmare monstrosity" that is "an offence to us," but it also praises Stowe's sense of humanity. With the outbreak of the war, however, the *Examiner* never wavered in its support for the cause of the Union and the end of slavery. In July 1861, it expressed this support, and it never weakened: "It is our duty, the duty of all patriots, to resist the new attempts which may be made to compromise, to concede, and to surrender principle for the sake of peace'' (77:114). The *Examiner* covered the political and intellectual issues of the war in depth.

After the war the *Examiner* was moved to New York, but it failed to make a success and was absorbed in 1869 by *Old and New*,* a new Unitarian magazine under Hale's editorship. Allen and Eddy explain that ''under Dr. Bellows's guidance, it aimed to do the work at once of a denominational organ and of an independent journal, absolutely open and free to the advanced criticism of the day. In this effort it lost the cordial support of one part without securing the full confidence of the other.''[6] The *Examiner*'s value lies in its moderate tone and open-minded, though conservative, reviews: ''[The *Examiner*] rather avoided than sought matter of controversy, giving far the larger space to questions of general moral or literary interest.''[7]

## Notes

1. Frank Luther Mott, "*Christian Disciple*, and *Christian Examiner*," *A History of American Magazines*, 4 vols. (Cambridge, Mass.: Belknap Press of Harvard University Press, 1957), 1:285.
2. Mott, 1:288.
3. Joseph Henry Allen and Richard Eddy. *A History of the Unitarians and the Universalists in the United States* (New York: The Christian Literature Co., 1894), p. 199.
4. Mott, 1:285.
5. Mott, 1:289.
6. Allen and Eddy, p. 231.
7. Allen and Eddy, p. 192.

## Information Sources

BIBLIOGRAPHY:
Allen, Joseph Henry, and Richard Eddy. *A History of the Unitarians and the Universalists in the United States*. New York: The Christian Literature Co., 1894.
Mott, Frank Luther. "*Christian Disciple*, and *Christian Examiner*." *A History of American Magazines*. 4 vols. Cambridge, Mass.: Belknap Press of Harvard University Press, 1957. 1:284–92.
INDEXES: Cushing, William. *Index to the Christian Examiner, Volumes I-LXXXVII, 1824–1869*. Boston: J. S. Cushing, 1879; rpt., in *Research Keys to the American Renaissance: Scarce Indexes of The Christian Examiner, The North American Review, and The New Jerusalem Magazine for Students of American Literature, Culture History, and New England Transcendentalism*. Ed. Kenneth Walter Cameron. Hartford, Conn.: Transcendental Books, 1967.
REPRINT EDITIONS: American Periodicals: Series II, 1800–1850. University Microfilms, Ann Arbor. Reels 79, 449–63.
LOCATION SOURCES: Widely available.

## Publication History

MAGAZINE TITLE AND TITLE CHANGES: *The Christian Examiner and Theological Review*, 1824–1828. *The Christian Examiner and General Review*, 1829-January

1844. *The Christian Examiner and Religious Miscellany*, March 1844-May 1857. *The Christian Examiner*, July 1857-November 1869.

VOLUME AND ISSUE DATA: Annual volumes 1–5, 1824–1828; semiannual volumes 6–87, 1829–1869 (In volume 9, December 1830 is substituted for January 1831. There were two January 1844 numbers, one in volume 35 and one in volume 36.) first series] volumes 1–4, 1824–1828; new series 1–13, 1829-July 1835; third series 1–17, September 1835-January 1844; fourth series 1–27, January 1844-May 1857; fifth series 1–17, July 1857–1865; sixth series 1–8, 1866–1869.

FREQUENCY OF PUBLICATION: Bimonthly.

PUBLISHERS: 1824–1826: Cummings, Hilliard Co., Boston. 1827–1829: Bowles & Dearborn, Boston. 1830–1832: Gray & Bowen, Boston. 1833–1837: Charles Bowen, Boston. 1837–1843: James Munroe & Co., Boston. 1844–1848: William Crosby, Boston. 1848–1857: William Crosby and H. P. Nichols, Boston. 1857–1863: Thomas B. Fox, Boston. 1863–1869: Joseph H. Allen, with Fox, then Alger, then Alger, Miller, and Bellows as partners, Boston. 1865–1869: W. R. Alger, Boston. 1866–1869: James Miller and H. W. Bellows, New York.

EDITORS: John G. Palfrey, 1824–1825; Francis Jenks, 1826–1830; James Walker and F.W.P. Greenwood, 1831-March 1839; William Ware, May 1839-January 1844; Alvan Lamson and Ezra S. Gannett, January 1844-May 1849; George Putnam and G. E. Ellis, July 1849-May 1857; Frederick H. Hedge and Edward Everett Hale, July 1857–1861; Thomas B. Fox, 1862; Thomas B. Fox and Joseph Henry Allen, 1863–1864; Joseph Henry Allen, 1865; Henry W. Bellows, 1866–1869.

*Edward Chielens*


# THE COLUMBIAN LADY'S AND GENTLEMAN'S MAGAZINE

When the first issue of the *Columbian Lady's and Gentleman's Magazine* appeared in January 1844, its new editor, John Inman, sounded a note of high enthusiasm. In his lead essay, "Magazine Literature," Inman indicated plans to bring some changes to periodical publication. Most startlingly, he intended to pay unknown contributors, musing how the "first compensation . . . may afford that stimulus which alone was wanting to bring out talents of the highest order" (1:5). Indeed, he can lay fair claim to publishing Emily Chubbuck before she became "Fanny Forrester," Walter Whitman before he became "Walt," and G. Wilkins Kendall before he became editor of the *New Orleans Picayune*.[1] His rate of payment, if the case of Mrs. Emma C. Embury is representative, was also unusual in its generosity. In paying her $30 apiece for six tales, the *Columbian* paid better than *Graham's** and *Godey's*,* both of which often editorially crowed at their payments.[2] Inman also hoped to avoid what he termed "that objectionable phrase, 'To be continued,' " high-mindedly expecting to attract and keep subscribers solely on the merits of each issue rather than through the strategy of serialization (2:93). He and his coeditor, Robert A. West, nevertheless abandoned this policy early in 1847.

Despite his professed interest in changes, however, Inman was a writer and practicing editor, and he consulted closely the prevailing fashion in magazine tastes. In truth, he created a magazine modeled so closely after the chief successes of the day that Poe even noted how *Godey's*, *Graham's*, and the *Columbian* "are so nearly alike that if the covers were changed it would not be easy to distinguish one from the other; they nearly all have the same contributors and the same embellishers."[3] The *Columbian*'s full title explicitly echoes that of *Graham's Lady's and Gentleman's Magazine. Embracing Every Department of Literature: Embellished with Engravings, Fashions, and Music*, etc. Its editorial policy quickly evolved into one that made *Godey's* so successful: "Our . . . aim is to sustain a periodical," wrote Inman, " . . . that should be a teacher of good taste and inculcate sound morals. If it shall speak of love it shall be that love that is true to nature. If fanciful and imaginative, [it shall] illustrate truth . . . elevate the soul and refine the heart" (2:283). Clearly, Inman was pursuing the most promising path to a respectful and respectable hearing. So much for planned innovations. He judged his readers well. Within the first year he boasted that the *Columbian* received "frank and honest praise from all quarters of the country" (2:283) and within the second year claimed a subscription list of "twenty odd thousand" (5:2).

In attracting a veritable who's who in popular mid-nineteenth century writers, Inman and his successors aimed at the best in periodical publication.[4] The *Columbian* also published a well-balanced variety of stories. For instance, each issue contained at least two domestic tales; Mrs. E. F. Ellet, Mrs. Caroline H. Butler, H. Hastings Weld, and T. S. Arthur (he wrote a total of eighteen tales in five years for the *Columbian*) contributed many of them. Some tales transported readers to foreign or exotic settings: Embury's "The Transplanted Flower; or, The Florentine Bride," H. W. Herbert's "Honor O'Neill; or, the Days of the Armada," and Ellet's "The Castilian Princess." Other tales explored the purely imaginative: Maria Child's "Thot and Freia—A Romance of the Spirit Land," Walter Whitman's "Eris; A Spirit Record," and E. A. Poe's "The Angel of the Odd." Others explored specific locales, such as John Neal's "The Little Fat Quakeress" and Caroline Kirkland's "A Bride's Trials." A notable number of tales retold well-known legends: Child's "Elizabeth Wilson," Frances S. Osgood's "Mabel—A German Legend," and Forrester's "The Demon of the Bush." Most issues also had a story based on biblical characters or set in biblical lands.

Despite such variety the stories read with numbing uniformity. Whatever the setting or subject matter, whether ancient Peking or contemporary Poughkeepsie, the heroes' and heroines' language is ornate and melodramatic, and their behavior vindicates this age's moral imperatives. Stories invariably end with uplifting reconciliations or moral treacle. The diction rigidly adheres to what sentimental America regarded as decorous and elevated: houses are "cottages," streams "rivulets," fishing "angling," and sleep "slumber." Predictable adjectives regularly precede certain nouns: boundless sea, busy multitudes, pious duties, laughing rivulets, and tender affections. The contributions by better writers made no difference. Whitman's four stories are appalling, Poe's tales are undistinguished, and James Kirke Paulding's six stories are summarized by one critic as "canned, stereotyped nonsense."[5] Two other satiric sketches by Paulding, "Peter Pettifog" and "A Panegyric," are clever and shrewdly observant; their inclusion, however, is unusual. While Inman aimed "to elevate and purify as well as to amuse," he also rejected manuscripts deficient in "taste"; namely, those that "cast ridicule upon qualities or classes entitled rather to respect or at least to forbearance" (2:96). His understanding of "amuse," however, admitted little latitude, judging from the rarity of such pieces in the *Columbian*.

Instead, Inman doggedly chose pieces that he felt "the old and young may read with profit to head and heart" (2:283). Here he gave himself too much latitude. The poets he published were among the most popular and prolific of the day, but their subject matter and themes were conventional and their treatment moralistic and lachrymose. In short, the poetry, like the tales, was too safe and accessible to readers of all ages. By far, the most popular subject was death, and children its most popular victims: "The Boy and the Wreck" and "Epitaph on a Young Lady" by Lydia Sigourney, "The Good Angel" by Frances Osgood, and "The Dying Boy" by Jerome A. Mabey. Next to children, death took its toll on Indians: "The Mohawk's Death-Song" by Miss Sarah L. Cahoone; next on wives: "The Husband to His Dying Wife" by William Wallace; then on maidens: "Verses on the Death of a Young Girl" by J. S. Ridney; and lastly on young husbands: "Young Widow's Lament" by Robert A. West. The more fortunate children died; many of the unfortunate remaining children were orphaned or maimed to serve the interests of such sentimental folderol: "Eyes to the Blind—The Blind Girl" by the blind hymn writer Frances J. Crosby, "The Widow's Child" by Miss A. Blackwell, and "The Blind Boy" by O. H. Mildeberger. Such poems revolved around endless variations on stock triadic rhymes: bloom, gloom, tomb; lay, decay, day; shine, shrine, divine; breast, rest, blest; and tears, fears, years. A reader perusing this poetry might do well to heed the title of a poem by Mrs. D. Ellen Goodman—"Bring a Wreath." Other poems evoke nostalgic recollections of home, and others apostrophize the seasons (most often spring and fall) and the vices and virtues this generation either shunned or embraced. The poetry suffers from the defects characteristic of a debased romanticism, drawing on a stock of wornout poetic diction and imagery to convey emotion and thought that was neither felt nor authentic.

The *Columbian*'s essays met well the requirements of a miscellany; they touched on diverse and interesting subjects, and their treatment was lively without being demanding, their tone invariably agreeable, and their style polished. Paulding's travelogue, "Sketch of the Great Western Lakes," combines amusing anecdotes and good descriptions with Democratic party propaganda. The locale of Caroline H. Butler's serialized essays, "Recollections on China," is more exotic. Closer to home, Mrs. James G. Brooks and Caroline Sedgwick satirized the follies of fashion and social life in "A Chapter on Woman" and "Varieties of Social Life in New York" respectively, while Ellet wrote a nostalgic piece on "Olden Traditions." Some essays had topical interest: "The Dead of the Princeton" by Rev. J. N. Danforth; other historical: Child's "The Northmen"; and others political: Forrester's "The Republic in Danger." Other essays were just sheer fluff: Embury's "Genius and Its Rewards" and "Extracts from the Diary of a Poor Man" by "A Starving Philosopher." Essays related to the arts and literature by far outnumber those in other groups. They range from "The Vision and Creed of Piers Ploughman" by Clara Kirkland to Mrs. E. R. Steel's "The Poetry of Ossian." These and most of the other essays, however, bear evidences of the *Columbian*'s editorial policies; namely, to inculcate some profitable thought or wholesome moral. In the first essay of his series "Thoughts on the Poets," Henry Tuckerman praises the sculptor Shobal Vail Clevenger for his industry, patience, generosity, and devotion to "the cause of elevated and progressive taste" (1:11). Lacking hard content and thoughtful analysis, these essays substituted graceful generalizations overlaid with hortatory wisdom.

The embellishments were also pleasantly diverting. As the *Columbian*'s subtitle promised, each issue offered original music and lyrics, engravings, and colored fashion plates. Here the influence of *Graham's* is strongly felt, the *Columbian* using some of the same talent as its rival: lyrics to songs and ballads by Ann S. Stephens and engravings by H. S. Sadd, A. L. Dick, W. L. Ormsby, and James Smillie. Each engraving bore the legend, "Engraved expressly for the *Columbian Magazine*." Many of the engravings were taken from original paintings to accompany the text of a sketch or tale; at other times commissioned poems or prose passages were paired with an engraving. The engravings are either sentimental or edifying: "Washington Crossing the Allegheny," "The Virgin and Child," and "The Bridal Prayer." The reflections on "View Near Cold-Spring," showing a generic Greek temple overlooking a bay that includes a dhow and a party of men in nineteenth-century dress overcrowding a rowboat, are typical: "I can never stand on such an eminence . . . without being filled with thoughts of Almighty power and of the consummate wisdom by which the plastic hand of that power was guided in the formation of hill, river, mountain, plain and valley—all designed by Almighty goodness also to delight the eye and subserve the varied interests of man" (2:43). The colored fashion plates, usually three to four figures in each issue, showed the latest Paris fashions. "Books of the Month" merely offered brief summaries of recent publications.

The *Columbian*'s contents remained consistent throughout the first four years of its existence under Inman and later under his coeditor, Robert A. West. Its most marked change occurred during 1848 when a new editor, Stephen M. Chester, made changes to quicken the *Columbian*'s expiring fortunes. He only hastened their decline. His more vigorous book-reviewing policies and his acceptance of three "bush-whacking articles" only antagonized subscribers; his initiating a hackneyed series of the graveyard variety, "Glances at Greenwood," and his increased acceptance of contributions from "reverends" mired the magazine deeper in a slough of writing that was stereotypical, pure, and pious.[6] Unable to reverse the magazine's fortunes, Chester resigned. Purchased and subsequently edited by the Reverend Darius Mead, the *Columbian* quickly died within two issues from a killing dose of moralistic excess.

The *Columbian* was too average to earn special distinction as an important nineteenth-century periodical. At best, the chief value of its contents lies in providing historians studying the popular mind of the period with source materials. The literature it published probably nudged Poe into the contemplation of writing free from a confining didacticism and provided Henry James with the impetus later in the century to formulate an art of fiction.

## Notes

1. Mentor L. Williams, "Portrait of a Popular Journal," *Bulletin of the New York Public Library* 56 (1952): 7–8.

2. Williams, p. 6.

3. *Broadway Journal* 1 (25 January 1845):60. As quoted by Williams, "Portrait," pp. 4–5.

4. Williams, "Portrait," p. 6.

5. Mentor L. Williams, "Paulding's Contributions to the *Columbian Magazine*," *American Literature* 21 (1949): 227.

6. Williams, "Portrait," p. 13.

## Information Sources

BIBLIOGRAPHY:

Mott, Frank Luther. *"The Columbian Lady's and Gentleman's Magazine."* A History of American Magazines 1741–1850. New York: D. Appleton and Company, 1930. Pp. 743–44.

Williams, Mentor L. "Paulding's Contributions to the *Columbian Magazine*." *American Literature* 21 (1949):222–27.

———. "Portrait of a Popular Journal: *The Columbian Lady's and Gentleman's Magazine*." *Bulletin of the New York Public Library* 56 (1952): 3–17.

INDEXES: None.

REPRINT EDITIONS: American Periodicals: Series II, 1800–1850. University Microfilms, Ann Arbor. Reel 313.

LOCATION SOURCES: Widely available.

## Publication History

MAGAZINE TITLE AND TITLE CHANGES: *The Columbian Lady's and Gentleman's Magazine, Embracing Literature in Every Department: Embellished with the Finest Steel and Mezzotint Engravings, Music, and Colored Fashions*, January 1844-June 1846. *The Columbian Lady's and Gentleman's Magazine, Embracing Literature in Every Department; Embellished with Fine Steel and Mezzotint Engravings, Music and Fashions*, July 1846-December 1847. *The Columbian Lady's and Gentleman's Magazine, Embracing Literature in Every Department; Embellished with Steel Line and Mezzotint Engravings, Music and Fashions*, January-December 1848. *The Columbian Magazine*, January-February 1849.

VOLUME AND ISSUE DATA: Volumes 1–10, January 1844-February 1849.

FREQUENCY OF PUBLICATION: Monthly.

PUBLISHERS: January 1844-December 1846: Israel Post, New York. January-December
     1847: Ormsby & Hackett, New York. January-December 1848: John S. Taylor,
     New York. January-February 1849: Darius Mead, New York.
EDITORS: John Inman, 1844; John Inman and Robert A. West, 1845-March 1848;
     Stephen M. Chester, April-December 1848; Darius Mead, January-February 1849.

*Arthur Wrobel*

## THE COLUMBIAN MAGAZINE (New York). See THE COLUMBIAN LADY'S AND GENTLEMAN'S MAGAZINE

## THE COLUMBIAN MAGAZINE (Philadelphia)

On 9 August 1786 the *Pennsylvania Gazette* announced the forthcoming publication at Philadelphia of the *Columbian Magazine*, wherein the publishers
promise, "No endeavours shall be spared to procure as great a variety of original
essays, instructive and entertaining, as the nature and extent of the work will
admit. . . . This design has been taken up, after mature deliberation: we shall
not, therefore, rashly abandon it. We are fully determined so to conduct the
undertaking, as to merit the public attention." Mathew Carey, who was the
magazine's first editor but would leave this post at the end of the year to establish
the *American Museum*,* declares in the opening Preface (September 1786) that
"the great purpose of the Columbian Magazine has been to communicate essays
of entertainment, without sacrificing decency to wit, and to disseminate the works
of science, without sacrificing intrinsic utility to a critical consideration of style
and composition." He promises, "The admission of political and theological
controversy, has . . . been studiously declined"; the first part of this promise was
occasionally broken, especially at the time of the Constitutional Convention of
1787 and the debate over ratification.

When James Trenchard became publisher in January 1789, he declared, "No
pains, no cost will be spared to render the *COLUMBIAN MAGAZINE* the most
elegant, entertaining and valuable repository of the kind that has ever appeared
in America." In all but a few months between October 1786 and July 1791 one
or more copperplate engravings, usually one as the frontispiece, adorn the magazine. And in all but two months between March 1790, when the title was
changed to the *Universal Asylum, and Columbian Magazine*, and June 1791,
every issue carried the music and words of a popular song or operatic aria of
the day. In view of features like these one can understand why the *Columbian*
has been called "the handsomest American magazine of its century."[1]

The range of nonliterary writing in the *Columbian* is great. Special attention
is paid "to geography, agriculture, manufactures, science, and invention; and
it was with reference to these subjects that the copperplate engravings were
chiefly concerned."[2] The magazine sought original American material and to

this end paid some of its contributors like Benjamin Rush and Jeremy Belknap; however, "original contributions proved scarce."[3] Benjamin Rush, physician, patriot, humanitarian, contributed no fewer than nine essays on such social problems as antislavery, temperance, and free schools. "The Paradise of Negro-Slaves—*a dream*" (January 1787) gives voice to his strong antislavery senti-ments. The Negroes in this paradise appear happy and cheerful. The narrator's presence is cause for panic, though, because he is white; he is told that "that colour which is an emblem of innocence in every other creature of God, is to us a sign of guilt in man" (1:236). When the narrator says he is their friend and identifies himself, he is embraced. Three Negroes describe the circumstances of their deaths at the hands of their masters; as a fourth is relating hers, a small white man approaches and is greeted as Anthony Benezet. In another essay the German inhabitants of Pennsylvania are praised as "industrious, frugal, punctual and just" (3:25). This is the time, writes Rush in "Causes Which Produced the Ruin of States" (December 1787), to inquire why other states were ruined "in order to avoid the cause of their calamities in the construction of our American government" (1:816). Rome, for example, came to ruin through luxury and corruption. "When a man loses his liberty, he loses all which should engage his affections to his country" (1:818). No writer for the *Columbian* ranges more widely and knowledgeably and displays a livelier humanitarian impulse than Rush.

Literary writing in the *Columbian* covers fiction, the essay, biography, history, and poetry. In "Rules for Forming a Just and Elegant Style" (November-De-cember 1792) the British rhetorician Henry Felton sets down stylistic ideals subscribed to by the editors of the *Columbian*: "A composition is then perfect, when the matter rises out of the subject; when the thoughts are agreeable to the matter, and the expression suitable to the thoughts" (9:294). "After this regard to the purity of our language, the next quality of a just style, is its plainness and perspicuity" (9:296). Finally, "there is no inconsistency between the plain-ness and perspicuity, and the ornament of writing" (9:369). By far the most impressive work of fiction in the magazine is Jeremy Belknap's *The Foresters*, a satiric allegory in narrative form in the tradition of John Arbuthnot's *History of John Bull* (1712) and Francis Hopkinson's *A Pretty Story* (1774). It appeared in nine installments (June-December 1787, February, April 1788) and traces Anglo-American history from the settlement of Virginia down to the Townshend Revenue Act. (Belknap recast the work in epistolary form and, expanding it from nine letters to sixteen, carried the story forward to 1792, the year in which he published it as a book). In the course of this familiar story John Bull (England) enlists the support of the Foresters (Americans) in his lawsuit with Lewis (France) and Lord Strut (Spain). As a result he finds himself in debt, and on the advice of his wife (Parliament) seeks to tax the Foresters, who resist, holding John's wife and steward (prime minister), not himself, responsible. In constructing *The Foresters* Belknap was shrewd enough to select homely ingredients and place them in a familiar context; he casts an allegorical haze over the entire work.

Essay writing, especially in the tradition of Addison and Steele, was popular throughout the eighteenth century on both sides of the Atlantic. The most ambitious example in the *Columbian* is Charles Brockden Brown's *The Rhapsodist* (August-November 1789). This earliest of Brown's prose works foreshadows his novels; favoring Sterne over Addison, Brown modifies the spectator mask in the direction of the whimsical and dreamy, defining a rhapsodist as "one who delivers the sentiments suggested by the moment in artless and unpremeditated language" (3:467), and does little more in this short serial than flesh out his persona. "I intend that the sincerity of my character shall be the principal characteristic of these papers" (3:464), declares the Rhapsodist; "truth is with me the test of every man's character" (3:465). The Rhapsodist "is an enemy to conversation" (3:537). "Love and friendship, and all the social passions, are excluded from his bosom" (3:538). "Since, in a black moment of despair, I forsook my wonted habitation, and transported myself from the solitary banks of the Ohio, into the thronged streets of this metropolis [Philadelphia]; I have been compelled to wage perpetual war with my inclination, and to wear the garb not of reason or convenience, but of fashion" (3:599). Finally he confesses, "I love the pompous and the gay, the copious and diffuse in writing . . . nor can I prevail on myself to treat with approbation or applause, an affected obscurity and studied brevity" (3:663–64). Francis Hopkinson was one of the most successful American essayists of the late eighteenth century. "Nitidia's Defense of Women and White-Washing" (April 1787) is his response to an essay, also by him, in Carey's *Museum* ridiculing women for white-washing (q.v.). Nitidia observes that "men are naturally . . . nasty beasts: if it were not that their connection with the refined sex, polished their manners . . . these lords of the creation would wallow in filth" (1:375–76). Her scientist husband's melted rosin and vitriol have damaged her marble hearth and carpet, and he has invited to dinner friends who will spit tobacco juice on her carpet. "But we will not be laughed out of our cleanliness. . . . we are just preparing to white-wash" (1:377).

"To instruct and to amuse are the two grand objects intended by authors," writes Dr. Henry Stüber. "It is, perhaps, for this reason that Biography has been a favourite species of writing in all ages, and in all countries" (4:268). With these words Stüber begins his "History of the Life and Character of Benjamin Franklin" (May-July, September-November 1790, February-March, May-June 1791). The first six installments cover Franklin's life up to 1757, that is to say, to the point at which he broke off writing the *Autobiography*; it is possible that Stüber saw Part I of the *Autogbiography*, which brings Franklin's life story as far as 1730. Of particular interest is Stüber's lengthy discussion in the fourth installment of Franklin's electrical experiments. The remaining four installments, which conclude with an account of Franklin's death in April 1790, cover the last thirty-three years of his life in England, America, France, and back in America. Belknap contributed to the *Columbian* biographical sketches of John Winthrop (January-March 1788), Sir Ferdinando Gorges (April-July 1788), and John Smith (August, October-December, and Supplement 1788); these sketches were later incorporated into his two-volume *American Biography* (1794, 1798). To shift from biography to history, the anonymous "History of the American Revolution" ran from March 1789 through November 1792, being "forced to end with the Battle of King's Mountain because of the death of the magazine."[4]

"Four types composed approximately eighty percent of the poetry in the magazine: odes and ode-like occasional verse, *vers de société*, elegies, and didactic and philosophical verse. The remaining twenty percent included satire, beast fables, topographical verse, versifications of Ossian, sonnets, excerpts from epics, and miscellaneous curiosities."[5] The most prolific poets in the *Columbian* whom we know by name are Elizabeth Graeme Ferguson and Francis Hopkinson. Hopkinson's "The Birds, the Beasts and the Bat," reprinted in the March 1787 issue from the *Pennsylvania Packet* of 6 May 1778, depicts a trimming bat who, when war breaks out between the birds (Americans) and the beasts (British), throws in his lot with the victorious side, that is to say, first the birds, then the beasts, and finally the birds again, only to be ordered by the birds from their sight. "The bat disown'd, in some old shed, / Now seeks to hide his exil'd head; . . . In dark retreats, he shuns the light, / To hide his mongrel form from sight" (1:346). John Trumbull's "Epithalamium" (June 1789) is a scatological Hudibrastic poem occasioned by the wedding on 2 August 1769 of the Yale tutor Stephen Mix Mitchell to the heiress Hannah Grant and patterned on Spenser's "Epithalamion." Of several eighteenth- and nineteenth-century printings of the poem, only the *Columbian* text carries all 278 lines.

Book reviewing began in the June 1790 issue. Among American literary works reviewed are Royall Tyler's *The Contrast* (August 1790), Noah Webster's *Collection of Essays and Fugitiv Writings* (November 1790), Hugh Henry Brackenridge's *Modern Chivalry*, Part I, Volumes I-II (February, August 1792), and *The Miscellaneous Essays and Occasional Writings of Francis Hopkinson* (August 1792).

The Postal Act of 1792 spelled the doom of the *Columbian Magazine*, as it did of the *American Museum*. William Young, then editor of the magazine, explains at the head of the December 1792 issue, which was the final one to appear, "The principal motive . . . is to be sought in the present law respecting the establishment of the post-office, which totally *prohibits* the circulation of *monthly* publications, through that channel, on any other terms than that of paying the highest postage on private letters or packages." Young concludes that because "this *unequal* and *oppressive* law" has "rendered it impossible for the proprietors to convey this miscellany to their numerous subscribers in the interior part of the country, but at the expense of losing a great proportion of them through a bad conveyance, they have determined to relinquish their undertaking; and to employ their time and capital, in a way which may be more conducive to their private interest."

## Notes

1. Frank Luther Mott, *A History of American Magazines, 1741–1850* (New York and London: D. Appleton and Company, 1930), p. 99.

2.  Lyon N. Richardson, *A History of Early American Magazines, 1741–1789* (1931; rpt., New York: Octagon, 1966), p. 289.

3.  William J. Free, *The Columbian Magazine and American Literary Nationalism* (The Hague and Paris: Mouton, 1968), p. 16.

4.  Free, p. 110.

5.  Free, pp. 78–79.

## Information Sources

BIBLIOGRAPHY:

Free, William J. *The Columbian Magazine and American Literary Nationalism*. The Hague and Paris: Mouton, 1968.

Mott, Frank Luther. *A History of American Magazines, 1741–1850*. New York and London: D. Appleton and Company, 1930. Pp. 94–99.

Richardson, Lyon N. *A History of Early American Magazines, 1741–1789*. 1931; rpt., New York: Octagon, 1966. Pp. 276–93.

Smyth, Albert H. *The Philadelphia Magazines and Their Contributors, 1741–1850*. 1892; rpt., Detroit: Gale, 1970. Pp. 61–67.

INDEXES: None.

REPRINT EDITIONS: Microfilm edition in *American Periodicals: 18th Century—1800–1850*. Ann Arbor: University Microfilms, 1956. Reel 11; Reel 30, item 4.

LOCATION SOURCES: Widely available.

## Publication History

MAGAZINE TITLE AND TITLE CHANGES: *The Columbian Magazine, or Monthly Miscellany*. In March 1790 the title was changed to *The Universal Asylum, and Columbian Magazine*.

VOLUME AND ISSUE DATA: Volumes 1–9, September 1786-December 1792.

FREQUENCY OF PUBLICATION: Monthly.

PUBLISHERS: September 1786-December 1787: Thomas Seddon, William Spotswood, Charles Cist, James Trenchard, Philadelphia. January-December 1788: William Spotswood, Philadelphia. January-April 1789: James Trenchard, Philadelphia. May-June 1789: Trenchard and Stewart, Philadelphia. July-November 1789: James Trenchard, Philadelphia. December 1789–1790: William Spotswood, Philadelphia. March 1790-December 1792: William Young, Philadelphia.

EDITORS: Mathew Carey, September-December 1786; editor unknown, January-February 1787; Francis Hopkinson, March-April 1787; John O'Connor (?), May-June 1787; Alexander James Dallas, July 1787-December 1788; editor unknown, January-April 1789; James Trenchard, May-November 1789; William Spotswood, December 1789-February 1790; William Young, March 1790-December 1792.

*Bruce Granger*

# THE CONTINENT

Albion Tourgée was "an interpreter of the Negro's dilemmas in the post-bellum South."[1] He consistently supported civil rights for the freed slaves, defended federal control of Southern states, and approved of the disenfranchisement of the rebels. In his first novel, *A Fool's Errand, by One of the Fools* (1879), he created a carpetbagger hero and drew an uncomplimentary picture of the Ku Klux Klan, which had threatened him while he was a judge in North Carolina during Reconstruction. In his second and equally romantic novel, *Bricks without Straw* (1880), Tourgée portrayed blacks as outcast, independent men, actively fighting for their rights and refusing to return to their prewar condition. Tourgée's romanticism and desire to reform carried over into other areas of his life. In 1881, he formed the Our Continent Publishing Company with Robert S. Davis, a wealthy Philadelphian. Daniel G. Brinton, an ethnologist and editor and owner of the *Medical and Surgical Reporter*, was named secretary of the $150,000 corporation, and $50 shares were sold to influential men, mostly friends of Tourgée; Ulysses S. Grant, for example, invested $1,000.

Tourgée stated that he intended to assemble the best thoughts expressed in the best words of the best writers illustrated by the best artists. The magazine would be American, expressing a "healthy and self-respecting sentiment of Americanism in literature and art" in order to show that our literary productions were not simply "a barnacle of English intellectual life" (1:8). The first issue was sixteen small folio pages with many excellent illustrations to the serials, short stories, poetry, literary notes, and columns.

Continuity in readership insures the success of any periodical publication. Two devices available to an editor are columns and serials, and *Our Continent* had plenty of both. With C. L. Norton as managing editor, Tourgée assembled an interesting staff: Helen Campbell wrote "The Household," a homemakers' column; Louise Chandler Moulton wrote "Our Society" about manners and etiquette; Kate Field did "The Art of Adornment" with advice on how to dress; Max Adeler collected and wrote humor in "In a Lighter Vein"; and J. L. Russel assembled religious material for "The Still Hour." Later F. A. Benson added "Home Horticulture."

After 6 December 1882, when Tourgée declared himself sole editor and manager, the columns were unsigned. A new column, "Current Events," which had appeared first the previous July, had become by August the "Reference Calendar," a selective list of events deemed important by the editor and arranged by date and subject. "The Bookshelf," also done by Tourgée, was another early addition, but the most notable and interesting column of the *Continent*'s mature years first appeared 25 April 1883. "Notes and Queries," sometimes "Notandum et Inquiredum," appeared irregularly. Readers were invited to send in questions and, if they wished, answers; the editor answered those he could. Readers asked for Latin quotations appropriate for a seventy-year-old's birthday, the proper pronunciation of new words, the name of the best encyclopedia, the origin of skating, whether women were permitted in Turkish mosques, whether Warren Chase was still alive, and whether Israel Putnam was plowing with horses or oxen when he heard of the battle of Lexington. (The editor did not know.)

The reviews and other literary criticism published in the *Continent* reflected the editorial position of the magazine. William Dean Howells, Henry James, and Thomas Hardy, realists all, were intensely disliked. In describing the "New Fiction," Anna B. McMahan, lecturer and later editorial contributor to the *Chicago Tribune*, wrote that realism tended to "avoid the great passions, the stirring emotions, and to deal with life in its minor and insignificant relations only" (1:618). Elsewhere, Tourgée said that Howells chose "hopelessly common and uninteresting subjects," that he drew "every shade of vulgarity and meanness and narrowness." In the works of George Eliot, "spiritual forces conquer"; in Howells they did not (2:796–97). James, the editor wrote, "lacks spirituality" (3:508). James Lane Allen in "Henry James on American Traits" observed that James's view of art was based on "French canons of art . . . human life that is agnostic . . . pessimistic . . . undidactic . . . without spirituality and religiousness. It is freighted with magnificent analyses, but . . . light in deeds" (5:363). A review of Hardy's 1882 novel *Two on a Tower* took the author to task for creating a portrait of womankind "artistically and morally at fault," a "travesty of womankind." Hardy had "overstepped the bounds of nature" (3:733). In short, the realists contended that "all the good and pleasant and agreeable people . . . are immensely rich," while all who are not rich "have some defect of character or training" (5:125).

The better view, the truer vision, the more accurate presentation of life was to be found in the writers of romances. In a review of Robert Louis Stevenson's *New Arabian Nights*, the editor saw "a new departure in romance writing, and perhaps the keynote of a new era." Stevenson's work was "deliciously and consistently impossible" (3:91). Likewise, Francis Marion Crawford's first novel, *Mr. Isaacs* (1882), was "the most powerful the season has produced" (3:188). Christian Reid's work had "no taint of the realistic school" (3:348), and E. P. Roe was "a good man who has made the world a better place by having lived in it" (3:669).

Serials, important magazine fare well past the middle of the twentieth century, were well represented in the *Continent*. In early issues Tourgée ran as many as three concurrently, but during the final six months, when he was writing weekly installments and repeatedly falling behind, he reduced the number to one per issue. Many of the authors and their works, well received in the 1880s, have fallen into deserved oblivion. Overall, however, the literary content was good, and many of the authors, if not their particular works, are remembered today. The Englishwoman Annie French Hector, writing under the pen name "Mrs. Alexander," contributed "Valerie's Fate," one of her more than forty novels. Harriet Prescott Spofford, better known for her short stories, wrote "The Marquis of Carabas" for Tourgée. Helen Campbell had both "Under Green Apple Blossoms" and "Her Family Tree" published. Julian Hawthorne's "Dust" appeared here. Three pseudonymous works, Marion Harland's "Judith: A Chronicle of Old Virginia," Orpheus C. Kerr's "Once There was a Man," and Nathan Ben Nathan's "Dorcas, the Daughter of Faustia," were written by Mary Virginia Terhune, Robert Henry Newell, and Nathan Chapman Kouns respectively. Tourgée contributed "Hot Plowshares," a story of miscegenation, toleration, and justice, written in time stolen from his editorial duties. As the titles suggest, the majority of the stories had either romantic or local-color content.

Toward the end of the *Continent*'s existence, Tourgée invented an interesting alternative to the serial: a series of different stories written by famous authors of the day. He enlisted Charles Bernard, Rose Terry Cook, Edgar Fawcett, James R. Gilmore, Anna K. Green, John Habberton, Edward Everett Hale, H. H. Jacobs, Sarah Orne Jewett, Kouns, Philip Bourke Marston, L. C. Martin, Roe, and Harriet Beecher Stowe. Modestly, Tourgée listed himself among the authors. To add spice and an air of mystery, the stories were published anonymously. Readers, drawing upon their knowledge of the contributors, were challenged to match author with sketch. Prizes—Tourgée novels and subscriptions to the *Continent*—would be awarded to those who guessed ten, twenty, or thirty correctly. The "Too True for Fiction" series died with the magazine before any prizes could be awarded.

Poetry, often printed on the front page with accompanying illustration, was as sentimental and romantic as the fiction. Among the poets appearing were George Parsons Lathrop, Sidney Lanier, J. T. Trowbridge, Campbell, Moulton, John Bannister Tabb, Celia Thaxter, John Greenleaf Whittier, Joel Chandler Harris, Jewett, Spofford, Mary B. Dodge, and, of course, Tourgée.

The magazine was profusely illustrated. Columns had logos; fiction and non-fiction often had full page art. Only a few illustrators' names are familiar today: Henry Wolf, Kenyon Cox, H. F. Farney, Howard Pyle, and Joseph Pennel. More famous in their own time were Frank H. T. Bellow, J. P. Gipson, Frederick Juengling, Gustav Kruell, Will H. Low, William Miller, Walter Satterlee, F. Cresson Schell, and William Thomas Smedley.

Nonfiction was given an important place in Tourgée's experiment. Articles ranged in topic from "The Cotton Worm," "Charms and Amulets," "Curiosities of Heraldry," and "The Sea Otter," to "The Mexican Railroad" and "Training a Canary." Henry Christopher McCook, a Presbyterian minister and prominent entomologist, contributed articles on "Honey Ants" and a series on spiders called "Tenants of an Old Farm." Felix Oswald, a Belgian-born naturalist, wrote a number of travel articles on the national parks. Eugene C. Gardner, architect and editor of the *Builder*, wrote a humorous series called "The House that Jill Built after Jack Had Proved a Failure," in which, weekly he discussed in simple dialogue form "Drains," "Stairs and Ballisters," "Mouldings," and "Fireplace and Flues." Another series, more concerned with decorating than building, was Donald Grant Mitchell's "From Lobby to Peak," which gave suggestions for the "Breakfast Room," the "Library Corner," and "Over the Mantle." Hester Poole discussed the "Concord School of Philosophy," E. A. Barber "The Philadelphia Post Office," Sheridan Hood "The Bypaths of Tuscany," and William Desmond O'Brien "The Tenure of Land and Landlordism in Ireland." The *Continent* did not fail for lack of variety.

But it did fail. In the 31 October 1881 issue, Tourgée announced he had moved the editorial offices to 23 Park View in New York to be at the "centre of our

American thought and enterprise''; he would continue, however, to maintain the Philadelphia office (4:571). Privately, Tourgée wrote that the old ties must not be broken because his chief sources of funds—"A liquor dealer, an infidel, and two Democrats''[2]—were there. But the change could not arrest the slide. The cost of producing the *Continent* was greater than the income it generated. When one of the largest investors, Charles H. Blair, demanded payment on his loan, the *Continent* collapsed. The last issue appeared on 20 August 1884. Later Tourgée wrote to a friend, "A very rich man induced me in 1881 to engage with him in publishing the *Continent* magazine. When his extravagance and pretense had swamped what ought to have been a success, he dug out and I very foolishly undertook to resuscitate the corpse. Had I been brave enough to cut expenses down to bed-rock, I should have succeeded. But I was not.''[3] The *Continent* failed because it was too soon and too late. The means of producing such a slick magazine were not yet economical, but no matter how modern the appearance, the contents were still too old-fashioned. In an age that wanted realism, Tourgée held on to his romantic view of life and literature; in an age of objective, pessimistic determinism, Tourgée was bound by his "prudery, his moral didacticism, and his exalted view of mankind.''[4]

## Notes

1. Theodore Gross, *Albion W. Tourgée* (New York: Twayne, 1963), p. 17.
2. Roy F. Dibble, *Albion W. Tourgée* (1921; rpt., Port Washington, N.Y.: Kennikat, 1968), p. 89.
3. Dibble, p. 90.
4. Otto H. Olsen, *Carpetbagger's Crusade; The Life of Albion Winegar Tourgée* (Baltimore: Johns Hopkins Press, 1965), p. 258.

## Information Sources

BIBLIOGRAPHY:
Dibble, Roy F. *Albion W. Tourgée.* 1921; rpt., Port Washington, N.Y.: Kennikat, 1968.
Gross, Theodore. *Albion W. Tourgée.* New York: Twayne, 1963.
Mott, Frank Luther. *A History of American Magazines.* 4 vols. Cambridge, Mass.: Belknap Press of Harvard University Press, 1957. 3:557–59.
Olsen, Otto H. *Carpetbagger's Crusade: The Life of Albion Winegar Tourgée.* Baltimore: Johns Hopkins Press, 1965.
INDEXES: Indexed at the end of each volume.
REPRINT EDITIONS: American Periodicals: Series III, 1850–1900. University Microfilms, Ann Arbor. Reels 99–100. Lost Cause Press.
LOCATION SOURCES: Widely available.

## Publication History

MAGAZINE TITLE AND TITLE CHANGES: *Our Continent*, volumes 1–2. *The Continent: An Illustrated Weekly Magazine*, volumes 3–6.
VOLUME AND ISSUE DATA: Volumes 1–6, 15 February 1882–20 August 1884.
FREQUENCY OF PUBLICATION: Weekly.

PUBLISHER: Our Continent Publishing Company.
EDITOR: Albion W. Tourgée.

*E. Bruce Kirkham*

# THE CRITIC

"One of the things of which I am most proud," wrote Jeannette Gilder, editor of the *Critic*, "is that the *Critic* was the first publication of its class to invite Walt Whitman to contribute to its pages."[1] Though other contributors included Joel Chandler Harris, Julia Ward Howe, and John Burroughs, the publication of Whitman's several essays and the series "How I Get Around at Sixty, and Take Notes" is, in retrospect, the greatest measure of the *Critic*'s fame. Operating on a small budget and never rising above a circulation of 5,000 during its life, the *Critic* attained a reputation for literary merit and quality due mainly to the persistence of its editor Jeannette Gilder.[2] When she began the magazine in 1881, with the assistance of her brother Joseph, it was considered by their elder brother Richard Watson Gilder, editor of *Century* (see *Scribner's Monthly**), to be a "wild thing to do," but, he added, "they have had . . . lots of encouragement," no doubt his own.[3] The *Critic* was begun with an aim of capturing some of the increasing number of subscribers to magazines in the 1880s. The magazine was first published as a "Fortnightly Review of Literature, Fine Arts, Music, and The Drama," but became a weekly publication after the first year, remaining unchanged in its format and content until it was purchased by the Putnams in 1898.

The first number (29 January 1881) set the standard for the quality of contributions that were to come and established a format consisting of essays, reviews, poetry, fiction, and in each issue notes on literature, music, fine arts, and drama. It contained articles on "William Blake: Poet and Painter," by Edward G. Stedman, and "The Date of Forefather's Day," by Sidney Howard Gay. A highlight of the number was the publication of Charles DeKay's "chapter from an Oriental Romance," "The Vision of Nimrod." In the second number began Whitman's series and in the fourth number the first of Joel Chandler Harris's contributions.

The Gilders recorded the generally favorable reception of their magazine in an attempt to show it had a national rather than a regional appeal. "It starts under the best auspices to act as an encouragement and check upon American literature and Art" (*New York Times*). "Discerning criticism marks every paragraph, and full of good performance" (*Boston Evening Gazette*). "It is refreshing, like a sea-breeze at midsummer noon, or the stream of the brown March furrows, to meet Walt Whitman's fresh talk . . . in the second number of *The Critic*" (*Springfield Republican*). "We commend *The Critic* to people of taste in the South" (*Atlanta Constitution*) (1:42).

Though sister and brother shared credit for editing the *Critic*, Jeannette Gilder apparently was in charge and continued as sole editor after her brother retired in 1901. A veteran reviewer, she "had been literary editor for *The New York Herald* and several other papers" before she undertook the establishment of her own magazine.[4] As one might expect, then, book reviewing was not just a sideline of the *Critic*. Its large staff of reviewers soon developed a type of review that was "usually bright, incisive and impartial, with a tendency to be conservative in judgements."[5] The book reviewing department eventually numbered among its staff James A. Harrison, Tudor Jenks, G. Stanley Lee, W. J. Rolfe, N. S. Shaler, W. I. Fletcher, Charles DeKay, J. Ranken Towse, Thomas Bailey Aldrich, Richard Watson Gilder, Edward Everett Hale, Noah Brooks, and Thomas R. Lounsbury, all to some degree specialists, and a few, like the Shakespearean scholar Rolfe, experts in their fields.

Another interesting feature of the *Critic* was its frontispieces and their accompanying essays. Each frontispiece consisted of a woodcut illustration of a well-known artist, usually literary, and each number began with an essay on that personage. Although woodcut illustrations were soon dropped after the first year because of their inferior quality and the problems they caused in printing, the fortnightly issues of the *Critic* offered portraits and essays on William Blake, Henry David Thoreau, Victor Hugo, Anthony Trollope, Nathaniel Hawthorne, and Edward Bulwer Lytton among others. Later, special numbers were sometimes issued on occasions such as the centenary of Washington Irving's birth, James Russell Lowell's seventieth birthday, and Alfred Lord Tennyson's death. Deaths of note were often accorded special attention, as in the third issue of the magazine where Whitman's essay on "The Death of Carlyle" (3:30) replaced the previously scheduled publication of Joel Chandler Harris's first contribution.

Whitman and Harris, of course, are today the most well known of the *Critic*'s more frequent contributors. Besides his series of six essays on "How I Get Around," the last of which ran on 15 July 1882, Whitman, over the next year and a half, contributed the essays "Death of Longfellow," "By Emerson's Grave," "Edgar Poe's Significance," "Robert Burns," "The Bible as Poetry," "Walt Whitman on the Santa Fe Celebration," as well as others on Shakespeare and Tennyson. Nearly all of his essays for the *Critic* were later included in either *Specimen Days* or *Democratic Vistas*.[6]

Under the name of George Selwyn, Whitman contributed the essay "Walt Whitman in Camden" to the *Critic*'s series *Authors at Home*, which began in 1885. The essay was included in *Authors at Home: Personal and Biographical Sketches of Well-Known American Writers*, edited by Jeannette Gilder (1888). Whitman's authorship was soon detected, however, and the essay was reprinted as " 'Walt Whitman at Home,' by Himself," in *Critic Pamphlet No. 2* (1898) and in *The Uncollected Poetry and Prose of Walt Whitman* (1972). Among other notables visited at home (by essayists other than themselves) were John Greenleaf Whittier, John Burroughs, Francis Lathrop, George William Curtis, Oliver Wendell Holmes, Sr., George Bancroft, and Mark Twain.

The *Critic*'s infatuation with Whitman apparently caused some confusion to its second most widely recognized author, Joel Chandler Harris. The Gilders had contracted with Harris to contribute some Uncle Remus stories that had not been included in his first collection, *Uncle Remus, His Songs and His Sayings* (1881). When his first contribution to the *Critic*, "How Mr. Fox Failed to Get His Grapes," was pulled in favor of Whitman's "The Death of Carlyle," Harris published the story in his own paper the *Atlanta Constitution*. Thus, in the fourth issue of the *Critic*, we find the editors, obviously embarrassed, attaching a note to the end of Harris's story to explain that it is a reprint rather than "gathered here for the first time" (1:46). Harris also published "Mr. Fox Figures as an Incendiary" (1:104) and "A Dream and a Story" (1:347) in the *Critic*. These three stories, along with "A Rainy Day with Uncle Remus," published in the *Century* (April 1881), are accounted the first Uncle Remus stories to appear in Northern publications and were collected in the volume *Nights With Uncle Remus* (1883),[7] Harris was also a frequent contributor of essays, one of which stirred up the "great banjo controversy." Harris claimed, in an article on "Plantation Music" (3:505–6), that he had never seen a Negro play a banjo on a Southern plantation. The response that "Uncle Remus doesn't know what he's talking about" was so great that the controversy continued for another year. Finally, George Washington Cable ended the debate when he wrote in defense of Harris that the fiddle was one hundred times more popular than any other instrument on plantations and it was possible that Harris had not ever seen a Negro play a banjo (4:309).

The *Critic*, though it disclaimed bias, had a decidedly nationalistic slant, insisting, for instance, that "we have novelists whose merit is as great as that of Messrs. [Thomas] Hardy, [William] Black, and [Richard Doddridge] Blackmore" (2:72). Essays and reviews of English literature, with certain exceptions such as those praising Alfred, Lord Tennyson, William Morris, and Anthony Trollope, were usually moderate in tone, although one of the *Critic*'s contributors accused Thomas Hardy of plagiarizing portions of his novel *Trumpet Major* from Augustus Baldwin Longstreet's *Georgia Scenes* (2:25–26). Continental literature, on the other hand, received little attention at all.[8]

The Gilders tried to make a popular as well as critical success of their magazine. They established, at various times, a "London Letter," "Special Boston Correspondence," and a "Chicago Letter on Art and Literature." The *Critic* also did not shy from dealing with fads, literary or otherwise. Articles on "the bicycle craze," "the Kipling madness," the popularity of E. P. Roe's novels, and the scandalous success of Amelie Rives's *The Quick and the Dead* were prominently featured.[9]

Though Jeannette Gilder remained editor for the entire life of the *Critic*, the magazine's look, publication frequency, and editorial policies were altered when it was purchased by the Putnams in 1898. Book reviews were de-emphasized, although a "Bookbuyers' Guide" consisting of many brief reviews was added. Longer articles on literature, which remained the primary topic of the magazine, were encouraged, along with greater publication of poetry. The *Critic* became a true magazine. It shifted to monthly publication, its "page . . . was reduced to the normal size for monthlies at the time," and illustrations were reinstituted, much improved "with the advent of halftones." "The Lounger," a "book chat" column by Jeannette Gilder, was also given a more prominent position, leading off each issue of the magazine.[10] The first issue with this new look was published in July 1898.

Though the *Critic* absorbed *Good Literature* in 1884, and the *Literary World of Boston* in 1905, it continued to have very little financial success and failed to increase its circulation. Accordingly, the Putnams decided to merge the *Critic* with a revived version of its own *Putnam's Monthly\** beginning with the October issue of 1906.

## Notes

 1. Quoted in *Walt Whitman As Man, Poet, and Friend*, ed. Charles N. Elliot (Boston: R. G. Badger, 1915), p. 97.

 2. Frank Luther Mott, *A History of American Magazines*, 4 vols. (Cambridge, Mass.: Harvard University Press, 1938), 3:551.

 3. *The Letters of Richard Watson Gilder*, ed. Rosamund Gilder (Boston: Houghton Mifflin, 1916), p. 106.

 4. Mott, 3:548.

 5. Mott, 3:549.

 6. William White, *Walt Whitman's Journalism: A Bibliography* (Detroit: Wayne State University Press, 1969), pp. 68–70.

 7. Julia Collier Harris, *The Life and Letters of Joel Chandler Harris* (Boston: Houghton Mifflin, 1918), p. 167.

 8. Mott, 3:549.

 9. Mott, 3:550.

 10. Mott, 3:551.

## Information Sources

BIBLIOGRAPHY:

Harris, Julia Collier. *The Life and Letters of Joel Chandler Harris*. Boston: Houghton Mifflin, 1918.

*The Letters of Richard Watson Gilder*. Ed. Rosamund Gilder. Boston: Houghton Mifflin, 1916.

Mott, Frank Luther. *"The Critic." A History of American Magazines*. 4 vols. Cambridge, Mass.: Harvard University Press, 1938. 3:548–51.

*Walt Whitman As Man, Poet, and Friend*. Ed. Charles N. Elliot. Boston: R. G. Badger, 1915.

White, William. *Walt Whitman's Journalism: A Bibliography*. Detroit: Wayne State University Press, 1969.

INDEXES: *A.L.A. Portrait Index, Contents-Subject Index, Cumulative Index, Poole's Index to Periodical Literature, Reader's Guide to Periodical Literature, Review of Reviews.*

REPRINT EDITIONS: American Periodicals: Series III, 1850–1900. University Microfilms, Ann Arbor. Reels 101–108.
LOCATION SOURCES: Widely available.

## Publication History

MAGAZINE TITLE AND TITLE CHANGES: *The Critic: An Illustrated Fortnightly
 Review of Literature, Fine Arts, Music and The Drama*, January-December 1881.
 *The Critic: A Fortnightly Review of Literature, Science, the Fine Arts, Music,
 and The Drama*, January-December 1882. *The Critic: A Weekly Review of Lit-
 erature, Science, The Fine Arts, Music and The Drama*, January-December 1883.
 *The Critic and Good Literature*, January-December 1884. *The Critic: A Literary
 Weekly, Critical and Eclectic*, January-December 1885. *The Critic: A Weekly
 Review of Literature and The Arts*, January 1886-June 1898. *The Critic: An
 Illustrated Monthly Review of Literature, Art, and Life*, July 1898-December 1904.
 *The Critic and The Literary World*, January 1905-December 1905. *The Critic*,
 January-September 1906.
VOLUME AND ISSUE DATA: Volumes 1–3, January 1881-December 1883; volumes
 1–29 (new series), 4–32 (old series), January 1884-June 1898; volumes 30–45
 (new series), 33–48 (old series), July 1898-June 1906; volume 46 (new series),
 49 (old series), July, August, September 1906.
FREQUENCY OF PUBLICATION: Biweekly, January 1881-December 1882; weekly,
 January 1883-June 1898; monthly, July 1898-September 1906.
PUBLISHERS: January-March 1881: Jeannette and Joseph Gilder, New York. March
 1881-January 1884: The Critic Publishing Company, New York. February-De-
 cember 1884: Good Literature Publishing Company, New York. January 1885-
 June 1898: The Critic Company, New York. July 1898-September 1906: G. P.
 Putnam and Company, New York.
EDITORS: Jeannette Gilder and Joseph Gilder, January 1881-December 1901; Jeannette
 Gilder, January 1902-September 1906.

*Leonard Butts*

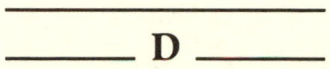

## D

**THE DEL MONTE WAVE.** See THE WAVE

**THE DEMOCRATIC REVIEW.** See THE UNITED STATES
MAGAZINE AND DEMOCRATIC REVIEW

## THE DIAL (Boston)

When the first issue of the *Dial* appeared in July 1840, it was the culmination
of planning by members of the Transcendental Club, who felt a need for their
own publication because of the inadequacy of other New England journals as
vehicles for their writing. The *Christian Examiner\** was conservative and unsympathetic, and, as Bronson Alcott stated in his diary on 27 March 1839,
Orestes Brownson's *Boston Quarterly Review,\** although "the best journal now
current on this side of the Atlantic . . . falls far below the idea of the best minds
among us. . . . Some of the freest pens now lie idle for want of a channel."[1] At
a meeting on 8 September 1839, the club decided to begin the new journal, and
soon thereafter Margaret Fuller agreed to serve as editor on the condition that
George Ripley serve as her assistant and business manager. Brownson, a former
member of the group, then offered to open his journal to their work, but because
his editorial views were considered too politically and philosophically narrow,
his offer was rejected. After some debate the new journal received the name that
Alcott had given his own diary.

Both Fuller and Ralph Waldo Emerson held high expectations that the *Dial*
would embody new literary and critical standards. The opening address to the
reader, written by Fuller and extensively revised by Emerson, declares an in-

tention to "give expression to that spirit which lifts men to a higher platform, restores them to the religious sentiment . . . makes life less desultory . . . and reconciles the practical with the speculative powers" (1:3). In "A Short Essay to Critics" immediately following, Fuller calls for a criticism less restrictive and partisan than that found in the *Dial*'s contemporaries: "The use of criticism in periodical writing is to sift, not to stamp a work. Yet should they not be 'sieves and drainers for the use of luxurious readers,' but for the use of earnest inquirers giving voice and being to their objections, as well as stimulus to their sympathies" (1:8). Opening the second issue with "Thoughts on Modern Literature," Emerson expresses hope for a new literature reflecting American culture. This was a guiding principle for the *Dial* and the reason Fuller and Emerson were willing to take editorial risks promoting unknown and unorthodox writers.

Predictably, from its first appearance the *Dial* was subjected to criticism and even ridicule. Alcott's "Orphic Sayings," spiritual and moralistic apothegms, caused hilarity in those who already considered the Transcendentalists an odd and extremist group. But even those in sympathy with the movement expressed disappointment. Brownson stated in his *Boston Quarterly Review* that the *Dial* writers "are too vague, evanescent, aerial."[2] Thomas Carlyle expressed to Emerson from England his disappointment in the *Dial*'s abstract, ethereal quality, and he repeated this criticism throughout its career. Even William Ellery Channing, Transcendental editor of the *Western Messenger*\* in Cincinnati, was mildly disappointed at first, although in the last issue of his journal in April 1841 he urged his readers to ignore "the Geese, who had hissed their loudest at this new comer" and to subscribe to this new "Era in American literature."[3]

Even members of the *Dial* group itself expressed disillusionment with the journal throughout its four-year life, in part because of their initial unrealistic expectations. After the first issue appeared, Fuller wrote to Emerson, "I feel myself how far it is from that eaglet motion I wanted. I suffer in looking over it now."[4] Although her spirits improved after the second issue, the *Dial* never fulfilled her expectations. Emerson's attitude vacillated. He feared that the journal would become too practical and reformist and thus lose its Transcendental identity, but he also sensed at times that it was too removed from everyday life. Theodore Parker and Alcott, both major contributors, held opposite views. Parker, himself a reformer of a more practical strain, expected "hoofs and horns, while it proved as gentle as any sucking dove," while Alcott felt that the *Dial* "measures not the meridian, but the morning ray," that it was not the Transcendentalist journal he had expected.[5] In the April 1842 issue Alcott stated in an introductory letter to his "Days from a Diary," "A fit organ for such as myself is not yet, but is to be. The times require a free speech, a wise, humane, and brave sincerity, unlike all examples in literature, of which the Dial is but the precursor" (2:409).

Fuller's publication of this criticism, by a writer whose ideas she herself distrusted, exemplifies her policy of publishing a wide range of opinion and philosophy with a minimum of editorial restriction. She was willing to publish untried writers and poets, some of whom never appeared in print again. When

Emerson became editor and began exercising a stricter editorial control, she protested to him in a letter: "You will sometimes reject pieces that I should not. For you have always had in view to make a good periodical and represent your own tastes; while I have had in view to let all kinds of people have freedom to say their say, for better, for worse."[6] Emerson and Parker were her most frequent contributors; other contributors included William Ellery Channing, Elizabeth Peabody, Henry David Thoreau, and Christopher Pearse Cranch. But frequently she had to draw material from her own private notebooks when contributions failed to fill an issue. The October 1841 *Dial* contains 85 pages of her own writing out of a total of 136, and the first two issues include 28 of her own pieces. Working without the pay promised her, she found the difficulty of reluctant contributors and publication deadlines exhausting. Her most important *Dial* contribution, "The Great Lawsuit. Man Versus Men. Woman Versus Women," appeared in the July 1843 issue under Emerson's editorship. Later expanded in her book *Woman in the Nineteenth Century*, this essay was one of the first calls in America for equal treatment of women. In spite of difficulties Fuller did exercise strict editorial control when she felt it to be necessary. She excluded Alcott's "Orphic Sayings" after two installments, in spite of Emerson's opinion. After publishing in the first issue a poem and a critique of Persius the satirist by Thoreau, she rejected later contributions, thus apparently cooling his interest in the *Dial*. She even criticized Emerson's "Thoughts on Modern Literature," suggesting to him that "I think when you look again, you will think you have not said what you meant to say."[7] He changed the wording.

Emerson took over the editorship reluctantly in 1842. Fuller was forced to resign because of exhaustion and ill health, Ripley had left for Brook Farm, and, with legal complications for the *Dial*, its publisher, Weeks, Jordan, and Company, had gone bankrupt. Elizabeth Peabody became publisher, and Emerson, in order to promote the work of Channing, Thoreau, and Alcott and to prevent the "Reform men" from taking control of the *Dial*, became editor. Under Emerson's editorship, Thoreau and Channing appeared more frequently. The July 1842 issue contained eight poems by Channing and Thoreau's essay "Natural History of Massachusetts." A number of Thoreau's translations of Greek classical writers were published, beginning with "The Prometheus Bound" (3:363–86), and these proved to be popular with *Dial* readers. Emerson's confidence in Thoreau culminated in Thoreau's editing the *Dial* for April 1843 while Emerson was on a lecture tour. Although Emerson had not wanted Parker, one of the "Reform men," to control the *Dial*, he did realize that Parker's articles were among the most popular in the journal, and he encouraged his faithful contributions. Parker's controversial essay on the "Hollis Street Council" defending John Pierpont, a minister under attack for reformist, including abolitionist, views, helped to sell the October 1842 issue. Nevertheless, Emerson found that he had to supply his own writing to fill the *Dial*'s pages, as Fuller had before him. He published a number of his lectures, including "The Transcendentalist" (3:297–313) and "The Conservative" (3:181–97), as well as poems. In articles such as "Fourierism and the Socialists" (3:86–96), "Chardon Street and Bible Conventions" (3:100–112), and "English Reformers" (3:227–47), Emerson reported on and evaluated contemporary reform movements.

Although the *Dial*'s character remained essentially unchanged, Emerson did make editorial changes. Consistent with his criticism of early issues, he included more of the Transcendentalists' poetry, which he felt most distinguished the journal from its contemporaries. Also, in his first issue of July 1842, he published a translation of the "Veeshnoo Sarma," announcing that "We commence in the present number the printing of a series of selections from the oldest ethical and religious writings of men, exclusive of the Hebrew and Greek Scriptures" (3:82). This series, later entitled "Ethnical Scriptures," reflected the Transcendentalists' pioneering interest in Oriental religions and philosophies. Thoreau selected five of the scriptures. Emerson continued Fuller's practice of reviewing books by or of interest to the group and of reporting cultural events in Boston. However, he added a section variously entitled "Intelligence," "Literary Intelligence," and "Editor's Table," which included more detailed reports of cultural activities in Europe and America. Here Emerson published letters of literary news from Germany by Charles S. Wheeler (3:388–98, 541–44) and a report on Fruitlands by Alcott and Charles Lane (4:135–36).

In spite of Emerson's efforts, though, the number of subscribers, never over 300, shrunk to 220. The *Dial*'s publisher in its last year, James Monroe & Company, charged one-third of the selling price, and this finally ended the journal. In a letter to his wife, Lidian, Emerson expressed relief at the prospect that his editorship would end: "Henry, whose name is a good omen, writes me good tidings for the Dial. It seems that we shall quickly see to the end of that labor."[8] He did continue publishing in the face of deficits that finally cost him $300 out of his own pocket. Emerson's experience with the *Dial* may be reflected in his refusal to become editor of the *Massachusetts Quarterly Review*,* for which he did, instead, supply an opening address. Both Emerson and Fuller discovered in their later travels to England that the *Dial* was known and even treasured there by a few people, and Alcott's letters indicate the demand in later years for complete sets. Nevertheless, a number of unsold copies made their way from Peabody's to Emerson's attic and finally, in 1872, to the ragman. Joel Myerson gives one reason for the *Dial*'s lack of readership: "The fact that Transcendentalism had been and would continue to be discredited, and the fact that the *Dial* and the names of its editors were irrevocably linked to that Boston movement, resulted in the *Dial*'s continued fall from serious attention as time went on."[9] But the *Dial* did serve as the only appropriate outlet for the Transcendentalists during an important period in their history.

### Notes

1. Quoted in Thomas Wentworth Higginson, *Margaret Fuller Ossoli* (Boston: Houghton, Mifflin, 1884), p. 143.

2. Quoted in Joel Myerson, *The New England Transcendentalists and the Dial: A History of the Magazine and Its Contributors* (Rutherford, N.J.: Fairleigh Dickinson University Press, 1980), p. 58.

3. Myerson, p. 64.

4. Higginson, p. 155.

5. Quoted in Charles R. Anderson, "Thoreau and *The Dial*: The Apprentice Years," *Essays Mostly on Periodical Publishing in America: A Collection in Honor of Clarence Gohdes* (Durham, N.C.: Duke University Press, 1973), p. 93.

6. James Elliot Cabot, *A Memoir of Ralph Waldo Emerson* (Boston: Houghton, Mifflin, 1887), p. 404.

7. Higginson, pp. 157–58.

8. *The Letters of Ralph Waldo Emerson*, ed. Ralph L. Rusk, 6 vols. (New York: Columbia University Press, 1939): 3:154.

9. Myerson, p. 53.

## Information Sources

BIBLIOGRAPHY:

Anderson, Charles R. "Thoreau and *The Dial*: The Apprentice Years." *Essays Mostly on Periodical Publishing in America: A Collection in Honor of Clarence Gohdes.* Durham, N.C.: Duke University Press, 1973. Pp. 92–120.

Cabot, James Elliot. *A Memoir of Ralph Waldo Emerson.* Boston: Houghton, Mifflin, 1887.

Cooke, George Willis. *An Historical and Biographical Introduction to Accompany The Dial As Reprinted in Numbers for the Rowfant Club.* 2 vols. 1902; rpt., Russell & Russell, 1961; expanded from " 'The Dial': An Historical and Biographical Introduction, with a List of the Contributors." *The Journal of Speculative Philosophy* 19 (1885): 225–65.

Hennessy, Helen. The *Dial*: Its Poetry and Poetic Criticism." *New England Quarterly* 31 (1958): 66–87.

Higginson, Thomas Wentworth. *Margaret Fuller Ossoli.* Boston: Houghton, Mifflin, 1884.

*The Letters of Ralph Waldo Emerson.* 6 vols. Ed. Ralph L. Rusk. New York: Columbia University Press, 1939.

Mott, Frank Luther. "*The Dial.*" *A History of American Magazines.* 4 vols. Cambridge, Mass.: Belknap Press of Harvard University Press, 1957. 1: 702–10.

Myerson, Joel. "The Contemporary Reception of the Boston *Dial.*" *Resources for American Literary Study* 3 (1973):203–20.

———. " 'In the Transcendental Emporium': Bronson Alcott's 'Orphic Sayings' in the *Dial.*" *English Language Notes* (10) 1972: 31–38.

———. *The New England Transcendentalists and the Dial: A History of the Magazine and Its Contributors.* Rutherford, N.J.: Fairleigh Dickinson University Press, 1980.

INDEXES: Cooke, George Willis, *An Historical and Biographical Introduction to Accompany The Dial.* Myerson, Joel, "An Annotated List of Contributions to the Boston *Dial*"; *The New England Transcendentalists and the Dial: A History of the Magazine and Its Contributors.*

REPRINT EDITIONS: American Periodicals: Series II, 1800–1850. University Micro-
    films, Ann Arbor. Reel 546. Rowfant Club. Cleveland, 1902. Russell & Russell,
    Inc. New York, 1961.
LOCATION SOURCES: Widely available.

## Publication History

MAGAZINE TITLE AND TITLE CHANGES: *The Dial: A Magazine for Literature,
    Philosophy, and Religion.*
VOLUME AND ISSUE DATA: Volumes 1–4, July 1840-April 1844.
FREQUENCY OF PUBLICATION: Quarterly.
PUBLISHERS: July 1840-April 1841: Weeks, Jordan & Company, Boston. July-October
    1841: Jordan & Company, Boston. January 1842-April 1843: Elizabeth Peabody,
    Boston. July 1843-April 1844: James Monroe & Company, Boston.
EDITORS: Margaret Fuller, July 1840-April 1842; Ralph Waldo Emerson, July 1842-
    April 1844.

*Edward Chielens*

## THE DIAL (Chicago and New York). See *American Literary Magazines: The Twentieth Century*

## THE DIAL (Cincinnati)

Moncure Daniel Conway began the *Dial* in January 1860 as an outlet for the
radical views of himself and his friends. Born in Virginia in 1832, Conway
graduated from Dickinson College, a Methodist school in Pennsylvania, and
became a Methodist circuit rider. In the early 1850s he became interested in
abolitionism and read Ralph Waldo Emerson's essays, both of which drew him
toward New England. There, he visited Emerson and Henry David Thoreau in
Concord, met Nathaniel Hawthorne, and heard Theodore Parker preach. He
eventually entered Harvard Divinity School, graduating in 1854. Two years later
he accepted a post as minister of the First Congregational Church of Cincinnati.
While in Cincinnati, his liberal leanings increased, and he became a leading
spokesman in the West for Hegelianism, natural supernaturalism, and Darwinian
thought. As he wrote in his autobiography, "My theological and philosophical
heresies . . . excited discussion far and near. The papers teemed with controversial
letters, and a magazine became inevitable."[1]

In his "A Word to Our Readers" in the first number of the *Dial*, the twenty-
eight-year-old Conway gave the reasons why he started his periodical:

The *DIAL* stands before you, reader, a legitimation of the spirit of the
Age, which *ASPIRES TO BE FREE*: free in thought, doubt, utterance,
love and knowledge. It is, in our minds, symbolized not so much by the
sun-clock in the yard, as by the floral dial of Linnæus, which recorded

the advancing day by the opening of some flowers and the closing of others: it would report the Day of God as recorded in the unfolding of higher life and thought, and the closing up of old superstitions and evils; it would be a Dial measuring time by growth (1:11).

If this passage brings to mind the language of the prospectus of the original *Dial* (Boston)* of 1840–1844, it was intended to, even as the subtitles of both *Dial*s were the same, for Conway saw his periodical as heavily influenced by its predecessor. As he wrote Emerson on 16 November 1859, "Very long has this revival of the Dial been my dream."[2] This new *Dial* attracted three of the old *Dial*'s contributors—Bronson Alcott, Charles T. Brooks, and Emerson—and published articles on two others—Margaret Fuller and Parker. It also recast the "Ethnical Scriptures" of the old *Dial* into an omnium gathering of "The Catholic Chapter."

Conway's *Dial* dealt with a wide variety of topics, including religion, women's rights, geology, German literature and theology, phrenology, politics, spontaneous generation, Swedenborgianism, physiology, prostitution, and atheism. In addition to "The Catholic Chapter," which presented quotations from Emerson, Hegel, Shakespeare, Goethe, John Ruskin, Jean Paul Richter, Newman, Coleridge, Fenelon, Carlyle, and the Hindu Scriptures, there were also long translations from French and German authors.

Conway himself wrote approximately thirty articles and seventy reviews for his *Dial*, including notices of books by Henry Ward Beecher, Elizabeth Barrett Browning, George Eliot, Emerson, Fuller, Hawthorne, Oliver Wendell Holmes, Julia Ward Howe, William Dean Howells, and Walt Whitman. He called the latter's 1860 *Leaves of Grass* a "remarkable work," and its author "never frivolous, his profanity is reverently meant, and he speaks what is unspeakable with the simple unreserve of a child" (1:518, 519). Conway was primarily responsible for the articles on religious subjects, including two long pieces on Parker, and Octavius Brooks Frothingham wrote a nine-part work on "The Christianity of Christ," which traced the various ways in which Christ's dogma had been perverted over the centuries. He also published verse by Myron Benton, Franklin Benjamin Sanborn, and a number of young Ohio poets, including William Dean Howells. Marx Edgeworth Lazarus, a contributor to the *Harbinger** of Brook Farm, sent in numerous translations and an article on utopianism, all of which made him, after Conway, the main contributor to the *Dial*. From the old *Dial* Alcott was represented by some new "Orphic Sayings," Brooks by some translations from German literature, and Emerson by the first publication of "Domestic Life" and some dozen poems and translations (which he later collected in *May-Day* [1867]), and by a reprinting of his 1844 address on "Emancipation in the West Indies."

Although Conway later wrote that the *Dial* "received good notices from the press" throughout Ohio,[3] there is evidence of mixed reviews of the *Dial*. At one end was the comment by the *Cincinnati Daily Gazette* (11 February 1860) that "Thus far the Dial has disgraced the name of the respectable, if erratic, periodical which it is a clumsy attempt to revive."[4] But Howells, writing in the *Ohio State Journal*, said,

> Until now Boston has been the only place in the land where the inalienable right to think what you please has been practised and upheld. . . . 'The Dial' is an attempt on the part of intellectual Cincinnati to do this, and the attempt is a noble one. We do not ask anybody to endorse the views of M. D. Conway, but we hold up his course as one of brilliant success, in everything that makes success honourable,—as that of a man singularly unselfish and devoted to what he believes the truth. He is the editor of 'The Dial,' but 'The Dial,' while it represents his views, shows the time of day by every intellectual light that shines upon it. . . . It is the organ of profound thinkers, merciless logicians, and polished writers.[5]

Conway, who had not yet met Howells when this review appeared, later wrote that something like "an old Methodist hallelujah rose to my lips" as he read it.[6]

The *Dial* seemed to have a respectable number of subscribers—Conway referred to "a large subscription list"[7]—probably a couple hundred. It came to a halt after only one year because Conway did not have the time to keep it going. As he wrote in the last number in "A Parting Word," "With this number the publication of the *Dial* ceases. The simple reason for this is, that the Editor is unable to bear the labor it adds to his usual and necessary duties" (1:713). Conway was becoming more involved with the abolitionist cause (as his favorable comments on John Brown in the *Dial* had shown), and the Civil War was on the horizon. Also, he was having trouble finding quality original contributions to the *Dial*, as seen by the many reprintings and translations present in the last few numbers, and, as he wrote Benton, "Subscribers are coming in very slowly."[8] By 1862, Conway was back in Boston, where he worked for a short time on the antislavery *Boston Commonwealth*, before going to England, where he remained for most of the rest of his life.

The great value of Conway's *Dial* is, in Clarence Gohdes's words, "that it reflects . . . the spirit of the last group of transcendentalists."[9]

## Notes

1. Moncure Daniel Conway, *Autobiography, Memories and Experiences*, 2 vols. (Boston: Houghton, Mifflin, 1904), 1:306.
2. *The Letters of Ralph Waldo Emerson*, ed. Ralph L. Rusk, 6 vols. (New York: Columbia University Press, 1939), 5:181.
3. Conway, 1:307.
4. Quoted in Clarence L. F. Gohdes, *The Periodicals of American Transcendentalism* (Durham: Duke University Press, 1931), p. 199.
5. Quoted in Conway, 1:307–8.
6. Conway, 1:308.

7. Conway, 1:307.

8. *A Troutbeck Letter-Book*, ed. George Edward Woodberry (Amenia, N.Y.: Troutbeck Press, 1925), p. 8.

9. Gohdes, p. 208.

## Information Sources

BIBLIOGRAPHY:

Burtis, Mary Elizabeth. *Moncure Conway*. New Brunswick, N.J.: Rutgers University Press, 1952.

Conway, Moncure Daniel. *Autobiography, Memories and Experiences*. 2 vols. Boston: Houghton, Mifflin, 1904.

Easton, Loyd D. "Religious Naturalism and Reform in the Thought of Moncure Conway." *Hegel's First American Followers*. Athens: Ohio University Press, 1966. Pp. 123–58.

Gohdes, Clarence L. F. "*The Dial* (Cincinnati)." *The Periodicals of American Transcendentalism*. Durham: Duke University Press, 1931. Pp. 194–209.

Mott, Frank Luther. "*The Dial* (of Cincinnati)." *A History of American Magazines*. 4 vols. Cambridge: Harvard University Press, 1957. 2:534–36.

Venable, W. H. "Conway's *Dial*." *Beginnings of Literary Culture in the Ohio Valley*. Cincinnati: Robert Clarke, 1891. Pp. 118–23.

INDEXES: None.

REPRINT EDITIONS: American Periodicals: Series III, 1850–1900. University Microfilms, Ann Arbor. Reel 7. AMS Press, Inc., New York, 1965.

LOCATION SOURCES: Widely available.

## Publication History

MAGAZINE TITLE AND TITLE CHANGES: *The Dial: A Monthly Magazine for Literature, Philosophy, and Religion*.

VOLUME AND ISSUE DATA: Volume 1, January-December 1860.

FREQUENCY OF PUBLICATION: Monthly.

PUBLISHER: Moncure Daniel Conway (implied, though not stated on title page).

EDITOR: Moncure Daniel Conway.

*Joel Myerson*

## THE DOLLAR MAGAZINE. See HOLDEN'S DOLLAR MAGAZINE

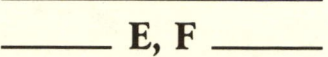

## E, F

**EPI-LARK.** See THE LARK

**THE EVENING MIRROR.** See THE NEW-YORK MIRROR, AND LADIES' LITERARY GAZETTE

**FEDERAL AMERICAN MONTHLY.** See THE KNICKERBOCKER

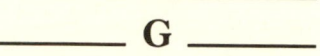

# G

## THE GALAXY

When Colonel William Conant Church and his brother Francis Pharcellus Church, experienced and successful editors of the *Army and Navy Journal*, founded the *Galaxy* in 1866 in New York, the enterprise was greeted by a number of writers as a necessary alternative to those keepers of genteel culture, *Scribner's Monthly*,* *Harper's Monthly*,* and, especially, the *Atlantic Monthly*.*[1] Even the Southern writer John Esten Cooke wrote from Winchester, Virginia, "I have never known a period in American letters when there was so plain and unmistakable a *demand* for a good magazine—*Harper* being sectional and dull—the *Atlantic* a New England coterie altogether."[2] Thus, as Robert J. Scholnick notes, "Founded as it was out of a local pride not entirely free of boosterism, the *Galaxy* was challenged to become a truly national magazine, hospitable to the thought of every section."[3] Indeed, although the *Galaxy* reflected New York culture in its diversity and tolerance, the Churches sought and accepted contributions from all sections. Approximately a third of the contributions were from New York writers, a third from New England, and a third from elsewhere.[4] The editors also made a policy of accepting contributions from little-known writers, basing their decisions on quality and not reputation. Contributions could be on "any subject except *party* politics or *sectarian* theology" (1:707). The Churches also were willing to publish views with which they disagreed, although at times they expressed editorial dissent. For example, they took exception to the "earnest protest, in our last number, against reserve and decency," of Eugene Benson, a regular contributor. " 'How far from Heine is our best and most ardent man of letters?' asks Mr. Benson. A very great way, we sincerely hope, as far as he is from Poe; else our national intellect is in a perilous state" (1:657–58).

The quality of the fiction in the *Galaxy* was high, especially in the later years, although from the beginning the editors sought manuscripts from the best writers.

They did not hesitate to solicit the *Atlantic*'s authors, although they were usually disappointed in those attempts, and William Church went abroad in 1867 and 1868 seeking contributions.[5] At least one and sometimes two serialized novels were running at all times, many of these by English authors. Anthony Trollope's *The Claverings* began with the first issue, and the *Galaxy* also eventually serialized *The Eustace Diamonds* and *An Editor's Tales*. The editors' taste for the sentimental and trite is evidenced by their running six novels of Mrs. Annie Edwards. It therefore seems ironic that in their editorial department, "Nebulae," for 1 July 1866 the editors praised American writers over English: "The souls of the literary future have come westward along with the Star of Empire. They will fitly embody themselves in due season. As long as we may believe ourselves encompassed by a bevy of such angels, we need not envy a Sennacherib's army of well-made dead corpses" (1:468). The main reason for this discrepancy, however, may be an economic one. The advance sheets for English novels or stories could be had for about $2 per page, while the going rate for a work by J. W. DeForest or Rebecca Harding Davis was about $5 per page, a difference that caused difficulties for American writers during this period.[6] However, the editors' solicitations of work by American writers eventually resulted in more and more of their work being published in the *Galaxy*. Davis's novel *Waiting for the Verdict* began in the issue of 15 February 1867, and the stories and novels of other realistic American writers, such as Henry James, Jr., DeForest, Rose Terry Cooke, H. H. Boyesen, and Constance Fenimore Woolson, appeared. Scholnick points out that this was a time of "trial and testing in American fiction" when realistic writers were beginning their careers. "The *Galaxy*'s contribution was in providing a congenial arena in which, to cite a notable example, a writer of the talent of Henry James, who published ten stories in its pages, could develop his craft."[7]

Another of the *Galaxy*'s important contributions to American literature was its editors' willingness to publish works by and about Walt Whitman, a daring policy considering the hostility generally expressed toward the poet. John Burroughs's essay "Walt Whitman and His 'Drum Taps' " appeared 1 December 1866, after having already been rejected by the *Atlantic*. The Churches themselves had reservations and took the piece only at the urging of William Douglas O'Connor.[8] Burroughs declares that the poetry's "primitive untaught ways are entirely new in literature. With all our profuse sentimentalism, there is no deep human solemnity—the solemnity of a strong, earnest, affectionate, unconventional man—in our literature" (2:606). The *Galaxy* went on to publish six contributions by Whitman, including the first two parts of what was to become *Democratic Vistas*, "Democracy," in December 1867, and "Personalism," in May 1868. However, their rejection of the third part, "Orbic Literature," has led to critical speculation. The hostility toward the first two essays may have led the Churches to conclude that they should "not . . . get too far away from the magazine-reading public."[9] In 1876 the poet complained bitterly in the *New Jersey Press* that the *Galaxy* along with the other important monthlies had treated him insultingly. However, evidence shows that the *Galaxy* remained receptive to Whitman even though he apparently submitted nothing after 1871.[10] In fact, Joaquin Miller's poem "To Walt Whitman" appeared there in January 1877. Scholnick concludes that the *Galaxy* treated Whitman much better than did the other monthlies: "The *Galaxy* paid Whitman well for almost everything which he submitted and opened its columns regularly to John Burroughs, perhaps Whitman's most articulate disciple."[11]

The Churches attempted to infuse humor into their magazine by hiring Mark Twain, whose "Memoranda" column appeared in every issue from May 1871 to April 1872 except for the March number. Twain introduces his column humorously, but he does state, "I would always prefer to have the privilege of printing a serious and sensible remark, in case one occurred to me, without the reader's feeling obliged to consider himself outraged" (9:720). Indeed, in the same column in an item entitled "Disgraceful Persecution of a Boy," Twain attacks the persecution of the Chinese in California, a theme he continues later with fictitious letters sent home by a Chinese immigrant. Other injustices were subject to ridicule or attack as well. In the second installment (June 1870), under the title "Hogwash," he reprints "the sickliest specimen of sham sentimentality that exists" (9:862), and he follows with "Post-Mortem Poetry" from the *Philadelphia Ledger* that is no less hilarious than the "Ode to Stephen Dowling Botts." This proved very popular, and in later "Memoranda" Twain included examples sent in by readers. Indeed, during Twain's year with the *Galaxy* circulation reached its high of over 23,000. But in April 1871 Twain said farewell, citing illness and death in his family. The editors announced in the same issue that a humorous department run by Don Piatt would begin accepting contributions, but "The Galaxy Club Room" proved a dreary successor to Twain, and it disappeared in 1873.

A third important figure to appear frequently in the *Galaxy* was Henry James, who contributed a dozen stories and a number of critical articles. After publishing "A Day of Days" in the issue for 15 June 1866, the editors recognized James's importance and pursued him to the point of irritation.[12] However, their pursuit paid off. For example, from July to December of 1875 James contributed to every issue. The Churches were later offered the opportunity to serialize *The American* and *The Europeans*. Negotiations for both works failed, however, because of financial restrictions imposed on the Churches by their partners, Sheldon & Co.

The cultural and historical writing and the departments were also of unusually high quality. Eugene Benson first appeared in the 1 June 1866 issue with "The Pagan Element in France," praising French culture as superior to the oppressive gentility of American culture, and in September in "Literary Frondeurs" he accused James Russell Lowell of a narrow, provincial attitude in his attack on Thoreau. Benson continued his attacks on America's prevailing culture until he left the country in 1869. Scholnick notes that "Benson, more than any other writer, set the tone of the *Galaxy* during its first few years."[13] The Churches published much of value on the Civil War, causing their magazine to be "recognized by many historians . . . as a printed source of much important information."[14] Beginning in November 1870 with "Fort Sumter," former Secretary of the Navy Gideon Welles began his series of articles relating war-policy decisions. Another view of the war was offered by James Franklin Fitts, a lawyer from Lockport, New York, and a former Union soldier, beginning with "The Last Battle of Winchester" in the issue for 15 October 1866. Fitts, whose battle descriptions are riveting and at times shockingly realistic, was "virtually unknown outside the *Galaxy*."[15] General George Custer's "Life on the Plains" appeared from January 1872 to October 1874, and his "War Memoirs" from March to November 1876, the last series cut short by his death at Little Big Horn. An interesting example of the *Galaxy*'s social analysis and its local focus is the series by Edward Crapsey on "The Nether Side of New York." Articles on philology ran throughout the *Galaxy*'s career by the humorist George Wakefield and William Grant White. In 1871 Edward L. Youmans began the regular "Scientific Miscellany," which covered a wide range of issues and developments. The "Drift-Wood" department was written by George E. Pond under the pseudonym of Philip Quilibet. In November 1870, he began a detailed and perceptive analysis of the Franco-Prussian War.

A number of reasons have been offered for the *Galaxy*'s demise. Pearson notes the partnership entered into in 1868 by the Churches with Sheldon & Company, a book publishing firm, in order to obtain greater financial stability. Sheldon restricted the Churches' financial dealings with contributors, as in the situation with James, prevented a possible merger with *Putnam's*\* and enraged contributors with late or diminished payments.[16] Circulation declined to 7,000 by 1878, and, ironically, the *Galaxy*'s subscription list was sold to the owners of the *Atlantic*. Scholnick concludes that New York society was not well enough established to support the sophisticated magazine. In addition, as political and economic corruption increased in the 1870s and the social and cultural atmosphere grew more reactionary, the *Galaxy* "could not survive in this conservative atmosphere. In a sense, its absorption by the *Atlantic* was symbolic of the new social and political reality."[17]

## Notes

1. Frank Luther Mott, *A History of American Magazines*, 4 vols. (Cambridge, Mass.: Belknap Press of Harvard University Press, 1957), 3:361.

2. Quoted in Justus R. Pearson, Jr., "The Story of a Magazine: New York's *Galaxy* 1866–1878: A study based on the unpublished correspondence of its editors," *Bulletin of the New York Public Library* 61 (1957):218.

3. Robert J. Scholnick, "*The Galaxy* and American Democratic Culture, 1866–1878," *Journal of American Studies* 16 (1982):71.

4. Pearson, p. 220.

5. Pearson, pp. 224, 223.

6. Mott, 3:372; Pearson, pp. 228–29.

7. Scholnick, *"The Galaxy,"* p. 77.

8. Edward F. Grier, "Walt Whitman, the *Galaxy*, and *Democratic Vistas*," *American Literature* 23 (1951):333.

9. Grier, p. 348.

10. Robert J. Scholnick, "Whitman and the Magazines: Some Documentary Evidence," *American Literature* 44 (1972):240.

11. Scholnick, "Whitman and the Magazines," p. 226.

12. Pearson, p. 225.

13. *"The Galaxy* and American Democratic Culture, 1866–1878," p. 73.

14. Pearson, p. 284.

15. Scholnick, *"The Galaxy,"* p. 72.

16. Pearson, pp. 292–94.

17. Scholnick, *"The Galaxy,"* p. 80.

## Information Sources

BIBLIOGRAPHY:

Grier, Edward F. "Walt Whitman, the *Galaxy*, and *Democratic Vistas*." *American Literature* 23 (1951):332–50.

Mott, Frank Luther. *"The Galaxy." A History of American Magazines*. 4 vols. Cambridge, Mass.: Belknap Press of Harvard University Press, 1957. 3:361–81.

———. "The *Galaxy*: An Important American Magazine." *Sewanee Review* 36 (1928):86–103.

Pearson, Justus R., Jr. "The Story of a Magazine: New York's *Galaxy* 1866–1878: A study based on the unpublished correspondence of its editors." *Bulletin of the New York Public Library* 61 (1957):217–37, 281–302.

Scholnick, Robert J. *"The Galaxy* and American Democratic Culture, 1866–1878." *Journal of American Studies* 16 (1982):69–80.

———. "Whitman and the Magazines: Some Documentary Evidence." *American Literature* 44 (1972):222–46.

INDEXES: An author-title index is included in each bound volume.

REPRINT EDITIONS: American Periodicals: Series III, 1850–1900. University Microfilms, Ann Arbor. Reels 7–12. Bell & Howell, Micro Photo Division.

LOCATION SOURCES: Widely available.

## Publication History

MAGAZINE TITLE AND TITLE CHANGES: *The Galaxy. An Illustrated Magazine of Entertaining Reading*. 1 May 1866-March 1872. *The Galaxy. A Magazine of Entertaining Reading*. April 1872-January 1878.

VOLUME AND ISSUE DATA: Volume 1, May-August 1866; volume 2, September-December 1866; volume 3, January-April 1867; volume 4, May-December 1867; volumes 5–24, 1868–1877 (regular semiannual volumes); volume 25, January 1878 (one number only).

FREQUENCY OF PUBLICATION: Semimonthly, 1 May 1866–15 April 1867. Monthly, May 1867-January 1878.

PUBLISHERS: 1 May 1866-January 1868: W. C. & F. P. Church, New York. February
    1868-January 1878: Sheldon & Co., New York.
EDITORS: William Conant Church and Francis Pharcellus Church.

*Edward Chielens*


**THE GENTLEMAN'S MAGAZINE.** See BURTON'S
GENTLEMAN'S MAGAZINE


**THE GENTLEMAN'S MAGAZINE AND MONTHLY
AMERICAN REVIEW.** See BURTON'S GENTLEMAN'S
MAGAZINE


## GODEY'S LADY'S BOOK

Louis Godey affectionately—and with no little nerve, given the era—referred
to it as "The Book." He could do so because his magazine for ladies was "the"
book for his subscribers as well, though none would have been so brazen as to
suggest as much. From 1830 to 1898 *Godey's Lady's Book* guided, comforted,
chastised, entertained, and enlightened thousands of American readers. "The
mirror of woman's mind,"[1] established in 1830 by Louis Antoine Godey, published material that ran the gamut from clothing to hair styles, from music to
domestic economy, from mawkish, moralistic fiction to doubly mawkish, moralistic poetry. Yet among the magazine's pages—liberally "embellished" by
the engravings and fashion plates for which *Godey's* became famous—readers
also found original contributions from Oliver Wendell Holmes Sr., Henry Wadsworth Longfellow, Nathaniel Hawthorne, Edgar Allan Poe, and several other
notables whose reputations have weathered changing literary climates. The importance of *Godey's Lady's Book* to students of the nineteenth century is, therefore, twofold: as an index to popular culture and as a friend to some of the
country's best writers, helping them to establish their careers.

*Godey's Lady's Book* came to possess a magical blend of business and editorial
acumen that its predecessors, such as *The Lady's Magazine and Repository of
Entertaining Knowledge* (Philadelphia, 1792) had not enjoyed. Louis Godey,
born in New York City in 1804, built his publishing career from the ground up,
working first as a newspaper journalist and then as an assistant in the paper's
business office. The essential difference between this portly, "Pickwickian"[2]
man and many another periodical publisher lay in his willingness to take risks.
Indeed, he seems to have delighted in them. Thus, after moving to Philadelphia
in 1828, he launched his publishing enterprise in 1830 with little capital but
much ambition. His audience would be the somewhat neglected "fairer sex,"
so he titled his magazine *The Lady's Book*. A similar operation already underway

in Boston had claimed Godey's attention, as had the woman who served as its editor; Sarah Josepha Hale's *Ladies' Magazine* (1828) may even have given Godey the idea with which he set out to make publishing history. He could do so, however, only after he managed to procure in 1837 the Boston periodical and "the Lady Editor" herself.

This widow and mother of five now occupies only a vague, misty place in the national memory. Sarah Josepha Hale lived many years, wielding her editorial pen in the cause of a healthier, more refined, and more equitable American life. Women's education, marriage and family, exercise and hygiene, social action (particularly in the name of patriotism), literature, and even the culinary arts were her subjects. At the height of *Godey's* popularity in 1861, her advice in these and other matters was reaching an estimated 150,000 readers—astounding numbers for those relatively early days of periodical literature. The woman who wrote "Mary Had a Little Lamb" and who successfully urged President Lincoln to proclaim Thanksgiving a national holiday also championed equal opportunity for aspiring women doctors, teachers, and missionaries. Mrs. Hale was instrumental in the founding of Vassar College (the first for women), the completion of the Bunker Hill Monument, and the preservation of Mount Vernon; she had also written a successful novel (*Northwood*, 1827), one of the first to prophesy that America would come to civil strife over economic difficulties. She served as editor-in-chief of *Godey's Lady's Book*, as it came to be called, a full forty years, building it into "an American institution."[3]

The years preceding *The Ladies' Magazine*'s 1837 merger with its Philadelphia counterpart now appear rather unremarkable ones for *Godey's*. Reprints from British periodicals filled its pages, only infrequently upstaged by American contributions. Until 1891 the absence of an international copyright law invited the pirating of English material by American publishers despite loud and frequent protests from authors on both sides of the Atlantic. American letters lost much, too, as the nation's publishers continued to pass over burgeoning local talent in favor of British authors, whose already printed work could be obtained for nothing. One of the first American magazine editors to disparage this publishing myopia was Mrs. Hale; as early as 1828 she determined to print contributions only from American authors in her *Ladies' Magazine*, and from her Godey eventually took his cue.

By the time Mrs. Hale joined *Godey's Lady's Book* in January of 1837, the publisher was making good his promise to pay generously for contributions from talented American writers. Not that he paid for everything he printed; a beginner then as now had usually to be content with mere honor. Nevertheless, Godey's willingness to compensate professional writers—as yet a rare practice in the periodical sphere—doubtless attracted several who otherwise might never have associated themselves with the magazine. James Russell Lowell and Hawthorne both published their work alongside the "thrice diluted trash in the shape of namby-pamby love tales and sketches" produced by "the d___d mob of scribbling women" (Lowell's and Hawthorne's valuations, respectively),[4] whose literary profusions composed the bulk of the *Lady's Book's* material. *Godey's* also published essays and sketches by Edward Everett and Washington Irving, as well as poems by Ralph Waldo Emerson. Holmes and Poe, both personal acquaintances of Mrs. Hale, saw much of their work appear within various *Godey's* issues, particularly throughout the 1840s. Godey printed Poe's "The Cask of Amontillado," "The Oblong Box," and one of his last stories, "Mellonta Tauta," and reprinted his famous review of Hawthorne's *Twice-Told Tales* in November of 1847.

By the 1840s and 50s Louis Godey could legitimately add to his claim for his "Book"—and he loved to sing its praises—that it was leading the way toward a richer body of American periodical literature than had previously existed. So successful were his efforts to secure native contributions that other American magazines began to reprint material from *Godey's* even as they still pirated British works. Although Godey found this circumstance flattering, his business sense found it threatening; he therefore courageously broke new ground by becoming, in 1845, the first American publisher to copyright his own magazine. His chief competitor, *Graham's Lady's and Gentleman's Magazine\** (formerly the *Casket* of Philadelphia), quickly followed suit, despite the loud uproar Godey had provoked within the periodical publishing community. The move won a measure of immediate support, however, and in time the American copyrighting of magazines became a matter of course.

Godey endeavored to make his magazine "the guiding star of female education, the beacon light of refined taste, pure morals and practical wisdom";[5] accordingly, *Godey's* ran various regular departments, some of which are germane to most women's magazines even today. Matters of domestic economy—sewing, cooking, and the like—were considered each month along with those of etiquette, beauty, health, and hygiene. Sheet music was staple, as were articles on geography, travel, history, and the arts. Biographical pieces on notable women, book reviews, and "The Editor's Table" also appeared in most issues. This last department, printed near the end of each number, gave Mrs. Hale a forum for advice and comments that had perhaps not found their way into her editorials. These remarks were frequently followed by a few more written by Godey, who eventually called his place at the back of the magazine "The Arm Chair." Of politics or current controversy there was little or no mention throughout the magazine's 68 years—such would never do among pages destined for female perusal. Indeed, *Godey's Lady's Book* all but ignored the Civil War.

From his "Arm Chair" Godey gloated over publishing promises made and fulfilled, often reminding readers that he produced his magazine at no small cost to himself. Each issue was usually on time, too—a commendable feat on Godey's part, given an unsophisticated postal service and the wide lack of passable roads. But then, no effort was too great for the sake of "the ladies": "We would like it noticed, that in addition to the steel engraving in each number . . . we also give a Plate of Fashion richly coloured. The latter . . . is intended for the ladies, and is very expensive. There is not a magazine in Europe or America, that gives so many and such beautiful embellishments'' (21:144). Extensive though his financial investment may have been, the *Lady's Book* nevertheless rewarded Godey handsomely. He was probably the first American magazine publisher ever to become a millionaire.

Appearing during the periodical's early years only once every three months, the fashion plates to which the publisher alluded became the *Godey's* hallmark. As circulation increased, so did the frequency with which these illustrations of family attire adorned the magazine, so that by 1849 twenty plates appeared in one year. Hand painted by a hundred and fifty women whom Godey employed for the purpose, the plates became collectors' items, homemakers often removing them from the magazine for framing. By 1861 *Godey's* went so far as to publish ''extension plates,'' which were double the width of a single page, and which folded out. Besides the colored fashion plates, the *Lady's Book* also published, from the beginning, copper and steel engravings of the works of various artists. The number of these that Godey could afford to include in each issue also increased over the years. The Sartain mezzotint was perhaps the best; but by 1888 the engravings yielded to half-toned electrotypes, which remained for the life of the magazine.[6]

Whereas pictures and engravings in most periodicals were (and still are) intended to illustrate the text, Godey preferred that the text illustrate the *Lady's Book*'s ''embellishments.'' Even the literature he typically published seemed to do so, presenting morals and life lessons that, presumably, accounted for the expressions of sweet content worn by man, woman, and child in most of the plates and engravings. Joseph N. Satterwhite offers a valuable analysis of the fiction that characterized the magazine. Because conceptions of the short story as a unique art form unto itself were not yet widely recognized, mediocre writers dabbling in the genre only saw it as an abbreviated version of the same story one might tell in a novel—the ''domestic'' novel, that is. Most *Godey's* fiction dealt in the scenes of domestic bliss threatened by a wayward husband, wife, child, fiancé, or sometimes a villainous relative or employer. An author typically devoted several pages of a story to wreaking havoc in the lives of flat, predictably virtuous Christian characters. Then in the last few paragraphs the author restored order, and because she had to do so briefly (as she frequently interrupted the narrative to inform the reader), the story closed with an amazing coincidence, liberally spiced with moralizing sentiment, that the tale might prove sufficiently ''educational.''[7]

*Godey's* poetry was of a similar stamp; E. Merriot's ''The Broken Heart'' is typical: ''I saw that the glow of her beauty had faded, / The eye that illum'd it gaz'd wildly and drear, / Her tresses neglected, hung loose and unbraided, / And shrouded a cheek dew'd with memory's tear'' (21:90). And so on, for three more stanzas. These lines were set to piano music, but whether found in song or poetry, *Godey's* verse rarely left the beaten track of literary sentimentality.

Literature of this nature bore the signatures (sometimes pseudonyms, particularly of women authors, though Mrs. Hale discouraged this practice) of many a popular nineteenth-century writer: Miss Eliza Leslie, Caroline Lee Hentz, Mrs.

E.D.E.N. Southworth (not a pseudonym), Mrs. Anne Stephens, Mrs. Caroline M. S. Kirkland, Catherine M. Sedgwick, "Grace Greenwood" (Sarah Jane Lippincott, who for a time edited Louis Godey's *Lady's Dollar Newspaper*), Mrs. E. F. Ellet, Miss Gooch, and the notoriously prolific poet Mrs. Lydia H. Sigourney. Similar edifying works flowed from the pens of a few men as well: T. S. Arthur (much loved among Prohibitionists for his *Ten Nights in a Barroom*), George P. Morris, Thomas Buchanan Read, Joseph C. Neal, James Kirke Paulding, Park Benjamin, and H. T. Tuckerman. Other contributors included N. T. Brooks, Charles Fenno Hoffman, William Henry Herbert, James T. Fields, R. Penn Smith, Charles Sprague, Mrs. Frances M. Whitcher, Metta Victoria Fuller, and Harriet Beecher Stowe. Such minor poets as Miss Hannah F. Gould and Mrs. Frances Osgood published in *Godey's*, as did the more noteworthy William Cullen Bryant, Bayard Taylor, and N. P. Willis. During the fruitful middle decades of the century and beyond, *Godey's* printed the work of Virginia S. Townsend, the Reverend H. H. Weld, A.J.H. Duganna, Mrs. Mary Janvrin, Fannie E. Hodgson, Marion Harland, Caroline Orne, and S. Annie Frost (Mrs. S. A. Shields, who became chief editor of the *Lady's Book* in 1878)—all much better known in their century than in ours.

The greatest stir *Godey's Lady's Book* ever made in literary circles resulted from the publication in 1846 of a series entitled "The Literati of New York," by Edgar Allan Poe. In these essays Poe offered "Some Honest Opinions" regarding several writers, and the sketches demonstrate what many in contemporary letters already knew, that Poe was not squeamish nor particularly selective about whose reputation he trounced. The series excited such immediate response that Godey had to reprint in June the first essay, which had appeared in May. Godey also felt it necessary to assure his genteel readers that "We have nothing to do but publish Mr. Poe's opinions—not our own" (32:288). To Poe, Hawthorne "evince[d] extraordinary genius" but Longfellow was "a dexterous adapter of the ideas of other people" (32:194–95); many other writers whom Poe praised or condemned have since faded into obscurity.

By the time of the deaths of Louis Godey and Sarah Josepha Hale (in 1878 and 1879, respectively), *Godey's Lady's Book*, though still appearing punctually every month, was no longer the bright star it had once been among the popular magazines. It had outlasted one rival, *Graham's*, but another, *Peterson's Magazine* (Philadelphia, 1842), had caught up to and surpassed it. *Godey's* ran another twenty years, however; various editors attempted to keep circulation figures up by reducing subscriptions from three dollars to two (and much later, to one), and by trying such publishing twists as "novelettes," written by John Habberton and Julian Hawthorne, among others. Nevertheless, in 1898 *Godey's Magazine* (the "Lady's Book" had dropped out of the title in 1892) was absorbed by Frank Munsey's *Puritan* (New York, 1897).

*Godey's Lady's Book* grew up and grew old with the century—more accurately, with the century's women, who used the magazine to exchange more than recipes and words of moral wisdom. In its era *Godey's* both shaped and reflected the tastes of these women; and with their help, it carved a respectable if not exceptional niche for itself in American literary history.

## Notes

1. Cited by Ruth E. Finley, *The Lady of "Godey's": Sarah Josepha Hale* (Philadelphia: J. B. Lippincott Company, 1931), p. 62.

2. Finley, p. 41.

3. James Playsted Wood, *Magazines of the United States*, 2d ed. (New York: The Ronald Press Company, 1956), p. 54.

4. Cited by Frank Luther Mott, *A History of American Magazines, 1741–1850* (New York: D. Appleton and Company, 1930), p. 736; cited by Alexander Cowie, *The Rise of the American Novel* (New York: American Book Company, 1951), p. 361.

5. Finley, p. 42.

6. Mott, pp. 592–93.

7. Joseph N. Satterwhite, "The Tremulous Formula: Form and Technique in *Godey's* Fiction," *American Quarterly* 8 (1956):99–113. See also Richard Fay Warner, "*Godey's Lady's Book*," *American Mercury* 2 (1924):399–405.

## Information Sources

BIBLIOGRAPHY:

Davenport, Walter, and James C. Derieux. *Ladies, Gentlemen and Editors*. Garden City, N.Y.: Doubleday and Company, 1960.

Finley, Ruth E. *The Lady of "Godey's": Sarah Josepha Hale*. Philadelphia: J. B. Lippincott Company, 1931.

Mott, Frank Luther. "*Godey's Lady's Book*." *A History of American Magazines, 1741–1850*. New York: D. Appleton and Company, 1930. Pp. 580–94.

Riegel, Robert E. *American Women: A Story of Social Change*. Cranbury, N.J.: Associated University Presses, 1970.

Satterwhite, Joseph N. "The Tremulous Formula: Form and Technique in *Godey's* Fiction." *American Quarterly* 8 (1956):99–113.

Warner, Richard Fay. "*Godey's Lady's Book*." *American Mercury* 2 (1924):399–405.

Woodward, Helen. *The Lady Persuaders*. New York: Ivan Obolensky, 1960.

INDEXES: None.

REPRINT EDITIONS: American Periodicals: Series II, 1800–1850. University Microfilms, Ann Arbor. Reels 772–76, 862–80.

LOCATION SOURCES: A complete run is available at the Connecticut Historical Society, Hartford. Partial runs are widely available.

## Publication History

MAGAZINE TITLE AND TITLE CHANGES: *The Lady's Book*, July 1830-June 1833. *Monthly Magazine of Belles-Lettres and the Arts, the Lady's Book*, July 1833-December 1834. *Lady's Book*, January 1835-December 1839. *Godey's Lady's Book, and Ladies' American Magazine*, January 1840-December 1843. *Godey's Magazine and Lady's Book*, January 1844-June 1848. *Godey's Lady's Book*, July 1848-June 1854. *Godey's Lady's Book and Magazine*, July 1854-December 1882. *Godey's Lady's Book*, January 1883-September 1892. *Godey's Magazine*, October 1892-August 1898.

VOLUME AND ISSUE DATA: Volumes 1–137, July 1830-August 1898. Two volumes
    each year; the last is incomplete.
FREQUENCY OF PUBLICATION: Monthly.
PUBLISHERS: 1830–1877: Louis A. Godey and Company. 1877–1883: Godey's Lady's
    Book Publishing Company. 1883–1886: J. H. Haulenbeek and Company. 1886–
    1887: William E. Striker. 1887–1888: Croly Publishing Company. 1888–1898:
    Godey Publishing Company (Philadelphia, 1830–1892; New York, 1892–1898).
EDITORS: Louis A. Godey, 1830–1836; Sarah Josepha Hale and Louis A. Godey, 1837–
    1838; Sara Josepha Hale, Lydia H. Sigourney, and Louis A. Godey, 1839–1840;
    Sarah Josepha Hale and Lydia H. Sigourney, 1841; Sarah Josepha Hale, Lydia
    H. Sigourney, Morton McMichael, and Louis A. Godey, 1842; Sarah Josepha
    Hale, Morton McMichael, and Louis A. Godey, 1843–1846; Sarah Josepha Hale
    and Louis A. Godey, 1846–1877; J.G.L. Brown, Charles W. Frost, and Mrs.
    S. A. Shields, 1878; J. Hannum Jones, A. E. Brown, and Mrs. S. A. Shields,
    1878–1881; J. Hannum Jones and A. E. Brown, 1881–1883; J. H. Haulenbeek,
    1883–1885; J. H. Haulenbeek and Eleanor Moore Hiestand, 1885–1886; Mrs.
    D. G. Croly, 1887–1888; Albert H. Hardy, 1892–1893; Harry Wakefield Bates,
    1894–1895(?); Harold Wilkinson (?).

*Allison Bulsterbaum*

# THE GOLDEN ERA

By 1852 San Francisco newspapers, which in 1847 had numbered only two,
were flourishing. Although the weekday editions were largely given over to
news, Sunday editions often contained poetry, short stories, and drama reviews
designed to satisfy a growing interest in literature and cultural affairs. Encouraged
by this interest in literature and unsuccessful at mining, Rollin M. Daggett and
J. Macdonough Foard published the first issue of the *Golden Era*, a weekly
periodical that became the most popular literary magazine in nineteenth-century
California.

    The youthful editors clearly aimed at a broad audience and set forth their
objectives in the first issue; the *Golden Era* was to be "a Good Family newspaper;
calculated for circulation in every parlor and miners' cabin; that would be of
interest to the merchant, the farmer and the mechanic; untainted with politics,
and unbiased by religious prejudices" (1:1). They did not attempt to publish a
polished literary magazine such as *Harper's Monthly*\* or *Blackwood's Magazine*
but rather sought to develop a Western literature which, in the 1850s, would
spring from "the incidents and characters of mining camps, the novelty and
peculiarity of which sufficed to impart a special stamp to the narration."[1] This
dedication to Western writing is mentioned in the first number of the *Golden
Era* and then more forcibly in a subsequent issue: "We do contend that foreign
writers should not be brought into daily, weekly, or monthly contact with the
people . . . to the exclusion of native writers. We contend further that in order
to secure a healthy literature, 'racy of the soil,' these native writers should

receive all possible encouragement.''[2] The editors of the *Golden Era* did realize their dream and did produce an informal literary magazine supportive of local authors. While critics often complained that the *Golden Era* was best "suited rather for the taste of the less exacting portions of the rural and mining population,''[3] they were forced to conclude that, "of similar papers, none have equalled it in popularity.''[4]

The popularity of the *Golden Era* was maintained by the careful way in which the editors courted their audience. From 1852 to 1866 the editors (first Daggett and Foard, who were succeeded in 1860 by Joseph E. Lawrence and James Brooks) were very successful; it was during these years that the *Golden Era* enjoyed its greatest popularity.

The *Golden Era* of the 1850s was written for and, to a large extent, by the miners of the California Gold Rush. Daggett and Foard began this tradition by writing of their own experiences while travelling to California as well as their adventures and misadventures in the mines. Daggett, dressed as a rather colorful miner, toured the mines soliciting subscriptions and encouraging the local residents to contribute poetry, short stories, and descriptions of mines and mining communities. Eager to publish original material and thereby reduce the amount of reprinted material, the editors established what amounted to a "Notes and Queries" column, "To Our Correspondents," which became a staple of the *Golden Era*. "To Our Correspondents," in which submission of poetry figured prominently, helped give the *Golden Era* its informal tone. Through this chatty column the editors also accepted or rejected pieces, gave encouragement to would-be authors, and provided lively reading for their subscribers. Items in the column varied from praise ("Lida Woodvale—You will see one of your favors on the 1st page of this issue. It is musical and pretty. We will make use of the others as we find proper space for them" [3:46]) to humorous rejections ("Brick— That 'brick-bat' tossed on our table won't stand fire. We can't exactly discover what it is all about. Men, women, cats, dogs, and horses are promiscuously mingled, jumbled and tangled together, and we are unable to separate them. Declined" [3:48]). The column was also used to answer questions from subscribers about grammar, history, geography, and many other subjects.

If a poem was selected for publication, it appeared in the "Poetry Column," which for many years was on page one, column one. Generally the poetry was characterized by optimism. The editors preferred verse that celebrated California and sang her praises. Although poetry received the most prominent position, the reputation of the *Golden Era* was built upon its prose. In the 1850s most of the prose pieces were concerned with travel to California or life in California, especially the mines. Daggett, under the pseudonym "Blunderbuss," wrote many of the better features about life in California. Other contributors included Joseph T. Downey ("Old Saw"), John R. Ridge ("Yellow Bird"), Robert F. Greely, and E. Gould Buffum, all of whom wrote about the Golden State. Most prose pieces had a vitality that was lost in later years when the experiences of early life in California were not freshly in mind.[5] Drama reviews, news summaries (both national and local), vital statistics, reprinted material on various subjects, and, of course, advertisements were also featured.

In 1860, when Brooks and Lawrence purchased the *Golden Era*,[6] San Francisco's burgeoning population had so grown that the new editors and proprietors, while anxious to maintain their support from rural areas, began to focus their attention on the urban population.[7] The new editors continued the "To Our Correspondents" column and maintained the friendly tone of the magazine, as well as the large number of agents throughout the state who obtained subscriptions and solicited material. To attract more effectively a cosmopolitan readership, however, Lawrence, the senior partner, deemphasized local color sketches in favor of serialized romances (Western and non-Western) and social satire. Under his leadership the *Golden Era* gave young authors a chance to develop and display their writing skills. As its focus shifted to more urban interests, the magazine began to publish many women authors.[8] Lawrence hired young San Francisco women and men such as Frances Fuller Victor, Bret Harte, Charles Warren Stoddard, and Mark Twain. Victor wrote a column and regularly commented on local events, from recent publications to social gatherings. Hubert Howe Bancroft credits her short stories, written under the pseudonym "Florence Fane," with helping to maintain the popularity of the magazine. In 1857 Bret Harte began his association with the *Golden Era* as a compositor and occasional contributor. Lawrence soon made him a columnist and regularly published Harte's short stories. Harte gave the *Golden Era* its best remembered prose work, "M'liss," which was later published in book form. In 1864 he left to join Charles Henry Webb as coeditor of the *Californian*, which was to be a more sophisticated literary journal than the *Golden Era*. Charles Warren Stoddard, perhaps too shy to use his name, submitted his first writing to the *Golden Era* pseudonymously as "Pip Pepperpod." In 1863, while in San Francisco, Mark Twain, who was making a name for himself as correspondent for the *Territorial Enterprise*, began contributing satirical pieces to the *Golden Era*. Twain soon felt he had outgrown the magazine and, in a letter written in 1864, states that, "I have been engaged to write for the new literary paper—the 'Californian'— same pay I used to receive on the 'Golden Era'—one article a week, fifty dollars a month. I quit the 'Era' long ago. It wasn't high-toned enough."[9]

Eager to bring some "high-tone" to the *Golden Era*, Lawrence pursued other authors with established reputations who were visiting or had come to live in San Francisco. He set himself up in the popular Occidental House and waged a "campaign of geniality and gin,"[10] which snared such notables as Artemus Ward, Adah Isaacs Menken (best known for her role in *Mazeppa*), Charles Henry Webb, and Ada Claire. The new sophistication was able to coexist with the informal style of the *Golden Era* while Lawrence was guiding the magazine. Critics generally believed, however, that the *Golden Era*, with its eight-column, eight-page newspaper format, was too popular and too successful to be a good magazine, and that it was not as polished as it should be. At various times during the *Golden Era*'s life, magazines with more refinement, such as the *Pioneer* or the *Californian*, were established as competition, but they were not able to find a sufficient number of readers or advertisers to survive.

After Lawrence's retirement in 1867, the *Golden Era* had a precarious existence. It lacked good authors and leadership and between 1867 and 1882 had fifteen different editors and proprietors. They dropped most of the local color sketches but continued to publish poetry and sensational stories. As in earlier times, much of the material was reprinted from other magazines.

The magazine, which was merged with *Vanity Fair* in November 1881, continued to drift until 1882, when Harr Wagner and Edward T. Bunyan purchased it. In January 1883, they changed the name back to the *Golden Era*.[11] The new editors, while continuing to publish poetry and serialized stories, once again included descriptions of places in California, accounts of California historical events, and wilderness sketches. The venturesome editors moved the *Golden Era* in new directions also. Travel articles began to proliferate, particularly after Wagner's *Ranch, Field & Fireside* and *Town and Country* merged with the *Golden Era* in August 1886. Most notable in its later life were the articles on spiritualism that formed a significant part of many issues. Of one contributor, David Lesser Lezinsky, Ella Sterling Cummins writes, "His verse is rather unconventional, and is a combination of the mystical and vague and too-deep-to-be-understood classifications."[12] Wagner held contests to encourage would-be authors to submit pieces. As in earlier years, critics charged that the *Golden Era* was too crude, but Wagner answered, "The *Golden Era* aspires to no more than to represent this great new country in all its primitiveness. . . . There are not enough cultivated people west of the Rockies to support a magazine like the *Edinburgh Review*" (35:10).

Although Wagner generated interest in the *Golden Era* and succeeded in persuading Joaquin Miller to serve briefly on its editorial board, the magazine remained in debt. In April 1884 Wagner changed the *Golden Era* into a magazine format and began issuing it monthly. In March 1887, after the city fathers of San Diego, then a "boom town," promised his support, Wagner moved the *Golden Era* to San Diego. The move meant a change from a San Francisco literary magazine to a San Diego historical and promotional magazine with some literature. Wagner eagerly began his new task and was moderately successful until 1890. As San Diego's prosperity declined, Wagner, who had become interested in education, was elected County Superintendent of Schools and his wife, Madge Morris Wagner, served as editor of the *Golden Era*. During the last four years of its existence, the *Golden Era* gradually became an educational journal, and when the Wagners returned to San Francisco in 1895, the *Golden Era* was succeeded by the *Western Journal of Education*, edited by Wagner and published by the Whitaker-Ray Company.

## Notes

1. Hubert Howe Bancroft, *Essays and Miscellany, Works* vol. 38 (San Francisco: The History Company, 1890), p. 627.

2. "Home Literature," *The Golden Era*, 6:15, as quoted in Lawrence E. Mobley, "San Francisco's *Golden Era*: 1852 to 1860," (Ph.D. diss., Michigan State University, 1961), p. 151.

3. Bancroft, p. 599.

4. Bancroft, p. 599.

5. Mobley, p. 174.

6. Both men had worked on the editorial staff of the *Golden Era* prior to purchasing the magazine, but it was not until they had complete control that their full influence was seen in the magazine.

7. Franklin Walker, *San Francisco's Literary Frontier* (New York: Alfred A. Knopf, 1943), p. 121.

8. Ella Sterling Cummins, *The Story of the Files: A Review of Californian Writers and Literature* ([San Francisco]: Issued under the auspices of the World's Fair Commission of California, Columbian Exposition, 1893) contains a chapter on the women writers of the *Golden Era*.

9. Twain to unknown correspondent [1864], as quoted in Walker, *San Francisco's Literary Frontier*, p. 179.

10. Walker, p. 122.

11. While published as *Vanity Fair and Golden Era* the magazine adopted the numbering sequence of *Vanity Fair*, and when the name was changed to the *Golden Era*, the numbering sequence of the *Golden Era* was resumed.

12. Cummins, p. 242.

## Information Sources

BIBLIOGRAPHY:

Bancroft, Hubert Howe. *Essays and Miscellany, Works* vol. 38. San Francisco: The History Company, 1890.

Bepler, Doris West. "Descriptive Catalogue of Western Historical Materials in California Periodicals, 1854–1890; With Introduction on the History and Character of the Magazines." M.A. thesis University of California, Berkeley, 1920.

Cummins, Ella Sterling. *The Story of the Files*: *A Review of Californian Writers and Literature*. [San Francisco]: Issued under the auspices of the World's Fair Commission of California, Columbian Exposition, 1893.

Granstaff, Viola. "Harr Wagner, California Educational Publicist." Ph.D. diss., University of California, Los Angeles, 1956.

Kemble, Edward C. *A History of California Newspapers: 1846–1858*. Ed. Helen Harding Bretnor. Los Gatos, Cal.: The Talisman Press, 1962.

Mobley, Lawrence. "San Francisco's *Golden Era*: 1852 to 1860." Ph.D. diss., Michigan State University, 1961.

Shinn, Charles Howard. "Early Books, Magazines and Book-making." *Overland Monthly* 12(1888):337–52.

Walker, Franklin. *San Francisco's Literary Frontier*. New York: Alfred A. Knopf, 1943.

INDEXES: None.

REPRINT EDITIONS: Microform: Bell & Howell, [1859]–1871.

LOCATION SOURCES: Widely available.

## Publication History

MAGAZINE TITLE AND TITLE CHANGES: *Golden Era*, 19 December 1852–29 October 1881. *Vanity Fair and Golden Era*, 12 November 1881–30 December 1882. *Golden Era*, 7 January 1883-April(?) 1894.

VOLUME AND ISSUE DATA: Volumes 1–29, numbers 1–49, 19 December 1852–29 October 1881; volumes 2–3, numbers 3–44, 12 November 1881–30 December 1882; volumes 31–43, numbers 1–4, 7 January 1883-April(?) 1894.

FREQUENCY OF PUBLICATION: Weekly, 19 December 1852–8 March 1884. Monthly, April 1884-April(?) 1894.

PUBLISHERS: 19 December 1852–26 March 1854: J. Macdonough Foard and Rollin M. Daggett. 2 April 1854–14 May 1854: Foard, Daggett, and John McCombe. 21 May 1854–6 August 1854: Foard, Daggett and M. M. Noah. 13 August 1854–10 December 1854: Foard and Daggett. 17 December 1854–25 January 1857: Joseph E. Lawrence, Foard, and Daggett. 1 February 1857–7 June 1857: Foard and Daggett. 14 June 1857–15 April 1860: James Brooks, Foard, and Daggett. 22 April 1860–27 May 1860: Brooks, Lawrence, and Foard. 3 June 1860–14 July 1867: Brooks and Lawrence. 21 July 1867–12 April 1868: Brooks and Charles S. Capp. 18 April 1868–28 August 1869: Capp. 5 September 1869–7 June 1874: G. B. Densmore & Co. 13 June 1874–15 November 1874: J. C. Johnson. 22 November 1874–17(?) January 1875: Lawrence and Johnson. 24(?) January 1875–31 December 1876: Golden Era Publishing Co. 7 January 1877–1 April 1877: Edward K. Chapman & Co. 8 April 1877–13 May 1877: Byron Adonis. 20 May(?) 1877–17 November 1878: B. F. Josselyn. 23 November 1878–29 October 1881: J. M. Bassett. 12 November 1881–31 December 1881: Vanity Fair Publishing Co. 7 January 1882-July 1884: Harr Wagner and Edward T. Bunyan. August 1884-October 1885: Wagner. November 1885-April 1887: Wagner and Walter E. Adams. May 1887-August 1887: Wagner. September 1887-June 1888: Wagner and P. W. Magrath. July 1888-April(?) 1894: Wagner.

EDITORS: J. Macdonough Foard and Rollin M. Daggett, 19 December 1852–10 December 1854; Joseph E. Lawrence, Foard, and Daggett, 17 December 1854–25 January1857; Foard and Daggett, 1 February 1857–7 June 1857; James Brooks, Foard, and Daggett, 14 June 1857–15 April 1860; Brooks, Lawrence, and Foard, 22 April 1860–27 May 1860; Brooks and Lawrence, 3 June 1860–14 July 1867; Brooks and Charles S. Capp, 21 July 1867–12 April 1868; Capp and N. Mullendorf, 18 April(?) 1868–28 August 1869; Gilbert B. Densmore, John B. Gilmore, and John J. Hutchinson, 5 September 1869–19 March 1871; Densmore and Hutchinson, 26 March 1871–8 September 1872; Densmore and Walter Gale, 15 September 1872–7 June 1874; John M. Foard, 13 June 1874–15 November 1874; Lawrence and J. C. Johnson, 22 November 1874–17(?) January 1875; Thomas J. Foard, 24(?) January 1875–31 December 1876; Edward K. Chapman and Byron Adonis, 7 January 1877–1 April 1877; Adonis, 8 April 1877–13 May 1877; B. F. Josselyn, 20 May(?) 1877–17 November 1878; J. M. Bassett, 23 November 1878–29 October 1881; M. R. Levenson and Browni Conner, 12 November 1881–31 December 1881; Harr Wagner and Edward T. Bunyan, 7 January 1882-July 1884. Wagner, August 1884-October 1885; Wagner and Walter E. Adams, November 1885-July 1886; Wagner, Adams, and Joaquin Miller, August 1886-February 1887; Wagner and Adams, April 1887; Wagner, May 1887-August 1887; Wagner and P. W. Magrath, September 1887-June 1888; Wagner, July 1888-June 1890; Wagner and C. S. Sprecher, July 1890-December 1890; Madge Morris Wagner and C. S. Sprecher, January 1891-September 1891; Madge Morris Wagner, October 1891-April(?) 1894.

*Glenn E. Humphreys*

## GRAHAM'S LADY'S AND GENTLEMAN'S MAGAZINE

*Graham's Lady's and Gentleman's Magazine* was the brilliant offspring of two relatively unprepossessing parent publications. George Rex Graham, a lawyer by training but a magazinist by choice, purchased the *Casket* in 1839 and *Burton's Gentleman's Magazine* in November 1840, united these two monthlies, and issued the first number of his new magazine in January 1841.[1] By January 1842, *Graham's* boasted a circulation of more than thirty thousand (37:44); by year's end, fifty thousand.[2]

The immediate reasons for *Graham's* appeal are obvious: original art and popular literature. At a time when the few illustrations appearing in periodicals were reprints from used plates, *Graham's* reproduced or commissioned original woodcuts, steel and copper engravings, and mezzotints. Though adding considerably to publication costs, Graham discovered that artwork enhanced circulation, and he alone made illustrations a distinctive feature of American magazines.[3] In addition to an art staff that variously included A. L. Dick, H. S. Sadd, Devereaux Rawdon, Thomas B. Welch, and James Smillie, *Graham's* secured the exclusive service of London-born John Sartain, a well-known painter and engraver, whose mezzotints and fashion plates rivalled those appearing in *Godey's*.* Avowedly as much a pictorial as a literary magazine, *Graham's* announced in 1845 that its art staff was engaged in *"the most elegant series of American subjects"* and "American beauty" (27:96). A few years later, *Graham's* even sent W. E. Tucker abroad to engrave Europe's masterpieces. Such engravings, however, were exceptions. Most issues were largely overwhelmed by the welter of artwork whose subject matter was decidedly romantic and sentimental: scenes of domestic concord, sublime beauty (both geographic and feminine), decorous courtship, and mothers with children and children with pets. The quality of artwork, however, always remained outstanding.

In their tone and subject matter, most of these plates also reflected the popular literary tastes of the day. Across the pages of *Graham's* many stories and poems fluttered a veritable aviary of Keatsian birds; here quailed armies of orphans and widows beleaguered by Saracenic Misfortune and there grew copses of sublime trees. The forest sheltered tribes of noble but safely expiring Indians; the hearts and villages welcomed back contrite souls who had wandered from middle-class verities. Poems taught that "perfect love is woman's dower" (19:9); essays mused how life is a "desperate encounter between the world, which is Time's eldest champion, and the soul of man, which is the offspring of Eternity" (27:1).

Stories recorded the temporary loss of illusions: "I fancied you . . . all that was chivalrous and courteous. I worshipped you almost as a god; my eyes are opened, and I find you—a mere man!" (30:285–86) *Graham's* was never avowedly a ladies' magazine. Still, its literature and its embossed, colored designs or ballads reflect *Graham's* bid for the same market *Godey's* found so lucrative. Indeed, *Graham's* published most of the tribe of prolific female writers: Lydia H. Sigourney, Mrs. Seba Smith, Frances S. Osgood, E. C. Embury, M.T.W. Chandler, Sarah J. Hale, "Grace Greenwood," Lydia J. Pierson, and Ann S. Stephens.

Such literature, however, is not what inspired Frank Luther Mott to laud *Graham's* as "one of the three or four most important magazines in the United States . . . [which] in the years 1841–1845, displayed a brilliance which has seldom been matched in American publishing history."[4] Instead, *Graham's* is remembered for publishing major works by classic American writers. During his literary editorship Poe published many of those works that insured his niche in American letters. Here he continued his campaign, begun at the *Southern Literary Messenger*,* against critics who indiscriminately puffed native writers or assessed literature without any conscious principles of literary theory. In 1842, the year Robert D. Jacobs called "Poe's *annus mirabilis* as a critic,"[5] he defined the role of criticism as that of mediator between a work of genius and an untutored public. He validated poetic feeling as an innate human need, repudiating Longfellow's didacticism. Finally, in the May review of Hawthorne's *Twice-Told Tales*, Poe made his theoretical statement about the unity of effect a short tale must achieve. Though his editorial tenure with *Graham's* was short (he resigned in April 1842), Poe published in its pages an impressive literary output, both in quantity and importance. Between the years 1841 and 1848, Poe published *Marginalia*, "The Philosophy of Composition," "The Murders in the Rue Morgue," "The Masque of the Red Death," "The Imp of the Perverse," and poems such as "Dream-Land," "To Helen," "Israfel," "To One Departed," and "The Conqueror Worm."

But Edgar Allan Poe was just one of the major writers publishing in *Graham's*. Its readers were also the first to have Hawthorne's "Earth's Holocaust"; Longfellow's "The Arsenal at Springfield," "King Witlaf's Drinking Horn," *The Spanish Student*, and his essay on "Dante's Divina Commedia"; as well as James Fenimore Cooper's *Autobiography of a Pocket-handkerchief*. Other writers—John Greenleaf Whittier, James Russell Lowell, Oliver Wendell Holmes, William Cullen Bryant, George Boker, Dr. T. H. Chivers, William Gilmore Simms, Henry T. Tuckerman, Joseph C. Neal, Park Benjamin, and James Kirke Paulding—published an enormous quantity of literature in *Graham's*.

For a nine-year period, *Graham's* thus reigned as America's leading popular miscellany. Unlike the often arid and intellectually severe *North American Review*,* *Graham's* was diverse and intelligent, its writing lively and fresh. Because it paid contributors handsomely (only *Godey's* could compare), *Graham's* editors selected from a wide range of unsolicited submissions to accompany those by writers and artists under exclusive engagement. For prose *Graham's* paid contributors between four to twelve dollars a page, and poems earned from ten to fifty dollars. This scale depended on the contributor's reputation.[6] Cooper, for example, was paid a thousand dollars for his biographies of naval commanders that filled but one hundred pages, and he was paid eighteen hundred dollars for *The Islets of the Gulf*, a deservedly overlooked novel (43:552). Longfellow's rate quickly increased from twenty-five to fifty dollars per poem, while Lowell's increased in three years from ten to thirty dollars.[7] Attracted by the lure of liberal payment, Hawthorne approached *Graham's* on plain terms: "I should make no difficulty in forswearing all other periodicals for a specified time—and so much more readily on account of the safety of your magazine in a financial point of view."[8] An 1853 editorial crowed, "We have spent as high as $1,500 on a single number *for authorship* alone . . . which is more than twice the sum that has ever been paid by any other magazine in America" (43:554). Generous payments made possible the emergence of "magazinists," as the parlance of the day referred to those who lived by the pen and their editorial skills.[9] Among them, *Graham's* published the foremost: T. S. Arthur, William Gilmore Simms, E. A. Poe, Lydia H. Sigourney, and Nathaniel P. Willis, the master of light sketches and a lively, entertaining style. Years later Willis recalled that "the burst on author-land of Graham's and Godey's liberal prices was like a sunrise without a dawn."[10]

Perhaps so, but shining payments were not enough to dispel a gathering darkness. *Graham's* long sunset took nine years, but shadows lengthened as early as 1845, when the *Editor's Table* began shrilly urging subscribers to pay their bills. In particular, the decline could be seen in *Graham's* fruitless attempts to model itself after more successful competitors. Inspired by *Godey's* robust success, for instance, J. R. Chandler announced in the January 1849 issue his intention to scrutinize carefully contributions for their moral content. For a time thereafter *Graham's* art and literature was freighted with leaden moral embroidery that did nothing to lift its fortunes. Neither could *Graham's* be saved by doubling the number of pages to 112; this move, in January 1852, was designed to make room for reprints from English magazines. In fact, however, that expansion really signalled an attempt to keep pace with *Harper's*,* the foremost of those magazines which, without copyright laws, not only avoided payments to British authors but was making a grand success of it all.[11]

In the meantime, the quality of native literature sharply declined. While *Graham's* front covers for 1852 blazoned the names of Bryant, Richard Henry Dana, Paulding, Longfellow, Willis, and Lowell, none of their work was published inside those covers. Instead, readers found sentimental clap-trap, written by undistinguished hacks both male and female. It was dross. Any hopes that such work might restore *Graham's* its gold were desperate. New departments and features surfaced constantly: "Foreign Literature," "Ladies' Department," "Flowers and Garden Hints," "The Cabinet of Kisses," "Literary Gossip," "Monthly Summary," and "The Ladies' Work-Table." Just as quickly they sank out of sight, evidence of how rudderless were the last years at *Graham's*.

The panic of 1857, with its widespread bank failures and unemployment, broke *Graham's* financially.[12] More important, its morale was broken, or so George Graham later felt, by the angry controversy he generated with his unfavorable review of *Uncle Tom's Cabin*.[13] Stung by morally self-righteous critics, Graham only made matters worse. In the next issue under the title "Black Letters or Uncle Tom-Foolery in Literature," he attacked all—publishers, critics, and the public—for abandoning questions of literary merit in their embrace of a "new hobby"—"an intense love of black people." He especially excoriated publishers of all "Cabin Literature," claiming they reduced matters of "slavery and liberty" to "a question of dollars and cents" (42:209–15, passim).

The controversy earned *Graham's* more notoriety than subscribers. The December 1858 issue quietly announced *Graham's* demise under the inauspicious heading of "Note": "Graham's Magazine will be incorporated with a new publication to be entitled The American Monthly" (53:567). *Graham's* long, poignant decline finally ended.

During its golden years, especially under George Rex Graham's editorship, *Graham's* numbers achieved that rare balance characteristic of significant periodicals—it published works that had popular appeal and those of lasting literary and critical merit. The latter consideration interests us the most. In its liberal payments and commitment to providing an outlet for native writers, *Graham's* nourished the roots of America's earliest flowering of an indigenous literature. Charles J. Peterson's brief biographical tribute to George R. Graham succinctly summarizes the importance of *Graham's* for American periodical history: "Having spared no expense to procure able writers and elegant embellishments, the result was . . . a periodical of unexampled merit and beauty. . . . A new spirit was infused into magazines" (37:44).

### Notes

1. John Tebbel, *The American Magazine: A Compact History* (New York: Hawthorn Books, 1969), pp. 48–49; James Playsted Wood, *Magazines in the United States*, 3d. ed. (New York: The Ronald Press Company, 1971), pp. 44–45; Frank Luther Mott, *A History of American Magazines, 1741–1850* (New York: D. Appleton and Company, 1930), pp. 545–46; and Frank Luther Mott, "A Brief History of *Graham's Magazine*," *Studies in Philology* 25 (1928):364.

2. J. Albert Robbins, "George R. Graham, Philadelphia Publisher," *Pennsylvania Magazine of History and Biography* 75 (1951):283.

3. Wood, p. 45. See also Mott, *A History, 1741–1850*, pp. 547–48.

4. Mott, *A History, 1741–1850* p. 344.

5. Robert D. Jacobs, *Poe: Journalist & Critic* (Baton Rouge: Louisiana State University Press, 1969), p. 273.

6. Tebbel, p. 71.

7. Mott, *A History, 1741–1850*, pp. 506–7.

8. Algernon de Vivier Tassin, *The Magazine in America* (New York: Dodd, Mead and Company, 1916), p. 97.

9. Wood, pp. 60–65, passim; and Tebbel, pp. 67–74, passim.

10. As quoted in Tassin, p. 102.

11. Wood, p. 49; Mott, p.553.

12. Tebbel, p. 93; Mott, *A History of American Magazines*, 3 vols. (Cambridge, Mass.: Harvard University Press, 1938), 2:5.

13. Mott, p. 553.

## Information Sources

BIBLIOGRAPHY:

Jacobs, Robert D. *Poe: Journalist & Critic*. Baton Rouge, La.: Louisiana State University Press, 1969. Pp. 249–73.

Mott, Frank Luther. "A Brief History of *Graham's Magazine*." *Studies in Philology* 25 (1928):362–75.

———. "*Graham's Magazine*, and *The Casket*." *A History of American Magazines, 1741–1850*. New York: D. Appleton and Company, 1930. Pp. 544–55.

Robbins, J. Albert, Jr. "George R. Graham, Philadelphia Publisher," *Pennsylvania Magazine of History and Biography* 75 (1951):279–94.

———. "The History of *Graham's Magazine*: A Study in Periodical Publication." Ph.D. diss., University of Pennsylvania, 1947.

Tassin, Algernon de Vivier. *The Magazine in America*. New York: Dodd, Mead and Company, 1916. Pp. 91–103.

Tebbel, John. *The American Magazine: A Compact History*. New York: Hawthorn Books, 1969. Pp. 70–72.

Thompson, Lawrence R. "Longfellow Sells *The Spanish Student*." *American Literature* 6 (1934):141–50.

Wood, James Playsted. *Magazines in the United States*. 3d ed. New York: The Ronald Press, 1971. Pp. 44–49.

INDEXES: None.

REPRINT EDITIONS: American Periodicals: Series II, 1800–1850. University Microfilms, Ann Arbor. Reels 546–60. Reprint edition. AMS Press, Inc., New York, 1967.

LOCATION SOURCES: Widely available.

## Publication History

MAGAZINE TITLE AND TITLE CHANGES: *Graham's Lady's and Gentleman's Magazine (The Casket and Gentleman's United)*, January 1841-December 1841. *Graham's Lady's and Gentleman's Magazine*, January 1842-December 1842. *Graham's Magazine of Literature and Art*, January 1843-June 1843. *Graham's Lady's and Gentleman's Magazine*, July 1843-June 1844. *Graham's American Monthly Magazine of Literature and Art*, July 1844-June 1855. *Graham's American Monthly Magazine of Literature, Art, and Fashion*, July 1855-December 1855. *Graham's Illustrated Magazine of Literature, Romance, Art, and Fashion*, January 1856-December 1858.

VOLUME AND ISSUE DATA: Continued the volume numbering of the *Casket*. Volumes 19–53, January 1841-July 1858. Starting with the September 1843 issue of volume 23, the caption volume information incorrectly reads volume 24, a discrepancy that continues until the December 1845 issue of volume 27, when it is corrected.

FREQUENCY OF PUBLICATION: Monthly.

PUBLISHERS: January 1841-July 1848: George R. Graham, Philadelphia. August 1848-March 1850: Samuel D. Patterson & Company, Philadelphia. April 1850-December 1853: George R. Graham. January 1854-June 1856: R. H. See & Company, Philadelphia. July 1856-December 1858: Watson & Company, Philadelphia.

EDITORS: George R. Graham, Charles J. Peterson, Edgar Allan Poe, 1841; George R. Graham, Charles J. Peterson, Edgar Allan Poe, Mrs. Emma C. Embury, Mrs. Ann S. Stephens, Rufus W. Griswold, 1842 (Poe resigned as literary editor in April and was succeeded by Griswold); George R. Graham and Rufus W. Griswold, 1843 (Griswold resigned in October); George R. Graham, 1843–1847; George R. Graham, Robert T. Conrad, J. R. Chandler, and J. B.[ayard] Taylor, 1848–1849 (Conrad is on the title page of xxxii only; Taylor joined in September and Chandler in October); George R. Graham, 1850–1857; Charles Godfrey Leland, 1857(?)–1858.

*Arthur Wrobel*

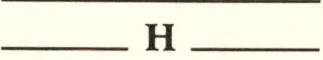

# H

## THE HARBINGER

In 1844, when the transcendental experiment in communal living called Brook Farm converted to Fourierist socialism, Albert Brisbane decided to move his New York monthly magazine the *Phalanx* to the Brook Farm commune located near West Roxbury, Massachusetts. He named George Ripley its editor-in-chief, assisted by Charles A. Dana as associate editor and John Sullivan Dwight as literary and music editor. Renamed the *Harbinger*, the sixteen-page quarto was published weekly from 14 June 1845 to 10 February 1849. While its official ancestor was the Fourierist *Phalanx*, the *Harbinger* was the spiritual successor to the transcendental *Dial* (Boston),* for it eschewed dogma and promoted radical inquiry of whatever stripe.

One risk of such eclecticism is that it encouraged a dimly defined idealism, as when Ripley promised that as long as he was editor the *Harbinger* would welcome any articles which "in any way indicate the unity of Man with Man, with Nature, and with God. . . . It is the duty of all persons who sincerely desire to aid in the progress of the human race not to abandon themselves blindly to one particular doctrine, but to try all and to hold fast to that which is good" (1:16). Despite this rather ethereal editorial policy, the *Harbinger* rapidly became one of the most read and readable of the American radical periodicals, in no small measure because the Brook Farm press produced such clean copy. Ripley hoped for too much in seeking to give the *Harbinger* "a place in American literature, in American history—shall I not say in the progress of Humanity— which no publication ever enjoyed before."[1] However, contemporary accounts of the inspirational quality of the journal, such as that by Caroline H. Dall (*Margaret Fuller and Her Friends*, 1897), should not be dismissed. Perhaps the most balanced appraisal comes from Frank L. Mott, the dean of nineteenth-century American magazine history, who said the *Harbinger* "was vigorous and rather lively, and always high-minded."[2]

The *Harbinger*'s charge was to promote socialism, particularly in its Fourierist variety. Fourierism, deeply rooted in Rousseau, argued that people were essentially good and only the external circumstances need be kind, honest, fair, and orderly for this nascent goodness to flourish. Communes were established to that end—over forty such phalanxes by the late 1840s. Brisbane, for one, dreamed that a network of communes and phalanxes would one day supplant the town and city system, and a socialist revolution by peaceful means would thereby take place. However, the *Harbinger* under Ripley in the 1840s, when about 200,000 Americans had declared themselves socialists, emphasized Fourierism as but one possible solution among many socialist approaches. Probably Ripley's finest single essay on this score was "Andrew Jackson" (1:45–47), written shortly after the president's death. While Jackson is praised as "the unflinching opponent of monopoly and privilege" and as a favorite of the common man motivated by a "genuine spirit of equality," he is blamed for causing as many ills as he cured because he did not change the system but merely erected "a new edifice on the crumbling ruins of the antique structure." Instead, the *Harbinger* argued, all American institutions had to be revamped. "This is a work," the journal asserted, "that no political reforms can effect. We need an organic change in the structure of society; the substitution of justice for fraud, of love for force. . . . Society must be made to revolve on a new pivot."

Yet the *Harbinger*'s self-declared role as a leader of radical causes ran hard aground against a contradiction when it discussed specific matters of liberal reform. As a spokesman for progressive issues, it championed labor unions, one of whose leaders was John Cheever, a former Brook Farmer, and argued against the inordinate power of corporation magnates. While the *Harbinger* staff praised antislavery organizations, they had no hope that slavery could be solved through legislation. The only solution was war, a condition the *Harbinger* equally opposed. The feminist movement also gained the *Harbinger*'s support, but again its articles pointed out that women's rights were a mainstay of communal-phalanstery life where equality was already a reality. In short, many of the tough, specific issues of the times were brought up in the *Harbinger*'s pages, often in contradiction to Fourierist doctrine. Socialism would cure slavery, as well as poverty, war, sexism, worker exploitation, and other social ills: "The axe must be laid to the root of the tree, or no universal good can be hoped for from the sincerest of reforms" (4:16). While the *Harbinger* threw its full weight behind individual reforms, it would fail to attract adherents to socialism should these individual reforms prove successful.

A further problem that plagued the *Harbinger*'s staff was the difficulty of developing a radical stance while at the same time demonstrating that socialism, although revolutionary, was nevertheless consistent with established American traditions. Frequently articles would appear in the *Harbinger* attempting to explain how Fourierism was consonant with, for example, the basic tenets of

Christianity and American culture (4:11, 4:25). Since science was rapidly looming as the acid test of realism, science too was dragooned into articles as a further basis of Fourierist socialism. The *Harbinger* staff saw themselves as revolutionaries, but only insofar as the sanctions established by Christianity, American civilization, and science allowed.

But the most severe contradiction inherent in the phenomenon of the *Harbinger* is that, though it spoke for an idealistic democracy which would benefit the working class and the bourgeoisie, its backers were wealthy. The *Harbinger* could not have existed without the financial support of rich New Yorkers such as Horace Greeley, Albert Brisbane, Marcus Spring, E. G. Loring, and T. B. Curtis. Ripley appealed with paltry success to the middle class for more general support (28 February 1846), but in fact the *Harbinger* remained a journal espousing radical causes but supported by a small core of powerful individuals.

The *Harbinger* flourished and died with the times. The 1840s were a period of radical interest and social experimentation in America. The coming decade, however, would see far less such activity. Two historical causes are in large part responsible. First, the failed revolutions in Europe in 1848 were blamed on socialism by newspapers like the *New York Herald* and the *New York Express*. " . . . poor Fourierism," Ripley lamented to George Bancroft in a personal letter, "poor Fourierism which points out the cure must be reproached as the cause." The second historical event was the discovery of gold in California in January 1848, a fact that caused Karl Marx to admit that revolutionary possibilities would have to be postponed in America. Even Horace Greeley, one of the staunchest Fourierist advocates, advised young men to go West. Closer to home, Brook Farm had suffered a smallpox scare in the fall of 1845 and then a devastating fire on 3 March 1846. While the *Harbinger* for a time continued to be published on the premises despite the exodus from Brook Farm, its staff's spirit was sapped, and the journal was moved to New York in October 1847. Its backers, seeking a purer Fourierist publication with a less eclectic editorial policy, appointed E. P. Allen as managing editor and demoted Ripley to one of several general editors. Because the *Harbinger* was losing money, some of the editors, led by Parke Godwin, wanted to tone down the magazine to make it more palatable to the rising conservatism in America, a proposal that Ripley staunchly opposed. But soon Ripley lost the debate. In March 1849, the decision was made to convert the weekly into a monthly, to change its name to either "The New Times" or "The Spirit of the Age," and, most importantly, to transform its tenor from a radical to a liberal periodical. The *Harbinger* published its last issue on 10 February 1849.

### Notes

1. Henry Golemba, *George Ripley* (Boston: Twayne Publishers, 1977), p. 99.
2. Frank Luther Mott, *A History of American Magazines*, 4 vols. (Cambridge, Mass.: Belknap Press of Harvard University Press, 1957), 1:764.

## Information Sources

BIBLIOGRAPHY:

Brownson, Orestes. "Brook Farm." *Democratic Review* 123 (1842):481–96.

Crowe, Charles. *George Ripley: Transcendentalist and Utopian Socialist.* Athens: University of Georgia Press, 1967.

Dall, Caroline Healy. *Margaret and Her Friends, or Ten Conversations with Margaret Fuller.* Boston: Roberts, 1897.

Frothingham, Octavius. *George Ripley.* Boston: Houghton Mifflin, 1882.

Gohdes, Clarence. "*The Harbinger.*" *The Periodicals of American Transcendentalism.* Durham, N.C.: Duke University Press, 1931. Pp. 101–31.

Golemba, Henry. *George Ripley.* Boston: Twayne Publishers, 1977.

Kirby, Georgiana B. *Years of Experience.* 1887; rpt., New York: American Missionary Society Press, 1971.

Mott, Frank Luther. "*The Harbinger.*" *A History of American Magazines.* 4 vols. Cambridge, Mass.: Belknap Press of Harvard University Press, 1957. 1:763–65.

Schultz, Arthur R., and Henry A. Pochmann. "George Ripley: Unitarian, Transcendentalist, or Infidel?" *American Literature* 14 (1942):1–19.

Sears, John V.D.Z. *My Friends at Brook Farm.* New York: Desmond, Fitzgerald, 1912.

Wilson, Howard Aaron. "George Ripley: Social and Literary Critic." Ph.D. diss., University of Wisconsin, 1941.

INDEXES: Indexes are at the end of each volume (26 issues) excepting the last, incomplete volume 8. Delano, Sterling F., and Rita Colanzi, "An Index to Volume VIII of *The Harbinger,*" *Resources for American Literary Study* 10 (1980):173–86.

REPRINT EDITIONS: American Periodicals: Series II, 1800–1850. University Microfilms, Ann Arbor. Reel 674. AMS Press. New York.

LOCATION SOURCES: Widely available.

## Publication History

MAGAZINE TITLE AND TITLE CHANGES: *The Harbinger: devoted to social and political progress.*

VOLUME AND ISSUE DATA: Volumes 1–8, 14 June 1845–10 February 1849.

FREQUENCY OF PUBLICATION: Weekly.

PUBLISHERS: 1845–1847: Brook Farm Phalanx, West Roxbury, Massachusetts. 1847–1849: American Union of Associationists, New York.

EDITORS: George Ripley, 1845–1846; George Ripley and John S. Dwight, 1846–1847; Parke Godwin, George Ripley, and John S. Dwight, 1847–1849.

*Henry Golemba*

# HARPER'S MONTHLY MAGAZINE

*Harper's Monthly Magazine* began as an accessory to the profitable book publishing firm presided over by the four Harper brothers: James, John, Joseph Wesley, and Fletcher. The new venture was mentioned in a letter to Henry W. Longfellow dated 1 October 1849, and the first number appeared in June of 1850 with an initial press run of 7,500 copies. Bound in royal-octavo size (6″ x 9″), the first issue contained over 60 articles on 144 pages of double columns. The subscription price was $3.00 per year.

The fiction in the first issue, all by British writers, included three short stories, two of them by Charles Dickens, and a pair of serialized novels. Also printed were popular science articles, travel accounts, discussions of the literary careers of William Hickling Prescott and Longfellow, three engravings depicting historians Prescott, Archibald Alison, and Thomas B. Macaulay, and an illustrated section on ladies' fashions. A "Monthly Record of Current Events" compiled by the editor-in-chief, Henry J. Raymond, appeared in this first issue and became a popular feature.

The eclectic contents of this inaugural number established the pattern for *Harper's* in the nineteenth century. As managing editor for the first quarter century of publication, Fletcher Harper defined the role of *Harper's* as a popular educator of the general public that would "place within the reach of the great mass of the American people the unbounded treasures of the Periodical Literature of the present day."[1]

The Harper publishing company, one of the largest in the world, had prospered by offering cheap reprints of popular English novels. Because no international copyright law existed, works from abroad could be reprinted at no cost, but the Harper brothers usually paid the author or printer for the privilege of printing from "advance sheets" that were brought to New York by special messengers on the fastest boats. Typically these novels would run first in successive numbers of the *Monthly* and then be printed as books. The prices paid for advance sheets included both forms of publication. The new magazine was originally thought of as "a tender to our business;"[2] no advertisements except for other Harper publications appeared for the first thirty years.

Although Hawthorne published *The Scarlet Letter* the same year the *Monthly* began publication, and Harpers printed Melville's *Moby-Dick* in book form in 1851, American writers did not command the readership of Dickens, Thackeray, and Bulwer-Lytton. The publication of Dickens's *Bleak House* and *Little Dorrit*, Thackeray's *The Newcomers* and *The Virginians*, Bulwer-Lytton's *My Novel*, and George Eliot's *Romola* in early volumes of *Harper's* clearly helped to assure the magazine's popularity.

Rival publishers resented the Harpers' entrance into the periodical field and their expanded reprinting of English writers. In addition to the numerous weeklies printing English fiction, there were already over 100 monthlies, including the successful Philadelphia publications *Graham's,** *Godey's,** *Sartain's,* and *Peterson's.* Some of these publications had shown a commitment to printing the work of American writers; George R. Graham estimated in 1853 that his magazine was spending as much as $1,500 per issue in fees to authors. A year earlier *Sartain's,* in an editorial printed in its final number, claimed to have paid American authors over $15,000. *Putnam's Monthly** (1853–1857), printed some of the best of American writers, but it soon failed.

American literature was clearly being hurt by lack of copyright protection and competition from immensely popular British novelists. The *American (Whig) Review**  labeled the Harpers "anti-American in feeling as concerns literary development,"[3] and Graham called the *Monthly* "a good foreign magazine" and predicted, "the veriest worshiper of the dust of Europe will tire of the dead level of silly praise of John Bull upon every page."[4] The *Monthly* prospered, however; at the end of six months a press run of 50,000 copies was being sold. In the period 1850 to 1865, sales averaged 110,000 copies per issue.

Some American writing appeared in *Harper's* from 1851 on, and after the Civil War the magazine followed a policy of encouraging native prose. Among the first sections to show American influence were the "departments," columns by staff writers that appeared in every issue. A humor feature, "The Editor's Drawer," began in the third volume. "The Editor's Easy Chair," begun in 1851 and presided over for forty years by George William Curtis, was unusually successful. William Dean Howells began writing "The Editor's Study" in 1886 and used it for six years to disseminate his theory of realistic fiction.

In its first quarter century, *Harper's* withstood a disastrous fire (1853), loss of Southern readers during the Civil War, and strong competition from the *Atlantic Monthly** and *Scribner's.** The founding of the *Atlantic Monthly* (James Russell Lowell, editor) in November of 1857 brought the first real competition from America's finest writers. In competition for illustrations, *Scribner's** (founded 1870, known as the *Century* after 1881) was foremost.

Charles Parsons, a watercolorist, became art editor in 1863. Many well-known artists, including Howard Pyle, N. C. Wyeth, Winslow Homer, Frederic Remington, and John Singer Sargent were attracted to work for *Harper's*. The English edition, begun in 1880, printed some English writing not found in the New York edition and drew European admiration for its reproduction of art. When Andrew Lang assumed the British editorship in 1884, it had a circulation of 25,000.

The moral self-censorship epitomized by writers like Howells was *Harper's* policy—no vulgarity. Thomas Hardy rewrote one chapter of *Hearts Insurgent* (book title, *Jude the Obscure*), and the editors made other changes during publication so as not to violate the house policy of printing only material that could be read aloud in any family circle.[5]

*Harper's* reached its high point in the 1890s. George duMaurier's *Trilby* (1894) created a national sensation; Twain's *Personal Recollections of Joan of Arc* was serialized (1895–1896); Woodrow Wilson and Theodore Roosevelt both contributed historical series. By the turn of the century, *Harper's* was printing the finest native fiction. The fiftieth anniversary issue (May 1900) contained pieces by Stephen Crane, Howard Pyle, Mary E. Wilkins Freeman, Frederic Remington, Owen Wister, Mark Twain, William Dean Howells, and Theodore Dreiser, as well as work by the British Kipling and Hardy and the French Benjamin Constant and Victor Hugo. The bulk of Howell's writing, beginning with *Indian Summer* in 1885, ran in *Harper's*. Twain began writing for it in the 1890s. Though he complained that "the company one keeps in their magazine is of a paralyzing dreariness,"[6] Henry James published *Washington Square* there in serial form (1880). Perhaps the fact that of all James's work only this easy and realistic novel appeared in *Harper's* is evidence of the lingering effect of Fletcher Harper's commitment to popular writing for the general public.

The greatest increase in circulation took place in the decade 1900–1910. During that period color illustrations became a regular feature, and issues averaged two hundred pages. Although every number still contained seven or eight short stories, and there was usually one novel running in serial, the trend was clear. The editorial policy emphasized "timely interest," and articles on popular science, exploration, and sociology were dominant; sports, politics, and crime were not treated.

By 1908 editor Henry Mills Alden was stating that readers now preferred scientific, historical, biographical, and critical writing and noting that even in fiction the preference was for "such imaginative literature as creates reality and reflects truth" (117:961–64). He characterized *Harper's* readers as a group more "advanced in culture than the average constituency of the public library" (117:961). An abrupt change took place after World War I. The emphasis switched to analysis of current affairs, and in 1925 the format was drastically changed. Illustration was eliminated, the proportion of fiction was sharply reduced, and *Harper's* became a "magazine of ideas, free and tranquil discussion, and editorial comment" (181:112). In the ninetieth anniversary issue, (June 1940), Bernard DeVoto described the audience as "the intellectual aristocracy" (181:112). In the early 1940s line drawings again appeared and articles dealt with current events. In the Centennial Issue (October 1950), editor Frederick Lewis Allen listed his goals for the magazine: to be interesting and to provide news, interpretation, and discussion of important issues, a platform for original and inventive thinkers, and a vehicle for the artist in literature.

In September 1958, on the basis of a poll, editor John Fischer described the readers of *Harper's* as 'the decisionmakers, opinion-formers, and taste-makers" (217:14). The circulation at that time was about 200,000. Most readers were urban dwellers and college-educated professionals earning nearly twice the national average. In sharp contrast to the founding principle of catering to a mass audience, Fischer described his readers as "the minority who feed on different meat, and have a hard time finding enough of it elsewhere" (217:20). In 1965 Cowles Magazine and Broadcasting bought a half interest in the publication, which in seven years had increased its subscription lists by 80,000 and tripled its advertising rates. Under Fischer's editorship *Harper's* had evolved into a journal that accented politics, sociology, science, and economics. Fischer announced that the Cowles purchase would allow the editorial staff to invest more money in the publication and pay higher prices to contributors.

Willie Morris became editor-in-chief in 1967 with a "mandate to revitalize a literary magazine that had grown stodgy, predictable and tediously middle-brow."[7] He hired new staff and printed sections from controversial works like William

Styron's *Confessions of Nat Turner* and Norman Mailer's *Armies of the Night*. Morris resigned in 1971 in a controversy partially precipitated by the printing of Mailer's "The Prisoner of Sex," an essay critical of the women's movement. Several staff members also resigned. At that time *Harper's* had lost ground to its arch-rival the *Atlantic* in both circulation and advertising revenue. Taking over the editor's post, Robert Shnayerson announced his intent to change *Harper's* from a "writer's magazine" to one that would expand its readership and introduce "a little reason into American life."[8]

During the first tenure of Lewis Lapham (1976–1981), the magazine offered a mix of political commentary, essays, fiction, and book reviews. Financial problems continued, and in June of 1980 the editors announced that *Harper's* would cease publication. Twenty-three days later the MacArthur Foundation bought it for $250,000. The Atlantic Richfield Corporation agreed to provide three million dollars in operating expenses so that the magazine could continue as a nonprofit venture. Roderick MacArthur, Chair of the Foundation, defined his role as "the fierce defender of *Harper's* independence."[9]

Michael Kinsley, a young lawyer and editor of the *New Republic*, became the new editor. *Harper's* slashed its subscription rolls from 325,000 to 140,000 in an attempt to contain costs. The result was a smaller loss, but advertising revenues also declined. Meanwhile the *Atlantic*, buoyed by an infusion of money from Mortimer Zuckerman, had increased its circulation by a third to over 400,000. After several clashes with the board of directors, Kinsley resigned in July 1983.

Lewis Lapham, reappointed editor, promised a radical change of direction that would establish a new identity for *Harper's* distinctive from the *Atlantic*. In February 1984, he characterized the editorial staff as believing that "it is their business to open things out, not to wrap them neatly up" and said they would try to become "a means of interpretation, a drawing together of increasingly diffuse elements" in the belief that *Harper's* readers are people who "would rather have the tools to work the American grain into a knowledge of their own making" (268:10). Ironically, the summary of current events, opinion page, and major essay he proposed for each issue echoed features found in the first number of this long-lived publication.

## Notes

1. "A Word at the Start," *Harper's New Monthly Magazine* 1 (June 1850):1–2.
2. Eugene Exman, *The Brothers Harper* (New York: Harper and Row, 1965), p. 304.
3. *The American (Whig) Review* 16 (July 1852):17.
4. *Graham's Magazine* 38(March 1851):280.
5. Algernon Tassin, *The Magazine in America* (New York: Dodd, Mead, 1916), p. 248.
6. John A. Kouwenhoven, "Personal and Otherwise," *Harper's*, October 1950, p. 8.
7. *Newsweek*, 22 May 1967, p. 68.
8. *Newsweek*, 28 June 1971, p. 61.
9. *Newsweek*, 21 July 1980, p. 84.

## Information Sources

BIBLIOGRAPHY:

Alden, H. M. "An Anniversary Retrospect." *Harper's* 121 (June 1910):38–45.

————. "Fifty Years of Harper's Magazine." *Harper's* 100 (May 1900):947–62.

Allen, Frederick Lewis. "100 Years of *Harper's.*" *Harper's*, October 1950, pp. 23–36.

DeVoto, Bernard. "Ninetieth Anniversary." *Harper's*, 181 (June 1940):109–12.

Exman, Eugene. *The Brothers Harper*. New York: Harper and Row, 1965.

Fischer, John. "Self-Portrait of the Harper Reader." *Harper's*, September 1958. Pp. 14–20.

Harper, Joseph Henry. *The House of Harper: A Century of Publishing in Franklin Square*. New York and London: Harper's, 1912.

Mott, Frank Luther. *A History of American Magazines. 1850–1865*. Cambridge, Mass.: Harvard University Press, 1938. Pp. 383–405.

Tassin, Algernon de Vivier. *The Magazine in America*. New York: Dodd, Mead and Company, 1916. Pp. 232–55.

Wood, James Playsted. *Magazines in the United States*. New York: Ronald Press, 1956. Pp. 76–80.

INDEXES: General indexes, each cumulative to date, were published by *Harper's* in 1870, 1875, 1886, and 1893.

REPRINT EDITIONS: University Microfilms International. Princeton Microfilm Corporation (Volumes 1–138).

LOCATION SOURCES: Widely available.

## Publication History

MAGAZINE TITLE AND TITLE CHANGES: *Harper's New Monthly Magazine*, 1850–1900. *Harper's Monthly Magazine*, 1900–1925. *Harper's Magazine*, 1925-current.

VOLUME AND ISSUE DATA: Volumes 1–268, June 1850-current. Semiannual volumes. Volume 67 (December 1880-May 1881) is volume 1 of the English edition.

PUBLISHERS: 1850–1965: Harper and Brothers. 1965–1980: Harper's and Cowles, Inc. 1980-current: MacArthur Foundation.

EDITORS: Henry J. Raymond, 1850–1856; Alfred H. Guernsey, 1856–1869; Henry Mills Alden, 1869–1919; Thomas Bucklin Wells, 1919–1931; Lee Foster Hartman, 1931–1941; Frederick Lewis Allen, 1941–1953; John Fischer, 1953–1967; Willie Morris, 1967–1971; Robert Shnayerson, 1971–1976; Lewis Lapham, 1976–1981; Michael Kinsley, 1982–1983; Lewis Lapham, 1983-current.

*Barbara M. Perkins*

# THE HESPERIAN

One of the most distinguished early Western magazines, the *Hesperian* represented the flowering of its editor's ten-year effort to place the literature and culture of the Ohio Valley on a par with those of the East. Born in Philadelphia, William Davis Gallagher (1808–1894) moved as a child to Mount Pleasant, Ohio, where at age eighteen he took his first editorial job as a general assistant on the staff of the *Western Tiller*, an agricultural magazine. Publishing verse and nonfiction, Gallagher worked on a succession of short-lived Western magazines and newspapers, accumulating the journeyman experience in the press that led in 1831 to an offer to edit the *Cincinnati Mirror* (1831–1836). As editor Gallagher made the *Mirror* a voice for the promotion of temperance, religious moderation, and above all an indigenous literary life. By 1838 he had established himself as a tireless promoter of Western literature and one of the area's most promising young poets and essayists.[1] Yet he found the outlets for his work limited and the reception for it spotty, especially in the East. Sustained and profitable Western periodicals, he recalled years later, were "rendered *necessary* by the ignorance which has prevailed east of the Alleghenies and elsewhere, with reference to the West and its People and Institutions, and demanded by a community that has been in a measure debarred by distance from the great book marts of the Atlantic cities."[2]

To remedy those problems, Gallagher launched the *Hesperian; or, Western Monthly Magazine* in 1838. Published in Columbus, Ohio, the first number of the *Hesperian* appeared in May in a climate of optimism. "We have embarked in no trivial or temporary enterprise," Gallagher told readers; "we anticipate for our magazine, a long life of usefulness and honor" (1:93). Joining Gallagher as assistant editor was the Ohio poet Otway Curry (1804–1855), who appears to have contributed little to the editorial work but who offered poetry and essays in abundance.[3] Together, Gallagher and Curry planned a truly regional magazine that would provide opportunities to "*all* of our fellow valleymen who have the capability of imparting by their writings, either instruction or amusement" (1:93). Roughly half of each issue would be devoted to "original papers" by Westerners or about the West, with the remaining half divided between material selected from foreign and domestic magazines and literary notices by the editors—Gallagher, primarily. That combination, its editors wrote in the "Notice" preceding the first issue, would make the *Hesperian* appealing to a broad range of readers: "friends of education, morality, general intelligence, and polite literature."

Among the variety of articles that appeared in the *Hesperian*, certain emphases emerge. Gallagher recognized the need to record the achievements of the frontier before they vanished from memory, and much of the magazine is thus devoted to history and civic affairs. "Ohio in Eighteen Hundred Thirty-Eight," which appeared in the first three numbers, is Gallagher's attempt to present the state in all its facets, from its "literary statistics" and the common school system to its industries and mineral resources. Valuable for their historical data, too, are essays on common roads (2:40–41), internal trade (1:115–19; 2:42–49, 347–52), and early Indian history, notably a sketch of the Sac Indian chief Keokuk (1:199–204). "Friends of education" could find the full texts of addresses and lectures on that subject. And those interested in science could read essays on, for instance, soil analysis (3:287–92), ligneous plants in Ohio (2:257–63), and the origins of bituminous coal.

While the *Hesperian* treated history, education, and science at greater length and with greater vigor than most other magazines in the region, it is best remembered for its attention to literature and to literary criticism. In its pages appeared dozens of poems and tales, some of them by the editors themselves (Gallagher's most mature short story, "The Dutchman's Daughter," was serialized throughout volume three), but many others by literary men and women of at least historical importance in the Ohio Valley: Thomas H. Shreve, Charles A. Jones, E. D. Mansfield, Frederick W. Thomas, Amelia Welby, and James Handasyd Perkins. Besides these original compositions, the magazine introduced its readers to the variety of American and European literature in its selections from other periodicals. Dickens's *Nicholas Nickleby* was excerpted several times, as was the fiction of Robert M. Bird, Washington Irving, and Nathaniel Hawthorne. Isaac Appleton Jewett, in his time a respected man of letters, contributed travel essays and reviews; the young Transcendentalist Christopher Pearse Cranch provided poetry.

Even more impressive than its original contributions are the literary reviews that appeared in the *Hesperian*. To be sure, in an age when criticism rarely rose above the carping or the insipid, Gallagher's magazine often descended to both. Accepted authors were dismissed with a sniff—authors like Bulwer-Lytton, whose novel *Alice* was called "as insidiously corrupt, and as seductively dangerous, as any of the virtue-sapping volumes with which its author has so long and so rapidly supplied a morbid taste and a craving appetite" (1:178). The popular gift book the *Token* was criticized for containing too much "European grain"; the reviewer remarked that a half-hour's reading of it would induce sleep as quickly as "the choicest narcotic ever administered to suffering humanity" (2:325–26). And the prolific James Hall's latest book on the West was hooted down in an epigrammatic "dialog" between the author and his ruminating cow, whose cud-chewing suggests an unflattering comparison: "I grant the likeness; I, my dear, / Make new *books* out of old, / And sell again, the present year, / The work I last year sold" (2:171).

At their best, though, the reviews in the *Hesperian* were discerning and fair. Most contemporary criticism, Gallagher wrote, was "very much a matter of favoritism." Instead of short notices and general remarks, he called for "close, sober, *analytical criticism*—that which shows an author he is read, and felt, and understood" (1:265). While it is not always possible to defend the taste of the *Hesperian*'s critics—far too many "sweet singers" of the West were puffed for having written "flowers from the highest height of Poesy" (2:179)—they were often sensitive enough to praise major authors not yet fully appreciated in the 1830s. Jewett called Thomas Carlyle "the most remarkable thinker of the present century" (2:5); Curry defended Percy Bysshe Shelley as a poet "of the most eloquent meaning" whose low reputation derived less from his own faults than from the "negligence, indifference, or incapacity" of his critics (2:445). Longfellow, Irving, and Hawthorne were also reviewed repeatedly and thoroughly.

Despite its editors' initial optimism, the *Hesperian* was beset with problems from the beginning. Curry left the magazine's staff at the end of volume one—though he remained a contributor—and Gallagher found publication in Columbus a troublesome task. Paper was in short supply, and the difficulty of getting current books and journals in central Ohio prevented him from giving sufficient "spirit and variety" to the magazine. In March 1839 Gallagher decided to transfer the magazine to Cincinnati, where the improved facilities—including a new press—and the more varied cultural life would, he hoped, result in a more interesting periodical and one more attractive to new readers (2:412–13).

From a critical standpoint, the magazine had always been a success. As Gallagher reported at the close of the second volume, the *Hesperian*'s reception had been enthusiastic in the West (2:493), and he pledged that the third volume would continue the high tone of the first two: "industrious in its researches, deliberate in its judgments, candid in its opinions, and dignified in its tone— carefully eschewing evil, honestly aiming to do good" (3:iii-iv). Yet the tardiness of subscribers made money a constant worry. There were other problems as well, some of them common to all periodicals in the area: the indifference of publishers to local talent and issues, the "backwardness of many of our abler and more experienced writers," the negligence of subscribers, and—most important—the need for editors to attend to day-to-day business matters that the publishers frequently ignored.[4] Gallagher had little aptitude for the financial management of the magazine, and by the end of the volume he was several thousand dollars in debt (3:500).

When volume three closed in November 1839, the editor promised that the *Hesperian* would resume publication in January 1840. But the "grossest remissness and most culpable mismanagement on the part of its publisher" prevented the magazine from ever reappearing, a fact that Gallagher remembered years later with mortification. Discouraged and almost penniless, Gallagher accepted a job as assistant editor of Charles Hammond's prestigious *Cincinnati Gazette*.[5] Surely the magazine's financial troubles were an immediate cause for its failure; but its character itself most likely played an equal part. An "agreeable melange . . . of tales, sketches, poetry, biographies, anecdotes, literary reviews, and essays," the *Hesperian* lost definition and direction by its sheer diversity. The issue for January 1839 is representative. Its original contents include a long review of the regional poet Amelia Welby, a conservative essay on the role of women, a history of Ohio's common roads, a travel narrative about Texas, a tale to illustrate the need for public charities, and a technical paper on the vegetable origins of bituminous coal. In an age when periodicals were generally polemical and topical, the "elaborate medley" of literature, science, history, and insistent sectionalism that today makes the *Hesperian* one of the most historically valuable products of the early Western press may at last have proved too rich and rarified for its readers.[6]

## Notes

1. James A. Tague, "William D. Gallagher, Champion of Western Literary Periodicals," *Ohio Historical Quarterly* 69 (1960):257–64. The fullest discussion of Gallagher's

long career remains chapter 15 in William H. Venable, *Beginnings of Literary Culture in the Ohio Valley* (Cincinnati: Robert Clarke, 1891).

2. Gallagher, "Periodical Literature," *Western Literary Journal and Monthly Review* 1 (1844):2.

3. *Ohio Authors and Their Books*, ed. William Coyle (Cleveland: World, 1962), pp. 148–49.

4. Gallagher, pp. 6–9.

5. Gallagher, p. 5; Venable, pp. 450–51.

6. Ralph L. Rusk, *The Literature of the Middle Western Frontier*, 2 vols. (New York: Columbia University Press, 1925), 1:177.

## Information Sources

BIBLIOGRAPHY:

Gallagher, William Davis. "Periodical Literature." *Western Literary Journal and Monthly Review* 1 (1844):1–9.

Mott, Frank Luther. "*The Hesperian*." *A History of American Magazines*, 4 vols. Cambridge, Mass.: Belknap Press of Harvard University Press, 1957. 1:692–93.

Rusk, Ralph L. *The Literature of the Middle Western Frontier*. 2 vols. New York: Columbia University Press, 1925. 1:177–78.

Tague, James A. "William D. Gallagher, Champion of Western Literary Periodicals." *Ohio Historical Quarterly* 69 (1960):257–71.

Venable, William H. *Beginnings of Literary Culture in the Ohio Valley*. Cincinnati: Robert Clarke, 1891. Pp. 436–70.

INDEXES: Following the last number of each volume.

REPRINT EDITIONS: American Periodicals: Series II, 1800–1850. University Microfilms, Ann Arbor. Reel 417.

LOCATION SOURCES: Widely available.

## Publication History

MAGAZINE TITLE AND TITLE CHANGES: *The Hesperian; or, Western Monthly Magazine*, May 1838-April 1839. *The Hesperian; A Monthly Miscellany of General Literature, Original and Select*, June-November 1839.

VOLUME AND ISSUE DATA: Volume 1, May-October 1838; volume 2, November 1838-April 1839; volume 3, June-November 1839.

FREQUENCY OF PUBLICATION: Monthly.

PUBLISHERS: May 1838-April 1839: John D. Nichols, Columbus. June-November 1839: John D. Nichols, Cincinnati.

EDITORS: William D. Gallagher and Otway Curry, May-October 1838; William D. Gallagher, November 1838-November 1839.

*Robert D. Habich*

# HOLDEN'S DOLLAR MAGAZINE

The names and faces of many popular American and British personalities would grace the pages of *Holden's Dollar Magazine*, but the periodical is probably better known today for one writer's refusal to lend either pen or portrait to it.

The *Dollar Magazine* was important in the careers of Charles F. Briggs and
Evert A. Duyckinck, for Duyckinck's lack of success with *Holden's* would
lengthen the list of his associations with failed magazines, while Briggs would
hone his editorial skills at *Holden's* to go on to achieve acclaim with his next
editorial endeavor at *Putnam's Magazine*.* However, any repute the *Dollar
Magazine* still sustains is more likely to be connected with Herman Melville's
parody of it in *Pierre*.

As Evert Duyckinck was preparing to assume the editorship of the *Dollar
Magazine* early in 1851, Melville rejected his friend's invitation to become a
contributor: "I can not write the thing you want . . . ; I am not in the humor to
write the kind of thing you need—and I am not in the humor to write for Holden's
Magazine." And as for a picture—"a Daguerretype (what a devel [*sic*] of an
unspellable word?)"—well, since "almost everybody is having his 'mug' engraved nowadays" for magazine publication, Melville prefers not to.[1] His reluctance to show his face in the magazine is understandable. Engraved portraits
had been accompanied by such effusions as, "A fine eye, a lofty stature, and a
prematurely grey head, are the noticeable outer marks of the soul of George
Burrow" (7:146), and by such blunt description as, the Reverend Thomas P.
Hunt's "personal appearance . . . is peculiar" (6:490). While Melville was not
inclined to set aside the manuscript of *Moby-Dick* to write for *Holden's*, he
would recall the magazine in his next romance. There Duyckinck's request
appears exaggerated in the importunings of the "joint editor of the 'Captain
Kidd Monthly,' " and Melville's own refusal reappears as his protagonist Pierre's,
now reinforced with brandishings of a "determinately double fist" and a threat
to "drop" the editor.[2] Melville's "no" to Duyckinck, though no less decisive,
is more civilized; he regrets whatever there might be of "unkindness" in his
letter of refusal and hopes that he might "yet be of some better service . . . than
merely jotting a paragraph for Holden's."[3] Perhaps he thought of himself as
beginning in a small way to make good this promise when he arranged for a
friend's subscription to the magazine in the following month.[4] But Duyckinck
reprinted his unsympathetic review of *Moby-Dick* from the *Literary World** in
the December *Holden's*, and Melville's thoughts turned from obligation to re-
taliation as he drafted *Pierre*.

By the time he wrote *Pierre*, Melville's familiarity with *Holden's* enabled
him to reflect the magazine's attitudes in Pierre's career as a magazinist. The
nineteen-year-old Pierre has already achieved fame and the "unqualified admiration" of numerous magazine editors as the author of "The Tropical Summer," a single sonnet.[5] Indeed, *Holden's* had argued in one article that a poetic
reputation might be built on the strength of the lyric (though the writer had in
mind a larger production than Pierre's): "The praise of the poet . . . is to be
determined, not by the nature of the work he undertakes, but by the kind of
mastery which he shows. . . . 'Scorn not the Song!' "(4:238) Also, the *Dollar
Magazine*'s sometimes inflated assessment of its favored authors parallels the
growing "literary enthusiasm" for Pierre, "the illustrious Glendinning."[6] For

example, *Holden's* praises one Edward P. Clark, a recent graduate of Yale, whose prize-winning English composition on Irving and Goldsmith appears in revised form in the magazine: "Mr. Clark is only 19 years of age, yet he has already written articles which have won the attention of some of the first literary men of the country. . . . we have no doubt that he will be 'heard from' in after years" (7:139). Pierre earns a reputation for "genteelness" in his writing; fictional editors celebrate his literary talent for appearing as "the unruffled gentleman from the drawing-room" in his works, avoiding any trace of "vulgarity."[7] *Holden's* advertised itself as "free from . . . grossness" and appropriate for "persons of the utmost refinement" (4:[706]); one editorial celebrates George Cruickshank as a model for the satirist of both genius and gentility, crediting his talent for his genteelness: he "is a genius, and men of genius are always gentlemen" (5:126). Melville borrows a tone of magazine genteelness himself to describe Pierre's readers as "the always intelligent and extremely discriminating public,"[8] ironically echoing *Holden's* principle (quoting a commendation from the *Literary World*) that "Publishers of magazines should not underrate the intelligence of the public." (3:191).

Charles W. Holden began the *Dollar Magazine* in January 1848 and served as publisher until his death in June of the following year. Holden left his native Barre, Massachusetts, at sixteen to spend two years, according to Henry Fowler's "Tribute" to him in *Holden's*, in "wanderings, privations, and fruitless undertakings at the West" before making his way to New York, "determined to be a good writer" (5:35). A series of jobs with city newspapers, while having a debatable impact on the quality of his writing, brought him enough capital to start the monthly that would bear his name and publish his poems and sketches of Western adventure. One such job at the *New-York Mirror** also introduced him to Charles F. Briggs, who became the longest-lived editor of the *Dollar Magazine*.

Briggs had moved to the *Mirror* as writer and editor from the *Broadway Journal*,* which he had founded, when some combination of his coeditor Edgar Allan Poe's drunken antics, political intriguings, and conflicts over plagiarism had forced him away. Briggs would continue his contributions to the *Mirror*, notably the satirical Fernando Mendez Pinto letters, throughout his tenure at *Holden's*, regarding his work for *Holden's* as "an aside employment from other engagements which afforded greater emolument, if not greater pleasure" (5:380). Able to give only "slight care" to the magazine, Briggs divided editorial duties with its publishers. His "duties were confined almost entirely to the review department and the brief editorial communications with readers and correspondents," while the publisher should be given "more credit . . . for the discrimination and judgment shown in the general arrangement of the Magazine" (5:380–81). The division of talent and labor apparently worked well, for Briggs noted on resigning a "steadily increasing circulation of a most gratifying character" (5:380).

A large circulation was the essential factor in the success of Holden's "bold experiment" of offering a literary monthly for only one dollar. Basing its "calculations'' on mutual profit—a bargain for the reader and a lucrative return on his investment for the publisher—the magazine anticipated ''with perfect confidence'' the subscription list of fifty thousand necessary to turn a profit, for a popular audience of ''live Yankees'' could be counted on to refuse to pay three to five dollars—the going rate of most competitors—for what might be had for one. Literary merit figured as secondary. While the *Dollar Magazine* did plan to become ''twice as good'' as its first number, the projected improvement was merely part of a larger plan ''to double our circulation'' to a hundred thousand ''before long'' (1:57). The wager on ''the shrewdness of the people,'' backed by the magazine's design for popular appeal, proved successful yet did not yield the hoped-for profit. Consistently increasing subscriptions did enable the *Dollar Magazine* to change its format on a number of occasions, for example, adding engraved illustrations in the second volume (see 1:379). Also, the name of Briggs's editorial ''gossipiad'' was changed in the fifth volume because ''circulation of the magazine having increased so largely as to render it necessary to issue it before the month is half expired, in order to enable our far-flung subscribers to receive it before it is a month old and out of date, the [former title] 'topics of the month' became a misnomer'' (5:61). *Holden's* editorials and prospectuses repeatedly notice the magazine's growing circulation throughout Briggs's editorship, on one occasion counting its ''success . . . wholly unprecedented in the history of publishing'' (3:[386]). Perry Miller speculates that the extent of the *Dollar Magazine*'s subscription list prompted the Duyckinck brothers to buy the magazine in 1851.[9] The monthly claimed ''30,000 readers'' after two years of publication, far short of initial hopes but still competitive with the widely circulating *Godey's Lady's Book*\* (with a subscription list of forty thousand) and significantly superior to the average circulation figure of 7,400 for monthlies in 1850.[10] Impatient for financial success, Holden did not live to see his magazine at the height of its achievement; joining the Gold Rush, he died of typhoid fever in California in June of 1849. His magazine would survive him for a total of eight volumes in four years, another testimony to its relative success in a market where the average life of a periodical was probably only half that of *Holden's*.[11]

Briggs must be credited with much of what success the *Dollar Magazine* achieved, in spite of his modest disavowal. *Holden's* reflects Briggs's ability to recognize and supply what a popular audience wanted to read. The ability earned him an enduring reputation as a journalist and some celebrity as a humorist. With nearly a decade as a magazinist behind him, Briggs came to *Holden's* knowing that ''the Public'' can be as ''fickle'' as ''Fortune, or weathercocks,'' or even ''women,'' if not given what it desired (1:1). Accordingly the format of *Holden's* is broadly miscellaneous, with enough variety in its content to offer something for the whim of every reader: ''Criticisms, Biographies, Sketches, Essays, Tales, Reviews, Poetry, Etc., Etc.,'' as its subtitle proclaims. Briggs also aimed to affront as few readers as possible. The editorial policy he announces on the first page of the new *Dollar Magazine* pledges, in a tone at once conciliatory and droll, to shun sectarianism in politics, religion, and philosophy; and an editorial note prefacing the series of "Living Pictures of American Not-abilities, Literary and Scientific," begun in the fourth issue, promises literary nonsectarianism as well: the author has no affiliation with any "clique" and "is confederated with no literary party" (1:193). Going beyond the conventional disclaimer of the miscellanies, Briggs's stance of conciliation and independence characterizes his editorial career at *Holden's*.

In this stance, Briggs speaks in his editorials for institution of an international copyright, for support of the Art Union, and for a greater audience for the poetry of his friend James Russell Lowell, even when it is appearing in the radical *Anti-Slavery Standard*, from whose abolitionist "politics and designs" he is careful to dissociate himself (3:313–14). The independence of mind that earned Briggs the epithet "Ishmael" from Duyckinck and the label "conscience Whig" from Perry Miller[12] combines with his editorial sense of what "*morceaux* more prop-erly belong to magazines" (5:316) to exclude from *Holden's* political or literary-political issues of unavoidably partisan nature: "The death of the great south-erner, Calhoun, the talk about disunion, the compromising speeches of Webster, Benton, and Clay, and the uncompromising speeches of Senator Seward, are tabooed subjects for such humble laborers as ourselves" (5:316).

Briggs's editorial columns thus betray more of his personal biases than divulge any alignment with the literary-political factions into which Miller has divided New York's mid-nineteenth-century magazine world. If Briggs joins in the nearly universal deprecation of any attempt made at writing by Cornelius Mathews, Duyckinck's favorite (1:251), and if he finds another Duyckinck associate, Wil-liam Gilmore Simms, guilty of producing "the most melancholy examples of dismal writing that it has ever been [his] lot to encounter . . . [composed] in a more wretched, unskilful, and beggarly manner than [he] had supposed possible in these days of universal education" (1:182), Briggs nonetheless admires Duyck-inck's own "excellent weekly," the *Literary World* (3:191), and carries his advocacy of another Duyckinck associate, Herman Melville, through several essentially favorable reviews—of *Mardi* (3:370–72), *Redburn* (5:55–56), and *White-Jacket* (5:313–14)—to endorse him as one of "the two most popular writers among us just now" (5:123). When he does not like a book, Briggs details specific literary reasons. He criticizes *The Sea Lions* because James Fen-imore Cooper buries his adventures in polemic, producing "more of a sermon than a romance" (3:369); he criticizes *The Forgery* because G.P.R. James buries his story in verbiage, using in one exemplary sentence "78 words of which 61 are entirely unnecessary to the expression of his idea" (3:119). However, policy in editorials and the monthly "Holden's Review" section—"brief but discrim-inating notes on new books" (1:62)—advocates praising writers, especially American writers, whenever their merit makes it possible. Thus he reserves criticism of Rufus Griswold's *Poets and Poetry of America* (tenth edition), for "It would be an ungracious office to point out defects in a work which we must confess, after all, was the best of the kind to be had; let us . . . be grateful to the author for it and, until we can either produce or point to a better one, speak of it only in terms of praise'' (5:183). Since taste varies—''Johnson thought Milton no great shakes of a poet''—and since ''it can injure none but a churl to hear another overpraised,'' Briggs lectures one correspondent who objected to a eulogistic article calling General George P. Morris ''a great poet . . . and literary creator of a high order'' for his songs ''I Have Never Been False to Thee'' and ''Woodman, Spare that Tree'' (''one of those accidents of genius which . . . never happen but to consummate artists'' [4:740–41]).

Another of Briggs's personal biases—one common to his era—surfaces in his monthly chats with *Holden's* readers where on a number of occasions he reminds his female reader of her rightful sphere and gives tips to his male reader on how to keep her in it. An excerpt from one of those ''strong minded ladies'' who are '' 'riled up' about women's rights'' is offered for the amusement of the *Dollar Magazine*'s audience in the April 1849 number, along with the editorial analysis that this particular lady must be ''undoubtedly, a screamer'' and an editorial expression of compassion for her husband, should she have one (3:251). Four issues later Briggs is reminding readers that ''You must not reason with a woman,'' because logic exceeds female capabilities: women ''probably . . . cannot reason'' (4:510). The comic, ''earnest'' tone of the ''strenuous opposition'' to ''female pantaloonery'' in one Miss F. L. Townsend's article arguing against ''Women in Male Attire'' sounds suspiciously like Briggs's own; at any rate, the article urging ''the female sex to retain the garments which the experience of centuries has proved to be proper to their condition'' appears during his editorship and reflects his conservatism (5:178–79). He notes with satisfaction Grace Greenwood's retirement from ''the responsible post of editor of a newspaper'' since he is unable to see how women ''were accomplishing their mission in the world while editing papers, any more than in farming or shoeing horses'' (2:509). However, a woman's natural role and ''mission'' could very well include writing, and *Holden's* reflects Briggs's attitude toward female writers, a compound of honest admiration of what he considered good writing and self-congratulation for his magazine and his own discernment in giving talented women their due recognition. Literary ability supercedes the question of sex in Briggs's review of *Shirley*: ''Currer Bell—whether man or woman—is the greatest living writer of fiction'' (5:57). Briggs, in reviewing Caroline May's collection of *American Female Poets*, finds among the ''lady scribblers'' and ''most sinful and incurable plagiarists'' some few writers who can express ''thoughts of which no poet need be ashamed'' (4:697–98). He estimates that at the beginning of 1850 America's ''most brilliant'' as well as most ''popular authors are sailors and women,'' and he discovers that ''among our own contributors those that we take the most pride in, and whose fresh, lively, and vigorous thoughts, have gained the attention of the public already, are two ladies who made their literary debut in our columns. We allude to Caroline C—, of Canandaigua, and the author of Susy L—'s Diary'' (5:61). Apparently these ladies shared Briggs's notion of woman's proper sphere, for the heroine of ''Susy L—'s Diary,'' in the concluding episode of the serial tale, puts down her pen after her wedding at her husband's request and declares (at his prompting) that he is "Worth more to [her] than five hundred diaries! more than anything, *everything* else in the wide world!" The denouement sees her concluding that "the only superiority [she] *would* have over [her] husband" is the virtue of superior tidiness, which the tale was designed to inculcate in her and—presumably—in female readers (5:148). Caroline C—'s satirical and admonitory sketch of a heroine (Mrs. Masters) who harries her husband to an early grave with her advocacy of women's rights and other faddish philosophies ends with a quote Briggs would approve: "The Rights of Woman! what are they? / The right to labor and to pray; / The right to watch while others sleep, / The right o'er others woes to weep; / The right to succor in distress, / The right while others curse, to bless" (4:735).[13]

Under Briggs, *Holden's* became increasingly committed to giving the general reading public what it wanted in popular entertainment from new writers. He saw the "mission of our magazines to develop . . . [the] immense amount of available literary talent lying dormant, unemployed, and unappreciated" rather than to "beslobber great names with compliments" as was all too often the case in other journals (3:377). Accordingly, he paid unknown writers well (he said) and continued doing so even after a public squabble with one writer who claimed not to have been compensated for his contribution.[14] Caroline C— debuted in the October 1848 *Holden's* with the first in her series of "Talks with You" published under the name of Evangeline Scroggs. Her moral and allegorical sketches and her poems (signed variously Caroline C— and C. C., Canandaigua) became a staple of the magazine. Encouraged by the reception *Holden's* readers and editor gave her pieces, she began signing her own name, Caroline Chesebro', in the February 1850 issue with "Shades and Sunbeams: A Transparent Story" (5:68). After her apprenticeship at the *Dollar Magazine*, Chesebro' would continue writing fiction enough to fill almost twenty books, including *Peter Carradine* (1863), her final novel, which Nina Baym rates as "a minor masterpiece" in spite of Chesebro's predilection for an exaggerated style and her tendency toward "wearisome lecturing at the reader."[15] Briggs was a good judge of what nineteenth-century magazine readers would pay their dollar for, and, as they wanted didacticism in a high literary mode, he gave it to them regularly over Chesebro's many signatures. In fact, Briggs complained that a British periodical pirated one of Chesebro's "pleasant articles . . . bodily from our magazine without any acknowledgment whatever of the source from whence it was derived" (5:317). Less frequently the names of other popular writers—John T. Headley, Dr. Augustus Kinsley Gardner, once even Nathaniel Hawthorne—appear on *Holden's* sketches, essays, and tales. Verse contributions, in addition to Holden's own rhymed philosophical meditations and Chesebro's sentimental lines, come from the popular writers Dr. T[homas] H. Chivers, Alice Cary, Phoebe Cary (signing her parodies "By the Muse"), and Mrs. Elizabeth Jessup Eames. Briggs reprints many of his friend Lowell's "effusions" (5:125).

The contents of the magazine reflected little change when Henry Fowler and William Dietz took over from Briggs in July 1850. But when the Duyckinck brothers began their brief editorial reign, they altered the nature of the *Dollar Magazine*. Although the *Literary World* promised "entirely distinct and separate publications,"[16] the *Dollar Magazine* soon began carrying much of the same material as the Duyckincks' weekly, while claiming to be a "strictly original publication" (7:144). Although their first issue reprinted Hawthorne's "Ethan Brand,"[17] their apparent plan to refine the literary quality of the magazine may have met with disappointments similar to Melville's refusal to contribute; at any rate, they soon lapsed into reprinting articles, poems, and feature-length reviews from their other journal and ended by turning what remained of their subscribers over to the *North American Miscellany* after only nine issues.

With few exceptions, Evert Duyckinck lacked Briggs's inclination and ability to speak to a popular audience. He betrays a certain condescension to what his friend Melville called "the tribe of 'general readers' "[18] who sustained the *Dollar Magazine*. An advertisement for the magazine quotes a puff from the *Albany State Register* that originally anticipated the Duyckincks' success but can now ironically explain their failure: "The editors have no idea of writing down to the popular level, and therefore will endeavor to cultivate an elevation in style, topics, and even illustrations which will render this periodical a source of intellectual improvement to any family circle."[19] At the end of 1851 the Duyckincks concluded the futility of their endeavor and went back to their *Literary World*, while the *Dollar Magazine* subscribers went on to the *North American Miscellany*, not for any intellectual improvement they might need, but for the kind of entertainment they wanted for their dollar.

**Notes**

1. *The Letters of Herman Melville*, ed. Merell R. Davis and William H. Gilman (New Haven: Yale University Press, 1960), pp. 120–22.

2. *The Writings of Herman Melville*, vol. 7, *Pierre; or, The Ambiguities*, ed. Harrison Hayford, Hershel Parker, and G. Thomas Tanselle (Evanston: Northwestern University Press, 1971), pp. 253–54.

3. *Letters of Herman Melville*, p. 122.

4. *Letters of Herman Melville*, pp. 122–23.

5. *Pierre*, p. 245.

6. *Pierre*, pp. 246, 248.

7. *Pierre*, p. 245.

8. *Pierre*, p. 245.

9. Perry Miller, *The Raven and the Whale: The War of Words and Wits in the Era of Poe and Melville* (New York: Harcourt, Brace and World, 1956), p. 294.

10. Frank Luther Mott, *A History of American Magazines*, 4 vols. (Cambridge, Mass.: Harvard University Press, 1938), 1:514. Mott thinks that even this figure may be high.

11. Mott, p. 342.

12. Miller, passim.

13. Barbara Welter identifies the author of these lines as Mrs. E. Little, who published them in the *Ladies' Wreath* 2 (1848–1849):133; see "The Cult of True Womanhood," *American Quarterly* 18 (Summer 1966):173.

14. The writer was Augustine Joseph Hickey Duganne. Briggs explained that *Holden's* paid when authors finished their contributions, which he said Duganne never did.

15. Nina Baym, *Women's Fiction: A Guide to Novels by and about Women in America, 1820—1870* (Ithaca: Cornell University Press, 1978), p. 207.

16. *The Literary World* no. 213 (1 March 1851):176.

17. The story first appeared in the *Boston Weekly Museum* 2 (5 January 1850):234–35, under the title "The Unpardonable Sin. From an Unpublished Work." See C. E. Frazer, Jr., *Nathaniel Hawthorne: A Descriptive Bibliography* (Pittsburgh: University of Pittsburgh Press, 1978), p. 423.

18. *Letters of Herman Melville*, p. 129. Melville uses the phrase in telling Hawthorne he read "Ethan Brand" in the *Dollar Magazine*.

19. Quoted in *The Literary World* no. 217 (29 March 1851):259.

## Information Sources

BIBLIOGRAPHY:

*American Women Writers: A Critical Reference Guide from Colonial Times to the Present.* Vol. 1. Ed. Lina Mainiero. New York: Frederick Ungar, 1979.

Baym, Nina. *Women's Fiction: A Guide to Novels by and about Women in America, 1820–1870.* Ithaca: Cornell University Press, 1978.

Miller, Perry. *The Raven and the Whale: The War of Words and Wits in the Era of Poe and Melville.* New York: Harcourt, Brace and World, 1956.

Mott, Frank Luther. *A History of American Magazines.* 4 vols. Cambridge, Mass.: Harvard University Press, 1938. 1:347–48.

INDEXES: None

REPRINT EDITIONS: American Periodicals: Series II, 1800–1850. University Microfilms, Ann Arbor. Reel 604.

LOCATION SOURCES: Widely available.

## Publication History

MAGAZINE TITLE AND TITLE CHANGES: *Holden's Dollar Magazine. Of Criticisms, Biographies, Sketches, Essays, Tales, Reviews, Poetry, Etc., Etc.*, January 1848-December 1850. *Holden's Dollar Magazine containing Original Criticisms, Biographies, Sketches, Essays, Tales, Reviews, Poetry, etc., etc.*, January-February 1851. *The Dollar Magazine*, March-December 1851.

VOLUME AND ISSUE DATA: Volumes 1–8, January 1848-December 1851.

FREQUENCY OF PUBLICATION: Monthly.

PUBLISHERS: January 1848-October 1849: Charles W. Holden, New York. November 1849-March 1851: William H. Dietz, New York. April-December 1851: Evert A. and George L. Duyckinck, New York.

EDITORS: Charles F. Briggs, January 1848-June 1850; William H. Dietz and Henry Fowler, July 1850-March 1851; Evert A. and George L. Duyckinck, April-December 1851.

*Charlene Avallone*

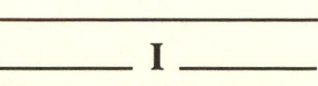

## THE ILLINOIS MONTHLY MAGAZINE

The first issue of the *Illinois Monthly Magazine* appeared in Vandalia in October 1830. Its founder and editor, Judge James Hall, had come West in 1820 from Philadelphia, and, combining writing with a career in politics and law, he had gained a modest reputation for his Western sketches and tales. A number of these had appeared in the *Port Folio*,* edited by his brother John Ewing Hall from 1816 until it ceased publication in 1827. Hall's *Illinois Monthly* was truly a pioneer effort, the first literary magazine west of the Ohio River. An announcement in the *Illinois Intelligencer* on 10 April 1830 indicated its regional focus: "The object of this work, will be to develope the character and resources of Illinois."[1]

Hall's "Preface" to the first issue indicated that the *Illinois Monthly* would serve to bring culture to the West. "Great as our country is becoming, and rapidly as it is advancing in every branch of physical development, our mental resources are yet but small. Literature is but little cultivated" (1:2). But paradoxically, Hall also intended to promote "the history, character, condition, and prospects of this great section of the union" since it is "little understood" in the East. This dual intention meant that the magazine would "embrace a great variety of topics," and Hall promised that "while we thus propose to give a prominent place to the *useful*, it is not our intention to neglect the lighter and more elegant branches of literature" (1:3). This was a tall order for a frontier magazine, and Hall was well aware of the difficulty of filling his pages with such variety. He readily admitted that "We shall partially avoid this difficulty, by selecting interesting articles from other works. The proportion which the selected shall bear to the original matter, will remain for the present undecided, and be determined by circumstances" (1:3). Circumstances indeed dictated that a large portion of the contents be selected. Hall's frank plea that "gentlemen of

literary acquirements, not . . . hide their lights under bushels" (1:4) did not result
in significant submissions. Later, in the *Western Monthly*, Hall looked back and
admitted of the *Illinois Monthly* that "of the five hundred and seventy-six pages
contained in each of the two first volumes, about two-thirds were written by the
editor, a very few were contributed by two or three friends, who had the kindness
to assist him occasionally, and the remainder were selected" (3:93).

Frank Luther Mott's statement that Hall achieved a "thoroughly magazinish
variety" is apt.[2] The first forty-eight page issue was typical. It included a tale
entitled "The Missionaries," a poem entitled "The Indian Wife's Lament,"
articles on "Railways" of the West, the "Geology of Illinois," humorous "Railroad Speech," and Yellowstone's "Petrified Forest," "Law Notices," an article
on current events entitled "Algiers," and an article on Illinois geography by
Governor Edward Coles, a friend of Hall. As Ralph Rusk notes, the weakest
aspect of the magazine was its literary criticism, and the reason is evident in
Hall's statement in his "Literary Intelligence" column for December 1830. He
notes that books are scarce in Vandalia, "Nor do we expect to be able, at any
time, to throw much light upon the passing events, of the literary world. But
we intend to pick up all we can; and for this purpose, have made arrangements
for procuring some of the best English and American periodicals, from which
we shall be able to extract much that will be interesting" (1:142). Consequently,
much of the literary criticism was reprinted. But the difficulty of obtaining quality
material became acute in the second volume of the *Illinois Monthly*. Book reviews
and literary criticism appeared much less frequently, and, as John Flanagan
notes, there was "noticeably more padding."[3]

Disheartened by his failure to achieve success with his magazine, and having
suffered financial loss in the attempt, Hall suspended publication in September
1832 and moved to Cincinnati, the cultural and literary center of the West. In
January 1833 he began the *Western Monthly Magazine, A Continuation of the
Illinois Monthly Magazine*. Stating in the first issue that his publication was
"devoted chiefly to elegant literature" and was "the medium for disseminating
valuable information and pure moral principles," Hall declared that "The literature of the West is still in its infancy, and we trust that we are not unconscious
of the responsibility which rests on those who attempt to direct it" (1:1). Although
the stated policy of the *Western Monthly* and the nature of its contents were
similar to those of Hall's earlier magazine, it was superior in important ways.
Hall no longer was forced to write the majority of the contents himself and
instead focused his writing talents on book reviews and critical notices. This,
plus the fact that he had greater access to recently published books, resulted in
a review department that was, unlike the *Illinois Monthly's*, "much more than
an affectation."[4] In February 1835 Hall noted that thirty-seven writers had
contributed to the last volume of the *Western Monthly* (3:94), one indication of
his success in drawing some of the best Western writers to his magazine. A
major reason for this was his unusual policy of paying contributors one dollar
per page. As Flanagan points out, "Since almost all of the early magazines

expected gratuitous contributions, there was a distinct advantage in writing for the *Western Monthly Magazine*, and as a result Hall commanded the best available talent."[5] Among the contributors were the poets Otway Curry and William D. Gallagher, editor of the *Cincinnati Mirror*. Harriet Beecher, daughter of Lyman Beecher, contributed a number of stories, including "The Prize Tale," entitled "A New England Sketch," in April 1834 (3:169–92). Ironically, Hall's success in attracting quality writing is reflected in his complaints about other editors stealing and reprinting his material.[6]

However, Hall became embroiled in two controversies that brought him into conflict with his publisher, Eli Taylor, owner of the *Cincinnati Journal* and a supporter of Lyman Beecher. First, he attacked abolitionism as a "vast scheme of anarchy and carnage . . . almost unprecedented in the annals of crime" (5:2), and, second, he spoke out against attacks on the Catholic Church, then occurring in Cincinnati, as unfounded and unjust, "Without a trial, without evidence, without exhibition of a single overt act of illegal tendency" (5:3). Citing threats against him, cancelled subscriptions, and "*prayers* . . . put up for the death of the magazine," Hall decided "to say to the publisher, that our connection with him must cease" (5:7). Hall resigned, and Joseph Reese Fry became editor. The *Western Monthly* was merged with Gallagher's *Western Monthly Review*, and the combined publication died in 1837 in Louisville. Hall thus ended an editorial career that cost him considerable financial loss. Flanagan concludes that "The major difficulty in Hall's editorship was that he was never able to give his publication his undivided attention."[7] His political, legal, and financial dealings took most of his time. Yet it is generally agreed that the *Illinois* and then *Western Monthly Magazine* was "one of the most important of the pioneer period," a major reason being its attention to literature, unique among Western magazines of the time.[8] And even though Hall never made money from it, to a great extent because of unpaid subscriptions, it is judged by Mott to be "one of the two or three most important literary magazines in the West before the Civil War."[9]

## Notes

1. Quoted in John T. Flanagan, *James Hall: Literary Pioneer of the Ohio Valley* (Minneapolis: University of Minnesota Press, 1941), p. 56.

2. Frank Luther Mott, "*The Illinois Monthly; The Western Monthly*," *A History of American Magazines*, 4 vols. (Cambridge, Mass.: Belknap Press of Harvard University Press, 1957), 1:596.

3. Flanagan, p. 59.

4. Flanagan, p. 68.

5. Flanagan, p. 68.

6. Flanagan, pp. 69–70.

7. Flanagan, p. 76.

8. Ralph Leslie Rusk, *The Literature of the Middle Western Frontier*, 2 vols. (New York: Columbia University Press, 1926), 1:172–73.

9. Mott, 1:387.

## Information Sources

BIBLIOGRAPHY:

Flanagan, John T. *James Hall: Literary Pioneer of the Ohio Valley*. Minneapolis: University of Minnesota Press, 1941.

Mott, Frank Luther. *"The Illinois Monthly*; *The Western Monthly." A History of American Magazines*. 4 vols. Cambridge, Mass.: Belknap Press of Harvard University Press, 1957. 1:595–98.

Rusk, Ralph Leslie. *The Literature of the Middle Western Frontier*. 2 vols. New York: Columbia University Press, 1926.

Shultz, Esther. "James Hall in Vandalia." *Journal of the Illinois State Historical Society* 23 (1930): 92–112.

INDEXES: Title index with each volume.

REPRINT EDITIONS: American Periodicals: Series II, 1800–1850. University Microfilms, Ann Arbor. Reels 389, 528.

LOCATION SOURCES: Widely available.

## Publication History

MAGAZINE TITLE AND TITLE CHANGES: *The Illinois Monthly Magazine*, October 1830-September 1832. *The Western Monthly Magazine, A Continuation of the Illinois Monthly Magazine*, January 1833-December 1835. *The Western Monthly Magazine*, January-December 1836. *The Western Monthly Magazine, and Literary Journal*, February-June 1837.

VOLUME AND ISSUE DATA: Volumes 1–2 (Illinois series), October 1830-September 1832; volumes 1–5 (Western series), January 1833-December 1836; volume 1 (new series), February-June 1837.

FREQUENCY OF PUBLICATION: Monthly.

PUBLISHERS: 1830–1831: Robert Blackwell and James Hall, Vandalia. 1831–1834: Corey and Fairbank, Cincinnati. 1834–1835: Taylor and Tracy, Cincinnati. 1836: Flash, Ryder and Company, Cincinnati. 1837: Marshall and Gallagher, Louisville.

EDITORS: James Hall, October 1830-June 1836; Joseph Reese Fry, July-December 1836; James B. Marshall and William D. Gallagher, February-June 1837.

*Edward Chielens*

# THE ILLUSTRATED WASP. See THE WASP

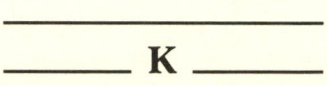

## THE KNICKERBOCKER

Begun in January 1833 to promote a genuinely national American literature, The *Knickerbocker* serves as a mirror to a significant segment of literary taste during the next thirty-odd years. Certain abortive potentialities prevented the magazine from attaining the summit of first-rate art throughout its contents. Nevertheless, its position as the major vehicle for expression of Knickerbocker sensibilities as well as for humor prevents its being ignored in histories of American literary periodicals. A broad awareness of contemporaneous cultural currents is also manifest in its pages. Above all else the *Knickerbocker* came to be associated with its long-time editor, Lewis Gaylord Clark. For better or worse he controlled the destinies of this magazine.

In the first number of the *Knickerbocker* a dialogue between the editor and the spirit of Peter Stuyvesant, the renowned crippled and crabbed governor of New York, unfolds wherein the latter questions the need for yet another American literary periodical. He vanishes rapidly when the editor names Washington Irving, from whose mellow combiner of history and legend, Diedrich Knickerbocker, the periodical drew its title. An aura of Knickerbocker auspices, for the old Dutch story-teller's name quickly came to dominate a group of writers associated with New York state and city, stamped the contents of The *Knickerbocker* throughout its career. Often "Knickerbocker" connotes genial, quiet literary comedy, although many writers among those termed Knickerbockers, such as William Cullen Bryant and James Fenimore Cooper, were not primarily humorists. Since many other New York authors numbered among those who first drew attention to our national literature, the editors chose enterprisingly in soliciting contributions from Washington Irving, John T. Irving ("Quod"), James Kirke Paulding, Fitz-Greene Halleck, Timothy Flint, Robert C. Sands, Gulian C. Verplanck, Park Benjamin, Henry Cary ("John Waters"), Willis Gaylord

Clark (the editor's twin, as well as associate editor until his early death in 1841), Nathaniel Parker Willis, and Charles Frederick Briggs ("Harry Franco"). From outside the New York area came William Dunlap, Robert Montgomery Bird, Henry Wadsworth Longfellow, John Greenleaf Whittier, Nathaniel Hawthorne, Oliver Wendell Holmes, James Hall, Francis Parkman, Charles Godfrey Leland, Albert Pike, and many others of greater or lesser literary fortunes. Notable British writers of the time were also asked to contribute, and consequently the names of William Wordsworth, Robert Southey, and Edward Bulwer-Lytton may be found.

A typical issue of the *Knickerbocker* reveals a miscellany in contents. Verse, fiction, essays, and literary notices regularly filled the pages. Illustrations were not prominent, as they were in many other periodicals of the day. A special feature that began in February 1833 and that later under editor Clark won fame for the magazine was "The Editor's Table," a section set in reduced type and featuring much chit-chat or zesty gossip about current personalities and literary works. Contributors generally were ill-paid or not paid. Subscribers, according to repeated notices, also only cavalierly paid for the journal.

No single long poem appeared in the *Knickerbocker*, although all forms of nonepic verse did. Many translations, especially ballads from Spanish and German, became a staple. Bryant published here his famous "The Prairies" in December 1833, one of the best examples of blank verse and of the poetic selections in general. Although other famous poets of the day contributed, like Longfellow, whose "A Psalm of Life" appeared in October 1838 and "The Skeleton in Armor" in January 1841, the overall contents in verse remained mediocre. Lachrymose effusions over ruins, the picturesque, or languishing fair maidens earmark verse in this journal. Lydia H. Sigourney, Charles Godfrey Leland, and altogether too many now-forgotten voices typify the versifiers. Although Clark liked verse and although some interesting comic verse appeared, one does not seek great American or other poetry here.

Fiction usually appeared as short stories, although serial novels of no great art or importance appeared later, when their vogue ensured increased circulation for a magazine. Paulding and Irving produced for "Old Knick" their customary blends of supernaturalism or fantasy with realism. Hawthorne's "The Fountain of Youth," later retitled "Dr. Heidigger's Experiment," and "Edward Fane's Rosebud" are among the best fiction in the *Knickerbocker*, although "John Waters's" "The Iron Footstep" in April 1840 was a one-time favorite, as was W. L. Stone's "The Skeleton Hand" in January 1834. In general this magazine's fiction remained either too close to older, inferior Gothic models in its early years, or it verged only timidly onto borders of the newer realistic fiction emerging during the 1850s and 1860s. Overdoses of sentimentality and too many cardboard figures rather than characters recur with monotony.

Nonfictional prose divides between essays of general interest and critical-notice material. Travel writing constitutes much of the former, and the outstanding title is Francis Parkman's *The Oregon Trail*, serialized during 1847. As did many other travel pieces, this one treated popular Western substance. Readers of the *Knickerbocker* also enjoyed articles about foreign places, as evinced by the works of C. G. Leland. Another signal item in this vein is Jeremiah N. Reynolds's "Mocha Dick," in May 1839. This essay provided inspiration for Herman Melville's novel *Moby-Dick* and in itself deftly mingles realism with suspense while detailing encounters with the fearsome white whale. The range of other articles ran the gamut from literary topics through political economy, and, as might be expected from a New York magazine, urban issues. In later years the number of abolition and anti-Southern articles increased. No great depth or critical acumen underlies the review sections. Characteristically, the notices print extracts accompanied by cursory commentary.

Another abiding concern in the *Knickerbocker*, manifested in varied ways, is humor. First, a considerable body of comic writing runs throughout the magazine. Albert Pike, C. G. Leland, Frederick S. Cozzens, Donald Grant Mitchell ("Ik Marvel"), "Harry Franco," and the Clark brothers are among the humorists in prose and verse who are remembered today, although there were many other lesser lights. A great limitation of *Knickerbocker* humor is that editor Clark continued to praise and to run items favorable to Oliver Goldsmith, Richard Steele, and Joseph Addison, as well as to elevate above all others Charles Lamb and Washington Irving. These writers furnished models, to be sure, of neoclass- ical wit and humor, but their wares paled in comparison with the humor arising from the American West and Southwest. Clark admired from afar this type of mirth, but his own predilections restricted pages of "Old Knick" for the more urban, more refined, and genteel comic elements. Thus he failed in part to keep up with changing tastes, and in that respect he brought about the demise of his own journal. To be fair, though, it must be said that humorous work of all sorts was reviewed in the *Knickerbocker* and that these notices allow us to chart courses of comic productions during the second third of the nineteenth century. Dickens, Thackeray, Douglas Jerrold, among British writers, and Irving, Haw- thorne, Melville, William Gilmore Simms, Thomas Bangs Thorpe, Charles F. Browne ("Artemus Ward"), James Morris ("K. N. Pepper"), among Ameri- cans, were reviewed with an eye toward their humor. Several longer articles on humor or laughter are also worthwhile for what they reveal about contempora- neous opinions about what was funny and in what ways. "The Editor's Table" embodied much that related to humor, either in terms of parody directed, for example, at Longfellow, Poe, Whitman, and Hawthorne, or in its burlesque of rural newspapers in the several "Bunkum" columns devised by Clark and run- ning recurringly for extended periods. Clark's personal inclinations in "The Editor's Table" were chiefly genial. Two exceptions stand out. Because William Gilmore Simms aligned for a time with the "Young America" cultural move- ment—of greater liberalism than Clark admitted—Clark attacked him via "The Editor's Table" and reviews of his books, finally denouncing this important Southern writer for a signal and deplorable lack of humor. Poe's falling out with Clark may have resulted from the former's jealousy over Clark's part in the moon hoax perpetrated in 1839 by the *New York Sun*. (The hoax resulted from an article in the *Sun*, supposedly reprinted from a scientific journal, claiming to reveal the discovery of humans and animals on the moon.) When Poe began to ridicule Clark, Clark used his status as editor of a powerful magazine along with his influence in prominent literary circles to bear down on yet another Southerner who dared to challenge Northern literary establishments, like that with which Clark was linked in New York. The journalistic wars of the 1840s are evident in strictures of merciless proportions levelled at Poe, those in the *Knickerbocker* being but one example. Ultimately, these attacks brought about his ruin as an editor and as a possible contributor to many leading periodicals. Clark especially resented Poe's negative criticism of Willis Gaylord Clark's "Ollapodiana" columns that had run in the *Knickerbocker* in 1835 and 1840, and his lampoons of "Old Knick" proper. What might have occurred, had Clark opened up the magazine to more of the coarse, bawdy humorists like those who frequently wrote for William T. Porter's *New York Spirit of the Times*,* which flourished in roughly the same years as "Old Knick," we may only conjecture. Clark instead opted to maintain such reputations as those of Lamb, and in consequence his journal faded as others took its place. In later years "The Editor's Table" came to occupy disproportionate space and to consist more of snippets from other writers. These qualities lessened its freshness and impact. His pages are still serviceable, however, in bringing to light identities of some of the more obscure American humorists of the period. We learn, for example, in March 1845 (25:262–64), that "Phazma," who enjoyed a vogue during the 1830s and 1840s, is Matthew Field, and elsewhere, but in a more general context, that "John Waters" was Henry Cary, and that "Hans Breitmann" was C. G. Leland.

In conclusion, then, the *Knickerbocker* will be remembered for many connections with American humor and its backgrounds. Had finances been better handled and contributors paid more and regularly, the magazine might have continued longer. By the mid–1860s, however, the Knickerbocker school of writing had diminished in popularity, Clark's cherished authors and causes had dimmed in reputation, and the temper of American humor had altered. After several attempts at recouping loss and redirecting its forces, the magazine ceased publication in October 1865.

## Information Sources

BIBLIOGRAPHY:

[Clark, Lewis Gaylord]. "Editorial Narrative of the *Knickerbocker Magazine*." *The Knickerbocker* 53–58 (February 1859-January 1861).

"Filching from Old Knick." *The Boston Aurora Borealis*, 24 February 1849. P. 38.

Francis, John W., George P. Morris, Rufus W. Griswold, Richard B. Kimball, and Frederick W. Shelton, eds. *The Knickerbocker Gallery: A Testimonial to the Editor of the Knickerbocker Magazine From Its Contributors*. New York: Samuel Hueston, 1855.

"Knickerbocker Literature." *Nation*, 5 December 1867. Pp. 459–61.

Leland, Charles G. *Memoirs*. London: Heinemann, 1893.

*The Letters of Willis Gaylord Clark and Lewis Gaylord Clark*. Ed. Leslie W. Dunlap. New York: The New York Public Library, 1840.

McHaney, Thomas L. "An Early 19th Century Literary Agent: James Lawson of New York." *Papers of the Bibliographical Society of America* 64 (1970): 177–92.

Miller, Perry. *The Raven and the Whale: The War of Words and Wits in the Era of Poe and Melville*. New York: Harcourt, Brace, and World, 1956.

Moss, Sidney P. *Poe's Literary Battles: The Critic In The Context of His Literary Milieu*. Durham, N.C.: Duke University Press, 1963; rpt., Carbondale and Edwardsville: Southern Illinois University Press, 1969; London and Amsterdam: Feffer & Simons, 1969.

Mott, Frank Luther. *"The Knickerbocker Magazine." A History of American Magazines, 1741–1850*. New York: D. Appleton, 1930. Pp. 606–13.

Nethery, Wallace. *Charles Lamb in America to 1848*. Worcester, Mass.: Achilles J. St. Onge, 1963.

"The Newspaper and Periodical Press." *Southern Quarterly Review* 1 (January 1842):28.

[Poe, Edgar Allan]. "The Magazines." *The Broadway Journal*, 12 July 1845. Pp. 10–11.

Pritchard, John Paul. *Literary Wise Men of Gotham: Criticism in New York, 1815–1860*. Baton Rouge: Louisiana State University Press, 1963.

Roche, Arthur John III. "A Literary Gentleman in New York: Evert A. Duyckinck's Relationship with Nathaniel Hawthorne, Herman Melville, Edgar Allan Poe, and William Gilmore Simms." Ph.D. diss., Duke University, 1973.

Sloane, David E. E., ed. *The Literary Humor of the Urban Northeast, 1830–1860*. Baton Rouge: Louisiana State University Press, 1983.

Spivey, Herman Everette. *"The Knickerbocker Magazine, 1833–1865: A Study of Its History, Contents, and Significance."* Ph.D. diss., University of North Carolina, 1938.

Tebbel, John. *The American Magazine: A Compact History*. New York: Hawthorn Books, 1969. Pp. 49, 61–62, 70–80, 82, 87, 96.

Thorpe, Thomas Bangs. "Lewis Gaylord Clark." *Harper's New Monthly Magazine*, March 1874. Pp. 587–92.

INDEXES: Title index bound at the beginning of each volume.

REPRINT EDITIONS: American Periodicals: Series II, 1800–1850. University Microfilms, Ann Arbor. Reels 349–61.

LOCATION SOURCES: Widely available.

## Publication History

MAGAZINE TITLE AND TITLE CHANGES: *The Knickerbocker; or, New-York Monthly Magazine*, January 1833-September 1862 [*Knickerbacker* in volume 1]. *The Knickerbocker Monthly; a National Magazine of Literature, Art, Politics, and Society*, October 1863-February 1864. *The American Monthly Knickerbocker. Devoted to Literature, Art, Society, and Politics*, March 1864-June 1865. *Federal American Monthly*, July-October 1865.

VOLUME AND ISSUE DATA: Volumes 1–66, January 1833-October 1865 (semiannual volumes).

FREQUENCY OF PUBLICATION: Monthly.

PUBLISHERS: 1833–1834: Peabody & Co. 1834–1839: L. G. Clark and Clement M. Edson. 1840–1841: L. G. Clark. 1841–1842: John Bisco. 1842–1849: John Allen. 1849–1857: Samuel Hueston. 1858–1860: John A. Gray. 1861: J. R. Gilmore. 1862: Morris Phillips. 1862–1863: J. H. Elliot. 1864–1865: J. H. Agnew (all in New York).

EDITORS: Charles Fenno Hoffman, January-March 1833; Samuel Daly Langtree, April-September 1833; Timothy Flint, October 1833; Samuel Daly Langtree, November 1833-April 1834; Lewis Gaylord Clark, May 1834-December 1860; Willis Gaylord Clark, Associate Editor, 1834–1841; James D. Noyes, Associate Editor, 1858–1859; Kinahan Cornwallis, January 1861-September 1863; Kinahan Cornwallis and Lewis Gaylord Clark [Charles Godfrey Leland assisted during part of 1861-September 1862], October-December 1863; J. Holmes Agnew, January 1864-October 1865.

*Benjamin Franklin Fisher IV*

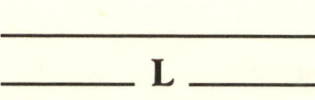

**L**

# THE LADY'S BOOK. See GODEY'S LADY'S BOOK

## THE LADIES' COMPANION

Publisher and editor William W. Snowden issued the first number of the *Ladies' Companion* in May 1834. The *Companion* was the first major periodical published in New York to be addressed primarily to women. Its chief rival was the Philadelphia-published *Godey's Lady's Book*\* (1830–1898). In a "To the Public" column in the first issue, Snowden promised that his monthly magazine would be "devoted to general literature in all its branches, embracing original and selected tales, sketches, poetry, the fine arts and the fashions" (1:1). Articles on travel and "Female Education" were also to be found, but there was nothing about politics or social and economic problems. This mixture helped the *Companion* to be a popular, middle-class periodical for ten and a half years.

From the first, Snowden filled his creation with some original writing, but most selections were pirated from other sources—both English and American. By 1837, however, Snowden was performing a genuine service to a growing native American literature by not only leaving out most British writers, but also, and more importantly, by paying for the material he printed—atypical editorial behavior in an era of no copyright laws. Snowden paid one dollar a page in 1834 and no doubt raised his scale as his magazine prospered. Many early articles were published anonymously, but soon initials began to appear. Further, Snowden recognized that some writers had established themselves, and he normally printed an author's name with the work. Most articles were signed by late 1837 and prefixed as "Original," a term that meant that the work had not been published before and that Snowden was paying its author. In fact, Snowden claimed "the honor of being the *first* to introduce to the public the plan of issuing a Magazine composed entirely of original articles'' (20:317). Snowden was justly proud of paying his contributors, and he certainly helped foster the principle of name value when many authors were struggling to make livings with their pens.

Snowden published the leading authors of the day: James Kirke Paulding (''The Eve of St. Andrew''), Lydia H. Sigourney (''Sailor's Hymn''), John Neal (''Value of Good Looks''), Captain Marryat (*Snarleyyow; or, The Dog Fiend*), Washington Irving (''Disappointed Affection''), William Gilmore Simms (''The Ship of the Palatines''), William Cullen Bryant (''Spring in Town''), Sarah Josepha Hale (''Accomplishments''), Nathaniel P. Willis (''The Undercliff''), Joseph Holt Ingraham (''Glimpses at Gotham''), Park Benjamin (''Lays of a Lover'') and Emma C. Embury (''The Exacting Lover''). Most of these pieces were not great works of literature by modern standards. More prose was published than poetry. Many works were frankly sentimental effusions of love and loss, but not all items fit these categories, and not all had uplifting endings. Edgar Allan Poe's ''The Mystery of Marie Roget,'' serialized from November 1842 through February 1843, is probably the most famous story; and Ann S. Stephens's *Malaeska*, which ran from February 1839 through April 1839, revised and enlarged, became the first ''Dime Novel'' published by Beadle and Adams (1860). Snowden also published articles of practical value—examples of embroidery, directions for making various types of caps, a recipe for preparing almond pudding.

As some of these foregoing authors and titles might suggest, there was much in the *Ladies' Companion* to attract male as well as female readers, although the *Ladies'* in the title would have worked against attracting male readers. Snowden charged three dollars a year for his magazine, twenty-five cents per issue. Each number usually contained fifty-two pages of small but clear letterpress printing on good quality rag-content paper; the page measured ten inches tall and six and three-eighths inches wide. In addition, each issue normally contained at least one steel engraving; from August 1841 on, two or three steel engravings were standard. The *Companion* was packed with reading material except for the usual two pages of sheet music. There were no advertisements, excepting an advertisement or two which might occasionally appear on the cover. Although Snowden took justifiable pride in paying his writers, he personally seemed most fond of the engravings. These were minutely detailed, printed on heavier stock than the rest of the *Companion* pages, and protected with tissue interleaving. Although a few periodicals of the era used color plates, Snowden explained that ''We don't color our plates because color would be incompatible with the extreme finish of the engraving. Plates prepared for coloring are mere outlines—ours are elaborate engravings'' (11:150). The plates were most often of detailed landscapes such as ''Byron Contemplating the Coliseum'' or ''Catskill Mountains,'' but the scope could also be smaller, such as the engraving of Benjamin West's painting ''The Last Supper.'' There were portraits of the famous like ''Lafayette'' and pictures showing domestic life such as ''The Invalid.'' Snowden published an engraving showing a bare breast in ''The Spirit Bride''; ''Sir Roger De Coverly and the Gypsies'' showed, in addition to Sir Roger having his palm read, a young mother breastfeeding her child. These were surely daring engravings for the time. Beginning in June 1839, Snowden added an occasional engraving which typically pictured four or five women modeling current fashions. These fashion engravings appeared monthly by August 1841. Snowden would name and describe the ladies' attire—morning dresses, evening dresses, full dresses, walking dresses, and ball costumes. He would note how much jewelry was worn and how a lady's hair was to be fixed to best complement her attire. The engravings were of American fashions until February 1843 when he started including an occasional plate devoted to Paris fashions. During the last six months of the periodical, when it was no longer owned by Snowden, the *Companion* did experiment with color in its fashion plates, which, while attractive, basically served to illustrate the editor's earliest comment that the black and white engravings were more carefully and elaborately finished. A. B. Durand was responsible for most of the engravings for the first few years of the *Companion*, and A. L. Dick was the principle engraver for the last few volumes. Such engravings were usually accompanied by a short poem or story to highlight the whole or a part of the picture. Ann S. Stephens wrote several of these short pieces as did Robert Hamilton and William Wallace.

Snowden was the principal editor throughout the *Companion's* history, but he seems to have had help from various other hands at different times. The terms that assistant editors served cannot be completely documented. Dramatist John Howard Payne helped to edit the July 1837 issue and presumably worked after that for a period; he left the country in 1842. Ann S. Stephens was apparently on the editorial board from November 1837 through April 1843. Henry F. Harrington served from approximately October 1838 through May 1843 and Frances S. Osgood from November 1839 through April 1843 (?). In May 1843, Lydia H. Sigourney and Emma C. Embury, both prolific *Companion* contributors, joined the editorial board. These two ladies saw their names printed on the title page of each volume; no other editors received such notice. These ladies served until April 1844. Poe reported that " 'Snowden pays his editresses $2 per week each for their names solely.' "[1] If Poe was correct it is rather obvious that Snowden had very definite ideas about what should and should not appear in his periodical.

In the "Editors' Column" would be found a note to the reader, reviews of New York stage productions, gossip about the actors and actresses, book reviews, and comments on coming attractions such as concerts in New York City. Here one could also find the descriptions of the ladies' fashions shown in the engravings.

One flaw in the *Companion* was the index at the end of each volume of six issues. The unique arrangement of these indexes, not to mention an occasional omission, makes them untrustworthy and remarkably frustrating to use. Each letter of the alphabet is followed by titles that are arranged in page number order; there is no alphabetical listing under each letter. Also, pieces that begin with *The*, such as Caroline Orne's "The Old Oak Chest" (starting on page 21 of volume 18), are listed under "T". Henry W. Herbert's "The Covenanter's Burial," starting on page 26 of volume 18, follows the Orne entry in the index.

In April 1844, Snowden reported that he had sold the *Companion* to a group referred to only as "a company of gentlemen" (20:317). He was apparently in great financial difficulty brought about by an unwise marketing technique. At its height of popularity in 1840, the *Companion* had 17,750 paying subscribers. It had many additional subscribers who refused to pay. Snowden did not insist on advance payment for the *Companion*. He would send the magazine to whoever requested it and send the bill later. Predictably, many people did not pay, so, in addition to publishing frequent pleas to subscribers to pay up, in October 1838 Snowden sent a Mr. Alexander Means into New York State on a collection tour. Snowden threatened, by May 1842, to start printing the names of delinquent subscribers on the cover of the *Companion*, and September 1842 found Snowden threatening to print the names of delinquents as a supplement to the magazine. But still so many did not pay when requested that by April 1843 Snowden admitted in the "Editors' Table" that he was owed over twenty thousand dollars. He followed this revelation by explaining why his accounts receivable were so high: "It is the duty of every subscriber to give notice at the office, *personally, or by letter post-paid*, if he desires the work stopped, and not to permit it to be forwarded to his address . . . after the year [subscription] has expired" (18:308). He had earlier written that "Persons receiving the *first* number of a *new volume* are considered as subscribers for the whole year, and payment will be insisted upon" (12:296). These two unsound business practices must have helped contribute to the *Companion*'s demise. The "company of gentlemen" could keep the magazine afloat only six months after they bought it in spite of such improvements as increasing the clarity of the print used for prose (but not the poetry) and adding color to the fashion engravings. Snowden did regain control of the periodical in October 1844 and did project a November number, but the history of the *Ladies' Companion* ended with the October 1844 issue.

Though the magazine is forgotten today, it was important enough in its time to earn a large readership and thus illustrate what readers of the 1830s and 1840s valued. Snowden himself deserves remembrance because he was a pioneer in his efforts to pay authors for their work and thus promote the spread of native American literature.

## Note

1. John Ward Ostrom, "Edgar A. Poe: His Income as Literary Entrepreneur." *Poe Studies* 15 (June 1982):3.

## Information Sources

BIBLIOGRAPHY:
Mott, Frank Luther. "*The Ladies' Companion*." *A History of American Magazines*, 4 vols. Cambridge, Mass.: Harvard University Press, 1938. 1:626–28.

Ostrom, John Ward. "Edgar A. Poe: His Income as Literary Entrepreneur." *Poe Studies* 15 (June 1982):1–7.

INDEXES: Each of the twenty-one volumes of the *Companion* includes an index, but each index is unreliable.

REPRINT EDITIONS: American Periodicals: Series II, 1800–1850. University Microfilms, Ann Arbor. Reels 738–40.

LOCATION SOURCES: A complete run is available at Smith College, Northhampton, Mass.; partial runs are widely available.

### Publication History

MAGAZINE TITLE AND TITLE CHANGES: *The Ladies' Companion, A Monthly Magazine; Devoted to Literature and the Fine Arts*, May 1834-April 1835. *The Ladies' Companion, A Monthly Magazine of Literature and the Arts; Embellished With Many Different Engravings, With Music Arranged for the Piano Forte, & c. & c.*, May 1835-April 1837. *The Ladies' Companion, A Monthly Magazine, Embracing Literature and the Arts, Embellished with Engravings, and Music Arranged for the Piano Forte, Guitar & c.*, May 1837-April 1838. *The Ladies' Companion. A Monthly Magazine, Embracing Every Department of Literature. Embellished With Original Engravings, and Music Arranged for the Piano-Forte, Guitar, & c.*, May 1838-October 1838. *The Ladies' Companion. A Monthly Magazine, Embracing Every Department of Literature. Embellished with Original Engravings, and Music Arranged for the Piano-Forte, Harp and Guitar*, November 1838-April 1843. *The Ladies' Companion, and Literary Expositor; A Monthly Magazine Embracing Every Department of Literature. Embellished with Original Engravings, and Music Arranged for the Piano Forte, Harp and Guitar*, May 1843-October 1844.

VOLUME AND ISSUE DATA: Volumes 1–20, May 1834-April 1844; new series, volume 1, May 1844-October 1844.

FREQUENCY OF PUBLICATION: Monthly.

PUBLISHERS: May 1834-April 1844: William W. Snowden, New York. May 1844-October 1844: Publishers called only "a company of gentlemen," New York.

EDITORS: Williiam W. Snowden, May 1834-October 1844; John Howard Payne, July 1837–1842?; Ann S. Stephens, November 1837?-April 1843?; Henry F. Harrington, October 1838?-April 1843?; Frances S. Osgood, November 1839-April 1843?; Lydia H. Sigourney, May 1843-April 1844; Emma C. Embury, May 1843-April 1844.

*Robert W. Weathersby, II*

# THE LAKESIDE MONTHLY

Although over sixty short-lived magazines had sprung up in young Chicago by about 1871, only one could lay some claim to providing a satisfactory frontier voice and publishing forum for scores of local writers, whose literary works had little or no chance in the then established Eastern magazines. Despite its burgeoning population and economic hustle, Chicago had little literary export capacity until after the Civil War. Even the opening of a Chicago branch of the

Western News Company in 1866 benefited East Coast publishers much more than their Midwestern counterparts, as only established publications with proven subscriptions were handled by that firm. For the Chicago entrepreneurial publisher setting out in magazine subscription, substantial upfront money had to be risked before the news companies would consider distributing local periodicals. Without advertising revenue, a magazine might need at least three or four years simply to stabilize its subscriber base without any thought of profit. First to prove its economic viability on a high literary level in Chicago was the *Lakeside Monthly*.

Begun in January of 1869 as the *Western Monthly* under the editorial supervision of H. V. Reed, this publication sought as its object the "Development of Western Intellect and Enterprise" (1: no. 1, front endpaper). Its early issues offered biographical sketches of prominent Westerners, poetry, essays, travelogues, and some natural science articles; book reviews were also included. Contributions from local writers were especially solicited, although an advertisement in the first issue also promised a column out of London by a travelling correspondent.

Reed was joined during the first few issues by Francis Fisher Browne, who rapidly became the sole editorial force behind the magazine's publication program. Born in Vermont but trained in the printing business of his father's western Massachusetts newspaper office, Browne had arrived in Chicago in 1867. His editorial talents, ambition, and quest for literary excellence propelled him to gain complete control of the young magazine (his name first appears in the imprint of the April 1869 issue). It was Browne who reshaped the journal by stressing literary contributions of sufficient merit to attract the attention of the Eastern literary circles. Quickly jettisoned were the early biographical snippets of local businessmen and manufacturers. A more dignified typographical layout was introduced, and (most significantly) a name change occurred that reflected less provincialism as the journal strove to expand its literary audience.

An advertising broadside appearing in the December 1870 issue announced the new name of the *Lakeside Monthly* (beginning with the January 1871 issue) and stressed that, although the magazine would "be no less distinctively a Western Publication than before," the title change reflected more accurately the future plans of its new organization, the Lakeside Publishing and Printing Company. That company, begun in 1864 by R. R. Donnelley and reorganized several times in the interim, had by 1870 undertaken a major recapitalization and was constructing its new Lakeside Building in Chicago. The firm foresaw the city as a new publishing center in the Midwest and correctly noted the increasing significance of Western writers and themes upon a broader American literary audience. Its increased financial and technical backing nicely matched Browne's aspirations of broadening the earlier "western" image of his struggling journal.

Circulation began to increase to about 9,000 in 1871 and reached its peak of 14,000 copies by 1873, with Lakeside Company production and marketing facilities (some production was also undertaken by a few other Chicago shops) promoting the increase and Browne continuing to maintain singlehandedly the editorial standards of the literary contributions. Not even the fire disruptions of October 1870 (a small in-house shop fire) and of the disastrous October 1871 Chicago fire could dampen the rising success of the new undertaking (despite the fact that both the old and newly constructed Donnelley buildings were destroyed in the latter conflagration and no issues of the *Lakeside Monthly* appeared in November and December of that year). Subscription prices rose to 35 cents per copy or four dollars annually (along with a larger number of contributions per issue), and local advertising revenues reached adequate levels such that the magazine could claim self-supporting status by 1873.

Disaster, however, struck in September of 1873 when the collapse of the great banking house of Jay Cooke precipitated the economic panic of 1873, a commercial depression that destroyed thousands of businesses. With its dependence upon much commercial printing and advertising, the Lakeside Company experienced severe shortfalls in revenue and dropping subscriptions and then began its production diversification into its directory business and (by 1875) the famed *Lakeside Library*. Browne, as both editor and business manager, could not endure the mounting pressures on the magazine, broke down physically, and was ordered out of the operation in early 1874 by his physician. With no qualified successor forthcoming, the final issue appeared in Feburary of that year; despite initial hopes for resuscitation and an offer for merger by *Scribner's Monthly** (rejected by Browne), the *Lakeside Monthly* ceased publishing totally. Browne later served briefly as literary editor for the weekly *Alliance* and edited the Chicago *Dial* (see *American Literary Magazines: The Twentieth Century*) for the McClurg Company until his death in 1913. (Founded in 1880 by Francis F. Browne, this *Dial* moved to New York in 1916, there to become a prominent modernist journal.)

That merger proposal itself reflected favorably upon the successful literary magazine that Browne had built into a potent medium for Midwestern literary output. Its critical style (Browne forced many revisions to be made by his contributors) and its pride in local writers caught the attention of many East Coast literary magazines, which began incorporating Western subjects and authors into their issues. An Eastern critic, reviewing the Chicago literary scene as late as 1893, could still begrudgingly admit that the *Lakeside Monthly* under Browne had assumed "high rank among the first-class magazines of the country."[1]

A glance through the contents of any given issue of the *Lakeside Monthly* confirms the local base of most of its contributors. Among the approximately twelve to fifteen articles per issue appeared literary and travel essays, a few short poems, and a section of book reviews. Local newspaper editors (George Putnam Upton, Frank Gilbert, and Benjamin F. Taylor), prominent clergymen (especially the Unitarian minister Robert Collyer), and college educators (David Hilton Wheeler of Northwestern and Edward P. Evans at the University of Michigan) contributed numerous essays during the life of the magazine. Historical popularizers such as Nathaniel Shotwell Dodge were also frequently represented. A substantial number of local women submitted articles, including many essays by Kate Doggett, who founded the Chicago Fortnightly Club in 1872, a literary salon for women. Very few of the poetical contributors achieved any fame, except for Joaquin Miller, the Indiana-born poet of the Far West, whose works began appearing during the final year of the magazine's existence.

Underscoring the local flavor of much of the writing was continued emphasis upon Chicago themes. This tendency was especially reflected in three issues devoted exclusively to both the literary and commercial activity of the city. The January 1872 issue analyzed the effects of the fire upon the economic and aesthetic progress of the city, while in the anniversary issue of the fire (October 1872) essayists concentrated upon the restoration of the city. Near the end of the magazine the October 1873 issue devoted much space to Chicago's influence upon various groups within its social structure, including comments on the city's literary circles and an essay by Simeon Gilbert entitled "The Chicago of the Reader," which addressed the role played by books and magazines in the city.

## Note

1. William Morton Payne, "Literary Chicago," *The New England Magazine*, n.s. 7 (1893):693.

## Information Sources

BIBLIOGRAPHY:

Manuscript materials: Francis Fisher Browne Papers, the Newberry Library, Chicago.

Donnelley, Gaylord. "The Beginning: 1864–1874" and "A Decade of Reorganization: 1874–1883." *The Donnelley Printer* (Spring 1965):38–44, and (Summer 1965):30–33.

Duncan, Hugh Dalziel. *The Rise of Chicago as a Literary Center from 1885 to 1920; a Sociological Essay in American Culture*. Totowa, N.J.: The Bedminster Press, 1964. Esp. pp. 42–46, 50–51.

Fleming, Herbert E. *Magazines of a Market-Metropolis, Being a History of the Literary Periodicals and Literary Interests of Chicago*. Chicago: University of Chicago Press, 1906. A reprint of papers entitled "The Literary Interests of Chicago" from *The American Journal of Sociology*, vols. 11 and 12.

"Francis Fisher Browne 1843–1913." *The Dial* 54, no. 647 (1 June 1913), 437–41.

Lewis, Lloyd. "Francis Fisher Browne." *The Newberry Library Bulletin*, no. 2 (September 1945):23–36.

"The Life-Story of a Magazine." *The Dial* 54, no. 648 (16 June 1913), 489–92.

Mott, Frank Luther. *A History of American Magazines*. 4 vols. Cambridge, Mass.: Belknap Press of Harvard University Press, 1938. 3:51–54.

Payne, William Morton. "Literary Chicago." *The New England Magazine*, n.s. 7 (1893): 683–700.

Pierce, Bessie Louise. *A History of Chicago*. Vol. 2: *From Town to City 1848–1871*. Vol. 3: *The Rise of a Modern City, 1871–1893*. Chicago: University of Chicago Press, 1940, 1957.

Shaver, Muriel. "Francis Fisher Browne." *Dictionary of American Biography* (1929).

Williams, Kenny J. *Prairie Voices: a Literary History of Chicago from the Frontier to 1893*. Nashville: Townsend Press, 1980.

INDEXES: None.
REPRINT EDITIONS: Microform: University Microfilms International.
LOCATION SOURCES: Complete runs: Newberry Library, Chicago Public Library,
    Library of Congress, New York Public Library.

## Publication History

MAGAZINE TITLE AND TITLE CHANGES: *The Western Monthly, Devoted to Lit-
    erature, Biography, and the Interests of the West*, 1869–1870. *The Lakeside
    Monthly*, 1871-February 1874.
VOLUME AND ISSUE DATA: Volume 1, number 1-volume 11, number 62 (January
    1869-February 1874). No issues for volume 4, number 21 (October 1870), volume
    6, numbers 35–36 (November-December 1871), volume 10, number 60 (December
    1873). A "Holiday no. 1873/4" appeared as volume 11, number 61 (January
    1874).
FREQUENCY: Monthly.
PUBLISHERS: January-March 1869: Reed & Tuttle, Chicago. April-December 1869:
    Reed, Browne & Co. January-December 1870: Western Monthly Company. Jan-
    uary-March 1871: Lakeside Publishing Co. April-October 1871: Reed, Browne
    & Co. January-September 1872: University Publishing Co. October-December
    1872: J. J. Spalding & Co. January 1873-February 1874: F. F. Browne & Co.
EDITORS: H. V. Reed, January-March 1869; Francis Fisher Browne, April (?) 1869-
    February 1874.

*Michael Hackenberg*

## THE LAND OF SUNSHINE

During the last quarter of the nineteenth century, the publishing industry in
Southern California concentrated primarily on the dissemination of materials
promoting the region's growth. Although occasionally a magazine of relatively
broad appeal such as the *Southern California Horticulturalist* (later renamed the
*Rural Californian*), which began in 1877, would appear, much more common
were pamphlets and brochures designed to lure prospective residents and investors to the commercial and agricultural opportunities offered by the booming
economy of Southern California.[1] Seemingly such a publishing milieu would be
inauspicious for the development of a periodical with goals beyond boosterism.
In fact, for the first half year of its existence, the *Land of Sunshine* was little
more than a forum for promotionalism. But after Charles Fletcher Lummis took
over as editor in 1895 and until he relinquished editorial responsibilities over a
decade later, this Los Angeles-based monthly enjoyed genuine stature as a mirror
of culture in Southern California and the Southwest. The *Land of Sunshine*,
which Lummis rechristened *Out West* in 1902, preserved a regional identity
while eschewing much of the unrestrained boosterism that characterized most
contemporary publishing ventures in Southern California.

The original conception for the *Land of Sunshine* was largely the work of Charles D. Willard, a Los Angeles newspaperman who had participated in the brief run of the *Pacific Monthly*, a Southern California magazine that had appeared irregularly in the late 1880s and early 1890s. Willard's talent for and interest in promoting the growth of Los Angeles and its environs resulted in his taking the position of secretary of the city's Chamber of Commerce in the 1890s.[2] Joined by Frank A. Pattee, who remained the magazine's nominal publisher until 1902, and by Harry Brook, an Englishman who had written a promotional tract entitled *The Land of Sunshine*, Willard launched a monthly magazine for "readers both here and in the East, among travelers, health seekers, and intending settlers." This editorial statement from the first issue, that for June 1894, continued, "The Land of Sunshine will be made . . . a reality rather than a dream, through the pages of this journal" (1:12). The contents of the magazine's early numbers reflect its goal of selling the region, for it featured laudatory articles on the commercial advantages of life in Southern California illustrated with plenty of appealing photographs. Fortunately for the magazine's place in American publishing history, though, Willard found his duties as Chamber of Commerce secretary too demanding to allow sufficient time for editing the *Land of Sunshine*. He turned to a friend and fellow journalist, Charles F. Lummis, who assumed the editorship with the January 1895 issue.

Lummis had attained celebrity status ten years earlier when he arrived in Los Angeles after making the 3,500-mile journey from Ohio on foot. His weekly letters to the *Los Angeles Times* had kept readers abreast of his progress, and when he reached his Southern California destination on 1 February 1885, he received a festive welcome. For awhile he served as city editor for the *Times* and then as the newspaper's on-the-scene correspondent in Arizona during the Apache outbreak of 1886. When his health failed in 1888, Lummis convalesced in New Mexico, where he became interested in the archaeology and ethnology of the Southwest. During the early 1890s, these interests, augmented by his association with the scientist Adolph Bandelier, with whom he made an expedition to Peru, resulted in a spate of books that brought Loomis a modicum of literary fame.[3] Thus, he was well known in Los Angeles publishing circles when Willard persuaded him to become editor of the *Land of Sunshine*.

The effects of Lummis's editorship were immediately apparent. Not only did the January 1895 issue contain a serious essay on Spanish influences in the New World and a poem by Lummis, but he also articulated an editorial policy that directed the *Land of Sunshine* away from narrowly economic promotionalism. In an early editorial Lummis argued that the magazine should place increasing emphasis on cultural and intellectual life in its region, which he extended beyond Southern California to include the Southwest. He asserted, "No equal area in the United States has so great a variety of interests for all minds" (2:21–22-January). Clearly boosterism would continue to characterize the magazine under Lummis, but commerce would not be the central concern as it had been under Willard. The breadth of topics treated in the *Land of Sunshine* reflected the "variety of interests" mentioned in Lummis's editorial. Published articles treated history, art, archaeology, ethnology, local and national affairs, and natural science. Moreover, Lummis took care to include at least one short story and some poetry in each issue. At the base of every published piece lay the magazine's regional focus, for virtually all articles, short stories, and poems dealt in some way with Southern California or the Southwest. Almost every author whose work appeared in the *Land of Sunshine* resided in or had travelled extensively in the region.

A typical issue of the magazine included at least one article of serious intent dealing with a historical or scientific topic. Another couple of articles would be lighter in tone, usually offering descriptions of people, places, or events in California and the Southwest. Photographs would accompany the articles, and frequently a photographic essay would appear, perhaps illustrating one of the region's scenic wonders such as the Petrified Forest in Arizona. One or two short stories and a like number of poems would probably be included. Several regular features appeared in each issue. One page was devoted to the activities— usually with a plea for financial contributions—of the Landmarks Club, an organization founded by Lummis to assist in restoring historic Franciscan missions that survived from California's Spanish days. An editorial section, "In the Lion's Den," allowed Lummis to discourse at some length on various matters that concerned him. Most often he dealt with issues of local or regional concern, but he frequently turned his attention to national issues. Lummis was dismayed by what he perceived as imperialism on the part of the United States and used his editor's department to speak out against the Spanish-American War and other manifestations of this imperialism. Finally, each issue of the *Land of Sunshine* contained a book review section, "That Which Is Written," which featured evaluations of volumes relating to Southern California and the Southwest.

Lummis himself was the chief contributor to the magazine. He wrote "In the Lion's Den" and most of the book reviews (until Charles Amadon Moody took over that task in the early 1900s), and almost every issue contained one of his articles or poems. Therefore, the *Land of Sunshine* reflected the editor's interests to a high degree. Lummis used the magazine to crusade for various causes that he championed, particularly the need to save the historic missions from destruction and an even more compelling need to ensure that the rights of the region's Native American inhabitants were secured. With the *Land of Sunshine* as a forum, Lummis and the Landmarks Club were able to raise sufficient funds to preserve significant portions of several Southern California missions, including San Juan Capistrano. The editor's partisanship on behalf of the Indians regularly characterized his commentaries in "In the Lion's Den." Moreover, beginning in the August 1899 issue of the *Land of Sunshine*, he wrote a seven-part series entitled "My Brother's Keeper," which fulminated against government treatment of Indians. His efforts resulted in the formation of the Sequoyah League for Indian rights, which addressed such matters as land allotment and ownership and the corruption-ridden Indian School System.[4] On a nonpolemical level, the

*Land of Sunshine* manifested Lummis's interests in archaeology and ethnology. More than any other periodical in the late nineteenth and early twentieth centuries, Lummis's magazine helped to popularize the discoveries of scholars in American Indian culture and prehistory.

The ultimate significance of the *Land of Sunshine*, though, was that Lummis managed to attract other writers, many of them first rate, who shared his regional commitment. In 1897, Lummis conceived a plan for creating a syndicate of Western writers who would regularly publish on Western topics in his magazine. Writers who joined the syndicate would become stockholders in the magazine and be designated contributing editors.[5] Over the next few years some of the most important names in Western letters appeared on the magazine's masthead. These included poets Joaquin Miller and Edwin Markham; ethnologists Washington Matthews and Frederick Webb Hodge; historian Theodore Hittel; and David Starr Jordan, president of Stanford University. Although these writers contributed to the magazine more occasionally than their status as contributing editors would imply, their acquiescence to Lummis's plan for a syndicate proved that his magazine had become more than a promotional publication or a polemical tract for the editor's crusades. Meanwhile, Lummis was helping to launch the careers of several regional writers of merit by publishing their early works and by encouraging them to maintain the regional focus in their writing. For example, Mary Austin, whose essays and short stories later came to characterize California and the Southwest, actually moved to Los Angeles so she could be near Lummis. The *Land of Sunshine* also published the first poetry and fiction of Eugene Manlove Rhodes, a New Mexico cowboy who became an important literary interpreter of the Southwest during the first quarter of the twentieth century. Another Lummis protégée was Sharlott Hall, who became official historian of Arizona Territory after working as the magazine's associate editor. Lummis also published the work of Jack London and Robinson Jeffers, although his influence on them as writers was probably minimal or nonexistent. The *Land of Sunshine* encouraged Western artists and illustrators as well. Gutzon Borglum designed the magazine's mountain lion logo, and Maynard Dixon and William Keith joined the contributors' syndicate.

With the January 1902 issue, Lummis engineered a final break with the magazine's origins as a promotional publication. He adopted a new title, *Out West, A Magazine of the Old Pacific and the New*, which he believed to reflect the magazine's regional identity without the boosterism connected with the older title. The new name heralded no change in editorial policy, but Lummis perceived that the magazine had definitely outgrown its origins. However, shortly after the name change, his interest in the periodical began to wane. In 1905 Lummis was appointed librarian for the city of Los Angeles, a position that consumed a good deal of time. Two years later the Southwest Society of the Archaeological Institute of America, which Lummis had founded in 1903, incorporated the Southwest Museum, a project to which the *Out West* editor devoted considerable energy for the next few years.[6] In July 1905, Lummis had promoted Charles Amadon

Moody from assistant editor to joint editor of *Out West*, and in November 1909 Lummis's name disappeared from the masthead completely. Thereafter the magazine languished under a succession of short-term editors. It ceased to appear regularly in June 1917 but was partially resurrected in May 1923 when it merged with the *Overland Monthly*,* the San Francisco-based periodical that had also deteriorated from its former preeminence. The result of this merger, *Overland Monthly and Out West Magazine*, disappeared completely in July 1935.

Charles F. Lummis's intent was for the magazine to be "local in color, yet broad in sympathy."[7] His careful maintenance of the regional focus of the *Land of Sunshine* faced two major obstacles, which he successfully surmounted. On the one hand, the temptation to allow the magazine to lapse into the commercial boosterism of its origins was ever present, especially given Lummis's own enthusiasm for Southern California and the Southwest. While the magazine definitely extolled the virtues of the region, Lummis did not permit the sort of uncritical praise that would characterize a purely promotional publication. At the same time, Lummis encountered the problem of sustaining high literary quality while not violating regional identity. By contributing heavily to each issue himself and by luring the region's top writers through such devices as the contributors' syndicate, he ensured that both quality and regionalism would be preserved. The result of his efforts was, in Lawrence Clark Powell's terms, a "California Classic,"[8] a model regional periodical that used a geographical locus as foundation for significant literary endeavor.

### Notes

1. Franklin Walker, *A Literary History of Southern California* (Berkeley: University of California Press, 1950), pp. 97–117.

2. Edwin R. Bingham, *Charles F. Lummis: Editor of the Southwest* (1955; rpt., Westport, Connecticut: Greenwood, 1973), pp. 38–40.

3. Bingham, pp. 3–20; Turbese Lummis Fiske and Keith Lummis, *Charles F. Lummis: The Man and His West* (Norman: University of Oklahoma Press, 1975), pp. 15–86; and Robert E. Fleming, *Charles F. Lummis*, Western Writers Series No. 50 (Boise, Idaho: Boise State University, 1981), pp. 6–11.

4. Dudley Gordon, *Charles F. Lummis: Crusader in Corduroy* (Los Angeles: Cultural Assets Press, 1972), passim.

5. Bingham, pp. 72–73.

6. Bingham, pp. 23–28; Fiske and Lummis, pp. 122–30; and Fleming, pp. 49–50.

7. Lawrence Clark Powell, "Charles Fletcher Lummis and *The Land of Sunshine*," *Westways* 62, no. 1 (January 1970):22.

8. Lawrence Clark Powell, *California Classics, The Creative Literature of the Golden State: Essays on the Books and Their Writers* (Santa Barbara: Capra Press, 1971), pp. 292–304.

### Information Sources

BIBLIOGRAPHY:

Bingham, Edwin R. *Charles F. Lummis: Editor of the Southwest*. 1955; rpt., Westport, Connecticut: Greenwood, 1973.

Fiske, Turbese Lummis, and Keith Lummis. *Charles F. Lummis: The Man and His West*. Norman: University of Oklahoma Press, 1975.

Fleming, Robert E. *Charles F. Lummis*. Western Writers Series No. 50. Boise, Idaho: Boise State University, 1981.

Gordon, Dudley. *Charles F. Lummis: Crusader in Corduroy*. Los Angeles: Cultural Assets Press, 1972.

James, George Wharton. "Founding of the Overland Monthly and History of the Out West Magazine." *Overland Monthly and Out West Magazine* 81 (May 1923):7–11.

Powell, Lawrence Clark. "Charles Fletcher Lummis and *The Land of Sunshine*." *Westways* 62, no. 1 (January 1970):20–23, 35; reprinted in *California Classics, The Creative Literature of the Golden State: Essays on the Books and Their Writers* (Santa Barbara: Capra Press, 1971). Pp. 292–304.

Walker, Franklin. *A Literary History of Southern California*. Berkeley: University of California Press, 1950.

INDEXES: None.

REPRINT EDITIONS: University Microfilms International.

LOCATION SOURCES: Widely available.

## Publication History

MAGAZINE TITLE AND TITLE CHANGES: *The Land of Sunshine, a Southern California Magazine*, June 1894-December 1901. *Out West, a Magazine of the Old Pacific and the New*, January 1902-September 1914. *Out West*, October 1914-June 1917. *Overland Monthly and Out West Magazine*, May 1923-July 1935.

VOLUME AND ISSUE DATA: Volumes 1–46, June 1894-June 1917; volume 81, May-December 1923; volumes 82–93, January 1924-July 1935 (after merger with *Overland Monthly* the San Francisco periodical's volume numbering was assumed).

FREQUENCY OF PUBLICATION: Monthly.

PUBLISHERS: 1894–1902: Frank A. Pattee, Los Angeles. 1903: Out West Company, Los Angeles. 1904–1917: Out West Magazine Company, Los Angeles. 1923: D. R. Lloyd and Mabel Moffitt, San Francisco. 1924–1925: Harry Noyes Pratt and Mabel Moffitt, San Francisco. 1925: V. V. Taylor and Hamilton Wayne, San Francisco. 1925–1926: B. Virginia Lee and S. Bert Cooksley, San Francisco. 1926–1928: R. D. Hart, San Francisco. 1928–1935: Arthur H. Chamberlain, Los Angeles.

EDITORS: Charles D. Willard, 1894; Charles F. Lummis, 1895–1905; Charles F. Lummis and Charles Amadon Moody, 1905–1909; Charles F. Edholm, 1909–1910; George Wharton James, 1910–1914; George Vail Steep, 1915; Lannie Haynes Martin and Cruse Carriell, 1915–1917; D. R. Lloyd and Mabel Moffitt, 1923; Harry Noyes Pratt and Mabel Moffitt, 1924–1925; V. V. Taylor and Hamilton Wayne, 1925; B. Virginia Lee and S. Bert Cooksley, 1925–1926; R. D. Hart, 1926–1928; Arthur H. Chamberlain, 1928–1935.

*William M. Clements*

# THE LARK

The English *Yellow Book* was the most influential and the most notorious of the "little magazines" that flourished during the 1890s. Published by John Lane, it featured the work of writers and artists including Aubrey Beardsley and Max Beerbohm. Although the *Chap-Book** was the best known of its American counterparts and imitators—the "fadazines," "freak periodicals," "ephemeral bibelots," and "dinkey magazines"—it is the *Lark* that has been judged "the most delightful," "the most brilliant and most original of the lot."[1] The *Lark* was essentially a one-man magazine, fastidiously edited and for the most part written, at times even illustrated, by its editor, Gelett Burgess, a Bostonian by birth, a draughtsman by training (MIT), and an antic iconoclast by temperament. He and the handful of men and women who contributed to the pages of the *Lark* dubbed themselves *Les Jeunes* in order to underscore their philosophy of youthful insouciance and to play upon the idea of their presumed decadence (*jaune* being the French word for yellow). *Les Jeunes* included many of fin-de-siècle San Francisco's most promising writers and artists: Bruce Porter, a respected muralist and maker of stained glass windows; architect Willis Polk; painters Ernest Peixotto, Maynard Dixon, and Florence Lundborg; popular fiction writer Juliet Wilbor Tompkins; Japanese poet Yone Noguchi; Porter Garnett, decorative artist and later a distinguished typographer; and, of course, Burgess, who went on to become a popular novelist and humorist.

From such diverse talents came a truly unusual journal that lasted well beyond the single-number expectations of its founding editors, Burgess and Porter. The twenty-five issues of the *Lark* (including the valedictory *Epi-Lark*) were printed on brownish bamboo paper so thin that after the first seven issues it was decided to print on only one side of each sheet, so embedded with bamboo chips as to occasionally cause the type to break, and so brittle as to make the original copies something of an endangered species. There was an abundance of facetious pseudonyms but few signed articles and no table of contents. The sixteen pages were left unnumbered and the lines of type unjustified, partly as an economy measure, partly because the editor "thought it artistic and degage."[2] Burgess chose his typographer, Charles Murdock, for his dedication to aesthetics, and the *Lark*'s typeface, Caslon Old Style, for its antiquated appearance. The publisher, William Doxey (who signed on in the middle of the first press run and underwrote Burgess's shoestring venture), was well known for his commitment to local authors and his awareness of current literary trends in England and on the Continent.[3]

The studied unconventionality of the *Lark*'s contents and physical appearance was characteristic of the little magazine movement in general, which in America took the form of a revolt against both "the dictates of the old literary tribunals" (no. 25) and the newer mass-circulation magazines such as *Munsey's* and *McClure's*. Like the literary realists (William Dean Howells in his *Criticism and Fiction*, for example, or Henry James in "The Art of Fiction"), the *Lark* demanded freedom for the artist. "Why try to set the limitations of art?" Porter asked in the first issue; "Why try to say what the poet may not sing—what the painter may not paint?" Opposing conventionality in any form, the *Lark* prized three qualities above all others: sincerity, spontaneity, and gaiety. Thus the publication of children's drawings under the title "Some Phases of Primitive Art" as examples of perfect and unrestrained aesthetic expression (no. 1).

The *Lark* was not simply another little magazine following in the *Yellow Book*'s *épater les bourgeoisie* footsteps, however, it was, as well, a critical response to—even in some respects a parody of—the little magazines themselves. Burgess began the *Lark* because he did not believe that the "new note of personal expression then becoming dominant" rang true in either the *Yellow Book* or the *Chap-Book*, both of which he and Porter found too sophisticated and stiff.[4] Preferring to "make an *original* contribution," they decided to eschew criticism, "timeliness," local color, and the fashionable decadence of Beardsley, the *Yellow Book*, and its imitators.[5] The *Lark*, they decided, would be unfashionably optimistic and light-hearted. Their rallying cry was not the decadent's "art for art's sake" but, instead, "Life is a bigger thing than art" (no. 1).

The same claim was being made by the literary realists, including the San Francisco novelist Frank Norris, one of Burgess's closest friends during the *Lark* years. Burgess, however, had little interest in either the methods or the goals of literary realism. For *Les Jeunes*, life was not a matter of Howellsian fidelity to the facts of contemporary existence; it was a matter of romance. Their aim was not to expose the reality of city life, as Norris was doing in his rewrite of *McTeague: A Story of San Francisco*; rather, it was to free man from "Care" so that he could partake of life in its more Western, which to Burgess and Porter meant romantic, aspect. As they explained in their *Epi-Lark*, "The absolute lack of realism in the *Lark*'s pages, needs no explanation other than the personal taste of its writers, moved to Romanticism by age, climate, and by all the traditions of Western life."

Humor served as the chief means by which the *Lark* sought to free its readers from the fetters of "Care," and the magazine's method and goal are summed up in its title. The cover poster, artwork, essays, verse, and stories all took the form of "larking," mixing "whimsicality with serious purpose," joi de vivre with "hilarious prank."[6] Only rarely is the serious purpose overtly stated, as in "The Diverting of Deighton," which concerns a minister who "had never committed an indiscretion. He had never gone larking," and as a result did not know that virtue is nothing more than a social varnish (no. 4). At times—Burgess's protestations to the contrary—the humor has a distinctly satirical edge; in most cases, however, the satire is directed at the *Lark* and its contributors in an effort to keep the magazine light and carefree. Usually the humor is intended solely as a spontaneous expression of gaiety, as in Burgess's own joyously funny and utterly nonsensical drawings, stories, and poems, especially his boneless humanoid Goops, "The Peculiar History of the Chewing-Gum Man," and his oft-parodied purple-cow quatrain: "I never saw a purple cow / I never hope to see one / But I can tell you anyhow / I'd rather see than be one" (no. 1). In the whimsical world of the *Lark*, one generally finds "sense in the guise of absurdity, and nonsense masquerading as reason" (no. 15). Nonsense, Burgess believed, is the purest type of humor and therefore the most universal—closest to spontaneous expression and furthest from conventionality. Significantly, Burgess claimed that his own nonsense works were too contrived and the most difficult to write: "I had to go into nothingness, divest my mind of every idea . . . and then perceive what came, like a wild thing, unused to reason, logic, creeping into my mind, and then tie it up with words."[7]

Once the *Lark*'s character had established itself, Burgess was reluctant to tamper with it, preferring to try out new ideas in altogether different magazines, spin-offs of the original *Lark*. When he wanted a forum for certain literary matters, he created *Phyllida; or, the Milkmaid*, in imitation of Addison and Steele's *Spectator* (two issues printed; a third set in type but never published); and when he wanted "to out-Lark the *Lark* itself," he fashioned the outrageous *Le Petit Journal des Refusées*, "the *reductio ad absurdum* of the 'freak' journal," trapezoidal in shape, sixteen cents in price, and printed on wallpaper (only one issue of this "quarterly" ever appeared).[8]

As noted earlier, Burgess and Porter assumed the *Lark* would have a similarly brief life. Although it was at first largely ignored or ridiculed in San Francisco, Burgess's $100 venture in the little magazine movement began to attract a fairly substantial, even national audience. As a result, press runs increased from 3,000 to 5,000 copies per issue (a sizable number even when compared with the more imposing circulation figures for the *Chap-Book*: 12,206 in 1894; 16,500 two years later).[9] To help meet expenses (the *Lark* did eventually become profitable), the single-copy price of all issues of the second volume was raised from five to ten cents, and "advertising wings" (in the form of an outer wrapper) were added to help "the Lark to fly another year." Readers were advised that the wings "may be easily removed from the Body of the Lark" if they "do not prove sufficiently amusing" (no. 12). But like the rest of the *Lark*, many of the advertisements were nothing but amusing. In addition to a number of generally straightforward ads for Doxey's and Harrold, Belsher and Allen, the furniture company for which Burgess did some design work, and a good many self-advertisements—approving notices about the *Lark* drawn from various newspapers and magazines—there were quite a few "pseudo-ads," as Oscar Lewis has called them, "clever take-offs on the style and methods of the copy writers of the day."[10]

The humor and irreverence of these "pseudo-ads" were, of course, characteristic of the magazine Burgess and Porter claimed would have "no more serious intention than to be gay" (no. 1). That gaiety, along with the youthful enthusiasm and carefree spontaneity that went with it, was both the *Lark*'s strength and its weakness. When Burgess decided to "kill" the magazine after its two-year run and while it was still "in its full freshness," one San Francisco weekly, the *Wasp**, danced on its grave, damning it as "a freak journal started by a few writers of very limited capacity who thought to make a short trip to fame by the most tawdry devices."[11] In another of the city's weeklies, the *Wave**, Frank Norris was more generous, though still critical, in his assessment of the magazine and its contributors; surveying the local literary talent, Norris pointed out that

"Yes, there are Les Jeunes, and the Lark was delightful—delightful fooling, but there's a graver note and a more virile to be sounded. Les Jeunes can do better than the Lark."[12] Burgess eventually came to agree with Norris, claiming *Les Jeunes* had been "too spontaneous . . . too enthusiastic" and had "dwelt overlong with gayety."[13]

Despite his later reservations, the *Lark* did play a significant role in establishing San Francisco as the literary center of the Pacific Coast. Moreover, the magazine and its contributors were involved in a larger cultural movement that was then only barely understood. As Burgess accurately prophesied in the May 1897 *Epi-Lark*, "When the history of Nineteenth Century decadence is written, these tiny eruptions of revolt [such as the *Lark*], these pamphleteering amateurs [such as *Les Jeunes*] cannot remain unnoticed, for their outbreak was a symptom of the discontent of the times." In such a light Burgess's nonsense becomes something of a forerunner of Dadaist art and the melancholy jesting of such recent writers as Donald Barthelme and Woody Allen.

## Notes

1. Sidney Kramer, *A History of Stone & Kimball and Herbert S. Stone & Co.* (Chicago: University of Chicago Press, 1940), p. 38; Claude Bragdon, "The Purple Cow Period," *Bookman* 69 (July 1929):475–78.

2. Carolyn Wells, "What a Lark," *Colophon* 22 (1931), part 8, n. pag.

3. Oscar Lewis, *Bay Window Bohemia* (Garden City, N.Y.: Doubleday & Co., 1956), pp. 80–81.

4. Gelett Burgess, *Bayside Bohemia: Fin de Siecle San Francisco & Its Little Magazines*, ed. James D. Hart (San Francisco: Book Club of California, 1954), p. 19.

5. Quoted in Wells.

6. Burgess, pp. 20, vi.

7. Quoted in Wells.

8. Burgess, pp. 25–33.

9. Wells; Kramer, p. 53.

10. Lewis, p. 85.

11. Wells; quoted in Gelett Burgess, *Behind the Scenes*, ed. Joseph M. Backus (San Francisco: Book Club of California, 1968), p. 13.

12. Frank Norris, "An Opening for Novelists: Great Opportunities for Fiction Writers in San Francisco," *The Wave* 16 (22 May 1897):7.

13. Burgess, p. 24.

## Information Sources

BIBLIOGRAPHY:

Backus, Joseph M. "Gelett Burgess: A Biography of the Man Who Wrote 'The Purple Cow.' " Ph.D. diss., University of California, Berkeley, 1961.

Bragdon, Claude. "The Purple Cow Period: The 'Dinkey Magazines' That Caught the Spirit of the Nineties." *Bookman* 69 (1929):475–78.

Burgess, Gelett. *Bayside Bohemia: Fin de Siecle San Francisco & Its Little Magazines*. Intro. James D. Hart. San Francisco: Book Club of California, 1954.

————. *Behind the Scenes: Glimpses of Fin de Siecle San Francisco*. Ed. Joseph M. Backus. San Francisco: Book Club of California, 1968.

Kramer, Sidney. *A History of Stone & Kimball and Herbert S. Stone & Co*. Chicago: University of Chicago Press, 1940.

Lewis, Oscar. *Bay Window Bohemia: The Brilliant Artistic World of Gaslit San Francisco*. Garden City, N.Y.: Doubleday & Co., 1956.

Starr, Kevin. *Americans and the California Dream 1850–1915*. New York: Oxford University Press, 1973.

Towne, Charles Hanson. "The One-Man Magazines." *The American Mercury* 63 (1946):104–8.

Wells, Carolyn. "What a Lark!" *Colophon* 22 (1931):Part 8 N. pag.

Ziff, Larzer. *The American 1890s: The Life and Times of a Lost Generation*. New York: Viking Press, 1966.

INDEXES: Published as supplements following each volume.
REPRINT EDITIONS: None.
LOCATION SOURCES: Widely available.

## Publication History

MAGAZINE TITLE AND TITLE CHANGES: *The Lark*; *Epi-Lark* (May 1897).
VOLUME AND ISSUE DATA: Volumes 1–2, May 1895-April 1897; *Epi-Lark* published May 1897.
FREQUENCY OF PUBLICATION: Monthly.
PUBLISHER: William Doxey, San Francisco.
EDITOR: Gelett Burgess.

*Robert A. Morace*


# LIFE

When John Ames Mitchell published the first issue of *Life* on 4 January 1883, he encountered an unpromising market for satirical magazines, especially for those with a literary bent. *Punchinello* and *Vanity Fair*, for example, had met with an early demise; *Our Continent* (see *The Continent**), for which Mitchell was illustrator before his own venture, was in weak financial condition. One initial difficulty was finding a printer willing to work with neophyte journalists to produce a competitor to the successful *Harper's Weekly*, *Puck*, and *Judge*. Guaranteed advance payment, Gilliss Brothers, accustomed to printing college magazines, agreed. The staff was assembled from a rising group of "university wits," as *Life*'s biographer Frank Luther Mott notes,[1] including Edward Sanford Martin, former editor of the *Harvard Lampoon*, who agreed to become literary editor, and Andrew Miller, also of Harvard, who became the first business manager.

Mitchell's plan was to produce a magazine that would become known for the quality of its satire and its illustrations. For this reason he decided to use the new zinc etching process, thereby achieving a lightness of touch and sophistication of line difficult to reproduce by the conventional wood engraving method.

As he writes in the jubilee issue published in January 1893, "For *Life*'s uses, such drawings, while being true to nature and clever artistically, must show a lightness of touch, an ease, brilliancy, and force of expression which are not demanded in other work. Moreover, a sense of humor, a playfulness, and a gentle exaggeration are indispensable to the perfect work." Much of the wit, then, was to be embodied in the graphics. The early cover design suggested not only the content but also the style and the point of view from which it was to be treated. The decorative border on top and left featured delicate roundels for society, literature, politics, and drama, all surmounted by the title embellished with a mascot cherub, an eagle, and the words "Americanus sum."

Initial circulation figures were erratic; it was nine months before the magazine stopped operating at a loss. After two years the circulation rose to 20,000, after seven years, to 50,000.[2] The rising figures reflect the development of the magazine's style, a mixture of the whimsical and sharply satirical, both furthered by the early influx of talent. Even by the end of the first year when Martin left the editorship for health reasons, Mitchell had attracted a fine group of illustrators, among them Francis Attwood, who specialized in monthly calendars embellished with figures of the day; Charles Kendrick, who became known as a skillful caricaturist; W. A. Rogers, who produced the bulk of *Life*'s covers and pictorial quips; and Oliver Herford, who drew "biographical primers" complete with verse. Perhaps the best known of *Life*'s illustrators was Charles Dana Gibson, whose first drawing appeared in 1887 and whose Gibson girl drawings of, as *Scribner's Magazine** puts it, "a woman of refinement and gentle breeding,"[3] became a cult in the 1890s.

*Life*'s literary content was never so far from the general public's point of view as to be elitist, primarily because of the liveliness of its writers. In 1884 John Kendrick Bangs came to *Life* as literary editor barely a year after graduating from Columbia University, where he edited the *Acta Columbiana*. He brought with him a witty perspective that became associated with the magazine's personality. Under the cognomen of Carlyle Smith, a pen name that represented both his literary and his middle-class leanings, he wrote columns, verse, and editorials. *Life* also attracted such lights as Robert Bridges (later the editor of *Scribner's Magazine* [see *American Literary Magazines: The Twentieth Century*]), who reviewed books as "Droch," and Henry A. Beers, who parodied contemporary novels. Brander Matthews, whom Mitchell had unsuccessfully approached as a partner in *Life*, wrote penetrating drama reviews. He was followed by Alfred J. Cohen writing as "Alan Dale," and then, in 1888, by James S. Metcalfe.

In the years before World War I the magazine became known for certain popular crusades as well as for certain political and literary views. *Life*'s editors attacked vivisection, for example, with the same gusto that they entered the lists against the Theatrical Syndicate. Indeed, Metcalfe, the drama critic, was so outspoken against Mark Klaw and Abe Erlanger's theatrical booking monopoly that he provoked a libel suit against *Life*. While *Life* never espoused a political party—as did *Judge* and *Puck*, for example—it did, in a lighthearted way, sponsor

Cleveland in the elections of 1884 and 1888. It betrayed a more consistent attitude toward the person it considered the archenemy to democracy—Queen Victoria— but even here the plethora of caricatures and jokes that enlived the pages until her death in 1901 were more whimsical than Hogarthian. Victoria was pictured sitting on a tuffet next to a purring British lion; she was interviewed by *Life*'s cherub; she was caricatured as an apple seller, writer, and impoverished tourist. In most cases Mrs. Wettin, as she was dubbed, was treated as a somewhat eccentric matriarch to be honored more for her domestic than for her political talents.

*Life*'s running argument with Queen Victoria was symptomatic of a larger issue; despite their gentle approach, the editors were completely serious about their attack on "Anglomania," the term they used to describe an adherence to British ideas and behavior to the detriment of the American ideal. Their attitude toward literary history and the contemporary movement of realism was a re- flection of their belief not only that the old way was to be defended but that the readership's literary taste needed to be educated so that a truly American style might be developed. For this reason "standard" authors such as William Make- peace Thackeray and Anthony Trollope were held up as models, while modern experimentalists such as Henry James and William Dean Howells were accused of deflecting the true course of the novel because their works lacked plot, focused on psychology, and provided unsatisfying endings. Amid the proliferation of satirical columns, parodies, and quips, the reviewer Robert Bridges alone quietly assessed James's importance in the development of narrative point of view.[4]

*Life* made capital of a number of social trends at the turn of the century. Always kindly toward the "summer girl," *Life* became more so as bathing suit styles changed. The 1893 Chicago exposition and the automobile both increased advertising revenues considerably. Before World War I, *Life*'s circulation had grown to 150,000. As Mott notes, *Life* had become more successful than ever.[5] After Mitchell's death in 1918, Charles Dana Gibson bought the magazine for one million dollars. However, while broadening its appeal with its new columns, among them "Neighborhood News" featuring homey anecdotes from other cit- ies, *Life* lost the individuality as well as the flavor of lighthearted intellectualism imposed upon it by the "university wits."

In 1929 the character of the magazine exhibited a decided change under the editorship of Norman Anthony, a former editor of *Judge*. In the "era of bootleg and legs," of the radio and the moving pictures, of the fluctuating stock market, *Life* adopted the flappers and circulation rose. Indeed, nonsubscription sales doubled, until Gibson forcibly reminded his editor of *Life*'s tradition of good taste and gentle satire. The consequent falling circulation figures were premon- itory of a greater crash. Its advertising seriously affected by the depression, *Life* became a monthly in 1932. Other factors were also at work. Competition from the *New Yorker* (see *American Literary Magazines*: *The Twentieth Century*), which came onto the field in 1925, and from *Esquire*, founded in 1933, attracted some of *Life*'s readership. Finally, in October 1936 *Life* was bought by Time

Inc. The subscription list was sold to *Judge*, while the name was given to the new twentieth-century *Life*. As Mott notes, ''in its last decade it was a strayed reveler, having lost its way in a confused world.''[6]

## Notes

1. Frank Luther Mott, *A History of American Magazines, 1885–1905* (Cambridge, Mass.: Belknap Press of Harvard University Press, 1957), Pp. 561. See also John Flautz, *Life: The Gentle Satirist* (Bowling Green, Ohio: Bowling Green University Popular Press, 1972).

2. Mott, pp. 558, 561.

3. Mott, p. 563.

4. E. R. Hagemann, '' 'Unexpected Light in Shady Places': Henry James and *Life*, 1883–1916,'' *Western Humanities Review* 24 (1970):250.

5. Mott, p. 565.

6. Mott, p. 568.

## Information Sources

BIBLIOGRAPHY:
Bangs, Francis Hyde. *John Kendrick Bangs: Humorist of the Nineties*. New York: Knopf, 1941.
Flautz, John. *Life: The Gentle Satirist*. Bowling Green, Ohio: Bowling Green University Popular Press, 1972.
Hagemann, E. R. ''*Life* Buffets (and Comforts) Henry James, 1883–1916.'' *Publications of the Bibliographic Society of America* 62 (1968):207–25.
———. '' 'Unexpected Light in Shady Places': Henry James and *Life*, 1883–1916.'' *Western Humanities Review* 24 (1970):241–50.
Marks, Patricia. ''Tennyson, One of *Life*'s 'Beauties.' '' *Tennyson Research Bulletin* 3, no. 2 (1979):80–82.
———. ''Mrs. Wettin Meets a Chum: *Life*'s View of Victoria, 1883–1901.'' *Journal of American Culture* 3 (1980):80–91.
Mott, Frank Luther. *A History of American Magazines, 1885–1905*. Cambridge, Mass.: Belknap Press of Harvard University Press, 1957. Pp. 556–68.
INDEXES: None.
REPRINT EDITION: American Periodicals: Series III, 1850–1900. University Microfilms, Ann Arbor. Reels 500–532.
LOCATION SOURCES: Widely available.

## Publication History

MAGAZINE TITLE AND TITLE CHANGES: *Life*.
VOLUME AND ISSUE DATA: Volumes 1–98, 1883–1931 (semiannual volumes); volumes 99–103, 1932–1936 (annual volumes).
FREQUENCY OF PUBLICATION: Weekly, 1883–1931; monthly, 1932–1936.
PUBLISHERS: 1883–1918: John Ames Mitchell and Andrew Miller. 1918–1919: Andrew Miller. 1920–1928: Charles Dana Gibson. 1928–1936: Clair Maxwell.
EDITORS: John Ames Mitchell, 1883–1918; Andrew Miller and James S. Metcalfe, 1918–1919; Edward Sanford Martin, 1920–1922; Louis Evan Shipman, 1922–

1924; Robert E. Sherwood, 1924–1928; Norman Anthony, 1929–1930; Bolton Mallory, 1930–1932; George T. Eggleston, 1932–1936.

*Patricia Marks*

## THE LITERARY AND SCIENTIFIC REPOSITORY, AND CRITICAL REVIEW

The *Literary and Scientific Repository, and Critical Review* got off to a rather inauspicious start in July 1820 with an issue that contained but three original articles filling only 36 of the 280 pages. The bulk of the issue was made up of fourteen articles selected from well-known British magazines: the *Monthly Review*, the *Edinburgh Review*, *Blackwood's Edinburgh Magazine*, the *New Monthly Magazine*, the *Quarterly Review*, the *Eclectic Review*, and the *British Critic*. Though these pieces were well chosen and contained material of interest to American readers—an article on Charles Brockden Brown and Washington Irving and reviews of Irving's *Sketch Book*, James Kirke Paulding's *The Backwoodsman*, and John Howard Payne's *Brutus, or The Fall of Tarquin*—it was hardly an impressive beginning for a magazine that sought to emulate the great British quarterlies. The second issue was only slightly better. Six original articles were offset by eight from the British magazines, and unlike the arrangement in the first issue, the original material was placed after the selections from the British journals. In all, only about a fourth of the first volume was written by American authors, and none of the original articles can be called in any sense literary.

Despite the paucity of original material in the first two issues, Charles K. Gardner, the editor, was able to establish his journal at once as the defender of the United States against attacks in the British magazines. The *Repository* appeared during the time of strong nationalistic feeling after the War of 1812, and Gardner, who had distinguished himself in that conflict and rose to the rank of colonel, threw his journal immediately into the "paper war" with the British press. The focus of attention was *An Appeal to the Judgement of Great Britain* by Robert Walsh, Jr. (1819). A patriotic book, it rehearsed the long history of British-American relations and defended the United States against the malicious attacks that British magazines, most particularly the *Edinburgh* and *Quarterly* reviews, leveled against it. Gardner selected British reviews of Walsh's book and reprinted them in his journal, one from the *British Critic* in the first issue, and one from the *Edinburgh Review* in the second. He also wrote a long rejoinder to the latter, defending *An Appeal* and affirming American support of its position. By these means Gardner brought his review squarely into the center of a major intellectual controversy.

Gardner's efforts alone were not enough, however, to insure the journal's success. Shortly after the second issue was published in October 1820, a circular appeared in New York seeking support for the quarterly, and some of the most influential citizens wrote letters in its behalf, including the mayor, Cadwallader

D. Colden; the editor of the *Evening Post*, William Coleman; and, among others, such well-known New Yorkers as Brockholst Livingston, Samuel L. Mitchell, and Gulian C. Verplanck.[1] The response must have been satisfactory, for the third issue appeared in January 1821. Two-thirds of the material in this issue still derived from British journals, but the patriotic theme continued with a circular letter describing the founding of the American Academy of Language and Belles Lettres, and the issue included important work by two aspiring American authors. James Fenimore Cooper reviewed Thomas Clark's *Naval History of the United States*, and Fitz-Greene Halleck contributed his now famous poem, "Lines on the late Doctor Joseph R. Drake." With the fourth issue (April 1821) original articles for the first time made up more than half the journal, a proportion that would continue in the four issues of the succeeding year.

In addition to Cooper, long a friend and once his "brother-officer . . . at Oswego in the winter of 1808–1809,"[2] Gardner turned to military men and well-known New Yorkers for articles and reviews. Among them, apparently, were General John Armstrong, Colonel William MacRae, Major John A. Dix, James Renwick, James De Peyster Ogden, and Benjamin U. Coles. All were influential men of their times. Armstrong, in particular, had served as Madison's secretary of war, and Dix was later to become secretary of the treasury.[3] Such men, as one might expect, contributed articles and reviews on a wide range of subjects: law, politics, economics, science, agriculture, travel, history, biography, and literature. Some of the books reviewed were of special interest to American readers, most notably Carlo Botta's history of the American Revolution, General James Wilkinson's *Memoirs of My Own Times*, and, of course, Clark's *Naval History* and Walsh's *An Appeal to the Judgment of Great Britain*. But others treated subjects that transcended national boundaries: accounts of the whale fisheries, of Arctic exploration, of travels in Europe, and even of farming in England and the corn laws of France. The *Repository* was a journal of wide intellectual appeal.

It also published a number of literary articles. Half were on British subjects and included some on older works of literature. In the April 1821 issue, for example, the leading articles were on Spenser's *Faerie Queene* and on two of Shakespeare's characters, Pistol and Sir Andrew Aguecheek. The following issue, for July, included a discussion of some English plays of the sixteenth and seventeenth centuries, most notably *The Four P's*, *Gammer Gurton's Needle*, *A Woman Killed with Kindness*, and *The Duchess of Malfi*. Other articles in both issues, however, discussed contemporary books and writers. The April issue contained an article on Maria Edgeworth and her father, Richard L. Edgeworth, and reviewed two recent British novels: Charles Robert Maturin's *Melmoth the Wanderer*, which the critic disliked because of its blasphemies and horror, and Sir Walter Scott's *Kenilworth*, which the reviewer thought inferior to such other novels by Scott as *Waverley*, *Old Mortality*, and *Ivanhoe*. In July the journal reviewed Byron's most recent works, *The Prophecy of Dante* and *Marino Faliero*. These two issues, for April and July 1821, were the most heavily literary that the *Repository* published and contained all its original essays on well-known British authors.

The journal noticed only a few American literary works. These were not banner years for American literature, which was only just entering its first important nineteenth-century phase, and most of the books reviewed are remembered today solely for their historical importance. The *Repository* printed only British reviews of *The Sketch Book*, and it missed the edition of William Cullen Bryant's poems that appeared in 1821. But it did review Cooper's *Precaution*, "the last American novel," in an article that paired it with *Melmoth the Wanderer*, which the critic thought inferior. He preferred "the solidity and healthful spirit of" Cooper's book to the "feverish imaginations" of Maturin's (2:364,371). The American poetry reviewed included *Yamoyden*, by James W. Eastburn and Robert C. Sands; the second, enlarged edition of *Fanny*, by Fitz-Greene Halleck; and a now forgotten poem, *Ontwa, The Son of the Forest*. Only in its final issue, for May 1822, did the *Repository* publish truly important reviews of American literary works. That number contained discussions of Catharine Maria Sedgwick's *A New-England Tale* and Washington Irving's *Bracebridge Hall*, articles that are especially significant not only for the books reviewed but also for the reviewer, who may have been James Fenimore Cooper.

When Cooper began to write for Gardner's journal, he was not the famous novelist we know today. *Precaution* had just been published when his first review, on Clark's *Naval History*, appeared in January 1821, and he was to publish reviews of two more books, *An Examination of the New Tariff Proposed by the Hon. Henry Baldwin* (April 1821) and William Scoresby's *An Account of the Arctic Regions* (July 1821), before the publication of *The Spy* in December established his reputation as a novelist. A fourth review, of Sir William Edward Parry's *Journal of a Voyage for the Discovery of a North-West Passage*, appeared the following month (January 1822). These four reviews, all certainly by Cooper, reveal his fine critical mind, his wide general knowledge, his understanding of significant issues, and his ability to write closely reasoned argument. He dismisses Clark's book as of little value, writes instead an essay on American naval action in the War of 1812, and makes an appeal for a strong American navy; he agrees with the author of *An Examination* that the proposed new tariff was not in the national interest; and he writes informed and appreciative reviews of Scoresby and Parry's accounts of their Arctic adventures.

From the literary point of view, of course, the reviews of Sedgwick and Irving's books are more significant, for they reveal contemporary critical attitudes toward the new American literature. The reviewer praises Sedgwick's *New-England Tale* for its use of native materials, the domestic manners of the New Englanders. It is the kind of book, he believes, that will give both pleasure and moral benefit to a wide popular audience. Irving's new book, however, does not fare so well at the hands of its reviewer. Though he approached *Bracebridge Hall* with great anticipation and was favorably disposed to its author as an American and a New Yorker, his expectations were not met. He admits that the book is without question a considerable one, but he sees it as no advance over *The Sketch Book*, and he is especially critical of the judicious praise of the British that he detects in it. Since the "idiosyncrasies of style and thought" in these two reviews "are identical with those Cooper elsewhere displays," James F. Beard has "tentatively assigned" them both to him,[4] but even without the attribution, they would demand our attention because of the critical principles they apply.

By the time these articles appeared, the *Repository* was already in trouble. The two final numbers were delayed, and, in a note appended to the last issue, Gardner pleaded his "absence, from unavoidable private avocations," as his excuse for the delay. He pointed out, however, that "the quantity of matter" had not been lessened, that subscribers had "four months' literature, instead of three," and that there was, therefore, "no loss of value . . . in respect to quantity," and "a gain with respect to time." He trusted that "the number of his original Articles in this No., and the diligence displayed in the Selections [would] be his evidence" (4:508). The issue was indeed a substantial one, but it proved to be the last. As Beard observes, "New York was not yet ready to support a quarterly. The list of subscribers probably contained fewer than five hundred names; and the roster of more or less regular contributors . . . fewer than a dozen."[5] Gardner was forced to suspend publication with the issue of May 1822. The *Literary and Scientific Repository* undoubtedly deserved, as Mott has suggested, "a longer life,"[6] but it did not receive the support that could have sustained it.

## Notes

1. James F. Beard, Jr., "Introduction," *Early Critical Essays (1820–1822)* by James Fenimore Cooper (Gainesville, Fla.: Scholars' Facsimiles & Reprints, 1955), p. [ix].

2. *The Letters and Journals of James Fenimore Cooper*, 6 vols. ed. James Franklin Beard (Cambridge, Mass.: Harvard University Press, 1960–1968), I,96. See also *Early Critical Essays*, p. [viii].

3. *Early Critical Essays*, pp. [viii], [xiv].

4. *Early Critical Essays*, p. [xiii].

5. *Early Critical Essays*, p. [xiv].

6. Frank Luther Mott, "*The Literary and Scientific Repository*," *A History of American Magazines, 1741–1850* (New York: D. Appleton and Company, 1930), p. 314.

## Information Sources

BIBLIOGRAPHY:

Cooper, James Fenimore. *Early Critical Essays (1820–1822)*. Ed. James F. Beard, Jr. Gainesville, Fla.: Scholars' Facsimiles & Reprints, 1955.

*The Letters and Journals of James Fenimore Cooper*. 6 vols. Ed. James Franklin Beard. Cambridge, Mass.: Harvard University Press, 1960–1968.

Mott, Frank Luther. "*The Literary and Scientific Repository*." *A History of American Magazines, 1741–1850*. New York: D. Appleton and Company, 1930. Pp. 313– 14.

INDEXES: None.

REPRINT EDITIONS: American Periodicals: Series II, 1800–1850. University Microfilms, Ann Arbor. Reel 126.
LOCATION SOURCES: Widely available.

### Publication History

MAGAZINE TITLE AND TITLE CHANGES: *The Literary and Scientific Repository,
and Critical Review*.
VOLUME AND ISSUE DATA: Volumes 1–4, July 1820-May 1822.
FREQUENCY OF PUBLICATION: Quarterly.
PUBLISHERS: Volumes 1–2: Wiley & Halsted, New York. Volumes 3–4: Wiley and
Halsted, and C. S. Van Winkle, New York.
EDITOR: Charles K. Gardner.

*Donald A. Ringe*


## THE LITERARY GAZETTE: OR, JOURNAL OF CRITICISM, SCIENCE, AND THE ARTS. See THE ANALECTIC MAGAZINE


## THE LITERARY MAGAZINE, AND AMERICAN REGISTER

From April 1799 to December 1800, Charles Brockden Brown edited *The Monthly
Magazine, and American Review*\* in New York City. In January 1801, he
followed with the quarterly *American Review, and Literary Journal*. After this
journal likewise failed, Brown returned to Philadelphia and, in October 1803,
issued the first number of the *Literary Magazine*, and *American Register*. Not
surprisingly, in that first issue's "Editor's Address to the Public," Brown admits
that "many are the works of this kind which have risen and fallen in America,
and many of them have enjoyed but a brief existence"(1:3).

Nonetheless, Brown relied on his own experience and energy—"As I possess
nothing but zeal, I can promise to exert nothing else" (1:3)—to fill a void in
American letters: "there is not, at present, any other monthly publication in
America, and . . . a plan of this kind, if well conducted, cannot fail of being
highly conducive to amusement and instruction"(1:6).

What Brown planned was a compendium of reviews, essays, and notes similar
to his earlier *Monthly Magazine*: "Useful information and rational amusement
being his [the editor's] objects, he will not scruple to collect materials from all
quarters. He will ransack the newest foreign publications, and extract from them
whatever can serve his purpose. He will not forget that a work, which solicits
the attention of many readers, must build its claim on the variety as well as the
copiousness of its contents"(1:5).

Brown thus styled the *Literary Magazine* as "an American Review," a "history of passing events," and a "repository of all those signal incidents in private

life, which mark the character of the age, and excite the liveliest curiosity"
(1:5).

That first issue included Brown's own "Extracts from a Student's Diary" (on
Swift's polite conversation, fire, yellow fever, authorship, etc.); "Critical Notices"; "Communications" (brief essays on "The Ascendancy of the French
Language" and "The Eloquence of Pitt, Fox and Erskine"); reviews of D'Is-
raeli's poems, W. P. Young's *A View of South Carolina*, and James Abercrom-
bie's educational treatise on eloquence and natural history; original and selected
poetry; "Summary of Politics"; "Remarkable Occurrences"; "Anecdotes" (on
"Republican Festivals in France" and the British population); and "Miscellaneous Extracts." Although Brown would later add a section on "Literary and
Philosophical Intelligence" (which in turn would become "Literary, Philosophical, and Agricultural Intelligence"), he maintained the arrangement of this first
issue for the remaining numbers. The *Literary Magazine* would feature a number
of biographical sketches, travel and familiar essays, and some fiction. In fact,
Brown published his own "Memoirs of Carwin the Biloquist" beginning with
the November 1803 issue. There were fewer book reviews than had appeared
in the *Monthly Magazine* and a very limited amount of original poetry. One
notable poem is Alexander Wilson's "A Rural Walk" in the August 1804 issue.

Contributors to the *Literary Magazine* included John Blair Linn (Philadelphia
minister and Brown's brother-in-law), John E. Hall (lawyer and author of the
"Adversaria" and "Melange" series in the magazine), and, apparently, Bishop
William White of Philadelphia.[1] As Mott notes, "about half the contents of the
eight semiannual volumes seems to be original"[2]—and typically Brown wrote
most of the original material. "You will find but a single communication in it
[the June 1804 issue]—all the rest original prose, I have been obliged to supply
myself—for which I am sorry, for the sake of the credit of the work as well as
of my own ease."[3] As early as his "Editor's Address" of the first issue, Brown
stated that "I trust merely to the zeal and liberality of my friends to supply me"
(1:3). In the November 1803 number he makes another of his many appeals for
assistance:

> The Editor of this work having engaged in a very arduous undertaking, is
> conscious that his success will in great measure depend upon the literary
> aid which he shall receive from his friends, and the Literati of this country.
> He, therefore, most earnestly solicits from the man of science, and from
> the polite scholar, the contributions of their genius and leisure; while the
> Editor performs all that is in his power, he hopes that they will not permit
> another attempt to extend abroad useful knowledge to perish (1:158).

Unfortunately, few answered Brown's call, and the *Literary Magazine* suffered
throughout its life from a lack of contributors.

Nonetheless, Brown maintained the scope and variety of topics in monthly
issues through December 1807. The April 1805 issue, for example, began with

an article on a "New Invention: An Improvement on Steam Engines," and followed with essays on "Naval Transactions in the Mediterranean," "Chinese Gardening," "Dr. Gall's System of Craniology," "Shakespeare's Similes," "Kotan Husbandry," "Dean Swift," and others. In addition, Hall's "Adversaria" column and the "Latest News, Literary and Philosophical" also appeared, as did a letter from "N.W." to the editor on "The Duties of an Editor": "I am a warm well-wisher to your work, and am sorry that it does not seem to have attained a popularity and circulation quite as extensive as I think it merits" (3:301).

Brown thus was fighting battles to secure both subscribers and contributors. He won neither and found that he could not continue supplying so much of the magazine's material. In January 1807, he announced a forthcoming prospectus for a semiannual *American Register*. No proposals appeared, but in November 1807, the first volume (for 1806–1807) was published. Brown then ceased publication of the *Literary Magazine* to turn his full attention to the *American Register, or General Repository of History, Politics and Science*.

## Notes

1. David Lee Clark in *Charles Brockden Brown: Pioneer Voice of America* (Durham, N.C.: Duke University Press, 1952), p. 223, suggests that White was the author of an "unusually liberal and forward-looking" essay on education in volume eight, August-October 1807.

2. Frank Luther Mott, *A History of American Magazines, 1741–1850* (Cambridge, Mass.: Harvard University Press, 1938), p. 221.

3. Quoted in Mott, p. 220.

## Information Sources

BIBLIOGRAPHY:

Clark, David Lee. *Charles Brockden Brown: Pioneer Voice of America*. Durham, N.C.: Duke University Press, 1952.

Dunlap, William. *The Life of Charles Brockden Brown*. Philadelphia: James P. Parke, 1815.

Marble, Annie Russell. *Heralds of American Literature: A Group of Patriot Writers of the Revolutionary and National Periods*. Chicago: University of Chicago Press, 1907.

Mott, Frank Luther. *A History of American Magazines, 1741–1850*. Cambridge, Mass.: Harvard University Press, 1930. Pp. 218–22.

INDEXES: No complete index available, but the *Literary Magazine* is indexed in Poole's and is included in Jayne Kribbs, *An Annotated Bibliography of American Literary Periodicals 1741–1850* (Boston: G. K. Hall, 1977), p. 89.

REPRINT EDITIONS: American Periodicals: Series II, 1800–1850. University Microfilms, Ann Arbor. Reels 22–23.

LOCATION SOURCES: Widely available.

## Publication History

MAGAZINE TITLE AND TITLE CHANGES: *The Literary Magazine, and American Register*.

VOLUME AND ISSUE DATA: Volumes 1–8, March 1803-December 1807.
FREQUENCY OF PUBLICATION: Monthly.
PUBLISHERS: 1803–1806: John Conrad & Co., Philadelphia. 1807: T. & G. Palmer,
    Philadelphia.
EDITOR: Charles Brockden Brown.

*Timothy K. Conley*

# THE LITERARY WORLD

Turning the pages of the *Literary World*, one is immediately impressed by the broad coverage offered in the New York weekly journal, especially during the first and third periods of its life when it was edited by Evert A. Duyckinck early in 1847, then by him and his brother, George Long Duyckinck, from late 1848 until its demise at the end of 1853; Cornelius Mathews apparently had a hand in the editing during at least part of 1853.[1] The *World*'s articles and reviews provided readers with timely and literate information about developments in publishing. And for most of its existence, particularly under the Duyckincks, it paid attention not only to period fiction, poetry, and nonfictional prose (history, science, medicine, and travel, for example) but to the struggling American drama and even music and art. This rich fare was spiced with columns about inhabitants of the world it monitored and on developments abroad, especially in the British Isles and on the Continent. The reading public was informed, and the publishing industry that sought its favor was provided a forum in its inexpensive advertising pages in addition to book notices. At a time when the distinctions between journalism and literary criticism were not as sharp as they were to become and when periodicals in democratic America could hope for a broad audience they could reach without patronizing, the *World* often blended a newsletter tone with intellectually responsible commentary. The high quality of the *Literary World*'s contents was as unique for the period as its omnibus coverage. Striving for fairness and objectivity and most often attaining these high standards, the *World*'s editors eschewed puffing. They developed and practiced solid principles of literary and cultural criticism even as they strove to encourage and promote American literature. This is all the more remarkable if one judges magazines of the period as cursory and the condition of American culture as sterile and stagnant. While harsh, these conclusions are probably not far off, as has been shown by an analysis of periodicals published in January 1847, the month prior to the birth of the *World*.[2] Wide-ranging in its coverage and focused in its editorial standards, the *Literary World* earned a well-deserved, high reputation and was almost universally respected and saluted in its day and has been since.

Its reputation was naturally due to the standards and purposes of the publishers and editors. Evert Duyckinck was hired by the first publishers, John Wiley, George P. Putnam, and Daniel Appleton. The "Articles of Agreement," signed by all of them on 15 January 1847, defined the sixteen-page quarto journal's appearance and contents quite explicitly. Modeled on the London *Athenaeum*, it was "to be made up of Reviews, Extracts from new books, essays, sketches, miscellany, register of new publications, booksellers intelligence and advertisements." Duyckinck's legal copy, which survives, granted him "the exclusive editorial charge of the journal,"[3] an agreement the publishers were to breach in fewer than three months after the journal's debut on 6 February 1847. Their ostensible reason for firing him was allowing Cornelius Mathews to contribute despite their insistence that he not.[4] Mathews, a vigorous and often strident nationalist, embraced strong commitments to the related causes of international copyright and autochthonous literature that Duyckinck had shared for some time. The Young America group of which they were part had championed these and related causes for almost a decade, and Duyckinck himself as well as other members of his circle expressed their strong opinions in the major essays of the first twelve issues, published through 24 April 1847. Crusading and reform-minded, promoting cultural nationalism, and bringing to bear an occasionally rigorous morality (for example, on sexual matters),[5] Duyckinck created an air of intense, high-minded integrity that hangs over the twelve issues. This is in marked contrast to the relatively bland and neutral editorial reign of Charles Fenno Hoffman who edited seventy-four issues of the *Literary World* from 8 May 1847 to 30 September 1848—the 1 May 1847 issue was transitional and lacked an editor of record. Committed to critical objectivity but prone to cultivate and encourage authors, Hoffman articulated his critical beliefs and standards clearly in his first issue, 8 May 1847 (14:315). His conservatism on the question of nationalism (no. 17:387) is a marked contrast to the *World*'s strong views under Duyckinck; while he was not reactionary, one has a sense of hearing from a different quarter in the period dialogue to define the relationship between emerging American culture and that of its parent, Europe. Hoffman, who was born in 1806, almost a decade before Evert A. Duyckinck, came to the *Literary World* with a substantial journalistic background, having been a contributor and/or editor for periodicals such as the *Knickerbocker*,* the *American Monthly*,* and Greeley's *New-Yorker*. Already an established and productive writer, he was a New York literatus who even maintained close ties with the first generation of Knickerbocker writers headed by Irving. Nevertheless, the *World* under Hoffman was significantly less provocative than it had been, and its quality—never high for a sustained period—diminished perceptibly toward the end of his tenure.[6]

Prior to owning and editing the *Literary World*, Evert A. Duyckinck was well established in New York literary and cultural circles. Among his credits were a number of journal articles and editorial work on *Arcturus** and the *United States Magazine and Democratic Review.** When he began the *World* in 1847, he was editing two series of books for Wiley and Putnam. A prime mover in the Young America group of authors, editors, and critics and close to many writers of the period, he was to concentrate on composing nonfictional prose on historical subjects during the last twenty years of his career. The *World* was his younger brother George's first important literary venture. He was to join Evert in compiling and composing their most important work, the *Cyclopaedia of American Literature* and before his death at thirty-nine wrote other prose, including four biographies. The *Literary World* began its full flowering when the Duyckincks purchased it and assumed editorial control on 7 October 1848, control they held until it closed on the last day of 1853. Promising immediately to relieve the "monotony" into which the *World* had slipped,[7] their program for renewal depended upon improving standards and taste by promoting the best the contemporary literary scene had to offer while rigorously judging that which did not measure up. Although the journal is perhaps best remembered for printing Melville's "Hawthorne and His Mosses" in the summer of 1850, his assertive nationalism is actually not in keeping with the *Literary World's* more moderate position on the nationalism issue and other concerns during the Duyckincks' more-than-five-year tenure as publisher.[8] This more temperate posture, a marked contrast to the vigor, even occasional stridency, of the first twelve issues of 1847, is not, however, so tame and neutral as to render the magazine the sort of saccharine affair it had been under Hoffman. Rather, one senses a more mature recognition and acceptance of the cultural heritage at the same time the editors search for the best. This is to be expected from editors as well educated, widely read, and culturally aware as the Duyckincks. Their drift toward moderation is analogous to Emerson's retreat from the boasts of his earlier writings. Among a number of statements, one might grasp the new posture by focusing on the retrospectives on nationalism and critical reviewing in the *World*'s last issue (361:355, 357). It is all the more telling when one considers that George and Cornelius Mathews edited the paper during the last part of 1853 and perhaps longer. Mathews, the insistent nationalist, would appear to have changed considerably, judging by the *World*'s style and tone in its later years.

Perhaps it was this very integrity, this controlled and deliberate guiding of the journal, that was key in earning its solid reputation. Among the foreign and American authors who were noticed or whose works were reviewed, we find the Brontes, Coleridge, James Fenimore Cooper, Emerson, Sara Payson Willis (Fanny Fern), Margaret Fuller, Goethe, Oliver Wendell Holmes, Leigh Hunt, Irving, Caroline Kirkland, Melville, Theodore Parker, Francis Parkman, James Kirke Paulding, Catherine Marie Sedgwick, Lydia Hunt Sigourney, E.D.E.N. Southworth, Harriet Beecher Stowe, Thackeray, Thoreau, and N. P. Willis. The heterodoxy of even this short list testifies to the *World*'s comprehensiveness. But these authors were not merely promoted or puffed. For example, however enthusiastic Evert A. Duyckinck may have been about Hawthorne's writing— proposing and nurturing *Mosses from an Old Manse* (1846)[9] and then printing Melville's belated and laudatory review of it—he, his brother, or some other reviewer expressed increasingly serious reservations about *The Scarlet Letter*, *The House of the Seven Gables*, and *The Blithedale Romance*. And though the *World* and its editors had been central in the early stages of Melville's career (his name was mentioned about twice as frequently as any other American author's)[10] the reviews of *Moby-Dick* and *Pierre* were significantly less than laudatory. Striving for a higher, honest critical tone, the Duyckincks most often refused to compromise their standards, even to accommodate a friend or protégé whose work failed to measure up. Their rigor is further in evidence when we note their harsh treatment of Dickens, whose work they and their circle had enjoyed enormously a decade before. Scattered through the miscellany sections of the Duyckinck Family Papers at the New York Public Library is correspondence, almost all of it unsolicited, proposing topics for the journal; some proposals were accepted, most appear not to have been. Since reviews were very rarely signed and even the authors of longer articles were infrequently recorded, identifying writers is difficult if not impossible. Among better-known American contributors, however, the *World* could list William Cullen Bryant, Margaret Fuller, Hawthorne, Holmes, Irving, Caroline Kirkland, Longfellow, Melville, Poe, William Gilmore Simms, and Whittier. Pieces by British and other foreign authors were almost without exception reprints from foreign publications. While Hoffman appears to have done virtually all the writing himself, the Duyckincks had their cadre that, at the time they were preparing to publish their newly acquired *Holden's Dollar Magazine*,* in 1851, led George to comment that "We have long had such an overflow of excellent matter for the Literary World that we have often thought of starting a magazine."[11] Their success in attracting such a galaxy and such volume was due to their prominence on the literary scene and the solid reputations they enjoyed. They were, however, worn out from the constant pressure of weekly deadlines and probably anxious to move on to other pursuits.

The *Literary World* did not attract enough subscribers. And unable to compensate sufficiently with its advertising revenues, it finally closed because of the financial distress it had long suffered. With a circulation that hovered around 1,500 to 1,750,[12] it was evidently unprofitable from at least 1852 and probably earlier, although records are incomplete. A few weeks after it closed, the printer, Robert Craighead, wrote to remind the Duyckincks that their outstanding bill was $3,200.[13] The Duyckincks wanted to produce a quality journal that also made a profit, reasonable goals also sought by their predecessors, Appleton, Wiley, and Putnam, who apparently had also found the *Literary World* unprofitable and whose partnership was about to end when they sold it to the Duyckincks. David Davidson was involved in the business end of the journal from late 1848, when he began serving as the *World*'s London agent;[14] after coming to the United States in 1850, he became even more absorbed in promoting its financial well being.[15] But George, who was much closer to its finances than Evert, was clearly dubious about continuing beyond 1852, and even Davidson was not entirely satisfied with the results of the canvassing trip he had taken late in the year. He was sufficiently optimistic, however, to look toward prospects in 1853 as being no worse than the 1852 performance. But the hopes did not materialize, and by the end of the venture disappointment and frustration had bred nastiness and bitterness as George Duyckinck and Davidson settled accounts and argued about who was responsible for paying the magazine's debts.[16] The

*World* gave way to those with greater resources and popular appeal, journals of moderate circulation such as *Harper's\** and *Putnam's\** and the emerging big sellers.

## Notes

1. David Davidson, Letter to George Long Duyckinck, 10 February 1854, Duyckinck Family Papers, New York Public Library, Box 46. All letters and manuscripts cited are from this collection; hereafter, only box or volume numbers will be offered.

Reviewing the *Literary World*'s fiscal situation to challenge George's claim that Davidson was liable for the journal's debts, he notes that "you would not allow my name to appear on it [the *World*] and . . . I had nothing to say as to the editing of it that being engrossed by yourself and Mr. Mathews." Mathews, a key figure in the Duyckinck crowd, had a reputation as one of the most abrasive, vocal, and insistent of the Young America group, of which the Duyckincks were part. Davidson, for whatever reasons, was another who did not share the Duyckincks' enthusiasm for Mathews and his work. Davidson continues: "I object to this old man of the mountain [Mathews was not yet forty] tied around my neck whether I will or no."

Davidson's language invites the speculation that Evert Duyckinck was editing the *World* during part of its last year—even more, perhaps—in name only. It certainly suggests he was less involved than has been assumed and establishes Mathews's involvement at least in the journal's waning days.

For more about Davidson's background and connection with the *World*, see the last paragraph and note 15, below.

2. Daniel Arthur Wells, "Evert Duyckinck's *Literary World*, 1847–1853: Its Views and Reviews of American Literature," (Ph.D. diss., Duke University, 1972), pp. 38–52.

3. Articles of Agreement MS, Box 35; the bottom right corner of this document has been torn away, leaving only Appleton's and Duyckinck's partial signatures and the "W" in Wiley and Putnam.

4. Consult, among other items, A Card MS, Box 35, where Duyckinck identifies Mathews's contributions as a principal issue, and D. Appleton and Wiley and Putnam, Letter to Evert A. Duyckinck, 21 April 1847, Box 18, as well as H[enry] P[anton?], Letter to Evert A. Duyckinck, 23 April 1847. See also George Edwin Mize, "The Contributions of Evert A. Duyckinck to the Cultural Development of Nineteenth Century America," (Ph.D. diss. New York University, 1954), pp. 117–22; and Donald Yannella and Kathleen M. Yannella, "Evert A. Duyckinck's 'Diary: May 20-November 8, 1847,' " in *Studies in the American Renaissance, 1978*, ed. Joel Myerson (Boston: Twayne, 1978), p. 208.

5. Wells, pp. 56–57, 346; and Mize, p. 140.

6. Wells, pp. 90, 103, 107–9, 119, 134, and 139.

7. Wells, p. 140.

8. Wells, pp. 346–48.

9. John J. McDonald, " 'The Old Manse' and Its Mosses: The Inception and Development of *Mosses from an Old Manse*," *Texas Studies in Language and Literature* 16 (1974):77–108.

10. Wells, p. 151.

11. George Long Duyckinck, Letter to Joann Miller, 8 February 1851, Box 49. Notice that he is apparently distinguishing between a "magazine" (which, among other characteristics, would reach a wider audience) and a journal or, as he and his brother often referred to it, a paper or newspaper.

12. Account Book, Vol. 37, p. 4. This 481-page book for 1847–1852 is one of the handful of documents scattered throughout the collection that contain information about the *Literary World*'s finances, circulation, contents, and contributors. Other useful items are: a ledger identifying subscribers principally from New York City; a subscription book, alphabetically arranged, for 1847–1851; a miscellaneous papers folder containing subscriptions information; a bound ledger listing subscribers, contributors, and the contents of numbers 127–66, as well as a list of books received between 1847 and 1849; a list of authors and articles for numbers 137–40 (all in Box 59); a pocket memorandum for 1850 which contains the contents for numbers 155–79 and an erratic and spotty record of accounts for January and February of that year; a pocket memorandum for 1851 which lists contents for numbers 216–36 (both in Box 25); a pocket memorandum book for 1851, listing contents for numbers 239–58; a pocket memorandum, undated, itemizing the contents of numbers 324–39 (both in Box 59); and a collection of manuscripts by various authors (Box 57), evidently the location of the Melville manuscripts when they were discovered.

13. Robert Craighead, Letter to Evert A. and George L. Duyckinck, 12 January 1854, Box 46. Other documents that suggest it was faltering as early as 1852 are: an undated memorandum in George L. Duyckinck's hand, which notes that the *World* had realized some $4,000 in advertising revenues, probably in 1852, and called upon advertisers to establish a budget for buying space at the same time it promised, or threatened, that the magazine would fold if income were not sufficient; and a second memorandum, dated 15 October 1852, noting a plan to increase advertising revenues and, as a result, increase the journal's size and influence. Mention is also made that David Davidson would take over the publishing department, apparently the business end as distinct from the editorial (both in Box 53).

14. David Davidson, Letters to George L. Duyckinck, 10 [?] November 1848 and 6 February 1849, Box 46.

15. David Davidson, Letters to George L. Duyckinck, 5 February 1852, 24 June 1852, and 10 February 1854. In the last two months of 1852 Davidson went on the road to solicit business, journeying to Boston and Providence, across New York State to Buffalo, and to Washington, D. C. (David Davidson, Letters to George L. Duyckinck, 9 November 1852, 22 November 1852, and 18 December 1852, all in Box 46). Washington Irving, one of the patriarchs of the New York literary scene, had befriended Davidson from boyhood and helped get him a position with Wiley and Putnam in 1841. He was working for them in 1843 (Washington Irving, *Letters: 1839–1845*, ed. Ralph M. Aderman, Herbert L. Kleinfield, and Jennifer S. Banks [Boston: Twayne, 1982], 3:156, 488, and 588), and after returning to London, reappeared in the United States in October 1850 "as an Agent for the London Booksellers" (Irving, *Letters: 1846–1859*, ed. Ralph M. Aderman, Herbert L. Kleinfield, and Jennifer S. Banks [Boston: Twayne, 1982], 4:229) and was well established at the *Literary World* by late 1851 (Irving, *Letters*, 4:272).

16. David Davidson, Letter to George L. Duyckinck, 10 February 1854, Box 46.

## Information Sources

BIBLIOGRAPHY:
Bergman, Harriet F. "Charles Fenno Hoffman." *Dictionary of Literary Biography: Antebellum Writers in New York and the South*. Ed. Joel Myerson. Detroit: Gale Research, 1979. Pp. 159–60.
Miller, Perry. *The Raven and the Whale: The War of Words and Wits in the Era of Poe and Melville*. New York: Harcourt, Brace, 1956.
Mize, George Edwin. "The Contributions of Evert A. Duyckinck to the Cultural Development of Nineteenth Century America." Ph.D. diss., New York University, 1954.
Mott, Frank Luther. "*The Literary World*." *A History of American Magazines, 1741–1850*. Cambridge, Mass.: The Belknap Press of Harvard University Press, 1957. Pp. 766–68.
Wells, Daniel Arthur. "Evert Duyckinck's *Literary World*, 1847–1853: Its Views and Reviews of American Literature." Ph.D. diss., Duke University, 1972.
Yannella, Donald. "Evert Augustus Duyckinck" and "George Long Duyckinck." *Dictionary of Literary Biography: Antebellum Writers in New York and the South*. Ed. Joel Myerson. Detroit: Gale Research, 1979. Pp. 101–9, 109–11.
INDEXES: Wells, Daniel A. "An Index to American Writers and Selected British Writers in Duyckinck's *Literary World*, 1847–1853." *Studies in the American Renaissance, 1978*. Ed. Joel Myerson. Boston: Twayne, 1978. Pp. 259–78; *The Literary Index to American Magazines, 1815–1865*. Metuchen, N.J.: Scarecrow Press, 1980.
REPRINT EDITIONS: American Periodicals: Series II, 1800–1850. University Microfilms, Ann Arbor. Reels 483–86.
LOCATION SOURCES: Widely available.

## Publication History

MAGAZINE TITLE AND TITLE CHANGES: *The Literary World: A Gazette for Authors, Readers, and Publishers*, 6 February 1847–29 January 1848. *The Literary World: A Journal of American and Foreign Literature, Science, and Art*, 5 February 1848–25 December 1852. *The Literary World*, 1 January 1853–31 December 1853.
VOLUME AND ISSUE DATA: Volumes 1–13, or numbers 1–361, 6 February 1847–31 December 1853.
FREQUENCY OF PUBLICATION: Weekly.
PUBLISHERS: 6 February 1847–30 September 1848: Osgood and Company, New York, the umbrella company in this venture for D. Appleton and the firm of Wiley and Putnam. 7 October 1848–31 December 1853: Evert A. and George L. Duyckinck.
EDITORS: Evert A. Duyckinck, 6 February 1847–24 April 1847; Charles Fenno Hoffman, 8 May 1847–30 September 1848; Evert A. Duyckinck, and George L. Duyckinck, 7 October 1848–31 December 1853; during at least part of 1853 and perhaps for even longer, Cornelius Mathews was a coeditor.

*Donald Yannella*

# THE LOWELL OFFERING

When editor Harriet Farley credited her *Lowell Offering* with making "a contribution to American literature which has not, probably, its counterpart in any
other country,"[1] she had less in mind any literary merit of the magazine than
the two unique features of its contributors that were to secure its fame: all writers
for the *Lowell Offering* were factory workers and all were women.

Among the first periodicals produced by female factory workers in New England, the *Offering* survived as one of the longest lived and most critically celebrated of the genre. While Harriet Martineau, Charles Dickens, and John
Greenleaf Whittier would all find a good word to say for the intrinsic merit of
the "girls'" writing, the primary value of the magazine lies in its status as an
historical and sociological document, no better or worse than many other contemporary magazines with which it was favorably compared. Most readers could
agree with Martineau that "the Offering improves much as it goes along" (3:216);
the distance is indeed measurable from the first article relating the "History of
a Hemlock Broom. Written by Itself" (1:1) to the serialization of editor Harriet
Curtis's romance *The Smugglers* in later issues. Yet even its fondest critics and
proudest contributors qualify their praise of the *Offering*; and modern commen-
tators bear out the attitude of nineteenth-century critics who admire the sketches,
essays, and poems in the *Offering* because they were written by self-educated
women who labored twelve and more hours six days weekly in the textile mills
rather than because they are necessarily commendable sketches, essays, or poems.
Readers found good enough writing in the magazine to lead them to doubt that
"mill girls" could produce it, however. Editorials routinely insist that all writing
is "exclusively, the productions of Females employed in the Mills" (1:iii),
"wholly the offering of Females" (1:6). Indeed, among the highest plaudits the
editors recognize in their own puffs for the magazine are the "rather complimentary . . . suspicions which have been expressed that the 'lawyers' of Lowell,
and not the factory operatives were the writers for the *Offering*" (4:167). Although the factory workers did author the *Offering*, those involved with the
magazine were not numerically representative of Lowell's labor force. Only a
few factory "girls" wrote for it (the figures vary from 54 up to 70), and not
enough of them subscribed to maintain the *Offering* beyond its five-volume run.

The initial conception of the *Offering* was far less ambitious than to attempt
to contribute to American literature; the first editor, the Reverend Abel C. Thomas,
rather wished to collect and print the best compositions that five or six female
operatives read in their "Improvement Circle" initiated by Harriot F. Curtis at
his Universalist church in Lowell, Massachusetts. One contributor recalls of the
project that the women "did not set [themselves] up to be literary,"[2] and one
*Offering* editorial would "entirely waive all considerations of literary excellence,
in our appeal to public patronage, for it is not upon these that our strongest
claims are founded" (3:24). Instead, the editors aim modestly "to please, if not

to edify and instruct'' (3:24), never expecting ''to be considered oracles, instructors, modern Minervas, &c.'' nor thinking ''our assistance was needed to
enlighten the community upon lofty or abstruse themes'' (1:377).

This concession would not mean that contributors eschew lofty themes in their
compositions, however. Descriptions and narratives of their own quotidian experiences consistently draw the most praise for the *Offering*'s writers; but while
their loftier flights inevitably draw criticism, authors continue to attempt them,
especially in the vehicle of verse. One British admirer of the *Offering*, the
Reverend William Scoresby, points up the inevitability of failure when the
magazine's writers attempt ''great and profound subjects'' without knowledge
or experience: ''By trying to write in fine language on sentimental topics, or to
clothe in pompous adornment, moderate ideas of sublime subjects, they, of
course, fail.''[3] The poems in the *Offering* doom themselves on all these counts.
The vast majority of verses meditate upon death or a related ''lofty'' motif,
many of them in the Emmeline Grangerford school of pathos-poetry. Some verses
immortalize patriotic figures who have died. ''Adelaide's'' (Lydia S. Hall) commemoration of the public's ''loud farewell'' at ''The Funeral of Harrison,'' for
example (1:84–85), or her meditation on ''The Tomb of Washington,'' which
was so esteemed by the editors that they included it in two issues of the *Offering*
(1:9 and 2:79–80). More of the verses are given to mourning—most in rhymed
couplets—the mortality of family and friends or even of strangers or the poet's
self. Each number of the magazine includes some such verse, as the following
partial list of titles suggests: ''A Sister's Tomb''; ''My Burial Place''; ''The
Graves of a Household''; ''Lament of the Little Hunchback''; ''Death''; ''On
a Young Man Lost at Sea''; ''Song of the Invalid Girl'' (''written by one who,
we fear, will never recover from her present disease''—3:88); ''The Murderer's
Request''; ''Eternity''; ''Room for the Dead,'' ''lines suggested'' to editor Farley
''by that beautiful Swedenborgian superstition, that the dead, though invisible,
are ever around us'' (3:266–67); ''The Stranger Maiden's Death''; ''The Early
Doomed''; and ''My Grave.'' Some poetry focuses on other themes—nature,
history, or fantasy—but the verses on death preponderate. Lucy Larcom, who
was to gain some stature as a poet later, served up many of these, notably eight
stanzas of ''Momento Mori,'' each of which punctuates its promise of a higher
life with the refrain ''Remember, *thou must die*'' (3:201). Larcom would note
in looking back at her early ''morbid verses'' that she tended ''needlessly to
dismalize.''[4] Farley also gained critical perspective from her experiences of
writing and editing for the *Lowell Offering*; when she became editor for the *New
England Offering* she encouraged prose contributions and qualified her requests
for verse, announcing ''We would not discourage poetical genius, but to *rhyme*,
we fear, is becoming sometimes a substitute for to *think*'' (7:277).

Although less strenuously than the poets, many writers of sketches pursue
lofty themes of mortality as well; but in that form more variety abounds. Short
sketches and essays translate moral and spiritual messages of Nature; recollect
historical figures and local legends; recall the pleasures of rural life, of childhood,

and of family associations; ponder "Friendship," "Happiness," and other abstract notions; instruct with "Chapters on the Sciences;" chronicle allegorical visits with "Genius," "Hope," and in a lower key, the "Improvement Circle;" dream a "Vision of Truth" or "A New Society." Occasionally sketches depict details of how the "girls" lived in the corporation houses where they were required to board; rarely does one depict the work they performed in the mills or describe the actual workplaces. After Farley and Curtis assume editorship, the magazine prints dramatized sketches and stories more frequently.

The longer, dramatic sketches repeatedly illustrate the duty of woman as worker and as daughter, sister, lover, wife, or mother. These fictionalized portraits bear out the conservative philosophy of the essays that more prosaically describe woman's role in her sphere. With the editorial aim of investing the public image of the factory "girls" with respectability, the *Offering* presents females who are models of industry, thrift, piety; of independence, filial responsibility, self-denial; and of usefulness, studiousness, sanguine stoicism; or the sketches show them repenting of venial lapses in these virtues. Each "girl" is exemplary in social as well as moral behavior. Many of the heroines are factory operatives or formerly worked in the mills. These Emmas and Ellens, Susans and Marys send wages home to parents; they support brothers through professional schooling; they save husbands or brothers from the demon bottle; they fondly tuck their infants into graves with unruffled faith in Providential care; they ease the final hours of beloved family and friends. The saintlier heroines sacrifice their own desires (for anything from a new bonnet to an education or a husband) or even sacrifice their lives for others. One example can serve to indicate the type of this paragon who varies from sketch to sketch only in circumstantial detail. Ellen Gray, in "The Cousins," not only puts her brother through law school with her wages from working in the mill, but she also distinguishes herself in her cousin's middle-class drawing room where her beauty and her talents for conversing, singing, and playing piano charm the gathered company. The sketch returns this particular paragon to the Lowell mills after her social coup, further to evince the dignity and the rewards of labor: "Ellen continued to work in the factory. She considered it no disgrace to labor for her own support: it was far preferable to eating the bread of idleness, or to be dependent on others. Her evenings were spent in study, or other useful employment, for she was never idle. Being cheerful and contented herself, she made everything pleasant about her. She was never heard to complain" (4:60). For her labor, Ellen earns the ultimate reward—a husband.

The examples of Ellen and other factory operatives, as described in "Abby's Year in Lowell," "Disasters Overcome," "Prejudice against Labor," and the two series "Tales of Factory Life" and "The Affections Illustrated in Factory Life" aim to educate the female worker in ideal conduct and, even more, to elevate her image in the public mind. The editorial objective in offering such sketches of the operative as idealized heroine is a defensive one against "the prejudice, which has long existed, against the manufacturing females of New

England'' (3:24). Editorials reiterate this ''object'' more consistently than any
other throughout the run of the magazine; and while this motive obviously
operates in the selection of fictional sketches for the *Offering*, surprisingly few
articles aside from short editorials argue directly against the public prejudice
against women working in the mills. The exceptions are notable. ''A Factory
Girl'' (probably by Farley) takes Orestes Brownson to task for exaggerating
widespread prejudice in his ''horrible'' slander against factory employ as ''sufficient to damn to infamy the most worthy and virtuous girl'' (2:17). A dialogue
on ''Factory Labor'' also directly vindicates mill workers; factory labor in itself
is neither ''degrading'' nor ''productive of vice,'' nor does it foster ignorance
(4:199–200). And in response to a slur from *Godey's Lady's Book*,\* an article
entitled ''Gold Watches'' exonerates the New England operative from any more
''folly of extravagance in dress'' than her unemployed sisters (3:44–45, reprinted
2:377–79).

Most writers for the *Offering*, however, sweeten their polemic with fiction.
In practice, apparently, those who wrote for the magazine preferred to combine
the two theories of writing set forth by ''Annette'' and ''Ella'' in ''Fiction. A
Dialogue,'' for most sketches seem designed to ''please others'' with their
narratives while they also ''aim to elevate, to instruct, and purify'' with their
pointed morals (2:251). In addition to this commonplace of Victorian aesthetics,
the pages of the *Offering* suggest other sources for the restraint with which the
magazine advocates the factory ''girl's'' cause. One source of restraint lies in
the editorial policy of avoiding argumentation—''all sectarianism'' and ''dis-
puted questions''—in favor of writing that would ''raise the humble'' through
''the all-pervading influence of true Christianity'' (5:248). The Christian spirit
behind the writers' exempla and the editors' mild chastisements reinforces another motive of their restraint, their concept of feminine delicacy, which produces
the periodical's characteristic tone: if Christians do not dispute with their neighbors in print, neither do ladies with their employers. One writer notes in her
autobiography that she ''always regarded it as a better ambition to be a true
woman than a successful writer.''[5] While biblical allusions function in many
pieces as direct reminders of Christian duty, few articles as directly describe
woman's role. But those few clearly draw out the assumptions behind the idealized portraits of women in the sketches, defining the role of woman as a moral,
circumscribed, and subservient one.

One can readily see ironic implications for the magazine's policy if the editors
agree with ''B'' (and their selection of her essay to appear in the *Offering* surely
indicates some degree of agreement) in delineating ''Woman's Proper Sphere''
within a circumference of silence: ''the silent rebuke with which she restrains
vice . . . acts more effectively than a thousand reproofs, uttered through a public
medium'' (1:3). ''Ella's'' definition of the role of ''Woman'' similarly excludes
the option of public address, in her case because she sees the female voice as
not ''suitable'' for preaching or lecturing and because a woman's ''domestic
duties should claim her first thoughts'' (1:133). For all the female operatives'

vaunted esteem for education, pointed up with paternal pride by corporation owners, the only scheme projected for an organized school for the women employees appears to have been "A Manual Labor School," its curriculum designed not to develop writing skills but to prevent the female operative from losing her touch with a pudding in spite of her twelve hours each day tending the mill loom (3:213). The editors warn that they reject any treatment of political issues in their *Offering* because "with regard to politics, we, as females should do, remain entirely neutral," that is, silent (4:24).

Indeed, the prospect of publishing their own journal overwhelmed the writers of the first issue, and they "shrank so sensitively from the proposal" of editing and publishing a journal that Reverend Thomas took on the job for the first six issues. Even when Curtis and Farley found their editorial voices, they would appeal for the success of their venture not to support from female-operative readers but to the patronage of "bachelors," for "we feel that we have peculiar claims on their gallantry," claims substantiated "if for no other reason, than that we were a band of *young* females—of laboring females—of *factory girls*" (3:24, 282). Contributors to the magazine seek beyond gallantry to the further protection of anonymity, signing their particular offerings with only initials or a fanciful pen-name (Ethelinda, Orianna, Adelaide, Grace Gayfeather); only some editorials bear Harriet Farley's full name. In the hesitancy and coyness of all this it might be difficult to discern how Harriot Curtis would establish a basis for her reputation as a feminist. But a sense of the boldness of these "girls" in undertaking the *Offering* at all can be restored by bearing in mind that America could claim only three, at most five, other women editing magazines during this period.[6] And the spirited editorial defense of Curtis's prerogative to print the phrases "d——d rascal" and "d——d knave" in the magazine's serialization of her *The Smugglers* suggests they resent their feminine restraint being stopped far short of the "namby-pamby" editorial policy of other nineteenth-century magazines that shared their moral objectives (4:120).

Behind the Christian reticence and feminine delicacy, some of the magazine's detractors saw another source of the *Offering*'s constraint, one which the editorials deny on several occasions: "an undue degree of deference to our employers" (3:283). The editors protest accusations that they are "tools, dupes, decoys, &c." manipulated by corporation owners, and they list rationalizations for their magazine's "design," which considers it outside "their provincee to discuss the manufacturing system" with its reputed exploitation of the workers who help sustain it (2:380). The women seem to protest too much their powerlessness to change the system; their reluctance to "expose . . . the evils and miseries, and mortifications, attendant upon a factory life" (1:376); their eagerness "to counteract the false impression" given of the mills by those seeking reforms (1:377); their determination to "have nothing to do" with "wages, board &c." in the pages of their magazine (3:48).

Some combination, then, of deferential attitudes toward capitalist bosses, toward male prerogative, toward contemporary Christian mores, all so evident in the *Offering*, underlies the magazine's general editorial policy. An "allegorical" motto at one time appearing on the cover to represent the "aspirations" of the literary millworkers and their magazine may indicate the extent to which those attitudes shaped the *Offering*: "The worm on earth may look up to the stars" (5:2).

The *Offering*'s emphasis on the priority of self-reform, however, needs also to be viewed in the context of literary history, where its affinities with the Yankee Transcendentalism then current provide another explanation for the journal's focus and tone. It is not surprising that the *Offering* could count among its special "friends" William Ellery Channing and Elizabeth Peabody (3:282). The editors of the periodical are as insistent as Emerson or Thoreau that true reform must begin with the moral reformation of the individual rather than with adjustments to any institutions; they waste no "sympathies . . . with that spirit which would reform its neighbor and leave its own heart the abode of every bitter, malignant passion" (5:284). And another editorial admonishes reformers "that those who are so ready to point to the beam in another's eye should first cast out that which is in their own" (3:283). The journal shared with much Transcendental philosophy the notion of work as a mode of effecting one's own reform or redemption. The successor to the *Lowell Offering*, the *New England Offering*, would quote paragraphs from Channing in defense of "Manual Labor" as a "school . . . of purpose and character" which justifies "sufferings and wants" and "vicissitudes" as necessary instructors of duty and wisdom: "these stern teachers do a work which no compassionate, indulgent friend could do for us; and true wisdom will bless Providence for their sharp ministry" (n.s. 5:102–3). Harriet Farley selected that article for the *New England Offering*, and she suggests that its assumptions also inform her earlier *Offering* when, in an autobiographical editorial, she counts as a "blessing for her own good" and "development of character" the deprivations, criticism, and problems she encountered earlier in her work as a Lowell operative and editor. If Emerson spoke on the topics of work and reform when he lectured in Lowell—some statement perhaps such as that in "Self-Reliance": "attend your own work and already the evil begins to be repaired"—his words would ring familiar to the "girls" raised "to work almost as if it were a religion"[7] by mothers of the same Yankee stock as his.

But although they proselytize in their pages an almost Transcendental faith in hard work, the "girls" came to see the Lowell factories as not the only altar to worship at nor the only shrine to bring their literary offerings to. As lower wages and worsening conditions in the boarding houses undermined the operatives' faith in the dignity of labor, they moved on to other work. Perhaps even more importantly, conditions no longer served the "girls" "for the promotion of the design for which we are collected, namely, to get money, as much of it and as fast as we can" (2:18). And although none of the former operatives managed to sustain herself solely by her writings for the remainder of her days, Curtis, Farley, and contributors Lucy Larcom, Harriet Hanson Robinson, Eliza Jane Cate, Abby A. Goddard, and Sarah Bagley authored books after the demise of their journal, including some of the best evaluations of their achievements in the *Lowell Offering*.

## Notes

1. *New England Offering*, n.s. 1 (April 1848):23.
2. Lucy Larcom, *A New England Girlhood* (Boston: Houghton, Mifflin, 1889), p. 221.
3. William Scoresby, *American Factories and their Female Operatives* (1845; rpt., New York: Burt Franklin, 1968), p. 71.
4. Larcom, p. 213.
5. Larcom, p. 272.
6. Figures differ in the sources: Harriet H. Robinson counts three (*Loom and Spindle* [1898; rpt., Kailua, Hawaii: Press Pacifica, 1976], p. 65); Hannah Josephson counts four (*The Golden Threads* [New York: Duell, Sloan and Pearce, 1949], p. 190); neither includes Margaret Fuller in her headcount.
7. Larcom, p. 9.

## Information Sources

BIBLIOGRAPHY:
Dickens, Charles. *American Notes and Pictures from Italy*. 1842 and 1846; rpt., London: Oxford University Press, 1957.
Josephson, Hannah. *The Golden Threads: New England's Mill Girls and Magnates*. New York: Duell, Sloan and Pearce, 1949.
Larcom, Lucy. *A New England Girlhood: Outlined from Memory*. Boston: Houghton, Mifflin, 1889.
*The Lowell Offering: Writings by New England Mill Women (1840–1845)*. Ed. Benita Eisler. Philadelphia: J. B. Lippincott, 1977.
*Mind Among the Spindles: A Selection from the Lowell Offering*. Ed. Charles Knight. London: 1844.
*New England Offering*. 1847–1850; rpt., Westport, Connecticut: Greenwood, 1970.
Robinson, Harriet H. *Loom and Spindle; or, Life Among the Early Mill Girls*. 1898; rpt., Kailua, Hawaii: Press Pacifica, 1976.
Scoresby, William. *American Factories and their Female Operatives; With an Appeal on Behalf of the British Factory Population, and Suggestions for the Improvement of their Condition*. 1845; rpt., New York: Burt Franklin, 1968.
*Shells from the Strand of the Sea of Genius*. Ed. Harriet Farley. Boston: J. Munroe and Co., 1847.
INDEXES: None.
REPRINT EDITIONS: American Periodicals: Series II, 1800–1850. University Microfilms, Ann Arbor. Reel 675. Greenwood Press. Westport, Connecticut, 1970.
LOCATION SOURCES: Widely available.

## Publication History

MAGAZINE TITLE AND TITLE CHANGES: *The Lowell Offering; A Repository of Original Articles, Written Exclusively by Females Actively Employed in the Mills*, 1840–1842. *The Lowell Offering and Magazine*, October 1842-September 1843. *The Lowell Offering*, November 1843-December 1845.

VOLUME AND ISSUE DATA: Numbers 1–4, October 1840-March 1841. Volumes 1–
    5, April 1841-December 1845.
FREQUENCY OF PUBLICATION: Numbers 1–4, bimonthly. Volumes 1–5, monthly.
PUBLISHERS: October 1840-September 1842: Powers and Bagley. October 1842-Oc-
    tober 1843: William Schouler. November 1843-December 1845: Harriot F. Curtis
    and Harriet Farley.
EDITORS: Abel C. Thomas, October 1840-September 1842; Harriot F. Curtis and Harriet
    Farley, October 1842-December 1844; Farley through December 1845.

*Charlene Avallone*

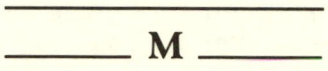

## THE MAGNOLIA

When his *Southern Post* failed in fall 1839, editor Philip C. Pendleton persuaded George F. Pierce, president of the new Georgia Female College, to coedit a magazine especially for Southern ladies, to be published, as was the *Post*, in Macon, Georgia, by Cornelius R. Hanleiter. Asked for aid by Pierce, Augustus Baldwin Longstreet replied, " 'The Southern Ladies' Book' will do for a name, if book it will be, which I doubt. . . . The plan is well conceived, will go into operation, progress twelve or eighteen months, and expire, because subscribers won't pay. . . . It will start pretty fair, grow lamer at every step until it expires; simply because your [contributors] won't write for it.''[1] In fact, the *Southern Ladies' Book* barely survived ten months, but, continued as the *Magnolia*, it achieved some success before being abandoned in June 1843.

In November 1839, Pendleton and Pierce addressed to ''the Ladies of Georgia, and of the South'' their prospectus, including a list of contributors heavy with ministers and educators—all Georgians and all males. Observing that the ''female mind'' was no longer ''held in thraldom . . . by the force of conventional arrangements,'' the editors offered their magazine as ''a useful aid to the young, and fair, and beautiful, in preparing themselves for the discharge of the noble and arduous duties which devolve on Woman, in her varied capacity of Daughter, Wife and Mother.''[2]

By the time the magazine appeared in February 1840, both women and non-Georgians, including Caroline Lee Hentz and Alexander B. Meek of Alabama and Caroline Gilman and William Gilmore Simms of South Carolina, had joined the listed contributors.[3] Actual contributors, however, were neither numerous nor well known. The longest piece was a borrowed tale by G.P.R. James; the next Pierce's ''Address on Female Education.'' Admitting satisfaction with ''neither paper, type, execution, or matter,'' the editors promised improvement and appealed to "State pride" and "Southern spirit" for support (1:54).

A change of publishers in May from Hanleiter to Benjamin Griffin had no more effect on production problems than repeated pleas had on nonpaying subscribers and on *"contributors, so called"* (2:189). Longstreet provided only his Inaugural Address as president of Emory College; Simms offered a few "Early Lays.'' The magazine carried a series of articles on female education and one on "The Right of Property of Married Women." Among numerous "selected" pieces were works by Longfellow, Irving, Cooper, and Lydia Sigourney. As proprietor, Pendleton managed all business arrangements; Pierce's duties as college president and popular Methodist preacher left little time. In September they promised that, despite discouragements, "the work will be continued to the end of the year'' (2:186–88, 192). The volume was completed but only with the issue of the November and December numbers from Savannah in July 1841.

By then six numbers of volume 3 had already been issued there as the *Magnolia; or Southern Monthly*, published by H. S. Bell and edited by Pendleton alone. The move was prompted by Savannah's superior printing facilities and by the hope "to enlist a greater number of literary gentlemen" as contributors. In changing the name, Pendleton hoped to escape comparison with *Godey's Lady's Book* * and to reach a wider audience with "sterner material" than might be appropriate to female "feelings and sentiments" (3:42–43).

Disavowing any intention to emulate "a work of like name, at the North," the *Southern Ladies' Book* prospectus declared, "We leave to our Northern contemporary pictorial representations of fashions and dress, for the embellishment of the person: be it ours to provide . . . for the adornment of the mind."[4] When *Godey's* dismissed their magazine as a vain attempt to trade on the popularity of *"The Lady's Book,"*[5] the editors, professing to "know little or nothing" of the elder work, suggested renaming it "Godey's Lady's *Picture Book*" (2:190). Eschewing "mawkish love tales and frothy sentimentalism, they would offer instead "Tracts on Science and the Arts" as well as "illustrations of the passions, in prose and verse" (1:2). While pleading for contributions, they rejected numerous submissions, including one characterized as "puerile enough for the fireside entertainment of children" (1:192). They denied that their work was "solely for the 'Fair' ": although its name guaranteed "nothing indelicate, impure, or offensive," the *Southern Ladies' Book* aimed at "the reading *public*" (1:127–28).

The *Magnolia*, Pendleton asserted, while making allowance for "young writers of merit or promise," had no place for "the effusions of every scribbler, who may conceive that he has become a prime favorite with Minerva or the Muses" (3:46). William Alexander Caruther's *The Knights of the Golden Horse-Shoe* inaugurated Pendleton's plan to run "stories of length continuing from month to month" (3:43). Other contributors to the 1841 *Magnolia* included Hentz, Meek, Simms, Mary E. Lee, and Richard Henry Wilde. The second number complained of lack of "room for the various good things sent us by our correspondents'' (3:96). After six issues, Pendleton boasted of exceeding ''our most sanguine expectations in securing the assistance of writers of genius'' (2:347). When a self-styled ''Puritan'' objected to James Edward Henry's ''Tales of the Packolette'' and Simms's ''The Loves of the Driver'' in a periodical ''designed in some degree for the Ladies'' (3:285), the editor published defenses by himself and the authors and continued both works (3:286–87, 334, 376–79).

Simms, in the lead article of the first *Magnolia*, declared from his own experience ''in the making of Southern Magazines'' that his conviction of their ''almost certain fate'' inspired him ''with a feeling, very like disgust'' at news ''of any new experiment of this kind'' (3:1). The following December Pendleton proposed to engage him as a coeditor (3:572). In January Pendleton became publisher, and in April ''co-editor'' Simms took charge of the ''Editor's Table,'' changing its title to ''Editor's Bureau.''[6]

In his first editorial he asserted, ''It is very evident that we shall have to depart very considerably from what is quite too much assumed to be the necessary character of a literary or ladies journal.'' Repudiating ''that disparaging estimate of their intellectual character, which supposed that they can enjoy and endure nothing but . . . nauseating and injurious sweets,'' Simms promised his women readers a ''rude'' but ''wholesome'' fare. The *Magnolia* would address women as ''in the noblest sense . . . help-mates for our men'' (4:248–49). Henceforth it would contain ''papers on legal, social, moral, and scientific subjects'' as well as ''poetry and romance, anecdote and jest, the sportive essay, and the gay rejoinder.'' Upon completion of Simms's ''Castle Dismal,'' the magazine would avoid serial fiction (4:320).

The June number, boasting ''accession of several hundred subscribers and more than thirty new contributors'' during Simms's coeditorship, announced ''arrangements . . . for making the Magnolia one of the neatest periodicals in the Union'' and the removal of the magazine from Savannah to Charleston (4:384). In the move to Charleston, with its ''prospects of greater literary and pecuniary patronage,'' printers James Burges and Robert James became publishers and proprietors along with Pendleton, and Simms became editor, assuming ''general supervision of the work.'' With no mention of its origin as the *Southern Ladies' Book*, the circular announcing these changes declared the new *Magnolia*, now subtitled *Southern Appalachian*, ''a work in which the tone shall be manly and the character and sentiment essentially and only Southern.''[7]

For Pendleton and Pierce the need for distinctively Southern literature was ''too clear and decisive for controversy.'' (1:1); for Simms it became a matter of continuing controversy. In September 1841 Pendleton, calling upon Southerners to support their own literature, asserted that ''the Northern Press cannot supply the South with such periodicals as the wants of a Southern community demand'' (3:431–32). When Lewis Gaylord Clark's *Knickerbocker Magazine*\* denounced such ''prating'' of literary sectionalism,[8] Pendleton conciliatorily replied, '' . . . as regards *sectional* literature, we repudiate the thought of such provincial distinctions'' (3:524).

Simms, however, in his first "Editorial Bureau," dismissed the *Knicker-bocker*, charging that Northern magazines were either "ignorant" of Southern concerns or "criminal, *for they do not represent them.*" "If there be not a sectional literature," he insisted, "there will be none national" (4:251–52). The quarrel culminated in August, when Simms, professing "some reluctance" (n.s. 1:128), published a scathing review of the "senseless stuff which disgraces" the *Knickerbocker* (n.s. 1:109–14). Clark, in the same month, blasted section-alism as "a device to secure an extrinsic and undue consideration for flimsy novels, and other of the least deserving elements of our national literature." "Least of all," would he recognize Simms as "a competent *arbiter literarum*" regardless of "his 'lots' of labored romances—upon which Time and the silent indifference of the public . . . are already doing their work."[9] The following month Simms expressed his "desire . . . to avoid bickering with our contem-poraries" and his willingness to "*forgive* . . . though it is only a becoming policy that we should not forget" (n.s. 1:194).

Simms boasted that "in assuming conduct of the Magnolia, I am rapidly accumulating about me, & in the cause of Southern Literature, a really able array of highly endowed and well educated men."[10] Such members of his circle as George F. Holmes and Benjamin F. Perry began contributing, and Pendleton finally secured a new series of Longstreet's "Georgia Scenes" (n.s. 1:61, 199–200). Simms himself became the major contributor. By fall 1842 he was crowding articles into unleaded columns,[11] unable to accommodate "the variety and abun-dance of our contributors" (n.s. 1:328). The "several hundred" subscribers added by the absorption of the *Chicora* (n.s. 1:328), together with "some fifteen hundred" that Simms claimed earlier, should have brought circulation near the 2,000 initially deemed "requisite" by Pendleton and Pierce.[12] In February 1843, the *Magnolia*'s publishers assured their readers "that it is now permanently established" (n.s. 2:144).

On the back cover of the following number, however, Pendleton admitted financial "embarrassment," due not to "want of subscribers" but to their failure to pay. As Simms explained to Perry in May, "Pendleton is over head & ears in debt." Moreover, Pendleton and Burges were "squabbling among them-selves." With Burges's proposed withdrawal from the magazine, Simms pre-dicted, " . . . it will stop for I very much doubt if the money credit of P. is sufficient to secure him a printer." Already owed "several hundred dollars" by Pendleton, Simms had reached his own "determination to withdraw."[13]

The "Editorial Bureau" for May announced, "With the forthcoming, or June, issue of the Magnolia, Mr. Simms withdraws from its Editorial management" (n.s. 2:336). A month earlier he had declared himself "half resolved" to do so, calling his situation "irksome" and his duties "disagreeable to me, fatiguing yet not likely to enhance my fame." Still, he later claimed, "But for the quarrels of the publishers . . . I should have continued." His later accounts lay the blame entirely on the publishers, through whose "perverseness . . . a work, in full favor and with an excellent subscription list was suffered to drop—actually dying of plethora.''[14]

With his withdrawl, for whatever reasons, the *Magnolia*, née *Southern Ladies' Book*, finally reached the end, prophesied at the outset by Longstreet and later by Simms himself.

## Notes

1. Quoted in George G. Smith, *The Life and Times of George Foster Pierce* (Sparta, Ga.: Hancock Publishing Co., 1888), p. 102.

2. Macon *Georgia Messenger*, 7 November 1839; *Macon Georgia Telegraph*, 24 December 1839. Some of the confusion attending the project is suggested by the editors' failure to include with their prospectus sent to the Charleston *Courier* any indication of where or by whom the magazine was to be published (*Courier*, 23 January 1840).

3. *Georgia Messenger*, 6 February, 13 February, 1840; *SLB*, 1 (January 1840), back cover.

4. *Georgia Messenger*, 7 November 1839; see also *SLB* 1 (January 1840), back cover. *The Southern Ladies' Book* could not, of course, afford the expensive engravings of *Godey's*. The *Magnolia* did introduce scenic engravings in March and in December 1842, suggesting that they would continue if response and resources warranted (4:188; n.s. 1:395).

5. *Godey's* 21 (October 1840):192.

6. *The Letters of William Gilmore Simms*, ed. Mary C. Simms Oliphant, Alfred Taylor Odell, and T. C. Duncan Eaves, 6 vols. (Columbia, S.C.: University of South Carolina Press, 1952–1982), 1:301–3, 306–8, (hereafter cited as *Letters*). Because of the death of his daughter in April, Simms had little part in the May number (4:320).

7. Circular, printed on back cover, n.s. 1 (July 1842); also in *Letters*, 1, facing p. 329.

8. *Knickerbocker* 18 (November 1841):461–62. The *Knickerbocker* earlier extended ''hearty sympathy and cordiality'' to the *Magnolia* (*Knickerbocker* 17 [April 1841]:357).

9. *Knickerbocker* 20 (August 1842):199–200. (See also *Knickerbocker* 19 [May 1842], 496; *Magnolia*, 4:377–78.)

10. *Letters*, 1:318. (For problems in compensating those contributors, see *Letters*, 1:307, 309, 318, 322; V, 368, 369, 373.)

11. *Letters* 5:369; see also *Magnolia*, 1:328.

12. *Letters* 1:326, 308; *Magnolia*, prospectus.

13. *Letters* 1:351–52. (On the *Magnolia*'s financial straits, see also 5:373.)

14. *Letters*, 1:346, 353, 371, 380.

## Information Sources

BIBLIOGRAPHY:

Cohen, Sidney J. *Three Notable Ante-Bellum Magazines of South Carolina*, *Bulletin of the University of South Carolina*, No. 42, part 2. Columbia, S.C.: The University Press, 1915. Pp. 26–38.

Flanders, Bertram Holland. *Early Georgia Literary Periodicals to 1865*. Athens, Ga.: University of Georgia Press, 1944. Pp. 38–61.

Guilds, John C. ''Simms as Editor and Prophet: The Flowering and Early Death of the Southern *Magnolia*.'' *Southern Literary Journal* 4 (Spring 1972):69–92.

———. ''William Gilmore Simms as Magazine Editor to 1845.'' Ph.D. diss., Duke University, 1954.

Herbert, Edward T. "William Gilmore Simms as Editor and Literary Critic." Ph.D. diss., University of Wisconsin, 1957.

Hoole, William Stanley. "William Gilmore Simms's Career as Editor." *Georgia Historical Quarterly* 19 (March 1935): 47–54.

*The Letters of William Gilmore Simms*. 6 vols. Ed. Mary C. Simms Oliphant, Alfred Taylor Odell, and T. C. Duncan Eaves. Columbia, S.C.: University of South Carolina Press, 1952–1982.

Stearns, Bertha-Monica. "Southern Magazines for Ladies (1819–1860)." *South Atlantic Quarterly* 31 (January 1932):79–81.

INDEXES: None.

REPRINT EDITIONS: American Periodicals: Series II, 1800–1850. University Microfilms, Ann Arbor. Reel 676. Gerritsen Collection of Women's History. Glen Rock, N.J.: Microfilming Corp. of America.

LOCATION SOURCES: Complete runs: Charleston Library Society. Partial runs: widely available.

## Publication History

MAGAZINE TITLE AND TITLE CHANGES: *The Southern Ladies' Book: A Magazine of Literature, Science and Arts*, January-December 1840. *The Magnolia; or, Southern Monthly*, January 1841-June 1842. *The Magnolia; or, Southern Apalachian. A Literary Magazine and Monthly Review*, July 1842-June 1843.

VOLUME AND ISSUE DATA: Volume 1, numbers 1–6, January-June 1840; volume 2, numbers 1–6, July-December 1840; volume 3, numbers 1–12, January-December 1841; volume 4, numbers 1–12, January-June 1842; volume 1 new series, numbers 1–6, July-December 1842; volume 2 new series, numbers 1–6, January-June 1843.

FREQUENCY OF PUBLICATION: Monthly.

PUBLISHERS: January-April 1840: Cornelius R. Hanleiter, Macon, Ga. May-October 1840: Benjamin F. Griffin, Macon. November 1840-December 1841: H. S. Bell, Savannah, Ga. January-June 1842: Philip C. Pendleton, Savannah. July 1842-June 1843: Philip C. Pendleton and [James] Burges & [Robert] James, Charleston, S.C.

EDITORS: Philip C. Pendleton and George F. Pierce, January-December 1840; Philip C. Pendleton, January 1841-March 1842, May 1842; Philip C. Pendleton and William Gilmore Simms, April 1842, June 1842; William Gilmore Simms, July 1842-June 1843.

*William M. Moss*


# THE MASSACHUSETTS MAGAZINE

Responding to "the complaint made for the Want of a Monthly Magazine in this Commonwealth [Massachusetts]," Isaiah Thomas, who has been called "the leading publisher of his day,"[1] determined "that nothing in our power shall be wanting to make it as complete and useful as any ever yet published in the United States" (*Massachusetts Spy*, 4 September 1788). In January 1789 the first issue of the *Massachusetts Magazine* appeared, the longest lived of all eighteenth-century American magazines; Thomas remained at the helm as publisher and sometime editor for the first five years of its eight-year history. "The editorial theory . . . was to compile a periodical not only for those whose cultural advantages had been considerable, but for a proletarian class which, until now, had neither supported or found reason for supporting magazines."[2] "I am one of those who have sincerely wished for a Magazine published in this Commonwealth," declares an anonymous contributor in the first issue. "Such a publication . . . would answer many valuable purposes. . . . It would give birth to literary emulation and effort. . . . It would improve the taste, the language and the manners of the age" (1:7–8). And in April 1795 another contributor maintains that periodical publications "tend at once to enliven our pleasures, increase our knowledge, polish our manners, and humanize our hearts" (7:3).

Thomas saw to it that his magazine, like the *Columbian*,* was ornamented with copperplate engravings and music. An engraving appeared as the frontispiece of each issue during the first six years and irregularly thereafter. Every issue between January 1789 and December 1791 carried one or two pieces of music with words, many of these being "original American compositions."[3] Also like the *Columbian*, albeit on a more modest scale, the *Massachusetts Magazine* reviewed books, beginning in July 1790 and continuing in every issue until October 1794 and sporadically thereafter.

The hope expressed by the editors at the beginning of 1793 that every page of the magazine for that year "may subserve the grand cause of Religion, Virtue, Reason" (5:iv) helps explain why the bulk of the poetry in the *Massachusetts Magazine* as a whole is sentimental and didactic. A handful of lighthearted poems escape this fate. For example, the author of "Chusing a Wife by a Pipe of Tobacco" (January 1789) writes:

> Tube, thy colour let me find,
> In her skin, and in her mind.
> Let her have a shape as fine;
>
> Let her breath be sweet as thine:
> Let her, when her lips I kiss,
> Burn like thee, to give me bliss;
> . . . . .
> Let her live to give delight,
> Ever warm and ever bright:
> Let her deeds, whene'er she dies,
> Mount as incense to the skies. (1:57)

And in "The Coquette" (June 1792) forty-five-year-old Corinna, not yet despairing of marriage, writes to Strephon, "You've conquer'd, Sir, I yield to you." To which he replies that while he's often admired the rising sun, when the sun declines at evening, "With ruddy face still, still he shines, / But ah! his heat and beams are gone.'' Reading this, Corinna no more frequents balls and routs, "A victim now to hips and spleen.'' The moral?

> Then let not slip, ye lovely fair!
> Youth's prime, and Beauty's blissful date,
> To generous lovers be sincere,
> Lest you should meet Corinna's fate. (4:395)

Far more important than the poetry in the *Massachusetts Magazine* is the prose, nonfiction and especially fiction. In "Account of the Ugly Club, in Charleston, (S.C.)'' (April 1791), an essay reminiscent of Steele's *Spectator* No. 17, the club room is furnished among other things with "a dutch looking glass, full of veins; one look into which would convince even a handsome man that he is a perfect fright'' (3:211). "When an ill favoured gentleman arrives'' (3:211) he is invited by the members to meet with them the next evening. When he does not appear, one of the members waits on him with a letter from the President. "Zounds!'' cries the strange gentleman, "I am not so ugly . . . as to attract the notice of the whole town almost at my first setting foot upon the wharf!'' (3:211) But the messenger charges that his nose is very long and that he has "so elegant a pair of lantern jaws'' (3:211). The gentleman "receives a letter from some pretended female (it being a trick of the club)'' (3:212), which reads in part: "I am now almost two years beyond my grand climacterick: And am four feet four inches in height; rather less in circumference; am a little dropsical; have lovely red hair and a fair complexion: . . . I am universally allowed to have charming eyes. They are indeed somewhat inclined to squinting'' (3:212). Enraged by this letter, the gentleman cries, "I must be ugly, it seems, whether I will or not'' (3:212). At this moment the president enters and, leading him to the club room, says, "Look into this Dutch glass,'' to which the gentleman replies: "God's will be done. Since there seems to be no avoiding it, I will even do as you say!'' (3:212) In "Criticism on Chesterfield's Letters'' (January 1790) Mercy Warren, acknowledging Chesterfield's virtues as a writer, warns her son,

> When he sacrifices truth to convenience, probity to pleasure, virtues to the graces, generosity, gratitude, and all the fine feelings of the soul, to a momentary gratification, we cannot but pity the man as much as we admire the author. . . . Can there be a portrait more unnatural or deformed, or an object more completely ridiculous, than that of a father, exerting all the powers of brilliant talents . . . to arouse the corrupt passions in the bosom of his son. [I am convinced that] had his Lordship laid a little more stress on purity of sentiment, and less on the efficacy of intrigue and gallantry, it might have corrected the errours of his raw traveller, and perhaps sooner have rubbed off the awkwardness inherent in his character, than the *un gout vie*, about which the careful parent is so solicitous. . . . I am happy

to have a son to whom I can disclose the full flow of sentiment, and the mixture of indignation, that arises in the maternal bosom (2:36, 37, 38).

In December 1789 the editors of the *Massachusetts Magazine* assured their readers that there had been nothing in their first volume "incompatible with pure morality, nor adverse to the grand principles of religion; neither has the blush of sensibility crimsoned the cheek, nor the lovers of wit received gratification at the pain of innocence" (Preface). The same can be said for the entire run of the magazine. As the eighteenth century drew to an end, literary taste in England and America increasingly favored writers of sensibility like the novelists Sterne, Henry Mackenzie, and Fanny Burney. Successful fiction was that which moralized at the same time that it appealed to the reader's sensibility. A favorite way to make such fiction respectable was to insist that the story was founded on fact. Here follow four examples from the large body of fiction that was published in the *Massachusetts Magazine*, the first being a sentimental tale, "The Inexorable Father" (October 1791). Clericus, who "acquired a considerable property by the demise of relations and his marriage with an opulent heiress" (3:619), has an only daugher Blandisia who he hopes will marry "where money, not merit, should be the magnet of sympathy" (3:619). When she is verging on thirty, a farmer's son, who has nearly completed his medical studies, courts her; Blandisia "determined to venture on the ocean of matrimony without ballasting the skiff in cash" (3:619). Clericus, when told of this plan, forbids the doctor to see his daughter again and confines her to her room where she sickens and languishes. Permitted to see the doctor one last time, "she prest his cheek to her quivering lips, and expired," and he rushes from the house in a state of distraction, "whilst Clericus stood, the unmoved spectator of the awful transaction" (3:620).

The Oriental tale was popular on both sides of the Atlantic in the eighteenth century. In "Hamet: Or the Insufficiency of Luxury to the Attainment of Happiness" (February 1790) Hamet, who has a fine house and gardens in Ispahan, feels a void in his life. As he is wandering alone abroad one day, a shepherd tells him the sources of his own happiness "are in a woman whom I tenderly love, and a faithful friend who regards me as himself" (2:75). A storm coming up, Hamet is taken in by a hermit who says, "Wouldst thou seek for love and friendship, fly the court, quit Ispahan, and seek them in some distant province. Lay by thy rich attire, and conceal thy grandeur" (2:75). When Hamet does this he is attacked by robbers only to be rescued by a young man, Heli, who takes him home. For the first time in his life Hamet tastes real friendship. Then he sees a beautiful woman, Abra, who is Heli's sister; shortly they are married. Hamet takes Abra and Heli to court and declares, "Learn that splendour may be attended with anxiety, and that without love and friendship there can be no true happiness" (2:76). The narrator in another Oriental tale, "The Talisman of Truth" (August 1795), declares "How plentiful a source of misfortunes is an extravagant imagination!" (7:259) and tells a story to illustrate his point. When a son is born to an Indian king, a good Genius endows him "with all possible gifts of person and understanding'' (7:259), to which the rival Genius adds ''that of the most ardent and extensive imagination'' (7:260). The first Genius gives the father the Talisman of Truth to put in the child's hands when he reaches the age of reason; the father dies suddenly before he can say where the stone is hidden. Soon the young prince ''began to display the immense riches of his mind'' (7:260), but likewise ''the fire of an excessive imagination was lighted up in his mind'' (7:260). Searching the palatial apartments, he comes across the last relics of his father, among them the talismanic stone, which he is to apply to his forehead. He does so, and in an instant ''truth spread its clear and constant light over his imagination'' (7:261).

Judith Sargent Murray's essay serial *The Gleaner* (February 1792-December 1794) contains imbedded within it an unfinished sentimental novel, the ''Story of Margaretta.'' The Vigilliuses adopt young Margaretta Melworth who, so far as they know, is an orphan and train her up to be on her guard against pride and affectation. When Margaretta visits a friend in New Haven, the fortune-seeking Sinisterus Courtland declares himself her lover; the Vigilliuses warn her against such a man and recommend instead Edward Hamilton, for whom her feelings at this time are only sisterly. Courtland pursues Margaretta, and finally she rejects him as unworthy. Shortly it is revealed that he got the defenseless orphan, Frances Wellwood, with three children out of wedlock, stripped her of a £2,000 patrimony, and then deserted her; humbled by his confinement in the county jail, he now agrees to make Miss Wellwood his lawful wife. Scarcely is Margaretta married to Edward Hamilton than she is distressed to see him frequently keeping intimate company with their friend Serafina Clifford; finally Serafina explains that she is Edward's illegitimate half sister, born of their father's indiscretion while abroad. One evening a stranger appears and embraces Margaretta as her long-lost father, Mr. Melworth; it seems that when his ship bound for the East Indies was wrecked, he managed to save himself and eventually returned to England only to find his wife dead. One day there caught his eye the *Massachusetts Magazine* for March 1792, which carried the first installment of the ''Story of Margaretta''; immediately he took a ship for America to hunt for his daughter.

Mrs. Murray shrewdly chooses to focus on the years when female sensibility is most acute. From the time she meets Courtland at age sixteen until her reunion with her father, Margaretta's heart is constantly aquiver. Although she experiences the familiar conflict between inclination and conscience, unlike Clarissa Harlowe and Charlotte Temple, filial duty prevails and she is never actually seduced. Whereas Clarissa and Charlotte are dishonored and die a lingering death, when last seen (in the book edition of 1798, which advances the narrative somewhat) Margaretta is the happy, useful wife, mother, and citizen. Like Pamela's, hers is the story of virtue rewarded. ''Sinisterus'' Courtland, though a less artful charmer than Lovelace, resembles him in being the seducer not of Margaretta, but of Frances Wellwood. He has designs on Margaretta's fortune and, had he won her love, would undoubtedly have deserted her too. However, he is reclaimed by the woman he seduced and makes her his wife, thus becoming an example of the reformed rake. By allowing the "Story of Margaretta" to unfold within the framework of a series of moral essays, Mrs. Murray achieves a balance between an appeal to sensibility and to morality so that she can have her cake and eat it too.

In December 1796 the editor William Biglow declared, "The Publishers of the Massachusetts Magazine have now completed the eighth volume of that publication." Should it "finally share the fate of all other American publications, of the kind; those who have been, and still are, interested in its success, will have, at least, the satisfaction of reflecting, that, in comparison with the rest, *'it died in a good old age'* " (Preface). With these words publication of the *Massachusetts Magazine* came to an end.

## Notes

1. Robert W. G. Vail, "Isaiah Thomas," *Dictionary of American Biography* (1936), 18:435.
2. Lyon N. Richardson, *A History of Early American Magazines, 1741–1789* (1931; rpt., New York: Octagon, 1966), p. 357.
3. Frank Luther Mott, *A History of American Magazines, 1741–1850* (New York and London: D. Appleton and Company, 1930), p. 110.

## Information Sources

BIBLIOGRAPHY:
Mott, Frank Luther. *A History of American Magazines, 1741–1850*. New York and London: D. Appleton and Company, 1930. Pp. 108–11.
Richardson, Lyon N. *A History of Early American Magazines, 1741–1789*. 1931; rpt., New York: Octagon, 1966. Pp. 354–61.
INDEXES: None.
REPRINT EDITIONS: Microfilm edition in *American Periodicals: 18th Century—1800–1850*. Ann Arbor: University Microfilms, 1956. Reels 15–16.
LOCATION SOURCES: Complete runs are to be found at the Library of Congress and the American Antiquarian Society; partial runs are widely available.

## Publication History

MAGAZINE TITLE AND TITLE CHANGES: *The Massachusetts Magazine: or, Monthly Museum of Knowledge and Rational Entertainment, Containing, Poetry, Musick, Biography, History, Physick, Geography, Morality, Criticism, Philosophy, Mathematicks, Agriculture, Architecture, Chymistry, Novels, Tales, Romances, Translations, News, Marriages, Deaths, Meteorological Observations, &c. &c.* In January 1790 the title was changed to *The Massachusetts Magazine, or Monthly Museum. Containing the Literature, History, Politics, Arts, Manners & Amusements of the Age.*
VOLUME AND ISSUE DATA: Volumes 1–8, January 1789-December 1796. The magazine was suspended during the first three months of 1795.
FREQUENCY OF PUBLICATION: Monthly.
PUBLISHERS: January 1789: Isaiah Thomas and Ebenezer T. Andrews, Boston. February-August 1789: Isaiah Thomas and Company, Boston. September 1789-December 1793: Isaiah Thomas and Ebenezer T. Andrews, Boston. January 1794:

Weld, Greenough, and Hill, Boston. February-December 1794: Erza W. Weld and William Greenough, Boston. April 1795: Alexander Martin, Boston. May-September 1795: William Greenough, Boston. October-December 1795: Alexander Martin, Boston. January 1796: James Cutler, Boston. February-June 1796: Alexander Martin, Boston. July-October 1796: Benjamin Sweetser, Boston. November-December 1796: James Cutler, Boston.

EDITORS: According to Richardson, p. 373, Isaiah Thomas and others (including possibly Jeremy Belknap) edited the magazine, January 1789-December 1793; again, according to Richardson, p. 373, the probable editors for January-December 1794 were the publishers, Ezra W. Weld and William Greenough; Thaddeus M. Harris, April-December 1795; William Biglow, January 1796; Thaddeus M. Harris, February-June 1796; William Biglow, July-December 1796.

*Bruce Granger*

# THE MASSACHUSETTS QUARTERLY REVIEW

The *Massachusetts Quarterly Review* was to be a mature *Dial** (Boston) a "Dial with a beard" in editor Theodore Parker's words.[1] Like the earlier *Dial*, the *Massachusetts Quarterly* arose out of impatience with the conservatism of leading American periodicals and a sense of community and shared purpose among liberal Unitarian ministers, New England literati, and social reformers. When the *Dial* discontinued publication in the spring of 1844, there was soon talk of a journal to replace it. As early as the summer of 1844, London bookseller John Chapman was unsuccessfully promoting the idea of a transatlantic successor.[2] Emerson, who had found his duties as editor of the *Dial* increasingly irksome, was understandably not enthusiastic. Three years later, however, both he and Parker were separately drawing up lists of possible contributors and subjects for a new magazine.[3] In April of 1847 a small group, composed mostly of writers from the *Dial*, gathered at Emerson's to lay the groundwork for the new journal. Though Henry Thoreau asked pointedly whether anyone present could not publish in existing journals, and enthusiasm was shared by few, plans went ahead, and a committee composed of Emerson, Parker, and Charles Sumner agreed to seek a publisher.[4] Subsequently both Emerson and Sumner flatly refused to head the new journal, and Parker became editor by default. Emerson "weakly" consented to assist with the editorial duties, and James Elliot Cabot agreed to be corresponding secretary and business manager.[5]

Under Parker the project took on the coloring of social reform. In May Parker convened a larger group, now called significantly a "Council of Reformers." William Lloyd Garrison and other antislavery friends outnumbered the former *Dial* writers.[6] After the meeting Parker, Cabot, and Samuel Gridley Howe prepared a prospectus for a new journal that would survey *"Literature, Politics, Religion, Humanity and the Humanities."* In a letter to a friend, however, Parker confessed his frankly didactic goal of promoting "the great Ideas of our day which are not yet incorporated into Institutions."[7] The "Editor's Address," coaxed out of the reluctant Emerson for the first number in December of 1847, echoed the reform spirit of Parker's circle. Lamenting that American "moral and intellectual effects are not on the same scale with trade and production," Emerson promised a journal with the "courage and power to solve the problems which the great groping society around us, stupid with perplexity, is dumbly exploring." (1:2, 5).

Reform interests dominated the first issues. Parker's indictment of the Mexican War, the first article and in a sense the real germ of the *Massachusetts Quarterly Review*, set the tone. Like the anti-slavery essays that followed in a nearly unbroken stream over the next three years, his essay avoided partisan politics but was bursting at the seams with Free-Soil principles. The war, to Parker, was symptomatic of America's shallow materialism, violating the Constitution and higher law and leading to "the debasement of her great men" (1:54). American soldiers killed in the war, Parker charged, were "murdered by slavery."

The first issues also reflected Parker's and Cabot's eclectic interests in science, history, law, biblical studies, and, to a lesser degree, literature and art. Cabot's timely review of the life and writings of Swiss biologist Louis Agassiz, who had just completed his triumphant residence in America by being appointed to the faculty of Harvard's new Lawrence Scientific School, was the article best calculated to attract a wide audience. In literature and the arts, however, the first issues made a revealingly weak showing with Samuel Gray Ward's diffuse meditation on sculptor Hiram Powers's enormously popular "Greek Slave" and Parker's brief essay on ballad literature. These were hardly the reputation-settling discussions promised in the "Editor's Address." Another sign of a shaky beginning, hidden by the anonymity of all the authors, was that half the pages in the first two issues were written by the editor himself. The first number ended heavily with a section of short reviews of new books, mostly scholarly and religious, and a two-page list of "Recent Publications in Continental Europe," not one in English.

The new journal attracted little notice and, at best, grudging approval. Writing in the Fourierist *Harbinger*,* Parker's friend George Ripley praised the "high and manly position" but found "more of the judicious composure of the venerable North American than the sparkling and salient freshness . . . in a new child of the morning."[8] "Beautiful paper and print," Thomas Carlyle wrote Emerson slyly from England, "and very promising otherwise."[9] The reaction among Emerson's circle was decidedly unfriendly. "Concordians are not quite content" wrote Amos Bronson Alcott with understatement, " . . . and would have a better or none."[10] Thoreau, who had been hostile from the start, observed caustically that "it is probably not so good a book as the Boston Almanac."[11] Emerson, too, was much dissatisfied. "Their journal is of a good spirit . . . but no intellectual tone . . . no literary skill even," he wrote after receiving the first number while still in England.[12] After another number he wrote Cabot from London to propose "dropping this Review form & obtaining short miscellanies also; prose & verse."[13] To his wife he added that "the M. Q. J. will fail unless Henry

Thoreau & Alcott & [Ellery] Channing and Charles Newcomb,—the fourfold-visaged four,—fly to the rescue."[14] There was little chance, however, that Parker would begin welcoming contributions from Emerson's circle. Before the *Quarterly* had begun, he had written off Channing and Thoreau under the heading, "Certain but not Valuable."[15] By the late summer of 1848 Emerson was pleading in the name of "the unwilling martyr contributors" to let the journal die in its infancy. "Who is it for?" he asked, and when he had dismissed all possibilities, concluded, "We are to work blindly for these poor publishers to the certain wasting of our wits."[16] After having expressed himself so strongly, Emerson was annoyed and angered to find that Parker had inserted an unauthorized announcement that the "Senior Editor" had returned from abroad "and will of course contribute to its columns" (1:528). Both Emerson and Cabot had had enough and withdrew entirely from all editorial responsibilities.

Following the defections Parker carried on the journal alone, but later issues showed the influence of Emerson's criticisms. In the first volume Parker had given literary subjects a scant twenty-three pages. In the second volume, he was to increase the literary matter to seventy-two pages, or one-seventh of the total, and then to almost a quarter of the third and final volume. Reviews and critical articles began appearing on such new English authors as Alfred Lord Tennyson, Arthur Hugh Clough (by Emerson), Robert Browning, and Walter Savage Landor (by James Russell Lowell). The third volume was marked by Parker's long review of Emerson's career and by two reviews of new American books, Lowell's qualified but generally favorable review of Henry Thoreau's first book, and George B. Loring's notice of Hawthorne's *Scarlet Letter*. But while the *Massachusetts Quarterly* began to show promise as a liberal review of rising English and American authors, Parker made only a half-hearted attempt to fulfill his promise of including original pieces in prose and verse. Aside from quotations in reviews the only poetry or fiction in the *Massachusetts Quarterly* was translations of a handful of German hymns and lyrics and of nearly a hundred aphoristic verses by seventeenth-century German mystic Johann Scheffler. Scheffler's verses, Cabot's article on Hindu philosophy, and a pair of articles on Swedenborg by Henry James, Sr., were as close as the *Massachusetts Quarterly* ever came to *Dial*'s fascination with mysticism and Oriental scriptures.

While literary subjects eventually eclipsed both scientific and religious concerns in the *Massachusetts Quarterly Review*, political and social criticism remained the journal's core. Parker found ready contributors for antislavery subjects, but on other reform topics he was the chief writer. Nearly every issue carried one of his weighty articles on politics or society, always infused with democratic, vaguely Jeffersonian values that constituted the magazine's ideology. Against the standard of ideal democracy he measured American public education, the career of John Quincy Adams, the Polk administration, the Free-Soil party, even the works of historians Richard Hildreth and William H. Prescott.

Other writers echoed Parker's democratic themes. Articles on cheap postage by Samuel Gridley Howe, on the Massachusetts Indians by Wendell Phillips, on the German Revolution of 1848, the economic status of Russia, "Panslavism," and the Irish question all joined in promoting democratic institutions and human rights while condemning political, economic, and social systems that favored class interests and restricted individual liberty.

Despite its promise as a liberal journal of literary and social criticism and its growing list of contributors, the *Massachusetts Quarterly* never found wide acceptance. As a reform publication it had to compete in a field already crowded with pamphlets, newspapers, and periodicals. As a literary jounral it had been slow to find its voice, and moreover, its failure to include original fiction and poetry ruled out a large portion of its potential public. When the publishers failed in 1850, Parker let the journal die quietly following the September issue. As he admitted in his farewell to his readers, the journal "never became what its projectors intended" (3:524). The public apparently agreed, for the demise of the *Massachusetts Quarterly* went virtually unnoticed.

Even without the support of Emerson and the *Dial* group, the *Massachusetts Quarterly Review* had kept alive much of the spirit of the *Dial*. Its idealism, having matured amid the disorder of American politics during the Mexican War, was more practical than the *Dial*'s. Although it lacked the youthful exuberance and freshness of the *Dial*, it still embodied the vigorous political, social, literary, and philosophical idealism of the Transcendental movement. In this sense it was the legitimate heir of Brook Farm, *Walden*, and the *Dial*.

## Notes

1. Thomas Wentworth Higginson, "Memoir of James Elliot Cabot," *Proceedings of the Massachusetts Historical Society*, n.s. 20 (December 1906), 530.

2. Theodore Parker to Ralph Waldo Emerson, 12 August 1844, MS. Houghton Library, Harvard University.

3. Clarence Gohdes, "Parker's Quarterly Review," *The Periodicals of American Transcendentalism*, (Durham, S.C.: Duke University Press, 1931), pp. 164–65; *The Journals and Miscellaneous Notebooks of Ralph Waldo Emerson*, ed. William H. Gilman et al. 16 vols. (Cambridge, Mass.: Belknap Press of Harvard University Press, 1960–1982), 10:46–47.

4. James Elliot Cabot, *A Memoir of Ralph Waldo Emerson*, 2 vols. (Boston: Houghton Mifflin, 1887), 2:497; Amos Bronson Alcott, journal entry for 14 April 1847, quoted in *The Letters of Ralph Waldo Emerson*, ed. Ralph L. Rusk, 6 vols. (New York: Columbia University Press, 1939), 3:392, n.82 (Hereafter cited as *Letters of RWE*).

5. Cabot, 2:496–97; Higginson, p. 530.

6. Samuel May, Jr., to Mary Carpenter, 29 May 1847, quoted in Wendell Phillips Garrison and Francis Jackson Garrison, *William Lloyd Garrison, 1805–1879: The Story of His Life, Told by His Children*, 4 vols. (New York: Century, 1885–1889), 3:188.

7. Theodore Parker to John P. Hale, 21 June 1847, printed in George E. Carter, "Theodore Parker and John P. Hale," *Dartmouth College Library Bulletin*, n.s.13 (November 1972):14.

8. George Ripley, "The Massachusetts Quarterly Review," *The Harbinger*, 11 March 1848.

9. Thomas Carlyle to Ralph Waldo Emerson, 30 December 1847, *The Correspondence of Emerson and Carlyle*, ed. Joseph Slater (New York: Columbia University Press, 1964), p. 437.

10. Amos Bronson Alcott to [Charles Lane], 30 May 1848, *The Letters of A. Bronson Alcott*, ed. Richard L. Herrnstadt (Ames: Iowa State University Press, 1969), p. 141.

11. Henry Thoreau to Ralph Waldo Emerson, 21 May 1848, *The Correspondence of Henry David Thoreau*, ed. Walter Harding and Carl Bode (New York: New York University Press, 1958), p. 227.

12. Ralph Waldo Emerson to Lidian Emerson, 8 January 1848, *Letters of RWE*, 4:4.

13. Ralph Waldo Emerson to James Elliot Cabot, 21 April 1848, *Letters of RWE*, 4:60.

14. Ralph Waldo Emerson to Lidian Emerson, 21 April 1848, *Letters of RWE*, 4:56.

15. Quoted in Gohdes, p. 165.

16. Ralph Waldo Emerson to Theodore Parker, 17? August 1848, *Letters of RWE*, 4:107.


## Information Sources

BIBLIOGRAPHY:

Cabot, James Elliot. *A Memoir of Ralph Waldo Emerson*. 2 vols. Boston: Houghton, Mifflin, 1887.

*The Correspondence of Henry David Thoreau*. Ed. Walter Harding and Carl Bode. New York: New York University Press, 1958.

*The Correspondence of Emerson and Carlyle*. Ed. Joseph Slater. New York: Columbia University Press, 1964.

Carter, George E. "Theodore Parker and John P. Hale." *Dartmouth College Library Bulletin*, n.s. 13 (November 1972):13–33.

Dorn, Minda Ruth Pearson. "Literary Criticism in the *Boston Quarterly Review*, the *Present*, and the *Massachusetts Quarterly Review*." Ph.D. diss., Southern Illinois University at Carbondale, 1976.

Garrison, Wendell P., and Francis Jackson Garrison. *William Lloyd Garrison, 1805–1879: The Story of His Life Told by His Children*. 4 vols. New York: Century, 1885–1889.

Gohdes, Clarence. "Parker's Quarterly Review." *The Periodicals of American Transcendentalism*. Durham: Duke University Press, 1931. Pp. 157–93.

Higginson, Thomas Wentworth. "Memoir of James Elliot Cabot." *Proceedings of the Massachusetts Historical Society*, n.s. 20 (December 1906):526–33.

*The Journals and Miscellaneous Notebooks of Ralph Waldo Emerson*. 16 vols. Ed. William H. Gilman et al. Cambridge, Mass.: The Belknap Press of Harvard University Press, 1960–1982.

*The Letters of A. Bronson Alcott*. Ed. Richard L. Herrnstadt. Ames, Iowa: Iowa State University Press, 1969.

*The Letters of Ralph Waldo Emerson*. 6 vols. Ed. Ralph R. Rusk. New York: Columbia University Press, 1939.

Mott, Frank Luther. "*The Massachusetts Quarterly Review*." *A History of American Magazines*. 4 vols. Cambridge, Mass.: Belknap Press of Harvard University Press, 1957. 1:775–79.

Ripley, George. "The Massachusetts Quarterly Review." *The Harbinger*, 11 March 1848, p. 151; 9 September 1848, p. 150.

Weiss, John. *The Life and Correspondence of Theodore Parker*. 2 vols. New York: Appleton, 1864.

INDEXES: Gohdes, Clarence. ''Parker's Quarterly Reivew.'' *The Periodicals of American Transcendentalism.* Durham: Duke University Press, 1931. Pp. 166–70.
REPRINT EDITIONS: American Periodicals: Series II, 1800–1850. University Microfilms, Ann Arbor. Reel 658. Library Resources, Inc. The Microbook Library of American Civilization. (LAC).
LOCATION SOURCES: Widely available.

## Publication History

MAGAZINE TITLE AND TITLE CHANGES: *Massachusetts Quarterly Review.*
VOLUME AND ISSUE DATA: Volumes 1–3, December 1847-September 1850.
FREQUENCY OF PUBLICATION: Quarterly.
PUBLISHERS: Coolidge & Wiley, Boston.
EDITORS: Theodore Parker, Ralph Waldo Emerson, James Elliot Cabot, 1847–1848; Theodore Parker, 1848–1850.

*Gary L. Collison*

## M'LLE NEW YORK

Conceived by Vance Thompson as a free-spirited romp through modern life and laced with intellectual pretentions, *M'lle New York* was the offspring of such European counterparts as the *Germ*, the *Century Guild Hobby Horse*, and the *Yellow Book*. As part of the fin de siècle Decadent movement, however, *M'lle New York* had largely missed its moment, as had America generally, despite the undeliberate influence of Edgar Allan Poe. In fact, the birth of the magazine had been motivated by editor Thompson's observation that New York of the 1890s was behind the times and needed a publication that would generate some controversy. First appearing in August 1895, three months after the Oscar Wilde trial (after which even such key figures of decadence as Arthur Symons were hastening to disassociate themselves from the movement), *M'lle New York* starts out in a position uncharacteristic of its European predecessors, who saw themselves at the forefront of the avant-garde. To *M'lle New York* and a handful of other small magazines of the 1890s (the *Knight Errant*, *Moods*, the *Lotus*, *John-A-Dreams*) was left the task of catching up.

Vance Thompson got together with J. G. Huneker, music critic for the *Recorder*, and cartoonists Tom Fleming and Tom Powers to form his staff immediately after his return from a stay in Europe that had been so stimulating as to doom anywhere else to dismal comparison. He often refers to those years in the pages of *M'lle New York*, mostly in the form of offhand name-dropping: ''I wish I had never known Paul Verlaine; had never lent him five francs, had never helped him up the hospital step'' (no. 1, n.p.) and so on. Thompson also knew Maeterlinck and Rodenbach, and the associations left him feeling not a little cocky and superior to the average man of learning in New York. It was in the spirit of that contempt for the average man of learning and for the masses as well that the Princeton graduate of 1883 conceived his editorial policy. In the forward to the premier issue, he dedicates *M'lle New York* to a sort of elitism that scorns the public in favor of an oddly conceived mob. "*M'lle New York* is not concerned with the public. Her only ambition is to disintegrate some small portion of the public into its original component parts—the aristocrat of birth, wit, learning and art and the joyously vulgar mob" (no. 1, n.p.). The most notable difference between the mob and the public is that the mob avows its ignorance and allows those who are superior to advance. Thompson of course placed himself and his cronies in the superior group. In this heightened sense of individual superiority and in most other respects *M'lle New York* is in step with the Decadent journals that precede it. Particularly characteristic is the Francophilia evident in the frequent publication of French verse and in the title of the magazine itself. For function "Miss New York" would have done nicely, but the connotation of Paris, amorality, and the courtesan, coupled with an enthusiasm for Baudelaire, Mallarmé, Verlaine, and Huysmans, dictates the "M'lle." The first number sums up the picture with an epilogue entitled "The Helen of Cities." "Bonjour M'lle New York! Sh, saperlipopette—b'jour, l'petit rat'. M'lle New York is awake. You have indulged in the innocent depravity of her morning kiss. Now ring the bell and bid your man bring you a toothbrush and a glass of water" (no. 1, n.p.). So Vance Thompson hoped to awaken a French Decadent consciousness in New York.

Another evident union with the Decadence is the pleasure these aristocrats of birth, wit, learning, and art take, like Huysmans's Des Esseintes, in slumming among the joyously vulgar mob, a pleasure often evoked in the contributions of novelist Edward W. Townsend, author of *Chimmie Fadden*, who provides the magazine with the inevitable 1890s New York tenement article, and its first short story, "By Whom the Offence Cometh," in which Lena, a nice girl, meets the wrong sort of boy and predictably spirals into a life of despair and opium addiction as a result.

Although bad things characteristically happen to female characters in Decadent texts, *M'lle New York* is singular in its celebration of misogyny. In "The Spider," the narrator has a hallucination that a spider resembles his "woman," and he concludes that she is a female fiend. He accuses her of trying to poison him, makes the sign of the cross, and kills her (no. 1, n.p.). Another misogynistic fantasy in which the female is similarly linked to the grotesque motivates the plot of "The Double-Headed Nightingale" (no. 4, n.p.), the tale of a two-headed chanteuse (she sings her own harmony) who is murdered by the narrator.

The implied misogyny of the fiction is reinforced overtly in the editorials, which provide "witticisms" such as "God alone has the right to be a misanthrope; for man there is only misogyny," as well as blatant assertions such as "woman is physically, mentally, and morally inferior to man" (no. 6, n.p.). For *M'lle New York*, it seems that woman's moral inferiority is most important, as indicated by numerous tales of women of fallen virtue as well as the large number of illustrations in this heavily illustrated journal, of loose or evil women. Add to this a fantasy interview with Jack the Ripper (no. 6, n.p.), an obsession with the image of the devil as a woman, Salome, and on and on. In a rebuttal to one of Thompson's particularly potent attacks on the female, entitled "Gynolatry," associate editor Huneker defends woman as a civilizing influence, man's equal except when she is "strong minded" (no. 8, n.p.). Thompson responds that he has published Huneker's "study in hysteria because it is at once an example and a warning."

The gynolatry versus misogyny debate between Huneker and Thompson is, according to Frank C. Hanighen, a hidden comedy, as "Thompson stood in immense awe of his wife," actress/playwright Lillian Spencer, "and never dared oppose her slightest wish," whereas "Huneker was said to be a brutal cave-man."[1] More importantly, it exemplifies a tendency toward either/or thinking, not only in *M'lle New York*, but in Decadent thought generally. Fleming's illustration of two women, one a laughing wench, the other a weeping nun (no. 4, n.p.), is typical— the virgin and the whore. One is either one or the other, as one is either modern or a philistine. This is the antithetical equation that explains the Decadent preoccupation with both religious images and satanism; the Catholic mass is easily reversed into the Black mass. Pieces such as "A Victim of Devil-Worshippers" (6: n.p.), which includes "blasphemous and awful litanies," illustrated with a drawing of Baudelaire, provide vivid examples.

Consistent with its Decadent sympathies, *M'lle New York* is obsessed with the underdeveloped world, Chinese opium dens, of course, but black women especially. A reader confronted by Hamlin's crude caricatures of Jews and Fleming's flattering portraits of Negro women is told, "It is a matter of pure prejudice. You prefer port, I prefer sherry; it is futile to debate questions of personal taste" (no. 2, n.p.) *M'lle New York* never questions the pleasures it takes—even at others' expense. The denigration of Jews is extraordinarily energetic and sophomoric. This has been credited to Thompson's snobbism and Huneker's admiration for the famed anti-Dreyfusard Edouard Drumont.[2] Whatever the case, the only fact about Jews that seems to be familiar to Thompson and his staff is that a kosher diet prohibits pork, prompting numerous cartoons of large-nosed businessmen cuddling up to pigs—an odd blend of anti-Semitism and misogyny. More pointedly, in an appeal based on biology and evolution common to Decadent-fatalistic thought, we read such commentaries as, "Jewish children are more intelligent than ours at the age of puberty; however, they lose as they grow. They are at once nearer Nature and the ape" (no. 13, n.p.).

At times, usually in its purely critical moments, *M'lle New York* does provide valuable insights. In it we find an introduction to numerous non-English writers, including the first American review of Norwegian novelist Knut Hamsun. Thompson's analysis of Mallarmé, "The Technique of the Symbolists," (no. 7, n.p.), almost keeps pace with the switch from Decadence to symbolism that had begun in Europe, as do pieces on Wagnerian poets and the celebrated Black-French poets Charles Cros and José Maria de Hérédia. *M'lle New York* laments in "Scalpel or Branding Iron" (no. 2, n.p.) that in "the age of criticism . . . young men do not write love verses . . . they write essays on Ibsen," and it also makes an interesting argument for a movement toward a science of criticism. But it also could turn its critique inward: "The average art or dramatic critique is made up in almost equal parts of middle-class opinions, uncertain axioms of the craft, and personal prejudices" (no. 2, n.p.).

When the magazine is most playful and least anarchically spiteful it is at its best, as in a poetic spoof of Max Nordau, the author of *Degeneration*, with whom the Decadents had a justifiable feud. The piece is accompanied by a drawing of Nordau with wild art-noveau hair (2: n.p). Also amusing is a fantasy piece describing the performance of "Dred," a romantic opera in four acts, performed by an all-black cast at the Metropolitan Opera in 1895. Like the piece on Cros and Hérédia, it borders on biting social commentary.

Overall, one gets the sense that *M'lle New York*'s main function was to provide an outlet for Americans who were frustrated by having had a glimpse of Europe. Vance Thompson was surely one of the Americans who, as the upper crust in Wilde's *Picture of Dorian Gray*, want to go to Paris when they die. Thompson did in fact spend most of his last twenty years in Europe and died in Nice in 1925.

The circulation of the magazine was understandably small. It is not unlikely that this fact kept its more outrageous ribaldries from attracting the attention of censors. It briefly provided its readers with an outlet for their cosmopolitan inclinations before it met financial trouble, began to appear irregularly, and finally disappeared entirely. To American letters *M'lle New York* gave very little, except as it helped bring little magazines into fashion, and as writers associated with it went on to other pursuits. Several writers for *M'lle New York* later wrote for the *Criterion*; Huneker continued to grow as an interesting literary figure and commentator on Nietzsche. Perhaps too *M'lle New York* helped weaken the puritanism of the nineteenth century, despite its repressive moments.

Vance Thompson, though his career covered a remarkable range and offered constant promise, never was to realize the achievement of an Arthur Symons. Although his serious effort, *French Portraits*, was fairly well received, Thompson was too willing to act on whims and to produce work purely for the cash; he died best remembered for his popular success *Eat and Grow Thin*, a work based on his wife's menus. The irony is perhaps appropriate.

## Notes

1. Frank Hanighen, "Vance Thompson and *M'lle New York*," *The Bookman* 75 (1932):477.
2. Hanighen, p. 475.

## Information Sources

BIBLIOGRAPHY:

Fletcher, Ian. "Decadence and the Little Magazines." *Decadence in the 1890's*. London: Edward Arnold Ltd., 1979.

Hanighen, Frank C. "Vance Thompson and *M'lle New York.*" *The Bookman* 75 (1932):472–81.

INDEXES: None.

REPRINT EDITIONS: None.

LOCATION SOURCES: Complete runs: Harvard University, Peabody Institute, Free Library of Philadelphia, University of Oregon, University of Chicago, Newberry Library. Partial runs: Yale University, Tulane University Howard-Tilton Memorial Library, American Antiquarian Society, New York Public Library, University of Minnesota, Princeton University.

### Publication History

MAGAZINE TITLE AND TITLE CHANGES: *M'lle New York.*

VOLUME AND ISSUE DATA: Volume 1, numbers 1–11, August 1895-April 1896; volume 2, numbers 1–4, November 1898–1899.

FREQUENCY OF PUBLICATION: Irregular.

PUBLISHERS: M'lle New York, 100 Nassau, New York, and 256 W. 23rd, New York.

EDITORS: Vance Thompson (October 1895–1899 with J. G. Huneker).

*Anthony Chase*

# THE MONTHLY ANTHOLOGY AND BOSTON REVIEW

Literary historians most often associate the *Monthly Anthology* with the Boston Athenaeum and the *North American Review.** The "society of gentlemen" that generated the *Anthology* also founded the library, and several members drew on their *Anthology* experience in creating the *North American*. The *Anthology*'s seven-and-a-half-year life was remarkable for its day, however, and its pages house a literate, sometimes provocative examination of society and culture during a transitional period of American life and literature.

David Phineas Adams, a young, Harvard-educated teacher and mathematician, initiated the *Anthology* in November 1803. Editing as Sylvanus Per-Se to invite comparison with the *Gentlemen's Magazine*, Adams aspired "to open to public notice some specimens of the literary skill in this country,—to offer such essays, as are furnished with sentimental instruction and rational amusement,—to remark on the progress of science and the fine arts, and, with various tongues, to plead in behalf of virtuous refinement" (1[242]).[1] His magazine offered essays on subjects from dueling to church music, original and reprinted verse, and reviews. Hoping to emphasize native works, Adams introduced a "Monthly Catalogue" of new American publications in the third number. He wrote for all three sections himself, but attracted only two frequent contributors, William Ellery Channing, the Elder, and his brother Francis Dana Channing. Forced to fill his *Anthology* with reprinted British material and unable to make money, Adams abandoned the enterprise after six months.

William Emerson, pastor of Boston's First Church and father of Ralph Waldo Emerson, assumed editorship with the seventh number in May 1804. Emerson hoped, even more expansively than Adams, to deal with "almost every art and science," especially "natural history and philosophy, . . . logick and theology, mathematicks and poetry, . . . law and medicine" (1:ii-iii). John T. Kirkland later defined the *Anthology*'s goal as "promoting useful knowledge and harmless amusement . . . sound principles . . . good morals . . . and correct taste" (4:1). By August 1804, Emerson had refined the magazine's format. An anthology of essays and poetry would be followed by an expanded *Boston Review*. The "Monthly Catalogue" would also be expanded and such almanac material as meteorological tables and notices of prominent deaths added as filler, perhaps at the request of the printers. Collections of state papers would be appended to most volumes.

Emerson did even more to revitalize the *Anthology*'s base of contributors. Forced to write much of his first number alone, the new editor sought help from friends. On 3 October 1805, the Anthology Society adopted a constitution, mandated weekly dinner meetings, and elected officers. The typical member, as described by M. A. DeWolfe Howe, was "a young graduate of Harvard, between twenty and thirty years of age. . . . representing that class of the community in which the traditions of intellectual leadership were most firmly established."[2] Among the fourteen charter members were John S. J. Gardiner, rector of Trinity Church; William Smith Shaw, clerk of the U.S. District Court; Joseph S. Buckminster, minister and later lecturer on biblical criticism at Harvard; and William Tudor, Jr., first editor of the *North American Review*. Members invited later included Kirkland, minister and future president of Harvard; James Savage, president of the Massachusetts Historical Society; poet Winthrop Sargent; Alexander Hill Everett; and George Ticknor. The society's constitution established shared responsibility for writing and selecting material. The annually elected editor, later called the superintending committee to reduce the suggestion of individualism, merely oversaw printing and read proofs. Members pledged to gather items for the "Silva" collection of short excerpts, to contribute "Remarker" essays periodically, and to pursue special interests in essays or poems. New books were assigned to members for their own or solicited review. All reviews, most essays and poems, and eventually all "Silva" and "Remarker" numbers were read and evaluated at the weekly dinners. Although society members often neglected their writing and editorial chores, the *Anthology* flourished on their blended talents.

Addresses to the *Anthology*'s readers insist that the society is "pledged to no party in religion or politicks," though acknowledging "opinions on both" (5:122). Their political opinion was decidedly Federalist, but they avoided controversy on the subject by relegating political discourse to asides within other contexts. Ardent Unitarianism was harder to mute, and the *Anthology* openly endorsed the Reverend Henry Ware's controversial appointment to the Hollis Professorship of Divinity at Harvard in 1803 (2:78-80, 152-57, and 211-16). Sectarian concerns faded as clergymen became less dominant in the society, though comments on morals and manners remained essential to the *Anthology*.

Both politics and religion took back seats to the society's neoclassical critical doctrine. Essays and reviews repeatedly assert the critic's duty to define universal standards of artistic form, standards inherited from classical writers and from the moderns who most ardently follow their lead. Samuel C. Thacher, for example, proposes Tacitus's *Life of Agricola* as a corrective model for John Marshall's *Life of George Washington* (5:261). Arthur M. Walter claims the *Spectator* and the *Rambler* as inspirations for the society's own "Remarker" series (2:451–54). Though disclaiming "deep erudition," Walter displays his own learning through Latin and French phrases and citations of Tasso, Sydney, and Greek historians. Such devices typify *Anthology* prose, and translations of Greek and Latin verse appear frequently. Purifying English is also important. Thacher ends his three-part review by attacking Marshall's style. The chief justice reveals "too many proofs that the study of a pure, logical, and classical style has not occupied enough of his attention" (5:437). A long list of linguistic inaccuracies illustrates that weakness. Not surprisingly, Noah Webster emerges as a major cultural villain.

Neoclassicism moderates the society's insistence on "raising the reputation of American literature" (5:122). Americans, they argued, must meet universal standards before claiming literary greatness, and few native writers had done so. "In literature we are yet in our infancy," Gardiner claims, "and to compare our authors, whether in prose or poetry, to those of the old world, can proceed only from the grossest ignorance or the most insufferable vanity" (2:632). On introducing a series of retrospective reviews of American books, Buckminster can hope to find only "a few rare and undescribed specimens which may . . . awaken . . . the regard of some future historian of literature" (5:54). Crude American manners, corrupt American language, and exaggerated claims of national excellence often bear the brunt of *Anthology* satire, as when Shaw proposes a native tongue "one part Indian, another Irish, and three fifths Negro" to embody "the origin and descent of those who guide the destinies of our nation" (3:400). But the society glimpses a hopeful future. William Cullen Bryant's *Embargo* shows considerable promise (5:339–40), and Tudor dubs Washington Irving's *History of New York* "the wittiest [book] our press has ever produced" (8:123).

An honest desire to foster responsible discussion prevented the *Anthology* from becoming a doctrinaire magazine. The society violated its ban on political discourse by accepting Fisher Ames's essay on republicanism (2:563–66), because they had asked Ames for a contribution.[3] Everett finds *Modern Chivalry* effective as a collection of opinionated essays while objecting to Hugh Henry Brackenridge's politics (5:508, 554–56). Jedidiah Morse, a theological conservative, rebuts the *Anthology*'s defense of the Ware appointment (2:206–11), and even Noah Webster gains a hearing (7:205–11). Dissenting critical views are also present. Benjamin Welles's "Remarker" invocation to "let him . . . , whose soul is pure and holy with the love of nature, take his position in the midst of creation, and commence the mighty work of eternal perfection of thoughts" (3:288) is openly romantic. Walter endorses "the creative energies of invention, the sublime soarings of thought, and the audacious struggles of imagination, bursting from the confinement of reason" (2:235). John Stickney finds Walter Scott "the finest poet of the age" (9:340).

The *Anthology*'s strengths and weaknesses may both be attributed to amateurism. As ministers, doctors, lawyers, and teachers, society members embraced literature as an adjunct to other professional endeavors. Modest hopes of paying for their weekly dinners with something left over to assist the Athenaeum proved futile. "Through their whole career," Tudor explains, "they wrote, and paid for the pleasure of writing."[4] Financial independence, however, gave them free reign over their magazine's content. The *Anthology* often presents the best their age had to offer in serious analyses of pressing cultural issues. Tudor provides a sound assessment of their accomplishment: "The work undoubtedly rendered service to our literature, and aided the discussion of good taste in the community. It was one of the first efforts of regular criticism on American books, and it suffered few productions of the day to escape its notice."[5]

## Notes

1. Authorial attribution of anonymous or pseudonymous articles in the *Anthology* is based on "Contributors to *The Monthly Anthology*," *Anthology Society: Journal of the Proceedings of the Society Which Conducts the Monthly Anthology and Boston Review, October 3, 1805, to July 2, 1811* (Boston: The Boston Athenaeum, 1910), pp. 317–28.

2. "The Anthology Society and Its Minutes," *Anthology Society*, pp. 11–12.

3. *Anthology Society*, p. 39.

4. [William Tudor, Jr.], "The Monthly Anthology," *Miscellanies* (Boston: Wells and Lilly, 1821), p. 4.

5. Tudor, p. 4.

## Information Sources

BIBLIOGRAPHY:

*Anthology Society: Journal of the Proceedings of the Society Which Conducts the Monthly Anthology and Boston Review, October 3, 1805, to July 2, 1811.* Boston: The Boston Athenaeum, 1910. [Apparatus includes an introduction by M. A. DeWolfe Howe, a collation of the *Anthology* by Albert Matthews, lists of members and officers of the society, a list identifying contributors by volume and page number, and a list of books mentioned in the *Journal*.]

Buell, Lawrence. "Identification of Contributors to the *Monthly Anthology and Boston Review*, 1804–1811." *ESQ* 23 (1977):99–105.

Mott, Frank Luther. "*The Monthly Anthology and Boston Review*." *A History of American Magazines*. 4 vols. Cambridge, Mass.: Belknap Press of Harvard University Press, 1957. 1:253–59.

Quincy, Josiah. *The History of the Boston Athenaeum, With Biographical Notices of Its Deceased Founders*. Cambridge, Mass.: Metcalf and Company, 1851.

Simpson, Lewis P., ed. *The Federalist Literary Mind: Selections from the Monthly Anthology and Boston Review, Including Documents Relating to the Boston Athenaeum*. Baton Rouge: Louisiana State University Press, 1962.

————. "A Literary Adventure of the Early Republic: The Anthology Society and the *Monthly Anthology*." *New England Quarterly* 27 (1954):168–90.

[Tudor, William, Jr.] "The Monthly Anthology." *Miscellanies*. (Boston: Wells and Lilly, 1821). Pp. 1–7.

INDEXES: None.

REPRINT EDITIONS: American Periodicals: Series II, 1800–1850. University Microfilms, Ann Arbor. Reels 30–32, 143–144.

LOCATION SOURCES: Widely available.

## Publication History

MAGAZINE TITLE AND TITLE CHANGES: *The Monthly Anthology; or Magazine of Polite Literature*, November 1803-April 1804. *The Monthly Anthology; or, Massachusetts Magazine*, May 1804-July 1804. *The Monthly Anthology, and Boston Review*, August 1804-June 1811.

VOLUME AND ISSUE DATA: Volumes 1–10, November 1803-June 1811.

FREQUENCY OF PUBLICATION: Monthly.

PUBLISHERS: November 1803-April 1804: E. Lincoln, Boston. May 1804-December 1807: Munroe and Francis, Boston. January 1808-December 1808: Snelling and Simons, Boston, and Hastings, Etheridge and Bliss, Boston. January 1809-December 1809: Hastings, Etheridge and Bliss, Boston. January 1810-June 1811: T. B. Wait & Company, Boston.

EDITORS: David Phineas Adams, November 1803-April 1804; William Emerson, May 1804-?; Samuel Cooper Thacher, ?-May 1806; William Smith Shaw, June 1806-October 1807; William Smith Shaw and James Savage, November 1807-November 1808; William Smith Shaw, James Savage, and Alexander Hill Everett, December 1808-July 1809; William Smith Shaw and James Savage, August 1809-June 1811. [After October 1805 most editorial selection was done by the Anthology Society as a whole, the editor serving primarily as a liaison with the printers.]

*Kennedy Williams, Jr.*


# THE MONTHLY MAGAZINE, AND AMERICAN REVIEW

The *Monthly Magazine, and American Review* was first published in April 1799 and ran through three volumes of six issues each until December 1800. Charles Brockden Brown was the chief editor and primary contributor to the *Monthly Magazine* until the journal altered its title (and format) to the *American Review and Literary Journal*, which was issued quarterly from January 1801 to December 1802 with Brown serving in a less prominent capacity. Brown's 1799 correspondence reveals that he had been persuaded by "eight friends" to start a magazine, which Brown did while depending for success upon certain promised "contributions and assistance" from his contemporaries.[1] When such assistance was not forthcoming, the effort to sustain the *Monthly Magazine* came largely from Brown himself, and eventually the strain and distractions of directing the journal caused him to modify and then finally abandon the publication altogether.

In the first issue of the *Monthly Magazine*, an article by Brown strikes a prophetic note. Addressed satirically to the editor, the article notes the ambitious promise of the *Monthly Magazine* to "extract the quintessence of European wisdom, to review and estimate the labors of all writers, domestic and foreign . . . to scrutinize the causes and deduce the consequences of contemporary events" so that, by reading the journal, "the taste of all may be gratified" (1:1). Through this article Brown accurately questioned the *Monthly Magazine*'s "power to perform" these roles, for the journal never did fully achieve its stated ambitions (1:2). Yet all critics agree that Brown's editorial guidance earned the *Monthly Magazine* "a high place in early American journalism."[2]

The first issue of the *Monthly Magazine* established four main sections that would remain as parts of the journal's standard format. The first of these, entitled "Original Communications," contains various essays and samples of American literature. An "American Review" section follows, filled with "critical notices of American publications" as well as speculative ideas about "the literary problems of the day."[3] After the "Review" a "Selections" section appears (largely containing excerpts taken from scientific publications), and the final two or three pages of the *Monthly Magazine* are given to "Poetry," where readers can find selections from William Cowper, John Davis, and Robert Southey. Brown added a fifth section in the second issue of the *Monthly Magazine* (May 1799) entitled "Miscellaneous Articles of Literary and Philosophical Intelligence." These five sections subsequently provided the main framework for all later issues of the *Monthly Magazine*.

One of Brown's primary objectives was to use the *Monthly Magazine* as a forum for the expression of chauvinistic ideas about America's ability to produce and sustain a native literature. In an early article, "On the State of American Literature," Brown expressed "a degree of pride in contemplating the bold, enterprising, and independent spirit of my contemporaries"; yet, at the same time, he described America's "literary character" as "extremely superficial" (1:15–19). The *Monthly Magazine*, Brown hoped, would "materially subserve the interests of letters and science" in America (1:19). It is notable that, during this time of intense political activity, Brown eschewed party politics: "there already exist a sufficient number of vehicles of political expression," he wrote, and "it is presumed readers will in general be best pleased with . . . scientific and literary topics" (1:80).

As Clark notes, the issue of establishing a native literature was always a "live one" in the *Monthly Magazine*, and all three volumes contain materials that vividly illustrate Brown's criticisms of and rather evangelical hopes for America's letters.[4] In another essay "On American Literature," Brown suggested that, in "the literary harvest of America," the "grain is neither vigorous nor plentiful" (1:339–42). A magazine like Brown's could offer at least a partial solution, as long as the journal adhered to a policy of discussing a "variety of topics . . . in a light, familiar, and attractive manner," which meant mixing "humor with pathos; seriousness with gaiety; poetry with narrative" (2:254). Brown also called for American newspapers to play a role in sophisticating the literary tastes of his countrymen. He looked to the newspapers as potentially an "effectual means of introducing" taste and "virtue . . . to the counters, desks, and tea-tables of every rank and profession in society" (3:264).

Brown's critical observations were complemented by samples of his own work, and the *Monthly Magazine* is distinguished by extracts from *Edgar Huntly* (1:21–44) and the *Memoirs of Stephen Calvert* that appeared regularly in the "Original Communications" section of the journal.[5] Donald Ringe also points out that a number of Brown's minor works were used to fill up the pages of the magazine, the most significant being "Thessalonia: A Roman Story" (1:99–117); "The Memoirs of Mary Selwyn" (2:174–207); and "The Trials of Arden" (3:19–36).[6] But the *Monthly Magazine* offered, by design, an eclectic fare for its readers, and the early issues are in particular distinguished by Brown's effort to incorporate a variety of materials into his journal. Therefore, readers looking for historical materials could be satisfied by reviews of and selections from Benjamin Turnbull's *A Complete History of Connecticut* (1:45–46) or Hannah Adams's *A Summary History of New England* (1:445–49). Passages from *Mr. Park's Journey to the Interior Parts of Africa* (1:62–75); Noah Webster's *A Brief History of Epidemic and Pestilential Diseases* (2:30–36); and Thomas Jefferson's "Description of a Quadruped of the Clawed Kind" (2:68–72) were included for readers interested in natural history. Despite Brown's avowed disinterest in political content, the *Monthly Magazine* occasionally printed abolitionist diatribes (2:81–84), and the journal was continually laced with eulogies and orations on George Washington that led to extremely chauvinistic ideas about America's evolving political system.[7] Testaments to such other "Distinguished Characters" as Timothy Dwight (1:388–90) and Joel Barlow (1:465–68) also aimed at developing a sharp pride in American national identity. In a different context one other valuable index to the cultural pulse of the age can be found in a short-lived column entitled the "Theatrical Register," which appeared late (and very rarely) in the magazine (2:143–45; 3:380–82, 455–56). This column surveyed the past two or three months of activity on the American stage in New York and Philadelphia, and as a result the "Register" offers a unique catalog (but not an analysis) of the theatrical fare available to Americans at the turn of the century.

This kind of content, especially when compared to the paucity of material offered in publications contemporary to Brown's, justifies Warfel's contention that the *Monthly Magazine* "deserved to live."[8] But Brown could not rid the magazine of the problems that continually plagued it. Throughout his issues Brown found it necessary to apologize to his readers. At first there were "unavoidable delays" (1:80); then, a series of abbreviated issues were necessitated by a forced "removal from the city during the late epidemic" (1:131); finally, "the many difficulties" that prevented "a prompt collection of the small funds which so cheap a publication demanded" forced Brown into a major alteration of the journal (3:iv). Beginning in January 1801, the *Monthly Magazine* would change its title to the *American Review and Literary Journal*, and the new publication would be issued quarterly.

The *American Review and Literary Journal* quite simply grew out of the *Monthly Magazine*'s "Review" section, which had always been "the most highly regarded feature" of Brown's first magazine.[9] The "Preface" to the first volume of the *American Review* predictably emphasized many of the same editorial sentiments as its predecessor: "with our national independence secured, and our government established," the *Review* aimed at directing more attention to "literature and science" (1:iii). The *Review* would attempt to "cultivate" the "intellectual soil of America" through "original essays on moral, literary, and scientific subjects," adding "biographical memoirs and anecdotes of remarkable and eminent persons, particularly in America" (1:v). Like the *Monthly Magazine*, the *Review* proposed to keep political discourse to a minimum, suggesting that "they who look for the ordinary effusions of party politics must turn from the pages of this Review" (1:v).

With this editorial policy the *Review* presented itself as an extension of the *Monthly Magazine*—not as a different publication. Yet significant differences separate the two titles. Whereas Brown was unquestionably the driving force behind the *Monthly Magazine*, he had "little close connection" with the *Review*, and, most critics agree, he served mainly as an occasional contributor and reviewer.[10] This made for significant alterations in the content and format of the *Review*. The journal was divided into three major sections, instead of the *Monthly Magazine*'s five. An "Articles" section presented excerpts from or reviews of such works as G. R. Minot's 1798 *History of Massachusetts Bay* (1:1–16); Noah Webster's *Elements of Useful Knowledge* (2:334–37); and Brown's own *Wieland*, which was reviewed in two volumes (1:333–39; 2:26–38). The following section, "Foreign Works Published," reviewed American or English editions of scientific works like Lavoisier's *Elements of Chemistry* (1:96–100). The *Review*'s third section was called the "Literary Journal," and it consisted of three subsections: "Intelligence" (dealing with scientific topics, or those of natural history); "New Patents, Inventions, and Discoveries"; and "New Publications Preparing for the Press." Scattered throughout these sections were materials dealing with science—such as "Discoveries in Mineralogy" (1:364–69)—natural history—A. Michaux's *History of American Oaks* (2:317–24)—religion—"A Catechism designed for the Instructing of the rising Generation into the principles of the Christian Religion (2:403–06)—or politics—John Quincy Adams's "Oration, Delivered at Plymouth" (3:479–83).

As these representative titles indicate, the *American Review* is, in Mott's words, filled with a lot of information but not much that is "very interesting" to literary or cultural historians; at best, with regard to Brown's career, it is possible to view the journal as paving the way for Brown's later "political pamphleteering."[11] But even this view is debatable, since Brown's precise involvement in the *Review* remains ambiguous. Obviously, the most striking dissimilarity between the *American Review* and the *Monthly Magazine* involves the former's near-total exclusion of literary pieces—Brown was no longer contributing his works as he had done for the *Monthly Magazine*. For literary historians the most interesting or useful part of the *American Review* is its "New Publications" subsection, where readers find notices regarding the publication of novels like *Clara Howard* (1:263), as well as summaries of the publishing activities of Mathew Carey and T. & J. Swords (2:378–79; 3:496–500).

Unable to sustain the spectrum of commentary he had managed in the *Monthly Magazine*, Brown surely must have become disillusioned with the *Review* when the journal could not satisfy its editorial ambitions. When the *Review* closed in 1802, it had indeed been transmogrified into a quasi-almanac repository of factual information. Thus, Brown's ambitious plans for his first magazine had failed. But the initial attempts of the *Monthly Magazine* to instill pride in America's literature—to function as a forum for the expression of American literature— were significant and inspiring enough to spur Brown into the editorship of another magazine, the Philadelphia *Literary Magazine, and American Register*,* with which Brown became involved in 1803.[12]

### Notes

1. Frank Luther Mott, *A History of American Magazines, 1741–1850* (Cambridge: Harvard University Press, 1957), p. 218.

2. David Lee Clark, *Charles Brockden Brown: Pioneer Voice in America* (Durham: Duke University Press, 1952), p. 154.

3. Harry R. Warfel, *Charles Brockden Brown: American Gothic Novelist* (Gainesville, Florida: University of Florida Press, 1949), p. 170.

4. Clark, p. 137.

5. *The Memoirs of Stephen Calvert* was serialized in the *Monthly Magazine*. In volume 1, see pp. 191–215, 267–82, 350–59, 424–34; in volume 2, see pp. 17–30, 256–84, 330–40, 415–23. This policy of serialization was a regular one in the *Magazine*, and articles and review essays as well as literary samples were continued from issue to issue.

6. A complete listing of Brown's minor works in the *Monthly Magazine* is provided by Donald Ringe, *Charles Brockden Brown* (New York: Twayne Publishers, 1966), p. 149.

7. Some representative examples of these eulogies and orations can be found in volume 2, pp. 120–24, and volume 3, pp. 128–36.

8. Warfel, p. 170. By far the best composite overview of the *Monthly Magazine*'s content is supplied by Clark, pp. 137–54.

9. Charles E. Bennett, "Charles Brockden Brown: Man of Letters," *Critical Essays on Charles Brockden Brown*, Bernard Rosenthal, ed. (Boston: G. K. Hall and Co., 1981), p. 212.

10. For the quotation see Ringe, p. 112, see also Bennett, p. 212.

11. The first quotation comes from Mott, pp. 219–20, the second from Warfel, p. 188.

12. On the details of the journal's final evolution, see Mott, pp. 220–21.

### Information Sources

BIBLIOGRAPHY:

Charvat, William. *The Profession of Authorship in America, 1800–1870*. M. J. Bruccoli, ed. Columbus: Ohio State University Press, 1968.

Clark, David Lee. *Charles Brockden Brown: Pioneer Voice in America*. Durham: University of North Carolina Press, 1952.

Marchand, Ernest. "The Literary Opinions of Charles Brockden Brown." *Studies in Philology* 31 (1934): 541–66.

Mott, Frank Luther. "*The Monthly Magazine and American Review*." *A History of American Magazines, 1741–1850*. Cambridge: Harvard University Press, 1957. Pp. 218–22.

Ringe, Donald. *Charles Brockden Brown*. New York: Twayne Publishers, 1966.

Rosenthal, Bernard, ed. *Critical Essays on Charles Brockden Brown*. Boston: G. K. Hall and Co., 1981.

Warfel, Harry. *Charles Brockden Brown: American Gothic Novelist*. Gainesville, Florida: University of Florida Press, 1949.

INDEXES: Indexes to the *Monthly Magazine* can be found at the beginning of each volume; the index is divided into "Articles" and "Poetry" sections.

REPRINT EDITIONS: American Periodicals: Series I and II, 1741–1800, 1800–1850. University Microfilms, Ann Arbor. Reels 17 and 3.

LOCATION SOURCES: Widely available.

## Publication History

MAGAZINE TITLE AND TITLE CHANGES: *The Monthly Magazine, and American Review*, April 1799-December 1800. *The American Review, and Literary Journal*, January 1801-December 1802.

VOLUME AND ISSUE DATA: *The Monthly Magazine, and American Review*: volume 1, April-December 1799; volume 2, January-June 1800; volume 3, July-December 1800. *The American Review and Literary Journal*: Volume 1, January-December 1801; Volume 2, January-December 1802.

FREQUENCY OF PUBLICATION: *The Monthly Magazine, and American Review*: Monthly. *The American Review and Literary Journal*: Quarterly.

PUBLISHER: April 1799-December 1802: T. & J. Swords, No. 99 and 160 Pearl Street, New York.

EDITOR: Charles Brockden Brown (January 1801-December 1802: conjectural).

*Christopher J. Forbes*


# MONTHLY MAGAZINE OF BELLES-LETTRES AND THE ARTS, THE LADY'S BOOK. See GODEY'S LADY'S BOOK

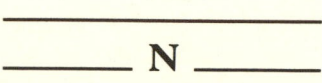

**THE NEW ECLECTIC MAGAZINE.** See THE SOUTHERN MAGAZINE

## THE NEW ENGLAND MAGAZINE

In 1831, Joseph T. Buckingham and his son Edwin founded the *New England Magazine*, hoping that the Boston monthly would attract contributions from burgeoning New England literary talent. With the help of a dollar a page offered as remuneration—a small but respectable reward, given that the practice of compensating writers for their work was yet a rare one—the effort met with considerable success throughout most of the magazine's brief run. In the beginning the triumph owed chiefly to Edwin's intelligence and energy, though his father's experience in editing and publishing surely provided the venture a measure of stability not often found among early periodicals. By the time of the last issue, December 1835, the *New England Magazine*'s pages attested the talent of another young editor, Park Benjamin. For the Buckinghams and later for Benjamin the key to success was essentially the same: the securing of stories, poems, essays, and sketches from highly qualified contributors.

Descended from Thomas Tinker, a passenger aboard the *Mayflower*, Joseph T. Buckingham had edited in turn *The Polyanthus*, *The Ordeal*, *The New England Galaxy and Masonic Magazine*, and *The Boston Courier*. A daily journal, this last paper remained his chief occupation before and after the period of the *New England Magazine*.[1] Buckingham and his son, then about twenty-one, commenced the magazine with no small enthusiasm—whch doubtless intensified the elder's sorrow at having to report in the July 1833 issue that young Edwin had died of tuberculosis while at sea. The announcement also gave Buckingham occasion to explain the inception of the magazine and the policy that had governed its birth: "The New England Magazine was the offspring and the property of Edwin Buckingham. . . . [who] sought this, as a field for improvement in the pleasanter departments of literature, for the cultivation of a better taste. . . . No promises were made, to win the favor of the public, except that it should be continued for one year, in order that none, who contracted to receive it for that period, should be disappointed. . . . No pledge was given that has not been amply redeemed" (5:1–2). Edwin's father continued to edit the magazine for a year and a half, though with waning enthusiasm. Early in 1834, the *New England Magazine* absorbed Sidney Willard's *American Monthly Review*, evidently to no measurable consequence. In the December 1834 number Buckingham announced that he was turning over his responsibilities to Samuel G. Howe and John O. Sargent, who had been "contributors to the pages of the Magazine from its commencement . . . known to the public as writers of ability and taste" (7:515). By February of the next year these men relinquished the editorship to Park Benjamin, who brought the periodical to what many have considered its prime.

The contributors' names read like a portion of the roll call of respected persons in nineteenth-century American letters: William Austin, Hanna Gould, Henry Wadsworth Longfellow, George Hillard, Samuel Kittell, H. T. Tuckerman, James Sheridan Knowles, Edward Everett, John Greenleaf Whittier, Richard Hildreth, Noah Webster, Mrs. Lydia Sigourney, John Neal, and the Reverend N. L. Frothingham. Oliver Wendell Holmes contributed several pieces, and his series *The Autocrat of the Breakfast Table* enjoyed a rather dubious introduction to print—but not long after, ceased to appear. Given time to ripen, the series eventually prospered some twenty years later in the *Atlantic*.[*2] With Benjamin at the helm, the *New England Magazine* published Albert Pike's "Letters from Arkansas" and Whittier's "Mogg Megone," as well as fifteen Hawthorne stories, signed with pseudonyms or unsigned altogether. Among these were "The Ambitious Guest," "Young Goodman Brown," "The Gray Champion," and "The Old Maid in the Winding Sheet" (later, "The White Old Maid").

The paper published serially the autobiography of Mathew Carey as well as biographical "portraits," sometimes illustrated, of such notaries as Daniel Webster, Fitz-Greene Halleck, Charles Sprague, James C. Percival, William Cullen Bryant, Gould, and Everett. Excerpts from Byron, Coleridge, Southey, Schiller, Dante, and Hugo were sprinkled throughout each issue. While the magazine was in Buckingham's hands there always appeared a department entitled "Literary Notices," which included reviews of the latest books, poetry, lectures, and addresses. Very little contemporary oratory or writing went unremarked—the efforts of Washington Irving, James Fenimore Cooper, N. P. Willis, Bryant, Nathan Hale (nephew of the Revolutionary War hero), William Ellery Channing, Elizabeth Peabody, Emma Willard, Jared Sparks, Richard Henry Dana, Caroline Lee Hentz, and Miss Eliza Leslie drew critical attention, not all of it favorable. Other articles commented on the work of Benjamin Franklin and Walter Scott. With Park Benjamin's editorship the department's name changed to "Critical Notices," continuing the tradition of insightful reviewing—with occasional splashes of humor, as when it considered the then recently published *Old Maids; Their Varieties, Characters, and Conditions*.

By the time of the last volume, one department had disappeared. "Politics and Statistics," regularly covering the proceedings of Congress and of the state legislatures, had perhaps been the brainchild of Federalist Joseph T. Buckingham, who at various times served in the Massachusetts legislature.[3] Despite the change of format, the *New England Magazine* continued to cover politics under the guidance of Benjamin, who also added an editorial department called "Cabinet Council." Benjamin delighted in printing selected correspondence and his own retorts; however, he seems to have tired of his sport with the *Christian Examiner*\*—the topic was phrenology—for subsequent to printing one of its letters Benjamin announced to his "Trusty and well-beloved Correspondents" that "[w]hile we wish you length of days, we deprecate your length of articles. We solemnly assure you, that if your papers must occupy over ten blessed pages of the eighty or ninety, which are our monthly dole, nobody will read them but yourselves and your maiden aunts" (March 1835, 8:233).

Despite the prestige the *New England Magazine* eventually claimed among contemporary periodicals of its kind, it was never immune to the financial problems that frequently beset nineteenth-century periodicals. Benjamin continued Buckingham's policy of offering a dollar a page for original prose contributions and double the sum for poetry. Subscriptions cost five dollars per year, but, owing to the magazine's nature, it probably sold—consistently, anyway—only to the erudite few. Benjamin merged his periodical with the New York *American Monthly Magazine*\* in January of 1836, remarking in the *New England Magazine*'s closing number that "[i]t could not be expected that a journal, affording, like this, very limited means of compensation to authors, could attain a very high standard of excellence. . . . Could the American publishers afford, like the English, to pay handsomely for articles, we should soon see our journals assuming a different character, and vieing successfully with the best transatlantic productions." The editor certainly knew American values; in the same paragraph he expressed his hope that "[a]uthorship may soon be as much thought of as ownership" and that "talents of mind may weigh against talents of silver" (December 1835, 9:479–80).

Benjamin's association with the *American Monthly* brought him an association with Charles Fenno Hoffman as well, and Benjamin's name long remained in periodical publishing. Though short-lived, the *New England Magazine* had been for him what it had been for several bright young writers, the first chapter of an illustrious career. Edwin Buckingham's desire to "cultivate a better taste" in New England letters was in some measure fulfilled.

### Notes

1. Evert A. Duyckinck and George L. Duyckinck, *Cyclopaedia of American Literature*, 2 vols. (New York: Charles Scribner, 1866), 2:19.

2. Frank Luther Mott, *A History of American Magazines*, 4 vols. (Cambridge: The Belknap Press of Harvard University Press, 1957), 1:601.

3. Duyckinck, p. 19.

### Information Sources

BIBLIOGRAPHY:

Cooke, George Willis. "The First *New England Magazine* and Its Editor." *The New England Magazine* 16 (1897):103–17.

Duyckinck, Evert A., and George L. Duyckinck. *Cyclopaedia of American Literature.* 2 vols. New York: Charles Scribner, 1866. 2:19–20.

Mott, Frank Luther. "*The New-England Magazine.*" *A History of American Magazines.* 4 vols. Cambridge, Mass.: Belknap Press of Harvard University Press, 1957. 1:599–603.

Tassin, Algernon. *The Magazine in America.* New York: Dodd, Mead and Company, 1916.

INDEXES: None.

REPRINT EDITIONS: American Periodicals: Series II, 1800–1850. University Microfilms, Ann Arbor. Reels 841–42.

LOCATION SOURCES: Widely available.

### Publication History

MAGAZINE TITLE AND TITLE CHANGES: *The New England Magazine.*

VOLUME AND ISSUE DATA: Volumes 1–9, July 1831-December 1835.

FREQUENCY OF PUBLICATION: Monthly.

PUBLISHERS: July 1831-May 1833: Joseph T. and Edwin Buckingham. June 1833-December 1834: Joseph T. Buckingham. January-December 1835: E. R. Broaders.

EDITORS: Joseph T. Buckingham and Edwin Buckingham, July 1831-May 1833; Joseph T. Buckingham, June 1833-December 1834; Samuel G. Howe and John O. Sargent, January-February 1835; Park Benjamin, March-December 1835.

*Allison Bulsterbaum*

## THE NEW MIRROR OF LITERATURE, AMUSEMENT, AND INSTRUCTION. See THE NEW-YORK MIRROR, AND LADIES' LITERARY GAZETTE

## THE NEW-YORK MIRROR, AND LADIES' LITERARY GAZETTE

In launching the *New-York Mirror* in August 1823, George Pope Morris and Samuel Woodworth were well aware of the pitfalls of literary periodicals in America. They had worked as journeyman printers and written for newspapers and magazines, and Woodworth had edited the short-lived *Ladies' Literary Cabinet* (1819–1822). "The lovers of American literature," Morris wrote in the "Prospectus" to the *Mirror*, "are always lamenting the fact, that our literary periodical works, even the best of them / 'Bloom but an hour, and then expire;' / and seeking the cause of this effect, they generally impugn either our taste, our munificence, or our talents.'' But the real cause, Morris suggested, was a national character "so strongly marked with the love of novelty, variety, and mystery, that . . . we are perpetually in search of something new.'' Morris promised something new, "a 'Mirror' for reflecting back to many, the intellectual treasures of the few, who may voluntarily throw them into one common stock for the general use'' (1:1). He was simply restating, however, the standard rationale of literary periodicals: they were supposed to disseminate elite culture more widely than books. What was new about the *Mirror* was that Morris made it a successful vehicle of popular rather than elite culture. Most of his predecessors claimed to serve "the many,'' but the contents of their periodicals were either too refined, too learned, or too narrow in political or religious outlook to satisfy more than "the few.'' The *Mirror* adapted itself more effectively to a general audience and thus anticipated mass-market periodicals later in the century. When the average run of literary periodicals was two years, it survived nearly twenty in its original form and claimed ten thousand subscribers, twice as many as most leading monthlies and quarterlies at that time.[1]

Morris and Woodworth appealed to the "national character'' only to the extent that it coincided with a growing audience of literate and leisured middle-class readers, mostly women. This audience, Morris thought, could best be served by a literary weekly, something light "to fill the intermediate rank between quarterlies and the daily papers'' (3:358). As its subtitle suggests, it was to be essentially an extension of Woodworth's *Ladies' Literary Cabinet* but with broader appeal. It would avoid "detailed reviews,'' which belonged in "well-conducted quarterly and monthly magazines,'' and specialize in miscellaneous literary subjects that "come within the cognisance of any person of taste and information'' and "tales and essays of such moderate length, as anyone possessing a common share of leisure may peruse with pleasure and profit'' (3:358). The brevity would foster a greater variety, making it possible to satisfy diverse tastes in every issue. Like many magazine editors, Morris relied upon Addison's formula in the *Spectator* to justify his miscellaneous weekly. The *Mirror* is intended "to combine instruction with amusement,'' and a "devotion . . . to the great interests of *morality*, is the governing principle which shall characterize it in every stage of its existence'' (1:1). In the *Spectator*, however, wit sharpened the morality; in the *Mirror*, morality dulled the wit. The difference suggests how literary periodicals were evolving in America to meet the demands of a popular audience.

For a yearly subscription of four dollars, Morris and Woodworth offered their readers eight "royal octavo'' pages every week. The first page was usually devoted to an "Original Moral Tale'' or featured essay. Pages two through six contained miscellaneous features, varied from week to week. Many of these were aimed explicitly at women, such as "Female Biography,'' "The Toilet,'' and "The Mirror Fashion,'' but some were of more general utility, such as "The Moralist,'' "The Reflector,'' "The Historian,'' "The Grammarian,'' and "Natural History." In these pages too, we find verse, travel letters, and occasional critical columns, such as "The Rambler," "The Censor," and "The Drama." Page seven was a forum for editorial comment and short notices of books, and page eight usually contained original or selected poetry, the music and lyrics of popular songs, or selections of quotations, epigrams, or other fillers.

The *Mirror*, Morris assured his readers, was intended to be "literally and emphatically" American, but it would not exclude articles of foreign origin as long as they "shall be in accordance with our national habits, patriotism, and modes of thinking" (1:1). He printed selections from a wide range of British, French, and German authors but nothing to offend a patriot.[2] For "native genius" Morris relied upon "voluntary" unpaid submissions from local versifiers and romancers and reprintings of well-known writers, such as Fitz-Greene Halleck, Washington Irving, and William Cullen Bryant. In addition, he enlisted the aid of salaried associate and subeditors, such as John Inman, William Cox, William Leggett, Theodore Fay, Charles Fenno Hoffman, Epes Sargent, and N. P. Willis. For a "Ladies' Literary Gazette," the *Mirror* published few women writers until late in its history, when contributions from Anna Cora Mowatt, Frances S. Osgood, Lydia Maria Child, Maria Brooks, and Emily Chubbuck ("Fanny Forester") became more frequent.

The contents of the *Mirror*, with few exceptions, were conventional and tame. Like most of his fellow editors, Morris believed that political and religious controversy had no place in a literary periodical, especially one which billed itself as a family or parlor magazine. Drawn into conflict with New York Catholics by N. P. Willis's irreverent description of Palm Sunday in Rome, Morris appealed to his "whole editorial career, as an evidence of the scrupulous care with which we have shunned a collision with the religious or political tenets of our numerous readers" (11:159). Noncombative by nature, Morris tried to stay out of literary squabbles too. He was sensitive to criticism but was inclined to be courteous even when provoked. The equanimity with which he met Park Benjamin's attacks in the *New-Yorker* and *New World* from 1838 to 1842, for example, ultimately drew an apology from Benjamin.[3] Although Morris used the *Mirror* to crusade for municipal improvements in New York, he commented sparingly on national issues and usually with a voice of moderation. He thought the proposal of an abolitionist paper to raise "the coloured people . . . to a perfect equality with the whites" rash and impractical (5:103). In the "paper war" with England, he followed the example of Irving's "English Writers on America" and adopted a conciliatory tone. "We are not among those," he wrote in a review of Sir Walter Scott's *Redgauntlet*, "who by a foolish national prejudice, or an ignorant selfishness, arrogate all merit to ourselves and deny it to others" (2:28). Nationalism, however, was often touted as a sign of merit in American works. Because there was no room for extended reviews, criticism in the *Mirror* was seldom significant. Notices of books were brief, impressionistic, and of the summary-and-extract variety.

Morris's business sense had as much, if not more, to do with the success of the *Mirror* as his editorial orthodoxy and appreciation of popular tastes. Having learned from Woodworth's failures, he supervised production carefully and promoted the weekly aggressively after Woodworth's departure in 1824. As promised in the prospectus, he paid particular attention to "external appearance," and the *Mirror* was often praised for its attractive typography and embellishments. In 1833, he reported paying six hundred dollars each month for an engraving (10:335), which rivalled what the more lavish monthlies were spending. Morris dunned his subscribers frequently, drove hard bargains with contributors, absorbed subscription lists of defunct periodicals, and fought off literary pirates. He made more frequent and effective use of literary prize contests than previous editors and was the first to send correspondents abroad to contribute exclusively to his periodical. The travel letters of N. P. Willis, William Cox, and Theodore Fay contributed greatly to the popularity of the *Mirror* in the 1830s.

Although he owned and edited the *Mirror* for most of its life, Morris was not alone in shaping its character. John Inman, brother of the famous portrait painter, served as associate editor from 1828 to 1831 and was succeeded that year by Theodore Fay and N. P. Willis, the former serving until 1833 and the latter until 1839. In addition, when Fay and Willis were abroad, Morris was aided by several subeditors, including William Cox, William Leggett, Charles Fenno Hoffman, and Epes Sargent. The combined efforts of these men, however, only reinforced the *Mirror*'s editorial orthodoxy. "Whoever draws on the stores of fancy for the amusement of the public," he wrote in a review of Sir Walter Scott's novels, "should remember that the highest end of authorship is the inculcation of virtuous precepts" (5:255). Thus he set the standard that governed selection of material for the *Mirror*. The problem was, however, that virtuous authors of Scott's ability were unlikely to volunteer their services for free. Much of what Morris and his associates published was third-rate, the sentimental, patriotic, and didactic outpourings of unpaid amateurs.

Morris's own verse is a good measure of the standard literary fare in the *Mirror*. By 1830 he was a respected poet and widely known lyricist of popular songs. Edgar Allan Poe allowed that Morris was "our best writer of songs" and, in saying this, meant to "assign him a high rank as a *poet*."[4] Like many others, Poe was acknowledging the popular appeal of Morris's simple, sentimental lyrics. Morris is still remembered for "Woodman, Spare That Tree!" but another that Poe praised will serve as a typical example of *Mirror* verse. "Near the lake where drooped the willow, / Long time ago! . . . Dwelt a maid, beloved and cherished / By high and low; / But with autumn's leaf she perished, / Long time ago! . . . Mingled were our hearts forever, / Long time ago! / Can I now forget her?—Never! / No—lost one—no!" (15:160) Clichéd and clumsy as this is in its evocation of romantic sorrow, it was rarely excelled in the *Mirror*.

The real value of the *Mirror*, however, resides in the work of a few authors who were closely associated with it as editors or regular contributors. William Leggett's tales of the sea, especially "The Main Truck" (8:60), are still worth reading, as are Charles Fenno Hoffman's "The Twin-Doomed" (14:329–30), "Effie Gay" (14:370–71), "The Last Arrow" (15:1–2), "The Haunted Inn" (15:30–31), and "Scenes at the Sources of the Hudson" (15:118–19, 124–25, 132, 140–41). Between 1824 and 1834, James Kirke Paulding wrote forty-three original tales and sketches for the *Mirror* and several more were reprinted from other periodicals.[5] Many of these are brief, hastily written satires in the Knickerbocker tradition or moral apologues, but several, such as "Un Faineant" (6:85), "The Ghost" (7:112), "Legend of an Ancient Tile-roofed Cottage" (8:156), "The History of Uncle Sam and His Boys" (8:259), "The Mother's Choice" (9:89–90), and "Claas Schlaschenschlinger" (10:241), compare favorably with the best work of Irving and Poe. The sketches and travel letters of William Cox and Theodore Fay add much to the literary stature of the *Mirror*. Cox's essays are in the manner of Irving's *Sketch Book*, urbane yet sentimental portraits of people and places in America and Europe. Fay's "Little Genius" essays, many of which describe New York and its inhabitants, and his travel writings, which appeared in 1835 and 1836 as "The Minute Book" and "Odds and Ends from a Notebook," also recall Irving's style.[6]

The writer, however, who gave the *Mirror* its mark of distinction was N. P. Willis. His voluminous contributions spanned the life of the periodical, but it was as Morris's first salaried correspondent abroad that he became one of America's most famous men of letters. Willis's first series of travel letters, 139 in all, appeared from February 1832 to January 1836. Later titled "Pencillings by the Way," they followed the example of the *Sketch Book* at first but soon evolved their own style. Less reflective and melancholy than Irving, Willis evoked the feeling of being on the spot with a casual, charming, and chatty travelling companion. Willis's prose was remarkably concise and lively for the time, and he had a talent for conveying to his American audience in a few brief strokes the strangeness and delight of being abroad. Willis followed up the European series with "Letters from Under a Bridge," written from his home in Pennsylvania; "Dashes at Life with a Free Pencil"; and "Letters from Saratoga." These lacked the novelty of "Pencillings by the Way," but they continued to draw readers to the *Mirror*.[7]

Willis's association with the *Mirror* suggests that quality does not come without controversy. His literary talent, as Poe recognized, was "impelled" by a desire for notoriety.[8] His gossipy letters often strained Morris's canons of literary propriety and drew fire from readers. Morris usually backed him, but in 1838, in a new series of "Letters from London," Willis openly discussed an illicit relationship between Letitia E. Landon ("L. E. L."), a popular writer whose work had appeared in the *Mirror*, and William Jordan, editor of the London *Literary Gazette* (16:133). Amid a storm of criticism, Morris issued an apology

(16:159) and was reluctant to defend his editor. Within a month Willis left the *Mirror* to start the *Corsair* with T. O. Porter.

Willis's departure accelerated a decline that began with the economic panic of 1837. Morris was struggling financially even though subscriptions increased and in 1840 turned over proprietorship to Daniel Fanshawe. Ironically, Fanshawe was more extravagant than Morris and was forced to cease publication in December 1842. Morris, however, was already planning a new series and in April 1843, having mended fences with Willis and tightened his belt, issued the first number of the *New Mirror*. The reunited editors hoped to stimulate circulation by reducing the subscription price to two dollars a year and, following the practice of other weeklies, by issuing supplements, composing the ''Mirror Library,'' for twelve and a half cents each. They also decided to focus more exclusively on fashionable society, hoping to capitalize on Willis's talent for arousing curiosity about the beau monde. High society could not save it, however, from a new postal regulation that no longer allowed weeklies to circulate at newspaper rates. The *New Mirror* became a dead letter in September 1844.

The very next month Morris, Willis, and Hiram Fuller issued the *Evening Mirror*, a daily in newspaper format, and the *Weekly Mirror*, a weekend edition composed of extracts from the daily. Thus they got around the postal regulation. The weekend edition looked like the *New Mirror*, except that it was twice as long, but the daily *Evening Mirror* was a radical change. There were no illustrations in the four folio pages of seven columns each, and the last two pages contained mostly advertisements. It continued, however, to cultivate an interest in fashionable society. Poe worked as a subeditor on the daily for a time, contributing essays on authors' pay in America (10 October 1844 and 12 October 1844) and ''The Raven'' (29 January 1845), but the *Evening Mirror* was inferior to the original. With Willis in Europe again in 1845, Hiram Fuller gradually assumed editorial control and joined the battle of New York literati. Never ones for combat, Morris and Willis withdrew in January 1846 to start the *Home Journal*. The *Mirror* lost its identity as a literary periodical under Fuller's direction. The last *Weekly Mirror* appeared in October 1847, and the daily, though it survived another decade, came to look more like a newspaper.

The *Mirror* compares favorably with its weekly competitors, Horace Greeley's *New Yorker*, the Philadelphia *Saturday Evening Post*, and the *New-England Galaxy*, but it does not rank among the best literary periodicals of the day. Taken as a whole, it pales next to the *Knickerbocker*,* *New-England Magazine*,* *United States Magazine and Democratic Review*\* and *Graham's*.\* Friends praised it for being ''uniformly chaste, varied, entertaining, and creditable to American literature.'' Critics condemned it for catering to popular tastes.[9] In suggesting to Hawthorne that he write for the *Mirror*, Horatio Bridge characterized Morris as ''a man of influence and standing in the literary world, although in my opinion he is not very deep.''[10] The same may be said of Morris's weekly.

## Notes

1. Morris was seldom specific about the number of his subscribers, but ten thousand is probably accurate for the late 1830s. See Cortland P. Auser, "The Contribution of George Pope Morris to American Journalism," Ph.D. diss., New York University, 1960, p. 51.

2. The works of foreign authors reprinted in the *Mirror* are listed in Auser, pp. 386–91.

3. See Auser, pp. 109–15 and Merle M. Hoover, *Park Benjamin: Poet and Editor* (New York: Columbia University Press, 1948), pp. 74–77.

4. *The Complete Works of Edgar Allan Poe*, ed. James A. Harrison, 17 vols. (New York: Thomas Y. Crowell & Co., 1902), 10:44.

5. Based on the listing in Amos L. Herold, *James Kirke Paulding: Versatile American* (New York: Columbia University Press, 1926), pp. 154–55.

6. William Cox collected many of his essays for the *Mirror* in *Crayon Sketches by an Amateur* (New York: Connor & Cooke, 1833) and Theodore S. Fay in *Dreams and Reveries of a Quiet Man, Consisting of the Little Genius and Other Essays* (New York: Harper, 1832).

7. Nathaniel Parker Willis collected his writings for the *Mirror* in *The Complete Works of N. P. Willis* (New York: J. S. Redfield, 1846).

8. "The Literati of New York City," *The Complete Works of Poe*, 16:9–10.

9. Quoted is Greeley's *New-Yorker* (2:269). For a sample of contemporary opinion of the *Mirror*, see Auser, pp. 184–88.

10. Julian Hawthorne, *Nathaniel Hawthorne and His Wife*, 2 vols. (Boston: Houghton, Mifflin & Co., 1884), 1:134.

## Information Sources

BIBLIOGRAPHY:

Auser, Cortland P. "The Contribution of George Pope Morris to American Journalism." Ph.D. diss., New York University, 1960.

————. *Nathaniel P. Willis*. New York: Twayne Publishers, 1969.

Beers, Henry A. *Nathaniel Parker Willis*. Boston: Houghton, Mifflin & Co., 1885.

Cox, William. *Crayon Sketches by an Amateur*. New York: Connor & Cooke, 1833.

Fay, Theodore S. *Dreams and Reveries of a Quiet Man, Consisting of the Little Genius and Other Essays*. New York: Harper, 1832.

Hawthorne, Julian. *Nathaniel Hawthorne and His Wife*. 2 vols. Boston: Houghton, Mifflin & Co., 1884.

Herold, Amos L. *James Kirke Paulding: Versatile American*. New York: Columbia University Press, 1926.

Hoover, Merle M. *Park Benjamin: Poet and Editor*. New York: Columbia University Press, 1948.

Johnson, Stanley. "How a New York Editor Was Accustomed to Give Out Advice." *The Bookman* 26 (1907): 421–23.

Mott, Frank Luther. "*The New York Mirror*." *A History of American Magazines, 1741–1850*. New York and London: D. Appleton & Co., 1930. Pp. 320–30.

Myers, Andrew B. "Washington Irving and Gilbert Stuart Newton: A *New-York Mirror* Contribution Identified." *Bulletin of the New York Public Library* 76 (1972): 237–41.

Poe, Edgar Allan. *The Complete Works of Edgar Allan Poe*. Ed. James A. Harrison. 17 vols. New York: Thomas Y. Crowell & Co., 1902.

Weideman, Bette S. "The Pinto Letters of Charles Frederick Briggs." *Studies in the American Renaissance* (1979): 93–157.

INDEXES: Wells, Daniel A. *The Literary Index to American Magazines, 1815–1865*. Metuchen, N.J.: Scarecrow Press, 1980. For listings of items in the *Mirror*, check Auser, Herold, Barnes and Weideman in the notes and bibliography above.

REPRINT EDITIONS: American Periodicals: Series II, 1800–1850. University Microfilms, Ann Arbor. Reels 164–65, 785–87.

LOCATION SOURCES: Partial runs: Widely available.

### Publication History

MAGAZINE TITLE AND TITLE CHANGES: *The New-York Mirror, and Ladies' Literary Gazette*, 2 August 1823–1831. *The New York Mirror. A Weekly Journal Devoted to Literature and the Fine Arts* (variations in subtitle), 1831–31 December 1842. *The New Mirror of Literature, Amusement, and Instruction*, 8 April 1843–28 September 1844. *The Evening Mirror*, 7 October 1844–1857(?). *The Weekly Mirror*, 12 October 1844–18 January 1845 (a weekly edition of the daily *Evening Mirror*, as are the following). *The New York Mirror, A Reflex of the News, Literature, Arts, and Elegancies of Our Time*, 25 January 1845–15 May 1847. *The American Literary Gazette and New York Weekly Mirror*, 22 May 1847–2 October 1847.

VOLUME AND ISSUE DATA: Volumes 1–17, 2 August 1823–20 June 1840; volume 18, 27 June–19 December 1840; volumes 19–20, 1841–1842; *New Mirror* series, volumes 1–3, 8 April 1843–28 September 1844, semiannual volumes beginning in April and October; *Weekly Mirror* series, volumes 1–6, 12 October 1844–2 October 1847, semiannual volumes beginning in October and April.

FREQUENCY OF PUBLICATION: Weekly, 2 August 1823–31 December 1842, 8 April 1843–28 September 1844, 12 October 1844–2 October 1847. Daily, 7 October 1844–1857(?).

PUBLISHERS: 2 August 1823-October 1840: George Pope Morris. October 1840–31 December 1842: Daniel Fanshawe. 8 April 1843–28 September 1844: George Pope Morris and Nathaniel Parker Willis. 7 October 1844-January 1846: Morris, Willis, and Hiram Fuller. January 1846–1857(?): Hiram Fuller.

EDITORS: Samuel Woodworth, 2 August 1823-July 1824; George Pope Morris, July 1824–1828; Morris and John Inman, 1828–1831; Morris, Theodore S. Fay and Nathaniel Parker Willis, 1831–1833; Morris and Willis, 1833-February 1839; Morris, February 1839–31 December 1842; Morris and Willis, 8 April 1843–28 September 1844; Morris, Willis, and Hiram Fuller, 7 October 1844-January 1846; Fuller, January 1846–1857(?). William Cox, William Leggett, Charles Fenno Hoffman and Epes Sargent may have also served as editors for brief periods of time on the original *Mirror*.

*Bruce I. Weiner*

# THE NEW-YORK REVIEW, AND ATHENEUM MAGAZINE

*The New-York Review, and Atheneum Magazine* had its inception in January 1825 when Elam Bliss and Elihu White, the New York publishers, issued a prospectus detailing the plans for a new journal to succeed their *Atlantic Magazine*. Apparently conceived by Henry J. Anderson, newly appointed professor of mathematics and astronomy at Columbia and successor to Robert C. Sands as editor of the *Atlantic*, the plan was to modify that journal by increasing the amount of space devoted to criticism. "The recent development and rapid progress of native literature and science," the prospectus announced, "have created a corresponding necessity and demand for such periodical publications, as aim at exhibiting comprehensive views of the increase of knowledge, the progress of opinion, and the vicissitudes of taste in the political world." To fill this need, the journal would include a review section in which those publications which have "a well-founded claim upon the notice, or a serious influence upon the interests of the people of this country" would be analyzed and evaluated. The magazine section would continue to present "such articles in the lighter and more attractive kinds of literature, as may serve to relieve the attention of the reader, and diversify the character of the work."[1]

While this prospectus was being prepared, other events took place that would help to shape the review. The New York Athenaeum, a recently founded lyceum, was interested in sponsoring a journal of its own, and William Cullen Bryant, already a well-known poet, was seeking a way to abandon the practice of law in Great Barrington, Massachusetts, and establish himself in a literary career in New York. Henry D. Sedgwick, one of Bryant's friends, learned of the poet's intent, and in January 1825, he invited Bryant to visit him in New York. Sedgwick told him all the news: of Anderson's projected review, of the Athenaeum's interest, and of Bliss and White's desire to have Bryant work with Anderson, who, Sedgwick believed, would not "be able to conduct the work alone."[2] Bryant arrived in New York in February to begin negotiations and wrote his wife on the twenty-first to report the progress he had made. Jonathan M. Wainwright, James A. Hillhouse, and Gulian C. Verplanck—all officers of the Athenaeum—were working on his behalf in a project to establish "a literary paper ... under [his] direction," and Bryant thought it "a pretty good prospect that they will succeed."[3]

Bryant returned to Great Barrington with nothing settled, but by 23 March he was again in New York negotiating with the *Atlantic Magazine*. All parties soon reached an accord. A week later, on 30 March, Bryant and Anderson signed an agreement that made them coeditors of the *New-York Review and Monthly Magazine*. The last issue of the *Atlantic* appeared in April, and by the end of May the first issue of its successor was published as the *New-York Review, and Atheneum Magazine*. Bryant and Anderson had reason to be proud of their work. They published reviews of recent books by well-known American authors: James A. Hillhouse's *Hadad*, Catherine M. Sedgwick's *The Travellers*, James Fenimore Cooper's *Lionel Lincoln*, and James Kirke Paulding's *John Bull in America*; and in the magazine section, they printed original poetry: Fitz-Greene Halleck's "Marco Bozzaris," Richard Henry Dana's "The Dying Raven," and Bryant's "A Song of Pitcairn's Island." The issue was a success. As Bryant wrote his wife, the newspaper notices were "favourable in the highest degree," and the subscription list went on very well. By 12 June, there were "more than 500 subscribers in the city besides 150 in the country," and this did not include "the Boston and Northampton subscribers."[4]

To launch a journal is one thing, however; to sustain it quite another. Bryant had no illusions about the difficulties. Reviewing books was "not the literary employment the most to [his] taste nor that for which [he was] best fitted,"[5] but like most journal editors at that time, he and Anderson had to provide much of the material themselves. Between them they wrote five of the eight reviews in the first number, and over the course of the year, Bryant contributed almost a third of the reviews, in some of the later numbers writing up to half.[6] Bryant was also concerned with finding material for the "magazine or miscellaneous department," the section that was to provide amusement for the readers. "A talent for such articles," Bryant confided to Dana, "is quite rare in this country and particularly in this city. There are many who can give grave sensible discussions on subjects of general utility—but few who can write an interesting or diverting article for a miscellany." Paulding contributed three humorous pieces and Bryant a sketch and a story, but Dana was certainly right when he noted the "want of *literary entertainment* in [the] Journal."[7]

Of the four to eight works reviewed in each issue, only a few were literary, and fewer still were distinguished. After the first issue, the only significant novel was Cooper's *The Last of the Mohicans*, reviewed by Sands; the only American poetry of note, works by Lydia Sigourney and James Gates Percival, though one omnibus review did include books by James McHenry and Edward C. Pinkney. Among literary works from England were Sir Walter Scott's *Lives of the Novelists*, Thomas Moore's *Life of Sheridan*, and the collected works of Lord Byron. For the most part, however, the review section was devoted to critiques of a wide variety of nonliterary works, some of them legal, scientific, mathematical, and religious. Among them were travel volumes, orations, and biographies, including works by Henry R. Schoolcraft, Daniel Webster, and Edward Everett. There was even a review of an annual, the *Atlantic Souvenir*, and of a rival journal, the *United States Literary Gazette*.* The *New-York Review* was not primarily a literary journal but, faithful to its prospectus, sought to be a general review of wide appeal, helping its readers keep abreast of recent advances in all branches of learning.

A noteworthy feature of the journal was its articles on the fine arts, both music and painting. By 1825, New York was already a center of artistic activity. Lorenzo da Ponte, the librettist of three of Mozart's operas and now Professor of Italian at Columbia College, had popularized Italian opera in the city, and a group of painters, among them Thomas Cole, Asher B. Durand, and Samuel F. B. Morse, were developing a landscape style that we recognize today as that of the Hudson River school. The *New-York Review* reflected these developments. In a pair of critical articles it discussed multiple performances of three Italian operas, including *The Barber of Seville*; it reviewed a published address on the fine arts delivered at the American Academy of Fine Arts; and in a two-part article it reviewed an exhibition of paintings at the American Academy that included William Dunlap's *Death on the Pale Horse* and many canvases by both European and American artists, some of which it briefly discussed. The *New-York Review* was friendly to the arts, and during its brief career, it sought to advance them.

Another important feature of the journal was its poetry. Bryant and Anderson secured poems from such capable writers as Fitz-Greene Halleck (''Marco Bozzaris'' and ''Connecticut'') and Richard Henry Dana (''The Dying Raven,'' ''Fragment of a Poetical Epistle,'' ''The Husband's and Wife's Grave,'' and ''To the Little Beach Bird''). They printed some early poems by Nathaniel Parker Willis and published translations of German, Spanish, and Italian verse, including poems by Goethe and Schiller rendered into English by George Bancroft. The best poetry, of course, was Bryant's own. ''The Skies'' (later called ''The Firmament''), ''Lines on Revisiting the Country,'' ''Hymn to Death,'' ''The Death of the Flowers,'' and ''Stanzas'' (later revised as ''I Cannot Forget with What Fervid Devotion'') all appeared in the journal.[8] So too did Bryant's humorous pieces, ''To a Musquito'' and ''A Meditation on Rhode-Island Coal.'' Some of these poems were no doubt needed to fill up space, since several had been written a number of years before, and one, ''Chorus of Ghosts,'' is a piece of juvenilia that Bryant did not include in his collected verse. But taken together the poems in the *New-York Review* reached a high level of quality for contemporary magazine verse.

Though not as distinguished, perhaps, as the poetry, the critical reviews in the journal were for the most part well written and judicious. They placed each book in an appropriate context, examined its virtues and faults, and, following the common practice of the time, usually included extended excerpts from the book to indicate its style and support the critical judgments. Half a century later the journal was criticized by Parke Godwin, Bryant's son-in-law and biographer, as lacking ''distinctiveness, perhaps aggressiveness of character. Many of the disquisitions were heavy, and the criticisms, though sensible, were not pungent.''[9] Although there is truth in this judgment, it reflects the critical standards of a later age when magazines were flourishing and literary work of high quality was readily available to them. It is surely more just to consider the *New-York Review* in terms of its own age. Granted the difficulties under which Bryant and Anderson labored, trying to publish a critical review and magazine when professional writers were few and public support wanting, it is perhaps enough that they managed to sustain a consistent level of good writing and sound critical judgment over the course of the year that the journal survived.

By early 1826, it was apparent to Bryant that the *New-York Review* could not long continue. According to Parke Godwin, the journal had ''found no public,'' and, as both he and Charles H. Brown observe, the financial crisis that hit New York contributed to its difficulties.[10] The situation was apparently so threatening that in March Bryant secured a license to practice law in New York. He also sought, in April, to save the review by merging it with the *United States Literary Gazette*,\* a Boston journal edited by James Gordon Carter, to which Bryant had formerly contributed. The plan, as it was finally worked out, was to publish a new magazine, the *United States Review and Literary Gazette*,\* in both New York and Boston and to divide responsibility between the two editors, each of whom would remain in his own city. By these means the editors hoped to reach a wider audience than either of their journals had been able to find alone. When Bryant and Carter came to terms, plans for the new magazine were set in motion, and the *New-York Review, and Atheneum Magazine* lost its identity as an independent journal. The last issue appeared in May 1826.

## Notes

1. *The Letters of William Cullen Bryant*, ed. William Cullen Bryant II and Thomas G. Voss, 3 vols. (New York: Fordham University Press, 1975–      ), 1:178.

2. Quoted in Charles H. Brown, *William Cullen Bryant* (New York: Charles Scribner's Sons, 1971), pp. 122–23.

3. *Letters*, 1:174.

4. *Letters*, 1:191.

5. *Letters*, 1:184.

6. Lists of Bryant's reviews may be found in *Letters*, 2:434–35; Parke Godwin, *A Biography of William Cullen Bryant, with Extracts from His Private Correspondence*, 2 vols. (New York: D. Appleton and Company, 1883), 1:227; and Tremaine McDowell, ed., *William Cullen Bryant, Representative Selections, with Introduction, Bibliography, and Notes*, American Writers Series (New York: American Book Co., 1935), pp. 359–60. Each list is somewhat different from the others.

7. *Letters*, 1:183, 201. For Paulding's contributions, see 1:202. Bryant wrote "A Literary Trifler" (July 1825) and "A Pennsylvanian Legend" (December 1825).

8. Other poems by Bryant are: "A Song of Pitcairn's Island," "The Indian Girl's Lament," a poem "From the Spanish" (later called "Romero"), and "The New Moon."

9. Godwin, 1:226.

10. Godwin, 1:228; Brown, p. 148.

## Information Sources

BIBLIOGRAPHY:

Brown, Charles H. *William Cullen Bryant*. New York: Charles Scribner's Sons, 1971.

Godwin, Parke. *A Biography of William Cullen Bryant, with Extracts from His Private Correspondence*. 2 vols. New York: D. Appleton and Company, 1883.

*The Letters of William Cullen Bryant*. 3 vols. to date. Ed. William Cullen Bryant II and Thomas G. Voss. New York: Fordham University Press, 1975–

McDowell, Tremaine, ed. *William Cullen Bryant, Representative Selections, with Introduction, Bibliography, and Notes*. American Writers Series. New York: American Book Co., 1935.

Mott, Frank Luther. "*The Atlantic Magazine*, and *The New-York Review, and Atheneum Magazine*." *A History of American Magazines, 1741–1850*. New York and London: D. Appleton and Company, 1930. Pp. 334–35.

INDEXES: None.

REPRINT EDITIONS: American Periodicals: Series II, 1800–1850. University Micro-
    films, Ann Arbor. Reels 166, 615.
LOCATION SOURCES: Widely available.

### Publication History

MAGAZINE TITLE AND TITLE CHANGES: *The New-York Review, and Atheneum
    Magazine*.
VOLUME AND ISSUE DATA: Volumes 1–2, June 1825-May 1826.
FREQUENCY OF PUBLICATION: Monthly.
PUBLISHER: E. Bliss & E. White, New York.
EDITORS: Henry J. Anderson and William Cullen Bryant, with the assistance of Robert
    C. Sands.

*Donald A. Ringe*


## THE NEW YORK SATURDAY PRESS. See THE
SATURDAY PRESS


## THE NEW YORK SPIRIT OF THE TIMES

The *New York Spirit of the Times* has earned a reputation as probably this country's most notable source of backwoods humor stories because of its publication of the works of nearly every prominent Southern humorist writing prior to the Civil War. A sporting weekly founded in December 1831 by two young journalists, William Trotter Porter and James Howe, the *Spirit* was modeled "on the plan of" an English sporting magazine, *Bell's Life in London* (1, no. 15:3). Despite this English influence, Porter, who served as editor of the *Spirit* from 1831 to 1832 and 1835 to 1856, sought material from his American audience from the beginning. As Richard Boyd Hauck has noted in an examination of its first issue, Porter clearly intended the *Spirit* to be "a medium in which an indigenous literature, largely comic and definitely realistic, would find its growth and circulation."[1]

The *Spirit* underwent numerous changes in titles, ownership, and editorship during the first four years and struggled for survival during much of its first decade of existence. Original contributions were meagre, and as a result Porter had to rely mainly on reprinted British materials to fill the pages of the *Spirit*. He also occasionally reprinted extracts from the works of popular American novelists. In 1836, however, Porter enlisted C.F.M. Noland of Arkansas as an "original correspondent" to the *Spirit*; Noland's "Pete Whetstone" letters—utilizing a rough Arkansas backwoodsman as a persona who related anecdotes in his own vernacular—subsequently became very popular and influenced many Old Southwest yarnspinners in the 1840s. And near the end of its first decade, in July 1839, the *Spirit* published "Tom Owen, the Bee-Hunter" (9:247), the first comic sketch of the Louisiana humorist Thomas Bangs Thorpe, whose story

"The Big Bear of Arkansas" (11:43–44) two years later represented a standard of excellence that other Southern humorists who followed strove to match.

Literary and sporting selections represented only a small portion of materials printed in the *Spirit* in the early days. Its masthead subtitle in 1832, describing it as "A Sporting Paper; devoted to the Turf, the Ring, the Angler, the Hunter—News, Literature, Fashion, Taste, the Drama, and the Scenes of Real Life" (1, no. 12:1), reflects the many categories of information the *Spirit* sought to include each week. The only fields of public interest consistently excluded from the *Spirit*'s columns were those of religion and politics.

Porter initiated a number of actions in the 1830s to promote the *Spirit* and to secure subscribers to it. He made three separate tours of the South—in the fall of 1837, 1839, and 1840—to enroll subscribers and to encourage amateur writers to submit their works to the *Spirit* for consideration for publication. Earlier, in 1835, he began hiring "special correspondents" to travel the Southern states for the purpose of gathering horseracing results and other information that would appeal to sportsmen. The sport of horseracing and the public's interest in it served as the basis for the *Spirit*'s growing popularity. One of the features Porter added to the *Spirit* to attract subscribers was the inclusion in select issues of expensive "steel engravings" of famous racehorses, engravings taken from portraits by renowned painters of animals. These fine engravings represented a kind of "bonus" for readers. This feature, along with the *Spirit*'s annual statistical summaries of American thoroughbreds winning races at various distances, made the *Spirit* an indispensable item in the true sportsman's home by 1840.

Reliable circulation figures for the *Spirit* are not known. Porter claimed that subscribers grew from 3,000 in 1833 (2, no. 138:2) to as many as 30,000 by 1840,[2] but he almost certainly inflated those figures. The *Spirit*'s size increased from its original four pages to eight pages in 1835 and then to twelve pages in 1839. These increases in size were accompanied by increases in the cost of subscription, from the original price of $3.00 a year in 1831 to $5.00 in 1836, and then to $10.00 a year in 1839;[3] this latter figure subsequently being lowered to $5.00 because of a depressed economy in the country.

In 1842, Porter relinquished the proprietorship of the *Spirit* to John Richards, but he remained as editor to usher in the most productive decade of the publication. In the 1840s, talented humorists from the Old Southwest, who previously had only local community newspapers as outlets for their stories, turned to the *Spirit of the Times* and the national circulation it offered. In addition to Thorpe of Louisiana, Porter started Johnson Jones Hooper of Alabama, George Washington Harris of Tennessee, and Henry Clay Lewis of Mississippi on their writing careers by publishing some of their earliest works. Other humorists whose works the *Spirit* helped to promote included William Tappan Thompson of Georgia and John S. Robb and Joseph M. Field of Missouri. In fact, as Norris Yates, the master chronicler of the *Spirit of the Times*, has pointed out, A. B. Longstreet and Joseph Glover Baldwin are the only humorists of Old Southwest fame "who owed little of their contemporary reputation" to the *Spirit*.[4] By the mid–1840s,

Porter had received enough first-rate comic stories from such notable writers and from less-renowned ones to publish two anthologies drawn from *Spirit* materials—*The Big Bear of Arkansas, and Other Sketches* (1845) and *A Quarter Race in Kentucky, and Other Sketches* (1846).

The increasing popularity of the *Spirit* can be seen from complimentary notices it printed from other magazines and newspapers. In a list of reviews published in it in 1843, for example, the *Spirit* received praise from newspapers as widely scattered as South Carolina, Virginia, Delaware, Pennsylvania, Georgia, Alabama, Massachusetts, Kentucky, Louisiana, Ohio, and Indiana (13:61). In 1844, the St. Louis *Reveille*, itself soon to become an important source of humorous stories, remarked on its dependence on *Spirit* materials: "It may yet be ten days before our valuable Eastern exchanges reach us, but we can edit the 'Reveille' any three days with nothing else before us than the 'Spirit' " (14:192). A Pennsylvania newspaper asserted that "[a]s a sporting periodical it [the *Spirit*] has no equal, while in the richness and raciness of its original articles it is 'a full team, and a yaller dog under the wagon' " (24:552). In 1846, even *Bell's Life in London*, the original model for the *Spirit*, lauded its American offspring, commenting that "[t]he paper ought to be in every sporting house in the United Kingdom" (15:578).

Subscribers also testified to the popularity of the *Spirit*. An Arkansas reader wrote Porter that the *Spirit* was in such demand in his isolated area that his neighbors had stolen nearly half of his issues; as a result, the exasperated Arkansan determined to keep his future issues "under lock and key" (18:462). A later Mississippi correspondent did not let even a flooded river keep him from enjoying the *Spirit*, as he explained to the editor: "In spite of the flood the 'Spirit' still came regularly, and every day when the mail boat came down I would get into my 'dug out' and paddle over to the office, a mile and a half through the woods, to get it; and then what a treat it was. I would take off my coat and light my pipe, and begin and read it regularly through, advertisements and all. This, and laying plans for future hunts, was about all the amusement of those two weeks" (28:486).

Porter himself took every opportunity to publicize the merits of the product he had to offer. In an 1846 *Spirit* issue, he boasted that seven of its twelve pages contained "original material" by at least thirty-three correspondents (16:277). He alerted his readers to the fact that a number of *Spirit* writers were important government officials, including at one point eighteen U.S. Congressmen (20:613). Porter also proudly noted that the *Spirit* was extremely popular outside the United States: "This paper has a Foreign circulation unequalled, probably, by any other in the country; it has found its way into all the European Capitals, into the East and West Indies, and is read with as much *gout* at Canton, Batavia, Sydney, the Sandwich Islands . . . as partial friends would induce us to believe it is at home" (20:1).

The *Spirit of the Times* had reached its height of popularity by 1850. An analysis by Eugene Current-Garcia of the *Spirit*'s annual indexes of contributions shows that the total number of stories and essays published by the *Spirit* fell from 1,225 in 1849–1850 to 845 in 1851–1852.[5] Statistics for the remainder of the decade are not available, but it is very doubtful any later two-year period could match the level of productivity measured in the 1849–1850 span. Only Hooper of the renowned group of Old Southwest humorists cited earlier continued to contribute much to the *Spirit* in the 1850s.

In September 1856, John Richards dismissed William T. Porter as editor and replaced him with Edward E. Jones. Richards claimed that he took this action because of Porter's "unavoidable absence from ill-health, and afterwards from a desire to become entirely master of all the details and authorities necessary to success" (26:354). Jones, the new editor, had been associated with the *Spirit* for the previous twenty-one years. He found himself in immediate journalistic competition with his predecessor, for Porter promptly joined with George Wilkes as editor of a new sporting publication called *Porter's Spirit of the Times*.[6] Jones tried to broaden the appeal of the original *Spirit* by introducing sentimental ladies' literature and educational natural history essays, but the changes apparently did not succeed in holding old subscribers or gaining new ones. After the death of Richards in 1859, Jones for a time shared the editorship of the *Spirit* with T. B.Thorpe, but no combination could stop the disintegration of the *Spirit* as the Civil War moved closer. The last issue of the *Spirit* appeared on 22 June 1861, two weeks after the U.S. Government ordered the halting of mail delivery to the Southern states and thereby cut off the *Spirit*'s main audience.

The significant role the *Spirit of the Times* played in nurturing the antebellum humor of the Old Southwest has been recognized in the twentieth century by an array of distinguished humor specialists, including Franklin Meine, Walter Blair, Arthur Palmer Hudson, Norris Yates, Eugene Current-Garcia, Milton Rickels, John Q. Anderson, Hennig Cohen, William B. Dillingham, and Richard Boyd Hauck. But perhaps no one has described the role the *Spirit* played in the day-to-day life of its readers more aptly than a correspondent writing in 1860: "When misfortune pressed heavily upon me, where have I found comfort? In the columns of the 'Spirit.' When my feelings are depressed, how elated by reading the side-splitting stories in the 'Spirit.' If I wanted to know the time of any race, the pedigree of any thoroughbred, or a cure for any disease to which the horse is incident, I found it in the 'Spirit of the Times.' Thus it has truly been my friend" (30:405).

## Notes

1. "Predicting a Native Literature: William T. Porter's First Issue of the *Spirit of the Times*," *Mississippi Quarterly* 22 (1968–1969):78.

2. Cited in Richard Boyd Hauck, "The Literary Content of the New York *Spirit of the Times*, 1831–1856" (Ph.D. diss., University of Illinois, 1965), p. 55.

3. Norris Yates, "*The Spirit of the Times*: Its Early History and Some of Its Contributors," *Papers of the Bibliographical Society of America* 48 (1954):126.

4. Yates, p. 127.

5. " 'York's Tall Son' and His Southern Correspondents," *American Quarterly* 8 (1955):381.

6. After Porter's death in 1858, Wilkes left *Porter's Spirit of the Times* to establish a third sporting publication with "Spirit of the Times" in the title—*Wilkes' Spirit of the Times*. Thus, for a period between September 1859 and June 1861, all three of these "Spirits" competed with one another [Carvel Collins, *"The Spirit of the Times," Papers of the Bibliographical Society of America* 40 (1946):168].

## Information Sources

BIBLIOGRAPHY:

Collins, Carvel. *"The Spirit of the Times." Papers of the Bibliographical Society of America* 40 (1946):164–68.

Current-Garcia, Eugene. " 'York's Tall Son' and His Southern Correspondents." *American Quarterly* 7 (1955):371–84.

Eberstadt, Lindley. "The Passing of a Noble 'Spirit.' " *Papers of the Bibliographical Society of America* 44 (1950):372–73.

Hauck, Richard Boyd. "The Literary Content of the New York *Spirit of the Times*, 1831–1856." Ph.D. diss., University of Illinois, 1965.

————. "Predicting a Native Literature: William T. Porter's First Issue of the *Spirit of the Times." Mississippi Quarterly* 22 (1968–1969):77–84.

Hauck, Richard Boyd, and Dean Margaret Hauck. "Panning for Gold: Researching Humor in the *Spirit of the Times." Studies in American Humor* 3 (1977):149–57.

Keller, Mark A. "Reputable Writers, Phony Names: Identifying Pseudonyms in the *Spirit of the Times." Papers of the Bibliographical Society of America* 75 (1981):198–209.

Yates, Norris W. *"The Spirit of the Times*: Its Early History and Some of Its Contributors." *Papers of the Bibliographical Society of America* 48 (1954):117–48.

————. *William T. Porter and the 'Spirit of the Times'*. Baton Rouge: Louisiana State University Press, 1957.

INDEXES: Annual indexes in the magazine, incomplete and unreliable.

REPRINT EDITIONS: American Periodicals: Series II, 1800–1850. University Microfilms, Ann Arbor. Reels 620–40.

LOCATION SOURCES: Widely available.

## Publication History

MAGAZINE TITLE AND TITLE CHANGES: 10 December 1831–24 November 1832: *Spirit of the Times & Life in New York*. 1 December 1832–26 January 1833: *The Traveller: Spirit of the Times and Life in New-York*. 2 February 1833–6 October 1833: *The Traveller, Family Journal, Spirit of the Times, and Life in New-York*. 13 October 1833–27 December 1834: Unknown. 3 January 1835–22 June 1861: *The New York Spirit of the Times*.

VOLUME AND ISSUE DATA: Volume 1–31, no. 20, 10 December 1831–22 June 1861; only seventy-two issues extant for volumes 1–5, 10 December 1831–13 February 1836.

FREQUENCY OF PUBLICATION: Weekly.

PUBLISHERS: 10 December 1831–2 March 1832: William T. Porter and James Howe. 3 March 1832–2 November 1832: Porter and Thomas W. Renne. 3 November

1832–30 November 1832: James D. Armstrong. 1 December 1832–15 March 1833: Freeman Hunt and John J. Adams. 16 March 1833–21 June 1833: Charles J. B. Fisher. 22 June 1833–6 October 1833: Charles J. B. Fisher and John Inman. 7 October 1833–2 January 1835: Unknown, but owned by Charles J. B.Fisher on 2 January 1835. 3 January 1835–31 December 1841: Unknown, but probably William T. Porter, George Porter, and others. 1 January 1842–11 February 1859: John Richards. 12 February 1859–23 November 1860: Edward E. Jones, T. B. Thorpe, and Richard Hays. 24 November 1860–15 March 1861: Jones and Thorpe. 16 March 1861–22 June 1861: Jones.

EDITORS: William T. Porter and James Howe, 10 December 1831–2 March 1832; Porter, 3 March 1832–30 November 1832; Freeman Hunt and John J. Adams, 1 December 1832–15 March 1833; Charles J. B. Fisher, 16 March 1833–21 June 1833; Fisher and John Inman, 22 June 1833–6 October 1833; Unknown, 7 October 1833–2 January 1835; William T. Porter, 3 January 1835–5 September 1856; Edward E. Jones, 13 September 1856–11 February 1859; Jones and T. B. Thorpe, 12 February 1859–15 March 1861; Jones, 16 March 1861–22 June 1861.

*Mark Keller*

# THE NORTH AMERICAN REVIEW

For much of its 125-year history, the *North American Review* enjoyed a reputation as the most important intellectual magazine in the United States, and it was the first to achieve an international reputation. Although there were times when the *Review* was deservedly chided for being too safe and too dull, it provided at various times during its long life a platform for some of the most exciting literary and social commentary in this country.

Since its beginnings in 1815, the *Review* had included discussions of American government, economics, and religion, but it was not until 1878, when its new owner and editor, Allen Thorndike Rice, moved the journal away from its ties to Boston intellectualism that it became a genuine arena for debate on contemporary affairs. Under Rice and settled in its new home in New York City, the *Review* plunged into controversy. For Rice, the more volatile the topic the better, and presidential elections, labor problems, divorce, evolution, and agnosticism were just some of the issues debated in the *Review*'s symposia of the 1880s. By 1891, this lively and contemporary approach had brought the magazine's circulation to 76,000, the largest it would ever have.

Certainly Rice had saved a magazine that was precariously close to being folded or merged, and his almost newspaper-like approach helped the *Review* to achieve an impressive circulation and financial sheet. However, circulation figures alone are an inadequate measure of the influence of any periodical (one can remember, for example, that the *Dial* [Boston]* never topped a circulation of 300), and one can look at the earlier history of the *Review* and see that, although the magazine then was far more conservative than it would be under Rice, it nevertheless did much to set the direction for a new nation's literature.

And it is for its contributions to literature and literary criticism that the *Review* retains its place of importance in the history of American periodicals.

The *Review*'s contributions to literature were twofold. First, it introduced its American readers to foreign literature and foreign ideas. Despite its repeated call for the creation of an indigenous literature and despite its longheld suspicion of French literature and its supposed libertinism, it sought to acquaint its readers with the best from abroad, especially from England, Germany, Spain, and Italy. Several of its early editors were themselves well traveled, and they were keenly aware that American literature could not thrive by its writers ignoring Europe. As the *Review*'s third editor, Edward Tyrrel Channing, said in an address entitled "Literary Independence," "Never let us wish for an absolute independence of any nation,—least of all, of that nation whose laws, character, language and religion are ours' [*sic*]."[1] The *Review*'s early editors were also aware that much of European literature was simply inaccessible to American readers, and thus they, like other journal editors in the early nineteenth century, gave "notice" to literature that was readily available to readers but reviewed, quoted, and summarized at length from foreign works hard to come by. Alexander Hill Everett in 1835 explained that the journal was reviewing Casanova's *Memoirs* because only three copies of it were in America (41:46). For several decades after its inception the *Review* argued that foreign literature should be read and studied by Americans. In 1817, Edward Everett, brother of Alexander Hill Everett, the journal's fourth editor, summarized at length from Goethe's autobiography as well as translated excerpts, providing one of the first introductions of the great German poet to America. German literature continued to receive much attention, especially under the editorship of Jared Sparks (1824–1830), and other foreign literatures, including the Scandinavian and modern Greek, were discussed at length. Henry Wadsworth Longfellow's first contribution to the *Review* was an article on the history of the French language (32:277–317), and he followed with articles on the Italian, Spanish, and Anglo-Saxon languages.

The international scope of the *Review* was no doubt part of the reason for the journal's acceptance abroad. The official stamp of approval came in 1820 from the prestigious *Edinburgh Review*, which termed the *North American Review* "the best and most promising production" of the American press. Until the mid-nineteenth century the circulation of British journals in America about equalled that of American journals, and it is significant that by 1824 the *Review* had achieved a circulation of about 4,000, the same as the American circulations of the *Edinburgh Review* and the *Quarterly Review*.[2] In 1826, the *Review*'s circulation included sales of one hundred copies a month in London and even twelve copies in Calcutta.[3]

Despite its international scope, the *Review* considered its foremost duty that of encouraging American writers and the developing of a unique American literature. Such an undertaking must have seemed ambitious in December 1814 and January 1815, when the founders of the journal met to discuss the possibility of forming a journal and picking up where the *Monthly Anthology** had left off when it had ceased publication after ten volumes. Most of the journals of the period had been short-lived, and there was little assurance of success for a new publication other than the talents of those committed to the project and the endorsement of John Thornton Kirkland, president of Harvard College. Inspired by Kirkland and Edward Channing, a professor at Harvard, several of the young men of Boston and Cambridge who had supported the parent journal made plans for the *New England Monthly Magazine and Review*, to be edited by Willard Phillips, a young tutor at Harvard. However, William Tudor, also one of the old *Anthology* group, had just returned from Europe with plans of his own for a new publication, and the group agreed to follow Tudor's lead. Thus, Tudor launched the *North American Review and Miscellaneous Journal* in May 1815, writing all of the first issue's 144 pages, except for one poem, himself.

At first the *Review* offered the potpourri that was typical of journals of the time. Early issues contained, in addition to review essays, a department of general intelligence and even meteorological tables. Missing, however, was the chatty correspondence typical of other journals, and the *Review*, for the most part, avoided the common practice of ''scissoring'' from other publications. Articles, most of which were submitted by members of the anthology club, covered such topics as travel, biography, law, and history. In December 1818, the news notes, general essays, and poetry were dropped, though the subtitle was retained for another three years. The *Edinburgh Review* was clearly the model, and the *Review* adopted both quarterly publication and, as its format, the review essay.

The review essays were not reviews at all in the modern sense. They sought less to assess the merits of the work or works being reviewed than they sought to explore the issues that the work had raised. Thus, the review essay provided the writer a chance to engage in a broad—and often lengthy—discussion. Titles can be misleading, and the famous essay by R. H. Dana, Sr., entitled ''Hazlitt's English Poets,'' turns out to be less a judgment of Hazlitt's commentary on poets than a defense of the English romantics and, in particular, a praise of Words-worth. As important as Dana's endorsement of Wordsworth is to the history of American critical thought, it is significant that the *Review* gave more attention to a writer such as the conventional novelist Catherine Sedgwick than it did to Wordsworth. The *Review* clearly saw its major charge that of encouraging Amer-ican literature, and it found several ways to do it.

American writers, first of all, found in the *Review* a place for their productions. The *Review* never published much poetry, but the editors took special pride in having first published William Cullen Bryant's ''Thanatopsis'' (5:338–40), even though the editor at the time, Jared Sparks, assumed the poem had been written by Bryant's father and even though lines that were intended as a separate piece were mistakenly printed as part of the poem. The poem's true authorship was soon discovered, and the *Review* sought out Bryant, asking for additional ma-terial. The *Review*, in fact, was largely responsible for Bryant's decision to continue with his writing.[4] In the next year, 1818, the *Review* published Bryant's ''To a Waterfowl,'' and during the next few years Bryant furnished several seminal essays on the topic of American literature. The *Review* also attracted Ralph Waldo Emerson, who supplied his lecture on Michaelangelo for the January 1837 isssue and his lecture on Milton the following year. Later James Russell Lowell would print two of Emerson's essays, and Rice would print three of his lectures. In the late nineteenth century, even as the *Atlantic** reigned supreme in its ability to attract prominent writers, the *Review* published some of the best. Several essays by Walt Whitman appeared in the 1880s and several by Mark Twain in the mid–1890s, including Twain's "In Defense of Harriet Shelley" and "Fenimore Cooper's Literary Offences." The first work of fiction in the *Review* appeared in 1903, when the journal serialized Henry James's *The Ambassadors*. James, as had his father, had already been supplying reviews and articles.

The *Review*'s judgment in printing original works was not always sound. Today's readers of James generally rank *The Ambassadors* as his finest novel if not the finest novel ever written in America, but the novel, as its editors knew, was bound to fail in appealing to most of the *Review*'s readers. And for all the pride the editors took in having first published Bryant's poetry, it is noteworthy that the same volume containing "Thanatopsis" also contained poems by Lydia Sigourney, one of the most pedestrian and sentimental poets of the nineteenth century, though also probably its most prolific. More significant to the development of American literature than was its publication of original works was the journal's reviewing, through which the *Review* praised American writers whenever possible and argued at length that American literature deserved both attention and cultivation. In the early years of the *Review*, critics, except for Bryant and Dana, were generally soft on all the writers under review, and especially the Americans. Edward Everett, writing to Sparks in 1821, complained that "the American books are too poor to praise, and to abuse them will not do."[5] The first issue contained Tudor's appreciation of the poems of Mrs. Sigourney (then Miss Huntley). In the 1820s, under Edward Everett, the *Review* printed Edward Channing's positive assessment of Charles Brockden Brown and Dana's early recognition of Washington Irving. In the first few decades of its history, the *Review*'s critics were mixed in their responses to the new English and German romanticism and its influence on American writing. Some, more neoclassical in orientation, were disdainful; others were enthusiastic.[6] In 1825, Sparks found encouragement in American novelists turning to Scott for their model, yet the next year Alvan Lamson praised Anna Barbauld, a British novelist, for avoiding the "mawkishness" of romanticism and choosing Addison as her model. Like most American critics, the *Review*'s had mixed reactions to Byron, whose personal life made objective analysis nearly impossible. On the other hand, a sense of Victorian propriety did not keep the *Review* from giving early recognition to the least genteel and most innovative American poet of the nineteenth century. Edward Everett Hale in 1856 reviewed a new and obscure book of poems by an unknown poet named Walt Whitman. Although Hale lamented that Whitman "should go out of the way to avoid the suspicion of being prudish"

(82:277), he did offer an astute explanation of Whitman's aims as well as lavish praise.

As the *Review* matured its criticism of American writers became less promotional than genuinely evaluative. Cooper, reviewed many times, fared less well in the hands of the *Review*'s critics as the years passed. Francis Bowen in January 1838 argued that Cooper was inept at characterization and that his nationalism had led him to appear undignified. Bowen, however, knew he was dealing with a writer of immense reputation, and he granted that "the beauties [of Cooper's writings] are so evident . . . that they needed no particular notice" (46:19). He was less generous in the October issue of the same year. Of Cooper's *Homeward Bound* he wrote, "Nothing redeems it from utter and deplorable dulness save a few descriptive passages, and two or three animated actions" (47:489). More judicious and balanced was Henry T. Tuckerman's October 1859 review of a half dozen works by Cooper. Such reviewing was typical of Tuckerman, who supplied the *Review* with some of its best writing in the three decades before the Civil War. Margaret Fuller's *Women in the Nineteenth Century* received positive comments and good summaries from Andrew Peabody in 1855. A *Review* critic in 1876, however, termed the book "singularly elementary" and complained against Fuller's "imperious personality, her exaggerating quality of mind, and her truly stupendous conceit" (123:473). Of the American writers to suffer the most at the hands of the *Review*'s critics were two Southerners. During his lifetime Edgar Allan Poe was never the subject of an article in the *Review*. After his death, upon the publication of a four-volume collection of his works, Mrs. E. Vale Smith praised some of Poe's fiction but condemned his poetry for being too obscure and too mechanical. "No mere revision," she wrote, "could make 'Al Aaraaf' coherent" (83:428). Like most of her contemporaries, Smith could not separate the man from the writer, and she dwelled at length on Poe's biography and his "dissipated" life. In the October 1846 issue, Cornelius C. Felton had no mercy on another Southerner—William Gilmore Simms, one of the century's most frequently published magazine writers and editor of the *Southern Quarterly Review*.* Simms, said Felton, was unoriginal in his fiction and overly nationalistic in his criticism (63:357–81).

That anyone writing for the *Review* should complain against a writer's being too nationalistic may seem at odds with the journal's commitment to advance American literature, but one needs to appreciate the extent to which the *Review*—and American critics in general—felt themselves in a defensive position. British critics were often merciless—or worse yet, indulgent—in their response to American writers, and critics such as Felton feared that Americans, should they protest too much, would appear immature and ludicrous. Thus Felton would argue that "An intense national self-consciousness, though the shallow may misname it patriotism, is the worst foe to the true and generous unfolding of national genius" (63:377).

An "unfolding of national genius" was exactly what the *Review* hoped to witness, and it believed it would if it made sure that Americans did not become insulated from the literature of other countries and if American writers could stand tall while somehow still reaching for their boot straps. Sometimes, however, the attacks from the British were too strong for Americans to remain aloof. Such was the case when Sidney Smith declared in the *Edinburgh Review*, "Who reads an American book?" Alexander Everett promptly took forty pages of the July 1830 *North American Review* to give an answer, and it was a poor one indeed. Everett first lists various American writers worthy of international attention, and he has more than a little difficulty, having to head his list with statesmen such as Hamilton, Jefferson, and Franklin. Then he defends William Ellery Channing and Washington Irving against the *Edinburgh Review*'s criticisms by arguing that it is bad manners to mistreat a minister of religion, such as Channing, and that Irving's feelings are bound to have been hurt. Following Everett's essay, many other American critics, in and out of the pages of the *Review*, added to the defense. The most successful were those with a sense of humor. In 1842, John Gorham Palfrey, then editor of the *Review*, found great fun in pointing out, with ample documentation, that the *Monthly Review*, even as it lamented the theft of British works by American journals, was stealing regularly from the *North American Review*. In the July 1849 issue, James Russell Lowell, in his review of Longfellow's *Kavanaugh*, attempted to put to rest once and for all the *Edinburgh Review*'s challenge, and Lowell's keen wit aided his purpose. He first joins a long list of critics who had to admit that Joel Barlow's nationalistic epic, *The Columbiad*, was a disaster. "One would think that the Barlow experiment should have been enough," he writes. "But we are still requested by critics, both native and foreign, to provide a national literature, as if it were some school exercise in composition to be handed in by a certain day" (69:203). Like Felton, Lowell found the best defense in no defense.

While Lowell would have freed Longfellow and all American writers from the necessity of being "American," he did commend Longfellow's faithful rendering of New England life. And it was subject matter that dominated the criticism of the *Review* as it urged on American writers. In the first issue, Tudor wrote, "We have in the way of subjects, a rich and various mine that has hardly been opened. Let it be remembered, how much the genius of Scott struck out from his Scottish highland chiefs. . . . How much more varied, how vastly superior in picturesque effect, the events that took place on our frontier" (1:120). The *Review*'s critics, especially those amenable to romanticism, urged American writers to choose as their subjects the American frontier, American scenery, and American Indians. Cooper was liked best when he was writing about home, and Sedgwick was praised for her use of native materials. As Robert E. Streeter has explained, the basis for this call for American subject matter was eighteenth-century associationalism, the belief that the mind works by a process of associated thought and that the process is affected by time and place.[7] Critics such as Bryant could argue for the use of American materials since those materials were likely to produce a unique chain of thought in both writer and reader.

The extent to which the *Review* relied upon associationalism has led some scholars to assume that the journal had no real critical base of its own. For example, Darwin Shrell writes, "Almost without exception the literary nationalists were concerned with things . . . rather than ideas. Aside from the theory of associationalism, which did little more than justify American settings, there was no new and basic philosophy about which the writer could weave his materials."[8] Shrell is overstating the case. In the first place, as Harry Hayden Clark has illustrated, even if Emerson did not draw directly upon the *Review* for his Transcendental and romantic ideas, all of those ideas were available to him in the *Review* prior to his publication of "Nature."[9] Secondly, the *Review*'s critics were relatively freed from their concern over American subject matter when they turned to one of their favorite topics—American oratory. Little attention has been given to the *Review*'s concern with oratory even though many of its editors and writers were deeply involved in public speaking and preaching. Edward Channing left his editorship to accept the Boylston Professorship of Rhetoric at Harvard, where he would be the teacher of Emerson and Thoreau and a long list of other prominent writers and speakers. Edward Everett, whose address at Gettysburg greatly overshadowed Lincoln's, was regarded as the foremost American public speaker. Many of those editing and writing for the *Review* were men deeply involved with oratory. Some were statesmen, lawyers, and Harvard lecturers, and some, such as Sparks and John Gorham Palfrey, were ministers. The *Review* printed several of the Phi Beta Kappa addresses given at Harvard, and many orators and preachers were reviewed. When it came to oratory, the *Review*'s writers felt that the Americans were without peer. Edward Everett, reviewing Daniel Webster's speeches in 1835, argued that the modern Americans were equal to the classical orators. Earlier, in 1820, Palfrey had written that American preachers had surpassed the French, who were too blunt, and the English, who were too didactic. For Palfrey, " . . . the standard of preaching is no where higher than with us" (10:214). What the critics in the *Review* found so praiseworthy in American speeches and sermons was not the choice of American subject matter, though that was encouraged. What they praised was the American orator's sincerity and democratic spirit. According to Palfrey, the American preacher "gains influence, if he deserves it, by contributing his opinions on equal ground with them [members of the audience] on subjects of common interest. More than all, he brings . . . the force of personal attachment, which breathes into his address that tone of sincerity and feeling, which cannot be counterfeited" (20:213–14). Alexander Hill Everett, like nearly everyone else connected with the *Review*, had the highest praise for William Ellery Channing, whom Everett elevated above all English and Scottish preachers because of his sincerity and accessibility. Of Channing, Everett wrote in 1835, " . . . there is no appearance about him of a wish to display his powers of oratory, or indeed to bring before his hearers in any way the idea of himself. You feel, on the contrary, that you are listening to a person, whose consciousness of self is absorbed in the deep interest with

which he enters into his subject, and whose only effort is to communicate"
(41:397).

In its reviewing of oratory the *Review* was freed from the defensiveness that
often encumbered its literary criticism, and it was also dealing with a subject
comfortable and close to home. Boston was the center of American education
and liberal religion, and until Rice moved the journal to New York, most of its
writers were drawn from the Boston circle. Consequently, the *Review* benefitted
from a ready supply of talent, but it also suffered from provincialism. The journal
was founded as a cooperative effort, and articles continued to be selected by
committee until during Everett's term as editor (1820–1823).[10] The insularity of
the Boston group led it to lose one of its most talented prospects. When Edward
Channing accepted the Boylston Professorship in 1819, both he and Dana, who
had been assisting Channing, assumed the editorship would go to Dana; but
Dana, who had been expelled from Harvard in 1807, was too much of a radical
for the association, and the editorship went to Edward Everett. Both Dana and
Channing left the association, though it is possible that Channing's major concern
was for his new teaching duties. (Many of the *Review*'s editors and contributors
complained they had too little time for both writing and teaching.) Dana was
lost not only as an editor but also as a contributor.

The *Review* was "safe" in Everett's hands, and the journal generally preferred
it that way. Its conservatism was apparent in the early issues' discussions of
social problems; politics were generally avoided. In the decades before the Civil
War, while American magazines were embroiled in the slavery issue, the *Review*
sought safe ground. In the 1820s Sparks argued for a hands-off policy to slavery.
When the problem was too great to ignore, the *Review* still sought to avoid
confrontation. Its writers argued against immediate emancipation and some argued that black Americans should be sent to Africa. W.B.O. Peabody, one of
the twin brothers to write regularly for the journal, wrote in 1846, "It passes
our comprehension to discover what they [free blacks] can find here, in the way
either of enjoyment or hope that should be so difficult to resign" (63:276).

In matters literary as well as social the *Review* was often too conservative. It
was slow—even slower than most journals—in recognizing fiction as a legitimate
genre. Before 1822, it did not even list novels among new books. Peabody in
the 1840s warned against the frivolous nature of fiction, and although the *Review*
was favorable to certain novelists, particularly to Nathaniel Hawthorne, it would
go almost a century before actually publishing any fiction.[11] And despite its
desire to encourage American authorship, its editorial practices worked to the
opposite. At first it paid nothing to contributors. Under Sparks it began to pay
one dollar per printed page (but no complimentary copy). Assuming its contributors were men of leisure, it maintained that rate for many years. After the Civil
War, when it began paying five dollars, the rate was still half that being paid
by comparable magazines.[12] Even less encouraging to the development of a
writing profession was the *Review*'s refusal to print names of contributors. In
1815 anonymity was the standard. By 1868, when it finally began to print names,

it was the last of the prominent magazines to do so. This was not just a matter of being stingy. The *Review* saw itself in service to the institution of belles-lettres, and it felt that writers were less important than the institution. Thus, Felton in 1850, even as he could praise Emerson's *Representative Men*, expressed concern over Emerson's popularity and warned against the "cult" growing up around him (70:520–24).

The *Review* suffered from isolation and conservatism, and under a few editors it suffered from sloppy work. John Gorham Palfrey, who edited from 1836 to 1842, was one of the least conscientious of the *Review*'s many editors. A professor of sacred literature at Harvard, Palfrey was especially interested in historical studies, and the *Review* featured long and often tedious historical pieces. Evidently some of them were even too dull for Palfrey. He confessed in the semicentenary issue that when he had been editor he had been so busy with his teaching and research that he once published a piece without first having read it. What is more amazing is that he did not even read it afterwards, until he was told the piece had libeled a man of good name.

The *Review*, however, also had some superb editors, notably James Russell Lowell (1863–1872), Charles Eliot Norton (coeditor with Lowell [1863–1868]), and Henry Adams (1872–1876). Lowell, who left most of the editing to Norton, contributed several of his important lectures on literature. After Lowell the *Review* continued to review works of literature, but its focus was on history and social issues. In the centennial issue of 1876, it reviewed the first hundred years of the United States in six different essays: one each on religion, politics, abstract science, economic science, law, and education. Literature was not included.

The *Review*'s history after its purchase in 1878 by Rice and its move to New York continued to be characterized by a lively interest in controversial current issues as well as in literature. But the end of the *North American Review* is a sad story for a magazine that had achieved such greatness. In September 1938 the *Review* was sold to Joseph Hilton Smyth, who later admitted to having bought the magazine with money given to him by the Japanese government to establish a propaganda instrument. He pleaded guilty in 1942 to having served as a foreign agent without having registered with the State Department. As a piece of propaganda, the *Review* in its last few years was tame. Books condemning Japanese imperialism were reviewed negatively, but the journal overall was merely radical. In contrast to John Pell, the previous editor, Smyth argued that Franklin Roosevelt was not a dictator. With an editorial policy that was markedly prolabor and antibig business, the *Review* concentrated on social and political issues, but it did print some original poetry. Its poetry editor, John Auslander, had stayed on from his days with Pell and continued his pledge to keep the *Review*'s poetry different from that in the "pure" poetry magazines of the day. He succeeded better than he might have realized. Propaganda aside, the magazine had become slapdash and embarrassing to anyone who remembered it from its days of greatness. One essay in the last issue stands as an apt though pathetic closing for a magazine that had only memories of significant victory in serving American society and literature: "Why I Believe in America" by Wendell Willkie.

## Notes

1. Channing's speech, a Phi Beta Kappa address at Harvard College, is reprinted in Richard Beal Davis's "Edward Tyrrel Channing's 'American Scholar' of 1818," *The Key Reporter* 26, no. 3 (1961):1ff. Ralph Waldo Emerson, then a freshman at Harvard, may well have been in the audience.

2. William Charvat, *The Origins of American Critical Thought, 1810–1835* (Philadelphia: University of Pennsylvania Press, 1936), p. 29.

3. Algernon Tassin, *The Magazine in America* (New York: Dodd, Mead, 1916), p. 28.

4. See Tremaine McDowell, "Bryant and *The North American Review*," *American Literature* 1 (1929):14–26.

5. See Darwin Shrell, "Nationalism and Aesthetics in the *North American Review*: 1815–1850," *Studies in American Literature*, eds. Waldo McNeir and Leo B. Levy (Baton Rouge: Louisiana State University Press, 1960), pp. 11–21.

6. Herbert B. Adams, *The Life and Writings of Jared Sparks*, 2 vols. (Boston: Houghton Mifflin, 1893), 1:243.

7. Robert E. Streeter, "Associational Psychology and Literary Nationalism in the *North American Review*, 1815–1825," *American Literature* 17 (1945):243–54.

8. Shrell, p. 21.

9. Harry Hayden Clark, "Literary Criticism in the *North American Review*, 1815–1835," *Transactions of the Wisconsin Academy of Science, Arts, and Letters* 32 (1940):299–300.

10. Why the practice of committee selection was abandoned is not entirely clear. Frank Luther Mott says that Everett resented the association's interference: *A History of American Magazines*, 4 vols. (Cambridge, Mass.: Belknap Press of Harvard University Press, 1957), 2:228. Mott has in mind a letter Everett wrote to Sparks in which he complained of having had to circulate manuscripts when he was editor. Quoted in Adams, p. 341.

11. Neal Frank Doubleday, however, contends that the *Review*'s arguments for nationalism in literature actually laid the groundwork for fictional realism. See "Doctrine for Fiction in the *North American Review*: 1815–1826," *Literature and Ideas in America: Essays in Memory of Harry Hayden Clark* (Athens: Ohio University Press, 1975), pp. 20–39.

12. Mott, 2:244.

## Information Sources

BIBLIOGRAPHY:

Adams, Herbert B. *The Life and Writings of Jared Sparks*. 2 vols. Boston: Houghton, Mifflin, 1893.

Charvat, William. *The Origins of American Critical Thought, 1810–1835*. Philadelphia: University of Pennsylvania Press, 1936.

Clark, Harry Hayden. "Literary Criticism in the *North American Review*, 1815–1835." *Transactions of the Wisconsin Academy of Sciences, Arts, and Letters* 32 (1940):299–350.

Cushing, William. *Index to the North American Review, Volumes I-CXXV, 1815–1877.* Cambridge, Mass.: John Wilson and Son, 1878. rpt. *Research Keys to the American Renaissance.* Ed. Kenneth W. Cameron Hartford, Conn.: Transcendental Books, 1967, pp. 83–160; rpt. *American Transcendental Quarterly* 4 (1969): 83–160.

DeMille, George E. "The Birth of the Brahmins." *Sewanee Review* 37 (1929):172–88.

Dennis, G. Rodney. "Attributions of Critical Notices in the 'North American Review.' " *Papers of the Bibliographical Society of America* 68 (1964):292–93.

Doubleday, Neal Frank. "Doctrine for Fiction in the *North American Review*: 1815–1826." *Literature and Ideas in America: Essays in Memory of Harry Hayden Clark.* Athens: Ohio University Press, 1975. Pp. 20–39.

Duberman, Martin. *James Russell Lowell.* Boston: Houghton, Mifflin, 1966.

Firda, Richard Arthus. "German Philosophy of History and Literature in the *North American Review*: 1815–1860." *Journal of the History of Ideas* 32 (1971):133–42.

Hale, Edward Everett. *James Russell Lowell and His Friends.* Boston: Houghton, Mifflin, 1899.

Kleinfield, H. L. "Infidel on Parnassus: Lord Byron and the *North American Review*." *New England Quarterly* 33 (1960):164–85.

Miller, F. DeWolfe. "Identification of Contributors to the *North American Review* under Lowell." *Studies in Bibliography* 6 (1953–1954):219–29.

Mott, Frank Luther. "*The North American Review*." *A History of American Magazines.* 4 vols. Cambridge, Mass.: Belknap Press of Harvard University Press, 1957. 2:219–61.

Paine, Gregory. "Cooper and the *North American Review*." *Studies in Philology* 27 (1931):799–809.

Shrell, Darwin. "Nationalism and Aesthetics in the *North American Review*: 1815–1850." *Studies in American Literature.* Eds. Waldo McNeir and Leo B. Levy. Baton Rouge: Louisiana State University Press, 1960. Pp. 11–21.

Streeter, Robert E. "Association Psychology and Literary Nationalism in the *North American Review*, 1815–1825." *American Literature* 17 (1945): 243–54.

Vanderbilt, Kermit. *Charles Eliot Norton: Apostle of Culture in a Democracy.* Cambridge, Mass.: Belknap Press of Harvard University Press, 1959.

INDEXES: Cushing, William, *Index to the North American Review, Volumes I-CXXV,1815–1877.* Dennis, G. Rodney, "Attributions of Critical Notices in the 'North American Review.' " Miller, F. DeWolfe, "Identification of Contributors to the *North American Review* under Lowell."

REPRINT EDITIONS: American Periodicals: Series II, 1800–1850. University Microfilms, Ann Arbor. Reels 177–83, 270–81, 1613–47. AMS Press. New York, 1965. Volumes 1–175. Microform: Library Resources Inc. Chicago, 1971. Volumes 1–173.

LOCATION SOURCES: Widely available.

## Publication History

MAGAZINE TITLE AND TITLE CHANGES: *The North American Review and Miscellaneous Journal*, May 1815-April 1821. *The North American Review*, July 1821-Winter 1939–1940.

VOLUME AND ISSUE DATA: Volumes 1–7, May 1815-September 1818 (semiannual, 3 numbers each); volume 8, December 1818, March 1819; volume 9, June, September 1819; volumes 10–183, 1820–1906 (semiannual volumes, 10–30 also called new series, volumes 1–21); volume 184, 4 January–19 April 1907; volume 185, 3 May–16 August 1907; volume 186, September-December 1907; volumes 187–221, January 1908-June 1925 (semiannual volumes); volume 222, September 1925-February 1926; volume 223, March 1926-February 1927; volume 224, March-December 1927; volumes 225–241, 1928-June 1936; volumes 242–243, Autumn 1936-Winter 1939–1940.

FREQUENCY OF PUBLICATION: Bimonthly, May 1815-September 1818; quarterly, December 1818-October 1876; bimonthly, January 1877-December 1878; monthly, January 1879-August 1906; fortnightly, 7 September 1906–16 August 1907; monthly, September 1907-June 1924; quarterly, September 1924-June 1927; monthly, September 1927-March 1935; quarterly, June 1935-Winter 1939–1940.

PUBLISHERS: 1815–1816: Wells & Lilly, Boston. 1817–1820: Cummings & Hilliard, Boston. 1821–1824: Oliver Everett, Boston. 1825–1828: Frederick T. Gray, Boston. 1828–1831: Gray & Bowen, Boston. 1832–1836: Charles Bowen, Boston. 1837–1838, 1843–1847: Otis, Broaders & Co., Boston. 1838–1840: Ferdinand Andrews, Boston. 1840–1841: James Munroe & Co., Boston. 1842: David H. Williams, Boston. 1848–1852: Charles C. Little & James Brown, Boston. 1853–1863: Crosby, Nichols & Co., Boston. 1864–1867: Ticknor & Fields, Boston. 1868–1869: Fields, Osgood & Co., Boston. 1870–1877: James R. Osgood & Co., Boston. 1878–1880: D. Appleton & Co., New York. 1881–1889: A. T. Rice, New York. 1889–1894: Lloyd Bruce, New York. 1895–1915: North American Review Publishing Co., New York. 1915–1940: North American Review Corp., New York.

EDITORS: William Tudor, 1815–1817; Jared Sparks, 1817–1818; Edward Tyrrel Channing, 1818–1819; Edward Everett, 1820–1823; Jared Sparks, 1824–1830; Alexander Hill Everett, 1830–1835; John Gorham Palfrey, 1836–1842; Francis Bowen, 1843–1853; Andrew Preston Peabody, 1853–1863; James Russell Lowell, 1863–1872 (with Charles Eliot Norton, 1863–1868; E. W. Gurney, 1868–1870, Henry Adams, 1870–1872); Henry Adams, 1872–1876; Allen Thorndike Rice, 1877–1889; Lloyd Bruce, 1889–1896; David A. Munro, 1896–1899; George B. M. Harvey, 1899–1926; Walter Butler Mahony, 1926–1935; John H. G. Pell, 1935–1938; Joseph Hilton Smyth, 1938–1940.

*John B. Mason*

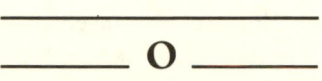

## OLD AND NEW

In its review of the first issue of *Old and New*, the *Western Monthly* saluted the birth of the new magazine with the witches' salutation to Macbeth: "All Hale! All Hale! All Hale!"[1] Edward Everett Hale was the founder, editor, and principal contributor to *Old and New* throughout its five-year run. If he was its guiding genius, his domination of the magazine was also a principal cause of its failure.

In the fall of 1869, Hale decided to start what he hoped would be the pride of his journalistic career. The monthly would combine the *Christian Examiner\** and *Journal of the American Unitarian Association* and would be like *Blackwood's* or the *Atlantic\** but would have a pervading tone of religion instead of *Blackwood's* "toryism" or the *Atlantic*'s literary emphasis.[2] The new magazine, Hale wrote, should have as much "criticism, religious and theological matter as the *Examiner* . . . yet have three times as much space devoted to literature, popular science, history and the rest." These additions should be more like "the better parts of Harper's . . . than . . . the Atlantic or the Galaxy."[3]

Writing to his brother Charles, Hale listed the projected contributors for the first issue: Henry Whitney Bellows; brother Charles; Calvin Stowe; Charles Carroll Everett; Samuel Longfellow; Mrs. Adeline Whitney, a summer neighbor; and an apostate Catholic named J. B. Torricelli.[4] The religious emphasis Hale sought is clearly evident. But by the time the first issue appeared, Hale's proposed contents had been modified. Torricelli, Bellows, and Everett were there, but Stowe's article on "The Religious Politics of Spain" had been replaced with a hymn by his wife, Harriet Beecher Stowe, who was also Hale's wife's aunt. Bellows wrote about Egypt, a topic originally assigned to brother Charles, instead of California. Everett, though, came through with the theology requested in the form of an article called "God the Father." William Tufts Brigham, botany instructor at Harvard, wrote on New England earthquakes, and Robert Collyer,

Unitarian minister and organizer the following year of the reconstruction of Chicago after the fire, contributed "Eternity in Time." James Freeman Clarke, Unitarian minister and early editor of the *Western Messenger*,* added "The Perfection of Jesus," while William Healey Dall, whose famous *Alaska and its Resources* would appear the following year, submitted "The First Day on the Yukon." Julia Ward Howe, Joseph Lovering, Mrs. Hannah E. Lunt, and Nathan Hale rounded out the contributors for the first issue. Editor Hale's purpose was to "interest all members of the home circle" with articles on "every subject of present importance" (1:723).

Hale was there, of course, with an introductory preface, a custom he would continue for several volumes. He also contributed a story, "The Surprise," and appeared in disguise as Colonel Frederic Ingram with part one of the first of several serials he wrote for *Old and New*. "Ten Times One Is Ten" is the story of the effect that one man had on the lives of ten people who, in turn, influenced another ten apiece. The "Lend a Hand Movement," which grew from this story, led to the formation of Hale's *Lend a Hand Magazine* after the death of *Old and New*, and ultimately to several religious societies, the most enduring of which was the Epworth League.[5]

Hale also wrote most of the reviews in a section called "The Examiner," brought over from the old magazine and given its title. Books were chosen "to show the great body of Americans . . . what are the books of the times which are best worth their buying and reading . . . and . . . what had best be neither bought nor read" and to encourage the formation of book and reading clubs. The reviews would be characterized by "calm judgment" and "fair criticism," for Hale said that he chose as reviewers persons "in sympathy with the author" (1:82–83). Hale's additional self-appointed task was the assembling of the "Record of Progress" which, each month, would tell of "discoveries, inventions, and social improvements . . . diminutions of disease . . . amelioration of morals and the growth of the kingdom of God" (1:111).

A name for the new venture was not arrived at without difficulty. The following were suggested over the two-month gestation period: The New Crusader, the Crusade, the Advance Guard, Guide Right, the Left Centre, the File Leader, Color Guard, the Round Head, the Two Worlds, Life, the Freeman, the Liberal, the American, Both Worlds, True Life, and the True World.[6] Eventually it was *Old and New* that won, but the uncertainty about the content and purpose is reflected in the variety of associations of the proposed names. Religion is prominent, clearly a kind of militant Christianity. But also suggested are a cosmopolitanism and an avant garde point of view, a collection both national and international, free and liberal yet round-headedly conservative. The dualism explicit in these sometimes antithetical ideas was one of the major reasons for the magazine's failure; Hale tried to reach and serve both worlds, the old and new, and failed.

When the first issue appeared early—the January issue was mailed in December—even Hale was astonished. He noted he had received permission to start the magazine on 15 November at nine in the evening, and exactly thirty days later, 15 December, "the proof of number one passed my eye and in twenty-four hours more than 1,500 copies were on their way to Chicago."[7] It was done, and he had done it, almost single-handedly. As *Old and New* ran its five-year span, the task of filling the pages fell more and more instead of less and less on Hale's shoulders. As he said early on, "A Monthly magazine makes the year very short."[8]

After "Ten Times One," Hale contributed a second serial, "John Whopper, the Newsboy," under the pseudonym of "a distinguished prelate," and later a third, "Ups and Downs." Elise Polko's novel, *Ein Frauleben*, was translated from the German and published serially as "She Writes" in the first volume. Later volumes presented George McDonald's "The Vicar's Daughter," Sara Dana Loring Greenough's "Pythonia," and "Scrope, or the Lost Library" by Hale's brother-in-law, Frederick B. Perkins. But the best serials were Harriet Beecher Stowe's "Pink and White Tyranny," a social satire; Charles Dudley Warner's "Sorrento Days;" and, as a result of a trip Hale made to England, Anthony Trollope's "The Way We Live Now." Hale had acquired exclusive American rights for the Trollope, but only seventy-two of the more than one hundred chapters had been published when *Old and New* folded.

Perhaps the most unusual serial was entitled "Six of One by a Half Dozen of the Other." Using the idea suggested by Frederick Loring, six authors—Mrs. Stowe, Mrs. Whitney, Lucretia Hale, Perkins, Loring, and Hale—contributed a story on the theme of three women and three men who are at first mismatched but eventually find their mates. When Loring died at the hands of Apaches in a stagecoach robbery, Hale, working from Loring's notes, completed his story.

The best series of articles published in *Old and New* was, as might be expected, on theology. James Martineau, an English Unitarian minister who had received an L.L.D. from Harvard, was paid one hundred dollars in gold for each essay in the series. The essays ran about 7,500 words[9] and were later collected as *The Transient and Permanent in Religion*. Although they were well argued, Martineau's deterministic position lost "five hundred subscribers in this country but gained . . . 150 in England."[10]

Pretty clearly speaking for the editors, William Weeden wrote on the subject of American poetry: "Photography is not art; realism is not truth . . . and can never be poetry." He found realism "vile," "worse than bad" (5:475), and guilty of "trifling with sacred things" (5:479). None of the newer poets, he concluded, were the equal of Lowell or Longfellow (5:480). Except for Joaquin Miller, whose poems only appeared once, the contributors—Constance Fenimore Woolson, Christina Rosetti, Mrs. Stowe, Paul Hamilton Hayne, and Sarah Whitmore—were not realists.

The essays were on various topics: Emon Converse wrote about language as fine art, Charles Beecher wrote about Florida, Julia Ward Howe contributed impressions of the American West, Sidney Andrews commented on the Negro and the Freedmen's Bureau, A. D. Mayo wrote on religion in school, James

Freeman Clarke on art and nature, and Austin Beerbower on socialism in Europe. Robert Dale Owen's "Looking Back Across the War Gulf," his memoirs of the recently ended war, ran for several numbers.

The magazine was funded by an $8,000 loan from the American Unitarian Association to be repaid at the rate of $1,000 a year if the circulation reached an average of 13,000 copies a month for a year. If 14,000 copies were sold, repayment would rise to $2,000 a year. The association took its interest in advertising at the going rate.[11] Despite subscription clubs and premiums of chromolithographs, croquet sets, and Christmas souvenir books, *Old and New* never produced the sales necessary to make a profit. It often attained 9,000 copies a month but fell as low as 7,000.[12] The first six months' sales totaled $14,500 and advertising revenue came to $2,500, but the total equaled almost exactly the printing and author costs. In December of 1872, the American Unitarian Association withdrew its support, never having been repaid its investment.

If *Old and New* was never "All Hale," it was, toward the end, too much Hale and too many of the same contributors over and over. Also, as the early title problem suggests, it was a magazine divided between the seminary and the fireside. Holloway has written that "the theological draw was ever the heaviest handicap" of the magazine,[13] yet Hale said he was "constantly abused for printing too little theology."[14] Too old for the readers who wanted the realism of Howells and Twain, it was still too innovative with its reviews of Turgenev, Taine, and Renan. Josiah Gilbert Holland said *Old and New* "was as pure as snow," to which Mott added "and as tasteless."[15] By the middle of 1875 the editor became "tired of the strain";[16] *Old and New* merged with *Scribner's Monthly** and passed out of existence.

## Notes

1. *Western Monthly Magazine*, 3 (January 1870), 80.

2. Edward Everett Hale, Jr., *The Life and Letters of Edward Everett Hale*, 2 vols. (Boston: Little, Brown, 1917), 2:100–101.

3. Jean Holloway, *Edward Everett Hale: A Biography* (Austin: University of Texas Press, 1956), p. 174.

4. Hale, 2:102.

5. Hale, vol. 2, Chapter 23.

6. Hale, 2:102–4, 106.

7. Hale, 2:110.

8. Hale, 2:112.

9. Hale, 2:113.

10. Hale, 2:184.

11. Hale, 2:106–8.

12. Hale, 2:114.

13. Holloway, p. 178.

14. Holloway, p. 184.

15. Frank Luther Mott, *A History of American Magazines*, 4 vols., (Cambridge, Mass.: Belknap Press of Harvard University Press, 1957), 3:438.

16. Mott, 3:439.

## Information Sources

BIBLIOGRAPHY:
Adams, John R. *Edward Everett Hale*. Boston: Twayne, 1977.
Coleman, Earle. "Edward Everett Hale: Preacher as Publisher." *Papers of the Biblio-graphical Society of America* 46 (1952):139–50.
Hale, Edward Everett. *A New England Boyhood and Other Bits of Autobiography*. Boston: Little, Brown, 1900.
Hale, Edward Everett, Jr. *The Life and Letters of Edward Everett Hale*. 2 vols. Boston: Little, Brown, 1917.
Holloway, Jean. *Edward Everett Hale: A Biography*. Austin: University of Texas Press, 1956.
Kennedy, William Sloane. "Edward Everett Hale." *Century Magazine* 29 (1885):338–43.
Mott, Frank Luther. *"Old and New." A History of American Magazines*. 4 vols. Cambridge, Mass.: Belknap Press of Harvard University Press, 1957. 3:436–39.
INDEXES: An author-title index appears at the end of each volume.
REPRINT EDITIONS: American Periodicals: Series III, 1850–1900. University Microfilms, Ann Arbor. Reels 130–32.
LOCATION SOURCES: Widely available.

## Publication History

MAGAZINE TITLE AND TITLE CHANGES: *Old and New*.
VOLUME AND ISSUE DATA: Volumes 1–11, number 5, January 1870-May 1875.
FREQUENCY OF PUBLICATION: Monthly.
PUBLISHERS: January-June 1870: H. O. Houghton, Boston. July 1870-December 1874: Roberts Brothers, Boston. January-May 1875: Lee and Shepard, Boston. (Hale and other owners).
EDITOR: Edward Everett Hale.

*E. Bruce Kirkham*

# THE ORION

In March 1842, William Carey Richards, a young man of twenty-four residing in the small town of Penfield, Georgia, edited and published the first number of a monthly magazine of "Literature, Science, and Art." As he stated in the "Prospectus" to the third volume, he intended to promote "the development of mind" and "the elevation of taste" in the South (3, no. 1: back cover). Titled the *Orion*—the "name of the most magnificent constellation in the southern hemisphere" (1:54) according to Richards—the magazine was more like a nova, surviving only for a period of a little more than two years. Today the *Orion* does not occupy a prominent position in literary history, but it is representative of many other small antebellum Southern magazines that sought to elevate the culture of their particular regions.

William C. Richards and his younger brother, Thomas Addison Richards, who joined the *Orion* venture as an illustrator, were born in London, the sons of a Baptist minister who moved his family to Hudson, New York, in 1831.[1] Subsequently, after living for a while in South Carolina, the Richards family moved to Penfield, Georgia, at that time the location of Mercer Baptist College. Following the failure of the *Orion*, the two sons returned to the North, William as a Baptist minister and Thomas as a professor of art at the University of the City of New York.

The prospectus for the third volume of the *Orion* described the role William C. Richards envisioned for it in the cultural life of the South. The editor sought "strictly original" articles—poems, stories, and essays. "Our aim," Richards commented, "is not to make a Magazine of Love Tales and Ghost Stories—the mere froth of Literature—but to contribute to the real mental wealth of our readers" (3, no. 1: back cover). One of the features that Richards emphasized in advertising the magazine was the "embellishments" of the *Orion*—"entirely devoted to the SCENERY OF THE SOUTH" (3, no. 1: back cover). The "original" "drawings" for these illustrations were to be done by Thomas Addison Richards, with the actual engravings done by James Smillie, "without question the best landscape engraver in the United States" (1:56). Because these engravings were not made from copies of English plates, William C. Richards claimed that the *Orion* was "the only Magazine in America which publishes original pictures of American Scenery" (3, no. 1: back cover).

Each number of the *Orion* usually consisted of forty-eight or fifty-six pages, so that each biannual volume contained about three hundred pages of reading material. The original cost of the magazine was $5.00 per year, but the subscription price was dropped to $3.00 in its second year of publication, a price more in line with that of the most popular Northern magazines of the time according to Richards (3:47).

In 1842, when Richards established his magazine, the *Orion* faced stiff competition from the prestigious and prosperous *Southern Literary Messenger*\* and from two struggling small regional publications—the *Magnolia*\* (begun in Savannah, Georgia, later moved to Charleston, South Carolina, and edited briefly by William Gilmore Simms) and the (Macon, Georgia) *Family Companion*. Therefore, Richards tried to reach as broad-based a readership as the *Orion*'s literary contributions would allow. As might be expected, the emphasis was on Southern materials: Simms of South Carolina, A. B. Meek of Alabama, and Georgians Richard Henry Wilde, R. M. Charlton, and Henry R. Jackson were some favorite "Southern sons" whose works appeared in the magazine. However, Northern writers were not excluded. E. G. Squier of New York, H. M. Spofford of Massachusetts, and others above the Mason-Dixon line found a welcome place in the *Orion*. Richards also gave much space to the literary productions of ladies from both regions, including the works of Lydia H. Sigourney, Mary E. Lee, Maria Gertrude Kyle, and Mrs. Anna L. Snelling, the latter a New Yorker whose romantic stories of the American Revolution received special praise from editor Richards.[2]

The Richards brothers used the *Orion* as an outlet for their own writings too. Thomas A. Richards specialized in serialized fiction that romanticized history. Typical of his contributions were "The Fulton Folley, or the First Steamboat" (published in six installments in vol. 3) and "The Trysting Rock: A Tale of Tallulah" (in five installments in vol. 1). William Richards wrote romantic poetry for the *Orion*, as well as some humorous stories in the same tradition as the comic stories of the Old Southwest; most notable in this latter category was his series of five "Smithville" stories, which satirized uneducated Georgia folk confronting the new fads and inventions of their day.

Regular features of the *Orion* were the "Editor's Department" and a book review section. From editorial remarks and the selections included in the magazine, one can glean that William Richards held a traditional Southern viewpoint on most issues of his time. He favored liberal education, supported the temperance movement, argued for an international copyright law, and defended the institution of slavery. However, he demonstrated a more independent spirit in his book reviews. Richards treated Charles Dickens much more kindly than most other American reviewers of the controversial *American Notes for General Circulation* (2:175), and he harshly attacked "To Allegra Florence in Heaven," a poem by the popular Georgia writer Thomas Holley Chivers (2:370–72).

Despite Richards's skill as an editor and the magazine's many attractive features, the *Orion* ultimately could not successfully compete with the firmly established *Southern Literary Messenger* or with Northern magazines popular in the South, such as the *Spirit of the Times*.* The *Orion*'s entire publishing life from 1842 to 1844 was a constant struggle for survival in the face of severe financial woes. In February 1844, William Richards moved the magazine from Georgia to Charleston, South Carolina, in a last-ditch effort to save it, but the *Orion* failed six months later. Richards's dream of establishing "an elevated literary Magazine in Georgia" (3:40) for the "advancement of literature in the South" (1:63) faded after only twenty-four numbers were published, and probably his only real satisfaction came from the fact that the *Family Companion* and the *Magnolia*, the *Orion*'s two contemporary Georgia rivals, failed earlier than his magazine.

## Notes

1. Biographical information concerning the Richards family is from Edward L. Tucker, "Two Young Brothers and Their *Orion*" *Southern Literary Journal* 11 (1978):65–66.

2. See, for example, "Agnes; A Tale of the Revolution" (2:101) and "Clarence Grahame, or the Capture of Burgoyne" (2:214).

## Information Sources

BIBLIOGRAPHY:

Abney, Beth. "The *Orion* as a Literary Publication." *Georgia Historical Quarterly* 48 (1964):411–24.

Tucker, Edward L. "Two Young Brothers and Their *Orion.*" *Southern Literary Journal*
     11 (1978):64–80.
INDEXES: Biannual indexes in the magazine.
REPRINT EDITIONS: American Periodicals: Series II, 1800–1850. University Micro-
     films, Ann Arbor. Reel 1216.
LOCATION SOURCES: Widely available.

### Publication History

MAGAZINE TITLE AND TITLE CHANGES: *The Orion: A Monthly Magazine of Lit-
     erature, Science, and Art*, March 1842-April 1843. *The Orion: A Monthly Mag-
     azine of Literature and Art*, September 1843-February 1844. *The Orion; or,
     Southern Monthly: A Magazine of Original Literature and Art*, March 1844-August
     1844.
VOLUME AND ISSUE DATA: Volumes 1–4, March 1842-August 1844; no numbers
     issued October 1842, May-August 1843.
FREQUENCY OF PUBLICATION: Monthly.
PUBLISHER: William C. Richards, Penfield, Ga., March 1842-April 1843; Penfield and
     Athens, Ga., September 1843-February 1844; Charleston, S.C., March 1844-
     August 1844.
EDITOR: William C. Richards, March 1842-August 1844.

*Mark Keller*

## OUR CONTINENT. See THE CONTINENT

## OUT WEST, A MAGAZINE OF THE OLD PACIFIC AND THE NEW. See THE LAND OF SUNSHINE

## OVERLAND MONTHLY

During the 1850s and 1860s, publishers in San Francisco were attempting to
devise a formula for a successful monthly magazine that would represent the
finest attributes of nature and culture in California. J. M. Hutchings, who founded
*Hutchings's Illustrated California Magazine* in 1856, believed such a magazine
should manifest a spirit of boosterism, and for five years his monthly included
pieces extolling the beauties of the California landscape and recounting great
events in the history of the West. On the other hand, the *Hesperian*, which began
its six-year run in 1858, attempted to transcend its locale by offering cosmopolitan
fare to its West Coast readers. Originally targeted at women, the *Hesperian*
brought news of Paris fashions and offered household hints to isolated, provincial
San Franciscans.[1] When the *Overland Monthly* appeared in 1868, its editorial
policy effected a compromise between the solutions to San Francisco's magazine
question represented by these two predecessors. But it also forged a new path

of its own and helped to establish the existence of and a market for serious literature in the Far West.

In 1859, Anton Roman, who had turned a profit selling books to the culture-starved miners in northern California, opened a bookstore in San Francisco. By the mid–1860s he had begun to publish occasional volumes, including an anthology of poems written by local authors and edited by Francis Bret Harte, secretary of the United States Mint. Roman was impressed enough by literary activities in San Francisco to be convinced he could publish a monthly magazine that featured local authors and would compare favorably with Eastern literary periodicals such as the *Atlantic Monthly*.*[2] He contacted some of his fellow businessmen in the city and amassed commitments amounting to nine hundred dollars per month for a year if he could produce three thousand copies of a monthly magazine designed primarily to "supply information on the development of the Pacific Coast and its vast unsettled back-country."[3] Roman's own vision for the periodical, though, extended beyond mere boosterism, for he wanted to include literary work produced by talented local writers.

Although he later confessed that he feared his choice for editor might prove much too literary for the tastes of his backers (n.s. 32:73), Roman selected Francis Bret Harte (who soon dropped his first name) to direct the new publishing venture. For the three years of his editorship, Harte was able to attract some of the West's finest writers to the pages of the magazine and to produce his own best short fiction and poems for it. Though reluctant to assume editorial chores, Harte was convinced by Roman's assurance of the availability of plenty of good material and of the assistance of two editorial associates, Noah Brooks of the *San Francisco Times* and later of *Alta California* and William C. Bartlett of the *San Francisco Bulletin*.[4] However, Harte took on virtually all of the editorial responsibilities, relying more on the other two members of the "Golden Gate Trinity,"[5] Charles Warren Stoddard and Ina Coolbrith, than on his coeditors.

On 1 July 1868, the first issue of the *Overland Monthly* appeared. According to Harte, the name chosen for the magazine had been deemed more appropriate than one referring to the place of publication. "Shall not the route be represented as well as the *termini*?" he asked in an editorial comment. He concluded, "And where our people travel, that is the highway of our thought" (1:99). On the tan cover of the new magazine were the motto "Devoted to the Development of the Country" and a logo representing a bear astride the tracks of the railway that would soon connect the West and the East by an overland route. Illustrator Charles Nahl had drawn the bear, and Harte himself had added parallel lines to suggest rails. In a letter to Thomas Bailey Aldrich written in 1871, Mark Twain explicated the iconography of the logo, which he praised as "the prettiest fancy and the neatest that ever shot through Harte's brain": "The ancient symbol of California savagery snarling at the approaching type of high and progressive Civilization, the first Overland locomotive!"[6] The contents of the first issue of the *Overland Monthly* reflected the dual nature of the magazine—its commitment to publicizing the West and its role as a forum for serious literature. Roman's financial backers must have responded favorably to the five articles that generally praised various aspects of life on the Pacific Coast, and lovers of literature, though they encountered nothing of exceptional merit, would have enjoyed poetry by Harte and Coolbrith and a travel sketch by Mark Twain, who was then on the journey that would yield his volume *Innocents Abroad*. Other features of the new monthly magazine included reviews of current literature and an editor's department called "Etc.," which allowed Harte to survey various topics in an informal, highly personal style. The whole product was a competent if none-too-exciting publication.

Not until the second number of the *Overland Monthly* did Eastern readers "recognize and openly acknowledge that a new star had arisen in the literary heavens," as George Wharton James characterized the phenomenon (n.s. 81:9-May). In that issue appeared "The Luck of Roaring Camp," a short story that propelled Bret Harte and with him the magazine to literary celebrity. Harte's first successful treatment of the California gold camps in fiction, "The Luck" also took "realism in American letters a significant step forward,"[7] for the *Overland Monthly* editor published his own story over the objections of a censorious proofreader who found offense in his using a prostitute as a major character and in his presentation of profanity in the discourse of the miners. The reader response to Harte's short story, though, justified his insistence that it be published as he wrote it. By the end of 1868, both Harte and the *Overland Monthly* had attained international fame largely due to "The Luck of Roaring Camp." During his editorial tenure, Harte wrote three other short stories for the magazine: "The Outcasts of Poker Flat," "Miggles," and "Tennessee's Partner." These provide the basis for his contemporary reputation as a local color writer and also helped to establish the formula for Western popular fiction in the twentieth century.

Harte's major contribution to the *Overland Monthly* though, was as editor rather than as writer of fiction. Early he established the policy of including enough Western material in each issue to maintain the magazine's commitment to its backers of being a locally oriented publication, while leavening the local material with enough to transcend regional interest and to prevent the magazine from being considered provincial. He assembled a group of regular contributors, members of what has been called the "*Overland* group,"[8] who notified the Eastern intellectual establishment that the life of the mind was flourishing on the West Coast. In addition to his friends Stoddard and Coolbrith, Harte published the work of such figures on the San Francisco literary scene as economist Henry George and entrepreneur J. Ross Browne. Other writers who contributed to the *Overland Monthly* during Harte's editorship included most of the major journalists of San Francisco, several noted clergymen, members of the faculty of the University of California across the bay in Berkeley, and a number of independent scholars and scientists. Harte's influence on the *Overland Monthly* was also evident in his book reviews and in his monthly commentary in "Etc." Although unsigned, most of the book reviews that appeared in the magazine between 1868 and 1872 were probably written by Harte, who cast himself as a "literary iconoclast"[9] in his critiques of such celebrated authors as James Russell Lowell, Benjamin Disraeli, and Harriet Beecher Stowe. "Etc." became the primary organ through which Harte expressed his views on a variety of topics, both local and national. Generally marked by a strong tone of sarcasm, his comments in this editorial department pilloried the boosterism that Anton Roman's original backers had probably hoped the *Overland Monthly* would espouse. While the magazine never abandoned a local focus during Harte's years as editor, his comments in "Etc." as well as the work of some other contributors prevented the publication from becoming merely a forum for San Francisco chauvinism.

Harte's stay with the *Overland Monthly* was brief, for although John H. Carmany, who had purchased the magazine from Roman in 1869, met his demands for salary and office space,[10] the appeal of the East was irresistible. Harte left San Francisco in 1872, his last major publication in the *Overland Monthly* being the antiracist poem "Plain Language from Truthful James" (sometimes called "The Heathen Chinee"). Harte's successor as editor was W. C. Bartlett, who served for only a year. Then Benjamin P. Avery became editor, and the magazine, clearly languishing in Harte's absence, showed some signs of recovering its waning prestige. But Avery was appointed minister to China in 1874, and his successor, Walt M. Fisher, presided over the magazine's demise in 1875. During the years after Harte's departure, the *Overland Monthly* continued to publish first-rate material and added such well-known figures as Ambrose Bierce and Joaquin Miller to its list of contributors. But its original luster left with the original editor.

In 1882, John Carmany offered the title, *Overland Monthly*, to Warren Cheney, who had been publishing a magazine called *California, A Western Monthly*. The next year Cheney inaugurated a second series of the *Overland Monthly* with Millicent W. Shinn as editor. The new version of the magazine lacked the glamor of its forebear, partly because magazine publishing had become a less innovative undertaking in the Far West. Moreover, it concentrated on local matter in a much more uncritical fashion than Harte had allowed his magazine to do. But for several decades the *Overland Monthly*, new series, published the work of many Western writers who eventually gained significant reputations. Even with its stated preference for local writers whose work might lack the polish of their Eastern counterparts (n.s. 10:443), the magazine's list of contributors during its second incarnation was impressive. For editor Shinn (who served until 1894) and her successors in the 1890s, 1900s, and 1910s included work by future notables such as Josiah Royce, Willa Cather, Gertrude Atherton, Edwin Markham, George Sterling, John G. Neihardt, and Jack London. In 1923 the *Overland Monthly* merged with *Out West*, a Los Angeles-based periodical, and for over a decade dealt almost exclusively with California topics. The final issue was that for July 1935.

During its history of "spectacular success, failure, death and resurrection, followed by total decline,"[11] the *Overland Monthly* accomplished several im-

portant feats. It showed that a locally published and edited periodical could have
real literary merit. Robert Glass Cleland has claimed that the authors who contributed to the magazine's early issues created the "Golden Age of California
letters."[12] The *Overland Monthly* also showed that the Eastern United States
had no monopoly on the country's intellectual life. Yet the magazine's career
reveals the dangers of relying too strongly on a single personality. For although
Bret Harte's place in American literary history may not be of the first rank, his
work for the *Overland Monthly* was largely responsible for the magazine's brief
but notable success. As editor and contributor he lifted the magazine above its
West Coast predecessors and contemporaries to become briefly one of the major
literary periodicals in nineteenth-century America.

## Notes

1. Franklin Walker, *San Francisco's Literary Frontier* (New York: Alfred A. Knopf,
1939), pp. 256–58.
2. Walker, pp. 259–60.
3. George R. Stewart, Jr., *Bret Harte: Argonaut and Exile* (1935; rpt. Port Washington, N.Y.: Kennikat Press, 1959), p. 155.
4. Ernest R. May, "Bret Harte and the *Overland Monthly*," *American Literature*
22, no. 3 (November 1950):260–61.
5. Richard O'Connor, *Bret Harte: A Biography* (Boston: Little, Brown, 1966), pp.
90–118.
6. Albert Bigelow Paine, ed., *Mark Twain's Letters* 2 vols. (New York: Harper and
Brothers, 1917), 1:183–84.
7. Patrick Morrow, *Bret Harte*, Western Writers Series No. 5 (Boise, Idaho: Boise
State College, 1972), p. 11.
8. Robert E. Spiller et al., *Literary History of the United States: History*, 4th ed.
(New York: Macmillan, 1974), p. 873.
9. May, p. 265.
10. Geoffrey Bret Harte, ed., *The Letters of Bret Harte* (Boston: Houghton Mifflin,
1926), p. 7.
11. Goldie Capers Smith, "*The Overland Monthly*: Landmark in American Literature," *New Mexico Quarterly* 33 (1963):340.
12. Robert Glass Cleland, *California in Our Time (1900–1940)* (New York: Alfred
A. Knopf, 1947), p. 289.

## Information Sources

BIBLIOGRAPHY:
Cleland, Robert Glass. *California in Our Time (1900–1940)*. New York: Alfred A. Knopf,
1947.
James, George Wharton. "Founding of the Overland Monthly and History of the Out
West Magazine." *Overland Monthly and Out West Magazine* 81 (May 1923):7–
11.
Marovitz, Sanford E. "Romance or Realism? Western Periodical Literature: 1893–1902."
*Western American Literature* 10, no. 1 (Spring 1975):45–58.

May, Ernest R. "Bret Harte and the *Overland Monthly*." *American Literature* 22 (1950):260–71.

Morrow, Patrick. *Bret Harte*. Western Writers Series No. 5. Boise, Idaho: Boise State College, 1972.

Mott, Frank Luther. *A History of American Magazines, 1865–1885*. Cambridge, Mass.: Harvard University Press, 1938. Pp. 402–9.

O'Connor, Richard. *Bret Harte: A Biography*. Boston: Little Brown, 1966.

Smith, Goldie Capers. "*The Overland Monthly*: Landmark in American Literature." *New Mexico Quarterly* 33 (1963):333–40.

Stewart, George R., Jr. *Bret Harte: Argonaut and Exile*. 1935; rpt., Port Washington, New York: Kennikat Press, 1959.

Walker, Franklin. *San Francisco's Literary Frontier*. New York: Alfred A. Knopf, 1939.

INDEXES: Eichelberger, Clayton L. *A Guide to Critical Reviews of United States Fiction, 1870–1910*. 2 vols. Metuchen, N.J.: Scarecrow Press, 1971.

REPRINT EDITIONS: American Periodicals: Series III, 1850–1900. University Microfilms, Ann Arbor. Reels 33–52. Bell and Howell Micro Photo Division. Microforms International.

LOCATION SOURCES: Widely available.

## Publication History

MAGAZINE TITLE AND TITLE CHANGES: *Overland Monthly*, July 1868-April 1923. *Overland Monthly and Out West Magazine*, May 1923-July 1935.

VOLUME AND ISSUE DATA: Volumes 1–15, July 1868-December 1875; suspended 1876–1882; volumes 1–79, January 1883-June 1922 (new series); volume 80, July 1922-April 1923; volume 81, May-December 1923; volumes 82–93, January 1924-July 1935.

FREQUENCY OF PUBLICATION: Monthly.

PUBLISHERS: 1868–1869: A. Roman and Company, San Francisco. 1869–1875: John H. Carmany. 1883: California Publishing Company, San Francisco. 1883–1885: Samuel Carson and Company, San Franciso. 1885–1900: Overland Monthly Publishing Company, San Francisco. 1900–1920: Frederick Marriott, San Francisco. 1920–1921: B.G. Barnett, San Francisco. 1921–1922: Almira Guild McKeon, San Francisco. 1923: D. R. Lloyd and Mabel Moffitt, San Francisco. 1924–1925: Harry Noyes Pratt and Mabel Moffitt, San Francisco. 1925: V. V. Taylor and Hamilton Wayne, San Francisco. 1925–1926: B. Virginia Lee and S. Bert Cooksley, San Francisco. 1926–1928: R. D. Hart, San Francisco. 1928–1935: Arthur H. Chamberlain, Los Angeles.

EDITORS: Francis Bret Harte, 1868–1870; W. C. Bartlett, 1871; Benjamin P. Avery, 1872–1873; Walt M. Fisher, 1874–1875; Millicent W. Shinn, 1883–1894; Rounsevelle Wildman, 1894–1897; James Howard Bridge, 1897–1900; Frederick Marriott, 1900–1903; Florence Jackman, 1903; P. N. Beringer, 1903–1905; Thomas B. Wilson, 1905; P. N. Beringer, 1906–1911; Frederick Marriott, 1911–1920; Herbert Bashford, 1921; Almira Guild McKeon, 1921–1922; D. R. Lloyd and Mabel Moffitt, 1923; Harry Noyes Pratt and Mabel Moffitt, 1924–1925; V. V. Taylor and Hamilton Wayne, 1925; B. Virginia Lee and S. Bert Cooksley, 1925–1926; R. D. Hart, 1926–1928; Arthur H. Chamberlain, 1928–1935.

*William M. Clements*

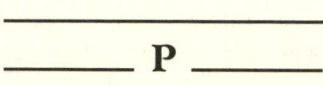

## THE PIONEER

James Russell Lowell began the *Pioneer* when he was only twenty-three years old. His youthfulness is reflected in both the high aims of the periodical and in its disastrous financial arrangements. Nevertheless, the *Pioneer*, which lasted for only three issues, attracted a surprisingly large number of quality contributions.

In late 1842, Lowell joined with Robert Carter, a man his own age who had had experience with printers, in founding the *Pioneer*. In the words of one of Lowell's biographers, he "had the double motive of making a vehicle for sound and generous literature, and of securing for himself a rational means of support."[1] Toward achieving the first end, Lowell wrote friends and acquaintances for assistance. To the Brook Farmer John S. Dwight, he announced,

> On the 1st of next January a magazine will be started in Boston, of which I am to be the editor. It is to be a *free* magazine, and is to take as high an aim in art as may be. I wish to notice every branch of art, and do it in an artistic way. To this end I wish to get those who know something to write for me in its several departments. I shall give them *carte blanche* as to what they say, not wishing to cut the opinions of those who know more than I do of the subjects on which they write down to my level.[2]

He also promised to give Edgar Allan Poe "*carte blanche* for prose or verse as may best please you," promising ten dollars "for every article at first with the understanding that, as soon as I am able I shall pay you more according to my opinion of your deserts."[3] By promising to pay contributors, Lowell showed he was ready to compete with the more popular magazines of the day and not, like the Transcendental *Dial* (Boston),* be dependent upon the good will of con-

tributors to sustain his venture. The prospectus for the *Pioneer* also rings with
faith:

> The contents of each number will be entirely Original, and will consist
> of articles chiefly from American authors of the highest reputation.
>
> The object of the Subscribers in establishing *The Pioneer*, is to furnish
> the intelligent and reflecting portion of the Reading Public with a rational
> substitute for the enormous quantity of thrice-diluted trash, in the shape
> of namby-pamby love tales and sketches, which is monthly poured out of
> them by many of our popular magazines,—and to offer instead thereof, a
> healthy and manly Periodical Literature, whose perusal will not necessarily
> involve a loss of time and a deterioration of every moral and intellectual
> faculty.
>
> The Critical Department of *The Pioneer* will be conducted with great
> care and impartiality, and while satire and personality will be sedulously
> avoided, opinions of merit or demerit will be candidly and fearlessly
> expressed.[4]

The arrangements that Lowell and Carter made with their publishers, Emerson
Leland and Willard J. Whiting, also showed the enthusiasm which both brought
to the *Pioneer*. The contract called for Lowell and Carter to deliver to the
publishers, on the twentieth of the month preceding publication, 5,000 copies
of a forty-eight page magazine, which Leland and Whiting would distribute,
paying the editors twelve-and-a-half cents for each copy sold.[5] In the flush of
enthusiasm shown by the prospectus, the neophyte editors signed a contract that
would, in the end, cause the downfall of the *Pioneer*.

The first number of the *Pioneer* in January 1843 got the magazine off to an
excellent start. Included were poems by Lowell, T. W. Parsons, William Wet-
more Story, and Jones Very; articles on Beethoven by John S. Dwight, on
Thomas Middleton by Lowell, on Aaron Burr by John Neal, and on the Boston
Athenæum by I. B. Wright; Poe's "The Tell-Tale Heart"; reviews by Lowell,
including books by Hawthorne and Dickens; and a department of "Foreign
Literary Intelligence." Preparations for the second number were hampered by
Lowell's ill-health; troubled by a problem with his eyes, he left Boston for New
York, arriving there on 10 January. But the February number of the *Pioneer*
also had good contributions, including Hawthorne's "The Hall of Fantasy";
articles on Beethoven by Dwight, on songwriting by Lowell, and on newspapers
by Neal; poems by Lowell, T. W. Parsons, Poe ("Lenore"), and John Greenleaf
Whittier; reviews by Lowell of DeQuincey, Longfellow, and Macaulay; and
more "Foreign Literary Intelligence."

Despite this excellent start, the preparation of the third number was severely
hindered by the state of Lowell's health. Before taking ill, Lowell had complained
to a friend that "I have been harassed more than you can well think with the
*business* of my magazine. . . . I have not felt at leisure enough to write."[6] Now,

as Carter announced in the next issue of the *Pioneer*, "A severe disease of the eyes . . . precludes the use of his sight except to a very limited extent" (1:144). With Lowell being in New York, where he was forced to stay until the end of February, without the use of his eyesight, much of the job of getting out the March issue was left up to Carter. The March number included Elizabeth Palmer Peabody's Transcendental "A Vision"; poems by Elizabeth Barrett, Lowell, Parsons, Story, and Maria White (Lowell's fiancee); Hawthorne's "The Birth-Mark" and Poe's "Notes Upon English Verse"; an article on John Flaxman by Story; and literary intelligence from Germany by Charles Stearns Wheeler. But the rush and confusion to print took its toll. The news from Germany was inadvertently published from the same information submitted to and published by the *Dial*, which caused Lowell an embarrassing confrontation with Emerson, the *Dial*'s editor, and the issue was delivered late to the publishers.

Although the reviews of the *Pioneer* had been good, the sales had not met the high expectations of its editors. Moreover, Lowell and Carter had set up a system whereby they paid for all the costs before a single copy had been sold and were dependent upon the monies received from sales by their publishers to meet the expenses of printing future issues. Thus, when the March issue was delivered to Leland and Whiting after February 20, the contracted date, the publishers invoked the penalty clause of the contract, calling for a $500 penalty fee and for the editors to purchase, at ten cents a copy, all numbers left unsold after six months. And, to make matters worse, the publishers stopped payment on their original promissory note for the first number, which represented all the monies Lowell and Carter had seen to date from sales. The result was predictable. With no funds to pay printers, engravers, authors, and binders, the *Pioneer* collapsed.

From the first, the contract had doomed the *Pioneer* to failure. In Leon Howard's words, "Such a contract was an extraordinary one because it provided, in effect, that Lowell and Carter should do all the work, take all the risk, and still publish their periodical without any likelihood of profit."[7] In fact, given the terms of the contract, even had all 5,000 copies sold out, after expenses Lowell and Carter could hope to make no more than about thirty dollars profit per issue, demonstrating that their contract showed more faith than common sense. Suits and countersuits flew, and when everything was settled, it appears that Lowell and Carter lost about one thousand dollars on the three issues of the *Pioneer* that were published.[8] Lowell later wrote that "I was not legally bound but felt myself so in honour," and thus he personally paid off all the "papermakers, printers and engravers . . . to the last penny."[9] It took Lowell three years before he was back on sound financial footing, by which time he had married and was pursuing full time his career as a poet.

## Notes

1. Horace Elisha Scudder, *James Russell Lowell: A Biography*, 2 vols. (Boston: Houghton, Mifflin, 1901), 1:106.

2. 7 October 1842, George Willis Cooke, *John Sullivan Dwight: Brook-Farmer, Editor, and Critic of Music* (Boston: Small, Maynard, 1898), p. 70.

3. 19 November 1842, George E. Woodberry, "Lowell's Letters to Poe," *Scribner's Magazine* 16 (1894):170.

4. Quoted in Scudder, 1:99–100.

5. In addition, the publisher's payment was to be made in three equal monthly promissory notes. Information on the business aspects of the *Pioneer* is from Leon Howard, *Victorian Knight-Errant: A Study of the Early Literary Career of James Russell Lowell* (Berkeley: University of California Press, 1952), pp. 123–33. Howard's information is more accurate than that presented by Sculley Bradley in his "Introduction" to the facsimile reprinting of the *Pioneer* (New York: Scholars' Facsimiles & Reprints, 1947), pp. v-xxix.

6. Letter of 30 November 1842 to G. B. Loring, *Letters of James Russell Lowell*, ed. Charles Eliot Norton, 2 vols. (New York: Harpers, 1894), 1:71.

7. Howard, p. 123.

8. In a letter to Poe of 24 March 1843, Lowell put the sum at $1,800, but this was probably before all the lawsuits were settled and he got the final figures (Woodberry, p. 171).

9. Letter of 12 March 1884 to George Edward Woodberry, *New Letters of James Russell Lowell*, ed. M. A. DeWolfe Howe (New York: Harpers, 1932), p. 274.

## Information Sources

BIBLIOGRAPHY:
Bradley, Sculley. "Introduction." *The Pioneer: A Literary Magazine*. New York: Scholars' Facsimiles & Reprints, 1947. Pages v-xxix.
———. "Lowell, Emerson, and *The Pioneer*," *American Literature* 19 (1947):231–34.
Howard, Leon. *Victorian Knight-Errant: A Study of the Early Literary Career of James Russell Lowell* (Berkeley: University of California Press, 1952).
Mead, Edwin D. "Lowell's *Pioneer*," *New England Magazine*, n.s. 5 (1891):235–48.
Mott, Frank Luther. "*The Pioneer* (Lowell's)." *A History of American Magazines*. 4 vols. Cambridge: Harvard University Press, 1957. 1:735–38.
Scudder, Horace Elisha. *James Russell Lowell: A Biography*. 2 vols. Boston: Houghton, Mifflin, 1901.
INDEXES: None.
REPRINT EDITIONS: American Periodicals: Series II, 1800–1850. University Microfilms, Ann Arbor. Reel 745. Scholars' Facsimiles & Reprints. New York, 1947.
LOCATION SOURCES: Widely available.

## Publication History

MAGAZINE TITLE AND TITLE CHANGES: *The Pioneer: A Literary and Critical Magazine*.
VOLUME AND ISSUE DATA: Volume 1, January-March 1843.
FREQUENCY OF PUBLICATION: Monthly.

PUBLISHERS: Boston: Leland and Whiting. Copies have also been located with the imprints New York: Drew and Scammel, and New York: James Stringer.
EDITORS: Robert Carter and James Russell Lowell.

*Joel Myerson*

## THE POCKET CARPET-BAG. See THE CARPET-BAG

## THE PORT FOLIO

When Joseph Dennie, a Harvard graduate, founded the *Port Folio* in Philadelphia in January 1801, he brought to it a significant amount of previous editorial experience. From 1795 to 1799 Dennie had served as editor of the *Farmer's Museum* in Walpole, New Hampshire, and in 1800 he was literary editor of the *Gazette of the United States* in Philadelphia. An urbane Federalist of aristocratic leanings, Dennie felt that the American Revolution had been a disastrous victory of the mob over civilized men, and as "Oliver Oldschool, Esq." he said so in the *Port Folio*. He was even indicted for seditious libel in 1803 for remarks made in a series of articles on "The Progress of Democracy," although he was acquitted.[1] But in his "Prospectus" "Oldschool" states that his name is "indicative of his moral, political, and literary creed," and indeed politics and literature are mixed in the *Port Folio*. The core of Dennie's regular contributors were members of the Tuesday Club, to which he himself belonged. "Most of them were graduates of the University of Pennsylvania or other colleges, most of them were Federalist in politics, and all were imbued with a love of literature, and ambitious of gaining literary fame."[2] This is the "Confederacy of Men of Letters" mentioned by Dennie when he announced that his magazine would be changed from a weekly to a monthly in 1809. The contributors to the *Port Folio* are identified by Randolph C. Randall and Harold Milton Ellis, including Tuesday Club members Charles Brockden Brown, Charles J. Ingersoll, and Philip Hamilton, son of Alexander Hamilton.[3] But many of the contributors were less prominent friends and neighbors of Dennie, and many of their contributions were poems of the sentimental, forgettable variety. In the department called "To Readers and Correspondents," he often communicated his judgments to contributors and would-be contributors. But the *Port Folio*'s personality for its first nine years was a projection of its editor's, who apparently wrote most of the political articles as well as a department called "An Author's Evenings," consisting of lively criticism of current literature.

Dennie expressed a conservative view of language in the *Port Folio*, and he connected corrupt language with corrupt politics, even as one of its causes. As Randall states, Dennie felt that "the crudities of the Republicans were the exaggeration and boastfulness of their language, their weak logic, and their in-

novations in words and pronunciations."[4] Thomas Jefferson came under especially severe attack. The language and intent of the Declaration of Independence
is criticized more than once in 1801. From 1802 to 1804 Dennie even published
poems slandering Jefferson's personal morality, specifically concerning his relations with "Sally," a slave. This series of poems, some of which Randall has
ascertained were written by John Quincy Adams, "remains the darkest stain on
the pages of a usually refined journal."[5] Dennie also repeatedly criticized Noah
Webster for his interest in American English, which Dennie saw as merely a
corruption of the mother tongue. To confront this deterioration of language, he
proposed a number of schemes, such as an academy of authors, to uphold the
standards and purity of English, even suggesting that political as well as linguistic
change could thus be prevented.

Under Dennie the *Port Folio* looked to the works of English neoclassical
writers, especially Addison and Goldsmith, as exemplars of purity and clarity.
His own essay series "The Lay Preacher," which began in the *Farmer's Museum*,
and the work for which he is best known today, is Addisonian in style and tone.
It was one of a number of such essay series to appear in the *Port Folio*. Randall
even notes that "Whoever lays the first volumes of the original *Spectator* and
the *Port Folio* side by side is struck by the similarity of their appearance in spite
of the ninety years that separates them."[6] Rejecting Webster's view of language,
Dennie turned to Dr. Johnson's *Dictionary* as the ultimate authority on spelling,
syntax, and etymology.

The *Port Folio*'s attitude toward the romantics was much more ambiguous.
Dennie did reprint twelve of Wordsworth's poems from *Lyrical Ballads* between
1801 and 1804, and he also praised the poet in a number of short, critical
comments.[7] However, Dennie's interest appears to have peaked early, as nine
of the poems appeared in 1801, one in 1803, and two in 1804. Randall speculates
that the basis of Dennie's initial admiration was Wordsworth's simplicity of
language, but that the poet's doctrine that purity of language and passion reside
in rustic folk was finally incompatible with Dennie's aristocratic views. In the
14 November 1807 issue, after stating that *The Lay of the Last Minstrel* by Sir
Walter Scott was "the most beautiful poem that has appeared since the days of
Goldsmith," Dennie recognized a new edition of Wordsworth's poems by saying,
"Wm. Wordsworth has published two volumes of poems. We hope that he does
not *continue to strike the very base string of humility*."[8] By May 1810, Dennie
introduced a burlesque of Wordworth's poetry as follows: "Some of Mr. Wordsworth's earlier effusions of poetical genius were certainly not unworthy of the
muse. But, of late, he has extended so far his theory of simplicity in writing,
that it degenerates into burlesque and puerility" (n.s. 3, 3:438).

Dennie's attitude toward Coleridge was similarly ambiguous, but the ambiguity
was caused by Dennie's reaction to Coleridge's political views. For one example,
in the "An Author's Evenings" column for 29 August 1801, while reviewing
Robert Southey's play *Joan of Arc*, Dennie mentions Coleridge: "It appears that
SOUTHEY and a Mr. Coleridge, another *democratic* poet, were educated to-

gether and mutually inflamed with French liberty.''[9] Such comments, as well as Dennie's reprinting of only one, very early, sonnet of the poet, leads Randall to conclude that ''This neglect and his expressed antipathy to Coleridge's politics reveal Dennie's biases and inevitably weaken his authority as a literary critic.''[10] All in all, however, under Dennie the *Port Folio* paid a good amount of critical attention to current English writers and poets, and although Brown, Royall Tyler, and William Dunlap, all contributors to the magazine, were praised, Dennie was not a promoter of American literature.

Plagued by ill health for years, Dennie's personal control over the *Port Folio* declined. In 1809, it became a monthly. Dennie was forced in that year for financial reasons to sell the magazine to the Philadelphia publishers Bradford & Inskeep. Although he remained editor until his death in January 1812, the magazine's critical outlook and tone changed, as is evidenced by the editor's using his own name instead of ''Oliver Oldschool.'' Critics agree that the liveliness, urbanity, and wit of the weekly *Port Folio* were never recaptured. Mott, for instance, concludes that as a weekly ''it was a greater and more important literary periodical than it ever was in its later career of nearly two decades as a monthly.''[11]

Under later editors the *Port Folio* also focused more attention on American writers and joined the campaign for the promotion of American literature. Ironically, considering Dennie's views, the *Port Folio* declared in 1814 that ''Americans are the only people on earth who uniformly undervalue the efforts of literary genius in their own country and hold in undue estimation much feebler efforts when received from abroad.''[12] Dennie was succeeded by Nicholas Biddle, a young Philadelphian who later became president of the United States Bank, the position for which he is known today. Under Biddle's two-year editorship, the *Port Folio* became primarily a review. After two years under Dr. Charles Caldwell, who recorded much on the War of 1812 and boosted circulation, the magazine was purchased by Harrison Hall, and his brother John Ewing Hall became editor. John Hall edited the *Port Folio* until its cessation in 1827 for financial reasons. Under Hall the magazine avoided political controversy and slowly became more and more eclectic. Another brother, James Hall, founded the *Illinois Monthly Magazine*,* and he was one of several contributors of fiction and travel literature, the best material to appear in the *Port Folio* in its later years. But it never achieved the excellence it had enjoyed under Dennie, as his successor Biddle noted in a tribute to him in the *Port Folio* upon his death: ''The attention of the people was excited by his brilliancy—the purest scholars of the country flocked to his standard, and the nation was seduced at once into the luxury of literature.''[13]

## Notes

1. Frank Luther Mott, ''*The Port Folio*,'' *A History of American Magazines*, 4 vols. (Cambridge, Mass.: Belknap Press of Harvard University Press, 1957), 1:229–30.

2. Harold Milton Ellis, *Joseph Dennie and His Circle: A Study in American Literature from 1792 to 1812*. Bulletin of the University of Texas No. 40. (Austin: University of Texas, 1915), p. 157.

3. See Ellis, and Randolph C. Randall, "Authors of the *Port Folio* Revealed by the Hall Files," *American Literature* 11 (1940):379–416.

4. "Joseph Dennie's Literary Attitudes in the *Port Folio*, 1801–1812," *Essays Mostly on Periodical Publishing in America*, ed. James Woodress (Durham, N.C.: Duke University Press, 1973), p. 64.

5. "Joseph Dennie's Literary Attitudes in the *Port Folio*, 1801–1812," p. 60.

6. "Joseph Dennie's Literary Attitudes in the *Port Folio*, 1801–1812," p. 83.

7. For treatment of this entire issue, see Randall, "Joseph Dennie's Literary Attitudes in the *Port Folio*, 1801–1812," pp. 69–76.

8. N.s. 2, 4:306, 310. Quoted in Randall, "Joseph Dennie's Literary Attitudes in the *Port Folio*, 1801–1812."

9. 1:274. Quoted in Randall, "Joseph Dennie's Literary Attitudes in the *Port Folio*, 1801–1812," p. 79.

10. "Joseph Dennie's Literary Attitudes in the *Port Folio*, 1801–1812," p. 82.

11. Mott, 1:227.

12. Third series, 3:387. Quoted in Mott, p. 232.

13. Third series, 7:187. Quoted in Randall, "Joseph Dennie's Literary Attitudes in the *Port Folio*, 1801–1812," pp. 90–91.

## Information Sources

BIBLIOGRAPHY:

Bent, S. Arthur. "Damon and Pythias Among Our Early Journalists." *New England Magazine* 14 (1896):666–75.

Ellis, Harold Milton. *Joseph Dennie and His Circle: A Study in American Literature from 1792 to 1812*. Bulletin of the University of Texas No. 40. Austin: University of Texas, 1915.

Kerber, Linda K., and Walter John Morris. "Politics and Literature: The Adams Family and the *Port Folio*." *William and Mary Quarterly* 3rd. Ser., 23 (1966):450–76.

Mott, Frank Luther. "*The Port Folio*." *A History of American Magazines*. 4 vols. Cambridge, Mass.: Belknap Press of Harvard University Press, 1957. 1:223–46.

Queenan, John T. "*The Port Folio*: A Study of the History and Significance of an Early American Magazine." Ph.D. diss., University of Pennsylvania, 1954.

Randall, Randolph C. "Authors of the *Port Folio* Revealed by the Hall Files." *American Literature* 11 (1940):379–416.

———. "Joseph Dennie's Literary Attitudes in the *Port Folio*, 1801–1812." *Essays Mostly on Periodical Publishing in America*. Ed. James Woodress. Durham, N.C.: Duke University Press, 1973. Pp. 57–91.

Woodall, Guy R. "The Relationship of Robert Walsh, Jr., to the *Port Folio* and the Dennie Circle: 1803–1812." *Pennsylvania Magazine of History and Biography* 92 (1968):195–219.

INDEXES: See Ellis, and Randall, "Authors of the *Port Folio* Revealed by the Hall Files." 1816–1825 indexed in volume 20.

REPRINT EDITIONS: American Periodicals: Series II, 1800–1850. University Microfilms, Ann Arbor. Reels 40–42, 220–28, 915.

LOCATION SOURCES: Widely available.

## Publication History

MAGAZINE TITLE AND TITLE CHANGES: *The Port Folio*.

VOLUME AND ISSUE DATA: First series, volumes 1–5, 1801–1805; second series, volumes 1–6 [6–11], 1806–1808; third series, volumes 1–8 [12–19], 1809–1812; fourth series, volumes 1–6 [20–25], 1813–1815; fifth series, [26–45], 1816–1825; sixth series, volumes 1–2 [46–47], 1826–1827 (suspended January-July 1826 and January-July 1827).

FREQUENCY OF PUBLICATION: Weekly, 1801–1809. Monthly, 1809–1819. Quarterly, 1820–1821. Monthly, 1822–1827.

PUBLISHERS: 1801–1808: Joseph Dennie (with Asbury Dickins, 1801, Elizabeth Dickins, 1802), Philadelphia. 1809–1815: Bradford and Inskeep, Philadelphia. 1815: Thomas Silver, Philadelphia. 1816–1827: Harrison Hall, Philadelphia.

EDITORS: Joseph Dennie, 1801–1811; Nicholas Biddle, 1812–1814; Charles Caldwell, 1814–1816; John Ewing Hall, 1816–1827.

*Edward Chielens*

# THE PORTICO

Born in the years after America's involvement in the War of 1812, the *Portico*, a literary magazine published in Baltimore, appeared from 1816 to 1818. Under the editorship of Tobias Watkins, who later became assistant surgeon general of the U.S. Army during the Adams administration, the *Portico* printed a chronicle of interesting national events, a repository of original poetry, selected criticism, and essays on literature and manners. In its balance of serious subject matter and lighter fare, it provided a varied regimen of reading for its subscribers in Baltimore and its environs.

Initial publication of the *Portico* stemmed from a spate of literary activity in Baltimore in 1816. Much of this activity centered on a literary society, named the Delphian Club, founded on 31 August 1816.[1] Many of the members of the Delphian Club contributed to the *Portico*, and the magazine often referred to club activities in its columns. Part of a tradition of literary coteries that prevailed in the nineteenth century, the Delphians convened for meals at the homes of members, heard presentations on poetry and the fine arts, and devoted the remainder of their gatherings to puns, jokes, and satire. A group of young professionals, the Delphians included editors of the *Portico* to whom they applied comic pseudonyms. Editor-in-chief and president of the club, Watkins received the name Pertinax Particular. Vice President John Pierpont, called Hiero Heptaglott, wrote a poem called *Airs of Palestine* that was reviewed in the *Portico*. Doctor John Didier Readel, club secretary, received the cognomen Blearix von Crambograph and the attendant title Professor of Crambography. William Gwynn, an editor to whom the young Edgar Allan Poe once applied for employment, won the nickname Odopoeus Oligosticous. The brilliant and erratic John Neal, who adopted the name Jehu O'Cataract, served to bring the latest romantic verse to the attention of club members. Paul Allen, the reputable editor of the *Baltimore Telegraph and Federal Republican*, was called Solomon Fitz Quizz.

Delphian activities served to lighten the tone of the otherwise sober *Portico*. Under the labels "Delphian Amusements" and "The Club Room," columns appeared that debunked the literary and social fashions of the day. The latter series centered on a figure named Horace Du Monde, who introduced himself as a member of every possible club, a posture that served to expose the cliquishness of literary societies. Many of these columns were undoubtedly written by Neal, who regaled the reader with a dizzying spectrum of puns, jokes, and epigrams. Not all the Delphian contributions, however, carried comic overtones, as an essay "On the Rules of Poetry" (3:461–75) and Readel's "Anniversary Ode" (4:140–45) indicate. With zany tag names and other assorted humor, nevertheless, the Delphians displayed enough comic proportion to twit their own literary propensities. The *Portico* surely established a wider audience for club activities; the club, moreover, asserted enough sustained influence to have caused speculation that it influenced Poe's projected volume *Tales of the Folio Club*, a later satire on literary coteries.[2] Much of Poe's humor, in fact, may derive from comic traditions in early magazines like the *Portico*, its satire on "Female Antiquarian Societies and Philosophies" reminiscent of Poe's "Mellonta Tauta," and its female antiquary, Pundita.

Despite close connections with the Delphians, comic pieces made up only a small percentage of contributions to the *Portico*. The magazine also reflected the wave of nationalism that swept the United States in the years after the War of 1812.[3] Works celebrating American naval combat, including "Perry's Victory—A Song" (4:148–50) by Neal, appeared, and a *History of the Late War* by H. M. Brackenridge won favorable review (3:188–92). Military pride and political advocacy inevitably led to expressions of literary nationalism in the pages of the *Portico*.[4] The most explicit articulation of such sentiments occurred in "The Pilgrim" and "The Swiss Traveler," both appearing in serial form. The former, in all likelihood written by the staunchly democratic Stephen Simpson, counselled patience for the development of an emerging national literature:

> But our country has scarcely begun to lisp in numbers. No Orpheus has bowed our tufted forests, in listening admiration to his lyre; and our bees have never swarmed upon the lips of a favourite Bard. To measure relative excellence, by subjecting American productions to so high a scale [English], would surely neither be agreeable to reason nor favourable to exertion. (1:132–39)

Such comments directly countered the position of the *North American Review*\* and *American Register*. Robert Walsh, editor of the *Register*, argued that America had to adopt its cultural tone from the superior, advanced models of the Old World. For such a position, Walsh took his lumps from a *Portico* reviewer in May 1817 (3:352–66). According to the reviewer, "Dependence, whether literary or political, is a state of degradation, fraught with disgrace; and to be dependent on a foreign mind, for what we can ourselves produce, is to add to the crime of indolence, the weakness of stupidity." Taking issue with Walsh's stance as well as with the aspersions cast on American letters by the Edinburgh critics, "The Swiss Traveler," detailing the adventures of a thirty-year-old Byronic wanderer, posited direct arguments for an indigenous national literature.

The postwar atmosphere influenced even those pieces that did not explicitly address political matters. A review of Eustace's *Classical Tour Through Italy* (1:269–82) focused on Rome by reflectng on "ancient monuments of its glory, that had been spared the violence of war, or the waste of time; and of contrasting its present beauties, with its former splendour. Indeed, there seems to have existed a general opinion, that the subject, and the country, were long since exhausted of their literary materials, except as it relates to their actual condition." The connection between nineteenth-century America and ancient Rome became explicit when the reviewer further pondered the significance of Roman ruins and monuments: "The bosom of every American, glowing with the fires of ancient freedom, must pant in sympathy with his [Eustace's] indignant lamentation of a brother patriot, whose language, laws, habits, and constitution, so closely assimilated our own." Thus, writers in the *Portico* reflected not only the nationalistic pride that permeated political circles but also the sense of lassitude and anticlimax that attended the expenditure of energy and resources demanded by the war. Calls for a distinctive national literature struck an upbeat note, but a series in the *Portico* on the decline of learning (1:106–121) attested to the sense of exhaustion, self-examination, and internal scrutiny that probed America's weakness, its possible fall from previous glory.

John Neal asserted himself as a leader among the magazine's authors in the campaign for a national literature.[5] His novel, *Keep Cool*, garnered praise from a reviewer who opined: "The conversation at the family fire-side of an American farmer, may supply as many subjects to the moralist as those in the drawing room of a noble lord" (4:160–69). *Keep Cool* merited attention, the reviewer continued, not just because of the nascent appetite for fiction, but also out of respect for one's countryman. The *Portico* sanctioned the appeal of Neal's fiction as well as that of John Pierpont's *Airs of Palestine*, works called by another reviewer a boon to those supposedly "doomed to depend upon materials from abroad." Somewhat disingenuously claiming that admiration for Pierpont did not stem from patriotic feelings, the same reviewer observed that Pierpont, despite his exotic subject matter, had struck a rich poetic ore "from an American mine" (2:448–55).

For all his effusive praise for native productions, Neal, perhaps the most significant literary figure among contributors to the *Portico*, did not remain indifferent to the positive values of British literary importation. He championed, in particular, the cause of Lord Byron, who had received castigation from many American reviewers for irregularities in his personal life. Cleverly separating the Byronic persona from the author, Neal argued that literature should be judged for its intrinsic merits rather than for the author's alleged misconduct. In addition to writing a 150-page essay on Byron for the *Portico*, Neal also contributed two poems, "To Byron" and "Fragment in Imitation of Byron" (4:148–50). He reviewed works by Byron as they appeared and thus served to establish the British poet as a model among the Delphians. Other poetic contributors aped the Byronic mode, as "The Paradise of Poets—A Vision" (4:132–36), in which Byron is granted the crown of genius over Campbell, Scott, and Moore, attests. In addition, an anonymous "Lady from Boston" contributed an untitled poem inspired by a picture of Newstead Park, the late country seat of Byron (4:316–20). The original poetry in the *Portico* has, on the whole, more significance for its assimilation of Byronic motifs than for its own literary quality, although Pierpont's "Della Cruscan Ode upon—anything" (4:413–14) displayed the characteristics of a flowery, ornamental verse that remained popular well into the 1800s.[6]

In his autobiography, *Wandering Recollections of a Somewhat Busy Life* (1869), Neal recalled several reasons for the eventual failure of the *Portico*. Indicating that he had been forced to write almost one-half of the final number, he suggested that Dr. Watkins had not been sufficiently scrupulous about the costs of the magazine. In addition to nagging editorial problems, lack of patronage, and financial reverses, he cited the yellow fever epidemic that afflicted Baltimore from 1818 to 1821.[7] In its brief duration, nevertheless, the *Portico* had established a political forum for thoroughgoing democrats in the mold of Stephen Simpson and provided a training ground for Neal and the young literati of the Delphian Club. As a vehicle for literary and cultural nationalism, the *Portico* asserted its most lasting influence, an impact that would be sustained in the subsequent decades.

## Notes

1. For an account of the club's history, see John Earle Uhler, "The Delphian Club: A Contribution to the Literary History of Baltimore in the Early Nineteenth Century," *Maryland Historical Magazine* 10 (1925):305–46.

2. For a survey of Poe's possible borrowings from literary coteries like the Delphian Club, see John C. French, "Poe's Literary Baltimore," *Maryland Historical Magazine* 32 (1937):101–12. Alexander H. Hammond minimizes the Delphian impact in "A Reconstruction of Poe's 1833 *Tales of the Folio Club*: Preliminary Notes," *Poe Studies* 5 (1972):25–32.

3. See Benjamin T. Spencer, *The Quest for Nationality: An American Literary Campaign* (Syracuse: Syracuse University Press, 1957), pp. 75ff. and J. C. McCloskey, "The Campaign of Periodicals after the War of 1812 for National Literature," *PMLA* 10 (1935):262–72.

4. See M. W. Fishwick, "*The Portico* and Literary Nationalism after the War of 1812," *William and Mary Quarterly* 8 (1951):238–45 and McCloskey, "A Note on *The Portico*," *American Literature* 8 (1936):300–304.

5. See Benjamin Lease, *That Wild Fellow John Neal and the American Literary Revolution* (Chicago: University of Chicago Press, 1972), pp. 18–20, 69–70.

6. See M. Ray Adams, "Della Cruscanism in America," *PMLA* 79 (1964):259–64.

7. Neal, *Wandering Recollections of a Somewhat Busy Life: An Autobiography* (Boston: Roberts Brothers, 1869), pp. 208ff.

## Information Sources

BIBLIOGRAPHY:

Adams, M. Ray. "Della Cruscanism in America." *PMLA* 79 (1964): 259–65.

Fishwick, M. W. "*The Portico* and Literary Nationalism after the War of 1812." *William and Mary Quarterly* 8 (1951):238–45.

French, John C. "Poe's Literary Baltimore." *Maryland Historical Magazine* 32 (1937):101–12.

Hammond, Alexander. "A Reconstruction of Poe's 1833 *Tales of the Folio Club*: Preliminary Notes." *Poe Studies* 5 (1972):25–32.

Mott, Frank Luther. "*The Portico*." *A History of American Magazines, 1741–1850*. New York and London: D. Appleton & Company, 1930. Pp. 293–96.

Neal, John. "John Pierpont." *Atlantic Monthly* 18 (1866):649–65.

————. *Wandering Recollections of a Somewhat Busy Life: An Autobiography*. Boston: Roberts Brothers, 1869.

Lease, Benjamin. *That Wild Fellow John Neal and the American Literary Revolution*. Chicago: University of Chicago Press, 1972.

McCloskey, J. C. "The Campaign of Periodicals after the War of 1812 for National Literature." *PMLA* 50 (1935):262–73.

————. "A Note on *The Portico*." *American Literature* 8 (1936):300–304.

Spencer, Benjamin T. *The Quest for Nationality: An American Literary Campaign*. Syracuse: Syracuse University Press, 1957.

Uhler, John Earle. "The Delphian Club." *Maryland Historical Magazine* 20 (1925):305–46.

INDEXES: Index at end of each volume.

REPRINT EDITIONS: American Periodicals: Series II, 1800–1850. University Microfilms, Ann Arbor. Reels 192–93.

LOCATION SOURCES: Complete runs: American Antiquarian Society, Library of Congress, Huntington Library, Georgetown University Library, State University of Iowa, Harvard University, Peabody Institute, New York Public Library, Ohio Wesleyan University, American Philosophical Society. Partial runs: Widely available.

## Publication History

MAGAZINE TITLE AND TITLE CHANGES: *The Portico*. 1816 volume has subtitle: *A Repository of Science and Literature*.

VOLUME AND ISSUE DATA: Volumes 1–5, January 1816-April, May, and June 1818.

FREQUENCY OF PUBLICATION: Monthly, but July-December 1817 is divided into three double issues, and January-June 1818 into two triple or quarterly issues.

PUBLISHERS: 1816: Neal Wills and Company, Baltimore. 1817–1818: E. J. Coale and
    Cushing and Jewett, Baltimore.
EDITORS: Tobias Watkins and Stephen Simpson ("Two Men of Padua").

*Kent Ljungquist*

## PUTNAM'S MONTHLY MAGAZINE

William Makepeace Thackeray thought *Putnam's Monthly Magazine* "much the
best Mag. in the world . . . better than Blackwood is or ever was."[1] Henry James
recalled his "very young pleasure" in basking in the prose "as mild as an Indian
summer in the woods" as he read the works of Herman Melville, George William
Curtis, and Donald Grant Mitchell in the "charming *Putnam*"[2] of the early
1850s. Such effusive, retrospective praise reflects the authoritative stature held
by *Putnam's Monthly Magazine* throughout the nineteenth century,[3] a position
of eminence in magazine publishing that could only be matched by *Harper's*\*
and the *Atlantic Monthly.*\* If a later series of the magazine (1868–1870) did not
approach the consistent excellence of its predecessor (1853–1857), the sustained,
pioneering efforts of *Putnam's* on behalf of native authors represented a major
contribution to American letters.

The appeal to literary nationalism could not have been more explicit than in
the magazine's first number.[4] One of the motivations for initiating a new journal
was to showcase America's cultural resources:

> It is because we are confident neither Greece nor Guinea can offer the
> American reader a richer variety of instruction and amusement in every
> kind, than the country whose pulses throb with his, and whose every interest
> is his own, that this magazine presents itself today. The genius of the old
> world is affluent; we owe much to it, and we hope to owe more. But we
> have no less faith in the opulence of our own resources (1:1).

The editor-in-chief, Charles Briggs (also known as "Harry Franco"); the three
working editors (Curtis, Charles A. Dana, and Frederick Law Olmsted); and the
contributing editor (Parke Godwin) followed through on this charge by providing
a forum for a wide range of American authors.[5] In the early numbers of *Putnam's*,
works of the following American writers appeared: Henry David Thoreau, Henry
Wadsworth Longfellow, Herman Melville, James Fenimore Cooper, Bayard
Taylor, John Pendleton Kennedy, Charles Dudley Warner, William Cullen Bryant,
and James Russell Lowell. A review of *Homes of American Authors* sustained
the nationalistic tone by suggesting that American writers had laid "a foundation
of a peculiar literature, not yet copious, not yet comparable for richness, depth,
variety, or grace, with either the ancient or modern literatures, but still full of
native freshness and vigor" (1:23–30). Even an essay on the popular reception
of *Uncle Tom's Cabin*, while acknowledging its fostering of antislavery senti-

ment, claimed that Stowe's novel opened a "new literary era" by applying American genius to native subjects (1:97–102). Other contributions that highlighted American subject matter included Lowell's "A Moosehead Journal" and Thoreau's "Cape Cod" (three numbers in 1855).

Although often criticized for his challenging style and metaphysical speculations, Melville was the most significant literary contributor to *Putnam's* in its early years. Inviting contributions in 1852, George Palmer Putnam had sent a personal request for material to Melville, who responded with installments of *Israel Potter* as well as some of his finest tales. During a period in his career when he tried his hand at short fiction, Melville's tales regaled *Putnam's* subscribers with a wealth and range of topical allusions.[6] A 3 December column in the *Literary World*\* congratulated *Putnam's* for completing a stellar first year, and singled out "Mr. Melville's 'Bartleby, the Scrivener,' a Poeish tale" infused with fine sentiment.[7] Conforming to the magazine's charge to deal with New York settings, Melville had just completed his two-part story of Wall Street in the December 1853 number (2:546–57, 609–15). Of *Benito Cereno*, editor Curtis offered an evaluation of "very good," though he wished that Melville had eliminated "the dreary documents at the end."[8] "I and My Chimney," with its rural setting and domestic scenes handled with deft comedy, recalled similar fare in *Putnam's*, such as Frederick Gould Cozzens's *The Sparrowgrass Papers*. Curtis found it "a capital, genial, humorous sketch . . . thoroughly magazinish."[9]

Melville's contributions to *Putnam's* provided him with necessary income,[10] and in addition to the publication of *Israel Potter* in book form, connections with the firm ultimately led to the appearance of *The Piazza Tales* as a collection. By 1856, Curtis had soured somewhat on Melville's commercial promise; a *Putnam's* reviewer in the following year, nevertheless, claimed that Maga, as the periodical was affectionately called, "loved its step-son Melville, as if he were her own" (9:384–93).

His name linked to Melville because of their common interest in travel writing, Curtis contributed material in diverse forms to *Putnam's*. In addition to regular musical and dramatic criticism and some forgettable poetry, he published reviews of *Hiawatha* and *Bleak House*, essays on the Brontes and Victorian poetry, and an assortment of descriptive sketches. Maintaining a busy schedule of public lecturing, Curtis kept his editing activities somewhat out of the public eye, while Godwin and Dana advised on manuscripts and Olmsted (known as "Mr. Law") dealt with rejected authors. Curtis still managed to commence his notorious series on the escapades of the Potiphar family, his fictional satires in the vogue of Thackeray. Beginning with a chapter entitled "Our Best Society" (1:170–79), this series exposed the money grubbing and false luxury of New York society. Inviting speculation about the real-life counterparts to Mesdames Potiphar, Croesus, and Gnu, Mr. Gauche Boosey, and Miss Caroline Petitoes, *The Potiphar Papers* may have lost much of their satirical zest because of the modern reader's distance from their topical source. Even in their own time, James Russell Lowell found that the papers relied too much on "monologizing and dialogizing thoughts," that they were "not flesh and blood enough."[11] Such strictures probably carry even more authority today, a criticism less applicable to Curtis's other series in *Putnam's: Prue and I.* "A Cruise in the Flying Dutchman" (5:516–25), in particular, records effectively the fanciful adventures of Curtis's home-bound, wife-doting narrator, who imagines himself at sea in the company of fantastic figures enveloped in spectral shrouds and a mysterious, smoky haze.

In addition to these ventures into belles lettres, Curtis kept some of his favorite topics before the attention of *Putnam's* readers. In all likelihood, he contributed an essay on "Lectures and Lecturing" (9:317–21), which provides a lively perspective on the nineteenth-century lyceum. Reflecting his predisposition to label Melville a travel writer, he also offered a penetrating estimation of the whole genre of travel literature ("American Travelers," 5:561–76).

Cozzens's *Sparrowgrass Papers*, an amusing series on rural and suburban life, sustained *Putnam's* interest in the nineteenth-century vogue of the picturesque. These sketches on "Living in the Country" followed a simple formula of presenting a comic domestic episode attended by a loving description of natural landscape. While Cozzens's efforts served to lighten the tone of *Putnam's*, John Hanson's "Have We a Bourbon Among Us" (1:194–217) won the most sustained amount of reader response. Hanson claimed that the Reverend Eleazar Williams was actually Louis XVII, the lost dauphin of France. The controversy attracted wide reader interest as a follow-up essay, "The Bourbon Question" (1:442–62), attests.

Focus on this issue indicated that *Putnam's* would not turn away from historical, literary, or political controversy. Delia Bacon, calling attention to the discrepancy between the sordid world of the playhouse and the lofty tone of courtly culture in Shakespeare's plays, launched her ill-fated attempt to question the authenticity of their authorship (7:1–19). In the sphere of politics Parke Godwin was *Putnam's* most articulate spokesman, a review of his *Political Essays* appearing in 1856 (8:441–42). *Putnam's*, on the whole, expressed the principles of republicanism, its championship of John Fremont's presidential candidacy emerging in a series of political pieces by Godwin.

Buoyed by interest in "The Bourbon Question," an 1855 editorial note acknowledged that *Putnam's* was still in the "bloom and freshness of youth" (5:545). Achievements of *Putnam's* had "not been paralleled in the history of periodical literature," a success resulting from a wealth of literary material in the country and the magazine's ability to nurture such a resource. The magazine had cleared $14,000 from 1855 to 1857, and circulation had peaked at 19,000 in 1855. Despite such obvious success, Putnam had sold the magazine to Dix & Edwards, or J. H. Dix & Company, in March 1855. Offered exclusive editorship at this point, Curtis turned down the position. Circulation subsided to 17,000 in 1856 and to 14,000 in 1857, a steady decline that augured the magazine's termination in its existent form. In October 1857, *Putnam's* merged with *Emerson's United States Magazine* to form *Emerson's Magazine and Putnam's Monthly*, a hybrid publication that feebly imitated the old series.

Under the editorship of Charles Briggs, *Putnam's* was revitalized in 1868. Briggs's opening column, "The Old and the New" (1:1–8), provided a retrospective on the former series and an update on some of its contributors. The explicit aim of the new series was to support a broad nationality of letters, to sustain the progress of American literature begun by the old series. Occupying a position in between a weekly and a quarterly review, the new *Putnam's* did attract some notable contributors. The first volume published contributions by Evert Duyckinck, William Douglas O'Connor, Bayard Taylor, Henry T. Tuckerman, E. C. Stedman, John W. DeForest, and John Neal. Advice to contributors outlined the requirements for a periodical of high quality: "A good magazine article, indeed, on whatever subject, should be condensed, pithy, pointed; it should be handled in a certain practical way." Potential authors should eschew rarefied subjects in favor of the mundane: "Home topics must generally be preferred . . . life and society in America; or the development of natural resources; industrial pursuits; incidents of travel; descriptions of unfamiliar occurrences, etc." (1:137). Perhaps because of such explicit encouragement of quotidian fare, the new *Putnam's* did not achieve the level of quality of the earlier series. The new series, however, did present a compendium of articles on everyday life and society in post-Civil War America. Essays appeared on the following commonplace topics: paper production, foreign travel, urban postal service, partisan politics, national finances, the copyright law, and women and work.

More self-conscious than its predecessor about its role in the burgeoning periodical milieu, the new *Putnam's* measured itself against the formidable competition: the *North American Review*,* the *Galaxy*,* and the *Atlantic Monthly*. While a magazine represented "just another form of book publication" in its reliance on the serial novels of popular authors, a good periodical could still establish its own distinctive features: the "convenience of an unbound book," the "variety of entertainment" available in the periodical format, and "frequent visits from authors whose writings are esteemed." The editors articulated explicitly the possible connection between author and audience, magazine and marketplace: "The model subscriber to a magazine, in fact, has a personal interest in the work; is a species of partner in the enterprise; has a community of interest with others, and enjoys a welcome sense of continuity, of a pleasure that ends not with an hour, but has a promise of renewal from month to month" (1:120–22).

Despite such concerted attempts to reach out to the literary marketplace, few individual pieces in the new series carried the unique character of those in the old *Putnam's*. Previously unpublished manuscripts of James Fenimore Cooper appeared, Putnam's own "Leaves from a Publisher's Letter Book" (4:467–74) recounted the glory years of a great publishing house, and C. F. Robertson attempted unsuccessfully to resurrect interest in the "Bourbon Controversy." E. C. Stedman, who assisted with some editing duties and reviewed widely, raised the level of literary analysis in the new *Putnam's* with his searching evaluations of American authors and the Victorian poets.[12]

At the end of the sixth volume, Parke Godwin announced "A Change of Base," a transformation rather than a suspension of the magazine's operations: *Putnam's* would join forces with its previous competitors to form the new *Scribner's Monthly*.\* High monetary outlays and substantial payments to contributors had invited unforeseen financial problems, and *Putnam's* was forced into this merger.[13] Nevertheless, in its encouragement of the finest qualities in a developing national literature, the old and new *Putnam's* had established a standard of excellence that few nineteenth-century magazines could rival.

## Notes

1. Apparently a comment made by Thackeray in conversation, as recollected by George William Curtis and cited in Laura Wood Roper, " 'Mr. Law' and *Putnam's Monthly*: A Note on a Phase in the Career of Frederick Law Olmsted," *American Literature* 26 (1954):92.

2. Henry James, "American Letters," *Literature* 2 (1898):676–77, reprinted in Henry James, *Literary Criticism: Essays on Literature, American Writers, English Writers* (New York: Literary Classics of the United States, 1984), p. 683.

3. A published incidence of *Putnam's* influence well into the latter half of the century is recorded by George Monteiro, " 'Bartleby the Scrivener' and Melville's Contemporary Reputation," *Studies in Bibliography* 24 (1971):195–96.

4. See Notley S. Maddox, "Literary Nationalism in *Putnam's Magazine*, 1853–1857," *American Literature* 14 (1942):117–25.

5. Roper provides an overview of the various editorial duties and how they were divided—with Olmsted's role, Dana's contributions, and Curtis's direction kept from the public eye.

6. Melville's topicality appealed to both the readers and editors of *Putnam's*, according to William Dillingham, *Melville's Short Fiction, 1853–1856* (Athens: University of Georgia Press, 1977), p. 15.

7. Cited in Jay Leyda, *The Melville Log: A Documentary Life, 1819–1891*, 2 vols. (New York: Gordian Press, 1969), 1:482.

8. Leyda, 2:50.

9. Leyda, 2:507.

10. A more detailed overview of Melville's sources of income is provided in Merton Sealts, "The Chronology of Melville's Short Fiction, 1853–1856," in *Pursuing Melville, 1940–1980* (Madison: University of Wisconsin Press, 1982), pp. 221–31. Melville also contributed "The Encantadas," "The Apple-Tree Table," and "The Lightning-Rod Man" to *Putnam's*. "The Two Temples" was rejected by *Putnam's* because of its supposed attitude toward the church, a rejection that won an apology for Melville from Charles Briggs.

11. *Letters of James Russell Lowell*, ed. Charles Eliot Norton, 2 vols. (New York: Harper & Bros., 1894): 1:211.

12. Contrary to what Mott claims, Stedman never assumed editorial control over *Putnam's*, as Stedman himself notes in a letter quoted in Robert Scholnick, *Edmund Clarence Stedman* (Boston: Twayne, 1977), p. 34.

13. See George Haven Putnam, *George Palmer Putnam: A Profile* (New York: G. P. Putnam & Sons, 1912), pp. 171–91, for fuller details on financial reverses.

## Information Sources

BIBLIOGRAPHY:

Cary, Edward. "Lecturer and Magazine Writer." *George William Curtis*. Boston: Houghton, Mifflin and Company, 1894. Pp. 74–90.

Dillingham, William. *Melville's Short Fiction, 1853–1856*. Athens: University of Georgia Press, 1977.

Emery, Alan Moore. "The Topicality of Depravity in 'Benito Cereno.' " *American Literature* 55 (1983):316–31.

*Letters of James Russell Lowell*. Ed. Charles Eliot Norton. 2 vols. New York: Harper & Brothers, 1893.

Leyda, Jay. *The Melville Log: A Documentary Life, 1819–1891*. 2 vols. New York: Gordian Press, 1969.

Maddox, Notley S. "Literary Nationalism in *Putnam's Magazine*, 1853–1857." *American Literature* 14 (1942):117–25.

Milne, Gordon. "The Magazine World." *George William Curtis and the Genteel Tradition*. Bloomington: Indiana University Press, 1956. Pp. 64–69.

Monteiro, George. " 'Bartleby the Scrivener' and Melville's Contemporary Reputation." *Studies in Bibliography* 24 (1971):195–96.

Mott, Frank Luther. "*Putnam's Monthly Magazine*." *A History of American Magazines*. 4 vols. Cambridge, Mass.: Harvard University Press, 1938. 2:419–31.

Putnam, George Haven. *George Palmer Putnam: A Memoir*. New York: G. P. Putnam's & Son, 1912.

Roper, Laura Wood. " 'Mr. Law' and *Putnam's Monthly*: A Note on a Phase in the Career of Frederick Law Olmsted." *American Literature* 26 (1954):88–93.

St. Armand, Barton Levi. "Curtis's 'Bartleby': An Unrecorded Melville Reference." *Papers of the Bibliographical Society of America* 71 (1977):219–20.

Scholnick, Robert. *Edmund Clarence Stedman*. Boston: Twayne, 1977.

Sealts, Merton. "The Chronology of Melville's Short Fiction, 1853–1856." *Pursuing Melville, 1940–1980*. Madison: University of Wisconsin Press, 1982. Pp. 221–31.

INDEXES: Indexed at end of each volume.

LOCATION SOURCES: American Periodicals: Series III, 1850–1900. University Microfilms, Ann Arbor. Reels 164–67.

## Publication History

MAGAZINE TITLE AND TITLE CHANGES: *Putnam's Monthly Magazine of American Literature, Science and Art*, 1853–1857. *Putnam's Magazine: Original Papers on Literature, Science, Art, and National Interests*, 1868–1870.

VOLUME AND ISSUE DATA: Volumes 1–9, January 1853-September 1857, semiannual volumes; volume 10 ends series with only 3 numbers; new series, volumes 1–6, January 1868-November 1870, semiannual volumes.

FREQUENCY OF PUBLICATION: Monthly.

PUBLISHERS: 1853–1855: G. P. Putnam & Company. 1855–1857: Dix & Edwards. 1857: Miller & Company. 1868–1870: G. P. Putnam & Son (all in New York).

EDITORS: Charles Briggs (George William Curtis, Charles A. Dana, Parke Godwin, and Frederick Law Olmsted, associate editors), 1853–1857; Charles Briggs, 1868–1869; Parke Godwin, 1870.

*Kent Ljungquist*

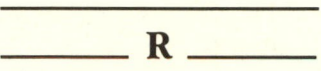

## THE RADICAL

The Civil War removed antislavery from its right-of-way role among reform movements in the United States. Transcendentalists, long active abolitionists, returned to what had been their primary target in the 1830s, the Unitarian establishment. They picked up the banner that had been sewn by Emerson and passed by George Ripley to Theodore Parker and charged forth again against the foe. Allying themselves with science, which they frequently equated with Emersonian Reason, they sought to universalize religion from its narrow sectarian state into a worldwide "Free Religion which was to embody the spiritual intuition of humanity at large."[1]

They rejected the "supernaturalism" of their contemporaries and insisted on the "naturalism" of Parker and Emerson. Man, not God, was the center of their lives; now, not then, was the focus of their attention; man's intuition was the only source of religious truth. The authority of the Bible and Jesus was to be replaced by the authority of each person's ability to behold God directly.

In September of 1865 appeared in Boston the first issue of the *Radical: A Monthly Magazine Devoted to Religion*, edited by Sidney Morse. Unlike the popular periodicals of the period, it featured no monthly columns, serials, sketches, travelogues, editorials, or illustrations. Clearly a serious publication, it looked more to the *Bibliotheca Sacra* than *Harper's Weekly*. Thirty-two pages in length, the first issue loudly proclaimed its position and purpose. Jesus divided the world into now and eternity, surface and reality. "Tear down the partition wall and there is One World and Eternity already present. To live in this Great Eternity . . . must be for man, his *Religion*." The editor stated that "in devoting our magazine to RELIGION . . . we have not drawn any excluding lines to bar our entrance into whatever field. . . . We included all departments of thought and work, which have for mankind any real worth or significance" (1:3–4).

For the first six issues Samuel Johnson, graduate of Harvard Divinity School, classmate of Samuel Longfellow, and pastor of the Free Church of Lynn, Massachusetts, wrote a series of "Discourses Concerning the Foundations of Religious Belief." He concluded that "the voice of nature is the voice of God. Miracle in the theological sense is impossible. We can have no other commandment than Natural Law; we can know no other gospel than Natural Inspiration; we can possess no other guarantee of Truth than Intuition and Recognition which in every case prove to be the native element and proper force of Man" (1:401).

The other two principal contributors to the early volumes were David Atwood Wasson and John Weiss. Wasson had filled pulpits at the churches of Thomas Wentworth Higginson and Parker, but because of ill health was unable to preach full time. Weiss graduated from Harvard Divinity School and succeeded Converse Francis at the Unitarian Church in Watertown, Massachusetts. Like his colleagues, he argued modern man's ability to attain the brotherhood of man and the Fatherhood of God. In "The Essential Jesus," an essay review of the proliferation of lives of Jesus, Weiss wrote, "Jesus himself is dead. . . . The best intelligible life of Jesus will be written by faith upon the face of human society, and all men will read there his essential truths converted into the body and the blood of everytime" (3:467).

On 30 May 1867, in Horticultural Hall in Boston, Octavius Brooks Frothingham, pastor of the Third Congregational Church in New York and intellectual heir of Theodore Parker, chaired the organizational meeting of the Free Religious Association. The purpose of the group was "to provide for a non-sectarian religion to which any intelligent person could subscribe despite condition of race and birth."[2] The association approached Morse and asked if the *Radical* might become their voice, as all the prewar Transcendental magazines had ceased publication. Morse, sympathetic, agreed.

Among the more frequent contributors to the *Radical* were Cyrus A. Bartol, Moncure Daniel Conway, Frothingham, Samuel Longfellow, and Higginson. Bartol was the leader of religious thought and life in Boston in the last half of the nineteenth century. His West Church had been the center of liberal religious influence since its founding in 1737, and his Chestnut Street house was for years the meeting place for those writers and thinkers who made Boston the center of literary life during the period. Bartol allowed several of his sermons to be printed in the early issues of the *Radical*, including a challenging address to the Harvard Divinity students (3:65).

Moncure Conway became the pastor of a Unitarian church in Washington after his graduation from Harvard Divinity School. Offered the pastorate of a church in London, he accepted and lived in England until 1884. At first he sent the *Radical* several letters describing the state of religion in England (1:110, 256, 426; 7:301, 335); later came other essays on topics such as "The Ethics of the Will" and "The Human Sacrifices of Christendom."

Frothingham's beliefs were even further to the left than those of his friend and mentor Theodore Parker. In numerous contributions such as "The Radical's Attitude Towards the Bible," "The Historical Position of Jesus," "The Ethics of Sentiment and of Science," and "What Is Religion and What Is It For?" he attacked the conservative position with vigor and wit.

Made up of "mystics, skeptics, and dyspeptics,"[3] Harvard Divinity School was not immediately attractive to Thomas Wentworth Higginson. Author of a novel and a collection of biographical sketches of Harvard men who died for the Union, Higginson combined religion and history in his early contributions to the *Radical*: "Charlotte Prince Hawes" and "The Pedigree of Liberalism;" his later pieces, "The Sympathy of Religions" and "The Buddist Path of Virtue," were more theological.

Samuel Longfellow, brother of the poet, was a classmate of Johnson, Frothingham, and Higginson at Harvard. "The clearest and most methodic in thought"[4] of the Transcendentalists, his arguments were always careful, gentle, and charming. "Some Radical Doctrines," "The Unity and Universality of the Religious Ideas," "Liberal Religion in Europe," "Scripture Lesson," and "Theism" are representative. In the last, he wrote, God "is not a deduction of the understanding, but a conviction of the reason" (10:180).

Although Amos Bronson Alcott's work had been given little attention in the early Transcendental periodicals, the *Radical* gave considerable space to his thoughts, reflecting perhaps "at least a sympathetic effort to understand what he said."[5] Three poems, "The Patriot," "The Chase," and "Misrule," appeared in the early volumes; his critical estimates of various writers, "Wendell Phillips," "Montaigne," "Plotinus," "Coleridge," "Berkley," "Boehme," and "Hermes Trismegistus," later collected in *Concord Days*, followed.

Most of the poetry that appeared in the *Radical* was either anonymous or signed with initials. Of those who signed their work, many were, not surprisingly, Unitarian clergy. James Vola Blake and John White Chadwick were both graduates of Harvard Divinity School and were lumped with three other ministers under the title "The Big Five" by the conservative Unitarians. One of Blake's poems, "The Hermit," appeared in the magazine, and two of Chadwick's, "Self-Possession" and "Insight." The most prolific contributor of verse was also the best of the minor poets the *Radical* published. Edward Rowland Sill was a Yale graduate who attended Harvard Divinity School for a year. Among his *Radical* poems were "Dare You?" "In Reply," "Five Lives," "The Secret," and "Truant." Characterized by doubt, the poems are the product of a sensitive, questioning mind obsessed with the conflict of religion and science.

Apparently because the magazine was criticized for its attack on the establishment, the editor printed a restatement of the credo given in the first number in the issue for March 1867. "THE RADICAL is a medium for the freest expression of thought on all religious and social topics. No subject important enough to be discussed in its pages is to be pronounced settled, and arbitrarily closed in deference to the popular sentiment. . . . The Radical will not covertly suppress error, but openly, with full faith in human nature under the sway of freedom, win the day against it'' (2:48). But the critics would not be pacified.

Three phrases are common to the biographies of most of those involved in the *Radical*: ''attended Harvard Divinity School,'' ''was a disciple of Theodore Parker,'' and ''held beliefs outside the bounds of orthodox Unitarianism.'' Such a group, consciously iconoclastic, embracing Darwin and evolution, accepting science as the partner of religion, and urging their readers to probe further and further from the established comfortable beliefs, inevitably had to alienate what was not a large readership to begin with. When more and more writers urged a search to find a replacement for the Bible, more and more subscribers cancelled.

In the spring of 1872 an attempt was made to raise funds to save the magazine. Five members of the Radical Association formed a corporation called The Radical Publishing Company and issued $50,000 of stock at $100 a share (10:319). Only ninety-three shares were sold, many to the magazine's contributors, and the attempt to save the *Radical* failed. In his valedictory, Morse wrote, ''The magazine has made a fair record and done good work'' (10:468).

## Notes

1. Clarence L. F. Gohdes, *The Periodicals of American Transcendentalism* (Durham, N.C.: Duke University Press, 1931), p. 212.

2. Gohdes, pp. 230–31.

3. M. A. DeWolfe Howe, ''Higginson, Thomas Wentworth,'' *Dictionary of American Biography*, vol. 9 (1932), pp. 16–18.

4. Francis A. Christie, ''Longfellow, Samuel,'' *Dictionary of American Biography*, vol. 11 (1933), pp. 387–88.

5. Gohdes, p. 223.

## Information Sources

BIBLIOGRAPHY:

Cooke, George Willis. *An Historical and Bibliographical Introduction to Accompany the Dial*. Cleveland: Rowfant Club, 1902.

Gohdes, Clarence L.F. *The Periodicals of American Transcendentalism*. Durham, N.C.: Duke University Press, 1931.

Mott, Frank Luther, *A History of American Magazines, 1865–1885*. Cambridge, Mass.: Harvard University Press, 1957.

Sargent, Mary E. *Sketches and Reminiscences of the Radical Club*. Boston, Mass.: Roberts, 1880.

Warders, Donald F. ''Transcendentalist Periodicals.'' *The Transcendentalists*. Ed. Joel Myerson. New York: MLA, 1984. Pp. 69–83.

INDEXES: Indexes at the end of each volume; volumes 1 and 2, title entries, volumes 4–10, author and title.

REPRINT EDITIONS: American Periodicals: Series III, 1850–1900. University Microfilms, Ann Arbor. Reels 15–17. AMS Press, Inc., New York.

LOCATION SOURCES: Widely available.

## Publication History

MAGAZINE TITLE AND TITLE CHANGES: *The Radical: A Monthly Magazine Devoted to Religion*, September 1865-June 1869. *The Radical*, July 1869-June 1872.

VOLUME AND ISSUE DATA: Volumes 1–10, September 1865-June 1872; suspended July 1870-January 1871.

FREQUENCY OF PUBLICATION: Monthly.

PUBLISHERS: September 1865-June 1867: A. Williams and Company, Boston. July 1867-June 1868: Adams and Company, Boston. July 1868-June 1872: n.p., Boston.

EDITORS: Sidney H. Morse, September 1865-August 1867; Sidney H. Morse and Joseph B. Marvin, September 1867-June 1869; Sidney H. Morse, July 1869-June 1872.

*E. Bruce Kirkham*


**REEDY'S MIRROR.** See *American Literary Magazines: The Twentieth Century*


**RICHARDS' WEEKLY GAZETTE.** See THE SOUTHERN LITERARY GAZETTE


**THE RICHMOND ECLECTIC.** See THE SOUTHERN MAGAZINE


**THE ROSE BUD, OR YOUTH'S GAZETTE.** See THE SOUTHERN ROSE


## THE ROUND TABLE

In 1863 the brothers Charles and Henry Sweetser established the *Round Table*, a New York weekly journal of opinion, in response to the intellectual challenge of the Civil War. "Our American life has hitherto been so full of sunshine and action, so buoyant and untrammeled, that the most serious problems of national existence have come upon us like a thief in the night," the editors observed in the first number, 19 December 1863 (1:4). The Sweetsers recognized that the Civil War had brought to the national consciousness questions of such complexity that a new, rigorously critical habit of mind was demanded: "While the dark cloud of trial and endurance which now rests upon the land throws its shadow upon us, it is well that we should learn to think," they wrote (1:4). The young editors sought to introduce into America the sort of high-powered magazine that was well known to English readers through the *Saturday Review* and other weeklies. It would "condense" for critical examination "whatever, in the crowded and varied life of each passing week, most merits or demands the thoughtful attention which it is impossible men should give to the facts of each day as they fly past them on the wings of the morning journal''(1:4).

The Sweetsers—perhaps with characteristic American idealism—assumed that their journal could succeed without establishing ties to a political faction, religious denomination, or publishing house, as was typical of American magazines. Of course, to do so would place external constraints on a journal that sought to approach all subjects in a free and open manner. ''Politics without partisanship, criticism without partiality or prejudice'' was its motto (2:8). But the difficulties of producing an independent magazine during the war forced the inexperienced editors to suspend publication with the number for 23 July 1864. They claimed that the *Round Table* had been a ''success,'' that its ''circulation and advertising patronage are greater than it was anticipated they would be at this date. . . . It has definitely proved that an independent, spirited and literary journal was an actual want in the country'' (2:88). But, the Sweetsers complained, they could not have anticipated the tremendous inflation caused by the war. On 9 September 1865 they made good their promise to resume publication, but it would not be long before each of the Sweetsers withdrew, Henry in April and Charles in November 1866. Their positions were assumed by Dorsey Gardner and Henry Sedley, who would turn the magazine sharply to the right and away from its strong American cultural nationalism.

Under the Sweetsers the *Round Table* was politically liberal, supporting a vigorous prosecution of the war as a means of ending the evil of slavery and restoring the Union. Unhesitatingly critical of the failures of both parties, it repeatedly warned against the dangers of factionalism. On the crucial issue of race, it was comparatively enlightened, praising the behavior of the Negroes, ''bond and free, North and South,'' during the war and urging that the Federal government assume the responsibility for caring for the recently manumitted slaves (1:100). The high-minded paper condemned the excessive profits of the few, and urged all citizens to share equally in the war's burdens. After the war it observed sadly that everywhere ''we see evidences that the desire for money has acquired a strength in our American nature which almost makes it now one of those passions before which all principle is powerless'' (2:25). A supporter of Lincoln, the *Round Table* campaigned for a wider democratization of American life, both in social policy and in the discussions of literature and the arts that figured prominently in its pages.

Attacking the ''deference'' paid to English cultural standards, the *Round Table* sought to stimulate ''a taste for American in preference to English books and periodicals'' (2:8). It criticized the ''elegant mediocrity'' of American literature and called for a ''rougher, stronger race of literary athletes'' to create a national literature expressive of the people themselves. Insisting that ''the one great requisite'' for such a national literature is ''trenchant, unsparing, vigorous criticism'' (2:18), the *Round Table* charged that fear of losing publishers' advertising had prevented most American periodicals from telling the truth about bad books

(1:55). It showed no such timidity in its own criticism of literature, drama, or the fine arts. For instance, its regular art critic, Eugene Benson, a self-styled "literary frondeur," brought a new outspokenness and thoroughness to art criticism in America.[1] "The first and last idea of the paper is free, independent, and hearty criticism," the editors asserted. However, the *Round Table* ran the risk, in its unrestrained and high-minded treatment of every aspect of American life—it was particularly harsh on the religious press—of becoming censorious. But refreshingly the editors admitted that "we should be graceless cowards if unwilling to receive that which we freely give" (3:344).

The Sweetsers did not establish an in-house corps of editors, but, in keeping with their goal of creating a truly national publication committed to informed discussion of all subjects, sought submissions from throughout the country. It subscribed to the policy of anonymous journalism, although it did permit the authors of "letters" from outside New York, such as Justin Winsor from Boston and Moncure Conway from London, to affix initials. Evidently, it was Charles Sweetser, an 1862 graduate of Amherst, who secured Emily Dickinson's "My Sabbath" ("Some Keep the Sabbath"), published anonymously in the number for 12 March 1863 (1:195). On 16 January 1864 the editors asserted that the policy of anonymous journalism had been no bar to their ability to secure contributions from writers "whose eminence in their respective departments, whether of belles-lettres, history, jurisprudence, metaphysics, warfare, science or art, is universally acknowledged" (1:67). However, in July 1866, they confessed their "disappointment" in not being able to enlist the aid of literary men who can and ought to aid in supporting the magazine and periodical literature of the day. "We believe that nearly half of the articles which have appeared in this journal from the date of commencement have been the production of writers comparatively unknown in the literary world" (3:440). The statement expresses both their dissatisfaction with the timidity of American literature and their disappointment in not attracting writers of established reputation, particularly from Boston. The editors refused to admit that their unrealistic policy of not identifying their writers had something to do with the reluctance of some writers to contribute. For instance, the New York poet and critic E. C. Stedman, despite his support of the Sweetsers' brave endeavor, decided not to send his best poems to the *Round Table* because its "impersonal" rule "hides its author's name, and where it can reach but a limited audience."[2] At the conclusion of the first volume the editors listed some sixty-seven writers who had contributed with some frequency, including such leading scholars as Daniel Gilman and Noah Porter of Yale, but New Yorkers, such as R. H. Stoddard, William Winter, C. B. Conant, Stedman, and T. B. Aldrich, composed the great majority, and it does appear that New York writers made up the bulk of the magazine's regular columns.

The resurgence of literary activity following the war brought with it a startling increase in the number of periodicals, most of which, the *Round Table* predicted, could not survive: "At no time have the expenses of publishing a paper been so great as now. . . . Our readers can get some idea of what it costs to make a paper when we state that the ordinary expenses of *The Round Table* vary not a great way from eight hundred dollars each week'' (3:89). The editors expressed confidence that the high quality of their weekly would attract increasing numbers of readers, but they also urged their regular subscribers to solicit new ones. Charles Sweetser's ''A Card.—Personal,'' published on 14 April 1866, the date of his withdrawal, gives us some insight into the extraordinary struggle that these editors regularly faced: ''None can so well know the great difficulties to be surmounted in establishing a literary adventure as those who have themselves attempted it; and it will, perhaps be considered just to say that no efforts have met more obstacles than this endeavor to create a critical periodical literature in our own country.'' Circulation, which, Charles Sweetser wrote, ''should not be less than 25,000'' (3:232), never exceeded 5,000, according to Frank Luther Mott.[3] There is, then, reason to be skeptical of the editors' claim at the end of 1866 that the magazine paid a ''handsome profit'' (4:357). With E. L. Godkin's establishment in New York of his well-financed *Nation* early in 1865, during its suspension, the *Round Table* faced a difficult competitor in a very limited market.

Much as the Sweetsers' *Round Table* reflected a Lincolnian commitment to democracy, so the *Round Table* under Gardner and Sedley became an expression of postwar disillusionment. Disgusted by widespread corruption in government, the magazine now propounded an immutable social law: ''In proportion as suffrage is extended downward the amount of ignorance and prejudice in the aggregate voting body is increased, with the direct consequence that politicians will become more and more demagogues—men who appeal to ignorance and prejudice and not knowledge and reason.'' And so, at a time of ''enormous influx of ignorant immigration, together with the proposed enfranchisement of an entire race, late a servile and now a semi-civilized one,'' the *Round Table* fastened on the threat from below, adamantly opposed Reconstruction, grew livid over the prospect of Negro suffrage, and questioned democracy itself (7:99). It spoke longingly of the advantages of a House of Lords as a conservative check on a popularly elected legislative body (8:19–20) and asserted that the absence of standards of proper behavior in social life was proof-positive of American provincialism (8:20–21). And whereas the old *Round Table* spoke out in favor of cultural nationalism, now the magazine adopted the stance of such English critics of American democracy as Carlyle and Arnold. Especially under Henry Sedley, who became sole editor and proprietor in December 1868, the magazine lost its earlier editorial openness, its willingness to consider tolerantly and critically all sides of any question, perhaps the most important contribution to American journalism of the Sweetsers' lively weekly. But under Sedley the magazine was no more popular with readers than earlier incarnations, and after the first number of volume 10, for 3 July 1869, the *Round Table* merged with the *Citizen* and ceased to exist.

## Notes

1. See Robert J. Scholnick, "Between Realism and Romanticism: The Curious Career of Eugene Benson," *American Literary Realism* 14 (1981):242–61.

2. *The Life and Letters of Edmund Clarence Stedman*, ed. Laura Stedman and George M. Gould, M.D. (New York: Moffat and Yard, 1910), 1:343.

3. Frank Luther Mott, *"The Round Table," A History of American Magazines*, 4 vols. (Cambridge, Mass.: The Belknap Press of Harvard University Press, 1957), 3:323.

### Information Sources

BIBLIOGRAPHY:

Mott, Frank Luther. *"The Round Table." A History of American Magazines*. 4 vols. Cambridge, Mass.: The Belknap Press of Harvard University Press, 1957. 3:319–24.

Tassin, Algernon. *The Magazine in America*. New York: Dodd, Mead & Co., 1916.

INDEXES: None.

REPRINT EDITIONS: American Periodicals: Series III, 1850–1900. University Microfilms, Ann Arbor. Reels 461–62.

LOCATION SOURCES: Complete runs: Library of Congress, New York State Library, Albany, Duke University Library, Library Company of Philadelphia, Boston Public Library, Harvard University Library. Partial runs: Widely available.

### Publication History

MAGAZINE TITLE AND TITLE CHANGES: *The Round Table*. Subtitles: *A Weekly Record of the Notable, the Useful and the Tasteful*, 1863–1864. *A Saturday Review of Literature, Society and Art*, 1866–1867. *A Saturday Review of Politics, Literature, Society and Art*, 1867–1868. *A Saturday Review of Politics, Finance, Literature, Society and Art*, 1868–1869.

VOLUME AND ISSUE DATA: Volumes 1–9, 19 December 1863–26 June 1869; volume 10, 3 July 1869 only. Suspended 30 July 1864–2 September 1865. Volume 2 begins new series with issue of 9 September 1865.

FREQUENCY OF PUBLICATION: Weekly.

PUBLISHERS: 1863–1866: H. C. and C. H. Sweetser, New York. 1866–1869: Round Table Association, New York.

EDITORS: H. C. and C. H. Sweetser, 11 December 1863–14 April 1866; C. H. Sweetser, 14 April 1866–30 April 1866; C. H. Sweetser and D. Gardner, 1 May 1866–25 August 1866; C. H. Sweetser, H. Sedley, and D. Gardner, 25 August 1866–12 November 1866; H. Sedley and D. Gardner, 12 November 1866–31 November 1868; H. Sedley, 1 December 1868–3 July 1869.

*Robert J. Scholnick*

# THE ROYAL AMERICAN MAGAZINE

Isaiah Thomas in January 1774 furthered the patriot cause when he launched the *Royal American Magazine* in the tense city of Boston. Remembered today for his brilliant publishing record, his standard *History of Printing in America*, and creation of the American Antiquarian Society, Thomas in 1774 was known mainly as a patriotic newspaperman. He had long pursued "high notions of liberty": he lost his position on the *Halifax* (Nova Scotia) *Gazette* after defying the Stamp Act, his newspaper the *Massachusetts Spy* presented violently anti-British material (in 1775 he placed atop his front page "Americans!—Liberty or Death!—Join or Die!"), he published such books as *The Revolution in New-England Justified, and the People There Vindicated*, he printed revolutionary handbills, and British soldiers threatened to tar and feather him.

External events dictated the magazine's course. The 24 June 1773 *Massachusetts Spy* contains proposals to publish the new monthly magazine. Advertising a subscription price of "*Ten Shillings* and *Four Pence* lawful money, or *Seven Shillings* and *Nine Pence* sterling, per annum," Thomas promises pages set in "a new and elegant type."[1] Unfortunately, late arrival of that "elegant" type delayed publication until the January 1774 issue. Thomas worked as publisher, editor, and printer until June, when he had to remove from Boston to Worcester. There he renewed the *Spy* but not the *Royal American Magazine*.

He instead sold the magazine to aging Joseph Greenleaf, who continued the enterprise through March 1775. A radical Whig, Greenleaf had earlier helped Thomas with the *Spy* as a financial partner and writer. Greenleaf had earned his friend's admiration for the "ardent zeal" demonstrated in his attacks upon Governor Thomas Hutchinson, whom he accused of usurping authority. Thomas left Greenleaf a respectable readership, but political unrest and absence of the younger man's publishing talents produced financial distress. Thus, the April Battle of Lexington immediately ended the venture, but the final issue's pleas for payments and apologies for missing articles show that the magazine had already run its course. Greenleaf thereupon retired from publishing.

Thomas enunciates in the proposals his overall selection policies. He feels that readers can learn all they should of the world through periodicals. Furthermore, "None is more wanted in America . . . than a MONTHLY one; . . . men of the greatest ingenuity in the American world . . . [will] undoubtedly much oftner favour the public with essays, instructive and entertaining to all classes of men."[2] He plans to rely greatly upon American contributions, including also entertaining items from other periodicals and miscellaneous news. He promises also to avoid political partisanship. However, as Thomas notes in his final issue, few original contributions materialized; also, the editors never strove for bipartisanship. The *Royal American Magazine* instead immediately became a combination of innocuous, often borrowed material and original revolutionary propaganda. We have in its fifteen issues a medley of tones within a miscellany of contents: pictures, political news and essays, history, fiction, literary essays, poetry, and science.

Thomas's advertising publicizes the visual appeal of readable type, fine paper, and copper engravings. Remarkably striking indeed are the engravings, five by Joseph Callender and seventeen by Paul Revere. Adept at careful draftsmanship,

Callender pleased Thomas with work such as "An Indian Gazette" (1:185), reproduced in Thomas's *History* to illustrate primitive people's artistry. But Revere's brilliantly exaggerated artwork makes the engravings truly memorable. Already notorious for his lurid pictures of the Boston Massacre, Revere created for the magazine mostly patriotic scenes and portraits. His renderings of John Hancock and Samuel Adams (March and April 1774), for instance, feature portraits surrounded by symbols of Roman liberty, the Magna Carta, fruitful labor, and crushed tyranny. The first issue boasts the well-known "View of the Town of Boston, with Several Ships of War in the Harbor." We find here a background packed with businesses, while British warships portentously occupy the foreground. Revere achieves power in his editorial cartoons when he pictures America being despoiled by the mother country. The June 1774 issue features "The able Doctor, or America Swallowing the Bitter Draught," wherein evil-faced physicians strip the maiden America and pour tea down her throat as ships cannonade Boston. Similarly, the final issue's frontispiece exhibits evil British doctors binding the maiden while flourishing weapons and remarking, "She must lose more blood." No earlier colonial magazine had employed illustrations with such effectiveness.

The premier number defines the *Royal American Magazine* as "a repository of such interesting events as occur from one month to another" (1:35). Such a purpose necessitated monthly recountings of political news. The "Historical Chronicle" and "Domestic Intelligence" sections thus include—along with weather forecasts, obituaries, and other miscellanea—notes on current events that in their very sequence take us inexorably into revolution. Reprinted documents and lists reveal the tension: Philadelphia resolutions against taxes, Hutchinson's speech against troublemakers, public reactions to the Port Bill, the multiplication of government proclamations and citizens' committees, statistics on goods smuggled into Boston, altercations between soldiers and citizens. Ever tenser events push us toward Lexington and Concord. The editors usually let verbatim texts and statistics imply antigovernment viewpoints without editorial elaboration. But Thomas in particular sometimes emotionally breaks in, especially against the Port Bill. He waxes eloquent: "One great Soul now animates the American World, unites all the Colonies in one Band of Brothers, and every Pulse beats Ardour for American Freedom" (1:234).

The political philosophy inherent in selecting such news items assumes direct statement in the many political essays. Even when essays come from English magazines, the central topic is nearly always liberty. The essays—again, particularly during Thomas's months—ripple with patriotic logic and emotion. Original political essays include animated tributes to patriotic genius and patriots' character. Finer still are Hancock's fiery speech castigating "Ye dark designing knaves" (1:85) and John Lathrop's "Artillery Election Sermon" espousing Thomas Paine's call to citizens to "take up arms against their Kings, when they made dangerous encroachments on their rights and liberties" (1:205).

Although the magazine seldom broadens its perspective to embrace historical material, the editors include one notable exception. Each issue reprints a section of Hutchinson's *History of the Colony of Massachusetts-Bay*, which Thomas considered worth the magazine's price. Thomas and Greenleaf realized several benefits from printing their archenemy's *History*. They appeared fair-minded, for while in the *Spy* they railed against the governor, here they promoted him. They did not compromise their revolutionary principles, because Hutchinson had not yet released his account for years past 1750. The public got attractive monthly supplements containing lucid, clear-headed American history. And the *History* brought profits. Thomas did not pay for printing plates, since he had published the volumes earlier, and Greenleaf notes in December 1774 numerous requests for separate reprints.

The editors contributed little to the evolution of magazine fiction. As E. W. Pitcher indicates, most of their stories are European borrowings drawn especially from London magazines.[3] But unlike other colonial editors, they printed a large proportion of sensationalist tales of sex and sentimentality. "Hamet," an Oriental tale, offers fast-paced action and exotic names (1:173–75). "The Stage-Coach" presents Delia, a seemingly innocent nymph who specializes in seducing men and absconding with their cash (1:378–80). More interesting than the pure fiction is the dream or vision essay, an allegorical subgenre. In one vision troops enforcing revenue taxes shoot a boy and are quickly judged innocent. To ensure our grasping the point, "an American" explains that the soldiers represent Parliamentary omnipotence, the boy and his mother brave Bostonians (1:414–16). Other contributions portray King Tyranny's court and an Edenic garden featuring a dying serpent. These allegories combine the magazine's emphases upon graphics and political commentary.

Thomas appreciated literary essays, but this magazine was not his place to exercise that interest. In the first issue "To the Literati of America" optimistically proposes an American Society of Language (1:6–7). Thereafter little appears to further serious linguistic or literary study. Many original contributions appear as essays or letters on personal conduct. We find opinions proffered on idolatry, love, slavery, time, public spirit, prostitution, chastity, and flattery. While many items abound with clichés, many others delight us in their nimble thought and style. "Leander," for instance, derides women's mastering sciences: "How must it disgust the refined ear, when introduced to . . . the *polite* sex, to . . . [hear] learned discourses on *abstract ideas* and *mixed modes*!" (1:132) A popular running feature is the "Directory of Love," offering advice on penning love letters and choosing mates. Such material contributed to the growing tendency of magazines to involve their readers.

Every issue contains a department of "Poetical Essays," as do many other contemporary magazines. These approximately one hundred poems represent typical eighteenth-century poetic types: biblical translation, funeral elegy, mock praise, congratulation, rebus, prayer, allegory, ode to nature, patriotic hymn, animal fable, and epithet. Humorous poems afford some pleasant reading, as when an author sensually praises a tobacco pipe with "Lips of wax" or birds celebrate the death of a bird-eating feline (2:70–71). Most serious verse yields turgidity and technically undistinguished writing like "If you'd be truly blest in love, / Be constant as the turtle dove" (1:151). More memorable poems extol patriotism. "Song for America" urges patriots to drive "sons of blood" from the land (1:429). Except for Phillis Wheatley, represented by two minor poems, the poets are either anonymous or insignificant.

Like most colonial editors wishing to increase readers' knowledge, Thomas and Greenleaf provide generous portions of science. Readers curious about unusual phenomena find elephant bones described, while agriculturists learn how to plant madder. Amateur physicians discover how to cure consumption or "tenacious slime" with rhubarb and herbs. And through the issues appear numerous mathematical puzzles. Unlike most other contributors, these scientific authors usually sound intrigued by their discoveries. They write in the spirit of inquiry announced in Thomas's proposals.

The periodical did little to promote fine poetry, fiction, or literary criticism. But it showed some possibilities for exciting visual effects. And it showed how independent political thought could function as a magazine's prime moving force. With all its inconsistencies, the *Royal American Magazine* caught the essence of a city and a continent in upheaval.

## Notes

1. *Massachusetts Spy*, 24 June 1773, p. 1.
2. *Massachusetts Spy*, p. 1.
3. E. W. Pitcher, "Sources for Fiction in *The Royal American Magazine* (Boston, 1774–5)," *American Notes and Queries* 17, no. 1 (September 1978):6–7.

## Information Sources

BIBLIOGRAPHY:
Marble, Annie Russell. *From 'Prentice to Patron: The Life Story of Isaiah Thomas*. New York: D. Appleton-Century, 1935.
Mott, Frank Luther. "*The Royal American Magazine*." *A History of American Magazines 1741–1850*. 4 vols. Cambridge, Mass.: Belknap Press of Harvard University Press, 1957. 1:83–86.
Pitcher, E. W. "Sources for Fiction in *The Royal American Magazine* (Boston, 1774–5)." *American Notes and Queries* 17, no. 1 (September 1978):6–7.
Richardson, Lyon N. *A History of Early American Magazines 1741–1789*. 1931; rpt., New York: Octagon Books, 1966.
Shipton, Clifford K. *Isaiah Thomas: Printer, Patriot and Philanthropist 1749–1831*. Rochester, New York: Leo Hart, 1948.
Thomas, Isaiah. *The History of Printing in America, with a Biography of Printers, and an Account of Newspapers*. 2d ed. 2 vols. Worcester, Mass.: American Antiquarian Society, 1874.
———. "Proposals for Printing by Subscription . . . *The Royal American Magazine, Or, Universal Repository*." *Massachusetts Spy*, 24 June 1773, p. 1.
INDEXES: None.

REPRINT EDITIONS: American Periodicals: Series I, 1741–1800. University Micro-
films, Ann Arbor. Reel 26.
LOCATION SOURCES: Complete runs: Henry E. Huntington Library (San Marino,
Cal.), Yale University, Library of Congress, Massachusetts State Library (Boston),
Boston Public Library, Boston Athenaeum, American Antiquarian Society
(Worcester, Mass.), New York State Library (Albany), New York Public Library.
Partial runs: Widely available.

### Publication History

MAGAZINE TITLE AND TITLE CHANGES: *The Royal American Magazine, or Uni-
versal Repository of Instruction and Amusement.*
VOLUME AND ISSUE DATA: Volumes 1 (numbers 1–12)–2(numbers 1–3), January
1774-March 1775.
FREQUENCY OF PUBLICATION: Monthly.
PUBLISHERS: January-June 1774: Isaiah Thomas, Boston. July 1774-March 1775:
Greenleaf's Printing-Office, Boston.
EDITORS: Isaiah Thomas, January-June 1774; Joseph Greenleaf, July 1774-March 1775.

*Avon Jack Murphy*


# RUSSELL'S MAGAZINE

The premier issue of *Russell's Magazine* appeared in Charleston in April 1857.
For a fledgling the journal possessed a singularly mature and professional look;
its initial number included the first installment of a novel by John Esten Cooke
(*Estcourt: or the Memoirs of a Virginia Gentleman*), a laudatory review of the
latest volume of Poe's works, a gothic tale of adventure in Iceland, a humorous
essay on cats, and an editorial pronouncement that *Russell's* would be "another
depository for Southern genius, and a new incentive . . . for its active exercise"
(1:82). It was apparent that *Russell's* had begun with a clear sense of purpose
and with every confidence that "the hearts, intellect, and purses of all Southern
men and women will be open for the triumphant progress of *Russell's Magazine*"
(1:82).

Rare indeed is the literary magazine that does not launch itself on the wings
of hope. For *Russell's* such an attitude seemed justified. Its seat was Charleston,
the cultural and intellectual center of the antebellum South. At the helm was a
capable gentleman of some literary reputation, Paul Hamilton Hayne, whose
credentials included the editorship of the *Southern Literary Gazette** (1852–54)
and publication in respectable journals north and south. Behind Hayne stood a
brilliant, diversified coterie of literary men and women led by the dean of
antebellum Southern letters, William Gilmore Simms. The time for such a venture, Hayne insisted, was "auspicious," for "surely it is not for the South, with
its lofty aspirations, fine taste, and subtle intellect, to neglect the noblest of all
fields of enterprise—that of Letters and the Arts" (1:82). Hayne, with his knowledge of the Southern literary milieu, doubtless knew this sanguine hope would

eventually be dashed. Yet throughout its four years of publication *Russell's* struggled valiantly against its own inevitable fate, maintaining to the last its elevated tone and remaining faithful to Hayne's pledge that the periodical would be "truly representative of the mind, the morals, the social and political position of a nation" (1:178).

Hayne was referring, of course, to the Southern "nation," that geographical region soon to comprise the Confederacy; a region keenly sensible of its own culture and of the myriad ways in which that culture lay at odds with its neighbor to the north. By 1856, the fissure in the great wall of the Republic had widened beyond repair, and the political banners behind which men were rallying would soon become the martial standards of regiments and brigades. In this last uneasy twilight the voice of *Russell's* arose to champion "the opinions, doctrines and arguments of the educated mind of the South," and to proclaim the "self-reliance, energy, courage, and all the resources of independent nationality" whereby the Southern states would soon attain "the station which God designed that they should occupy and adorn" (1:178). It was the sentiment of a nation and a culture already doomed.

But in 1856, men could still dream of an independent South. In that year *Russell's Magazine* was conceived in John Russell's bookstore on King Street in Charleston. Here were regularly gathered, in the best Johnsonian coffee-house tradition, some of the keenest intellects of Charleston and the South. Here, among others, met Simms, Hayne, and the poet Henry Timrod, three "littera-teurs" of no small reputation; Basil Gildersleeve, graduate of Gottingen and classical scholar; attorneys James L. Petigru and Mitchell King; Dr. Samuel Dickson of the Charleston Medical College and his namesake, Dr. J. Dickson Bruns; William R. Tabor of the *Charleston Mercury* and Samuel Lord, destined for a brilliant career at the South Carolina bar. While Simms was the acknowl-edged mentor of the group, their host was the flamboyant John Russell, "Lord John" to his friends, whose establishment had come to be the South's most distinguished literary rendezvous. The Russell's coterie was unique in the South, where the profession of letters was regarded as suspect save for the purposes of polemics. It was inevitable that such a gathering would produce what Hayne would call "a representative organ, not merely of local, but of *Southern* intellect, taste, and opinions."[1] The result was *Russell's Magazine*.

Hayne was asked to be the editor of the new journal; he would reflect years later that he "coolly and cheerfully accepted one of the most difficult, exacting, and thankless positions imaginable."[2] The position of coeditor was filled by Charleston journalist W. B. Carlisle, but that gentleman left the magazine after the second issue. In December 1858, George C. Hurlbut joined the staff, and Russell himself functioned as coeditor from time to time. Nevertheless, the editorial burden was always heaviest on Hayne.[3]

One of Hayne's first duties was to canvass the state for funds to support the venture. Russell had agreed to help financially, but outside sources of revenue, in the form of stocks and contributions, were essential. Predictably, Hayne's success was limited despite his wide-ranging itineraries.[4] Even so, he managed to generate considerable interest in the project, and on one occasion was approached by James Henley Thornwell with an offer to merge the new magazine with Thornwell's *Southern Quarterly Review*.* Hayne was flattered, but declined.[5]

The first issue of *Russell's* appeared in April 1857. In February Hayne had written John Esten Cooke: "I am anxious & fearful in the extreme about this first number—People are expecting altogether *too much* & that looks *squally*."[6] But the magazine met with favorable reviews in the Southern press. The *Southern Literary Messenger** was especially effusive in its praise. As early as October 1856, the *Messenger* had predicted that the new periodical would be of the first rank and had lauded both Hayne and Carlisle. Now, after the first issue, the *Messenger* greeted *Russell's* as a "coadjutor in the defense of Southern institutions and the reflection of Southern sentiment."[7] Hayne must have been somewhat consoled by this comradely gesture from one of the South's leading literary journals.

Though *Russell's* was never to receive the monetary support Hayne so earnestly hoped for, it nevertheless deserved the critical praise of its contemporaries. The typography was excellent, the writing was of a high caliber, and the content was varied and interesting. Modelled on *Blackwood's*, to which it looked as "an exemplar" (2:91), *Russell's* was published in octavo at twenty-five cents the issue. From the first there were two regular features: "The Editor's Table," written by Hayne, touching on a variety of subjects and always reflecting the genteel nature of its author; and "Literary Notices," a compendium of criticism and reviews written by divers members of the "Charleston School." In accordance with Hayne's editorial statement the journal sought to express attitudes and problems common to all areas of the South, though much content was devoted to Charleston and Charleston society. Beyond its primary interest in the arts, *Russell's* delved into the areas of politics, religion, and social institutions as well.

In the latter category, two of the leading citizens of Charleston met in the pages of *Russell's* to exchange volleys over the propriety of the duelling code. The celebrated William Grayson, statesman, planter, and scholar, condemned the system; the eminent physician S. H. Dickson ardently defended it. Another Southern phenomenon, the "peculiar institution" of slavery, found a consistent champion in *Russell's*. Indeed, the leading article of the first issue was an attack by Grayson on the antislavery doctrines of the *Edinburgh Review*. Throughout its existence *Russell's*, committed to "the defense of Southern institutions," would, through the pens of various authors, continue to voice its support of slavery.

In spite of Hayne's protest that it was not the policy of *Russell's* "to touch, however superficially, upon the question of politics" (6:360), no Southern journal of the period could leave this ground untilled. Sectional feelings were too strong and political antagonisms too bitter for the subject to be ignored. Admittedly Hayne, in his editorials, tried to steer clear of political comment, but his writers felt no such restraint. The political implications of slavery, the invective of the Northern press, and the excesses of "Black Republicans" found antagonists in the pages of *Russell's*. Still, Hayne would later recall with pride that Northern as well as Southern writers contributed to *Russell's*, particularly John William DeForest and Richard Henry Stoddard.[8]

Much poetry found its way into *Russell's*, a natural result of the association of Hayne, Simms, and Timrod with the journal. There was also much discussion of poetry and poetic principles, as in Hayne's two-part "The Poets and Poetry of the South" in the November and December 1857 numbers. Fiction had less prominence in *Russell's*, though the magazine could claim Cooke's *Estcourt* and a number of short tales, serials, and sketches by the Charleston group. Among the steadiest contributors of fiction to *Russell's* were two female authors, Mrs. H. C. King and Miss Essie Cheeseborough. Miss Cheeseborough's work was quite sentimental, written in what Mott calls "the worst perfervid style of the broken-heart school."[9] Mrs. King struck a more didactic note in her tales and sketches; her situations were less intense and reflected her complacency as one of the leading society matrons of Charleston. Another of *Russell's* serialized novels, *Silvia's World*, came from the pen of Mrs. King.

In spite of its diversity and the reputations of its contributors, *Russell's* was plagued throughout its short history by a lack of funds. Southern readers simply would not support the magazine, for all Hayne's appeals to their patriotism. In a letter to John Esten Cooke, in which Hayne apologizes for the magazine's inability to pay for *Estcourt*, the frustrated editor adds: "I am tempted . . . to *turn*—Yankee, and write exclusively for Yankee publications. All this talk about [Southern] patriotism is gammon & moonshine. May the Devil sieze the *whole* of the degenerate *race*!"[10] In the end Cooke received only fifty of the four hundred dollars promised for *Estcourt*, and *Russell's* went the way of so many literary magazines before and since. As Hayne was to write in 1885: "*Russell's* . . . which had long been sailing the ocean of literature under difficulties, chief among them the lack of golden ballast, at the close of the fourth [*sic*] volume struck upon breakers and sunk, like a shot, to 'Davy Jones' Locker,' where she rests in peace among the fragments of a hundred similar ventures."[11]

Thus ended, in 1860, the best of the Charleston monthlies. Its contributors were scattered by the war and many of them, Hayne included, were virtually ruined by it. Russell's bookstore was devastated; its stock of rare volumes, hidden away in the upcountry, had been discovered and carted off by Sherman's "bummers," and the store was only a melancholy shadow of its former self when Hayne visited it in 1873.[12] Yet the six volumes of *Russell's Magazine* remain as an elegant and varied account of Southern thought and feeling in the final years before the war.

## Notes

1. Paul Hamilton Hayne, "Antebellum Charleston," *Southern Bivouac* 4 (November 1885):330.

2. Hayne, p. 330.

3. Frank L. Mott, *A History of American Magazines, 1850–1865*. 4 vols. (Cambridge: Harvard University Press, 1938), p. 489.

4. Hayne details one of his canvassing trips in a letter to his wife on 17 January 1857. *See* Rayburn S. Moore, ed., *A Man of Letters in the Nineteenth Century South: Selected Letters of Paul Hamilton Hayne* (Baton Rouge: Louisiana State University Press, 1982), pp. 46–47.

5. Moore, p. 45.

6. Moore, p. 51.

7. Quoted in Fronde Kennedy, "Russell's Magazine," *South Atlantic Quarterly* 18 (April 1919):127.

8. Hayne, p. 330.

9. Mott, p. 490.

10. Moore, p. 52.

11. Hayne, p. 334.

12. Hayne, p. 335.

## Information Sources

BIBLIOGRAPHY:

Calhoun, Richard J. "The Antebellum Literary Twilight: Russell's Magazine." *Southern Literary Journal* 3 (Fall 1970):89–110.

Hayne, Paul Hamilton. "Antebellum Charleston." *Southern Bivouac* 4 (1885):327–36.

Kennedy, Fronde. "Russell's Magazine." *South Atlantic Quarterly* 18 (April 1919):124–44.

Loftis, Alan T. "A Study of Russell's Magazine: Antebellum Charleston's Last Literary Periodical." Ph.D. diss., Duke University, 1973.

Moore, Rayburn S., ed. *A Man of Letters in the Nineteenth Century South: Selected Letters of Paul Hamilton Hayne*. Baton Rouge: University of Louisiana Press, 1982.

Mott, Frank L. *"Russell's Magazine." A History of American Magazines*, 1850–1865 4 vols. Cambridge, Mass.: Harvard University Press, 1938. Pp.:488–92.

INDEXES: None. However, the *Russell's* volumes in the New York Public and Duke University libraries are annotated in pencil, presumably by William A. Courtnay, who was involved in publishing *Russell's*, or perhaps by John Russell himself.

REPRINT EDITIONS: American Periodicals: Series III, 1850–1900. University Micro-films, Ann Arbor. Reel 17. AMS Press, Inc. New York.

LOCATION SOURCES: Widely available.

## Publication History

MAGAZINE TITLE AND TITLE CHANGES: *Russell's Magazine*.
VOLUME AND ISSUE DATA: Volumes 1–6, April 1857-March 1860.
FREQUENCY OF PUBLICATION: Monthly.
PUBLISHERS: Russell & Jones, Charleston.
EDITOR: Paul Hamilton Hayne.

*Howard L. Bahr*

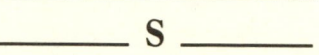

# S

## ST. NICHOLAS

In antebellum America children characters were few and usually allegorical, like Hawthorne's Pearl, and so-called children's magazines like N. P. Willis's the *Youth's Companion* (1827–1940) were written largely for and entirely by adults. After the Civil War, for reasons hard to determine, children became the cynosure of American literature. Children suddenly appeared in fiction portrayed fairly realistically, as in Louisa May Alcott's *Little Women* (1868–1869) and Thomas Bailey Aldrich's *The Story of a Bad Boy* (1869–1870). Capitalizing on this fascination with children, the author Josiah Gilbert Holland approached one of the directors of Scribner and Company, suggesting that they establish a children's magazine of stories, poetry, and essays with the same high standards as their adult periodical, *Scribner's Monthly.*\* Roswell Smith, a Scribner's director, agreed and asked Mary Mapes Dodge, famous for her *Hans Brinker; or, The Silver Skates* (1865), to be editor-in-chief. She accepted and immediately suggested the title *St. Nicholas; A Magazine for Boys and Girls*, thereby launching in 1873 an enterprise that can only be described as a cultural phenomenon, both because of the popularity and affection demonstrated by the monthly's young recipients and because contributors had a respected outlet to experiment with this new form of literature.

An index to *St. Nicholas* reads like a list of famous nineteenth-century and early twentieth-century writers. Established authors were represented; poems by William Cullen Bryant, John Greenleaf Whittier, and Henry Wadsworth Longfellow as well as selections from Ralph Waldo Emerson and Henry David Thoreau were reproduced. Newer, already successful authors such as Mark Twain, Sarah Orne Jewett, T. B. Aldrich, and Edward Everett Hale also contributed. However, *St. Nicholas* is more impressive for the number of well-known children's works that began in its pages. Howard Pyle, later famous for his Robin Hood and knightly romances, began both as an illustrator and author with *St. Nicholas*. Louisa May Alcott's *Jo's Boys* appeared as a serial, as did her *An Old-Fashioned Girl* and *Eight Cousins*. From November 1885 to October 1886, story episodes appeared by Frances Hodgson Burnett called *Little Lord Fauntleroy*, illustrated by Reginald Birch. For *St. Nicholas*'s first issue Lucretia P. Hale wrote a story called "Anna's Doll," which inaugurated *The Peterkin Papers*. Mrs. Dodge cultivated Rudyard Kipling's friendship, and at a social gathering in her apartment persuaded him to write a story for her magazine.[1] Kipling did submit "The Potted Princess" and "Polly Cha," followed by "Toomai of the Elephants," and *St. Nicholas* published the first of his Indian stories, which would later appear as *The Jungle Book* and *The Second Jungle Book*. Another anecdote is that Jack London, while leading a lawless life on the San Francisco waterfront, happened across the 1884 volume of *St. Nicholas* in the Oakland Public Library and was so impressed by a story by E. M. White that London gave up his wild ways, joined the state fish patrol, and dedicated himself to becoming a writer. Whatever the veracity of this legend, the fact is that London did publish "Cruise of the Dazzler" in *St. Nicholas* for 1902.

In 1898, the year that the Century Company bought *St. Nicholas*, a new feature inspired by Albert Bigelow Paine was begun that added a further dimension in the area of contribution. It was called "The St. Nicholas League," and its motto was "Learn to live, and live to learn." Its aims were "creative adventure for young people from five to eighteen which will stimulate them to strive toward higher ideals both in thought and living, to protect the oppressed, to grow in understanding of all forms of nature."[2] The league offered all sorts of juvenile paraphernalia: membership buttons, certificates of achievement, an honor roll, and gold and silver badges for prose and verse published in the St. Nicholas League Department. Eudora Welty was fifteen years old when she published a poem, as was Stephen Vincent Benet. E. Babette Deutsch was eleven when she published in *St. Nicholas*, and some other league contributors included Ring Lardner, Vita Sackville-West, Richard Bentley, Edna St. Vincent Millay, Deems Taylor, Alan Seeger, Cornelia Otis Skinner, Elinor Wylie, Bennett Cerf, and Edmund Wilson. Cornelia Meigs is certainly correct when she says in *A Critical History of Children's Literature* that "In the editors' realization of the desire that children have to create something, in the opportunity the League gave them to carry out their creative urge, there was a foreshadowing of the . . . freer education that was to come in the twentieth century."[3]

*St. Nicholas* became so popular that it absorbed five other magazines by 1893 and was translated into French, Arabic, and other tongues. Children from as far away as China and India wrote fan notes expressing their pleasure with the magazine. A major cause of this popularity was that *St. Nicholas* was a true "magazine," that is, a storehouse of a variety of items. Besides pictures, stories, and poetry, there were articles on science, technology, and biography. There was a "How to Do and Make" department, a section that reviewed and discussed books, and an editor's column called "Jack-in-the Pulpit," which explained how modern domestic items were made and praised children's projects such as cookbooks. Readers' suggestions for future issues were printed in the "Letter Box," and recitations were recommended for the children's local "Sunday School Tree." Each December *St. Nicholas* issued a special Christmas number that offered ideas for parlor performances and holiday activities.

A further cause for *St. Nicholas*'s early success was Mary Mapes Dodge herself. Although her assistant editors, Frank Stockton and William Fayal Clark, did most of the work, and even though she rarely came to the magazine's offices in the last seventeen years of her life, she loomed as the dowager empress of the periodical whose image was affectionately known by her readers. May Lamberton Becker, who was to become *St. Nicholas*'s last editor, records that when she was a young girl subscribing to the periodical Mary Mapes Dodge was "one of the fixed facts in our world: her name was on our magazine and we knew, from her picture, just how she looked."[4] When Dodge died in 1905, adoring children spontaneously formed a procession at her funeral.

But Dodge also made the magazine successful in an inadvertent fashion; that is, simply, she was confused. She wavered between a Victorian need to refine and cultivate children and a more realistic and modern desire to capture them as they are. In 1873, she wrote nine tenets of her editorial policy, completely unaware of the contradictions between didacticism and realism that she encoded. On one hand, she wanted to give children "genuine fun," but instruct them in moral examples of "the finest types of boyhood and girlhood." One of her principles is to "foster a love of country, home, nature, truth, beauty, and sincerity," but her very next goal is "To prepare boys and girls for life as it is." Even in a single sentence she was able to encode her confusion, as when she wrote: "To stimulate their ambitions—but along normally progressive lines."[5]

Dodge's confusion was most fortunate for the magazine because it enabled a contributor to do one or the other. A Longfellow poem and a Bret Harte story could be published side by side in the same issue. Burnett's sentimental Little Lord Fauntleroy would be balanced by a more realistic depiction of childhood by T. B. Aldrich or William Dean Howells. Sometimes these extremes can be seen in the work of a single author such as Frank Stockton, who, according to H. S. Commager, wrote "the best fairy tales (if you can call them that) of any one in the country."[6] The reason for Commager's parenthetical aside is that Stockton's stories are full of ambiguity, relativity, confusion of values, and approximations of children's anxieties and fears. Stockton's fairy tales verge constantly on the less idyllic versions of childhood that Bruno Bettelheim well describes in *The Uses of Enchantment* (1976). It is no coincidence that Maurice Sendak, whose *Where the Wild Things Are* (1964) was criticized for being too frightening for children, chose Stockton's stories to illustrate nearly a century after Stockton had first published them in *St. Nicholas*. Thus the magazine not only gave many writers a start; it broke ground for further famous interpretations of childhood, from Mark Twain's Huck Finn through Henry James's Maisie Farange to more modern conceptualizations.

As popular and as important as *St. Nicholas* proved to be, it ended in 1940, save for a brief revival in 1943. The causes of its demise are numerous. The appeal of radio was one factor. The Great Depression took its toll both in decreased birth rate and lower per capita income, as well as a more generally somber mood accentuated by the onset of World War II. *St. Nicholas* lived on only as a fond memory, such as the one tenderly described by M. L. Becker. But this memory too will soon fade, to persist only as nostalgia. Perhaps the last reference to *St. Nicholas* in literature was made by John McPhee, who in *The Survival of the Bark Canoe* (1975) describes a canoe trip with presumably the last of the Thoreauvians into the backwater wilds of the Maine woods. McPhee observes a scene that reminds him of an illustration in *St. Nicholas* from 1910 which depicts a man catching a loon from a now-obsolete birchbark canoe.

## Notes

1. Alice Barrett Howard, *Mary Mapes Dodge of St. Nicholas* (New York: Julian Messner, 1943), pp. 167–78.
2. Cornelia Meigs, Elizabeth Nesbitt, Anne Eaton, Ruth Hill Viguers, *A Critical History of Children's Literature* (New York: Macmillan, 1953), p. 283.
3. Cornelia Meigs et al. p. 283.
4. May Lamberton Becker, "Introduction," *The St. Nicholas Anthology*, ed. Henry Steele Commager (New York: Random House, 1948), p. xv.
5. Meigs et al., p. 280.
6. Henry Steele Commager, "Preface," *The St. Nicholas Anthology*, ed. Henry Steele Commager (New York: Random House, 1948), p. xx.

## Information Sources

BIBLIOGRAPHY:
Becker, May Lamberton. "Introduction." *The St. Nicholas Anthology*. Ed. Henry Steele Commager. New York: Random House, 1948.
Commager, Henry Steele. "Preface." *The St. Nicholas Anthology*. Ed. Henry Steele Commager. New York: Random House, 1948.
Golemba, Henry. *Frank Stockton*. Boston: Twayne Publishers, 1981.
Guthrie, Anna Lorraine. *Index to St. Nicholas: Vols. I-XLV (1873–1918)*. New York: H. W. Wilson, 1920.
Howard, Alice Barrett. *Mary Mapes Dodge of St. Nicholas*. New York: Julian Messner, 1943.
Jordan, Alice M. *From Rollo to Tom Sawyer*. Boston: Horn Book, 1948.
Meigs, Cornelia, Elizabeth Nesbitt, Anne Eaton, Ruth Hill Viguers. *A Critical History of Children's Literature*. New York: Macmillan, 1953.
Mott, Frank Luther. "*St. Nicholas.*" *A History of American Magazines*. 4 vols. Cambridge, Mass.: Belknap Press of Harvard University Press, 1957. 3:500–505.
Shaw, John MacKay. *The Poems, Poets & Illustrators of St. Nicholas Magazine, 1873–1943; an Index*. Tallahasee: Florida State University, Strozier Library, 1965.
INDEXES: Guthrie, Anna Lorraine, *Index to St. Nicholas: Vols. I-XLV (1873–1918)*. Shaw, John MacKay, *The Poems, Poets, & Illustrators of St. Nicholas Magazine, 1873–1943; an Index*.

REPRINT EDITIONS: AMS Press, New York. American Periodicals: Series III, 1850–
1900. University Microfilms, Ann Arbor. Reels 591–99. (November 1873-October
1907).
LOCATION SOURCES: Widely available.

### Publication History

MAGAZINE TITLE AND TITLE CHANGES: *St. Nicholas: Scribner's Illustrated Magazine for Girls and Boys*, 1873–1880. *St. Nicholas: An Illustrated Magazine for Young Folks*, 1881–1930. *St. Nicholas for Boys and Girls*, 1930–1943.
VOLUME AND ISSUE DATA: Volumes 1–67, number 4, November 1873-February
1940; volume 70, numbers 1–4, March-June 1943; suspended March 1940-February 1943.
FREQUENCY OF PUBLICATION: Monthly.
PUBLISHERS: 1873–1880: Scribner and Company, New York. 1881–1930: Century
Company, New York. 1930–1934: American Education Press, Columbus, Ohio.
1935–1940: Educational Publishing Corporation, New York.
EDITORS: Mary Mapes Dodge, 1873–1905; William Fayal Clarke, 1905–1927; George F.
Thompson, 1928–1929; Albert G. Lanier, 1930; May Lamberton Becker, 1930–1932;
Eric J. Bender, 1932–1934; Chelsa Sherlock, 1935; Vertie A. Coyne, 1936–1940.

*Henry Golemba*


## THE SAN FRANCISCO ILLUSTRATED WASP. See THE WASP


## SAN FRANCISCO NEWS-LETTER WASP. See THE WASP


## THE SATURDAY PRESS

In December 1859, the *Cincinnati Daily Commercial* hailed Henry Clapp's
*Saturday Press* as "the prince of literary weeklies, the *arbiter elegantiarum* of
dramatic and poetic taste." But the same article dismissed as "unmixed and
hopeless drivel" the *Press*'s "Christmas gift" to its readers—the first published
version of Walt Whitman's "Out of the Cradle Endlessly Rocking."[1] This
ambiguous reaction typifies the relation of the *Press* with its audience. The paper
remained financially insecure throughout its irregular publication between 23
October 1858 and 2 June 1866. Fiscal mismanagement and hard times contributed
to its lack of success. Some of the blame, however, must also fall on the character
of the paper itself, on its vehement sense of absolute independence; its self-
conscious policy making and breeding of controversy; its scathing, at times
insulting, commentary on conventional literary practices and attitudes in America;
its imported European frivolities; and its determination to represent the fringe
elements of American literary culture—not only the Bohemian circle from which

came its editors and chief contributors, but also budding authors like William Dean Howells; neglected writers like Walt Whitman; and Westerners mostly unknown to East Coast readers, the likes of Bret Harte and Mark Twain.

The early issues of the *Saturday Press* outlined its editorial policies. Noting that most papers deal only in "the squabbles of politicians" and publish only "flash stories," the *Press* complained that such papers narrow their appeal to "hack politicians and servant girls." One class of neglected readers demands "a more complete report of what is doing in the world of letters." The *Saturday Press* promised to meet this need, and in a rare moment of modesty announced that "by the publication of well written stories, such as appear in the English Reviews, and latterly in the 'Atlantic Monthly' and 'Harper's Magazine,' we hope to make at least a readable magazine." (1, no. 1:2). The paper's independence from politics and politicians extended to the politics of nineteenth-century publishing: "The *Saturday Press* is not the organ of any Bookseller, Publisher, Theatre Manager, or other Advertiser; nor of any clique of Authors or Artists." The editors claimed to be "irrecoverably opposed to the whole system of Puffing" (1, no. 10:1). Their reviews were to reflect honest principles of judgement regardless of literary associations and friendships.

But despite its avowed independence from any "party, sect, and . . . 'Ism,' " the paper was known, especially in its early years, as the organ of the Bohemian circle of authors and artists that gathered at Pfaff's Beer Cellar in New York City. The "King of Bohemia" was Henry Clapp, Jr., the founder, editor, main contributor, and guiding spirit of the *Press* from its beginning to its end. Born into a family of shopkeepers in Nantucket, Massachusetts, on 11 November 1814, Clapp grew restless as a young man, and he left home first to pursue a mercantile career in Boston. His career reached a turning point when he left America for Paris. There he developed an interest in Fourierism and socialism, which he would later introduce to America in association with Horace Greeley and Albert Brisbane. More important, his Parisian experience inspired in Clapp a taste for the brilliant and dissipated life of the street cafes. He honed the sharp wit for which he would achieve his measure of fame. After his death on 2 April 1875 an obituary in the *Boston Globe* observed, "His talent was essentially that of the French Feuilletonistes—bright, keen, and witty, but unsubstantial and ephemeral. In character, he was the essence of Bohemia—reckless and witty, caring and thinking little of the serious concerns of life."[2] In fact in the journalistic life he lived after his return to America, Clapp cultivated a disregard for the substantial seriousness of the middle-class world. He became known as the "arch-hater of 'brownstone morality.' "[3] He once suggested that the nation's motto "In God we trust" should be converted to "In Gold we trust"; he criticized Wall Street for its "lie-abilities"; and, upon hearing that Union College had conferred upon General Grant the honorary degree of LL.D., he commented, "Not that the General needed a degree, but the College needed a Grant" (4, no. 1:8).[4]

For all of his acerbity, however, Clapp was admired and even loved by his friends. Howells would remember, "He was kind to neglected talents, and befriended them with a vigor and zeal which he would have been the last to let you call generous."[5] Whitman would say, "Henry Clapp was always loyal. . . . [He] stepped out from the crowd of hooters—was my friend: a much needed ally at that time (having a paper of his own) when almost the whole press of America when it mentioned me at all treated me with derision or worse."[6] And William Winter, the *Press*'s "sub-editor" in 1865–1866, would recall that Clapp "was wayward and erratic; but he possessed both the faculty of taste and the instinctive love of beauty, and, essentially, he was the apostle of freedom of thought."[7]

Clapp's writings in the *Saturday Press* varied in kind and quality, though not in quantity; each week he filled as much as half of the column space with his reviews of books, plays, art, and cultural life. Occasionally he would try fiction as a vehicle for his sardonic humor or his Bohemian morosity. He wrote poetry, too: parodies like "Woman spare that Tea! / Touch not a single cup, / In youth it tempted thee, / But now, O give it up" (4, no. 2:26); satires on American life like "The Fourth of July" (2, no. 27:1) and on materialism (God's but a sterner name for gold, / Or gold a softer name for God" [2, no. 28:1]); and even an occasional gentle lyric sympathizing with social outcasts like "The Old Maid" (2, no. 48:1). His semi-fictionalized "A New Portrait of Paris," which was serialized in several early numbers (1, no. 4–2, no. 2), gave a humorous account of an American wit's first day in the city of the Bohemians. Clapp was a cosmopolitan who hoped that newspapers, telegraphs, and trends in communications could inspire a communion of cultures throughout the world. To this end he often reprinted accounts of the social and cultural habits of faraway places and furnished original and reprinted translations, especially of French writers like Balzac. He criticized other American papers for provinciality, sectionalism, and cliquishness, his favorite target being the Boston literary establishment. Howells said that Clapp "exposed all kinds of folly but his own,"[8] though he did his best in this regard as well, deriding his former pursuits in socialism and the temperance movement, gleefully reprinting criticisms of his own magazine, and even on one occasion exposing his own anti-Semitism. In his satirical article "A Night with a Mosquito," he had written, "Jews excepted, I have . . . a lively sympathy for all . . . victims of general persecution" (1, no. 2:4). In the very next issue he published an angry correspondence denouncing his bias and upholding the victimized Jew (1, no. 3:3).

In 1858, Clapp was assisted in the editorship of the *Saturday Press* by Fitz-James O'Brien and Thomas Bailey Aldrich. O'Brien wrote the weekly "Dramatic Feuilleton" and rivaled Clapp with his caustic and brilliant wit. His reviews chided the American theater for its overly elaborate and expensive sets, poor management, bad casting, and failure to do justice to good plays. Much of his writing attempted to create critical and appreciative American audiences like those found among the French, "the best dramatically educated people in the world" (1, no. 5:3). Aldrich's reviews tended to be short and predictable, especially in their derision of the Boston Philistines. He attacked Longfellow's "The Courtship of Miles Standish," for example, as a work which "besides not being poetry as it pretends to be, is neither instructive or agreeable prose" (1, no. 2:2). Ironically, Aldrich later went over to the other side and became the editor of the *Atlantic Monthly*.\* He resigned as associate editor of the *Saturday Press* in January 1859 for "private reasons" (2, no. 5:2), though he continued to be a frequent contributor of poems and stories. O'Brien was gone by the next issue and was replaced by the frivolous Ned Wilkins writng under the pseudonym "Personne." Other members of Clapp's Bohemian group, such as William Winter and George Arnold, furnished the bulk of the paper's poems in the early numbers.

Among the most interesting of the regular contributors was the failed actress "Ada Clare" (Jane McElheney), who came to be known as the "Queen of Bohemia" (though she had no intimate relations with Clapp, the "King"). Her "Thoughts and Things" column gave in fact the best definition of a "Bohemian" as the term applied to herself and her associates: "By nature, if not by habit, a Cosmopolite, with a general sympathy for the fine arts, and for all things above and beyond convention" (3, no. 6:2). She longed to free criticism from impersonality and academic frigidity. The critic must dare to be enthusiastic, to respond subjectively, to "love" art (3, no. 5:2); so in her reviews she mingled sad confessions, rash praise, and harsh denigration. She directed her diffuse imagery and flowing commentary to magazine poems and stories, musical events, plays, and life in general. One column expressed boredom with the earnestness and monotony of a women's rights convention in New York (3, no. 20:2). Not even her colleagues were safe from her critical eye. She took exception to the praise for William Winter's "Song of a Ruined Man" (published in the *Saturday Press*, 3, no. 1:1). It was, she claimed, the work of a mere technician, a "versifier" who "must go on rhyming till the seas were dry"; she preferred Walt Whitman's "A Child's Reminiscence," which "could only have been written by a poet, and versifying could not help it" (3, no. 2:2).

The spirit of the Bohemians affected a number of young New York writers not directly connected with Clapp's circle. They found a needed outlet for their work in the *Saturday Press*. William Dean Howells contributed a number of early lyrics much in the manner of those by Aldrich, Winter, and Arnold. The bittersweet "Under the Locusts" concluded that "Death is delight, and life is pain" (2, no. 25:1). "Drifting Away" spoke of riding "forlorn upon the sea of life" (2, no. 37:1). The young John Burroughs, later to become an important naturalist and literary essayist, contributed nostalgic poetry and an essay, "Fragments from the Table of an Intellectual Epicure," which he signed "All Souls" and which called for a literature that appealed to more than one faculty of the mind. He praised Plato, Shakespeare, Carlyle, and Emerson (2, no. 21:1). In his lifetime Burroughs would produce two books about Walt Whitman, whose works he first encountered in discussions with the Bohemians.

Clapp's own championing of Whitman was as close as he came to a departure from his antipuffing policy, though this promotion was effected not by unmitigated praise but by a method Clapp might have learned from Whitman himself— the stirring of controversy. Whitman met Clapp at Pfaff's in the late 1850s during the preparation of the greatly expanded 1860 *Leaves of Grass*. Among the new poems was "A Child's Reminiscence" (later titled "Out of the Cradle"), which was to become the most historically significant poem published in the *Saturday Press*. This "curious warble," the *Press* commented, "will bear reading many times"; "the purport of this wild and plaintive song . . . is positive and unquestionable, like the effect of music" (2, no. 52:2). When the Cincinnati paper did dare to question the poem's "purport," however, Clapp reprinted the article (3, no. 1:1). And, after publishing Whitman's "You and Me To-Day" with its cosmopolitan theme of the modern world as the sum of all advances through the ages (3, no. 2:1), the *Press* immediately ran a hilarious parody of it, "Yourn and Mine, and Any-Day" (3, no. 3:1) by "Saerasmid," a Philadelphia writer who would offer other parodies of Whitman in later issues (3, no. 5:1; 3, no. 11:1). Every reprint from or advertisement for *Leaves of Grass* was balanced by a parody or criticism. "The Song of the Dandelions (After Walt Whitman)" began, "I am going to write something gorgeous, / And you will believe every word I say" (3, no. 23:1). Clapp solicited a review from Whitman's admirer Juliette Hayward Beach, whose own poems were frequently published in the *Press*. But Beach's husband intercepted the article and substituted a rabid denouncement of Whitman, claiming that the poet was a sexual predator and suggesting that he commit suicide. A confused Clapp published the piece under Juliette's name and boasted that the *Press* welcomed "every variety of opinion" (3, no. 22:2–3). In compensation he reprinted from the Philadelphia *City Item* Henry P. Leland's laudatory article greeting Whitman as the Luther of modern poetry (3, no. 24:1). When Juliette's article finally arrived with an explanation, Clapp noted the error in authorship of the first piece and printed the new article signed "A Woman." It extravagantly praised the "immortal Whitman" and the "deep spiritual significance" of *Leaves of Grass* (3, no. 25:3). The "stew," as Whitman called it, continued throughout 1860 and brought the poet valuable national attention.[9]

Poetry for the *Press* also came from Richard Henry Stoddard, Charles D. Gardette, and Edmund C. Stedman. Stories were furnished by John H. Watson, Mrs. R. H. Stoddard, Horatio Alger, Jr., Thomas Hood, Mrs. S. W. Jewett, Mary S. Gove Nichols, and Harriet E. Prescott. Clapp was particularly proud of his women contributors. When the first issue of the *Nation* appeared, he chided the editors for including no work by women and suggested that "for this and other reasons its name be changed to the Stag-Nation."[10]

On 17 November 1860, the *Saturday Press* announced that it had "run through the small capital . . . with which it started" and that it would be discontinued after a few issues. Nevertheless it promised "not to sing like a dying swan, but to growl and snarl more like a moribund canine quadraped [*sic*], at the same time that it makes a whine for a little more life" (3, no. 46:1). Conceding that puffing may have given such life, it steadfastly maintained its independence and suspended publication after the 15 December 1860 issue.

Clapp revived the *Press* on 5 August 1865. In a dialogue with an "old subscriber" he explained that he had stopped the paper "for want of money" and began it again for the same reason (4, no. 1:8). The paper sported a handsome new magazine format, which, however, had to be abandoned on 3 March 1866 presumably because it was too expensive.

A new kind of subject matter also dominated its pages. Though favorite old articles by Clapp, Ada Clare, and other Bohemians were reprinted, much of the new material represented a pioneering effort to introduce a kind of humor that, as it turned out, would sweep the nation's magazines in the late 1860s and early 1870s. This was the dialect literature of the so-called "local colorists." Some of the earliest "sayings" of Josh Billings (H. W. Shaw) found their way into the *Saturday Press*, and Artemus Ward (C. F. Browne) became an almost regular feature. Ward, who was known to borrow jokes from Henry Clapp, furnished commentary on the Fenians (5, no. 17:1), the Shakers ("the strangest religious sex I ever met" [4, no. 4:59–60]), and himself ("His Autobiography" [4, no. 7:3–21]).

Encouraged by Artemus Ward and the success of this frontier-flavored postwar humor, Clapp opened his pages to West Coast Bohemians like Bret Harte, whose story "A Vernerable Imposter" appeared first in the *Saturday Press* (5, no. 5:66). Clapp also reprinted from the *Californian* many other pieces by Harte, who by 1871 was able to sign a lucrative contract with the *Atlantic Monthly*.*[11]

The *Saturday Press* found another Western contributor in Mark Twain. "Jim Smiley and His Jumping Frog" was published on 18 November 1865 (4, no. 16:248–49), having been sent to Clapp by Artemus Ward's publisher, G. W. Carleton.[12] It dazzled Eastern readers and was followed by a reprint of "The Ballad Infliction" (4, no. 19:298) and the original of "The Boy That Bore a Charmed Life" (5, no. 19:1). The very last issue of the paper contained a correspondence from Hawaii by Mark Twain; "A Strange Dream" was a humorous account of a mock dream-vision connected with the author's visit to the active volcano Kilauea (5, no. 11:1–2). The fact that the article was addressed to "My Dear Press" suggests that Mark Twain may have become a regular correspondent.

But on 2 June 1866 the struggling paper finally died, this time without an announcement. Clapp had grown increasingly embittered and had embarked on a course of suicidal drinking following the death of his friend George Arnold.[13] Nevertheless he had made a name for himself and had performed a valuable editorial and critical service for American literary culture. As Howells remembered, "The young writers throughout the country were ambitious to be seen in [the *Saturday Press*], and they gave their best to it; they gave liberally, for the *Saturday Press* never paid in anything but hopes of paying, vaguer even than promises. It is not too much to say that it was very nearly as well for one to be accepted by the *Press* as to be accepted by the *Atlantic*, and for the time there was no literary comparison. To be in it was to be in the company of . . . whoever . . . was liveliest in prose and loveliest in verse at that day in New York. It was a power."[14]

## Notes

1. Justin Kaplan, *Walt Whitman: A Life* (New York: Simon and Schuster, 1980), p. 241.

2. *National Cyclopedia of American Biography*, 63 vols. (New York: James T. White and Company, 1907), 9:121.

3. Fred Lewis Pattee, *The Feminine Fifties* (New York: Appleton-Century, 1940), p. 300.

4. Albert Parry, *Garrets and Pretenders: A History of Bohemianism in America* (New York: Covici-Friede, 1933), pp. 45–46.

5. Quoted in Chester L. Davis, "Jumping Frog and N.Y. *Saturday Press*," *Twainian* 18 (1959):3.

6. Horace Traubel, *With Walt Whitman in Camden*, 5 vols. (New York: Mitchell and Kennerly, 1914), 1:236.

7. Quoted in Frank Luther Mott, *A History of American Magazines*, 4 vols. (Cambridge, Mass.: Harvard University Press, 1938), 2:38.

8. Quoted in Parry, p. 44.

9. Kaplan, p. 242.

10. Quoted in Parry, p. 45.

11. Claude M. Simpson, *The Local Colorists* (New York: Harper and Brothers, 1960), p. 8.

12. Davis, p. 1.

13. Parry, p. 47.

14. Quoted in Pattee, p. 300.

## Information Sources

BIBLIOGRAPHY:
Davis, Chester L. "Jumping Frog and N.Y. *Saturday Press*." *Twainian* 18 (1959):1–4.
Howells, William Dean. *Literary Friends and Acquaintance*. New York: Harper and Brothers, 1900.
Kaplan, Justin. *Walt Whitman: A Life*. New York: Simon and Schuster, 1980.
Mott, Frank Luther. *A History of American Magazines*. 4 vols. Cambridge, Mass.: Harvard University Press, 1938.
Parry, Albert. *Garrets and Pretenders: A History of Bohemianism in America*. New York: Covici-Friede, 1933.
INDEXES: None.
REPRINT EDITIONS: *Source Newspapers in Microfilm: United States 1848–1972* (Washington, D.C.: Library of Congress, 1973).
LOCATION SOURCES: Complete runs: None. Partial runs: New York Public Library, U.S. Library of Congress.

**Publication History**

MAGAZINE TITLE AND TITLE CHANGES: *The Saturday Press*, 23 October 1858–27 November 1858. *The New York Saturday Press*, 4 December 1858–2 June 1866.

VOLUME AND ISSUE DATA: Volume 1, number 1-volume 3, number 50, 23 October 1858–15 December 1860; volume 4, number 1-volume 5, number 22, 5 August 1865–2 June 1866.

FREQUENCY OF PUBLICATION: Weekly.

PUBLISHER: Henry Clapp, Jr. (various printers not indicated)

EDITOR: Henry Clapp, Jr.

*M. Jimmie Killingsworth*

**THE SATURDAY WAVE.** See THE WAVE

**SCRIBNER'S MAGAZINE.** See *American Literary Magazines: The Twentieth Century*

## SCRIBNER'S MONTHLY

In the late nineteenth century *Scribner's Monthly* (later *Century Illustrated*) became a focal point of American culture. Along with its rivals, *Harper's\** and *Atlantic Monthly,\** it is a bellwether of the entire Gilded Age and a benchmark for the growth of American culture into this century. Charles Scribner, Roswell Smith, and Dr. Josiah Gilbert Holland founded the magazine in 1870 to be a direct competitor of *Harper's New Monthly*. *Scribner's* soon became highly popular, chiefly because its illustrations were of high quality from the beginning. Indeed, *Scribner's* is usually credited with leadership of the industry with regard to innovations in typesetting, engraving, and other forms of illustration as well as in advertising. Most of the famous illustrators of the time were featured in the magazine: Timothy Cole, George Kivell, E. W. Kemble, Francis G. Attwood, Winslow Homer, Frederick Remington, and others. Cole was art editor for many years, and Theodore Low De Vinne superintended the magazine's printing from its beginning until his death in 1914.[1]

*Scribner's-Century* had a religious and upright moral tone from the beginning, set by the founding editor, Josiah Gilbert Holland. He was one of the most popular of nineteenth-century American poets, author of the long poems *Bitter-Sweet* and *Kathrina*, and a man of enormous energy, talent, and devotion. Just after Holland's death, Edward Eggleston summed up the general opinion of this famous editor: "He was the most popular and effective preacher of social and domestic moralities of his age; the oracle of the active and ambitious young man and of the susceptible and enthusiastic young woman, the guide, philosopher and schoolmaster of humanity at large, touching all questions of life and character'' (23:164). Frank Luther Mott names Holland as one of the six greatest American magazine editors.[2] But it was Richard Watson Gilder who presided as editor over the magazine during the period of its greatest popularity (by 1890, the circulation was 200,000) and its greatest influence. Gilder had been Holland's assistant for eleven years. During his tenure (1881–1909) he continued the policies of Holland, though he was more liberal than Holland. For instance, Gilder published some poems by Walt Whitman, whom Holland had refused to publish, referring to the great poet as an "old wretch."[3]

Because of management disagreements with the book publishing house, *Scribner's* became the *Century* in 1881, with a new ownership and with Gilder as editor. The magazine actually changed little. Before the name change, the most popular feature had been Edward King's series *The Great South*, which spurred Northern interest in the South awakened during the Civil War and Reconstruction. After the break with Scribner's, the *Century* had enormous success with *Battles and Leaders of the Civil War*, featuring memoirs and debates authored by such old soldiers as Grant, Johnston, McClellan, Longstreet, Eads, Beauregard, Hill, Sherman, and many others. This long-running series of the 1880s caused a renaissance of interest in the Civil War. The other popular and successful series of the same period was George Kennan's exposé of Czarist oppression, *Russia and the Exile System*, which was an international sensation.

But it was fiction that was the mainstay of the magazine. During the *Scribner's* period (1870–1881), Holland had published many American authors, even though European writers were enormously popular with American readers: Mark Twain, Rebecca Harding Davis, H. H. Boyesen, Frances Hodgson Burnett, Bret Harte, George W. Cable, Henry James, Helen Hunt, Joel Chandler Harris, Thomas Nelson Page, Edward Eggleston, and Julian Hawthorne. He also published work by such writers as Joaquin Miller, T. W. Higginson, Charles Dudley Warner, William Cullen Bryant, John Burroughs, Sidney and Clifford Lanier, Edward Everett Hale, Emma Lazarus, John Muir, Edward Bellamy, Brander Matthews, and Ralph Waldo Emerson and Henry David Thoreau. The list of European authors includes Jules Verne, Ivan Turgenev, Christina Rosetti, Robert Louis Stevenson, and Hans Christian Andersen.

During Gilder's editorship, more poetry was featured in the magazine. This is an undistinguished period in American poetry, but Gilder published some first-class verse. Frequent contributors were Whitman, Henry Wadsworth Longfellow, James Russell Lowell, James Whitcomb Riley, Sidney Lanier, Charles Edwin Markham, Louise Imogen Guiney, Thomas Bailey Aldrich, Edith Wharton, Hayden Carruth, Herman Melville, Richard Henry Stoddard, Rudyard Kipling, Paul Lawrence Dunbar, Harriet Monroe, and Albert Bigelow Paine.

Gilder published fiction by the most eminent writers of the day, featuring James, William Dean Howells, Twain (a serialized and bowdlerized *Huckleberry Finn*), Bret Harte, F. Marion Crawford, Jack London, Lafcadio Hearn, Joel Chandler Harris's "Uncle Remus" stories, Frances Hodgson Burnett's *Little*

*Lord Fauntleroy*, Frank R. Stockton (author of the highly popular "The Lady or the Tiger?"), George W. Cable, Bill Nye, Hamlin Garland, Kate Chopin, Winston Churchill, Lew Wallace, and Stephen Crane.

Articles, reviews, memoirs, and arguments were contributed by such luminaries as Matthew Arnold, Frederick Douglass, George Bird Grinnell, Theodore Roosevelt, Thomas Carlyle, James A. Garfield, George Bancroft, Henry Cabot Lodge, John G. Nicolay and John Hay (a serialized life of Lincoln by his private secretaries), Julia Ward Howe, William T. Sherman, Frederick Remington, John La Farge, Henry George, Richard Harding Davis, Horace Greeley, E. W. Howe, Hiram Maxim, E. C. Stedman, John Muir, John Burroughs, Jacob Riis, Gifford Pinchot, Woodrow Wilson, Ernest Fenellosa, and Ernest Thompson Seton. U. S. Grant's memoirs were serialized in 1885–1886, and proved enormously popular.

Perhaps the *Century* had its greatest success and influence during the 1890s. Because of its enormous circulation, it could attract the best-known authors and pay them well. Its standards for artwork and illustrations remained quite high, and its staff was ambitious and energetic. Yet it remained nervous about its readership, practicing the sort of self-censorship common in late-Victorian America. Often, the editors explained to potential contributors that the *Century* would print nothing that might offend the sensibilities of the women in the family circle. Scholars have speculated that the *Century* was behind the times, underestimating the degree of social change for American women in the turn-of-the-century period and blindly insisting that American women continue to rely on the *Century* to tell them what was good for them and what to believe in.[4]

It was during the 1890s that the *Century* published some of its most popular works and authors: Frank Stockton's *Rudder Grange*; Bret Harte's *Gabriel Conroy*; Cable's *The Grandissimes*; Jack London's *The Sea-Wolf*; Edward Eggleston's *Roxy*; poems by Emma Lazarus, Sidney Lanier, Paul Hamilton Hayne, and Joaquin Miller; essays by John Muir, John Burroughs, and Charles Dudley Warner. Yet it was in 1890 that the *Century* rejected Richard Harding Davis's *Gallegher* because of its slanginess. A few years before editors stopped the presses because of a passage in Howells's *The Rise of Silas Lapham* that uses the word "dynamite" in reference to labor troubles and riots.[5] The *Century* walked the fine line between popularity and comstockery on the one hand and artistic integrity on the other. The line was marked by Richard Watson Gilder, one of the most influential American men of letters of the nineteenth century. Perhaps he was too frequently guilty of false delicacy, but so was the entire American culture.

In the 1890s, changes in printing technology and the development of a clear photoengraving technique made cheap illustrated magazines possible and caused the first serious challenges to the preeminence of the *Century* and *Harper's*. The *Century* began to lose readers to such inexpensive illustrated magazines as the journalistic *McClure's*, *Munsey's*, *Cosmopolitan*, *Everybody's*, *Collier's*, and *Ladies' Home Journal*.[6] Evidently, the new readership wanted reportage, analysis, and diversion, not art, philosophy, literary criticism, and serious literature.

By 1900, the *Century* reported a circulation down to 150,000 from its 1890 high of 200,000. *Munsey's* had 650,000 in 1900 and much more advertising than the *Century*, which, ironically, had always been considered ad-heavy by publishing insiders.

To respond to this challenge, Gilder made slight changes in the editorial policy, placing a bit more emphasis on nonfiction and opinion and featuring writing by famous Americans from nonliterary fields, such as General Shafter, Admiral Sampson, Grover Cleveland, and William Howard Taft. But the *Century* maintained its eminence untarnished, albeit slightly grayed, until well after the turn of the century. Its enormous influence remained, and it continued to publish the most famous writers of the day, such as James, Twain, Howells, Hamlin Garland, Harte, and Kipling. It also published many emerging major talents, such as Stephen Crane, Paul Lawrence Dunbar, Kate Chopin, Sarah Orne Jewett, and Harriet Monroe. And it continued to be a forum for such people as Theodore Roosevelt, Gifford Pinchot, and Frederick Law Olmsted.

Gilder's long stewardship of the magazine ended with his death in 1909. An eminent American of the Gilded Age, he had been in some ways the conscience of the American publishing industry. He was also a leader of New York society, a civic leader, and an artistic guardian.[7] The new editor, Robert Underwood Johnson, had been Gilder's longtime associate editor, so there was continuity in the editor's office. Johnson was a champion of causes, active in the fight for an international copyright law, in the push for a national park system, and in the movement to establish an American Academy of Arts and Letters. But Johnson's forty-year career with the magazine included a scant three and a half years as its chief editor; he resigned in 1913 to become ambassador to Italy. He probably resigned, at least in part, because of a disagreement with the publishers over the need for a more journalistic tone to meet the direct competition of the cheaper monthlies.[8] Curiously and ironically, under Johnson's chief editorship, the magazine did take a decided turn away from belles-lettres and increased its coverage of news events. For example, in volume 80 (May-October 1910), one sees feature articles on the German Zeppelin service, Bible study around the world, Russian politics, recent progress in chemistry, the growth of college athletics, and similar issues. No eminent authors appear in volume 80, but there are several articles about American politics and several photographs of President Taft playing golf. The magazine had obviously begun to change well before Johnson resigned.

In the remaining seventeen years of its existence, the years of its decline, the *Century* had six editors, three of whom served for only a year. During this period the magazine increased its coverage of world affairs and politics and published articles on travel, European history, science, and humor. The amount of fiction published lessens during this period, and it is noticeably more escapist. However, a number of poems and essays by the more important newer writers were published: G. K. Chesterton, Booker T. Washington, Louis Untermeyer, Adelaide Crapsey, Robert Graves, Joseph Hergesheimer, Thomas Beer, Alexander Woolcott, Frederick Lewis Allen, John Gould Fletcher, Rebecca West, Amy Lowell, George Santayana, Maxwell Bodenheim, Edna St. Vincent Millay, Henry Seidel Canby, Bertrand Russell, Witter Bynner, Sara Teasdale, Carl Van Doren, Floyd Dell, Arnold Bennett, James Branch Cabell, Mary Austin, Carl Sandburg, T. S. Stribling, James Weldon Johnson, Will Durant, and Edgar Lee Masters.

But by 1919, the *Century* had changed almost completely into a news commentary and public affairs monthly, merely larded and decorated with poems and belles-lettres. The number of illustrations trailed off to almost zero. A separate "literary editor," Carl Van Doren, was appointed by editor Glenn Frank in 1921. Frank resigned in 1925 to become president of the University of Wisconsin and was succeeded by Hewitt H. Howland, who promptly cut the number of poems and stories even further. Nevertheless, circulation continued to decline.

The *Century* became a quarterly in 1929–1930 in a last-ditch effort to continue, but circulation had sunk below 20,000 in 1930, and after the spring issue of 1930, the *Century Quarterly* merged with the *Forum* and disappeared. Once the *Century* had an almost incalculable influence on American society, and it reflects much of American life of the period 1870 to 1930. It regularly published a score of the greatest American authors and introduced several of them to the world. While never in the avant garde, the *Century* held to the highest aesthetic and moral ideals of its time and as such reflects much of the best as well as some of the worst of American literature and American society.

## Notes

1. Max J. Herzberg, ed., *The Reader's Encyclopedia of American Literature* (New York: Thomas Y. Crowell, 1962), p. 1008.

2. Frank Luther Mott, *A History of American Magazines*, 4 vols. (Cambridge, Mass.: Harvard University Press, 1957), 3:459.

3. Mott, 3:473.

4. Robert E. Spiller, Willard Thorp et. al., *Literary History of the United States* (New York: Macmillan, 1963), pp. 956–57.

5. Spiller, p. 953.

6. Spiller, p. 959.

7. James D. Hart, *The Oxford Companion to American Literature* (New York: Oxford University Press, 1965), p. 314.

8. Mott, 3:477.

## Information Sources

BIBLIOGRAPHY:

Hart, James D., ed. *The Oxford Companion to American Literature*. New York: Oxford University Press, 1965.

Herzberg, Max J., ed. *The Reader's Encyclopedia of American Literature*. New York: Thomas Y. Crowell, 1962.

*An Index to Volumes I-X of Scribner's Magazine*. (November 1870-October 1875). New York: Scribner and Co., 1876.

*An Index to Volumes I to XXX Inclusive*, 1870–1885. New York: The Century Co., 1886.

*Index, Volumes 31 to 84*. (November 1885-October 1912). New York: The Century Co., 1919.

*Letters of Richard Watson Gilder*. Ed. Rosamond Gilder. New York: Houghton, Mifflin, 1916.

Mott, Frank Luther. *American Journalism*. New York: Macmillan, 1962.

———. "*Scribner's Monthly-Century*." *A History of American Magazines*. 4 vols. Belknap Press of Harvard Univ. Press, 1957. 3:457–480.

Spiller, Robert E., Willard Thorp et. al. *Literary History of the United States*. New York: Macmillan, 1963.

INDEXES: Published as separate volumes by Scribner's in 1876 and by the Century Company in 1886 and 1919.

REPRINT EDITIONS: American Periodicals: Series III, 1850–1900. University Microfilms, Ann Arbor. Reels 548–66. Princeton Microfilm Corporation.

LOCATION SOURCES: Widely available.

## Publication History

MAGAZINE TITLE AND TITLE CHANGES: *Scribner's Monthly*, 1870–1881. *The Century Illustrated Monthly Magazine*, 1881-October 1925. *The Century*, November 1925-May 1929. *The Century, A Popular Quarterly*, 1929–1930; Autumn 1929, Winter 1930, Spring 1930.

VOLUME AND ISSUE DATA: Semiannual (volumes 1 to 117), November 1870-August 1929; quarterly, Autumn 1929-Spring 1930: 118, May-August 1929; 119, Autumn, 1929; 120, Winter and Spring 1930. New Series 1 to 46, same as whole numbers 23–118, November 1881-August 1929, reflecting title change from *Scribner's Monthly* to *The Century* and its variations.

FREQUENCY OF PUBLICATION: Monthly, except quarterly from fall 1929 to spring 1930.

PUBLISHERS: 1870–1881: Scribner and Company, New York. 1881–1930: The Century Company, New York.

EDITORS: Josiah Gilbert Holland, 1870–1881; Richard Watson Gilder, 1881–1909; Robert Underwood Johnson, 1909–1913; Robert Sterling Yard, 1913–1914; Douglas Zabriskie Doty, 1915–1918; Thomas R. Smith, 1919; W. Morgan Shuster, 1920–1921; Glenn Frank, 1921–1925; Hewitt H. Howland, 1925–1930. *Assistant Editors*: Gilder, Frank R. Stockton, Johnson, Clarence Clough Buel, L. Frank Tooker, William Carey, Sophie Bledsoe Herrick, Harriet Bliss, T. R. Smith, Carl Van Doren, Anna Lord Strauss.

*Fred W. Robbins*

## SIMMS'S MONTHLY MAGAZINE. See THE SOUTHERN AND WESTERN MONTHLY MAGAZINE AND REVIEW

## THE SOUTHERN AND WESTERN LITERARY MESSENGER AND REVIEW. See THE SOUTHERN LITERARY MESSENGER

## THE SOUTHERN AND WESTERN MONTHLY MAGAZINE AND REVIEW

In April 1842, before William Gilmore Simms announced his withdrawal from editorship of the *Magnolia*,\* publishers James Burges and Robert James spoke to him of a "cheaper and more popular" successor to it. In August 1844, their recently acquired *Orion*\* having joined the *Magnolia* in the dustbin of failed Southern periodicals, Burges and James offered Simms the editorship of a new "Politico Literary Magazine"; in November he accepted their offer with the promise of half the profits. On 1 December the prospectus announced "Simms's Southern Monthly Magazine," to be published in Charleston at $3.00 per year, and on 15 January appeared the *Southern and Western Monthly Magazine and Review*, popularly referred to as "Simms's Magazine" or "Simms's Monthly" during its year of publication.[1]

Introducing his magazine as a "restoration of the *Magnolia*," Simms characterized it as "a new journal as nearly on the plan of the old as possible" (1:67). He intended, however, "to impart to it a more decided political complexion . . . and if possible, to impress upon it more of those sectional aspects, South and West, which need development quite as much as advocacy." Yet, while emphasizing literature "made at home" and promising to address the magazine "particularly to the people of the South and West," he declared, "Some of our most valuable . . . contributors are citizens of the North,—men of that catholic sense which readily recognizes the necessity of many such journals . . . for the proper representation, in the world of literature, of every section of our common country" (1:67–68).

Simms's championing of literary nationalism was evident in the magazine's initial article, "Americanism in Literature." Here he denied the title "American" to those native writers who "think after European models" (1:1) and insisted on a literature embodying American character and institutions. The material for such a literature he explored in seven installments of "The Epochs and Events of American History, as Suited to the Purpose of Art in Fiction." In editorial remarks he repeatedly chastised American readers and publishers for their acquiescence to the nation's "colonial thraldom" (2:352, 356–57). Among unjustly ignored American writers "equal in real genius to . . . almost any that we import," he listed Bryant, Emerson, Lowell, Longfellow, and Hawthorne—and very few Southerners (2:357).

Simms nevertheless announced his principal aim to be the promotion of Southern literature (2:345). "Our humble efforts," he asserted, "are devoted to this object almost wholly" (1:263). The sectional bias is apparent in Simms's lead article for the second number, "Our Agricultural Condition," warning of the dangers of Northern economic and industrial domination, and in "Slavery," which opens the second volume, declaring "no subject more closely interwoven with the political and social well-being of the southern and south-western States of this confederacy, than that of slavery" (2:1).

In Simms's view the *Southern and Western*'s nationalism and its sectionalism were in no way incompatible. Insisting that a truly national literature could be made up only "of the literature of distinct sections,"[2] he dismissed charges of narrowness leveled at Southern magazines. For him the fault lay rather with those Northern periodicals that denounced sectionalism while promoting their own writers and ignoring those of the South. Thus in the *Southern and Western* he denounced equally those Southerners who subscribed to Northern periodicals to the neglect of Southern and those Americans who read and published British works to the neglect of American. His advocacy of such views in the *Magnolia* had involved Simms in a bitter feud with Lewis Gaylord Clark, whose *Knickerbocker Magazine**\* bore the standard for the Whig opposition to literary nationalism and to sectionalism.[3]

In the Young America group and its acknowledged leader Evert A. Duyckinck, whom he had met in New York just after leaving the *Magnolia*, Simms felt that he had found his natural allies. He shared with Duyckinck both the advocacy of literary nationalism and the enmity of Clark and his circle. Since Duyckinck and Cornelius Mathews's *Arcturus**\* had shared the fate of the *Magnolia*, Simms proposed his own new undertaking as a voice for Young America, suggesting to Duyckinck, "it will, in some measure afford us the organ we desire. Until you can get your press in N. Y. you must be content with a wing of it in Charleston."[4]

Recognizing the growing dominance of New York in the publishing trade, Simms sought an alliance for the magazine, for the South, and for himself. To Duyckinck he wrote, "All your affinities in New York are with the South rather than New England."[5] After a visit in late summer 1845, he editorialized, "New York will inevitably become the great central city, drawing into her capacious bosom the literary minds of future generations of this country, as certainly as she draws its trade and capital" (2:205). Already, he claimed, "hither tend writers from all quarters of the country, east and west, north and south" (2:352). Boston publishers, he observed, "do not often publish the works of any but New England authors" (2:347).

Thus, rather than renew his warfare with Clark and the *Knickerbocker*, Simms leveled his charge of literary exclusiveness at Boston's *North American Review*.\* In "A Passage with 'The Veteran Quarterly,' " he remarked that a circular claiming national status for the *North American* listed among contributors no Southerners and "not a single New-Yorker." "It is New England only and all over—nothing but New England" (1:297), he declaimed. "As for serving the national cause, and representing the national character, . . . the sectional and selfish partiality which it has always maintained,—asserting the one region to the wholesale neglect of all others,—was . . . calculated to do the national reputation more injury . . . than all the abuse of all the British Quarterlies" (1:306).

Editorial reactions to Simms's magazine often reflected the editors' positions on these issues. Both the *Southern Quarterly Review*\* and the *Southern Literary Messenger*\* warmly received the new venture, the latter particularly commending

Simms's stand "in favor of Americanism in Literature."[6] *Godey's*,* "pleased with every feature" of the magazine, noted, "the whole affair has a stamp of nationality which we decidedly approve."[7] Offering frequent encouragement in the *New York Morning News* and the *New York Weekly News*, Duyckinck pronounced Simms's attack on the *North American Review* "well calculated . . . to disturb even the thrice-drugged conservative North American."[8]

Clark, who had ignored the *Southern and Western* aside from excerpting the *Broadway Journal*'s* criticism of the first number, dismissed Simms's attack as a recent "example of labored debility" by one of those "small authors and smaller critics" unnoticed by the *North American*.[9] *Broadway Journal* editor Charles F. Briggs, reviewing that first number, ridiculed both Simms's "Americanism in Literature" and his complaint of Southern patronage of Northern works. Despite Simms's professed "desire to produce a Southern magazine," Briggs claimed, "The best things in the present number come from the North."[10] After the departure of Briggs (who split with Edgar Allan Poe over Poe's accusations of plagiarism against Longfellow—the Young Americans siding with Poe, and Briggs with the literary Whigs), Poe, now editing the *Journal*, declared the *Southern and Western* "as ably edited as any journal in America—if not more ably edited than any."[11]

In the midst of this literary warfare, Simms's editorial criticism remained fairly even-handed. He commended Catherine Maria Sedgwick as "one of our favorites" while chastising her for a "wanton fling at our [Southern] institutions" (1:434–35). In an issue carrying Duyckinck's highly favorable review of Cornelius Mathews's *Big Abel and the Little Manhattan*, Simms praised Duyckinck's "correct taste, and . . . genial sympathy with the delicate and graceful in authorship" (2:425) but declared the review "much more indulgent . . . than we should have been" (2:427).

Before accepting the editorship, Simms spoke of the magazine as an outlet for the "numerous conceptions" with which he was "teeming."[12] Although he solicited contributions from friends and literary acquaintances both North and South, the bulk of most issues was his own. Assuming his seat in the South Carolina legislature as he was beginning the *Southern and Western*, he complained frequently of the demands on his time.[13] Although, as he prepared his second number, he complained to Duyckinck, "In truth the work is quite too small for my purposes and does not give me sufficient room for my own utterance," he later protested, "You see how much of the drudgery of the magazine falls to my share. Of course, writing as I do, I can do no justice to the public and but little to myself."[14] Among this outpouring, some of it reprinted or revised from earlier publication, are some of Simms's better short fiction and criticism, including "Oaktibbe; or the Choctaw Sampson" and "The Snake in the Cabin," later included in *The Wigwam and the Cabin*, and most of the essays collected in *Views and Reviews in American Literature, History and Fiction*, First Series.

But the editor increasingly saw his work as "just so much hopeless drudgery" and began "to repent" the "sentiment of patriotism . . . half way at the bottom of my efforts.''[15] In June he complained, ''I long to shake it off, and to begin again independently. My mind is full of earnest and original projects, which, of course, I cannot touch, with the toils of a miscellany to encounter.''[16] In his November ''Editorial Bureau,'' he spoke of his recent sojourn in New York as ''a brief respite from the daily drudgery of making provision for the month'' (2:343). Later in the same ''Bureau'' he announced, ''With the close of the present volume of this periodical, we propose to withdraw from the conduct of its pages'' (2:344).

Before the appearance of that announcement, Simms had arranged for B. B. Minor to purchase the *Southern and Western* from Burges and James, and for himself to conduct the critical department of Minor's *Southern Literary Messenger.*\*[17] The December *Messenger* announced the merger and its own new name to commence with the January issue: the *Southern and Western Literary Messenger and Review.*[18] After one year, it resumed its former name.

In announcing his withdrawal from the *Southern and Western*, Simms confessed to his readers, ''It has not answered our expectation, and it takes too greatly from the time which we would find more profitably bestowed upon independent individual labors. Its duties are irksome, and it is compensative neither in money nor other reward'' (2:234). The magazine had afforded payment neither to its contributors nor, apparently, to its editor. Although Simms claimed in the second month of publication a circulation of ''something like 1,500 copies already'' and prospects of ''a large increase,''[19] the work never approached the 3,000 subscribers necessary to sustain it. (2:345).

Ending with a final plea to fellow Southerners to rouse themselves to confidence in their section and to support of Southern intellect, Simms declared, ''In withdrawing from this, we abandon the editorial chair, in all probability, forever'' (2:344). Little more than three years later, he would take on the editorship of the *Southern Quarterly Review.*

## Notes

1. *The Letters of William Gilmore Simms*, ed. Mary C. Simms Oliphant, Alfred Taylor Odell, and T. C. Duncan Eaves, 6 vols. (Columbia, S.C.: University of South Carolina Press, 1952–1982), 1:351, 400, 412, 430, 436, 439, 440, 446; 2:13; 5:373.

2. *Magnolia* 4 (April 1842):251.

3. For Simms's role in the literary wars of Young America, see C. Hugh Holman, ''Introduction'' to *Views and Reviews in American Literature, History and Fiction*, First Series, by Simms (Cambridge, Mass.: Belknap Press, 1962), pp. xxii-xxvi, and David Tomlinson, ''*Simms's Monthly Magazine: the Southern and Western Monthly Magazine and Review*,'' *Southern Literary Journal* 8 (Fall 1975):99–114. For broader discussions of the conflict, see John Stafford, *The Literary Criticism of ''Young America'': A Study in the Relationship of Politics and Literature, 1837–1850* (Berkeley and Los Angeles: The University of California Press, 1952) and Perry Miller, *The Raven and the Whale: The War of Words and Wit in the Era of Poe and Melville* (New York: Harcourt, Brace, 1956).

4. *Letters of William Gilmore Simms*, 1:440.

5. *Letters of William Gilmore Simms*, 1:438.

6. *Southern Quarterly Review* 7 (April 1845):529; *Southern Literary Messenger* 11 (February 1845):128.

7. *Godey's Lady's Book* 30 (March 1845):144; see also 30 (June 1845):281.

8. *New York Weekly News*, 24 May 1845.

9. *Knickerbocker* 25 (March 1845):281, 26 (August 1845), 174.

10. *Broadway Journal* 1 (1 February 1845):77. See also Briggs's attack on "A Passage with 'The Veteran Quarterly,' " *Broadway Journal* 1 (31 May 1845):337–39.

11. *Broadway Journal* 2 (30 August 1845), 121.

12. *Letters of William Gilmore Simms*, 1:436.

13. *Letters of William Gilmore Simms*, 1:443–44; 2:47, 70.

14. *Letters of William Gilmore Simms*, 2:69.

15. *Letters of William Gilmore Simms*, 5:388.

16. *Letters of William Gilmore Simms*, 2:69.

17. *Letters of William Gilmore Simms*, 2:109–10.

18. *Southern Literary Messenger* 11 (December 1845):760–62.

19. *Letters of William Gilmore Simms*, 2:29.

## Information Sources

BIBLIOGRAPHY:

Guilds, John C. "William Gilmore Simms as Magazine Editor to 1845." Ph.D. diss., Duke University, 1954.

Herbert, Edward T. "William Gilmore Simms as Editor and Literary Critic." Ph.D. diss., University of Wisconsin, 1957.

Hoole, William Stanley. "William Gilmore Simms's Career as Editor." *Georgia Historical Quarterly* 19 (March 1935):47–54.

*The Letters of William Gilmore Simms*. 6 vols. Ed. Mary C. Simms Oliphant, Alfred T. Odell, and T. C. Duncan Eaves. Columbia, S.C.: University of South Carolina Press, 1952–1982.

Tomlinson, David. *"Simms's Monthly Magazine: The Southern and Western Monthly Magazine and Review." Southern Literary Journal* 8 (Fall 1975):95–125.

INDEXES: None.

REPRINT EDITIONS: American Periodicals: Series II, 1800–1850. University Microfilms, Ann Arbor. Reel 1407.

LOCATION SOURCES: Complete runs: Charleston Library Society, Duke University, Emory University, Harvard University, New York Public Library, State Historical Society of Wisconsin, University of Minnesota. Partial runs: American Antiquarian Society, Library of Congress, New York Historical Society, New York State Library, Princeton University, Stanford College, University of Georgia, University of South Carolina, Yale University.

## Publication History

MAGAZINE TITLE AND TITLE CHANGES: *Simms's Monthly Magazine: The Southern and Western Monthly Magazine and Review* (inside: *Southern and Western Magazine and Review*).

VOLUME AND ISSUE DATA: Volume 1, January-December 1845.

FREQUENCY OF PUBLICATION: Monthly.

PUBLISHERS: [James] Burges & [Robert] James, Charleston.
EDITOR: William Gilmore Simms.

*William M. Moss*

# THE SOUTHERN BIVOUAC

Sponsored by the Southern Historical Association of Louisville, Kentucky, and published in that city, the *Bivouac* appeared in September 1882 and was not called the *Southern Bivouac* until the November issue. Conceived in the notion that firsthand accounts of the late war and of the principles for which it had been fought should be given by those who had espoused the cause of the Confederacy, the monthly published chiefly during its first year articles on various aspects of the war and the Confederacy.

At the end of this period the *Bivouac* changed editorial hands (it continued to be published under the "auspices" of the association, but its editorial control was assumed by William M. Marriner and William N. McDonald, both former Confederate officers) and announced to its readers in August, 1883 that the magazine's contents would include "the papers of historic value read before the Association, short stories of the war, sketches of soldiers distinguished in battle, poetry, notices of individual heroism on either side, and a select miscellany of other articles. . . . The *Bivouac*," the editorial continued, "means to reproduce and preserve in book form as far as practicable the life and body of Confederate times," for the "very bitterness" of the period "has its lessons, while the good and brave deeds that adorned it are the precious heritage of our common country." Moreover, the article concludes, "the survivors of the lost cause can least of all afford to be silent. The fairest history a victor may write never does justice to the cause of the conquered" (1:493).

This general purpose and editorial policy obtained for the next two years, and interestingly enough there was little animus expressed toward the North, an attitude clearly suggested in an advertisement in the May 1884 issue announcing that the *Southern Bivouac* and the *Bivouac*, a new Boston monthly published by Grand Army of the Republic veterans, were "clubbing" subscriptions at $2.50 per year! More accounts of battles and engagements appeared as well as sketches of Confederate leaders. Some original fiction (especially an irregular series of sketches in Negro dialect by McDonald) and verse were published, but the best poems were reprints of old favorites like "Florence Vane" and "Little Giffen." The circulation reached 3,000 in September 1884 and 7,500 by the end of 1885.[1] In the meantime, the McDonalds had sold the magazine and had given up control after bringing out the May number of 1885. (Marriner had retired from his editorship in September 1883, at which time E. H. McDonald as business manager had joined W. N. McDonald in the management of the enterprise.)

The general nature of the journal was changed by its new editors—Basil W. Duke, a Louisville attorney and a well-known Confederate brigadier, and Richard

W. Knott, editor of *Home and Farm*, an agricultural biweekly, and a Louisville journalist—and its new publisher, B. F. Avery and Sons, a Louisville firm that published the highly successful *Home and Farm*, whose circulation was 120,000 in 1885. An editorial in the June issue, the first to be brought out by the new team, describes the change of plan and emphasis:

> the managers . . . propose to publish a distinctively Southern Magazine. Southern in no merely political sense, but a magazine which, while appealing to the lovers of good literature every where, will deal chiefly with the aspects of Southern life, thought, action, with Southern history and scenery, with Southern traditions and prejudices in accordance with the accepted rules of art (n.s. 1:62).

Consequently, the writer (presumably Knott) declares, the magazine will devote "special attention . . . to papers relating to the war" and will seek to "illustrate in any way Southern life, manners, history, or tradition; Southern life not as something separate from the national but as an inseparable and integral part of it" (n.s. 1:62). This new blueprint of the journal might also be considered a reasonably accurate description of its content over the next two years. War papers were published and articles on Turner Ashby, John H. Morgan, Braxton Bragg, Robert Toombs, and Robert E. Lee.

Moreover, as if to underscore the South's relation to the rest of the world, there were also contributions by Northern and British writers. Tennyson, Swinburne, and Jean Ingelow were each reprinted once from other sources. The most intriguing criticism was an article in April 1886 by Henry W. Austin, a Massachusetts magazinist, which printed "Lilitha, Princess of Ghouls" and maintained on the basis of internal evidence that it was Poe's last poem. This ascription provoked a controversy that was finally resolved in October by Mariner J. Kent's "Poe's Last Poem," which demonstrates conclusively that the lyric had been written by a New York journalist in 1863. Austin is also responsible for "My Pilgrim Fathers," a three-installment account beginning in January 1887 that censures the Pilgrims for their harsh treatment of the Indians in the seventeenth century. Altogether, non-Southern writing makes up a small but not insignificant part of the *Bivouac*'s contribution to periodical literature, but the magazine's reputation is rightly based on its Southern offerings.

The new *Bivouac* was also faithful to its promise to deal with Southern life and literature apart from the war. Southern life, for example, comes in for its share of attention in pieces on oranges, sugar, cotton, rice, and summer resorts.

Southern literature is even more generously represented. There is fiction by Will Wallace Harney, Nannie M. Fitzhugh, and William Hamilton Hayne; poetry by Paul Hamilton Hayne, John Esten Cooke, Maurice Thompson, Margaret Junkin Preston, W. H. Hayne, Robert Burns Wilson, Harney, Danske Dandridge, and Lizette W. Reese; criticism by Paul Hayne, Wilson, Charles F. Smith, and Richard W. Knott; and nonfiction by Paul Hayne, R. T. Durrett,

Alexander H. Stephens, Charles Gayarré, Maurice Thompson, Thomas H. Hines, Mrs. Preston, and Lafcadio Hearn.

Southern fiction, however, was not a strong suit with the *Bivouac*, a fateful circumstance in the magazine world of the 1880s, when local-color fiction was a vital feature of all the great national monthlies. Several short serials were printed, including in 1885 Harney's "Wild Life in the 'Seventies,' " a story of Florida, concluding in January 1887, and O. B. Mayer's "The Two Marksmen of Ruff's Mountain," a three-part tale of German settlers in South Carolina during the Revolution. The short fiction, on the other hand, was generally better, if hardly more distinguished. In a period when George Washington Cable, Walter Hines Page, Joel Chandler Harris, and Mary Murfree, among others, were bringing out fiction in the chief Northern magazines, none contributed to the *Bivouac*, despite its obvious interest in dialect as manifested by the publication of Nannie Mayo Fitzhugh's "At Rickettses' Play Party," a piece in mountain dialect printed in December 1886; various anecdotes and tales in Negro dialect by Louis Pendleton and W. H. Hayne; and one of the best discussions of Southern idiom published during the period, Charles Forster Smith's "Southern Dialect in Life and Literature." To be sure, the best Northern magazines usually paid better, but the *Bivouac*'s rate of five dollars per printed page for prose was respectable if not always competitive, and its total circulation was about that of the *Atlantic Monthly*,* though it fell far below that of the *Century* (see *Scribner's Monthly*\*) and *Harper's Monthly*.\*[2] Still, the significant Southern writers of fiction failed to contribute, and the *Bivouac*'s offerings are not really comparable to those usually available in the important Northern monthlies.

Much the same may be said of the quality of the magazine's verse, but, in contrast to the absence of noteworthy Southern writers of fiction, a number of well-known Southern poets are represented, including Paul Hayne, Cooke, Thompson, and Mrs. Preston. And though these poets contributed only five poems among them, their names lent prestige to the *Bivouac*'s pages.

A number of younger Southern poets also appeared. William Hamilton Hayne, son of Paul Hamilton Hayne, presented ten of his brief polished lyrics; Robert Burns Wilson, a young Pennsylvanian of Southern forebears and leanings and later the author of "Remember the Maine," contributed several poems and translations; W. W. Harney, a Kentucky emigré in Florida and the author also of contributions in prose to the *Bivouac*, offered some verse; and Danske Dandridge, of Virginia antecedents, and Lizette W. Reese, of Maryland, demonstrated their lyrical wares.

Altogether, the poetry in the *Southern Bivouac* is generally of better quality than the fiction, and it is not far below the usual level of merit found in its chief Northern competitors, though this is not to suggest that any periodicals of the period published consistently superior verse. Paul Hayne's sonnet "Robert Lee" (February 1886) represents the magazine's verse at its best.

Actually, the most valuable contributions to the *Bivouac* were in the form of nonfiction, essays on a variety of topics not easily classified and often combining attributes of history, biography, criticism, and other genres. Among these should be mentioned Paul Hayne's "Ante-Bellum Charleston" and "Charles Gayarré"; R. T. Durrett's "Resolutions of 1798 and 1799"; Alexander H. Stephens's "My Impressions of General Robert E. Lee"; Charles Gayarré's "W. H. Seward on Reconstruction" and "The Famous Lafittes at Galveston"; J.T.L. Preston's "The Execution of John Brown"; Maurice Thompson's "Ceryle Alcyon"; Thomas H. Hines's "The Northwestern Conspiracy"; Margaret J. Preston's "Paul Hamilton Hayne"; and Lafcadio Hearn's "New Orleans Fencing Masters."

Several of these pieces are of some importance. Durrett's three-part article on the Kentucky Resolutions (March-May 1886), for example, is based on important papers of John Breckinridge recently acquired by the author and offers facsimile reproductions of the originals of the Resolutions of 1798 and 1799; Stephens's essay (February 1886) gives an objective appraisal of Lee's character by one whose knowledge and judgment may be considered authoritative; Gayarré's piece on Seward (February 1886) is a "strictly faithful account" of an interview on the subject of Reconstruction between the author and the secretary of state in October 1866; Mrs. Preston's sketch of Hayne (September 1886) is based on almost twenty years of a close and intimate literary correspondence; and Hayne's own three-part essays on Charleston (September-November 1885) and Charles Gayarré (June-August 1886) are spirited and informative.

Hayne, of course, was the most widely known American writer to appear in the *Bivouac*, and indeed he was the first literary figure of consequence Knott sought for contributions when B. F. Avery and Sons bought the magazine in 1885. As an old and favored contributor to *Home and Farm*, the firm's popular periodical, Hayne was urged by Knott, an editor of both publications, to furnish something to the new journal. Since *Home and Farm*'s compensation for poems was being reduced for various reasons, Hayne would have been interested even if Knott had not invited him to contribute; after all, the new management was paying five dollars a page for prose, if not so much per poem as *Home and Farm* had paid. Hayne thereupon put together the essays on his native city and on Gayarré and contributed also several other articles and the sonnet on Lee mentioned previously. For these items he received in a year's time between $375 and $400.[3]

Hayne's contributions to the *Southern Bivouac* do indeed constitute one of its chief claims to literary standing, and his death may be said in one sense to have presaged the journal's discontinuation a year later. There were, of course, other reasons for its sale to the *Century* in 1887, not the least of which was the New York monthly's apparent desire to eliminate its chief competitor in the publishing of war papers and sketches, but the *Bivouac* was surely less reluctant to quit the field after the loss of its main literary asset than it would have been otherwise. Moreover, the magazine's circulation had never exceeded 15,000, and as Knott had written Hayne in 1886, the firm would not really profit until the circulation reached 25,000.

Whatever the reasons, the editors announced in May 1887 that the *Southern Bivouac* and its "plates, engravings, subscription lists, copy-rights, and good will" had been purchased by the Century Company and that the magazine would be "discontinued." Thereupon, they continued, the periodical becomes a "milestone in the progress of Southern literature" and a "record" which shows that "the growth of literature in the South keeps pace with its progress in material affairs." The valedictory ends on a hopeful note:

> With the close of these volumes this work of making a distinct literature of the South—not as something apart from English literature, but enriching it as does the literature of New England—will not cease. It is in the hands of hundreds scattered every where. It will find its own channel of expression as surely as the rivers find their way to the sea. . . . It is not an epitaph we write, but a prediction of continued advancement (n.s. 2:773).

Thus the *Southern Bivouac* closed its last number. The editors and the publishing firm had made a valiant effort to produce a literary magazine with Southern roots and sympathies that would at the same time appeal to an audience beyond the region. The effort failed in the end, but there was consolation in the welcome Southern writers and materials received concurrently in Northern magazines and in the *Century* in particular. The *Century*, indeed, had been hospitable to Southern writers since the 1870s, when it was called *Scribner's Monthly*.[4] There was, then, a special appropriateness in the sale of the Louisville magazine to the New York periodical as far as Southern literature was concerned. In the pages of the *Century*, Southern writers could deal with Southern life and ideas before an audience composed of readers not just from the South but from all parts of the country. In effect, the "epitaph" of the *Bivouac* had to be written in order for the "advancement" of Southern writing to continue on a broader scale.

## Notes

1. For figures on circulation throughout the lifespan of the monthly, see the appropriate issues of *N. W. Ayer and Sons American Newspaper Annual*.

2. For the magazine's rates, see Paul Hamilton Hayne's letter of 19 October 1885 to Charles Gayarré in *A Man of Letters in the Nineteenth-Century South: Selected Letters of Paul Hamilton Hayne*, ed. Rayburn S. Moore (Baton Rouge: Louisiana State University Press, 1982), p. 286.

3. See the letters of this period of Richard W. Knott, William Hamilton Hayne, and Paul Hamilton Hayne in the Hayne Papers, Perkins Library, Duke University. For permission to use and quote from these papers, I am grateful to Mattie U. Russell, Curator of Manuscripts.

4. For the *Century*'s hospitality to Southern writers, see chapter two of Rayburn S. Moore's unpublished Ph.D. dissertation, "Southern Writers and Northern Literary Magazines, 1865–1890" (Duke University, 1956).

## Information Sources

BIBLIOGRAPHY:
Atchison, Ray M. "Southern Literary Magazines, 1865–1887." Ph.D. diss., Duke University, 1956.
Moore, Rayburn S. " 'A Distinctively Southern Magazine': The *Southern Bivouac*." *Southern Literary Journal* 2 (Spring 1970): 51–65.
Mott, Frank Luther. *A History of American Magazines*. 4 vols. Cambridge, Mass.: Belknap Press of Harvard University Press, 1957. 3:47.
Spaulding, Thomas M. "Basil Wilson Duke." *Dictionary of American Biography*, vol. 5 (1930), pp. 495–96.
INDEXES: None.
REPRINT EDITIONS: None.
LOCATION SOURCES: Widely available.

## Publication History

MAGAZINE TITLE AND TITLE CHANGES: *The Bivouac*, September, October 1882. *The Southern Bivouac*, November 1882-May 1885. *The Southern Bivouac: A Monthly Literary and Historical Magazine*, June 1885-May 1887.
VOLUME AND ISSUE DATA: Volumes 1–3, September 1882-May 1885; volumes 4–5 (New series 1–2), June 1885-May 1887.
FREQUENCY OF PUBLICATION: Monthly.
PUBLISHERS: September 1882-July 1883: Southern Historical Association, Louisville, Kentucky. August 1883-May 1885: W. N. McDonald and E. H. McDonald, Louisville. June 1885-May 1887: B. F. Avery and Sons, Louisville.
EDITORS: Editorial Committee, headed by W. M. Marriner, Southern Historical Association, September 1882-July 1883; W. M. Marriner and W. N. McDonald, August, September 1883; W. N. McDonald, October 1883-May 1885; Basil W. Duke and Richard W. Knott, June 1885-May 1887.

*Rayburn S. Moore*

## THE SOUTHERN LADIES' BOOK. See THE MAGNOLIA

## THE SOUTHERN LITERARY GAZETTE

Possibly the most important literary weekly of its period in the South, the *Southern Literary Gazette* provided an outlet for the publication of work by Southern writers, especially those from Georgia and South Carolina, encouraged William Gilmore Simms, Henry Timrod, and Paul Hamilton Hayne, among others, and gave Hayne in particular his first opportunity to edit a literary journal. The brainchild of William C. Richards (1818–1892), an English emigrant and bookseller in Athens, Georgia, who had earlier established the *Orion** (1842–1844), the *Gazette* was founded, as Richards remarked in his first editorial on 13 May 1848, to "develope and foster the intellectual capital of the South."

"We are avowedly and ostentatiously Southern," he continued, "because the South needs to be spurred on to diligent effort and high attainment in the noble departments of . . . Literature and the Arts," and, he added, "Strictly neutral in partisanship, we shall present our readers with a bare synopsis of political intelligence, possessing general interest. Literature is the staple of our Journal" (1:5). This policy concerning literature and the weekly's neutrality regarding contributions brought poetry and fiction from such Northern authors as Richard Henry Stoddard, John T. Trowbridge (under the pseudonym of Paul Creyton), and Ellen Louise Chandler (later Mrs. Louise Chandler Moulton), to say nothing of reprints of work by Irving, Cooper, Bryant, Longfellow, Whitman, and Melville, among others.

In the beginning the journal included both original and selected matter and published tales, poetry, essays, criticism, travel sketches, and a "General Miscellany of information in all departments of Literature, Art and Science" (1:8). Engravings were occasionally featured and were usually based upon the sketches and paintings of T. Addison Richards (1820–1900), one of the editor's younger brothers who had gone to New York in 1845 to study at the National Academy of Design and who also served the weekly as one of its New York correspondents. This was the general plan throughout the *Gazette*'s history, though after Hayne's departure in March 1855 there was much more coverage of news and politics than earlier, and there were few illustrations after 1851. Even in the last year of publication, however, tales and poetry (usually reprints) and essays continued to appear, and such old features as letters about cultural and current events in New York City were printed from time to time. Over the lifespan of the periodical Simms contributed poems and fiction, Timrod poems (usually over the name of Aglaus), and Hayne poems, tales, letters, and reviews (frequently over his initials). James Mathewes Legaré, Henry Rootes Jackson, and Thomas Holley Chivers also contributed poetry and Mrs. Caroline Lee Hentz, Mrs. Ann S. Stephens, and Joseph Addison Turner fiction. The most important contribution made by these writers was Simms's "The Sword and the Distaff" (later called *Woodcraft*), published in "semi-monthly supplements" from 28 February to 6 November 1852 and one of Simms's best novels.[1] Not only is *Woodcraft* significant intrinsically and as a contribution to the *Gazette*, but it is also a vital element in another aspect of the weekly's significance—its relationship to a Southern publishing firm. In December 1849 Richards had joined forces with Joseph Walker, a Charleston entrepreneur involved in the paper and printing business, established the publishing house of Richards and Walker, and moved the journal to Charleston in January 1850 with, as Richards once remarked, the purpose of publishing "Southern books and encourag[ing] Southern authors . . . after the fashion of Harper and Appleton."[2] The plan was also to publish periodicals such as Richards's *Gazette, The Southern Quarterly Review,** and *The Schoolfellow*, a juvenile monthly, and to print fiction in the *Gazette* that might subsequently appear in book form under the firm's imprint, but the house, after bringing out *The Golden Christmas* (1852), *The Sword and the Distaff* (1852), and a few other titles, "collapsed" when, as Richards expressed it many years later, a principal backer of the enterprise failed to put up the money he had promised.[3] Thus the *Gazette* was an integral part of the most important effort to date to establish a full-scale publishing enterprise and a literary center in a Southern city. Part of the significance of this attempt was that it failed, and a direct result of this failure was that Richards left Charleston for New York and Hayne purchased Richards's interest for a debt of $800 owed him and succeeded him as editor of the *Gazette* with the issue of 25 December 1852.[4] In January Hayne, in conjunction with William Y. Paxton, a partner in the firm that published the Charleston *Evening News*, merged the journal with the *Weekly News* and called it *The Weekly News and Southern Literary Gazette*, a title it retained until 1854.

The new editor immediately sought additional contributions from Simms and Timrod, and Timrod, in particular, contributed a number of poems, usually over his old nom de plume of Aglaus. Simms offered poems occasionally and avuncular advice. Hayne also procured work by such Northern writers as Richard Henry Stoddard and John T. Trowbridge and reprinted via the exchange poetry by Bryant, Poe, and Park Benjamin and prose by N. P. Willis, Poe, and Fredrika Bremer. Hayne himself provided poems, reviews, editorials, and two series of letters occasioned by his visits to Boston in the late summer and early fall of 1853 to arrange for the publication of his first collection of poems and again during the same season in 1854 to read and correct the proofs of the book. He encouraged local writers, at least one of whom, Essie B. Cheesborough, praised him years later for his "charming" treatment of contributions and his editorial "tolerance." "He gave us no advice," she observed after Hayne's death in 1886, "how we ought or ought not, to write. He was exceedingly tolerant of our opinions, and the language in which they were clothed. He never gave himself what may be termed, 'editorial airs.' "[5] Nevertheless, the weekly was not a financial success, and Hayne sold his interest in it in 1854. John Cunningham, editor of the *Evening News* and a staunch supporter of states' rights, became editor with the issue of 23 March. Hayne returned to his old post as assistant editor for another year, but though Timrod continued to contribute occasionally and Hayne's poems, reviews, and letters also appeared, the content and focus of the journal under Cunningham became more and more political, and Hayne closed his editorial association with the periodical on 22 March 1855. On 29 March, Jacob N. Cardozo, the founder of the *Evening News* and a well-known local journalist, became assistant editor. With Hayne's departure the literary content of the weekly gradually decreased until by 1856 there were few reviews or even brief mentions of new books or descriptions of new issues of magazines, and though original poetry still appeared from time to time, the poets were such unknowns as George M. Smith and W. Walmsley Bilby. Moreover, there were few original tales or sketches, and much of the fiction that was published was reprinted from the *New York Sunday Dispatch*. Thus the literary nature of the old *Gazette* changed and deteriorated, and the final stage of the printing history of the *Weekly News* clearly illustrates these transmutations.

Begun in Athens because of its proximity to the University of Georgia and moved to Charleston in order to seek the benefits associated with and the support inherent in a literary center, the *Gazette* had made a valiant attempt, especially under Richards and Hayne, to provide literary fare on a weekly basis. That it lasted for over eight years and that it printed work by leading Southern authors demonstrates its significance in the history of Southern periodicals. It was also briefly an integral part of a substantial publishing undertaking and provided one of its editors with the scope and experience he needed for the editing and nurturing of an even larger journalistic enterprise, the planning, establishment, supervision, and maintenance of *Russell's Magazine*,* the most important literary monthly published in Charleston. On the whole, the *Southern Literary Gazette* is intrinsically and historically the best literary weekly of its time and region.

### Notes

1. "The Sword and the Distaff" was scheduled to begin in the issue of 3 January 1852 but was delayed until February, and instead Simms's "The Golden Christmas" appeared on 10 January and in subsequent issues until "The Sword and the Distaff" began on 28 February and was concluded in the issue of 6 November.

2. See 2:3 (15 December 1849) for Richards's editorial concerning his partnership with Walker and the plans for moving the *Gazette* to Charleston. The firm's title changed to Walker and Richards in May 1850, and subsequently to Walker, Richards and Company in November 1851.

3. See Richards's letters of 21 July and 20 September 1886 to Mary Michel Hayne and William Hamilton Hayne, respectively, in the Paul Hamilton Hayne Papers, Perkins Library, Duke University. Richards maintained in his September letter that the venture failed because "Colonel [John E.] Carew of the 'Mercury' " did not provide his share of promised capital. These letters are quoted with the kind permission of Mattie U. Russell, Curator of Manuscripts.

4. In his valedictory to his readers in the issue of 18 December, Richards admitted that the "chief editorial management of the Gazette" had "devolved" upon Hayne for the previous six months. Though Hayne had contributed to the weekly as early as 1849, he did not join the staff until 21 May 1852. See Rayburn S. Moore, "Paul Hamilton Hayne as Editor, 1852–1860," *South Carolina Journals and Journalists*, ed. James B. Meriwether (Spartanburg, S.C.: The Reprint Company, 1975), pp. 92, 94.

5. "Recollections of Paul Hamilton Hayne," unpublished manuscript, Hayne Papers. Quoted in part in Rayburn S. Moore, *Paul Hamilton Hayne* (New York: Twayne Publishers, Inc., 1972), p. 17.

### Information Sources

BIBLIOGRAPHY:

Atwater, Katharine L., "Thomas Addison Richards." *Dictionary of American Biography*, vol. 15 (1935), 559–60.

Allibone, S. Austin. "William Carey Richards." *A Critical Dictionary of English Literature and British and American Authors*. 3 vols. Philadelphia: J. B. Lippincott Company, 1897. 2:1791.

Cardozo, Jacob N. *Reminiscences of Charleston*. Charleston: Joseph Walker, 1866.

Flanders, Bertram H. *Early Georgia Magazines: Literary Periodicals to 1865*. Athens: University of Georgia Press, 1944.

Hoole, William Stanley. *A Check-list and Finding-List of Charleston Periodicals 1732–1864*. Durham: Duke University Press, 1936.

King, William L. *The Newspaper Press of Charleston, S.C.* Charleston: Lucas & Richardson, 1882 (revised copyright edition).

Mitchell, Broadus, "Jacob Newton Cardozo." *Dictionary of American Biography*, vol. 3 (1929), pp. 486–87.

Moore, Rayburn S. "Paul Hamilton Hayne as Editor, 1852–1860." In *South Carolina Journals and Journalists*. Ed. James B. Meriwether. Spartanburg, S.C.: The Reprint Company, for the Southern Studies Program, University of South Carolina, 1975. Pp. 91–108.

INDEXES: None.

REPRINT EDITIONS: None.

LOCATION SOURCES: Complete runs: None. The University of Georgia Library has film of much of the run, but there are breaks and gaps in 1851, 1853, 1854, and 1856, and a number of supplements for 1852 are missing. Partial runs: Duke University, Georgia Historical Society, Library of Congress, University of Georgia, University of North Carolina, University of South Carolina, Yale University.

## Publication History

MAGAZINE TITLE AND TITLE CHANGES: *Southern Literary Gazette: An Illustrated Weekly Journal of Belles Lettres, Science and the Arts* [subtitle modified to *A Weekly Journal of Literature, and Art* on 4 November 1848], 13 May 1848–28 April 1849. *Richards' Weekly Gazette, A Southern Family Journal Devoted to Literature, the Arts and Sciences, and to General Intelligence*, 5 May 1849–27 April 1850. *Southern Literary Gazette: A Family Journal Devoted to Literature, the Arts and Sciences, and to General Intelligence* [subtitle changed to *A Journal of Thought and Event* on 3 January 1852], 4 May 1850–22 January 1853. *The Weekly News and Southern Literary Gazette: A Family Paper Devoted to Intelligence, Literature and the Arts*, 29 January 1853–4 March 1854. *The Weekly News and Gazette: A Family Paper Devoted to Intelligence, Literature and the Arts*, 11 March 1854–14 August 1856 [last known available issue].

VOLUME AND ISSUE DATA: Volumes 1–4, numbers 1–187, 13 May 1848–27 December 1851; new series, volumes 1–6, numbers 1–291, 3 January 1852–14 August 1856.

FREQUENCY OF PUBLICATION: Weekly (with semimonthly supplements in 1852).

PUBLISHERS: 13 May 1848–15 December 1849: William C. Richards, Athens, Georgia. 5 January 1850–27 April 1850: Richards & Walker, Charleston, S.C. 4 May 1850–(?) October 1851: Walker & Richards, Charleston. 1 November 1851–25 December 1852: Walker, Richards and Company, Charleston. 1 January 1853–18 March 1854: W. Y. Paxton, Charleston. 23 March 1854–8 November 1855: W. Y. Paxton and Company, Charleston. 15 November 1855–14 August 1856 (last available issue): John Cunningham and Company, Charleston.

EDITORS: William Carey Richards, 13 May 1848–18 December 1852 (assistant editors: D. L. Jacques, March 1849-April 1850; Edwin Heriot, October 1851-May 1852;

Paul Hamilton Hayne, May 1852-December 1852); Paul Hamilton Hayne, 1 January 1853–18 March 1854; John Cunningham, 23 March 1854–14 August 1856 (assistant editors: Paul Hamilton Hayne, 23 March 1854–22 March 1855; Jacob Newton Cardozo, 29 March 1855–14 August 1856).

*Rayburn S. Moore*

# THE SOUTHERN LITERARY JOURNAL

The *Southern Literary Journal* is the least known and least praised among Southern antebellum literary magazines. Its plight is due, in part, to the fact that on its founding in 1835 it was intended to be the successor to the *Southern Review*,* one of the most respected magazines in the antebellum period. The *Journal* fell short of its goal because it did not have as contributor or editor anyone of the scholarly reputation of Hugh Swinton Legaré. The *Southern Literary Messenger*,* which was destined to become the most acclaimed of all Southern magazines, emerged as its rival in the South largely because it had during this time the creative genius of Edgar Allan Poe as contributor and, for a brief and stormy time, as editor. The *Southern Literary Journal* had as proprietor and editor only Daniel K. Whitaker, an editor of poor reputation for success because he failed, not once, but four times.[1] It has also been remembered to Whitaker's detriment that William Gilmore Simms, his most important contributor, never liked him,[2] and that, though not a native Southerner, he quickly turned to ardent support of slavery.

Daniel K. Whitaker was a native of Massachusetts, born there in 1801. He was well educated, with an A.B. and M.A. from Harvard. He served briefly as a Congregational minister, and he edited for one year, 1822 to 1823, a religious magazine, the *Christian Philanthropist*. He moved South to Charleston in 1823; studied law with James L. Pettigru; married a Charleston lady of means, Mary H. Firth; and acquired thereby two large tracts of land and sixty-two slaves.[3] In September 1835 he added to his respectable positions as lawyer and slaveowner a third distinction as editor of a literary magazine.

For a man destined to fail Whitaker did the proper spade work for establishing a successful magazine. He secured the support of the prestigious Literary and Philosophical Society of South Carolina, and he received the promise of assistance from "the Faculty of at least five of our Southern colleges—from erudite members of the medical profession—from distinguished statesmen, eminent lawyers and learned clergymen through the South" (1:57). Whitaker had appraised the situation in Charleston well enough to know that, for lack of established writers, he must have the support of the professional men. Unlike Richmond there was in Charleston no Edgar Allan Poe to send contributions and to appear in person with a letter of recommendation or a Philip Pendleton Cooke to return home from Princeton with a desire to write. Although he came from the North,

Whitaker did not get from there the support that Thomas W. White was careful to cultivate for the *Messenger*.

This failure did not bother Whitaker because he intended to make do with what was available in the South. The *Southern Literary Journal* was a magazine "projected at the South, and chiefly supported by the citizens of the South. It will, at all times, breathe a Southern spirit, and sustain a strictly Southern character" (1:58). Southern editors who preceded and followed Whitaker also professed the regional mission of their magazines but with the intention of making distinctive contributions to American literature; Whitaker's goal was more clearly a magazine "strictly Southern." He recognized a problem in accomplishing this purpose that Simms and other editors were also to complain about: Southerners were "eminently a political people." Consequently, he dedicated the *Journal* to the proposition that the literary reputation of the South would someday match the political and appealed to those "who are no longer willing that the fair field of the South should be known only as a political debating ground" (1:60).

The *Southern Literary Journal* proved to be neither long-lived nor distinguished and emerged as a literary magazine that was quite willing politically to be part of a "debating ground" for stating the South's positions. It lasted only slightly more than three years, from September 1835 to December 1838. Whitaker did not stay around for the finish, announcing his resignation as editor in the January 1838 issue. He made only one important literary discovery, William Gilmore Simms, who was actually known but just not yet accepted in Charleston. Simms may not have liked Whitaker, but the *Journal* liked Simms, defending his early works and publishing everything that he offered. There was just one problem. The *Southern Literary Messenger* had also discovered Simms and promoted him so well that many readers thought after Poe left that Simms would be his successor as editor.[4] Next to publishing Simms, the *Journal* can be said to earn only the faint praise that it was "typical" and that in some ways it was not as bad as its utter neglect would imply. It showed an interest in the usual things that Southern antebellum magazines were interested in—essays on travel, articles on British and Continental (especially German) literature, articles on scientific topics like phrenology, and, above all, essays on history and politics. It included from its very first issues defenses of slavery without the fear of consequences in the North that worried the *Messenger*.

The *Journal*'s critical tastes were consistently conservative, reflecting Charleston tastes of the period, which meant they were more neoclassical and Scottish rhetorical judicial than representative of the new romantic sympathetic "appreciations" that were beginning to infect New York periodicals. A special target was uncritical puffery of works simply because they were of the nation or from the region. Southern editors were always tempted to believe this to be a Northern vice, since Southern works, unlike Northern, rarely received praise anywhere. The best critical essay published in the *Journal*, Simms's "American Criticism and Critics," a knowledgeable discussion of current periodical critical practices (2:393–404), came in the form of a letter supplementing an editorial on puffery

(2:312). In order to further his watchdog role of editor and judicial critic, Whitaker concluded each issue with editorial comment and critical advice for his readers, titled "From our Arm-Chair," in order to "rouse a spirit of inquiry, and improvement among our citizens" (1:57).

In his next issue Whitaker decreed for the benefit of potential contributors the kind of poetry he sought, "striking sentiments and harmonious numbers" (1:123), clearly the old rather than the new in literary taste, turn of the century rather than the new mode for the 1830s. Since "harmonious numbers" designated regular meter, he warned that "attention must be paid by our poets to their feet." Whitaker's exemplars were neoclassical, Pope and Dryden, with the addition of Byron, the romantic poet whose style Southern critics tended to like.

The *Southern Literary Journal* was even more positive about Byron than Legaré had been in the *Southern Review*, excusing the man as a genius far above the level of lesser men who slandered him, as well as praising the poet (3:19). Editorially, the same sympathy was expressed for the embattled James Fenimore Cooper, regretting that he stood little chance of receiving objective treatment because he "has erected himself into a public censor, scattered his opinions without fear of favor." Perhaps with empathy for anyone under attack in the North, the editorial concluded: "We are not disposed to join and swell the popular cry against him. . . . We believe that he has sinned on the right side" (n.s. 3:159). But when Cooper was reviewed, forgiveness did not extend to transgressions against unity. In a review of *Homeward Bound*, strong disapproval was expressed over interruptions of the narrative to allow Cooper opportunity to express his opinions on matters not clearly related to the plot (n.s. 4:307–11).

To Whitaker the novel was clearly the literary form for the age, and it was Simms who best exemplified what could be done with that form in American literature. His work satisfied the *Journal*'s characteristic neoclassical sense of propriety: he avoided "false views" of life (2:234), and his novel *The Partisan* adhered to historical truth (1:284–85). *Martin Faber* was generally attacked for dreariness and moralizing, but in the *Journal* it was defended in terms of *vraisemblance*: "The novelist or poet may imagine such beings and such events, beings and events which have no other existence than *in* his own imagination; but he must fit his fictitious creations to a strictly human standard, and not to one merely ideal" (1:40). And this was exactly what Simms did well. The moralizing was justified as "poetic justice," which demands in *Martin Faber* that "crime should draw after its natural consequence, misery" (1:42).

To explain to his readers what a critical review must do, Whitaker distinguished two ways of reading a novel, for "intellectual gratification," as his readers might read, and the way a critic must read, analytically and judicially. The critic takes "the whole frame work of the story to pieces and examines its parts separately. He ascertains whether or not they are all properly embraced in the leading design of the author and contribute to an imposing and important result" (3:331). Although the *Journal* was on record as sympathetic to Cooper, once again it could not accept bad form in a novel. *Wyandotte* was another disappointing work artistically, a "sort of hasty pudding, the ingredients tumbled in, and the whole miserably done up" (n.s. 1:573). Dickens's *Pickwick Papers* had received great acclaim in England, but to the *Journal* it was actually an overpraised work, "a creditable imitation" of the styles of Fielding and Smollett "without their wit" (n.s. 1:573). On the other hand, *Oliver Twist*, because it demonstrated "a connected and definite purpose" and paid more attention to the unities "than has been the peculiarity of his former productions," was judged Dickens's best work so far (n.s. 4:159). The *Southern Literary Journal* may not have published any major critical reviews, but it had, overall, less praise of sentimental or poor works than many other Southern periodicals because it consistently and rather rigorously applied its judicial standards.

The *Journal* played both sides of the question of the need for and feasibility of a distinctive American literature. The Rev. S. G. Bulfinch's proto-Whitman vision of a literature "of a manly, energetic, solid cast" in tune with "American temperament and character" was a feature of the first issue (1:1–6). The next year, James W. Simmons reported, without complete approval, that many Americans feel "they have no need of a separate literature," that "English literature is good enough at present; and may actually continue good enough for a century to come!" There was also a problem with subject matter: "We have nothing wherewithal to make it" (3:68).

Since Whitaker had not counted on Northern support for the *Southern Literary Journal*, he had no reservations about his magazine taking up the defense of slavery. In his inaugural editorial, he included the first of many proslavery comments. In the next issue he spelled out the advantages of a more aggressive defense on the part of the South. "The citizens of the South stand upon their right. They are able to protect their domestic institution by the shield of the Constitution, and could easily show, if they would condescend to do it, that slavery . . . has been practically recognized as lawful in every country" (1:128). Whitaker even extended his attack into the North, suggesting that in the factory system "there was more real slavery existing at the North than at the South" (1:63).

Whitaker was also quick to suggest ways that the South could maintain political and economic equity with the North. A special interest of the *Journal* was in building railroads linking the South and the West. In November the *Journal* printed a detailed report making a case for a financial investment that would produce political benefits:

> In every aspect of the question, it must be greatly beneficial to us to open a new channel of trade, and to find new customers in the people of the 'far West,' to give them a strong inducement for sustaining Southern institutions, thus binding together two quarters of the union by the endearing bond of mutual sympathies and common interests (1:168).

The history of antebellum Southern literary magazines is one of announced great expectations and early disillusionment. The *Southern Literary Journal* differed only in that its expectations were somewhat less, but even here there was disillusionment. A complaint about lethargy in supporting things Southern and about the Southern habit of buying things Northern appeared as early as September 1836 (3:3). By December Whitaker was attempting to improve a bleak situation for the *Journal* by promising changes for more popular appeal, more reviews, and more of "the lighter kinds of literature, those proper to a popular magazine or journal" (3:306). By June 1837 Whitaker began to doubt publicly the assumption that the leisure time expected from plantation life would result in a support of literature. Experience seemed to show that the growth of literature was compatible with the growth of city life.

In January 1838 the *Southern Literary Journal* printed an "Editor's Valedictory," in which Whitaker offered "private considerations as his reason for giving up the magazine (n.s. 4:75–76). Without him, with Bartholomew Rivers Carroll as the editor, the *Journal* survived only till the end of the year. More space was given to state and regional history, still more to political issues, and less to literature. New series on the lives of painters and autography, a popular interest of the time, appeared. It was to no avail. In the final issue, December 1838, Carroll announced: "The last attempt at reviving the dying energies of Southern literature has utterly failed. Out of a very large subscription list, scarce anything has been collected" (n.s. 4:47). It was by no means to be the last attempt; it was rather another early and short chapter in a long and consistent history of the failure of antebellum magazines, from the *Southern Review* to *Russell's Magazine*.*

## Notes

1. Whitaker edited the *Southern Literary Journal* (1835–1837); the *Southern Quarterly Review*\* (1842–1847), later edited more successfully by Simms; *Whitaker's Magazine* (1850–1853); and the *New Orleans Monthly Review* (1874–1876).

2. The charge was first made by William P. Trent, *William Gilmore Simms* (Boston: Houghton Mifflin, 1895).

3. Robert Bain, Joseph Flora, and Louis D. Rubin, Jr., *Southern Writers: A Biographical Directory* (Baton Rouge: Louisiana University Press, 1979), pp. 481–82.

4. Trent, p. 105.

## Information Sources

BIBLIOGRAPHY:

Bain, Robert, Joseph Flora, and Louis D. Rubin, Jr. *Southern Writers: A Biographical Directory*. Baton Rouge: Louisiana State University Press, 1979.

Hubbell, Jay Broadus. *The South in American Literature, 1607–1900*. Durham, N.C.: Duke University Press, 1954. Pp. 366–69.

Kane, Katherine Curnan. *William Gilmore Simms: A Biographical and Critical Study, 1806–1841*. Ph.D. diss., Yale University, 1943.

Mott, Frank Luther. *"The Southern Literary Journal." A History of American Magazines*. 4 vols. Cambridge, Mass.: Belknap Press of Harvard University Press, 1957. 1:664–65.

INDEXES: None.
REPRINT EDITIONS: American Periodicals: Series II, 1800–1850. University Microfilms, Ann Arbor. Reels 574–76. AMS Press, Inc., New York, 1967.
LOCATION SOURCES: Complete runs: Library of Congress, Chicago Public Library, University of North Carolina, University of South Carolina, Charleston Library Society.

## Publication History

MAGAZINE TITLE AND TITLE CHANGES: *The Southern Literary Journal and Monthly Magazine.*
VOLUME AND ISSUE DATA: Volume 1, September 1835-February 1836; volume 2, March-August 1836; volume 3, September 1836-February 1837; new series 1, March-August 1837 [new series 2, September-December 1837, omitted]; new series 3, January-June 1838; new series 4, July-December 1838.
FREQUENCY OF PUBLICATION: Monthly. Volume 2, September-December 1836, omitted.
PUBLISHERS: Daniel K. Whitaker, proprietor; J. S. Burges, printer.
EDITORS: Daniel K. Whitaker, September 1835-August 1837; Bartholomew R. Carroll, January-December 1838.

*Richard J. Calhoun*


# THE SOUTHERN LITERARY MESSENGER

In August 1834, Thomas Willis White, a Richmond, Virginia, printer, became founder, printer, and proprietor of the *Southern Literary Messenger: Devoted to Every Department of Literature and the Fine Arts*. A prospectus for the magazine had appeared in the *Daily National Intelligencer* (Washington, D.C.) on 15 May 1834 in which White proposed offering a wide and varying selection, pleasing not only to Southerners but also to the nation as a whole. White also pledged that "the best foreign, and all domestic reviews, and periodicals" would constantly be at the editorial department's disposal to insure interesting published matter.[1] White's practical knowledge as a printer, combined with other assets, created a sound base for success. His liberal view on national questions conciliated Northerners; his Southern loyalties strengthened much needed sectional support. Before the *Messenger* began no literary periodical had succeeded in the South. Although many had been attempted, Southerners tended to patronize Northern and English periodicals.

White's goal was to produce a first-rate magazine from the South, not necessarily about the South, that could rival the best Northern publications. He hoped to gain support from professional journalists, even if that meant going North, and he hoped to attract a Southern audience by publishing Southern writers, even if that meant printing what were often amateur "effusions." The August issue began White's campaign. The price for the magazine was five dollars per year. It was started as a bimonthly publication but changed to a monthly in November 1834. For the next thirty years various editors to varying degrees answered White's initial call to literary arms. During that time the *Messenger* published a wide range of material: travelogues, translations from foreign works, biography, history, addresses, essays, law cases, critical reviews, fiction, and poetry. Of the numerous authors it published, many for the first time, Edgar Allan Poe is today considered the most notable.

James E. Heath, a Virginia auditor and author of *Edge Hill* (1828), acted as editor, without pay, for the first nine numbers. Throughout White's close involvement with the magazine, he depended greatly on gratis contributions from others. The first number opened with excerpts from commendatory letters by Washington Irving, J. K. Paulding, J. Fenimore Cooper, J. P. Kennedy, John Quincy Adams, and Peter A. Browne. The letters, wrote White, "ought to stimulate the pride and genius of the south, and awaken from its long slumber the literary exertion of this portion of the country" (1:1). Heath's first editorial, "Southern Literature," followed the excerpts and initiated the *Messenger*'s friendly rivalry with the North. Heath exhorted Southerners by saying, "Hundreds of similar publications thrive and prosper north of the Potomac sustained . . . by the liberal hand of patronage. Shall not one be supported in the whole South? . . . Are we to be doomed forever to a kind of vassalage to our northern neighbors?" (1:1)

Heath and White immediately procured writings by Mrs. Lydia Sigourney (Connecticut) and R. H. Wilde (Georgia). Also, beginning with the first issue and continuing for many years, several prominent Virginians rendered assistance to White through their advice and numerous contributions. Thomas R. Dew of William and Mary College contributed several articles; the most notable was a serial on the characteristic differences between the sexes, which began with the May 1835 number. Lucian Minor's "Letters From New England" also profited White. Begun in the November 1834 number, the letters attempted to create fraternal feeling and mutual understanding between the people of the sections. As early as January 1835, however, Beverly Tucker, of the William and Mary law department, contributed "Notes to Blackstone's Commentaries," a defense of slavery (5:227–31). Heath dissented from Tucker's view, saying that "we regard [slavery] . . . as a great evil, which society, sooner or later, will remove or mitigate. . . . We must dissent from the opinion that it is either a moral or political benefit" (5:254). Nevertheless, a discussion began in which the *Messenger* was bound to take a leading part; the editorial department narrowed its view as Northern factions pressured the South to change.

Heath and White also wanted to maintain a work in accord with sound morals. In commenting on "The Doom," a revenge tale published in the January 1835 number, Heath told contributors that "the 'Messenger' shall not be a vehicle of sentiments at war with the interests of virtue and sound morals—the . . . solid foundation of human happiness" (5:255). The month before Heath had condemned William Beckford, author of *Vathek*, as "one whose heart was . . . polluted at its very core" (4:188). When discussing "Morella," the April 1835 issue criticized Poe for drinking too deeply at some "enchanted fountain, which seems to blend in his fancy the shadows of the tomb with the clouds and sunshine of life" (8:460).

Surprising, then, was the formal announcement of Poe as editor in "assistance" in the December 1835 issue. Before he became editor, however, Heath retired with the ninth number, Lucian Minor refused White's $800 per year offer to edit the magazine, and Edward V. Sparhawk was hired as editor from May through July. Shortly thereafter he became editor of the *Petersburg (Va.) Intelligencer*. For the August number Poe supplied all the critical notices, and the September issue included three tales and a poem by him. Obviously, Poe directly influenced the content of the *Messenger* before December. Before, during, and after his editorship, Poe contributed to the *Messenger* fourteen tales (eight for the first time), two segments of *Arthur Gordon Pym*, numerous poems (either original or revised), and more than one hundred critical reviews and articles. With each number during Poe's editorship (December 1835-January 1837), the reputation of the magazine increased, attributable more to his criticism than to his tales and poems. His critical contributions varied from ten to thirty pages in each number. However, except for Poe's brilliant critical department, the general make-up of the magazine did not drastically change.

Poe made a sensational debut with the December 1835 issue, including twenty-eight pages of critical reviews. The most memorable is Poe's blistering criticism of Theodore Fay's *Norman Leslie*. Needless to say, criticism of Fay, a New York editor and Knickerbocker, threatened White's delicate relations with the North and also dropped him into the fray that he had hoped to avoid. Seventeen pages of reviews and an eight-page supplement taken from newspapers' praise of the *Messenger* were included in the January 1836 issue. Poe could be trenchantly critical of his Southern brethren also, for he censured William Gilmore Simms's *The Partisan* in this issue. The April issue contained another supplement of praise and many reviews, one of which was "Drake-Halleck." In this review Poe expressed some of his ideas concerning American criticism and literature. He also defended his policy of fearless criticism. Actually, Poe's reviews were laudatory in most cases. In only three cases did he condemn works to the fires, all three by Northern writers. During Poe's editorship Paulding, P. P. Cooke, and Simms were also notable contributors.

In January 1837, White announced Poe's departure from the *Messenger*. White, very mindful of the direction he wanted his magazine to go, felt Poe to be too demonstrative and strenuous for his tastes. Although White listed himself as editor beginning with the March 1837 number, he was as ever dependent on old friends and advisers, Heath, Minor, Tucker, and later, in 1840, Lt. Matthew F. Maury, who wrote a great many military pieces for the *Messenger*. White rejoined several broken ties with the North, and from 1837 until 1843, the magazine printed contributions from writers such as James T. Fillas, Henry Tuckerman, Park Benjamin, and, for a short time, James Russell Lowell. On 19 January

1843 White died from a prolonged illness, having been struck by paralysis while in New York the previous September.

Maury struggled along as editor, acting from Washington, until Benjamin B. Minor, younger brother of Lucian, purchased the *Messenger* from White's estate in July 1843. The August 1843 issue announced the new editor and stated that "the usual variety of subjects will be maintained" (8:449). During his editorship, however, Minor tended to emphasize historical writings and a strong Southern bias. He stated, concerning slavery, that the *Messenger* was willing "to present the arguments in our favor in any proper form" (9:737). Also during Minor's editorship Campbell's history of Virginia, Smith's *True Relation*, and Conway Robinson's colonial history of Virginia were published or engaged to be published. Fiction did continue; among other writings, Beverly Tucker's third novel, *Gertrude*, appeared in 1844–1845, and Poe's "The Literary Life of Thingum Bob" came with the December 1844 issue.

In the fall of 1845, Minor bought Simms's magazine, and at his request changed the *Messenger*'s name to the *Southern and Western Literary Messenger and Review*. The new title headed the January 1846 issue. The association with Simms assisted Minor in acquiring poetry, almost exclusively from the South and West. The merger also loosened Minor's dependence on Northern patronage and allowed him to print material for the South and about the South first, before considering the North. The emphasis placed on Southerners' production of original work acted as a catalyst for regional writing.

John R. Thompson, a young lawyer more interested in literature than his studied profession, bought the *Messenger* from Minor and formally assumed editorial control in November 1847. In January the former title was restored. Thompson possessed a solid prose style, keen critical insight, and was a poet himself. He returned the *Messenger* to high literary standards. Where Minor failed to attract Northern contributors, Thompson succeeded. Besides Park Benjamin and others, he published Richard H. Stoddard and Thomas B. Aldrich. At the same time, he encouraged Southern contributions from Simms, Paul H. Hayne, Henry Timrod, Joseph G. Baldwin, John Esten Cooke, and others. Poe's "Marginalia" and "Rationale of Verse" were also published.

Thompson promoted an excellent national magazine until sectional animosities could no longer be avoided; the *Messenger* had to express its Southern loyalty. In January 1853, Thompson, faced with insufficient funds, sold the magazine to the printers, Macfarlane and Fergusson, although he remained as editor. From this time on the *Messenger* was committed to the Southern political cause. By 1854, the magazine had opened its columns to all articles dealing with the South, a policy that also pointed the way toward regional literature.

After thirteen years as editor, Thompson resigned, and George W. Bagby, an avowed secessionist, took over in June 1860. In December 1863, the printers sold the *Messenger* to Wedderburn and Alfriend, and in January 1864 Bagby resigned. Frank H. Alfriend worked as editor until June 1864 when the *Messenger*, the longest running antebellum Southern magazine, finally collapsed.

## Notes

1. Quoted in David K. Jackson, *The Contributors and Contributions to "The Southern Literary Messenger"* (Charlottesville, Va.: Historical Publishing Co., 1936), p. xii.

## Information Sources

BIBLIOGRAPHY:

Chielens, Edward E. *The Literary Journal in America to 1900: A Guide to Information Sources.* Detroit: Gale Research Co., 1975.

Gilmer, Gertrude C. *Checklist of Southern Periodicals to 1861.* Boston: F. W. Faxon Co., 1934.

Hughes, Robert M. "Inaccurate Numerations in *The Southern Literary Messenger.*" *William and Mary College Quarterly Historical Magazine* 9 (1929): 217.

Jackson, David K. *Poe and "The Southern Literary Messenger."* Richmond, Va.: Dietz Printing Co., 1934.

————. "Some Unpublished Letters of T. W. White to Lucian Minor." *Tyler's Quarterly Historical and Genealogical Magazine* 17 (1936):224–43; 18 (1936):32–49.

Jacobs, Robert D. "Campaign for a Southern Literature: *The Southern Literary Messenger.*" *The Southern Literary Journal* 2 (Fall 1969):66–93.

Kribbs, Jayne K., ed. *An Annotated Bibliography of American Literary Periodicals, 1741–1850.* Boston: G. K. Hall and Co., 1977.

Mims, Edwin. "Southern Magazines." *The South in the Building of a Nation.* 13 vols. Richmond, Va.: Southern Historical Publication Society, 1909. 7:437–69.

Minor, Benjamin Blake. *The Southern Literary Messenger, 1834–1864.* New York: Neale Publishing, 1905.

Mott, Frank Luther. *"The Southern Literary Messenger."* *A History of American Magazines, 1741–1850.* Cambridge, Mass.: Harvard University Press, 1938. Pp. 629–57.

Rogers, Edward R. *Four Southern Magazines.* Charlottesville, Va.: University of Virginia Press, 1902.

Tucker, Edward L. " 'A Rash and Perilous Enterprise': *The Southern Literary Messenger* and the Men Who Made It." *Virginia Cavalcade* 21 (Summer 1971):14–21.

INDEXES: Jackson, David K., comp. *The Contributors and Contributions to "The Southern Literary Messenger".* Charlottesville, Va.: Historical Publishing Co., 1936.

REPRINT EDITIONS: American Periodicals: Series II, 1800–1850. University Microfilms, Ann Arbor. Reels 438–47. AMS Press, Inc., New York, 1965.

LOCATION SOURCES: Widely available.

## Publication History

MAGAZINE TITLE AND TITLE CHANGES: *The Southern Literary Messenger: Devoted to Every Department of Literature and the Fine Arts*, August 1834-December 1845. *The Southern and Western Literary Messenger and Review: Devoted to Every Department of Literature and the Fine Arts*, January 1846-December 1847. *The Southern Literary Messenger: Devoted to Every Department of Literature and the Fine Arts*, January 1848–1856. *The Southern Literary Messenger: Devoted to Literature, Science, and Art*, 1856-June 1864.

VOLUME AND ISSUE DATA: Volume 1, August, October-December 1834-January-
    September 1835 (September 1834, October-November 1835 omitted); volume 2,
    December 1835-January-November 1836 (December 1836 omitted); volumes 3–
    21, 1837–1855 regular annual volumes (February, August, October 1840 omitted);
    preceding numbers were doubled (May-June 1841, single number); volumes 22–
    33 (New Series 1–12) 1856–1861, regular semiannual volumes (October-Novem-
    ber 1851, single issue); volume 34 (title page error says 36), 1862; volume 35
    (title page error says 37), November-December 1863, combined; volume 36 (title
    page error says 38), January-June 1864.
FREQUENCY OF PUBLICATION: Monthly.
PUBLISHERS: August 1834-July 1843: T. W. White. August 1843-October 1847: B. B.
    Minor. November 1847-December 1852: John R. Thompson. January 1853-De-
    cember 1863: Macfarlane and Fergusson. January 1864-June 1864: Wedderburn
    and Alfriend.
EDITORS: James E. Heath, August 1834-May 1835; Edward V. Sparhawk, May-July
    1835; T. W. White and others, August-September 1835; Edgar A. Poe, December
    1835-January 1837; White and others, February 1837-December 1839 (?); White
    and Matthew F. Maury, January 1840 (?)-September 1842; Matthew F. Maury,
    October 1842-July 1843; B. B. Minor, August 1843-October 1847; John R.
    Thompson, November 1847-May 1860; George W. Bagby, June 1860-January
    1864; Frank H. Alfriend, February 1864-June 1864.

*David T. Dodd, II*

# THE SOUTHERN MAGAZINE

A study of the *Southern Magazine* would be incomplete without mention of its
two forerunners—the *Richmond Eclectic* and the *New Eclectic Magazine*. The
*Richmond Eclectic*, which announced itself as "A Monthly Magazine of Foreign
Literature, Religious and Secular," was established in Richmond in November
1866 by two Presbyterian ministers, Moses Drury Hoge and William Brown.
True to its name, the *Richmond Eclectic* published only a small amount of original
material, confined for the most part to editorial comments and two sections,
"Books Lately Published or Forthcoming" and "Science and Art." Most of the
articles in this ninety-six page, two-column, octavo journal were selected from
standard British magazines, including *Blackwood's* and *Fraser's*. Included were
biographical sketches, travel accounts, religious or theological essays, essays on
literary subjects, and articles pertaining to science, art, and woman suffrage.
Only a few translations, literary criticisms, or poems were published.

   In December 1867, Brown disposed of his interest in the *Richmond Eclectic*,
and Hoge formed a partnership with a Baltimorean, Lawrence Turnbull, "a
gentleman," wrote Hoge, "who brings to the conduct of the Magazine, energy,
fine literary culture, practical acquaintance with business, and, what I never
possessed—capital" (3:191). The *Richmond Eclectic* was transplanted to Baltimore, where it was published in a new series under the title *New Eclectic*. The

names of Lawrence Turnbull and Fridge Murdoch now appeared as editors and proprietors. The title was changed in January 1869 to the *New Eclectic Magazine*, and some time within the year William Hand Browne joined the staff as coeditor. In April 1869, the *Land We Love* united with the *New Eclectic Magazine*, and General D. H. Hill's name was printed on the outside cover from April 1869 through February 1870 as a partner and coeditor. In December 1869, the *New Eclectic Magazine* became the official organ of the Southern Historical Society (6:118–19). A number of engravings of politicians and authors now appeared.

Reprints in the *New Eclectic Magazine* included poetry, fiction, translations, biographical sketches, scientific articles, literary criticism, and essays on art. Since the *New Eclectic Magazine* contained more pages per issue than the *Richmond Eclectic*, it naturally increased its range of authors and magazines as sources of material. For example, included were the poems "The Rosebuds" by Henry Timrod (4:631–32) and "She Came and Went" by James Russell Lowell (4:375), and fiction by Charles Dickens ("The Mystery of Edwin Drood" [6:603–21; 7:674–702]) and Bret Harte ("The Luck of Roaring Camp" [4:322–29]). From the *Round Table*\* were reprinted the biographical sketch "Gioacchino Rossini" (4:93–96) and the critical article "Democracy, Carlyle, and Whitman" (1:190–94).

There were no original articles published in volumes 1 and 2 of the *New Eclectic*, but beginning with volume 3 there were four essays; and thereafter the original contributions progressively increased. Original poetry was published chiefly in volumes 5 through 7. Some of the better poems were written by such well-known Southern authors as William Gilmore Simms, Paul Hamilton Hayne, John R. Thompson, Sidney Lanier, John Esten Cooke, Margaret J. Preston, and Basil L. Gildersleeve. These included Hayne's "The Wife of Brittany" (7:571–90), Lanier's "Nirvana" (6:294–96), Preston's "Gone Forward" (7:763), and Thompson's "Poem. Read before the Society of Alumni of the University of Virginia, at the Annual Meeting, July 1, 1869" (5:328–36). "Nirvana," an Oriental imaginative piece, is one of Lanier's earliest and best poems. "Gone Forward" is a tribute to General Robert E. Lee by one who had known him as a friend and neighbor.

Richard Malcolm Johnston (as "Philemon Perch") contributed the best original fiction that the *New Eclectic Magazine* printed. His *Dukesborough Tales*, nine realistic humorous sketches, began to appear in November 1869 and were concluded in the *Southern Magazine* in August 1872. In his *Autobiography* the former Georgian tells how important these sketches were in his development as a writer of local color short stories.

> After my removal to Baltimore [in June 1867, states Johnston], Mr. Henry C. Turnbull, Jr., between whom and myself arose a very cordial friendship, beginning publication of *The Southern Magazine*, asked me to allow him to print these stories, which had appeared in a Georgia journal and were not copyrighted. I consented to do so, supposing they were to be my last

essays on that line of endeavor. They were so well received that I began to write others, partly to assist my friend in his enterprise and partly to subdue as far as possible the feeling of homesickness for my native region. It never occurred to me that they were of any sort of value.[1]

The Turnbull brothers brought out an edition of *Dukesborough Tales* in 1871 and again in 1874. A copy came into the hands of Henry M. Alden, who expressed surprise that the author had not been paid for his stories. Alden then paid Johnston for some of his newer tales and printed them in *Harper's Monthly Magazine.** The firm of Harper & Brothers brought out in 1883 an enlarged edition of *Dukesborough Tales* and gave it a fairly wide circulation.

The literary essays and reviews were especially good features of the *New Eclectic Magazine*. William Hand Browne was the most prolific contributor of literary criticism. In separate reviews and editorial sections he advocated a just criticism of all books. His treatment of Northern magazines was generally fair, and he would not withhold adverse criticism of Southern literary magazines if he thought they deserved it. For example, Browne stated, "Though we not unfrequently find brilliant and able papers in our own magazines, we should say their general literary standard was decidedly inferior to that of the prominent Northern monthlies" (3:380). In addition to the verse, literary essays, and some war articles, the *New Eclectic Magazine* published a number of interesting historical essays written by Browne, John Esten Cooke, and others. However, contemporary subjects—travel, education, the Negro, women's rights, and science and religion—were given a large share of attention.

In December 1870, Turnbull withdrew as an editor. The magazine under the new title the *Southern Magazine*, owned by Browne, Murdoch, and William S. Hill, was given over almost completely to printing original contributions by Southern authors. Most of the South's professional authors wrote for the magazine during the years 1871 through 1875. As sole editor, Browne dropped the eclectic feature almost entirely, printing occasionally a few articles from the *Spectator*, *Saturday Review*, and *Virginia Educational Journal*. The first issue was given over largely to memorial addresses that eulogized the late General Robert E. Lee.

Verse was a regular feature of the *Southern Magazine*, much of it written by poets who contributed to the *New Eclectic Magazine*. Among the better poems were Preston's "The Shade of the Trees" (n.s. 3:695), Hayne's "Frida and Her Poet. A Scandinavian Legend" (n.s. 5:661–64), and Sidney and Clifford Lanier's "A Sea-shore Grave" (n.s. 2:127). Henry Timrod's "Why Silent?" (n.s. 4:766) and "Lines to R. L." (n.s. 4:766) were sent to the periodical by Hayne after Timrod's death. Fiction in the *Southern Magazine* was confined largely to serials, most of which have little value. In addition to Johnston's *Dukesborough Tales*, one other short story deserves mention. "Witched" (15:565–72), by "Jennie Woodville" (Mrs. Jennie Stabler), employs effectively Negro dialect spoken by an old plantation "mammy."

The bulk of the literary criticism in this magazine is much better than its poetry. The critical attempts of women are not very successful, though their essays were given prominent space beside, for example, such a notable contribution as Hayne's "Literature at the South. The Fungous School" (14:651–55). With penetrating insight Hayne criticized women scribblers—the novelists in particular—and pointed out the folly of indiscriminately praising their works. Such criticism, he felt, merely destroyed rather than helped to develop a Southern literature. Equally important with other essays in the *Southern Magazine* are a number of articles that illustrate Southern thinking on a variety of topics. John Esten Cooke's "The West Twenty Years Ago" (11:468–75) and Sidney Lanier's "San Antonio de Bexar" (13:83–99, 138–52) represent a large group of semi-historical pieces. George W. Bagby's humorous series entitled "A History uv the Waw" (8:70–72, 613–16) and Edwin De Leon's "Ruin and Reconstruction of the Southern States" (14:17–41, 453–82) dealt with more contemporary material. Other writers chose to discuss topics of current interest, including Herbert Barnes's "The Scalawag" (15:302–307) and the Reverend Robert L. Dabney's "Women's Rights Women" (8:322–34).

If the seventeen volumes of the *Southern Magazine* and its predecessors are compared with other postbellum literary magazines published in the South, one must agree with Hayne, who thought that it came "nearest to the right ideal standard" of a "really thoughtful and comprehensive 'organ' of our intellectual progress and learning."[2] During the eight years of its publication, the *Southern Magazine* drew to its pages contributions from the largest number of the South's best authors. The weakness in fiction was offset by much better literary criticism and poetry. Some of the literary essays written by James A. Harrison, Hayne, C. Woodward Hutson, Lanier, and Browne compare favorably with similar material in contemporary Northern magazines. Lanier's review of "Paul H. Hayne's Poetry" (16:40–48), a belated review of *Legends and Lyrics* (1872), is a very good evaluation of some of Hayne's poems. Many of the travel and historical essays are still interesting reading. Excluding a political series by P. C. Centz of London entitled "Sovereignty in the United States" (8:479–87; 10:641–53), the material is not as heavy as what one finds in the *Southern Review\** (1867–1879). It should be remembered, too, that the *Southern Magazine* was important in encouraging Sidney Lanier, Richard Malcolm Johnston, and Lizette Woodworth Reese. Any future biographical study of William Hand Browne will be incomplete without a close reading of his numerous contributions to this periodical. One might say that the *Southern Magazine* more than any other magazine came nearest to filling the vacancy left by the *Southern Literary Messenger.\**

### Notes

1. *Autobiography of Col. Richard Malcolm Johnston*, 2nd ed. (Washington, D.C.: The Neale Company, 1901), pp. 71–72.

2. Letter to Margaret J. Preston, 16 January 1872 (original in Duke University Library).

## Information Sources

BIBLIOGRAPHY:

Atchison, Ray Morris. "Southern Literary Magazines, 1865–1887." Ph.D. diss., Duke University, 1956.

Hubbell, Jay B. *The South in American Literature, 1607–1900*. Durham, N.C.: Duke University Press, 1954.

Mott, Frank Luther. *A History of American Magazines*. 4 vols. Cambridge, Mass.: Belknap Press of Harvard University Press, 1957. 3:46–47.

INDEXES: None.

REPRINT EDITIONS: None.

LOCATION SOURCES: Widely available.

## Publication History

MAGAZINE TITLE AND TITLE CHANGES: *The Richmond Eclectic, A Monthly Magazine of Foreign Literature, Religious and Secular*, November 1866-December 1867. *The New Eclectic, A Monthly Magazine of Select Literature*, January-December 1868. *The New Eclectic Magazine, A Magazine of Selected Foreign and American Literature*, April 1869-December 1870. *Southern Magazine*, January 1871-December 1875.

VOLUME AND ISSUE DATA: Volumes 1–3, November 1866-December 1867; volumes 1–17, January 1868-December 1875 (new series, volumes 1–9), January 1871-December 1875.

FREQUENCY OF PUBLICATION: Monthly.

PUBLISHERS: January 1868-December 1870: Lawrence Turnbull and Fridge Murdoch, Baltimore. January 1871-December 1875: William Hand Browne, Fridge Murdoch, and William S. Hill, Baltimore.

EDITORS: Moses Drury Hoge and William Brown, November 1866-December 1867; Lawrence Turnbull and Fridge Murdoch, January 1868-December 1870; William Hand Browne, coeditor, 1869–1870; General D. H. Hill, coeditor, April 1869-February(?) 1870; William Hand Browne, 1871–1875.

*Ray M. Atchison*


# THE SOUTHERN QUARTERLY REVIEW

The *Southern Quarterly Review* made clear from its opening issue of January 1842 that it intended to be the successor to the *Southern Review** (1828–1832), an erudite magazine that had espoused the Southern cause and had folded in February 1832 after four financially troubled years. The initial article in the first number praised the *Southern Review* as the best of its time, claiming that "the Southern part of the American confederacy is not destitute of scholars" (1:39). Daniel K. Whitaker, first editor of the *Southern Quarterly Review*, issued volume 1 from New Orleans with his cousin and partner James Ritchie.[1] The magazine started with 1,600 subscribers at $10 per year.[2] After the first volume Whitaker moved his journal to Charleston, home of the late *Southern Review* and publishing center of the South. With this move George Frederick Holmes assumed Ritchie's role.[3] Although Whitaker was assisted by James D. B. De Bow, especially during Whitaker's absence, Whitaker never considered him the junior editor as De Bow had claimed. After this conflict between the two men, De Bow quit the *Southern Quarterly* and began his own magazine.[4]

The editorial stance of the *Southern Quarterly Review*, which has been called "ardently sectional beyond anything known to the periodicals of other regions,"[5] was made clear in the opening number. The magazine was, in large measure, to be a response to Northern periodicals that promulgated Northern values. Thus, the *Review* would promote Southern causes such as states' rights and slavery, as well as "the cause of learning, arts, and literature" (1:63). Whitaker further announced that his magazine would avoid religious debate, accepting religious articles only when they dealt with religion in a strictly literary manner. Although the new quarterly was well received by the Charleston press, which also saw it as a long-awaited revival of the *Southern Review*, the *Charleston Courier* criticized Whitaker for representing only one Southern view rather than speaking for the entire South. Eventually Whitaker had to modify his policy somewhat to avoid alienating desperately needed subscribers.[6] Finally, however, financial difficulties, his Northern background, and an article in volume 10 criticizing John Calhoun caused Whitaker to relinquish his post.

The editorship passed to J. Milton Clapp in January 1847 and then to William Gilmore Simms in April 1849. Although promised a salary of $1,000 a year, Simms took over the *Southern Quarterly* because of his love for the South; he was familiar enough with the perils of editorship to realize he would not collect his salary very often. As the publisher hoped, Simms managed to rescue the periodical from the brink of ruin. He added about fifty new contributors, partly by promising the best of them $1.00 per page, whereupon the articles improved.

Finally, the usual pressures as well as the editorial interference of the new publisher, Charles Mortimer, a Northerner, caused Simms to resign at the end of 1854. Because of an epidemic in Charleston, Mortimer took the magazine to Columbia, South Carolina. The new publisher himself edited the issue for January 1855, which was delayed because of a fire at the Columbia location. He hired William W. Bunwell as editor for the March and October issues, which were actually published in Baltimore, in spite of their Charleston imprint.[7] Though Mortimer had been driven from Charleston and Columbia by disasters, he was criticized for moving the magazine from South Carolina. At the end of 1855, Mortimer's brief stint as publisher of the *Southern Quarterly Review* had ended, and the new publisher, Edward H. Britton & Company, chose James H. Thornwell as editor. Only this last editor altered editorial policy by seriously considering religious views.[8]

Numerous important Southerners contributed to the *Review*. Among them were secessionist Beverley Tucker, magazinist James D. B. De Bow, Major M.C.M. Hammond, Col. and Mrs. D. J. McCord, William H. Trescot, Dr. J. C. Nott, D. F. Jamison, Mitchell King, and ex-Governor Hammond of South Carolina.

Some non-Southerners also contributed: M. F. Maury, Brantz Mayer, Professor George Frederick Holmes, Henry T. Tuckerman, and William A. Jones.[9] One of the most important and prolific contributors, especially during his editorship, was Simms, who was so influential that he has been called "the Dr. Johnson of Southern letters."[10] He wrote many of the longer articles and, while editor, all of the reviews in the "Critical Notices."

Like its predecessor, the *Southern Quarterly* was a review rather than a magazine. Yet both magazines used books largely as an excuse for the contributors to express their own ideas on the subjects. Simms admitted that most of the subscribers would not have read the book being considered and therefore the reviewer should discuss the topic rather than criticize the work. One contributor had not even read the book he was reviewing because it had not yet been published.[11]

Although the magazine carried rather dull articles on such subjects as "Refrigeration and Ventilation of Cities," it also discussed far more of the finer literary figures of the day, both in its longer articles and especially in the shorter "Critical Notices" that concluded each number, than had the *Southern Review*. British writers such as Dickens, Byron, Coleridge, Macaulay, Browning, Tennyson, Wordsworth, and Carlyle were considered, as were an impressive number of newly emerging American figures, few of them Southerners. Longfellow was highly praised in the first volume. Hawthorne, who received numerous favorable reviews, was correctly estimated as destined for greatness. Other Americans did not receive such kind treatment. Of Poe's "The Raven" the reviewer concluded, "It has mistaken the new for the original, the unintelligible for the profound, and the ridiculous for the sublime" (14:119). In volume 4 Whittier's poetry is pronounced mediocre, and Cooper's *Wyandotte* is called "unquestionably one of the feeblest books that has ever issued from Mr. Cooper's pen" (4:515). Transcendentalism came under attack in the South, as it often did elsewhere, as too nebulous. One reviewer said Emerson, "after borrowing his philosophy from others, . . . has borrowed his poetry from his philosophy" (11:493). Simms gave Melville's writing considerable attention in "Critical Notices." He liked *Mardi*, despite its fantastical allegory, and felt it revealed more of Melville's "real powers in reserve" (17:260) than *Redburn*, which he found dull and faulty in characterization. He praised *White-Jacket* as a social treatise, not a story. Simms considered *Moby-Dick* "sad stuff, dull and dreary, or ridiculous," and called Ahab "a monstrous bore" (21:262). *Pierre* convinced Simms that both the main character and the author ought to be locked up in a mental institution.

A large part of the *Southern Quarterly Review* was devoted to political issues, especially slavery. Ironically, the first editor, Whitaker, a Northerner by birth, had denounced slavery while living in New England in 1822 in the *Christian Philanthropist*. By the time he became editor of the *Southern Quarterly Review* in 1842, however, he had changed his views, perhaps because of his marriage to a plantation- and slave-owning widow.[12] Whereas the earlier *Southern Review*, though defending the South's right to own slaves, had admitted that the practice was attended by considerable evil, the *Southern Quarterly Review* transformed slavery into a virtue. The opening number called slavery "a great physical good, and a great moral and political right" (1:54). To the charge that slavery was a sin and a crime, the next volume responded that it wasn't a sin because "it is not prohibited by Divine Revelation." Furthermore, the issue continued, since a sin or crime is by definition an act, and slavery is "an existing relation or condition of society," calling slavery a sin or a crime "is an utter abuse of language" (2:151).

Once Simms took over, the *Review* became increasingly vehement in its defense of slavery. Fourteen of the twenty-six issues that he edited contained at least one article on slavery.[13] The subject even tinged the literary reviews. Although Simms generally liked Melville's *Mardi*, he said the negative picture painted of Calhoun as a slave driver "spoils every thing to a Southern reader" (16:260–61). Simms used *White-Jacket* as evidence that the slaveholders of Europe and the free states were more cruel in their use of the whip than the Southerner, but he attacked the book's criticism of Southern slave owners.

He considered it a particularly clever stroke to let a Southern woman, Louisa S. McCord, respond to the Northern woman Harriet Beecher Stowe in a review of *Uncle Tom's Cabin*. Mrs. McCord's review concluded with this rather startling statement: "Christian slavery, in its full development, free from the fretting annoyance and galling bitterness of abolition interference, is the brightest sunbeam which Omniscience has destined for his [the Negro's] existence" (23:120).

The *Southern Quarterly Review* was finally forced to cease publication for many of the same reasons that so many other magazines in the South and elsewhere had failed—money. In the "Critical Notices" at the end of volume 9, the editor said that although he had 2,000 subscribers, the *Review* needed to collect the $10,000 many of them collectively owed. By the beginning of volume 15, the subscribers owed more than $13,000.

Other problems seemed more peculiar to the South. Because of the scattered Southern population, it was difficult to find reliable agents to collect the money owed, and distant subscribers often failed to receive their copies. Further, Southern mills were not a reliable source of paper, nor was it easy to get shipments from the North.[14] Because of the lack of funds to hire proofreaders, rampant typographical errors discouraged contributors.[15] Another problem was the Southerner's general lack of interest in literature and learning, as well as a preference for Northern journals. Even devoted Southerner Simms wanted to move North because "a literary man, residing in the South, may be likened to the blooded horse locked up in the stable, and miles away from the Course, at the moment when his rivals are at the starting post."[16] Finally, as states began to secede and war became more likely, Southerners had to turn their attention to more practical matters.

Yet despite all these difficulties, only two issues in fifteen years failed to appear: January 1849 and January 1856. And to make up for the missing issue in 1849, Simms produced an extra number in September 1850.[17] That the *Southern Quarterly Review* survived as long as it did can be attributed only to the dedication and personal sacrifice in time and money of its many publishers and editors. Had it not been for them, the South would not have been represented by one of the most important and influential periodicals to appear in this region before the war.

## Notes

1. William M. Moss, "Vindicator of Southern Intellect and Institutions: The *Southern Quarterly Review*," *The Southern Literary Journal* 13 (Fall 1980):72.

2. Moss, p. 74.

3. Moss, p. 82.

4. Moss, p. 83. Ottis Clark Skipper, *J. D. B. De Bow: Magazinist of the Old South* (Athens: University of Georgia Press, 1958), p. 14.

5. Frank Luther Mott, *A History of American Magazines*, 4 vols. (Cambridge, Mass.: Belknap Press of Harvard Univ. Press, 1957), 2:110. Mott also applied this comment to the *Southern Literary Messenger*\*, *Russell's Magazine*\*, and *De Bow's Review*.

6. Moss, pp. 74–78.

7. Moss, pp. 104–5.

8. Moss, p. 106.

9. William P. Trent, *William Gilmore Simms* (Boston: 1892; rpt., New York: Greenwood, 1969), pp. 164–65.

10. Edward Reinhold Rogers, "Four Southern Magazines" (Ph.D. diss., University of Virginia, 1902), p. 91.

11. Moss, p. 96.

12. Moss, pp. 72–73.

13. Jon L. Wakelyn, *The Politics of a Literary Man: William Gilmore Simms* (Westport, Conn.: Greenwood, 1973), p. 192.

14. These problems are discussed extensively in Susan B. Riley's "The Hazards of Periodical Publishing in the South during the Nineteenth Century," *Tennessee Historical Quarterly* 21 (December 1962):365–76.

15. Moss, p. 98.

16. Jay B. Hubbell, *The South in American Literature: 1607–1900* (Durham: Duke University Press, 1954), p. 579.

17. Moss, p. 99.

## Information Sources

BIBLIOGRAPHY:

Hubbell, Jay B. *The South in American Literature: 1607–1900*. Durham: Duke University Press, 1954.

————. "Southern Magazines," in *Culture in the South*. Ed. W. T. Couch. Chapel Hill: University of North Carolina Press, 1934. Pp. 159–82.

Moss, William M. "Vindicator of Southern Intellect and Institutions: The *Southern Quarterly Review*." *The Southern Literary Journal* 13 (Fall 1980):72–108.

Mott, Frank Luther. "The *Southern Quarterly Review*," in *A History of American Magazines*. 4 vols. Cambridge, Mass.: Belknap Press of Harvard Univ. Press, 1957. 1:721–27.

Riley, Susan B. "The Hazards of Periodical Publishing in the South during the Nineteenth Century." *Tennessee Historical Quarterly* 21 (December 1962):365–76.

Rogers, Edward Reinhold. "Four Southern Magazines". Ph.D. diss., University of
    Virginia, 1902.
Skipper, Ottis Clark. *J. D. B. De Bow: Magazinist of the Old South.* Athens: University
    of Georgia Press, 1958.
Trent, William P. *William Gilmore Simms.* Boston, 1892; rpt., New York: Greenwood,
    1969.
Wakelyn, Jon L. *The Politics of a Literary Man: William Gilmore Simms.* Westport,
    Conn.: Greenwood, 1973.
INDEXES: None.
REPRINT EDITIONS: American Periodicals: Series II, 1800–1850. University Micro-
    films, Ann Arbor. Reels 684–87. AMS Press, Inc., New York, 1965–1967.
LOCATION SOURCES: Widely available.

## Publication History

MAGAZINE TITLE AND TITLE CHANGES: *The Southern Quarterly Review.*
VOLUME AND ISSUE DATA: Volumes 1–16, nos. 1–32, January 1842-January 1850
    (January 1849 is omitted). New series, volumes 1–12, nos. 1–24 [volumes 17–
    28], April 1850-October 1855. New new series, volumes 1–2, nos. 1–3 [volumes
    29–30], April 1856-February 1857.
FREQUENCY OF PUBLICATION: Quarterly.
PUBLISHERS: January 1842-January 1847: Daniel K. Whitaker, New Orleans in 1842,
    thereafter in Charleston. January 1847-February 1850: Burges and James, Charleston.
    April 1850-October 1852: Walker and Richards, Charleston. January-October 1853:
    Walker and Burkes, Charleston. November 1853-October 1855: C. Mortimer,
    Charleston. April 1856-January 1857: Edward H. Britton & Co., Columbia, S.C.
EDITORS: Daniel K. Whitaker, January 1842-January 1847; J. Milton Clapp, February
    1847-December 1848; William Gilmore Simms, April 1849-October 1854; Charles
    Mortimer, January 1855; William W. Bunwell, March 1855-October 1855; James
    H. Thornwell, April 1856-February 1857.

*Janice L. Edens*

# THE SOUTHERN REVIEW (1828–1832)

Generally acknowledged in its own day and in ours as one of the best antebellum
Southern periodicals, the *Southern Review* began its four-year life in February
1828 in Charleston, which soon became the South's literary center. One of the
first Southern magazines, it was founded by Stephen Elliott, Sr., the sixty-seven-
year-old president of the South Carolina State Bank, and modeled on British
quarterlies such as the *Edinburgh Review.*

Its purpose, as stated in a prospectus published in the Charleston press during
the fall of 1827, had three main objects. The first was to defend the South against
its detractors and prove that the intellect and the institutions of the Southern
states were worthy of respect: "It shall be among our first objects to vindicate
the rights and privileges, the character of the Southern States, to arrest, if
possible, the current which has been directed so steadily against our country

generally, and the South in particular; and to offer to our fellow citizens one Journal which they may read without finding themselves the objects of perpetual sarcasm, or of affected commiseration."[1] The magazine was also intended to be a watchdog over the federal government and its attempts, according to the Southern view, to extend its powers beyond those granted by the Constitution. Though the prospectus vowed that the *Southern Review* would be impartial in its judgment of constitutional issues, it generally supported a states' rights position. The third object was to consider literature, science, agriculture, "the improvements of the age," and "national and local concerns."[2]

Elliott was able to secure some of South Carolina's best scholars as contributors to the journal, the foremost being Hugh Swinton Legaré, a man of high scholarly standards who knew the classics well and revered them highly. In the first issue of the *Southern Review*, he wrote the lead article, "Classical Learning," which was to set the tone for the magazine as a whole and Legaré's contributions in particular. Here he defended the study of the classics against the attack of Thomas Grimké, who advocated a scientific and practical education. Legaré brought to the familiar argument his great breadth of learning as well as a heavy, tedious style. In addition to numerous articles on the classics, Legaré, who was later to become attorney general of the United States, wrote on law and literature. Throughout the life of the *Southern Review*, Legaré contributed profusely, especially once he became editor in 1830. In the last issue, in fact, he wrote five of the eight articles.[3]

The second most important contributor was Stephen Elliott, Sr., the editor. Nineteen articles from the *Review* have been identified as his work,[4] most of them concerned with science and history. Dr. Robert Henry and Dr. Thomas Cooper were also significant contributors. Others included Robert Y. Hayne, Robert Henry, Professor T. C. Wallace, Josiah C. Nott, Thomas S. Grimké, David J. McCord, J. L. Petigru, Samuel Prioleau, Dr. S. H. Dickson, and Robert J. Turnbull.[5] Even Noah Webster provided one piece, a response to an article pointing out errors in his dictionary's etymology.

When Stephen Elliott, Sr., died in March 1830, his son briefly took over, although the exact dates of the younger Elliott's tenure as editor are uncertain. Next the editorship passed to Legaré, the magazine's chief contributor, probably also in 1830. Editorial policy remained essentially unaltered throughout these changes.

The *Southern Review* contained, as its name implies, reviews rather than original literary compositions, but more often than not the books being reviewed provided a stepping-stone to the reviewer's own ideas about the subject at hand. The reviewer usually summarized the book (or sometimes the speech) at great length, often with long quotations, and expressed his own opinions throughout. The subject matter treated was broad, from the purely intellectual articles on classical learning, mathematics, languages, and the fine arts to extremely practical discussions of agricultural methods and malaria. In the first issue, for example, Legaré's difficult and erudite discussion of classical learning was followed by an article explaining the advantages of deep plowing, pulverizing the soil, crop rotation, and manuring.

Although the *Southern Review*'s lofty goals kept it from becoming as blatantly political as its successor, the *Southern Quarterly Review*,* the earlier journal did include sectional issues. In keeping with much of the South, it opposed the trade tariff, which it saw as beneficial to Northern manufacturers but damaging to Southern interests. The *Review* also supported states' rights and frequently called the Union a "confederacy" or a "confederation of states." The South seemed to view itself almost as a separate country linked to the North only by what amounted to a treaty for mutual benefit. An article claiming that the War of 1812 was designed to aid Northern trade and navigation, not the South, suggested the extent of this feeling: "The South suffered by it [the war] most severely, but it has never repented of its sacrifices; and our citizens are still prepared to make *great concessions to friendship and to peace*" (1:320) [italics added]. The article went on to warn that when the federal government stopped benefitting the South as well as the North, the Union would dissolve. The last issue called for a convention of the states to amend the Constitution to protect Southern interests.

As one might expect, slavery was also an important topic. The *Southern Review* defended the South's right to and need for slavery and tried to show its advantages as well. The first issue said, "That the institution of slavery is attended with some evils, and those not inconsiderable ones, we readily admit; though we think it is also attended with advantages which, in some degree, compensate for them" (1:219). It attacked as "uninformed and misguided" the American and British reformers who wanted to free the Negroes and send them to a newly formed African nation, and it used as one piece of evidence the example of a freed slave in Philadelphia who wanted to return to his old Southern master because he had heard about poor conditions in Africa (1:219).

Reviews of literature concentrated heavily on established British and European writers such as Sir Walter Scott, Goethe, Sir Philip Sidney, Lord Byron, and Ben Jonson, though American writers such as Washington Irving, James Fenimore Cooper, and James Percival were also included. An article entitled "American Literature" denounced the growing call around the country to throw off British influence and establish a uniquely American literature as premature for a young, inexperienced nation. Despite this obvious bias, American work was given a fair hearing. Cooper's *The Bravo* was favorably reviewed, and Legaré called William Cullen Bryant's poems "upon the whole the best collection of American poetry which we have ever seen" (8:443), although the qualification "American poetry" is perhaps significant. Charleston poet William Crafts did not fare so well, nor did Cooper's *The Wept of Wish-Ton-Wish*, which Legaré called "a failure" (5:207).

After four years of what James D. B. De Bow called the "Augustan Age of Southern letters,"[6] the *Southern Review* issued its last volume in February 1832 when Legaré went to Brussels as chargé d'affairs. The reasons for its failure are various, many of them rooted in the very section it was designed to support and defend. Even staunch Southerner William Gilmore Simms said Southerners were "not . . . a reading people."[7] Though they liked the idea of having a learned journal to represent their section, they were notoriously lax in paying for their subscriptions.[8] A notice at the end of volume 6 stated that although the magazine had sufficient subscribers, "the scattered nature of the agricultural population of the South" made it difficult to collect, and thus because of lack of funds, publication would cease with that issue. The magazine held on, though, for a little over a year in spite of continuing financial difficulties. A notice at the beginning of volume 8 showed less tendency to make excuses for its subscribers' failure to pay: "On receipt of the 15th Number of the *Southern Review*, Subscribers in arrears, are requested to make immediate payment, as the Publisher is considerably in advance for the work; and as it requires all that is due to reimburse him."

Other reasons for the *Review*'s failure lie in the publication itself. The 11 August 1828 issue of the *Charleston Courier*, a newspaper usually sympathetic to the *Review*, called it "too learned."[9] Although excellent in scholarship, it had little appeal for the masses, whom it did not even attempt to please. Two early discussions on the subject agree that although Southerners were justly proud of the *Southern Review*, it is unlikely that they read much of it.[10] According to Edward Rogers, articles such as "Geometry and the Calculus" and Dr. Wallace's review of Stuart's *Hebrew Grammar* were too specialized to have much appeal to a general readership.[11] In addition to difficult subject matter, the style of the *Review* was often heavy and abstruse, and the articles were far too long. Another reason may be the lofty aims with which the *Review* began. In trying to prove to the North the culture and erudition of a region often considered backwards and uncouth, the editors perhaps overcompensated by making their magazine too stately, dignified, and learned.

When Legaré returned from Brussels, Stephen Elliott, Jr., tried to get him to reestablish the *Southern Review*, but Legaré refused. In addition to his new commitments, he had found the difficulties in getting both reliable contributors and paid subscribers too formidable and exhausting. In fact, he had become so discouraged that he even refused to contribute to the *Southern Quarterly Review*,[12] begun after the *Southern Review*'s demise as its successor. He had learned the lesson many after him were to discover—that editing a review in the South was a difficult and often unappreciated task.

## Notes

1. Linda Rhea, *Hugh Swinton Legaré: A Charleston Intellectual* (Chapel Hill: The University of North Carolina Press, 1934), pp. 236–37, n.20.
2. Rhea, pp. 237–38.
3. Rhea, p. 112.
4. Rhea, pp. 108–9.

5. Frank Luther Mott, "The *Southern Review*," in *A History of American Magazines*, 4 vols. (Cambridge, Mass.: Belknap Press of Harvard University Press, 1957), 1:574–75.

6. Mott, 1:575.

7. Jay B. Hubbell, *The South in American Literature: 1607–1900* (Durham: Duke University Press, 1954), p. 367.

8. These difficulties and others are covered extensively in Susan B. Riley's "The Hazards of Periodical Publishing in the South during the Nineteenth Century," *Tennessee Historical Quarterly* 21 (December 1962):365–76.

9. Rhea, p. 97.

10. Edward Reinhold Rogers, *Four Southern Magazines*. Ph.D. diss., University of Virginia, 1902, p. 51; William P. Trent, *William Gilmore Simms* (Boston, 1892; rpt., New York: Greenwood, 1969), pp. 51–52, 57.

11. Rogers, pp. 53, 57.

12. Rhea, pp. 148–49, 202–3.

## Information Sources

BIBLIOGRAPHY:

Hubbell, Jay B. *The South in American Literature: 1607–1900*. Durham: Duke University Press, 1954.

———. "Southern Magazines," in *Culture in the South*, ed. W. T. Couch. Chapel Hill: University of North Carolina Press, 1934. Pp. 159–82.

Mott, Frank Luther. "The *Southern Review*." *A History of American Magazines*. 4 vols. Cambridge, Mass.: Belknap Press of Harvard Univ. Press, 1957. 1:573–76.

Rhea, Linda. *Hugh Swinton Legaré: A Charleston Intellectual*. Chapel Hill: The University of North Carolina Press, 1934.

Riley, Susan B. "The Hazards of Periodical Publishing in the South during the Nineteenth Century." *Tennessee Historical Quarterly* 21 (December 1962):365–376.

Rogers, Edward Reinhold. *Four Southern Magazines*. Ph.D. diss., University of Virginia, 1902.

Trent, William P. *William Gilmore Simms*. Boston, 1892; rpt., New York: Greenwood, 1969.

INDEXES: None.

REPRINT EDITIONS: American Periodicals: Series II, 1800–1850. University Microfilms, Ann Arbor. Reel 325.

LOCATION SOURCES: Widely available.

## Publication History

MAGAZINE TITLE AND TITLE CHANGES: *The Southern Review*.

VOLUME AND ISSUE DATA: Volumes 1–6, numbers 1–12, February 1828-November 1830. Volume 7, numbers 13–14, May and August 1831 (February of 1831 was omitted). Volume 8, numbers 15–16, November 1831-February 1832.

FREQUENCY OF PUBLICATION: Quarterly.

PUBLISHER: A. E. Miller, Charleston, S.C.

EDITORS: Stephen Elliott, Sr., February 1828-November 1829(?); Stephen Elliott, Jr., February 1830(?); Hugh Swinton Legaré, May 1830(?)-February 1832.

*Janice L. Edens*


## THE SOUTHERN REVIEW (Bledsoe's)

While "the North is sending forth, by the tens of thousands, her *Monthlies* and *Quarterlies* exclusively devoted to her own views," Albert Taylor Bledsoe declared in the first issue of his new *Southern Review* (Baltimore, 1 January 1867), "it seems but fair and right that the South should also be heard" (back cover). But the *Review* was to be more than a Southern apologia, at least initially, for in his statement of editorial policy Bledsoe says the purpose of the magazine is "to supply a need long felt in the South, . . . an organ for Southern men of letters . . . and a high class of periodical literature for Southern readers" (back cover). Bledsoe welcomes contributions, from "all thinking men who are friends of the South," in the areas of literature, science, and philosophy, but the subject of education, especially, "will form a prominent topic." Bledsoe notes that the *Review* will not exclude politics, and will, in fact, present essays that deal directly with "the causes and consequences of the late war . . . not with the view of awakening acrimonious or vindictive feeling, but of drawing profit from the experience of the past" (back cover).

The first issue of Bledsoe's *Southern Review* remains true to its editor's word, containing eight essays on topics as different as American education, international politics and history, "mental physiology," and legal rights of the South before, during, and after the Civil War. Especially worth noting are the two essays on Southern rights, one on "The Legal Status of The Southern States," a summary of the Supreme Court's decisions on this topic from 1862 to 1865, and another on "The Imprisonment of [Jefferson] Davis," for they reveal the impassioned but carefully argued defense of the Southern cause that dominated Southern periodicals and newspapers after the war and they belie Bledsoe's claims of moderation in dealing with such issues. Both of these essays are by Bledsoe himself, and they reveal the kind of attitude in the *Review* that moved none other than Robert E. Lee to write to Bledsoe, "You must take care of yourself; you have a great work to do; we all look to you for our vindication."[1]

Albert Taylor Bledsoe (1809–1877) was a native of Kentucky and was educated at Transylvania College and West Point, graduating in 1830. Soon after graduation he entered the practice of law in Springfield, Illinois, where he was a colleague of Abraham Lincoln. He left the law for the Episcopal ministry but quarreled over theological questions and left the ministry to become a professor of mathematics, first at the University of Mississippi (1848–1854) and then at the University of Virginia (1854–1861).[2] During this time he published his proslavery tract *An Essay On Liberty and Slavery* (1856) and his scholarly treatises *A Theodicy* (1853) and *A Philosophy of Mathematics* (1858). With the

secession of the Southern states, he was made a colonel in the Confederate
Army, but was soon relieved of his command to serve as assistant secretary of
war. He spent most of the war in England, however, where he was sent to
research a constitutional defense of the Southern cause. Upon his return to
America after the war, he discovered his old friend Jefferson Davis imprisoned
and on trial for treason.[3] Using the material he had gathered in England, he
came to Davis's defense with *Is Davis a Traitor, or Was Secession a Constitutional Right Previous to 1861* (1866). In the first issue of his *Southern Review*,
he again drew on these materials, as I have already mentioned.

Bledsoe shared his editorship of the *Review* only twice.[4] He began the periodical with coeditor William Hand Browne, who left after a year and later became
editor of the *Southern Magazine*.* Bledsoe then edited the periodical alone until
two years before his death, when he appointed his daughter, Sophia Bledsoe
Herrick, associate editor. After Bledsoe's death in 1877, Herrick became sole
editor of the *Review* for a year and a half. C. J. Griffith edited the final two
numbers of the *Review* in Richmond.

*The Southern Review*, along with the *Southern Magazine* (Baltimore, 1871–
1875), the *New Eclectic* (see the *Southern Magazine**) (Baltimore, 1869–1871),
and the *Land We Love* (Charlotte, North Carolina, 1868–1869) began as moderate
publications. They were pro-South but preached reconciliation even when attempting to justify the Southern cause. By 1870, however, after Reconstruction
was firmly entrenched, all of these publications became vehemently anti-Yankee,
and Bledsoe's magazine is accorded a reputation as the "most militant" of these
periodicals.[5] Though the review continued to present essays and reviews on a
variety of topics—Rousseau, Hamilton, French culture, Roman history, British
and American literature, religion, and education—they began to have a decidedly
Southern slant. By 1869, Bledsoe paints a rather grim picture of North and South
as antithetical cultures that can never be reconciled. "Our gracious, benevolent
and loving fellow-citizens of the North are striving to accomplish for the South,
the same result the French philosophers accomplished for their country—a thorough depravation of the character and morals, and by the same means" (6:96).
"The North," he goes on to write, "is of the earth, earthy; and ignores the
spirituality of our nature" (6:110), while the South is "defective, doubtless,"
but "a civilisation seeking a spiritual elevation over matter and money" (6:110).
In condemning the North as the perpetuator of mammon and materialism, Bledsoe
even goes so far as to reiterate strongly his defense of slavery. "The civil war
in Rome . . . in which the slaves were emancipated and made citizens, destroyed
the liberties of Rome. The same means . . . must produce the same results in the
United States" (6:127).

Bledsoe did encourage American education, noting that Americans "can no
longer trust the mental and moral training of our sons and daughters to teachers
and books imported from abroad." However, his actual intent becomes clear
when we understand many Southern periodicals decried that only textbooks of
Northern writers were being used in schools in the South. Neither was the

Southern view much disguised in essays on topics such as science and American literature. For instance, one writer reveals errors in scientific articles published by the *Review*'s Northern competitors *Harper's Weekly* and the *Atlantic Monthly*,* and another attacks the inconsistencies in Indian lore in Longfellow's "Hiawatha," a poem in which "the hero is a Chippeway, but with a name which no Chippeway (or Ojibwayg) could pronounce. . . . *Hiawatha* is the work of a foreigner unacquainted with the forests in which his scenes are laid" (3:210). And, until 1871, there is hardly an issue of the review without an essay reflecting on the causes, major battles, and/or personalities of the Civil War. Such regional jingoism was, of course, a mainstay of Northern magazines of the time as well.

Nevertheless, for the first three years at least, the *Review* provided an "incomparable . . . interpretation of the postbellum mind of the intellectual South."[6] Perhaps the highlight of the *Review*'s belles-lettres contributions during this time was Paul Hamilton Hayne's "Daphles" (7:213–25). Hayne, who has been called the "Laureate of the South," also wrote numerous reviews for the *Review*, though he never forgave Bledsoe for not paying him for his contributions.[7]

Bledsoe's religious inclinations soon began to have a greater effect on his editorial policies than his political views. Though Bledsoe had left the Episcopal ministry, his religious faith had never abated, and he eventually became a Methodist minister.[8] In 1870, with the *Review* still struggling financially, Bledsoe appealed to the Methodist Church South to adopt his magazine as its official organ. Having had its own publication, the *Quarterly Review*, suspended at the beginning of the Civil War, the church decided to comply with Bledsoe's request in 1871. William Hand Browne's prediction in a letter to Paul Hamilton Hayne that the "result would be a marked decline in the quality of the *Review*"[9] soon became realized, for Bledsoe began to shift the target of the *Review* from the North in general to the Methodist Church North in particular. By 1877, the year of Bledsoe's death, nearly all of the essays in the *Review* were on religious topics. Only Sophia Bledsoe Herrick's contributions on literature, naturalism, and history provide a welcome relief from the not-so-credible attacks of her father on his Northern religious brethren.

Even with church backing, however, the *Southern Review* was never a financial success, and the resumption of publication of the Methodist Church South's *Quarterly Review* in 1879 brought an end to Bledsoe's magazine. Nevertheless, Bledsoe's efforts at the *Southern Review* have been compared favorably with Orestes Brownson's at the *Boston Quarterly Review*.* "Both were masters of nervous, effective style, both were thoroughly earnest, both were lovers of controversy, both felt the irresistible urge for self-expression . . . and both were profoundly and personally affected by the Civil War."[10] Even after the turn of the century, Bledsoe was still thought of by some as "The giant of Southern literature."[11]

Surprisingly, Sophia Bledsoe Herrick's reputation as an editor seems to have survived the years better than her father's. After she gave up the *Review* and it died quietly in the hands of Griffith, she worked on the staff of *Scribner's*

*Monthly** and *Century Magazine*. She is credited with "keen literary percep-
tions" and was said by a male colleague to have been "one of the wisest and
best women" he had ever known. Among her credits is the encouragement and
editing she provided for Thomas Nelson Page and Richard Malcolm Johnston.[12]

## Notes

1. Quoted in Edwin Mims, *The South in the Building of the Nation*, 13 vols. (Richmond, Va.: The Southern Historical Publication Society, 1909), 6:464.

2. Frank Luther Mott, *A History of American Magazines*, 4 vols. (Cambridge, Mass.:
Harvard University Press, 1938), 3:382.

3. Mott, 3:382.

4. Mott says William Hand Browne was replaced for a time by Major Richard Venable
(p. 383), but I can find no evidence in the *Review* of Venable as coeditor or associate
editor for the year following Browne's resignation.

5. Fred Hobson, *Tell About The South: The Southern Rage to Explain* (Baton Rouge,
La.: Louisiana State University Press, 1983), pp. 91–92.

6. Mott, 3:383.

7. Milfred Lewis Rutherford, *The South in History and Literature: A Handbook of
Southern Authors From The Settlement of Jamestown, 1607, to Living Writers* (Atlanta:
Franklin-Turner Co., 1906), p. 452.

8. Mott, 3:383.

9. Quoted in Jay B. Hubbell, *The South in American Literature* (Durham, N.C.:
Duke University Press, 1954), p. 176.

10. Mott, 3:384.

11. Rutherford, p. 822.

12. Hubbell, pp. 718, 727.

## Information Sources

BIBLIOGRAPHY:

Hobson, Fred. *Tell About The South: The Southern Rage To Explain*. Baton Rouge, La.:
    Louisiana State University Press, 1983.

Hubbell, Jay B. *The South in American Literature*. Durham, N.C.: Duke University
    Press, 1954.

*A Man of Letters in the Nineteenth-Century South: Selected Letters of Paul Hamilton
    Hayne*. Ed. Rayburn S. Moore. Baton Rouge, La.: Louisiana State University
    Press, 1972.

Mims, Edwin. *The South in the Building of the Nation*. Richmond, Va.: The Southern
    Historical Publication Society, 1909.

Mott, Frank Luther. "*The Southern Review*." *A History of American Magazines*. 4 vols.
    Cambridge, Mass.: Harvard University Press, 1938. 3:382–84.

Rutherford, Mildred Lewis. *The South in History and Literature: A Handbook of Southern
    Authors From The Settlement of Jamestown, 1607, to Living Writers*. Atlanta:
    Franklin-Turner Co., 1906.

INDEXES: None.

REPRINT EDITIONS: American Periodicals: Series III, 1850–1900. University Micro-
    films, Ann Arbor. Reels 18–20. AMS Press, Inc., New York. Microform: Bell
    & Howell, Micro Photo Division.

LOCATION SOURCES: Widely available.

## Publication History

MAGAZINE TITLE AND TITLE CHANGES: *The Southern Review*.

VOLUME AND ISSUE DATA: Volumes 1–8, January 1867-October 1870; volume 9,
  July 1871; volumes 10–15, January 1872-October 1874; volume 16, January 1875;
  volume 17, April 1875; volume 18, July, October 1875; volumes 19–25, January
  1876-October 1879.

FREQUENCY OF PUBLICATION: Quarterly.

PUBLISHERS: 1867–1868: Bledsoe and Browne, Baltimore. 1869: A. T. Bledsoe, Baltimore. 1870: Henry Taylor and Company, Baltimore. 1871: Poisal & Raszell,
  Baltimore. 1871–1875: Southwestern Book and Publishing Company, St. Louis.
  1875–1879: Bledsoe & Herrick, Baltimore.

EDITORS: Albert Taylor Bledsoe and William Hand Browne, January 1867-October
  1868; Albert Taylor Bledsoe, January 1869-December 1877; Sophia Bledsoe Herrick, December 1877-October 1879.

*Leonard Butts*

## THE SOUTHERN ROSE

The first four-page issue of Caroline Howard Gilman's the *Southern Rose* was
dated 11 August 1832. Appearing then under the title of the *Rose Bud, or Youth's
Gazette*, the publication was directed to children; however, there was a reference
to a time when the *Rose Bud* would be "fully blown." Appearing weekly, the
magazine resulted from Mrs. Gilman's knowledge of and concern for children.
Hers was one of the country's earliest publications for children, the early issues
containing "original prose works and poetry, notices of new books and toys,
extracts from children's books that are not common, and many other interesting
things" (1:1). Items of local interest were also included. There was a great effort
to teach children morals. Many of the works included were written for the
periodical by the editor herself, including 50 of the 110 poems in the first volume.
An interesting work begun in the first volume and continued in the second and
third was described in the periodical as "Authentic Letters, by Eliza Wilkinson.
Written during the invasion and possession of Charleston, by the British, in
1779, and copied by herself, for a friend in 1782" (1:55). These lively letters
were probably the most interesting feature of the whole first volume. Mrs. Gilman
also published tributes to the periodical by several noteworthy men, one of whom
was Thomas S. Grimké (1:204).

  The title was changed to the *Southern Rose Bud* with the beginning of the
second volume, and Mrs. Gilman included more mature material without relinquishing the juvenile department. Her husband, Samuel Gilman, a Unitarian
minister, contributed translations of French and German writings. S. G. Bulfinch,
a friend of the Gilmans, also contributed a translation of a German song. Series
of travel letters gave detailed descriptions of various public buildings and other
attractions visited by the chronicling travelers. One series written by a traveler

from the North is valuable for its description of Charleston life in that era. Mrs. Gilman reviewed various publications of the time, one of which was a new book by William Gilmore Simms, *Guy Rivers: A Tale of Georgia*, which she predicted would rank above his previous work, *Martin Faber* (2:185). One new section, "The Musical Observer," discussing various musical compositions, was added in the second volume. Mrs. Gilman's *Recollections of a Housekeeper* was begun in number 18. This work and the later *Recollections of a Southern Matron*, serialized in the periodical and afterward published as separate volumes, are probably the two works for which the editor is best known today.

Reflecting the periodical's attempt to interest more mature readers, the third volume doubled its number of pages per issue, but its issues now appeared every other Saturday rather than every Saturday. Mrs. Gilman's poetic contributions decreased markedly in the third volume to 15 out of the 103 published. A noteworthy review of Simms's *The Yemassee* appeared. "Local Sketches," a volume describing local scenes, was added. Another item of note, written by Samuel Gilman, was "A Day Among the Autographs," concerning the autograph collection of J. K. Tefft, Esq., of Savannah, Georgia, at that time one of the three largest collections in the United States.

With the beginning of the fourth volume came the *Southern Rose*. Its object was "to enlarge, and mature, and improve the *Rose Bud*" (3:206–7). The pages were somewhat larger than those of the previous volumes, and more translations and longer works were the chief improvements. An item of interest is "Extracts from a Journal Kept on Tour From Charleston, S.C., to New York In May, 18——, an account of one of the land routes from Charleston to New York," by two ladies and two gentlemen (4:173). The value of the article today lies in its description of the perils of land travel at the time. Another travel series by Mrs. Gilman begun in volume 4 was later republished as *Poetry of Travelling in the United States* (4:156). Religious articles and discussions of literary works and authors were included regularly. *The Partisan*, another of Simms's works, was reviewed in this volume, along with Robert Southey's *Roderick*, Tobias Smollett's *The Expedition of Humphry Clinker*, and Henry Fielding's *The History of Tom Jones*. Summaries and evaluations of Theodore Foster's American editions of the *London Quarterly Review*, the *Edinburgh Review*, the *Foreign Quarterly Review*, and the *Westminster Review* were valuable in their day in disseminating the contents of these great reviews to people who would not otherwise have been aware of them. Mrs. Gilman contributed 15 of the 102 poems in volume 4.

Reviews of literary works continued in volume 5, the most noteworthy of which was that of Nathaniel Hawthorne's *Twice-Told Tales* in number 23. Mrs. Gilman had published "The Minister's Black Veil" from this collection in number 22, and she published "David Swan, A Fantasy" with her review. Within the review she commented on her choice of tales: " 'The Minister's Black Veil,' selected for the last number of *The Rose*, is one of the most original, rather than the best story in the collection. Among the most exquisite are 'A

Sunday at Home,' and 'David Swan' (5:183). She compared Hawthorne's animation with that of Washington Irving, a statement probably thought at the time very bold. Mr. Gilman wrote "A Day of Disappointment in Salem, by an Admirer of *Twice-Told Tales*" for a later volume, and Mrs. Gilman published "The Lily's Quest. An Apologue," which Hawthorne had sent to her for first publication. Her continued support of Simms was noted in a review of his *Mellichampe, or a Legend of the Santee* (5:54). Samuel Gilman's "Fair Harvard," an ode that he wrote for "the centennial celebration of the foundation of Harvard College" (5:24), also appeared in volume 5.

The "Prospectus to the Sixth Volume of the *Southern Rose*" indicated the last major change in the periodical, a change from a quarto of eight to an octavo of sixteen pages. Poems were intermingled with prose rather than being in a separate section. Mrs. Gilman contributed thirteen poems and five tales and began publication of her last lengthy work of fiction, *Love's Progress, or Ruth Raymond*. Samuel Gilman took over the column reviewing Foster's republications of the British reviews. Frederick A. Porcher, Esq., of Charleston contributed two vividly written series to this volume. An original letter of Thomas Paine was published in number 19 (6:289). Several accounts of the destruction of Charleston by fire were included in this volume. The publisher announced on the cover of number 26 that he would stop printing and managing the business aspects of the *Southern Rose* because subscriptions were not being paid. Possibly it was realized as early as number 19 of volume 7 that collecting for subscriptions would be unsuccessful and that publication would soon cease, for there was a note to the author of "Reminiscences of a Voyage to Europe" that he should lengthen his installments so as to complete the work within the volume. Nevertheless, Mrs. Gilman in her "Editor's Valedictory Address" gave the impression that the publisher would have been willing to continue publication of the *Southern Rose*, indicating that she had decided for other reasons not to continue as editor.

Although the periodical was never purely literary, neither politics nor religious controversy was ever included. However, Mrs. Gilman's efforts to present the Southern side of the slavery issue were an attempt to rebut the views of people who had no firsthand knowledge of the slavery system (5:26, 109). After having developed from a magazine for children to one for adults, the *Southern Rose* was valuable for its reviews of books and periodicals, including reviews of the American reproductions of four great British reviews of the day. In addition, it offered a valuable outlet for Southern writers. Several who later published in more widely known sources, such as Mrs. Frances Sargent Osgood and Mrs. E. F. Ellet, had some of their earliest "effusions" printed in the *Southern Rose*.

## Information Sources

BIBLIOGRAPHY:
Cardwell, Guy Adams, Jr. "Charleston Periodicals, 1795–1860: A Study in Literary Influences with a Descriptive Check List of Seventy-Five Magazines." Ph.D. diss., University of North Carolina, Chapel Hill, 1936.

Clark, C. E. Frazer, Jr. "In Quest of a Southern Admirer of Nathaniel Hawthorne." *Nathaniel Hawthorne Journal* 2 (1971):208–12.

Gilman, Caroline Howard. "My Autobiography." *The Female Prose Writers of America.* Ed. John S. Hart. Philadelphia: E. H. Butler, 1852. Pp. 49–57.

————. *The Poetry of Travelling in the United States.* New York: S. Colman, 1838.

Gilman, Samuel. *Contributions to Literature; Descriptive, Critical, Humorous, Biographical, Philosophical, and Poetical.* Boston: Crosby, Nichols, and Company, 1856.

Hoole, William Stanley. "The Gilmans and the *Southern Rose.*" *North Carolina Historical Review* 11 (1934):116–28.

Kennedy, Fronde. "The *Southern Rose-Bud* and the *Southern Rose.*" *South Atlantic Quarterly* 23 (1924):10–19.

Thompson, Janice Joan. "Caroline Howard Gilman—Her Mind and Art." Ph.D. diss., University of North Carolina, Chapel Hill, 1975.

Wallace, David Duncan. *The History of South Carolina.* 4 vols. New York: American Historical Society, 1934.

INDEXES: None.

REPRINT EDITIONS: Microform: The Library of Congress Photoduplication Service.

LOCATION SOURCES: No complete runs. Partial runs: Widely available.

## Publication History

MAGAZINE TITLE AND TITLE CHANGES: *The Rose Bud, or Youth's Gazette,* 11 August 1832–24 August 1833. *The Southern Rose Bud,* 31 August 1833–22 August 1835. *The Southern Rose,* 5 September 1835–17 August 1839.

VOLUME AND ISSUE DATA: Volumes 1–7, 11 August 1832–17 August 1839.

FREQUENCY OF PUBLICATION: Weekly, 11 August 1832-August 1834. Biweekly, August 1834–17 August 1839.

PUBLISHERS: 11 August 1832–23 February 1833: William Estill, Charleston, S.C., 2 March 1833–12 December 1834: James S. Burges, Charleston, S.C., 27 December 1834–30 April 1836: E. J. Van Brunt, Charleston, S.C., 14 May 1836: Unknown. 28 May 1836–7 January 1837: Burges and Honour, Charleston, S.C., 21 January 1837–18 August 1838: J. S. Burges, Charleston, S.C., 1 September 1838–17 August 1839: B. B. Hussey, Charleston, S.C.

EDITOR: Caroline Howard Gilman.

*Janice Joan Thompson*


**THE SOUTHERN ROSE BUD.** See THE SOUTHERN ROSE


**SPIRIT OF THE TIMES & LIFE IN NEW YORK.** See
THE NEW YORK SPIRIT OF THE TIMES

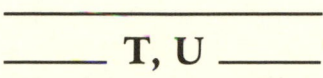

# T, U

## THE TRAVELLER: SPIRIT OF THE TIMES AND LIFE IN NEW-YORK. See THE NEW YORK SPIRIT OF THE TIMES

## THE UNITED STATES DEMOCRATIC REVIEW. See THE UNITED STATES MAGAZINE AND DEMOCRATIC REVIEW

## THE UNITED STATES LITERARY GAZETTE

The first issue of *The United States Literary Gazette* was dated 1 April 1824. According to the publisher's (Cummings, Hilliard, & Co.) prospectus, the *Gazette* would have *"a strictly national character,"* including "a large proportion of . . . reviews of works published here," "whatever information we can gather, concerning our national literature, education, and public opinion," and *"Literary and Scientific Intelligence"* (1:1). Although the publishers admitted that many periodicals "are now published in this country, and many more have been attempted and abandoned," they remained confident of their ability to produce a magazine "which shall be *highly useful* to the reading public of this country, and to all who are interested in matters relative to literature, either in the way of business or amusement" (1:1). To that end, the first issue included reviews of James Fenimore Cooper's *The Pilot*, *The Course of Instruction in Public Schools of Boston*, and William Cullen Bryant's collected poems; an essay on politics ("On the Growth of the United States"); Miscellany (a note on Niagara); poetry (including Bryant's "Ripzah"); Intelligence (notes on a variety of matters literary, scientific, and philosophical); and notices of new publications and works in press. This arrangement remained essentially the same for the first two years of the *Gazette*.

Theophilus Parsons, the first editor, felt that "no existing journal, at least none in this country, actually performs the uses of a General Review, and it will be a leading principle in the conduct of the Gazette to maintain this character" (1:1). Thus, Parsons sought out "gentlemen who stand high among the scholars and writers of our country" (1:1), and, as he wrote Bryant, "most of the best writers in Boston . . . have promised me their aid."[1] Parsons seemed eminently qualified for such a task. Son of the Massachusetts chief justice, Parsons in 1824 had been editor of the Taunton, Massachusetts, *Free Press*, in addition to his growing law practice. After relinquishing the editorship of the *Gazette* in early 1825, Parsons would continue his law practice, serve as editor of the *New-England Galaxy*, and, in 1848, begin a long career as professor in the Harvard Law School.

During Parsons's tenure as editor, the *Gazette* remained an eclectic journal, with reviews of religious tracts, travel literature, historical works, educational and self-improvement books, and leading prose and poetry (works by Byron, Irving, Perceval, Cooper, and Bryant). The Miscellany section included essays on "American Scholarship" and "Letters from a Traveller to Great Britain." The Intelligence notes covered a wide range of topics: from "The Effects of Lime Water in Preserving Eggs," to Greek newspapers, a Russian expedition to the North Pole, censorship in Austria, a mammoth skeleton, and Sicilian literature.

Parsons likewise featured a range of original poetry by popular American poets: Longfellow, Perceval, R. H. Dana, Rufus Dawes, and, particularly, William Cullen Bryant. In December of 1823, Parsons wrote Bryant that he was "very anxious that the work should have, in some measure, the support of your talents."[2] Parsons requested "ten or twenty pieces of poetry to be sent to Cummings, Hilliard, & Co. in the course of the ensuing year," and Bryant responded enthusiastically.[3] Through February 1825, the *Gazette* published some twenty-three poems by Bryant, an arrangement that ended when Parsons resigned his position.

On 18 February 1825, Parsons wrote Bryant that James G. Carter would become the editor of the *Gazette* beginning with the 1 April 1825 issue. Carter, an 1820 graduate of Harvard, conducted private schools at Cohasset and Lancaster, Massachusetts, and was a leading advocate of public education and the common school revival in Massachusetts. Later he helped to found the American Institute of Instruction, wrote several textbooks, and served in the Massachusetts legislature. In an "Introduction" to his first issue as editor of the *Gazette*, Carter announced a new form for the magazine (from quarto to octavo, number of pages increased to forty, and an eight-page "Literary Advertiser" added), but he remained faithful to the original prospectus: "the success of work is evidence that it could not be changed with a hope of improvement" (2:1). Later in 1825, a change in publishers would also occur. For the October issue Harrison Gray's name was added to the Cummings, Hilliard & Co. imprint; the 15 April 1826 edition would list only Gray as publisher.

At this same time in New York, Bryant was editing, with Columbia University Professor of Mathematics Henry Anderson, the *New York Review, and Atheneum\** (June 1825 to May 1826), a successor to Robert Sands's *Atlantic Magazine*. In April of 1826, Bryant suggested to Carter that the *Review* and the *Gazette* merge, with simultaneous publication in Boston and New York. Carter agreed, and the two prepared the first issue for 1 July 1826. Before the issue appeared, however, Harrison Gray wrote Bryant that Charles Folsom would replace Carter as editor of the *Gazette*. Folsom, an 1813 graduate of Harvard, had previously served as chaplain on the flagship of the Mediterranean squadron, as American consul at Tunis, and as tutor and librarian at Harvard. Although Bryant had some disagreements with Gray over the details of the merger, Bryant and Folsom initially appeared to work well together.

Under the terms of the final agreement, the magazine would be called *The United States Review and Literary Gazette*, with Bryant responsible for all poetry and for reviewing books published in New York and cities farther south, and Folsom responsible for reviewing all books published in Boston. Each had also one-quarter ownership, and Bryant served as nominal editor of the old *Gazette* for the July-September issues. The first issue of the new magazine, published simultaneously by Bowles and Dearborn in Boston and by G. and C. Carvil in New York, was dated 1 October 1826.

By merging and by increasing each issue to eighty octavo pages, Bryant and Folsom hoped to provide their readers with a greater variety of matter than had been possible with either the *New York Review* or the old *Gazette*. In some ways they succeeded. Although Bryant had begun his association with the *Saturday Evening Post*, he did find time to write many of the reviews, two short narratives, five original poems, and three Spanish translations for the *Review and Literary Gazette*.[4] He also secured original poetry from, among others, Fitz-Greene Halleck. At the end of October Bryant wrote Folsom that "the Review has been well received here in New York, and the subscription list is going on well in the city."[5] In March of 1827, Bryant wrote Folsom that he was "well-pleased" with the nature of the articles and "particularly gratified" with the business conduct of the magazine.[6]

Although the *Review and Literary Gazette* largely continued (and expanded) the contents of the old *Gazette*, Bryant grew uneasy with the Boston office's failure to communicate with him and with Folsom's tendency to introduce conservative political reviews into a literary journal. Although Bryant continued to write to Folsom, after April 1827 he had been receiving replies from Folsom's assistant, Edward Wigglesworth. In June of 1827, Willard Phillips wrote to Bryant that he had been offered the Boston editor's position—entirely without Bryant's knowledge. In July Bryant wrote simply to "the editor of the U.S. Review," expressing his doubts whether "a literary journal is the place for discussing the question concerning the propriety of Mr. Clay's appointment as Secretary of State."[7]

This uncertain editorial policy, combined with an insufficient number of subscribers and Bryant's increasing attention to the *Saturday Evening Post*, resulted in the failure of the *United States Review and Literary Gazette*. The final issue appeared in September 1827, only one year after the journal's inception.

## Notes

1. Quoted in *The Letters of William Cullen Bryant*, vol. 1 *1809–1834*, ed. William Cullen Bryant II and Thomas G. Voss (New York: Fordham University Press, 1975), p. 149.

2. Quoted in Charles H. Brown, *William Cullen Bryant* (New York: Charles Scribner's Sons, 1971), p. 109.

3. See Bryant, *Letters*, pp. 149–53 for an account of the negotiations. Parsons offered Bryant $200.00 a year for an average of 100 lines per month. Bryant found these terms "perfectly reasonable" (*Letters*, p. 152).

4. See Brown, p. 161.

5. Bryant, *Letters*, p. 221.

6. Bryant, *Letters*, p. 234.

7. Bryant, *Letters*, p. 247.

## Information Sources

BIBLIOGRAPHY:

Bigelow, John. *William Cullen Bryant*. Introd. John Hollander. 1890; rpt., New York: Chelsea, 1980.

Brown, Charles H. *William Cullen Bryant*. New York: Charles Scribner's Sons, 1971.

Bryant, William Cullen. *The Letters of William Cullen Bryant*. vol. 1: *1809–1836*. Ed. William Cullen Bryant II and Thomas G. Voss. New York: Fordham University Press, 1975.

Glicksberg, Charles. "Bryant and the *United States Review*." *New England Quarterly* 7 (1934):687–701.

Godwin, Parke. *A Biography of William Cullen Bryant*. New York: Appleton, 1883.

Mott, Frank Luther. *A History of American Magazines, 1741–1850*. Cambridge, Mass.: Harvard University Press, 1938. Pp. 331–33.

INDEXES: No complete index available, but the *Review* and the *Gazette* are indexed in Poole's and are included in Jayne Kribbs, *An Annotated Bibliography of American Literary Periodicals, 1741–1850* (Boston: G. K. Hall, 1977), p. 166.

REPRINT EDITIONS: American Periodicals: Series II, 1800–1850. University Microfilms, Ann Arbor. Reel 242.

LOCATION SOURCES: Widely available.

## Publication History

MAGAZINE TITLE AND TITLE CHANGES: *The United States Literary Gazette*, April 1824-September 1826. *The United States Review and Literary Gazette*, October 1826-September 1827.

VOLUME AND ISSUE DATA: Volumes 1–4, April 1824-September 1826; new series, volume 1, October 1826-September 1827.

FREQUENCY OF PUBLICATION: Monthly.

PUBLISHERS: April 1824-March 1826: Cummings, Hilliard & Co., Boston. April 1826-September 1826: Bowles and Dearborn, Boston. October 1826-September 1827: G. and C. Carvil, New York.

EDITORS: Theophilus Parsons, April 1824-March 1825; James G. Carter, April 1825-April 1826; Charles Folsom, May-June 1826; Folsom and William Cullen Bryant, July 1826-September 1827 (?).

*Timothy K. Conley*

## THE UNITED STATES MAGAZINE

The first issue of the *United States Magazine* appeared in January 1779, and like all subsequent issues reflected the strong editorial guidance of Hugh Henry Brackenridge. It was Brackenridge who convinced Francis Bailey, one of Philadelphia's best-known printers in the eighteenth century, to begin publication of the journal.[1] Brackenridge personally invested one thousand pounds "of continental currency" toward the initial production costs of the *Magazine*, and he was its primary contributor.[2] The underpinning egalitarian philosophy espoused by the *United States Magazine* came directly from Brackenridge, who wanted to offer the *Magazine* as "a library" and "literary coffee-house of public conversation" to such audiences as "the honest husbandman . . . the industrious laborer and mechanic" (1:10).

Brackenridge believed the *United States Magazine* would do more than cultivate "belles lettres" for the common man, however (1:4). The *Magazine* would also serve as a forum, of sorts, for expressions of revolutionary ideology, and Brackenridge loaded each issue with catalogs "of current events . . . foreign and domestic news" and editorials that called attention to America's revolutionary activities.[3] By collecting eighteenth-century examples of literary discourse and political ideology in the *United States Magazine*, Brackenridge hoped to document the "happy genius" of a "young and rising people" (1:3).

The political chauvinism of the *United States Magazine* has been widely noted by scholars of Brackenridge and America's publishing history; as a result, most estimates of the *Magazine*'s content begin either in an attraction or aversion to its regular patriotic displays of rhetoric. Enamored by Brackenridge's democratic fervor, Frank Luther Mott has described the *Magazine* as a "brilliant performance."[4] Yet Lewis Leary, being more interested in the *Magazine*'s literary content, dismisses the journal's "mishmash of political and patriotic scraps."[5] In its own time, despite Brackenridge's efforts, the *United States Magazine* never attracted a wide or enthusiastic audience. After a single year of twelve issues, the *Magazine* ceased publication in December 1779.

One reason for the short-lived history of the *Magazine* involved a weak publicity campaign. But the demise of the *Magazine* was typical, for "the times were not propitious" for any journals during the Revolutionary War period.[6]

The *Royal American Magazine*,* first published in January 1774, lasted thirteen months; the *Philadelphia Magazine, or American Monthly Museum*, edited by Thomas Paine, appeared in January 1775 and ceased publication after nineteen months. Like these journals, the *United States Magazine* was virtually ignored by critics in its own time, and even late into the nineteenth century it was given only cursory notices in publications like the *Southern Literary Messenger** or *Cyclopedia of American Literature*.[7] A further explanation for the failure of the *United States Magazine* to attract a loyal reading audience may stem from the somewhat scattered and disconnected format that characterizes all twelve issues. In the initial January number, for example, the only complete columns are Brackenridge's introductions to the *Magazine* (1:9–14), a section entitled "Poetical Essays" (1:43–45), and catalog-oriented entries listing military activities and information under such headings as "Captures at Sea" and "Captures by the State" (1:44–48).

A similar form of discontinuity often vitiated the flavor of the literary entries Brackenridge managed to include in the *United States Magazine*. Readers could find Philip Freneau's "Beauties of Vera Cruz" (1:84–88), the "House of Night" (1:155–63), and his "buccolic descriptions of tropical islands" in the *Magazine*'s "Poetic Essays" sections, while Brackenridge incorporated such literary pieces of his own as "The Cornwelliad" and "The Cave of Vanhest."[8] But the *Magazine* never fully solved the format problems that came with serializing such items. "The Cave of Vanhest" began to appear in January (1:14–15), was developed in small bits and pieces through the February, March, and April issues (1:61–63, 106–10, 149–50), and finally ended in July (1:253–55). Similarly, the "Cornwelliad" first appeared in March (1:133–34) but followed an irregular and unpredictable path to conclusion in October (1:431–33).

Brackenridge mixed political or topically oriented materials into the *Magazine* in much the same way. A series of political essays dealing with the problem of American inflation began to appear in January, for example, entitled "The Representation and Remonstrance of HARD MONEY" (1:28–31). The purpose of these essays was to support the idea of paper money as a method of controlling inflation, as was made clear in the "replies" to "HARD MONEY" that were printed in "The Adventures of a CONTINENTAL DOLLAR" and the "Reply of the CONTINENTAL CURRENCY" (1:72–81, 110–21, 385–87). Written entirely by Brackenridge, these essays undoubtedly "appealed to contemporary readers," as Bruce Granger notes, by borrowing several conventions from the "Addisonian periodical essay" and applying them to American topics.[9] Yet spread out in the *Magazine* from January through September (and not appearing at all from April through August), these examples illustrate the problems of fragmented copy that Brackenridge never fully solved. Although the reading audience of this period was naturally accustomed to serialization, it is still safe to assume that few readers of the *Magazine* were able to sustain an interest in a journal of such irregular content.

This is not to say that continuity was entirely lacking in the *United States Magazine*. The journal's "HARD MONEY" exchanges illustrate Brackenridge's successful fusion of the *Magazine*'s editorial, political, and literary purposes, and the January through August issues offer a fairly rich variety of materials that accompany the more or less regular "Foreign Affairs," "Domestic Affairs," "Poetical Essays," and "Political Diary" columns. Excerpts from political speeches, such as David Ramsey's "Oration on the Advantages of American Independence" (1:21–25, 53–58, 101–6), can be found in these issues. There are also treatises on scientific discoveries and areas of practical application (1:129–32), which provide interesting indices to the inquisitive and empirical spirit of eighteenth-century rationalism. In the later issues of the *United States Magazine* begin to appear circular letters from the Continental Congress authored by such persons as John Jay (1:408–10, 436–38, 448–50, 477–78). There were also a number of panegyrics to America as an emerging young nation. One of these, on "The Establishment of the United States," strikes a typical ideological note: "among the many revolutions . . . in the history of nations, there are none that can demand a greater compass of political investigation . . . than that of the United States (1:159–60).

This statement offers a good microcosmic assessment of the editorial principle operating behind the first six or seven issues of the *United States Magazine*, as these numbers reveal Brackenridge's sincere efforts to provide readers with a wide cultural and political "compass" of "investigation." Instruction occasionally formed a part of the *Magazine*'s design as well, as a number of columns offered ideas about the proper relations of church and state in America. Didactic in nature, entries like "The Contrast Between the Death of a Deist and a Christian" (1:65–72), "A Letter on the Danger and Evils of Religious Establishments" (1:155–59), and a final column on "Religious Enthusiasm" (1:411–21) all militate toward a shared ideological perception that is characteristic of Enlightenment religious perspectives: any legalized union of church and state will inevitably "foment bigotry . . . raise rancors . . . destroy civil and social happiness" (1:159).

The January through July issues of the *United States Magazine* most fully realize Brackenridge's hopes for an innovative American journal that would reflect the pulse of democratic life in revolutionary America. By August, however, Brackenridge appears to have lost his faith in the *Magazine*'s prospects. The August issue shrank to thirty-eight pages—compared to norms of forty-seven and forty-eight pages in prior issues—and after October no issue exceeded twenty-seven pages. Content also diminished in the later numbers, which were largely filled with texts of state constitutions. The last issues of the *United States Magazine* were but pale reflections of the first. Still, despite its rather short life, the *United States Magazine* for a time "exemplified an idealistic function of journalism in a democratic society."[10] In some of the "dulcet sounds for the listening ears" that Brackenridge provided (1:484), there is still a good deal of significant material in the *United States Magazine* for those readers interested in this critical period of America's cultural history.

## Notes

1. Lewis Leary, *Soundings: Some Early American Writers* (Athens: University of Georgia Press, 1975), p. 97.

2. Claude M. Newlin, *The Life and Writings of Hugh Henry Brackenridge* (1932; rpt., Mamaroneck, N.Y.: Paul P. Pappel, 1971), p. 45.

3. Daniel Marder, *Hugh Henry Brackenridge* (New York: Twayne Publishers, 1967), p. 75.

4. Frank Luther Mott, *A History of American Magazines, 1741–1850* (Cambridge, Mass.: Belknap Press of Harvard University Press, 1957), p. 27.

5. Leary, p. 164.

6. George O. Seilhammer, "Weekly Newspapers and Magazines," in *A Memorial History of the City of Philadelphia, from its First Settlement to the Year 1895*, ed. John Russell (New York: New York History Company, 1898), p. 271. The following details of publication history in my text also come from this page, as well as Mott, pp. 26–27.

7. See the "Biographical Notice of H. H. Brackenridge" in the *Southern Literary Messenger* 8 (January 1842): p. 3, and Evert A. Duyckinck, *Cyclopedia of American Literature*, 2 vols. (Philadelphia: T. E. Zell, 1856), 1:290–91.

8. Leary, pp. 139–41, discusses "The House of Night" in detail; he also refers to "The Cave of Vanhest" as "the first native tale set against a realistic background and the first fiction to use the realities of the American Revolution as a theme" (p. 164).

9. Bruce Granger, "The Addisonian Essay in the American Revolution," *Studies in the Literary Imagination 9* 2 (Fall 1976):43, 49.

10. Marder, p. 79.

## Information Sources

BIBLIOGRAPHY:

"Biographical Notice of Hugh Henry Brackenridge." *Southern Literary Messenger* 8 (January 1842):1–19.

Granger, Bruce. "The Addisonian Essay in the American Revolution." *Studies in the Literary Imagination 9* 2 (Fall 1976):43–52.

Leary, Lewis. *Soundings: Some Early American Writers*. Athens: University of Georgia Press, 1975.

Marder, Daniel. *Hugh Henry Brackenridge*. New York: Twayne Publishers, 1967.

———, ed. *A Hugh Henry Brackenridge Reader, 1770–1815*. Pittsburgh: University of Pittsburgh Press, 1970.

Mott, Frank Luther. *A History of American Magazines, 1741–1850*. Cambridge, Mass.: Belknap Press of Harvard University Press, 1957.

Newlin, Claude M. *The Life and Writings of Hugh Henry Brackenridge*. 1932; rpt., Mamaroneck, N.Y.: Paul P. Pappel, 1971.

Richardson, Lyon N. *A History of Early American Magazines, 1741–1789*. New York: Octagon Books, 1966.

Seilhammer, George O. "Weekly Newspapers and Magazines." *A Memorial History of the City of Philadelphia, From its First Settlement to the Year 1895*. Ed. John Russell. New York: New York History Company, 1898.

INDEXES: The only index is contained in the *Magazine* itself, in the last, December, issue, pp. 505–6. The index is partitioned into two sections: "Articles" (pp. 505–6), and "Poetry" (p. 506).

REPRINT EDITIONS: American Periodicals: Series I, 1741–1800. University Microfilms, Ann Arbor. Reel 30.
LOCATION SOURCES: Widely available.

### Publication History

MAGAZINE TITLE AND TITLE CHANGES: *The United States Magazine.*
VOLUME AND ISSUE DATA: Volume 1, January 1779-December 1779.
FREQUENCY OF PUBLICATION: Monthly.
PUBLISHER: Francis Bailey, Front Street, Philadelphia.
EDITOR: Hugh Henry Brackenridge.

*Christopher J. Forbes*


# THE UNITED STATES MAGAZINE AND DEMOCRATIC REVIEW

*The United States Magazine and Democratic Review* was first issued in October 1837 in Washington, D.C., by John L. O'Sullivan and Samuel D. Langtree. Unable to find scope for their political views in the *Georgetown Metropolitan*, a local newspaper they owned and edited, they conceived of a national periodical that would represent the interests of the Democratic party and combat the "literary toryism" of the nation's leading magazines. As its full title suggests, the *Democratic* was to combine the features of a quarterly review and monthly literary magazine, mixing scholarly articles on the issues of the day with light literature and miscellaneous features. The aim was to attract a wide audience to the liberal Democratic cause. The editors claimed to be partisan in politics and neutral in literary matters, recognizing where literature was concerned only "those universal principles of taste to which we are all alike subject." Thus they hoped to gain for the Democratic party, its fortunes sagging under the administration of Martin Van Buren, "a liberal and candid support from all parties, and from the large class of no party."[1]

A magazine of politics and literature was a bold and risky venture in 1837. Not since Joseph Dennie edited the *Port Folio** at the turn of the century had an American literary periodical engaged openly in partisan politics. As O'Sullivan and Langtree charged, the leading magazines in 1837 favored the Whigs, but they seldom avowed their partisanship when addressing public issues. Dennie's example had taught magazine editors to avoid controversy by feigning political neutrality. O'Sullivan and Langtree hoped, however, to rival the best British periodicals, in which political controversy and belles-lettres went hand in hand. They were, O'Sullivan later admitted, "very young, very sanguine, and very democratic."[2] They had the blessing of "Old Hickory" himself and the promise of patronage from Van Buren's administration in the form of government printing contracts.

Braving the economic panic of 1837, the sanguine editors attracted some six thousand subscribers by 1839, more than the *North American Review*,\* *New-York Review*, or *Knickerbocker Magazine*,\* but politics ultimately proved their undoing. Intending to serve the Democratic party at large, O'Sullivan and Langtree supported its "radical" liberal wing, alienating many moderates and conservatives. The radicals, or "Loco-Focos," as they came to be known, espoused a version of Jeffersonian democracy derived principally from John C. Calhoun, South Carolina senator and champion of states' rights. Their position is proclaimed in the motto of the *Democratic*, "The best government is that which governs least." The radicals sought to limit the power of the federal government, especially where it appeared to give advantage to a monied minority. The enemy, as they saw it, was the "aristocratic principle" of Whig policy, which sanctioned minority rule by the "better classes" and the imposition of "wholesome restraints" on the populace. The radicals advocated a "voluntary principle" of government, based upon the "virtue, intelligence, and full capacity for self-government, of the great mass of our people" (1:2). They held in principle that states, local communities, and individuals should do for themselves and that the popular will should initiate all legislation. In the wake of the Panic of 1837, political writers in the *Democratic* argued for the suspension of the National Bank and paper currency and the reduction of protective tariffs. On the important question of slavery, they adopted the policy of states' rights. Their antifederalism, however, did not prevent them from fanning the fires of American nationalism. They advocated the annexation of Texas and the Oregon Territory, and O'Sullivan is remembered today for having coined the phrase "manifest destiny" to justify American expansionism in the 1840s (17:5).

The political character of the *Democratic* was bound to alienate the conservative educated class, mostly Whigs, among whom a magazine with scholarly pretensions had to circulate in order to succeed. The Boston literati were so hostile to the magazine that they ostracized young George Sumner for contributing to it.[3] Longfellow had nothing but scorn for the "politico-literary system" of the Loco-Focos and thought O'Sullivan a "humbug."[4] Worse still was the indifference of many Democrats, who found the radical ideals of the magazine unpalatable. Even George Bancroft, the leading liberal in the party, was reluctant to write for it, no doubt because of his ties to Boston conservatives. Denied the government printing contracts by rival Democrat Francis P. Blair, editor of the *Washington Globe*, and facing financial failure, Langtree moved the magazine to New York, where, after his withdrawal and a hiatus of six months, O'Sullivan issued a new series in July 1841. Although he gave politics less prominence and sought to avoid intraparty squabbles, his views continued to be a liability. Especially as an advocate of territorial expansion and states' rights, O'Sullivan found himself increasingly out of step with Northern liberals, many of whom were joining ranks with the abolitionists. His attempts, moreover, to broaden his base of political support inevitably backfired. In 1842 he tried to consolidate liberal Democrats and boost circulation by purchasing the subscription list of the *Boston Quarterly Review** and making its editor, Orestes Brownson, a regular contributor to the *Democratic*. Brownson, however, who had tried unsuccessfully to rally liberal Democrats in New England, grew conservative after the Democratic defeat in 1840 and antagonized O'Sullivan's readers by questioning democratic principles in "Democracy and Liberty" (12:374–87) and "Origin and Source of Government" (13:129–47, 241–62, 353–77). After much controversy and some cancelled subscriptions, O'Sullivan was forced to end the arrangement. Before Brownson came aboard in 1842, subscriptions had dropped to 3,500, still a healthy figure. By 1845, when O'Sullivan was looking to sell the magazine, he could claim only 2,000 subscribers.[5]

After O'Sullivan's withdrawal in 1846, the *Democratic* suffered numerous changes in ownership, editorial staff, and format. Politically, it continued to be a force, and subscriptions swelled briefly in 1852 when editor George N. Sanders attacked the "Old Fogies" of the Democratic party in support of Stephen A. Douglas, but the literary quality of the magazine declined steadily. O'Sullivan's successor, Thomas P. Kettell, was an able editor but lacked the personality and influence to attract the best authors. Later editors, Theodore A. Foster, David W. Holly, Spencer W. Cone, and Conrad Swackhamer, published some good writing, much of it by the young Bohemians who frequented Pfaff's restaurant in New York—Fitz-James O'Brian, George Arnold, Henry Clapp, Ada Clare, William Winter, Louis Gottschalk, R. H. Stoddard, Bayard Taylor, Thomas Bailey Aldrich, and E. C. Stedman—but the magazine had achieved its high point of literary reputation and influence under O'Sullivan's direction. In 1843, Poe judged that there were only three magazines in the world superior to the *Democratic*, and in 1848, when O'Sullivan's imprint was still on the magazine, John Bristed singled it out in *Blackwood's* as the only American periodical worthy of praise. Walt Whitman recalled in 1858 that, under O'Sullivan, the *Democratic* was a "monthly magazine of a profounder quality of talent than any since."[6]

Although impractical, O'Sullivan was an able political writer and literary editor. During his association with the magazine, he wrote most of the political articles himself, getting help occasionally from Samuel J. Tilden, John Bigelow, Lewis Cass, Benjamin F. Butler, and Alexander H. Everett. O'Sullivan was opinionated, but he restrained himself in writing and gave his contributors plenty of latitude. His handling of the Brownson controversy demonstrates his editorial tact and fairness (12:387–91; 13:129, 262, 377). As a literary editor, O'Sullivan's tastes were catholic, although he preferred prose to verse. He warned James Russell Lowell not to "allow the vine of your genius to 'run too much to wood' " in magazine verse, and Lowell later complained that O'Sullivan "neither appreciates me nor the tendency of my poetry, nor the true worth of any real poetry."[7] Although a liberal literary editor, O'Sullivan was not afraid to exercise his authority, especially with unsigned articles. Emerson complained bitterly about the "interpolation" of his review of William Ellery Channing's poems (13:309–14), but such complaints were few.[8] O'Sullivan paid established contributors well by contemporary standards, five dollars a page for prose and five to fifteen dollars a poem, but like most magazine editors, he was frequently tardy. Even his good friend Nathaniel Hawthorne complained that he "is just as certain to disappoint me in money matters, as any pitiful little scoundrel among the booksellers."[9] Yet, the quality of the magazine in the 1840s resulted largely from O'Sullivan's ability to attract regular contributions from the likes of Hawthorne.

O'Sullivan and Langtree were sincere about their literary neutrality, inviting contributions from both Democrats and Whigs, liberals and conservatives. Longfellow was assured, for example, that his political views were of no concern to the editors, whose primary aim was to establish a magazine of "a higher order."[10] Yet, as Longfellow clearly saw, the magazine was the organ of a "politico-literary" clique. The editors were committed from the outset to the idea of a national literature based upon democratic principles. Once in New York, O'Sullivan joined Young America, a group of writers and editors, including Evert Duyckinck, William A. Jones, and Cornelius Mathews, whose manifesto became a unifying theme in the magazine: "The spirit of Literature and the spirit of Democracy are one" (11:196). The equation was so self-evident to Young America that it seemed to transcend politics. What American author was not a democrat in his writing? Even Longfellow would have agreed with William A. Jones that poetry in his day should be "Poetry for the People;" it should reflect the "predominant fact in the history of the nineteenth century thus far"—the elevation of the masses (13:266). He would have sympathized with James Russell Lowell's lines about the effect of reading Robert Burns's poetry in a crowded railway car: "It may be glorious to write / Thoughts that shall glad the two or three / High souls . . . that come in sight / Once in a century. / But better far it is . . . To write some earnest verse or line / Which, seeking not the praise of Art, / Shall make a clearer faith and manhood shine / In the unlearned heart" (11:432).

The aesthetic of democracy tended to produce sentimental and didactic verse and prose, calculated to stir and instruct the unlearned heart. Much of the literature in the *Democratic*, therefore, is typical of the day. American subjects and scenes serve as backdrop for the triumph of liberty and moral virtue. Even at its worst, some of it will interest literary historians. Take, for example, the eight melodramatic tales by young Walt Whitman that appeared between August 1841 and October 1842. Frequently, however, especially in the 1840s, the literature in the *Democratic* was better than the usual magazine fare. "A first-rate number," William A. Jones observed, "would have its poems by Bryant, Lowell and Whittier; its romances by Hawthorne; finished translations of German romance, or light sketches of manners from the French; criticism by [Parke] Godwin, or [John] Bigelow, or [Evert] Duyckinck; and politics by Mr. Editor [O'Sullivan] . . . or Mr. Everett" (15:246).

Despite O'Sullivan's distaste for magazine verse, the *Democratic* published some significant poetry during his editorship. Bryant contributed ten poems between 1837 and 1841, including "The Fountain" (5:404–8) and "The Winds" (6:269–70). Lowell wrote twelve poems for the magazine in the 1840s, some of which, like "Prometheus" (13:147–53), expressed his growing commitment to social reform. Many of the twenty-one poems that Whittier contributed comprise his "Songs of Labor and Reform." There are also twenty-two poems by William Gilmore Simms, mostly sonnets, and frequent contributions by more or less competent poets, such as Park Benjamin, Benjamin F. Butler, Henry T. Tuckerman, and Edward Maturin. Less frequently, we find poems by William Ellery Channing, Bayard Taylor, and Elizabeth Barrett, including her verse play, "The Drama of Exile" (15:72–88, 142–52). After 1850, poetry is less prominent in the magazine, although the occasional poems and parodies by Charles G. Rosenberg are notable.

The literary stature of the *Democratic* in its first decade was greatly enhanced by the presence of Hawthorne, who published more writing in O'Sullivan's magazine than in any other, some twenty-five essays and tales, including "Tales of the Province-House" (2:129–40, 360–69, 3:321–32, 5:51–59), "The Artist of the Beautiful" (14:605–17) and "Rappaccini's Daughter" (15:545–60). Whittier published legends of "New England Supernaturalism" (13:279–84, 389–93, 515–20) and Joseph C. Neal contributed a whimsical series of "Pennings and Pencillings, in and About Town," illustrated by F.O.C. Darley (13:89–96, 154–60, 521–27). There is also some notable historical and western fiction by more popular magazine writers, Joseph Holt Ingraham, John Treat Irving ("John Quod"), Henry William Herbert ("Frank Forester"), Charles Wilkins Webber ("C. Wilkins Eimi"), Mrs. L. Leslie, William Kirkland, and Samuel Adams Hammett. As Jones observed, literature in translation appears frequently in the *Democratic*, which was more hospitable to French and German writers than most American magazines. Johannes Zschokke, August Heinrich Hoffmann, Tieck, Goethe, Johann Ludwig Uhland, Schiller, Balzac, Theophile Gautier, Hugo, Joseph Berenger, and Alexandre Dumas Père, among others, were translated by Alexander Everett, Horatio Gates, William A. Butler, Nathaniel Green, Mrs. Elizabeth Ellet, Parke Godwin, and Thomas Kettell.

William A. Jones was the most prolific and prominent critic in the *Democratic*. His essays on "Poetry for the People" (13:266–79), "Female Novelists" (14:484–89), "British Critics and British Travellers" (14:335–43), "Critics and Criticism of the Nineteenth Century" (15:153–62), "Criticism in America" (15:241–49), "American Humor" (17:212–19), and "Nationality in Literature" (20:264–72, 316–20, 384–91) articulated the views of Young America and identified the literary trends in the 1840s. Also important in this regard are Parke Godwin's "Recent American Poetry" (5:523–41) and "American Poetry" (8:399–430) and Evert Duyckinck's "On Writing for the Magazines" (16:455–60). There are frequent short reviews of new American books in the *Democratic* but very few significant assessments of individual American writers; two essays on Emerson (1:319–29, 16:589–602), Duyckinck's essay on Hawthorne (16:376–84), John Savage's defense of Poe (27:542–44), (28:66–99, 162–72), and Whitman's review of his own *Leaves of Grass* (36:205–12) are notable exceptions. The criticism of foreign authors is usually derivative, although an essay by Jones on

"English Letter Writers" is unique (16:433–46). Several other critical features are worthy of note, such as James Fenimore Cooper's defense of his *Naval History* (10:411–35, 515–41); Poe's "Marginalia" (15:484–94, 580–94; 18:268–72; 19:30–32); J. S. Dwight's essays on Handel, Mozart, and Haydn (12:264–79; 13:465–73; 14:17–25); Horatio Greenough's essays on American art and architecture (13:45–48, 206–10) and Frederick Saunders's "Loose Leaves of a Literary Lounger," serialized in 1843 and 1844.

The weakness of the *Democratic* proved ultimately to be its strength. Political partisanship limited its circulation but gave it a distinct purpose and identity. Even the biographies in the *Democratic*, a standard magazine feature, assume importance as a record of prominent Democratic writers and politicians. The scope and quality of political writing in the magazine have made it a valuable resource for historians. The democratic zeal of its editors, moreover, attracted some of the best literary talent to the magazine. Especially during O'Sullivan's editorship, the *Democratic* may have been, as George Parsons Lathrop described it, "the most brilliant periodical of the time."[11]

## Notes

1. "Prospectus of *The United States Magazine and Democratic Review*," *Washington Globe*, 13 March 1837, p. 3.

2. *Passages from the Correspondence of Rufus W. Griswold*, ed. William M. Griswold (Cambridge, Mass.: W. M. Griswold, 1898), p. 123.

3. "Letters of George Sumner, 1837–1844," *Massachusetts Historical Society Proceedings* 46 (1913):359–60. For conservative reaction to the *Democratic*, see Sheldon Howard Harris, "The Public Career of John Louis O'Sullivan (Ph.D. diss., Columbia University, 1958), pp. 143–44.

4. *The Letters of Henry Wadsworth Longfellow*, ed. Andrew Hilen, 4 vols. (Cambridge, Mass.: Harvard University Press, Belknap Press, 1966), 2:162.

5. Harris, p. 145.

6. "Our Magazine Literature," *The New World* 6 (1843):302; "The Periodical Literature of America," *Blackwood's Edinburgh Magazine* 63 (1848):107–12; *The Uncollected Poetry and Prose of Walt Whitman*, ed. Emory Holloway, 2 vols. (New York: Doubleday, Page & Co., 1921), 2:15.

7. Martin Duberman, *James Russell Lowell* (Boston: Houghton Mifflin, 1966), pp. 121, 402 n.41.

8. *The Letters of Ralph Waldo Emerson*, ed. Ralph L. Rusk, 6 vols. (New York: Columbia University Press, 1939), 3:196–97.

9. Horatio Bridge, *Personal Recollections of Nathaniel Hawthorne* (New York: Harper and Brothers, 1893), p. 89.

10. O'Sullivan to Longfellow, 1 September 1837, Longfellow Papers, Harvard University, Houghton Library. Quoted by Harris, p. 62.

11. *A Study of Hawthorne* (Boston: J. R. Osgood, 1876), p. 199.

## Information Sources

BIBLIOGRAPHY:

Fuller, Landon Edward. "*The United States Magazine and Democratic Review*, 1837–1859: A Study of its History, Contents, and Significance." Ph.D. diss., University of North Carolina, 1948.

Harris, Sheldon Howard. "The Public Career of John Louis O'Sullivan." Ph.D. diss., Columbia University, 1958.

*The Letters of Henry Wadsworth Longfellow.* Ed. Andrew Hilen. 4 vols. Cambridge, Mass.: Harvard University Press, 1966.

*The Letters of Ralph Waldo Emerson.* Ed. Ralph L. Rusk. 6 vols. New York: Columbia University Press, 1939.

Miller, Perry. *The Raven and the Whale: The War of Words and Wits in the Era of Poe and Melville.* New York: Harcourt, Brace and Co., 1956.

Mott, Frank Luther. *"The Democratic Review." A History of American Magazines, 1741–1850.* New York: D. Appleton and Co., 1930. Pp. 677–84.

Pratt, Julius W. "John L. O'Sullivan and Manifest Destiny." *New York History* 14 (1933):213–34.

Schlesinger, Arthur M. *The Age of Jackson.* Boston: Little, Brown, 1945.

Stafford, John. *The Literary Criticism of "Young America": A Study of the Relationship of Politics and Literature, 1837–1850.* Berkeley: University of California Press, 1952.

*The Uncollected Poetry and Prose of Walt Whitman.* Ed. Emory Holloway. 2 vols. New York: Doubleday, Page & Co., 1921.

INDEXES: None.

REPRINT EDITIONS: American Periodicals: Series II, 1800–1850. University Microfilms, Ann Arbor. Reels 691–96.

LOCATION SOURCES: There is no complete run of the *Democratic* extant, since portions of the file for January-June 1857, when it was issued as a weekly, have not been located. Nearly complete and partial runs widely available.

## Publication History

MAGAZINE TITLE AND TITLE CHANGES: *The United States Magazine and Democratic Review*, October 1837-December 1851. *The Democratic Review*, January 1852-December 1852. *The United States Review*, January 1853-January 1856. *The United States Democratic Review*, February 1856-October 1859.

VOLUME AND ISSUE DATA: Volume 1, October 1837, January, February, March 1838; volume 2, April-July 1838; volume 3, September-December 1838; volume 4, "Historical Register," originally the ends of numbers 2, 3, 7, 10, 11, 15, 16, 19, 26, 27, and 36; volumes 5–8, 1839–1840, two volumes a year; new series, volume 9–29, July 1841-December 1851, two volumes a year; new series, volumes 1–2 [30–31], 1852; new series, volume 1 [32], January-June 1853; volume 2 [33], July, August, September 1853, June 1854; volumes 3–5 [34–36], July 1854-December 1855; new series, volume 6 [37], January-July 1856; volume 7 [38], August-December 1856; volume 39, January-June 1857; volumes 40–42, July 1857-December 1859; volume 43, April, October 1859. Omitted numbers: November, December 1837; August 1838; January-June 1841; October-May 1853; July 1859. Combination numbers: April-May 1840; November-December 1840; July-August 1845; November-December 1852; January-February 1855.

FREQUENCY OF PUBLICATION: Monthly, 1837–1856, July 1857–1858; weekly, January-June 1857; quarterly, 1859.

PUBLISHERS: October 1837-December 1839: Langtree and O'Sullivan, Washington, D.C. January 1840-December 1840: S. D. Langtree, Washington, D.C. July 1841-December 1843: J. and H. G. Langley, New York (as all the following). January 1844-June 1845: H. G. Langley. July 1845-May 1846: J. L. O'Sullivan and O. C.

Gardiner. June 1846-December 1847: John W. Moore. January-December 1848: Henry Wikoff. January-June 1849: Thomas Prentice Kettell. July 1849-December 1851: Kettell and Moore. January 1852-September 1853: D. W. Holly. June-December 1854: Lloyd and Brainard. January 1855-May 1856: Lloyd and Campbell. June-September 1856: Lloyd and Company. October 1856: L. F. Harrison and Spencer W. Cone. November 1856-June 1857: L. F. Harrison, Spenser W. Cone, and J. L. Benedict. July 1857-October 1859: Conrad Swackhamer.

EDITORS: John L. O'Sullivan and Samuel D. Langtree, October 1837-May 1839; Samuel D. Langtree, June 1839-December 1840; John L. O'Sullivan, July 1841-May 1846; Thomas Prentice Kettell, June 1846-December 1851; George N. Sanders and Thomas D. Reilly, January 1852-December 1852; Theodore A. Foster, January-April 1853; "Conductors" (editorial staff), May-September 1853; David W. Holly, June 1854-November 1855; Spencer W. Cone, December 1855-September 1856; L. F. Harrison and Spencer W. Cone, October 1856; L. F. Harrison, Spencer W. Cone, and J. L. Benedict, November 1856-June 1857; Conrad Swackhamer and Isaac Lawrence, October 1859.

*Bruce I. Weiner*


**THE UNITED STATES REVIEW.** See THE UNITED STATES MAGAZINE AND DEMOCRATIC REVIEW


**THE UNITED STATES REVIEW AND LITERARY GAZETTE.** See THE UNITED STATES LITERARY GAZETTE


**THE UNIVERSAL ASYLUM, AND COLUMBIAN MAGAZINE.** See THE COLUMBIAN MAGAZINE

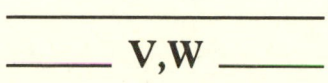

# V,W

**VANITY FAIR AND GOLDEN ERA.** See THE GOLDEN ERA

## THE WASP

The *Wasp*, a satirical weekly magazine published in San Francisco, is fondly remembered for its caustic and occasionally sarcastic cartoons, which were lithographically produced. It was reputedly the first cartoon magazine in color ever published for a significant length of time in the United States. The magazine was founded in 1876 by three brothers, Francis, Anton, and Joseph Korbel, who had immigrated from Czechoslovakia in the early 1860s. Their entry into the publishing business was circuitous. After several years of random employment, they had accumulated sufficient capital to establish a cigar-box factory. Redwood was used in the fabrication of the boxes, and a reliable supply was assured through the purchase of a mill in the redwood country of northern California; many acres of surrounding redwood land were also acquired by the Korbels.[1] The colored labels that were affixed on the boxes were printed lithographically by their firm in San Francisco. The success of this associated business rapidly out-paced box manufacturing, and F. Korbel & Brothers became well known for its lithographic printing.

The Korbel brothers had long been aware of the corruption that surrounded them in their adopted country. Economic depression, bossism, and lamentable conditions for the workingman were familiar themes both in California and in their homeland in central Europe. The brothers realized, however, that even though corruption in Europe was so intrenched that it was almost impossible to correct, in California they could at least speak out freely and agitate for change.

The *Wasp*, whose mission was to be "ever on the wing in search of news, and ever ready to inflict a justifiable sting upon those who may abuse public trust" (1:2) was their answer. The first issue appeared on 5 August 1876, and the combination of satire, humor, and literature, all "with brilliant artistic illustration of the topics of the day" (52:562), struck a responsive chord even in the crowded field of San Francisco journalism. John H. Carmany & Company printed the text portions of the *Wasp*. The colored cartoons and illustrations that made the *Wasp* famous, however, were rendered by "the Wasp's Practical Lithographic Establishment," owned by F. Korbel & Brothers, which also offered "Zincographing and Steam Press Printing."[2]

The *Wasp*, under the editorial guidance of George B. Mackrett, was less than a month old when fire razed the Korbel lithographic plant; "the stones and steam lithographic press, upon which the *Wasp* was [printed], suffered the same common fate which befel[l] the material in the construction of the buildings which now lie in ruins and one general mass of ashes" (5:2). Another lithographer in San Francisco, Britton & Rey, assisted the brothers in their ordeal and produced eight issues of the *Wasp*'s illustrations. Less than six weeks after the fire, Mackrett was able to announce the arrival of a new lithographic steam press from New York and the resumption of the *Wasp*'s printing by Korbel.

From its inception the *Wasp* was lavishly illustrated, at first with black and white lithographs, but, on 2 December 1876, the cover illustration was printed in black with a green background wash. The first three-color lithograph appeared on 26 May 1877, inaugurating a tradition that continued for two decades. The editor announced that "this new step of journalistic enterprise" by the Wasp Publishing Company was taken "to show to people of the Pacific Coast that the managers of the WASP are determined to leave no stone unturned whereby the success of their paper can be ensured [and] . . . also to place before the public an illustrated journal having no equal in artistic skill outside of New York" (18:156).

G. Frederick Keller, who had learned his art work under George H. Baker in San Francisco, was hired as staff cartoonist; he had already been working several years for the Korbels in designing and printing labels. For seven years Keller "was apparently his own 'idea man' and his satirical and powerful cartoons reflect ingenious concepts remarkably well drawn [and directly linked to the literary content of the publication]; much of his work is suggestive of the English artist . . . [Thomas] Rowlandson."[3] Political corruption (especially in local government as related to the Big Four, Collis P. Huntington, Leland Stanford, Charles Crocker, and Mark Hopkins of the Central Pacific Railroad), revolutionary social views (including those of organized labor), and Chinese immigration were only three targets at which the *Wasp*'s editors and illustrators pointed their barbs. Until his death in 1883, Keller was the major contributor of a remarkable series of biting cartoons and other illustrations, although work by J. Langstruth, Henry Barkhaus, and Joseph D. Strong also appeared occasionally.

George Mackrett was succeeded as editor by Joseph Carroll, then Richard Gibson. In August 1879, Salmi Morse, a religious zealot and pseudo-poet (but not a humorist), was named managing editor, and his selection proved a mixed blessing. Although Morse's editorial writing style did not measure up to that of his successors, he did have a critical eye in the selection of artwork, and he continued the use of colored cartoons and other illustrations that his predecessors had initiated.

The Korbel brothers secretly sold the *Wasp* in January 1881 to Charles Webb Howard, president of the Spring Valley Water Company, although the public was informed that Henry J. W. Dam, a San Francisco newspaperman, was the new owner. With the change in ownership came a change in editorial direction upon the hiring of Ambrose Bierce. The content of the *Wasp* had varied in nature and quality during its first five years. Political commentary was always the staple, however, and local, state, and national events seldom escaped the sting of the *Wasp*'s writers. But it was under Bierce's five-year editorship that the magazine achieved its greatest period of notoriety.

Bierce had earlier worked for Frank Pixley as associate editor of the *Argonaut*\* in San Francisco, but Pixley refused to reinstate Bierce after the latter returned from a gold-prospecting sojourn in the Black Hills of South Dakota. Perhaps because of this affront, when Bierce assumed his editorial duties with the *Wasp*, he revived his old "Prattle" column and from it "maintained a steady barrage against all other San Francisco editors, drawing freely from his arsenal of invective such epithets as congenital idiot, whimpering simpleton, gristle-brained contemporary, Colorado stone man, and royal Bengal jackass."[4] Bierce saved most of his vituperation, however, for Pixley, seeing to it that the *Argonaut*'s editor was unflatteringly depicted in many *Wasp* cartoons, repeatedly called "a sycophant and slanderer for hire," and ridiculed at every other opportunity. Bierce's mock-epitaph for Pixley was, "Here lies Frank Pixley, as usual."[5] It was also in the *Wasp* that Bierce first wrote what would later be published as *The Devil's Dictionary*, a collection of bitter, pessimistic, ironic definitions of words.

The names of most other literary contributors to the *Wasp* are today not usually recognized. Ella Sterling Cummins mentions several of the more notable contributors of the nineteenth century. The column "A Woman's Journal," written during the early 1880s by Annie Lake Townsend, "was the quintessence of woman's wit and philosophy." Dan O'Connell, who also contributed pieces to the *Argonaut* and other San Francisco magazines, saved his best work for the *Wasp*. Minnie Buchanan Unger "left the impress of her fervid pen in several of the Christmas stories," and in the late 1880s and early 1890s "Charlotte Perkins Stetson [later known as Charlotte Perkins Gilman] . . . contributed satires that sparkled, Lillian Plunkett, graceful verses with a little sting in them, [and] Ella Higginson . . . fanciful conceits in verse."[6]

When John P. Jackson became publisher of the *Wasp* in 1885, several changes were made, not the least of which was the departure of Ambrose Bierce. The sting of the *Wasp* gradually became less poisonous, criticism was muted, and original literary contributions became less important than "short jokes and small cartoons with a large amount of material reprinted from other journals."[7]

Ownership of the *Wasp* seemed to change with remarkable regularity, but through the remainder of the century its main claim to fame and notoriety, its colored lithographic cartoons, was in the hands of two firms: F. Korbel & Brothers, of course, which firm was eventually replaced by Schmidt Label and Lithograph Company in January 1885.

Under newspaperman Thomas E. Flynn in the 1890s, the *Wasp* became less of a satirical journal and began to concern itself with local news; its subtitle was "A Saturday Journal of Illustration and Comment Devoted to the Discussion of Public Affairs, Finance, Society and Art." Colored cartoons were also deemphasized, so that in 1899, when no cartoon in color at all was published, the omission passed by unnoticed. By 1901, the transformation was complete and the cartoons had disappeared. The *Wasp*, published as a review of events in San Francisco, covering especially social news, continued under its original title until 1928, although it never again reached the heights it had in the 1880s under Bierce. In its dwindling days it merged with the San Francisco *News-Letter* to become the *Wasp News-Letter*; the name was later changed to the *News-Letter Wasp*. The final issue was published on 25 April 1941.

## Notes

1. After the land was cleared of redwood trees, the Korbel brothers discovered that grape vines grew quite well in the soil. In time, the Korbels began to produce wine and sparkling wine, an enterprise that today survives as the Korbel Winery.

2. Henry C. Langley, *San Francisco City Directory for the Year Commencing February 1878*. (San Francisco: Henry C. Langley, 1878), p. 490.

3. Kenneth M. Johnson, *The Sting of the Wasp; Political & Satirical Cartoons from the Truculent Early San Francisco Weekly* (San Francisco: The Book Club of California, 1967), p. 3.

4. Franklin Walker, *Ambrose Bierce, the Wickedest Man in San Francisco* ([San Francisco]: The Colt Press, 1941), p. 20.

5. Walker, p. 20.

6. Ella Sterling Cummins, *The Story of the Files: A Review of Californian Writers and Literature* ([San Francisco]: World's Fair Commission of California, 1893), pp. 188–89.

7. Johnson, p. 11.

## Information Sources

BIBLIOGRAPHY:

Cummins, Ella Sterling. *The Story of the Files: A Review of Californian Writers and Literature*. [San Francisco]: World's Fair Commission of California, 1893.

Grattan, C. Hartley. *Bitter Bierce: A Mystery of American Letters*. New York: Doubleday, Doran & Company, 1929.

Johnson, Kenneth M. *The Sting of the Wasp; Political & Satirical Cartoons from the Truculent Early San Francisco Weekly*. San Francisco: The Book Club of California, 1967.

Langley, Henry C. *San Francisco City Directory for the Year Commencing February 1878*. San Francisco: Henry C. Langley, 1878.

McWilliams, Carey. *Ambrose Bierce: A Biography*. New York: Albert & Charles Boni, 1929.

Starrett, Vincent. *Ambrose Bierce: A Bibliography*. New York: The Centaur Book Shop, 1929.

Walker, Franklin. *Ambrose Bierce, the Wickedest Man in San Francisco*. [San Francisco]: The Colt Press, 1941.

INDEXES: None.

REPRINT EDITIONS: None.

LOCATION SOURCES: Widely available.

### Publication History

MAGAZINE TITLE AND TITLE CHANGES: *The Wasp*, 5 August 1876–20 January 1877. *The Illustrated Wasp*, 27 January–22 September 1877. *The San Francisco Illustrated Wasp*, 29 September 1877–11 December 1880. *The Wasp*, 17 December 1880–5 October 1895. *The Wasp: The Illustrated Weekly of the Pacific Coast*, 12 October 1895–3 April 1897. *The Wasp: A Journal of Illustration and Comment*, 10 April 1897–25 August 1928. *The Wasp News-Letter: A Weekly Journal of Illustration and Comment*, 1 September 1928–27 July 1935. *San Francisco News-Letter Wasp*, 3 August 1935–25 April 1941.

VOLUME AND ISSUE DATA: Volumes 1–57, 5 August 1876–27 July 1935; volumes 79–86, 3 August 1935–25 April 1941. Note that in 1935 the combined publications, the *Wasp* and the *News Letter*, began numbering volumes using that of the *News Letter*; volumes 58 through 85 of the *Wasp* were omitted.

FREQUENCY OF PUBLICATION: Weekly.

PUBLISHERS: 1876–1881: Wasp Publishing Company, F. Korbel & Brothers. 1881–1882: [Charles Webb Howard, silent publisher], Edward C. Macfarlane and H.J.W. Dam, publishers and proprietors. 1882–1885: Edward C. Macfarlane & Company, publishers and proprietors. 1885–1889: John P. Jackson. 1889–1941: Wasp Publishing Company, during which time the editor was also the publisher. Office of publication was invariably in San Francisco.

EDITORS: George B. Mackrett, 1876–1877; Joseph Carroll, 1878; Richard Gibson, 1879; Salmi Morse, 1879–1881; Ambrose Bierce, 1881–1886; John P. Jackson(?), 1887–1889; D. G. Waldron, 1889; S. W. Backus, 1890–1892. Thomas E. Flynn, 1892–1914; Martial Davoust, 1915–1941.

*Bruce L. Johnson*

# THE WAVE

The *Wave* began, humbly enough, in 1887 as the advertising organ for the Southern Pacific Railroad's newly rebuilt resort, the Del Monte Hotel near Monterey, California. Under the direction of its founding editor, Ben C. Truman, a press agent for the railroad, the *Wave* was, as its subtitle proclaimed, "A Journal for Those in the Swim"—"a bright and clever little paper . . . especially devoted to the amenities of the summer vacation and goings and comings of society, and published presumably in Monterey.''[1] For reasons that are still not clear, the magazine was sold in 1890 to two San Francisco newspapermen, Hugh Hume and John O'Hara Cosgrave, who moved the *Wave*'s editorial offices as well as its focus of attention north to the Bay City. Oscar Lewis and others have contended that Southern Pacific president Collis P. Huntington engineered the sale in order to establish a seemingly independent journal to counter the charges made by various antirailroad and anti-Huntington publications such as the *San Francisco Examiner* and the *Argonaut*.* Lewis's claim does little justice either to Huntington as a businessman or to Cosgrave as an editor. Although the *Wave*'s politics were certainly conservative, they were never expressed with the eloquent bitterness of the *Examiner*'s Ambrose Bierce. Moreover, the precarious financial situation that plagued the *Wave* throughout the decade strongly suggests that the only ''subsidy'' provided by the railroad took the form of the full-page advertisement for the Del Monte Hotel, which had been a regular feature since 1887.

Despite its humble beginnings, the *Wave* quickly established itself as a significant publication in a city inundated with printed matter. In 1896, for example, the ''West's leading citadel of culture'' boasted no fewer than 242 serial publications, including three major monthlies and seven principal weeklies. Frank Luther Mott has pointed out that San Francisco was noted for its weeklies, four of which had circulations of between fourteen and eighteen thousand: *Argonaut*, *News-Letter*, *Wasp*,* and *Wave*, the last of which was distributed by Brentano's in Paris, New York, Chicago, and Washington, D.C., chiefly (one assumes) to those touring or transplanted members of San Francisco's upper middle class, for which the *Wave* was intended.[2]

It was Cosgrave who was responsible for the *Wave*'s considerable success. Hume took little interest in the magazine, devoting most of his time to another of his and Cosgrave's jointly owned projects, the *San Francisco Evening Post* newspaper; he left the *Wave* entirely in 1894. As the *Wave*'s sole editor, Cosgrave not only committed himself to perpetuating the magazine in the face of strong established competition; he also transformed an advertising sheet into a lively reflection of the optimism, expansiveness, and pride of place that characterized California in general and San Francisco in particular during the 1890s. He seized on the new technology for reproducing clear but inexpensive halftone illustrations, thus marking the *Wave* as sprightly and distinctive. Cosgrave also recruited the best of the local literary talent in order to help realize his ambition of transforming the *Wave* into ''the *Collier*'s or *Harper's Weekly* of the Pacific Coast,'' as Will Irwin, the last of Cosgrave's assistant editors, recalled, perhaps hyperbolically.[3] (Another assistant editor compared the *Wave*—more accurately—to a smaller version of Clement Shorter's London journal the *Sketch*.[4]) There was no exaggeration, however, in Irwin's sweeping claim that ''nearly every writing man or woman who came out of California in that fecund period had published some or all of his maiden efforts in the *Wave*.''[5] John and Geraldine Bonner, Juliet Wilbor Tompkins, Arthur McEwen, Will and Wallace Irwin, James Hopper, F. Bailey Millard, Yone Noguchi, W. C. Morrow, Emma Frances

Dawson, and the painter Ernest Peixotto all contributed to the *Wave*, as did more recognizable figures such as Frank Norris, Gelett Burgess, Jack London, and the photographer Arnold Genthe. As early as 1893, Cosgrave's encouragement of local writers had become a discernible feature of his otherwise rather loose editorial policy. Cosgrave the editor, Irwin reported, was more an artist than a businessman. That his editorial style was responsible, at least in part, for the *Wave*'s persistent financial difficulties seems certain; however, it also resulted in a journal that, as one recent critic has noted, "rivaled *The Argonaut* and *The Overland Monthly**" in the quality of its literary material."[6]

Like the *Argonaut*, the *Wave* was not exclusively a literary magazine; rather it dealt with a variety of topics. There were editorials; paragraphs on people and news of local interest; interviews with visiting celebrities, from playwrights and actresses to vaudeville "artistes"; drama, music, and especially book reviews; society news; feature stories; exchange items; a generous supply of advertisements and halftones; and fiction (especially in the midsummer and Christmas issues) consisting of original stories by local authors, translations from the French, and items reprinted from various newspapers and magazines. The sixteen to twenty-four tabloid-size pages were written by a staff that expanded or contracted according to the *Wave*'s always uncertain finances. Cosgrave, a political writer, occasionally a sports writer, and a society columnist, supplied approximately half the copy; a harried and generally ill-paid assistant editor wrote nearly everything else. As might be expected, anonymous and pseudonymous contributions abounded.

The most notable of the *Wave*'s assistant editors was Frank Norris. As he later explained to Charles Lummis, editor of the California magazine *Land of Sunshine*,* he could think of "nothing better for [a] young man with 'literary aspirations' than [to] grind on this *kind of paper* (*not* a daily, but a weekly.)"[7] Norris's *Wave* period attests to the freedom Cosgrave allowed his most talented staff writer. From April to July 1896, while Norris was an active participant in San Francisco's literary life—election to the Bohemian Club and membership in the outer circle of Les Jeunes, the group of writers and artists who had given birth to Gelett Burgess's outrageous little magazine the *Lark**—Norris contributed chiefly stories, sketches, and reviews. After the first of three two-month absences, Norris immersed himself in the "hammer and tongs work" of weekly magazine journalism and contributed less literary and more conventional items such as articles and interviews from October 1896 to March 1897. Norris returned from his second leave invigorated and rededicated to a literary career, for which the *Wave* would be a stepping stone rather than a dead end. From May to November he wrote, on the average, one new story per week; just as important, his other contributions during this period provide dramatic evidence that the young author was absorbing as much of the city as he could for the fiction he was either writing or planning to write. His mood and method are neatly summed up in the title of one Norris article that appeared in the 22 May 1897 issue: "An Opening for Novelists: Great Opportunities for Fiction Writers" (p. 7). Norris used his third leave to revise the manuscript of his novel *McTeague*; he apparently resumed his editorial duties in November, having just one purpose in mind— moving on—and it was his *Wave* work that enabled him to do so. S. S. McClure, founder of *McClure's Magazine*, McClure's Syndicate, and the Doubleday & McClure publishing house, saw an early installment of Norris's novel *Moran of the "Lady Letty"* (serialized in the *Wave*, 8 January–9 April 1898) and invited Norris to New York. What McClure offered Norris was quite beyond the freedom (and grind) of his *Wave* work: a half-time editorial position and afternoons free to write his fiction.

Norris's *Wave* experience helped to shape his career as a novelist by forcing him to convert fact into fiction, to hone his aesthetic theories, and to write on demand as well as for a specific audience. By the same token, Norris left his mark on the *Wave*; for nearly two years his style, interests, point of view, and editorial decisions became, in large measure, characteristic of the entire magazine.

In going East, Norris was following in the footsteps of many other *Wave* writers whose ambitions outgrew the bounds of their lively but nonetheless provincial native city. Gelett Burgess had made the trek after serving a brief stint as assistant editor during his friend Norris's second leave (March-May 1897). Even in so brief a period, Burgess was able to transform the *Wave* and to be transformed by it. Just then in the process of "killing" his *Lark* after a two-year run, Burgess adapted his nonsense style (perfected in the *Lark*) to the demands of weekly journalism. The result was satire as different from the *Lark*'s "Goops" and "Purple Cow" as it was from Norris's naturalistic style. Significantly, both Norris and Burgess each thought enough of their *Wave* writings to prepare a selection for book publication (projects that were eventually realized after the authors' deaths).

Norris (as noted earlier) recalled his *Wave* experience in terms of his development as a writer. Burgess emphasized a different side, claiming "that were it not for the salary . . . I would rather write for *The Wave* than for any other paper alive."[8] At the time Burgess wrote these words, the *Wave* was only barely alive. When it became a weekly of two cities in 1899—San Francisco and Seattle—the change did not indicate growth but instead a desperate need to increase sales. The tactic failed, as did the reduction of the single-copy price from ten cents to five the following year. Publication was suspended for two months in late 1900, then started up again, but by that time Norris had already begun urging Cosgrave to come East. When Norris secured for him the position of managing editor of *Everybody's Magazine*, Cosgrave finally gave in and publication of the *Wave* ceased. Given the *Wave*'s importance in the development of so many California authors and in the establishment of literary tastes on the Pacific Coast (the earliest review of Stephen Crane's *Red Badge of Courage*, for example, appeared in the *Wave*), critical neglect of its history is dismaying. The actual demise of the *Wave*, however, cannot be mourned. It had been a journal of provincial concerns and local significance; in the century that was just then beginning, it could only have survived as an anachronism.[9]

## Notes

1. Ella Mighels, *The Story of the Files* (San Francisco: Co-operative Printing Co., 1893), p. 324.

2. Frank Luther Mott, *A History of American Magazines, 1885–1905* (Cambridge, Mass.: Harvard University Press, 1957), pp. 105–6.

3. Will Irwin, *The Making of a Reporter* (New York: G. P. Putnam's Sons, 1942), p. 39.

4. Gelett Burgess, *Bayside Bohemia: Fin de Siecle San Francisco & Its Little Magazines*, intro. James D. Hart (San Francisco: Book Club of California, 1954), p. 37.

5. Will Irwin, "Introduction," *The Third Circle* (New York: John Lane, 1909), pp. 8–9.

6. Joseph M. Backus, "Forepiece," of *Behind the Scenes: Glimpses of Fin de Siecle San Francisco*, by Gelett Burgess (San Francisco: Book Club of California, 1968), p. 9.

7. Donald Pizer, "Ten Letters by Frank Norris," *Book Club of California Quarterly News Letter* 27 (Summer 1962):55–56.

8. Burgess, *Bayside Bohemia*, p. 41.

9. Preparation of this essay would not have been possible without the kind assistance of James D. Hart, Director of the Bancroft Library, University of California—Berkeley, and L. Maxwell Taylor, City Archives, San Francisco Public Library.

## Information Sources

BIBLIOGRAPHY:

Burgess, Gelett. *Bayside Bohemia: Fin de Siecle San Francisco & Its Little Magazines.* Ed. Joseph M. Backus. San Francisco: Book Club of California, 1954.

Irwin, Will. "Introduction." *The Complete Edition of the Works of Frank Norris.* Vol. 4. Garden City, N.Y.: Doubleday, Doran and Co., 1928. Pp. vii–ix.

———. "Introduction." *The Third Circle*, by Frank Norris. New York: John Lane, 1909. Pp. 7–11.

———. *The Making of a Reporter.* New York: G. P. Putnam's Sons, 1952.

Lewis, Oscar. *Bay Window Bohemia: An Account of the Brilliant Artistic World of Gaslit San Francisco.* Garden City, N.Y.: Doubleday & Co., 1956.

———. "Introduction." *Frank Norris of "The Wave."* San Francisco: Westgate Press, 1931. Pp. 1–15.

Mighels, Ella. *The Story of the Files.* San Francisco: Co-operative Printing Co., 1893.

Morace, Robert A. "A Critical and Textual Study of Frank Norris's Writings from the San Francisco *Wave*." Ph.D. diss., University of South Carolina, 1976.

———. "The Writer and His Audience: Frank Norris, A Case in Point." *Critical Essays on Frank Norris.* Ed. Don B. Graham. Boston: G. K. Hall, 1980. Pp. 53–62.

Norris, Frank. *Blix.* New York: Doubleday & McClure, 1899.

Starr, Kevin. *Americans and the California Dream: 1850–1915.* New York: Oxford University Press, 1973.

INDEXES: None.

REPRINT EDITIONS: None.

LOCATION SOURCES: There is no complete run of the *Wave*. The San Francisco Public Library owns a representative selection of issues from the early years; the Bancroft Library of the University of California—Berkeley has assembled a nearly complete microfilm of the *Wave* for the years 1891 through 1901.

### Publication History

MAGAZINE TITLE AND TITLE CHANGES: *The Wave* (various subtitles) was originally titled *The Del Monte Wave*; from August to November 1900 the title was changed to the *Saturday Wave*.
VOLUME AND ISSUE DATA: Volumes 1–23, 1887–1901.
FREQUENCY OF PUBLICATION: Monthly until 1889(?); weekly thereafter.
PUBLISHER: None listed until 1890; thereafter The Wave Publishing Company.
EDITOR: John O'Hara Cosgrave.

*Robert A. Morace*


## THE WEEKLY NEWS AND GAZETTE. See THE
### SOUTHERN LITERARY GAZETTE


## THE WEEKLY NEWS AND SOUTHERN LITERARY
## GAZETTE. See THE SOUTHERN LITERARY GAZETTE


## THE WESTERN MAGAZINE AND REVIEW. See THE
### WESTERN MONTHLY REVIEW


## THE WESTERN MESSENGER

Published monthly in Louisville and Cincinnati by a group of New England Unitarians, the *Western Messenger; Devoted to Religion and Literature* was a product of the larger attempt to spread the liberal gospel in the Ohio Valley. Before 1835, the effort there had been a frustrated one; but by that year the young Western missionaries—among them Ephraim Peabody (1807–1856), William Greenleaf Eliot (1811–1887), and most importantly James Freeman Clarke (1810–1888)—saw evidence that the sectarianism that had blocked their efforts was beginning to crack under the strain of its own rhetoric: the Christian Connexion (later the Disciples of Christ) was making headway in the region with its antisectarian doctrines, and the cultural indefiniteness of the new settlements offered Unitarianism an opportunity in the religious life of the Valley. The West, Clarke wrote excitedly, was "all in a ferment, a perpetual boiling up and over. . . . nothing is stable, nothing is fixed."[1] With the encouragement of the American Unitarian Association, the three ministers and a layman, James Handasyd Perkins (1810–1849), launched the *Messenger* in June 1835.

According to the prospectus distributed the preceding February, the magazine would "explain and defend the misunderstood and denounced principles of Unitarianism" and "diffuse sound views on literature, education, schools, and benevolent enterprises."[2] But its editors conceived their mission broadly, as

Eliot made clear in the introduction to the first number: "We trust in God that our object is not to build up a sect, but to establish the truth" (1:2). Under the "special superintendence" of Peabody in Cincinnati, the magazine offered its readers a mixture of "practical religion" (moralistic warnings about gambling and mob violence), liberal theology (primarily essays refuting the biblical evidence for Trinitarianism), review essays on Western literature, and miscellaneous news of interest to Westerners. It was immediately clear, however, that the magazine's attacks on religious "bigotry and exclusiveness" would not be confined to its Calvinist opponents, for in the first issue Clarke contributed a scathing essay on the misplaced "Orthodoxy" of Eastern Unitarians, whose fear of German idealism had offended the budding transcendentalist (1:43–47).

Clarke's willingness to entertain the transcendental "new views" drove a wedge between him and the more conservative Peabody. In the fall of 1835, when both men returned East for visits, the *Messenger* fell to the care of Perkins and several other substitute editors. When Peabody and Clarke returned late in the year, the rift between them had grown wider; and Peabody, ill with tuberculosis and crushed by the recent death of his infant son, turned the magazine over to Clarke at Louisville.[3] The new editor, while affirming the magazine's opposition to "the Pharisaic spirit of bigotry, tyranny, and sectarianism" (1:730), opened its pages to "all who appear to write with a good purpose," both softening the *Messenger*'s anti-Calvinist rhetoric and broadening the scope of its interests. Gone were the strident attacks on local Presbyterians and the pandering reviews of regional poets; in their place Clarke printed mature essays on Tennyson, Keats (including a previously unpublished poem, the "Ode to Apollo"), Shelley, Wordsworth, Goethe, Schiller, and Irving. Henceforth, Clarke promised, the magazine would be devoted to Christian union and intellectual breadth—"a living mirror of the times" (3:853). With those new emphases came new contributors: the young minister Samuel Osgood and the poet Christopher Pearse Cranch, who helped edit the magazine; Margaret Fuller, who offered her earliest literary reviews; and Ralph Waldo Emerson, who contributed his first signed poetry.

The years of Clarke's editorship (1836–1839) were watershed years in American culture, a time of passionate extremes in politics, religion, literature, and social reform, and the magazine, pledged to be a "living mirror" of its age, participated fully in the shifting intellectual currents. Yet Clarke's commitment to avoid "ultraism"—he knew at firsthand how stifling dogmatism could be— prevented the magazine from allying itself with any of the contemporary "isms." On the issue of slavery, for instance, the magazine refused to condone slaveholding but would not endorse abolitionism; as a result, it drew criticism from both camps. In an age of party politics one contributor condemned the prevailing "reliance upon names" and encouraged men to cast aside party affiliations and vote with their consciences (4:94–98). Under a variety of names—"bigotry," "exclusiveness," "sectarianism," and "party spirit"—the *Messenger* opposed any adherence to human creeds or "isms" that delimited the individual's search for truth.

That editorial policy was never popular with readers. After reaching its peak of about 550 names in 1837, the *Messenger*'s subscription list fell steadily as the magazine alienated first one group, then another.[4] Clarke remained firm in his opposition to creeds, even in the face of the crisis for which the *Messenger* is most remembered today: its participation in the "Transcendental controversy."[5] Clarke, Cranch, Eliot, and Osgood each had affinities with New England Transcendentalism by the mid–1830s; Clarke's were the strongest of all, since he was a friend of Emerson and Fuller and had left Boston largely because of his disenchantment with conservative resistance to the "New School."[6] The *Messenger* contained positive review-essays on five of the earliest statements of transcendentalism: William Henry Furness's *Remarks on the Four Gospels*, George Ripley's *Discourses on the Philosophy of Religion*, Orestes Brownson's *New Views of Christianity, Society, and the Church*, Bronson Alcott's *Conversations with Children on the Gospels*, and Emerson's *Nature*. While defending these radicals, the magazine also offered vocal criticism of some Unitarian leaders for their lack of vitality and their unwillingness to change. The dispute came to a climax in the months following Emerson's inflammatory "Divinity School Address" in 1838. The transcendentalists' chief critic, Andrews Norton, had argued that the new views must be subject to approval "by those who are capable of judging of their correctness."[7] Clarke's response was a two-part essay in the *Messenger* on "R. W. Emerson and the New School" (6:37–47) in which he defended the "genius, life, and manliness" of Emerson's thought and accused Norton of being the true enemy of Unitarianism. To the *Messenger* writers, Unitarianism seemed in danger of becoming a "prison of Creed" every bit as restrictive as the Calvinist sects it had opposed for years (6:119). Eastern Unitarians were aghast, and Norton himself attacked the *Messenger* in the *Boston Daily Advertiser* (27 August 1838) as a "professedly religious magazine" that defended atheists and radicals while subverting the truly Christian.

The controversy left Clarke drained, mentally as well as physically, and in early 1839 he turned the editorship over to Perkins and William Henry Channing, who had lately come from New England to fill the pulpit at Cincinnati. Under the new editors, the *Messenger*'s ties to the theology of Unitarianism, already strained, were finally severed. Both were more interested in social reform than in promoting the denomination or elevating literary taste in the West. After a short volume of six issues, Perkins announced in the October 1839 number that the magazine would drop its consideration of theology altogether and concentrate instead on "vital, practical religion" (7:436). The eighth and final volume of the *Messenger* opened the following May with Channing's dismissal of Unitarianism as a "mere scholastic title" that held little interest for him (8:6). In place of the doctrinal matter were examinations of radical social and economic schemes from associationism to nonresistance. Even some of the magazine's supporters began to criticize the new policy: one of the most important contributors, Harm Jan Huidekoper of Pennsylvania (whose daughter had married Clarke in 1839), complained that the magazine had succumbed to "the ultra spirit of the times."[8]

Huidekoper had reason to worry, for the magazine that had defended Alcott, Emerson, and other "disorganizers" turned its attention to economic reform—the "view of property in all its relations" that Perkins called "Christian Economy" (7:221–25). Huidekoper defended the economic status quo in essays like his "Right and Duty of Accumulation" (8:145–49), a moral justification of free-market capitalism; but the *Messenger*'s other contributors continued to explore, sometimes uncritically, such radical schemes as chartism and associationism. When Orestes Brownson's explosive prediction of class conflict, "The Laboring Classes," appeared in the summer of 1840, the *Messenger* was almost the lone voice raised in his defense, and that proved to be a fatal mistake for the magazine. "We think [Brownson's] spirit unchristian, and his plan of action unwise," Perkins wrote cautiously, but the topic was an important one and the essay "worthy of careful study" (8:288). In the din that greeted "The Laboring Classes," not even this moderate response was considered a responsible position. Huidekoper called the *Messenger*'s defense "criminal indulgence" (8:316); what was left of the magazine's subscribers bolted. Channing, by now editing the magazine alone, openly endorsed the "cloudy raptures" of transcendentalism (8:452–61) and reminded his readers that the magazine was bound to no sect, only to the honest pursuit of truth (8:383). But the defection of readers, combined with his own sudden crisis of the spirit in early 1841, dealt the final blow to the *Messenger*. Channing closed the last number in April 1841 with a notice of the "bright signs of the times," including the impending "Age of Individuality" and the publication of a new Eastern magazine called the *Dial*\* (Boston) (8:570–72). For the *Messenger*, however, a victim at last of intolerance, neglect, and bankruptcy, there was no future at all.

Long associated with the transcendental movement in America, the *Western Messenger* remains the most sustained record of the literary and religious conflicts within Unitarianism in the late 1830s. Yet its opposition to all "isms" effectively prevented it from becoming an organ of the New School: to Unitarians it went too far, while to transcendentalists it did not go far enough. For the major writers of the *Western Messenger*, transcendentalism represented not a "creed, or philosophy, or party, or sect," but a "living and always new *spirit* of truth," as Cranch put it (8:407). In its dedication to that spirit, to "something beyond" the conventional in literature, religion, and social thought, the magazine can be said to be essentially, as well as literally, transcendental.

## Notes

1. James Freeman Clarke, "Liberal Christianity in the West," *Boston Observer*, 23 April 1835.

2. "Western Examiner," *Christian Register*, 21 March 1835.

3. Robert S. Peabody and Francis G. Peabody, *A New England Romance: The Story of Ephraim and Mary Jane Peabody* (Boston: Houghton, Mifflin, 1920), pp. 91–95.

4. Information about subscriptions was gathered primarily from the manuscript account books and records in the James Freeman Clarke papers at the Massachusetts Historical Society. For a full history, see Robert D. Habich, *Transcendentalism and the "Western Messenger": A History of the Magazine and Its Contributors, 1835–1841* (Rutherford, N.J.: Fairleigh Dickinson University Press, 1984).

5. Clarence L. F. Gohdes, for instance, has called the *Messenger* "a full-fledged organ of transcendental thought," in *The Periodicals of American Transcendentalism* (Durham, N.C.: Duke University Press, 1931), p. 18, and Elizabeth R. McKinsey cites it as "the first of all Transcendentalist periodicals" in *The Western Experiment: New England Transcendentalists in the Ohio Valley* (Cambridge, Mass.: Harvard University Press, 1973), p. 7.

6. Robert D. Habich, "James Freeman Clarke's 1833 Letter-journal for Margaret Fuller," *ESQ: A Journal of the American Renaissance* 27 (1981):47–56.

7. Letter to the Editor, *Boston Daily Advertiser*, 5 November 1836.

8. Letter to Frederick Huidekoper, 7 January 1841, in Nina Moore Tiffany and Francis Tiffany, *Harm Jan Huidekoper* (Cambridge, Mass.: Riverside, 1904), p. 281.

## Information Sources

BIBLIOGRAPHY:

Blackburn, Charles E. "Some New Light on the *Western Messenger*." *American Literature* 26 (1954): 320–26.

Gohdes, Clarence L. F. *The Periodicals of American Transcendentalism*. Durham, N.C.: Duke University Press, 1931. Pp. 17–37.

Green, Judith A. "Religion, Life, and Literature in the *Western Messenger*." Ph.D. diss., University of Wisconsin, Madison, 1982.

Habich, Robert D. *Transcendentalism and the "Western Messenger": A History of the Magazine and Its Contributors, 1835–1841*. Rutherford, N.J.: Fairleigh Dickinson University Press, 1984.

Miller, Perry. *The Transcendentalists: An Anthology*. Cambridge, Mass.: Harvard University Press, 1950.

Mott, Frank Luther. "*The Western Messenger*." *A History of American Magazines, 1741–1850*. Cambridge, Mass.: Belknap Press of Harvard University Press, 1957. Pp. 658–63.

Rusk, Ralph Leslie. *The Literature of the Middle Western Frontier*. 2 vols. New York: Columbia University Press, 1925. 1:178–85.

Venable, William H. *Beginnings of Literary Culture in the Ohio Valley*. Cincinnati: Robert Clarke, 1891. Pp. 71–80.

INDEXES: Habich, Robert D. "An Annotated List of Contributions to the *Western Messenger*." *Studies in the American Renaissance 1984*. Ed. Joel Myerson. Charlottesville: University Press of Virginia, 1984.

REPRINT EDITIONS: American Periodicals: Series II, 1800–1850. University Microfilms, Ann Arbor. Reels 489–90. Library Resources, Inc. (Library of American Civilization).

LOCATION SOURCES: Widely available.

## Publication History

MAGAZINE TITLE AND TITLE CHANGES: *The Western Messenger; Devoted to Religion and Literature* (Bound volume 8: *The Western Messenger; Devoted to Religion, Life, and Literature*).

VOLUME AND ISSUE DATA: Volume 1, June, August–December 1835, January-February, April–July 1836; volume 2, August–December 1836, January 1837; volume 3, February–July 1837; volume 4, September–December 1837, January-February 1838; volume 5, April-September 1838; volume 6, November-December 1838, January-April 1839; volume 7, May-October 1839; volume 8, May-December 1840, January-April 1841.

FREQUENCY OF PUBLICATION: Monthly.

PUBLISHERS: April-November 1835: T. H. Shreve & Co., Cincinnati. December 1835-February 1836: James B. Marshall, Cincinnati. April 1836-October 1837: Western Unitarian Association, Louisville. November 1837-April 1839: James F. Clarke, Louisville. May-October 1839: J. F. Clarke, W. H. Channing, and J. H. Perkins, Cincinnati. May 1840-April 1841: John B. Russell, Cincinnati.

EDITORS: Ephraim Peabody, June 1835; Peabody and U. Tracy Howe, August 1835; Howe, September 1835; James H. Perkins, October 1835; Perkins, William D. Gallagher, and Thomas H. Shreve, November 1835; Perkins and James F. Clarke, December 1835; Perkins, January-February 1836; Clarke, April-September 1836; Samuel Osgood, October-November 1836; Clarke and Osgood, December 1836; Osgood, January-February 1837; Clarke, March-July 1837; William Silsbee and Edward Jarvis, September 1837; Silsbee and Christopher P. Cranch, October 1837; Cranch, November 1837; Clarke, December 1837-November 1838; Cranch, December 1838; Clarke and Cranch, January 1839; Clarke, February-April 1839; Perkins and William H. Channing, May-August 1839; Perkins, September-October 1839; Channing, May-August 1840; Perkins, September-November 1840; Channing and Perkins, December 1840; Channing, January-April 1841.

*Robert D. Habich*

# THE WESTERN MONTHLY, DEVOTED TO LITERATURE, BIOGRAPHY, AND THE INTERESTS OF THE WEST. See THE LAKESIDE MONTHLY

# THE WESTERN MONTHLY MAGAZINE. See THE ILLINOIS MONTHLY MAGAZINE

# THE WESTERN MONTHLY MAGAZINE, AND LITERARY JOURNAL. See THE ILLINOIS MONTHLY MAGAZINE

# THE WESTERN MONTHLY REVIEW

When Timothy Flint, disgruntled at the failure of his earlier career as a minister, moved from his native Massachusetts to Cincinnati in 1815 he had—as had many pioneers, before and since—been almost overwhelmed by the roughness of the newly settled land he found surrounding him. Travel was primitive, accom-modations were often nonexistent and always of poor quality, and the food was bad; furthermore, sanitation was inadequate, and as a result disease was rife. After twelve years' sojourn in the West—he had lived in Missouri and then in Louisiana before returning to Cincinnati in 1827—his attitude had mellowed somewhat and the focus of his discontent had changed. Now the West still seemed a place of deprivation, but not so much physically as intellectually and spiritually. To remedy this condition, Flint, who for several years had been toying with the notion of some day establishing a literary journal, determined to establish a monthly review at Cincinnati loosely modeled on those he had known formerly in New England, but directed more specifically at the needs and interests of a Western audience. Accordingly, in 1827, he founded the *Western Monthly Review*, the first successful literary journal to appear in the United States west of the Appalachians. In the three years of its existence (the first issue appeared in May 1827, the last in June 1830) the *Review* made a major contribution to Western intellectual life. It also added much to the cultural enrichment of the recently settled areas of the Ohio River Valley and, to a lesser degree, of the Mississippi Valley considered as a whole.

The *Review*, published monthly as a fairly slim quarto volume, was intended to appeal primarily to a Western audience, whom Flint, in common with Western literary figures of every generation, saw as overlooked and neglected by existing journals controlled and published by, in today's phrase, the Eastern literary establishment. Flint hoped his new *Review* would become a kind of forum for the exchange of ideas primarily of interest to Westerners and for the publication of original work by them. Neither of these ideals was completely realized.

Flint's primary failure came in his lack of success in attracting contributors other than himself to the *Review*. The outpouring of native Western literary talent Flint had anticipated simply did not materialize. He himself wrote at least three-fourths of the material finally published, including all the fiction. Almost all the remainder was copied from other journals. Flint's son Micah, who wrote an occasional poem and presumably helped his father out with some of the other material, was the only regular contributor except for Flint himself.

The content of the *Review* was remarkably consistent from issue to issue. Most of the pieces were short and predominantly factual. They detailed progress in transportation and other improvements, both realized and anticipated, in the amenities of Western life. Much of this material would later appear in Flint's *History and Geography of the Mississippi Valley* (1832). Also included were local historical tidbits of a primarily anecdotal nature. One of these, "The Lost Child," a short account of a local kidnapping published in the first issue of May 1827, was so thoroughly confused with Flint's 1830 novel of the same name that the very existence of the latter was almost forgotten for years, until a copy was accidentally turned up in 1950. The contents were completed with homiletic moral essays, book reviews, and possibly a short story by Flint or a poem by his son Micah.

Flint himself published only six of his own stories in the *Review*, together with a brief excerpt from a forthcoming novel, *The Shoshonee Valley* (excerpt published 1828, novel, 1830). This, as much as any other single fact, indicates how far Flint's notion of the proper contents of a monthly literary review was from the modern conception of a literary magazine. Belles-lettres, though important, could not in themselves justify the existence of a monthly magazine either to Flint or, presumably, to the journal's readers. The specifically Western content of the *Western Monthly Review* consisted primarily in the rather boomerish reports of the present facts and future prospects for Western life, not in imaginative writing about these facts.

From its inception the *Review* was conceived as something of a family endeavor, and hence exact attribution of authorship is impossible. Besides Micah, another son, Ebenezer, who printed the *Review* from his shop in Cincinnati, quite possibly also had some hand in editing its contents; the role of Flint's sons in preparation of the material is analogous to that of a modern copy editor.

In 1830, the *Western Monthly Review* expired. Reasons for its demise are varied. The most obvious, though not necessarily the most important, is Flint's lack of success in attracting contributors. Financial reasons also should not be ignored. Flint had hoped to make a reasonable living from the *Review*, but the magazine could not at the best of times have done much more than break even. Flint was neither the first nor the last to see his dreams of journalistic success dissolve in a puddle of red ink. Another factor was Flint's declining health. Never robust, his physical state slowly deteriorated from the mid–1820s until his death at age sixty in 1840.

Most important, however, was a change for the better in Flint's literary fortunes. In 1827, he had been a virtual unknown. Although his first factual study of Western life, *Recollections of the Last Ten Years*, and his first novel, *Francis Berrian*, had been published the preceding year, neither had as yet made much of an impression on American literary life. The *Recollections* became a minor success, but *Francis Berrian* soon gained a considerable reputation as a literary curiosity. The first novel in English set in the American Southwest, it anticipates the plot of many later Westerns, in which the dastardly Hispanic villain and the clean-living Anglo hero battle for the affections of a beautiful Spanish maiden.

By 1830, the situation had changed. Flint had authored four more novels— *Arthur Clenning* (1828), *George Mason* (1829), *The Lost Child*, and *The Shoshonee Valley* (both 1830), together with *A Condensed Geography and History of the Western States* (1828). His reputation as a man of letters was, for the time being at least, secure, and the *Western Monthly Review* seemed more like a millstone around the neck than a banner before the eyes of genius. Flint would go on to expand his *Condensed Geography* into *The History and Geography of the Mississippi Valley* (1832), to edit and possibly largely write one of the best-known pioneer narratives of the early nineteenth century, *The Personal Narrative of James Ohio Pattie* (1831), and to write *Indian Wars of the West* and the most successful popular biography of early nineteenth-century America, the *Biograph-*

*ical Memoir of Daniel Boone* (both 1833). Today both Flint and his *Western Monthly Review* are forgotten, except by students of literary curiosa.

## Information Sources

BIBLIOGRAPHY:

Folsom, James K. *Timothy Flint*. New York: Twayne Publishers, 1965. See especially pages 61–73.

Kirkpatrick, John Ervin. *Timothy Flint. Pioneer, Missionary, Author, Editor. 1780–1840*. Cleveland: The Arthur H. Clark Company, 1911.

Mott, Frank Luther. "*The Western Monthly Review*." *A History of American Magazines*. 4 vols. Cambridge, Mass.: Belknap Press of Harvard University Press, 1957. 1:559–61.

Venable, William H. *Beginnings of Literary Culture in the Ohio Valley. Historical and Biographical Sketches*. Cincinnati: Robert Clarke & Co., 1891. Pages 323–60.

INDEXES: None.

REPRINT EDITIONS: American Periodicals: Series II, 1800–1850. University Microfilms, Ann Arbor. Reel 673.

LOCATION SOURCES: Widely available.

## Publication History

MAGAZINE TITLE AND TITLE CHANGES: *The Western Magazine and Review*, May–July 1827. *The Western Monthly Review*, August 1827–June 1830.

VOLUME AND ISSUE DATA: Volumes 1–3, May 1827–June 1830.

FREQUENCY OF PUBLICATION: Monthly.

PUBLISHER: Ebenezer H. Flint, Cincinnati.

EDITOR: Timothy Flint.

*James K. Folsom*

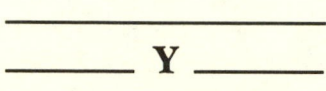

## Y

**THE YALE REVIEW.** See *American Literary Magazines: The Twentieth Century*

## YANKEE DOODLE

Writing in *A Fable for Critics* (1848), James Russell Lowell sentenced

Petty thieves, kept from flagranter crimes by their fears,
Shall peruse Yankee Doodle a blank term of years,—
That American Punch, like the English, no doubt—
Just the sugar and lemons and spirit left out.[1]

One may not agree with Lowell's harsh judgment, but it must be acknowledged that he understood *Yankee Doodle*'s purposes as did many of his contemporaries, including Evert A. Duyckinck, who was one of the enthusiasts who founded it late in 1846.[2] In Duyckinck's letter to his brother George on 15 September 1846, he called it "an American Punch," and two weeks later he reported to George that "the foundation was laid for a great deal of good humor." He realized, however, that "the success of the thing will depend upon the engagement of two or three well practiced writers to sustain it steadily."[3] The satire these New York literati strove for was perfectly in keeping with the long-established tradition of Knickerbocker literature initiated in the first decade of the nineteenth century by Irving's *Salmagundi* and the *History of New York* and perpetuated well into the 1850s. As Kendall Taft has asserted, "The New York newspapers and magazines fostered the taste for satire by opening their columns to every conceivable variety of skit, parody, burlesque, travesty, and caricature."[4] *Yankee Doodle* was conceived and born to continue this well-established New York tradition of humorous satirical writing, a heritage with roots in the eighteenth century as well as spin-offs and analogs in other sections of the new nation, such as the Old Southwest.

The ends and purposes for which the magazine was conceived were nowhere better articulated than in the preface to the first volume, anonymously contributed probably by George G. Foster, its prime mover and first editor. Establishing "Yankee Doodle" as the "Laughing Divinity" of the nation, he proclaimed that "rich and poor, famous and obscure, young and old, juvenile age and aged childhood, shall enjoy the inestimable blessings of a constant intercouse [sic] with their laughter-loving, mirth-provoking deity, who every week will present them with a fresh leaf from his inexhaustible library of fun" (1:iii–iv). Cornelius Mathews, who was to edit the weekly during the last several months of its one-year life and was also in on its founding, perhaps even as a coeditor, made similar assertions in the lead piece for the first number, "Yankee Doodle Come to Town." Personifying the American spirit in the figure of "Yankee Doodle," Mathews announced his arrival and presented, in a brief and witty catalog with a Southwestern humor tone, the mythical figure's history, interests, and aspirations: "From the moment of his birth he has been a spry child—brim-full of smartness, ready to turn his hand to psalm-singing, wood-chopping, witch-hanging, Indian-hunting, sarse, spouting and other vegetables, revolutionizing, town-building, canal-making, steamboating, railroading, [and] telegraphing." "Yankee" himself announced that the object of the paper will be "the propagation of true, genuine Yankee-Doodleism; and the utter extirpation of old Fudge-ism and Monkeyism in ART, LITERATURE, SOCIETY, THE DRAMA, and all other provinces of national labor." And Mathews concluded by more specifically identifying some of the objects of the journal's satire: "A wrong-built church, a domineering, blustering press, a filthy theatre or other house of entertainment, a hypocrite divine, a publisher of base degree, a mis-managing manager, an apish author, a vulgar statue, not any trickster of any class or kind staining the good name of the land" (1:3).

The assessment of *Yankee Doodle*'s fortunes by Evert A. Duyckinck—its close observer, supporter, and occasional contributor—are the most complete and judicious. Enthusiasm was first generated in September 1846, and two weeks later he reported to George in his next letter: "There were not a vast many good things said [at the "rich and tasty" dinner for planning] but the foundation was laid for a great deal of good humor in and towards the undertaking. Some excellent papers are ready and several very spirited wood cuts for the first numbers. . . . The success of the thing will depend upon the engagement of two or three well practiced writers to sustain it steadily."[5] But Evert's excitement was to wane during the following week. Writing to George on 14 October, he rather lamented his involvement with the "cub magazine." Reporting that the first issue had sold some eight thousand copies during the first two days it was on sale, he was both amazed at the success and critical of the publication: "The engravings are bad—that is admitted. The matter is too grave for a Punch. . . . There is not working material enough here for a paper answering to the London Clarion and for my part I wanted to see a vigorous, spirited and not merely a funny paper but people look for a thing with jokes." Even more significantly he wrote of the editorial power held by George G. Foster and Richard Grant White and reported tensions between them and Mathews: "They fight Mathews mightily about his leads [or leaders] and think he has too strong a mouth for them." (Mathews was his usual assertive, abrasive self.) By late November Evert was apologetic for his connection with the journal: "You must not hold me responsible for any personalities or [undeciphered word] that may strike you in Yankee Doodle. I am merely an outside contributor. Foster has the management of it pretty much in his own hands. . . . Looking at Y.D. critically there has been coarseness and not seldom a 'plentiful lack of wit.' "[6] And in mid-December he announced the withdrawal of himself and Mathews from the venture: "Neither Mathews nor myself have written anything for YD since I wrote you [probably the 30 November letter]. It has been a great deal attacked, has had a great deal of advice given it in the newspapers and upon the whole has made no reputation for wit & humor. Much in it is very flat. Mathews has not been drawn out & I was for a journal of a different kind."[7] In his 30 June 1847 letter to George, Evert indicated the level to which *Yankee Doodle* had fallen during Foster's editorship (White evidently had ceased editing it much earlier) and conjectured whether it could be revitalized: "The woodcuts are now very rude and cheap. The paper has been failing . . . and it may be doubted whether a new captain & crew can bring back popular gales of laughter [?]."[8] Two weeks later, after Mathews had taken over completely with the fortieth number (issued on 10 July 1847), Evert was again waxing enthusiastic about the magazine. That Mathews was doing the job Evert had hoped for was indicated on the day the third number under Mathews's control was issued: "Mathews is away with Yankee Doodle and [deleted word] spiking [?] the gun of the Mosquito Fleet of Sunday papers. Some of them are filled with this gigantic CM."[9] The Young America group, the Duyckinck Circle, was in control.

The more important phase of *Yankee Doodle*'s existence was during Mathews's editorship when Herman Melville, the most famous writer to be associated with the magazine, contributed some satiric sketches.[10] Melville's "Authentic Anecdotes of Old Zack" were published in seven installments beginning in number 42 (24 July 1847) and continuing through number 49 (11 September) except in number 48 (4 September). In addition, several additional items have been attributed to Melville by Merton M. Sealts, Jr., and will be published in the volume of his shorter works, forthcoming in the standard edition of *The Writings of Herman Melville* (Northwestern University Press and The Newberry Library). There were a number of other contributors, few of them remembered today. In keeping with period conventions, contributions were anonymous. However, Evert A. Duyckinck identified a number of contributors,[11] including: Jedediah Auld, Lemuel Bangs, Thomas Delf, Evert A. Duyckinck, George G. Foster, Charles

Fenno Hoffman, Caroline Kirkland, Cornelius Mathews, Charles W. Webber, and Richard Grant White. Possible contributors are Parke Godwin, John Keese, and John L. W. McCracken. Naturally, Foster, Mathews, and perhaps White did the lion's share of writing during their editorships.

Mathews, whose correspondence during this period has largely disappeared, had high hopes for the new venture. Late in August he wrote George, asking him to contact a Mr. C. H. Peabody in London and solicit him to act as "agent for *Yankee Doodle* London."[12] But such hopes for prospects were not realized. On 6 October 1847, several days after *Yankee Doodle*'s last appearance, Evert wrote George that "the last year [had] reduced them [literary matters] to their lowest terms. Even Yankee Doodle is in process of rapid evaporation. It concluded the second volume last week and the publisher's last [undeciphered word] this is to continue it for a monthly hereafter in the same size, a few more pages [deleted word] if it appears."[13] And he went on to lament the lack of profit realized from the project by Mathews, Melville, and Bangs. Three days later Evert amplified on the arrangement for the monthly in his *Diary*: "The publisher promises the latter [a monthly] on the first of December. He says he has extended more than $4000 upon the engravings of the year but having no Cruickshank or even the tenth part of one they have gone for nothing."[14] But a week later (14 October 1847) he advised George that *Yankee Doodle*'s failure or passage into the monthly state had "hardly excited a word." Referring to Mathews's proposal for a "*Yankee Doodle* London," George Duyckinck wrote what was the magazine's epitaph: "Y.D. being past surgery it is of course useless for me to call on Mr. Peabody, Norfolk St.—about it."[15] Nevertheless, for students of literature or popular culture, especially those willing to ferret out the meanings of topical allusions, it is a useful periodical. And for those concerned with the history of American humor, as well as with this facet of Herman Melville's early career, it is valuable.

## Notes

1. *The Poetical Works of James Russell Lowell* (Boston: Houghton Mifflin, 1897), pp. 124–28.

2. The most thorough as well as only account of the birth, maturity, and death of *Yankee Doodle* was recorded by Evert A. Duyckinck in his letters to his brother, George, who was in Europe; in his *Diary: May 29–November 8, 1847* (Donald Yannella and Kathleen M. Yannella, "Evert A. Duyckinck's 'Diary: May 29–November 8, 1847,' " *Studies in the American Renaissance, 1978* [Boston: Twayne, 1978], pp. 207–58); and in his copy of both volumes of the journal itself which has evidently disappeared from the New York Public Library; a microfilm copy has been put on deposit at The Newberry Library by Donald Yannella.

3. Evert A. Duyckinck, Letter to George Long Duyckinck, 30 September 1846, Duyckinck Family Papers, New York Public Library. All manuscripts cited are from this collection.

4. *Minor Knickerbockers* (New York: American Book Co., 1947), p. xci.

5. Evert A. Duyckinck, Letter to George Long Duyckinck, 30 September 1846.

6. Evert A. Duyckinck, Letter to George Long Duyckinck, 30 November 1846.

7. Evert A. Duyckinck, Letter to George Long Duyckinck, 15 December 1846.

8. Evert A. Duyckinck, Letter to George Long Duyckinck, 30 June 1847.

9. Evert A. Duyckinck, Letter to George Long Duyckinck, 24 July 1847.

10. Despite the statement in the preface for the bound trade edition of volume 2, written in all likelihood by Mathews in late September or during October 1847, that "ever since No. 40, when *Yankee Doodle*'s affairs went into the hands of a new management, things have worn a new face" (2:iii), it appears that the editorial transition began with number 39, issued on 3 July 1847. Luther Mansfield ("Melville's Comic Articles on Zachary Taylor," *American Literature* 9 [1938]:413 n. 3) has suggested that "Mathews did not take charge as soon as [Evert] Duyckinck had expected" in his 30 June 1847 letter to George. However, the last article in number 39, "A Little More Grape, Captain Bragg," asked the reader to notice that with "our present number (39) that *Yankee Doodle* has not fallen asleep in his old age," but is rather "just cutting his best teeth" (2:130). In his "Diary" for 30 June 1847, Evert indicated that he had seen the "proof sheets" for number 39, to be issued on 3 July, and also identified Jerry Auld as the author of three pieces and himself as having written one (Yannella and Yannella, p. 224). And writing to George on the same day, he announced Mathews's control: "Yankee Doodle . . . by the way appears this week under the direction of Mathews— Fraetas [the publisher] in his destitution having come back a prodigal to the home of wit humor entertainment and intellectual feasting—the Tetractys."

11. All his atttributions are included in Donald Yannella, "Cornelius Mathews: Knickerbocker Satirist" (Ph.D. diss., Fordham University, 1971), pp. 202–39. Duyckinck's identifications are in his letters to George during the period, his copy of *Yankee Doodle* (now missing from the New York Public Library, but on deposit, in microfilm, at The Newberry Library), and in Yannella and Yannella, pp. 212–58.

12. Cornelius Mathews, Letter to George Long Duyckinck, 31 August 1847.

13. Evert A. Duyckinck, Letter to George Long Duyckinck, 6 October 1847.

14. Yannella and Yannella, p. 242.

15. George Long Duyckinck, Letter to Evert A. Duyckinck, 2 November 1847.

## Information Sources

BIBLIOGRAPHY:

Genzmer, George Harvey. "Richard Grant White." *Dictionary of American Biography* (1936)19:113–14.

Mansfield, Luther S. "Melville's Comic Articles on Zachary Taylor." *American Literature* 9 (1938):411–18.

Miller, Perry. *The Raven and the Whale: The War of Words and Wits in the Era of Poe and Melville*. New York: Harcourt, Brace, 1956.

Stein, Allen F. *Cornelius Mathews*. New York: Twayne, 1974.

Yannella, Donald. "Cornelius Mathews: Knickerbocker Satirist." Ph.D. diss., Fordham, 1971.

Yannella, Donald, and Kathleen M. Yannella. "Evert A. Duyckinck's 'Diary: May 29– November 8, 1847.' " *Studies in the American Renaissance, 1978*. Boston: Twayne, 1978. Pp. 207–58.

INDEXES: None.

REPRINT EDITIONS: American Periodicals: Series II, 1800–1850. University Microfilms, Ann Arbor. Reel 1408.

LOCATION SOURCES: Widely available.

## Publication History

MAGAZINE TITLE AND TITLE CHANGES: *Yankee Doodle*.
VOLUME AND ISSUE DATA: Volumes 1–2, 10 October 1846–2 October 1847.
FREQUENCY OF PUBLICATION: Weekly.
PUBLISHERS: 10 October 1846–1 May 1847: William H. Graham, New York. 8 May
    1847–2 October 1847: Josiah A. Fraetas, New York. Fraetas printed all issues
    and during the second period noted there is a suggestion that there were silent
    publishers; notices and advertisements state that Fraetas "Published [it] for the
    Proprietors" (e.g. 2:200).
EDITORS: George G. Foster, Richard Grant White, and perhaps Cornelius Mathews,
    10 October 1846–26 June 1847; Foster served during this entire period, White
    evidently ceased in early 1847, and Mathews severed connections by late No-
    vember or early December 1846. Mathews was sole editor, 3 July 1847–2 October
    1847.

*Donald Yannella*

# Minor Literary Magazines and Nonliterary Magazines with Literary Contents

The following list is selective and includes magazines that, for various reasons, did not warrant study in full profiles. Some of them were literary and published interesting work but failed to survive beyond a few issues. Others, such as *Peterson's*, lived long and financially successful but undistinguished lives. Many were primarily political or religious magazines that included literature as a minor element. The *Nation*, with its distinguished literary criticism and book reviews, is an example. A few, including the *Home Journal* and the *Farmer's Weekly Museum*, were really newspapers, although the differentiation of journalistic types is difficult, especially early in the nineteenth century. The annotations focus on the magazines' literary significance. The listing is chronological.

*The American Magazine and Monthly Chronicle for the British Colonies*. October 1757–October 1758. Philadelphia. Although primarily political, William Bradford's monthly included poetry by Francis Hopkinson and Thomas Godfrey, Jr.

*The New American Magazine*. January 1758–March 1760. Woodbridge, N.J. Editor Samuel Nevill's magazine reflected his interest in current history. In 1780 Joel Barlow was advised to use it as a source for his *Columbiad*.

*The New-England Magazine of Knowledge and Pleasure*. August 1758–March 1759. Boston. Editor Benjamin Mecom, nephew of Benjamin Franklin, included poetry, moralistic fiction, and dramatic dialogue.

*The American Magazine, or General Repository*. January–September 1769. Philadelphia. Editor Lewis Nicola, a member of the American Philosophical Society, published many scientific articles along with the usual sentimental and moralistic tales and poems.

*The Pennsylvania Magazine; or, American Monthly Museum*. January 1775–July 1776. Philadelphia. Thomas Paine was the editor of and most prolific contributor to this monthly founded by Robert Aitken.

*The Gentleman and Lady's Town and Country Magazine*. May–December 1784. Boston. For the first time an appeal to women readers is reflected in a magazine's title.

*The New-York Magazine; or, Literary Repository*. January 1790–December 1797. New York. Most of the contents of this monthly were reprinted from other publications, as was typical of the period, but William Dunlap, Charles Brockden Brown, and Noah Webster were occasional contributors.

*The New-Hampshire Journal: or Farmer's Weekly Museum.* 11 April 1793–15 October 1810. Walpole, New Hampshire. Although classified as a newspaper, this weekly was edited by Joseph Dennie from 1796 to 1799 and included literary contributions from Dennie, Royall Tyler, and Thomas Green Fessenden.

*The Tablet.* 9 May 1795–11 August 1795. Boston. This was Dennie's first and unsuccessful attempt to establish his own literary magazine. It reflects his interest in the Addisonian essay.

*The New-York Weekly Magazine.* 1 July 1795–23 August 1797. New York. Later appropriately titled the *Sentimental and Literary Magazine*, this publication was one of the first to include significant amounts of fiction.

*The South Carolina Weekly Museum.* January 1797–July 1798. Charleston. This was the first Southern magazine, published in the city that would become the antebellum South's center of literary publication.

*The Time Piece and Literary Companion.* 13 March 1797–30 August 1798. New York. This political and literary triweekly was Philip Freneau's only such editorial venture; its failure discouraged him from any further attempts.

*The Weekly Magazine of Original Essays, Fugitive Pieces, and Interesting Intelligence.* 3 February 1798–1 June 1799. Philadelphia. This magazine published Charles Brockden Brown's essay series "The Man at Home" and excerpts from his *Sky-Walk* and *Arthur Mervyn*. Included was the section of *Arthur Mervyn* depicting the yellow-fever epidemic of 1797, the very epidemic that killed the *Weekly*'s first editor, James Watters.

*The Boston Weekly Magazine.* 30 October 1802–26 April 1806. *The Emerald.* 3 May 1806–15 October 1808. Boston. Primarily a ladies' magazine, with much discussion of manners and fashions, this magazine paid close attention to the early theater.

*The Monthly Register, and Review of the United States.* January 1805–December 1807. Charleston and New York. Stephen C. Carpenter's magazine consisted of two sections, one containing a chronicle of the recent revolution and the other containing essay and fiction series.

*Polyanthos.* December 1805–July 1807, February 1812–September 1814. Boston. This early venture by Joseph Buckingham provided dramatic reviews and commentary. Royall Tyler was among the contributors.

*Salmagundi; or, the Whim-Whams and Opinions of Launcelot Langstaff, Esq., and Others.* 24 January 1807–25 January 1808. New York. This satirical essay periodical contains the early work of Washington Irving, William Irving, and James Kirke Paulding. It was revived briefly by Paulding in 1819.

*The American Review of History and Politics.* January 1811–October 1812. Philadelphia. Robert Walsh's first quarterly review focused primarily on politics, and he wrote most of it himself. It was the first American quarterly patterned on the English reviews.

*The General Repository and Review.* January 1812–October 1813. Cambridge, Massachusetts. Founded by Andrews Norton and intended as a defense of Unitarianism, this quarterly was considered by James G. Palfrey to be the forerunner of the *North American Review*.*

*The American Monthly Magazine and Critical Review*. May 1817–April 1819. New York. One of a number of publications edited by Horatio Bigelow, this monthly combined reviews with a variety of contents, including poetry and scientific articles.

*The New-England Galaxy*. 10 October 1817–29 March 1839. Boston. Joseph Buckingham wanted his weekly to be "chiefly of a literary and miscellaneous character, eschewing entirely all political partizanship." He wrote much of the contents himself, with Susanna Rowson and Edward Everett among his contributors. In 1828, Buckingham sold the *Galaxy* and turned his attention to the *Boston Courier*.

*The Christian Spectator*. January 1819–November 1838. New Haven. Entitled the *Quarterly Christian Spectator* from March 1829. The views of orthodox Presbyterianism were presented in this religious magazine. Philosophically, it agreed with the Scotch Realists, and it judged contemporary poetry primarily from a didactic viewpoint.

*The Western Review and Miscellaneous Magazine*. August 1819–July 1821. Lexington, Kentucky. Founded by newspaper editor William Gibbes Hunt, this monthly drew some of its contributors from Transylvania University.

*The Idle Man*. 1821–1822. New York. Charles Henry Dana, Sr., moved to New York and founded and edited this miscellany after he was removed from the editorial board of the *North American Review*.* He was assisted by William Cullen Bryant and Washington Allston, but the venture lasted for only six issues.

*The Saturday Evening Post*. 4 August 1821–current. Philadelphia. In the nineteenth century the *Post* reached its greatest literary prominence during the editorship of Henry Peterson (1846–1873). Peterson obtained the work of such popular writers as Mrs. E.D.E.N. Southworth, Grace Greenwood, and Fanny Fern.

*The Atlantic Magazine*. May 1824–April 1825. New York. This monthly was founded by Robert C. Sands, magazinist, poet, and member of the Knickerbocker group, who wrote much of the contents himself. The *Atlantic* was the precursor of the *New-York Review, and Atheneum Magazine*.*

*The Casket*. January 1826–December 1840. Philadelphia. This illustrated monthly, a competitor of *Godey's*,* took most of its fiction and articles from other publications. George R. Graham purchased it from owner and editor Samuel C. Atkinson, combining it with *Burton's Gentleman's Magazine*\* to form *Graham's*.*

*The Youth's Companion*. 16 April 1827–September 1929. Boston. Founded by Nathaniel Willis, father of Nathaniel Parker Willis, this weekly included over the years stories, poems, and essays by prominent figures from many fields.

*The Southern Literary Gazette*. September 1828–15 October 1829. Charleston. This short-lived publication was the first of a number of ventures into magazine editing by William Gilmore Simms.

*The Critic.* 1 November 1828–2 May 1829. New York. Editor William Leggett wrote many of the essays, dramatic reviews, and fiction in this literary weekly himself. The *New-York Mirror** soon absorbed the *Critic.*

*The American Monthly Magazine.* April 1829–July 1831. Boston. The young Nathaniel Parker Willis edited and wrote most of the contents of this lively Boston monthly after the demise of which he joined the staff of the *New-York Mirror.**

*The Saturday Visiter.* 1832–1850. Baltimore. One of the longer-lived weekly miscellanies, the *Visiter* awarded a hundred-dollar prize in 1833 for best short story to the young Edgar Allan Poe for "A Manuscript Found in a Bottle." Poe published poems in it as well.

*The American Monthly Review.* January 1832–December 1833. Cambridge, Massachusetts. Modelling his magazine after the English reviews, editor Sidney Willard drew on the talents of Harvard intellectuals. The *American Monthly* was absorbed by the *New England Magazine.**

*The North American Magazine.* November 1832–April 1835. *The North American Quarterly.* 1835–June 1838. Philadelphia. The poet Sumner Lincoln Fairfield founded this magazine, struggled to keep it going, and then gave up in despair. His wife travelled extensively to gather subscriptions.

*The Select Journal of Foreign Periodical Literature.* January 1833–October 1834. Boston. Edited by Charles Folsom and Andrews Norton, conservative spokesmen for Unitarianism, this eclectic quarterly published material from the best foreign publications.

*The New-Yorker.* 26 March 1836–11 September 1841. New York. Horace Greeley's editorial assistants on this general weekly were the young Park Benjamin and Rufus Wilmot Griswold. The *New-Yorker* was absorbed as the weekly edition of Greeley's *Tribune.*

*The New York Review.* March 1837–April 1842. New York. Founded by Caleb S. Henry, professor of philosophy at New York University, this quarterly briefly rivaled the *North American** in quality.

*The Corsair.* 16 March 1839–7 March 1840. New York. The most urbane of the many eclectic magazines, the *Corsair* included witty and sophisticated contributions from Nathaniel Parker Willis. Willis edited it along with Dr. T. O. Porter, brother of William T. Porter of the *New York Spirit of the Times.**

*The Ladies' Repository, and Gatherings of the West.* January 1841–December 1876. Cincinnati. Subtitle dropped in 1849. A more strict and moralistic ladies' magazine than *Godey's,** the monthly *Repository* was edited by Methodist ministers. At various times

Alice and Phoebe Cary, Moncure D. Conway, and Mrs. Lydia Sigourney appeared in its pages.

*The Western Literary Messenger*. August 1841–April 1857. Buffalo. Edited by Jesse Clements, this monthly included contributions by Mrs. Sigourney and R. H. Stoddard.

*Peterson's Magazine*. January 1842–April 1898. Philadelphia. Various titles. This was the most successful competitor of *Godey's*,\* although its contents tended much more to the sentimental and undistinguished.

*The New York Ledger*. 1851–22 October 1898. New York. Under owner and editor Robert Bonner, the dull *Merchant's Ledger* was transformed into the best-selling magazine of its day. Bonner paid well for the work of popular writers such as Fanny Fern and Sylvanus Cobb, Jr.

*Miss Leslie's Magazine*. January–December 1843. *Arthur's Ladies' Magazine*. January 1844–July 1846. Philadelphia. Miss Eliza Leslie and then T. S. Arthur edited this rival of *Godey's*,\* and some well-known contributors appeared in it. Longfellow's "The Village Blacksmith" was included in August 1844. *Godey's* finally absorbed its short-lived rival.

*The New Englander*. January 1843–September 1885. *The New Englander and Yale Review*. November 1885–March 1892. New Haven. Founded by Edward Royall Tyler, this quarterly (later bimonthly and monthly) represented conservative New England Congregationalist thought. It was the precursor of the *Yale Review*.

*The Eclectic Magazine of Foreign Literature, Science and Art*. January 1844–December 1898. New York. This monthly eclectic was the best illustrated magazine of its type, including in its early years many engravings by John Sartain. It was taken over by the rival *Living Age*.

*The Christian Parlor Magazine*. May 1844–April 1854. New York. This was a religiously oriented alternative to the popular ladies' magazines. A number of the usual magazinists appeared here, including Mrs. Sigourney and T. S. Arthur.

*Littell's Living Age*. 11 May 1844–26 December 1896. *The Living Age*. 2 January 1897–August 1941. Under Eliakim Littell, his son Robert, and Frank Foxcroft, for its first eighty years this eclectic published serious material from the great English quarterlies mixed with lighter fare from publications such as Dickens's *Household Words*.

*The Flag of Our Union*. January 1846–October 1870(?). Frederick Gleason's weekly story paper was one of the best of its kind. The work of Poe, Park Benjamin, Horatio Alger, and Mrs. Sigourney appeared in it.

*The Home Journal*. 14 February 1846–23 March 1901. New York. Founded by Nathaniel Parker Willis and George Pope Morris, this witty weekly paper of fashion and manners was most lively before Willis's death in 1867.

*The Ladies' Wreath*. May 1846–August 1855. New York. Typical of ladies' magazines intended for binding as gift books, this *Wreath* included the work of T. S. Arthur, Mrs. Ann Stephens, and Mrs. Sigourney.

*The National Era*. January 1847–March 1860. Washington, D.C. Among the works published in this antislavery paper were *Uncle Tom's Cabin*, in serial form, Hawthorne's

"The Great Stone Face," and, in response to Daniel Webster's involvement in the Compromise of 1850, Whittier's poem "Ichabod."

*The Union Magazine of Literature and Art.* July 1847–December 1848. *Sartain's Union Magazine of Literature and Art.* January 1849–June 1852. New York and Philadelphia. An unsuccessful competitor to *Graham's** and *Godey's,** this monthly did publish some major writers, including Poe, Longfellow, and Lowell, as well as sentimental favorites, among them Mrs. Sigourney and T. S. Arthur.

*The Independent.* 7 December 1848–13 October 1928. New York. This Congregationalist weekly was fiercely antislavery. Among its editors after the war were Henry Ward Beecher and Theodore Tilton. It published the work of Harriet Beecher Stowe, and after the war it published poetry by Longfellow, Holmes, Emily Dickinson, Bryant, and other major figures.

*The International Weekly Miscellany of Literature, Art, and Science.* 1 July–26 August 1850. *The International Miscellany of Literature, Art, and Science.* October–November 1850. *The International Monthly Magazine of Literature, Art, and Science.* December 1850–April 1852. New York. Edited by Rufus Wilmot Griswold, who was assisted by Charles Godfrey Leland, this rival to *Harper's** also reprinted extensively the works of English writers. It was absorbed by its rival, however.

*To-Day: A Boston Literary Journal.* January–December 1852. Boston. Many of the literary and artistic essays and book reviews in this weekly were written by the editor himself, Charles Hale, brother of Edward Everett Hale.

*Arthur's Home Magazine.* October 1852–December 1898. Philadelphia. Owned and edited by the author of *Ten Nights in a Bar Room*, this ladies' magazine was a weak but solvent competitor to *Godey's** and *Peterson's*, also of Philadelphia. Arthur and Virginia F. Townsend, his coeditor until 1872, did much of the writing.

*The Crayon.* 3 January 1855–July 1861. New York. This high-quality art magazine also included literary contributions, among them pieces by Bryant and Lowell.

*The Criterion.* 3 November 1855–July 1856. New York. This conservative critical weekly edited by Charles R. Rode joined the attack on *Leaves of Grass* by labelling it "a mass of stupid filth."

*Hutching's Illustrated California Magazine.* July 1856–June 1861. San Francisco. This early Western magazine featured stories of gold prospecting.

*Mrs. Stephens' Illustrated New Monthly.* July 1856–June 1858. New York. Mrs. Ann Stephens was one of the most popular novelists of the day, her work much sought after by contemporary editors. Her own magazine, published by her husband, Edward Stephens, contained mostly her own fiction and essays.

*Harper's Weekly.* 3 January 1857–13 May 1916. New York. This political arm of the Harper & Brothers publishing house did include some literature, especially serial fiction by prominent English writers such as Dickens, Wilkie Collins, Edward Bulwer-Lytton, and Mrs. Elizabeth Gaskell.

*The Great Republic Monthly.* January 1859–November 1859. New York. This magazine featured travel literature and included literary reviews and poetry.

*The National Quarterly Review.* June 1860–October 1880. New York. Edward I. Sears founded and then edited for 16 years this conservative quarterly. Sears wrote many of its articles himself, thus impressing upon it his traditionalist personality.

*The Countryman.* 4 March 1862–8 May 1866. Turnwold, Georgia. Suspended from 30 June 1865–30 January 1866. The young Joel Chandler Harris wrote for and assisted in the printing of this literary weekly published on J. A. Turner's plantation. Harris's experiences there served as the basis for the *Uncle Remus* stories.

*The Old Guard.* June 1862–December 1870. New York. This Copperhead monthly published, after the war, poetry and fiction by Southerners William Gilmore Simms, John Esten Cooke, and John R. Thompson.

*The Magnolia: A Southern Home Journal.* 27 September 1862–1 April 1865(?). The leading writers of the South, William Gilmore Simms, Paul Hamilton Hayne, John R. Thompson, and John Esten Cooke, contributed to this weekly wartime magazine.

*The United States Service Magazine.* January 1864–June 1866. New York. A graduate of West Point, a veteran of the Mexican War, and a professor of English at the University of Pennsylvania, editor Henry Coppée included literature in his serviceman's magazine. *Love and Loyalty* by Louisa May Alcott was published serially in 1864, and the work of Charles Godfrey Leland and Charles Astor Bristed also appeared.

*The Californian.* 28 May 1864–1868. San Francisco. Charles H. Webb was owner and editor and Bret Harte the most frequent contributor. Both left the *Golden Era*\* to found this literary weekly. Mark Twain also left the *Golden Era* for the *Californian*, where he gained experience and the advice of Harte. Twain and Harte contributed parodies, satires, sketches, and essays. Ambrose Bierce and Henry George also were contributors.

*Demorest's Monthly Magazine.* January 1865–December 1899. New York. When W. Jennings Demorest's sons Henry and William took over their father's women's fashion monthly in 1885, they improved the quality of its literature. Among the contributors were Louisa May Alcott, Thomas Hardy, and Robert Louis Stevenson.

*The Catholic World.* April 1865–current. New York. Under its first editor, Father Isaac T. Hecker, this general monthly achieved its highest literary distinction. Among its contributors were Orestes Brownson, Joyce Kilmer, Hilaire Belloc, Agnes Repplier, and Louise Imogen Guiney.

*Hours at Home.* May 1865–October 1870. New York. This literary monthly published by Scribner was first edited by James Manning Sherwood, a Presbyterian minister, and then by Richard Watson Gilder. It was succeeded by *Scribner's Monthly.*\*

*The Nation.* 6 July 1865–current. New York. E. L. Godkin's weekly focused on political and social issues. However, its book reviews and literary criticism, written by leading scholars, were of high quality.

*Scott's Monthly Magazine.* December 1865–December 1869. Atlanta. W. J. Scott, a bookseller, published accounts of the war. He also offered an outlet for the early writing of Southerners Paul Hamilton Hayne, Sidney Lanier, and Maurice Thompson.

*Every Saturday.* 6 January 1866–31 October 1874. Boston. Founded by Ticknor and Fields, owners of the *Atlantic*,\* this weekly in its first years featured reprints of English novels. In 1870 it changed its focus to politics and social commentary, and, with more illustrations, it resembled and became a rival of *Harper's Weekly*.

*The Land We Love*. May 1866–March 1869. Charlotte, North Carolina. Founded by General Daniel Harvey Hill, this monthly published accounts of the war by Confederate officers but argued for reconciliation with the North. Its literature was generally unremarkable, but Paul Hamilton Hayne and John R. Thompson were among the contributors.

*Journal of Speculative Philosophy*. January 1867–December 1893. St. Louis. Although not literary, William Torrey Harris's journal did publish some philosophical articles by literary figures. These included Bronson Alcott, William Ellery Channing, and Frederick H. Hedge.

*The New Jersey Magazine*. May–June 1867. *The Northern Monthly*. July 1867–June 1868. Newark. Captain Allen Lee Bassett edited this magazine established by the New Jersey State Literary Union. Although some professional writers contributed, the contents were mostly leisurely essays on history and biography by amateur writers.

*Harper's Bazaar*. 2 November 1867–current. New York. Harper's women's magazine did include some literature along with its clothing fashions and patterns. English novels were serialized, and Thomas Wentworth Higginson and George William Curtis contributed essay series.

*Lippincott's Magazine*. January 1868–April 1916. Philadelphia. This monthly was a struggling and ultimately unsuccessful competitor to *Scribner's*\* and the *Atlantic*.\* However, it published much good literature throughout its career. After 1887 it included an entire short novel in each issue, one of them Oscar Wilde's *The Picture of Dorian Gray*.

*Hearth and Home*. 26 December 1868–25 December 1875. New York. Focusing on agriculture and literature, this weekly was at first edited by Donald Grant Mitchell and Harriet Beecher Stowe, with Mary Mapes Dodge an associate editor. Later, when Frank Stockton and Edward and George Cary Eggleston were editors, the amount of literature increased and its quality was high. Edward Eggleston's *The Hoosier Schoolmaster* was serialized.

*The Christian Union*. January 1870–June 1893. New York. Under the editorship of Henry Ward Beecher from its founding until 1881, this weekly published the work of some well-known writers, including Harriet Beecher Stowe and Edward Eggleston. It became the *Outlook* in July 1893.

*Penn Monthly*. January 1870–July 1882. Philadelphia. Edited by Professor Robert Ellis Thompson of the University of Pennsylvania, this general magazine drew contributors from that institution. Literature was not a major element.

*The Literary World*. June 1870–December 1904. Boston. This conservative monthly's main purpose was to review new books, but it also featured literary news and European correspondence. Never financially successful, it was absorbed by its rival review the *Critic*.\*

*Cottage Hearth*. 1874–1894. Boston. Contributors to this women's magazine included Edward Everett Hale, Joaquin Miller, and Lucy Larcom.

*The International Review*. January 1874–June 1883. New York. Foreign contributors to this monthly included Justin McCarthy and J. A. Froude. The list of American contributors was distinguished and included Henry James, John Greenleaf Whittier, Oliver Wendell Holmes, Thomas Wentworth Higginson, and William Cullen Bryant. A special effort was made to cover foreign literature.

*The American.* 16 October 1880–8 December 1900. Philadelphia. Suspended 1891–1894. This political and literary weekly published such well-known writers as Walt Whitman, Paul Hamilton Hayne, and H. H. Boyesen.

*Manhattan.* January 1883–September 1884. New York. John W. Orr, a professional illustrator, joined an already crowded field by establishing this high-quality illustrated monthly. Its contributors included Whittier, Brander Matthews, Julia Ward Howe, and Edmund Clarence Stedman.

*The Current.* 22 December 1883–13 October 1888. Chicago. This political and literary weekly published work by John Burroughs, Joaquin Miller, Paul Hamilton Hayne, and Opie Read.

*Cosmopolitan Magazine.* March 1886–April 1925. New York. Combined with *Hearst's International.* Under the brief coeditorship of William Dean Howells in 1890, this lively general mass-circulation monthly was at its most literary. However, millionaire owner and editor John Brisben Walker often included the work of the best writers of the time in order to boost circulation. He sold out to Hearst in 1905.

*The Forum.* March 1886–June 1930. New York. Absorbed by the *Century* as *Forum and Century.* Primarily a magazine of opinion on current issues, the monthly *Forum* did publish articles by prominent writers including Thomas Hardy, Jules Verne, and Charles Dudley Warner. Under the editorship of Mitchell Kennerley from 1910 to 1916, the works of the young H. L. Mencken, Sherwood Anderson, and Witter Bynner were published.

*Collier's.* 28 April 1888–4 January 1957. New York. The early years of this mass-circulation general weekly contained much fiction, including contributions by prominent writers such as H. Rider Haggard, O. Henry, Jack London, Frank Norris, and Booth Tarkington.

*Current Literature.* July 1888–December 1912. *Current Opinion.* January 1913–April 1925. New York. In its early years under founder and editor Frederick Somers, formerly of the San Francisco *Argonaut,*\* this eclectic reprinted material mostly from American sources. It successfully rivaled the best of its type, including *Littell's Living Age.*

*Poet-Lore.* January 1889–Spring 1953. Washington, D.C., and elsewhere. Promoting the study of Browning, Shakespeare, and comparative literature, this quarterly (after 1896) focused on modern drama, especially Ibsen and Russian playwrights, and contemporary poetry.

*The Arena.* December 1889–August 1909. Boston and New York. Benjamin O. Flower's monthly was a reform magazine focusing on social and political issues, but he did review and publish fiction, including the early stories of Hamlin Garland.

*McClure's Magazine.* June 1893–March 1929. New York. One of the ten-cent monthlies that successfully challenged the old "quality" monthlies, *McClure's* included fiction in its early years by prominent writers such as Rudyard Kipling, Conan Doyle, Thomas

Hardy, and Joel Chandler Harris. Its contents generally were of higher quality than *Munsey's*, another magazine of its type.

*The Midland Monthly*. January 1894–June 1899. Des Moines, Iowa. Johnson Brigham's magazine was regional in focus. Its most well-known contributors were Hamlin Garland and Octave Thanet.

*The Rolling Stone*. 14 April 1894–27 April 1895. Austin, Texas. Almost all of the contents of this satirical little magazine were written by its young editor William Sidney Porter, who received valuable training in preparation for his work as "O. Henry."

*The Basis*. March 1895–April 1896. Buffalo. This primarily political and historical magazine was edited by Albion W. Tourgée, founder of the *Continent*.* Tourgée and his daughter, Aimee, contributed fiction and poetry.

*The Literary Review*. January 1897–April 1901. Boston. This early little magazine founded by Edwin Ruthven Lamson published work by Edwin Arlington Robinson, Vance Thompson, and Elbert Hubbard.

# A Chronology of Social and Literary Events and American Literary Magazines, 1774–1900

| American Literary Magazines | Year | Social and Literary Events |
|---|---|---|
| | 1774 | |
| Isaiah Thomas establishes the *Royal American Magazine* to further the patriot cause. | | |
| | 1779 | |
| Hugh Henry Brackenridge's *United States Magazine* reflects America's revolutionary fervor. | | On 17 October, Cornwallis surrenders at Yorktown. |
| | 1786 | |
| The *Columbian Magazine* is founded with Mathew Carey as its first editor. | | |
| | 1787 | |
| Noah Webster starts the *American Magazine* in New York, hoping to transcend regional rivalries with a publication national in scope. | | On 17 September, the Constitution is signed. |
| The *American Museum* is founded by Mathew Carey in Philadelphia. | | |
| | 1789 | |
| Isaiah Thomas starts his *Massachusetts Magazine*. | | George Washington is sworn in as first president on 30 April. |

**1792**

The *Columbian Magazine* and the *American Museum* cease publication primarily because of prohibitive mailing costs created by the Postal Act of 1792.

**1799**

With the short-lived *Monthly Magazine and American Review*, Charles Brockden Brown begins his series of personally disappointing magazine ventures.

**1801**

Federalist Joseph Dennie begins his conservative weekly, the *Port Folio*.

**1803**

David Phineas Adams founds the *Monthly Anthology* in Boston.

Charles Brockden Brown begins his *Literary Magazine, and American Register* in Philadelphia.

On 20 December, the Louisiana Purchase is completed.

**1812**

On 18 June, war is declared against England for "Free Trade and Sailors' Rights."

**1813**

Bookseller Moses Thomas founds the *Analectic Magazine* with Washington Irving as editor.

The *Christian Disciple* is established in Boston as an outlet for the Unitarian views of Noah Worcester.

**1814**

The Treaty of Ghent, ending the war with England, is signed on Christmas Eve.

**1815**

Under editor William Tudor, the *North American Review* begins its distinguished 125-year career in Boston.

**1816**

The *Portico*, founded in Baltimore by members of the Delphian literary club, becomes a champion of cultural and literary nationalism.

**1820**

In an attempt to emulate the great British quarterlies, Charles K. Gardner founds the *Literary and Scientific Repository, and Critical Review*.

Washington Irving publishes *The Sketch Book of Geoffrey Crayon, Gent.*

Congress passes the Missouri Compromise.

**1823**

In his annual message, President Monroe elucidates principles later called the Monroe Doctrine.

**1824**

The *Christian Disciple* becomes the *Christian Examiner*, as Henry Ware, Jr., turns over editorial control to John Gorham Palfrey.

The *United States Literary Gazette* is founded in Boston. It became the *United States Review and Literary Gazette* under William Cullen Bryant.

**1825**

The *New-York Review, and Atheneum Magazine* is founded as a successor to the *Atlantic Magazine*, with William Cullen Bryant as coeditor.

The *Album*, founded in Charleston by William Gilmore Simms and others, is the first Southern magazine devoted exclusively to literature.

**1826**

Bryant and James Gordon Carter co-edit the *United States Review and Literary Gazette*, thus ending Bryant's *New-York Review, and Atheneum Magazine*.

James Fenimore Cooper publishes *The Last of the Mohicans* in the middle of the most prolific decade of his career.

**1827**

Timothy Flint founds the *Western Monthly Review* in Cincinnati, the first successful literary journal west of the Appalachians.

Veteran editor Robert Walsh starts his nationalistic *American Quarterly Review*.

**1828**

Stephen Elliott, Sr., founds the *Southern Review* in Charleston, modeling it on the *Edinburgh Review*.

Andrew Jackson is elected president.

Sarah Josepha Hale founds the *Ladies' Magazine* in Boston, determined to print the work only of American authors.

**1830**

With little capital and much ambition, Louis Godey launches his *Lady's Book*.

Judge James Hall founds the *Illinois Monthly* in Vandalia.

**1831**

William Trotter Porter and James Howe found the *Spirit of the Times* in New York, modeled on the English sporting magazine *Bell's Life of London*.

Joseph T. Buckingham and his son Edwin, hoping to attract contributions from burgeoning talent in the area, found the *New England Magazine*.

**1832**

Caroline Howard Gilman founds her children's magazine the *Rose Bud, or Youth's Gazette*, later to become the *Southern Rose Bud*, in Charleston.

**1833**

Henry William Herbert and Andrew D. Patterson found the *American Monthly Magazine* in New York.

Under editor Charles Fenno Hoffman, the *Knickerbocker* begins its long career.

Jackson stops funds to the Bank of the United States, thus defeating Nicholas Biddle.

**1834**

Thomas Willis White founds the *Southern Literary Messenger*, intending that it rival the best Northern magazines.

William W. Snowden founds the *Ladies' Companion*, the first major magazine in New York addressed primarily to women.

After his *New England Magazine* absorbs Sidney Willard's *American Monthly Review*, Joseph T. Buckingham turns over his editorship to Samuel G. Howe and John O. Sargent.

**1835**

With the encouragement of the American Unitarian Association, the *Western Messenger* is launched in Cincinnati.

Daniel K. Whitaker founds the *Southern Literary Journal* in Charleston, dedicating it to the proposition that the literary reputation of the South would one day match its political reputation.

Harper's publishes William Gilmore Simms's *The Yemassee*.

**1836**

The *New England Magazine* merges with the *American Monthly*, Park Benjamin joining Charles Fenno Hoffman as coeditor of the new, livelier *American Monthly*.

Ralph Waldo Emerson publishes *Nature*.

**1837**

The actor William E. Burton founds his *Gentleman's Magazine* in Philadelphia.

*Godey's Lady's Book* absorbs the *Ladies' Magazine*, and Sarah Josepha Hale becomes its editor, a position she will hold for 40 years.

Intending to combine scholarly writing with lighter fare, John L. O'Sullivan and Samuel D. Langtree found the *United States Magazine and Democratic Review*.

Emerson delivers his Phi Beta Kappa oration on "The American Scholar."

Nathaniel Hawthorne publishes his *Twice Told Tales*.

**1838**

Orestes Brownson founds the *Boston Quarterly Review* as an outlet for his reformist views.

William Davis Gallagher launches the *Hesperian* in Columbus, Ohio, in order to promote Western writers and culture.

Emerson delivers his "Divinity School Address."

**1839**

George Roberts founds the *Boston Notion*, a prominent example of the "mammoth weeklies" that flourished to the mid–1840s.

Philip C. Pendleton and George F. Pierce found the *Southern Ladies' Book* in Macon, Georgia.

**1840**

After Edgar Allan Poe resigns as coeditor, Burton sells his *Gentleman's Magazine* to George R. Graham, editor and owner of the *Casket*, who combines the two publications as *Graham's Magazine*.

The *Lowell Offering*, best known of the periodicals produced by female factory workers in New England, is founded.

1840 *Cont*

The *Dial* is published in Boston, the culmination of planning by the Transcendentalist Club, with Margaret Fuller as editor.

Evert A. Duyckinck and Cornelius Mathews found *Arcturus* as an organ that would speak for Young America.

1841

George Ripley establishes Brook Farm.

1842

Orestes Brownson's *Boston Quarterly Review* merges with the *Democratic Review*.

Daniel K. Whitaker begins the *Southern Quarterly Review*, intending it to be the successor to the earlier *Southern Review*.

William Carey Richards starts the short-lived *Orion* in Penfield, Georgia, one of many antebellum magazines intended to promote regional literary culture.

The new *Boston Miscellany of Literature and Fashion*, edited by Nathan Hale, Jr., absorbs the *Arcturus*.

1843

In January, James Russell Lowell and Robert Carter introduce the *Pioneer*, but it lives for only three monthly issues.

1844

Albert Brisbane founds the *Harbinger* at Brook Farm as the successor to his *Phalanx* and names George Ripley editor.

Brook Farm converts to Fourierist socialism.

Orestes Brownson founds *Brownson's Quarterly Review* in order to present and defend his new conservative philosophy.

John Inman founds the *Columbian Lady's and Gentleman's Magazine* as a rival to *Godey's* and *Graham's*.

**1845**

William Gilmore Simms edits the short-lived *Southern and Western Monthly Magazine and Review*.

Benjamin B. Minor buys Simms's magazine, changing the title of his own magazine to the *Southern and Western Literary Messenger and Review*.

The *American [Whig] Review* is founded in New York.

Charles Briggs, author of *Harry Franco*, is editor of the new *Broadway Journal*.

Henry David Thoreau sets up housekeeping at Walden Pond.

**1846**

After purchasing the *Broadway Journal* and struggling to make it succeed, Poe gives up, and the magazine ceases publication.

War is declared against Mexico.

**1847**

A group composed mostly of writers from the *Dial* help to found the *Massachusetts Quarterly Review*, with Theodore Parker as editor.

Evert Duyckinck's *Literary World* is founded in New York, its main purpose the review of new books.

**1848**

Charles W. Holden begins his *Dollar Magazine* in New York.

William C. Richards founds the *Southern Literary Gazette* in Athens, Georgia, the most important literary weekly in the South.

**1849**

Elizabeth Peabody publishes the only issue of *Aesthetic Papers*, including pieces by Emerson, Thoreau, and Hawthorne.

The Gold Rush begins, and San Francisco becomes a boom town.

**1850**

Harper Brothers begin *Harper's New Monthly Magazine* as an accessory to their book publishing business.

Hawthorne publishes *The Scarlet Letter*.

The Compromise of 1850 saves the peace for ten years, and the Fugitive Slave Act is passed.

**1851**

The *Carpet-Bag* begins publication in Boston, Samuel Clemens and Charles Farrar Browne (Artemus Ward) soon to appear among its contributors.

Melville publishes *Moby Dick*, and Hawthorne *The House of the Seven Gables*.

**1852**

In San Francisco Rollin M. Daggett and J. Macdonough Foard found the *Golden Era* in order to promote a Western literature that would spring from "the incidents and characters of mining camps."

Harriet Beecher Stowe publishes *Uncle Tom's Cabin*.

**1853**

*Putnam's Monthly* is established with Charles Briggs as editor and Herman Melville its most important contributor.

**1854**

Thoreau publishes *Walden*.

Admiral Perry opens Japan.

The Kansas-Nebraska bill is passed.

**1855**

Whitman publishes the first edition of *Leaves of Grass*.

Longfellow publishes *Hiawatha*.

**1856**

William T. Porter, dismissed as editor of the *Spirit of the Times*, founds the rival *Porter's Spirit of the Times*.

**1857**

*Russell's Magazine* is launched by a group of Charleston intellectuals with Paul Hamilton Hayne as editor.

In order to promote good literature and speak out against slavery, a group of New England writers led by Francis Underwood found the *Atlantic Monthly* in Boston.

*Putnam's* merges with *Emerson's United States Magazine*.

Economic panic results in widespread bank failures and unemployment.

The Supreme Court renders the Dred Scott decision.

**1858**

The "King of Bohemia," Henry Clapp, Jr., founds the New York *Saturday Press*.

**1860**

In January Moncure Daniel Conway founds the *Dial* in Cincinnati as an outlet for his radical views and those of his friends. Its last issue appeared in December.

Whitman's greatly expanded third edition of *Leaves of Grass* is published.

Lincoln is elected, and South Carolina becomes the first state to secede from the Union.

**1861**

On 12 April, Fort Sumter is fired upon.

**1862**

Lincoln makes the Emancipation Proclamation.

**1863**

Charles and Henry Sweetser establish the *Round Table*, a New York weekly journal of opinion, in response to the intellectual challenge of the Civil War.

The Battle of Gettysburg, the turning point of the War, is fought on July 1–3.

**1865**

Sidney Morse founds the transcendental *Radical: A Monthly Magazine Devoted to Religion*.

Lee surrenders at Appomattox.

Lincoln is assassinated.

Whitman publishes *Drum Taps*, including "When Lilacs Last in the Dooryard Bloom'd."

**1866**

The *Richmond Eclectic* is founded by two Presbyterian ministers.

John Greenleaf Whittier publishes *Snow-Bound*.

Beadle and Adams found *Beadle's Monthly*, but it never is able to compete successfully against *Harper's Monthly*.

The Church brothers start the *Galaxy* as a New York rival to the *Atlantic*.

**1867**

Intending to provide an outlet for Southern views, Albert Taylor Bledsoe establishes his *Southern Review*, with William Hand Browne as coeditor.

**1868**

The *Overland Monthly* is published in San Francisco, with Bret Harte as editor and a major contributor.

The Fourteenth Amendment to the Constitution is adopted.

*Putnam's* is revived for two years, but it never achieves the quality of its first series.

**1869**

The *Western Monthly* is founded in Chicago by H. V. Reed, soon to be joined by Francis Fisher Browne, its object the "Development of Western Intellect and Enterprise."

The transcontinental railroad is completed at Promontory Point, Utah.

Edward Livingston Youmans, interested in the popularization of science, begins his one-year editorship of the newly established *Appleton's Journal*.

**1870**

*Scribner's Monthly* is founded as a direct competitor of *Harper's Monthly*, with Josiah Gilbert Holland as editor.

With financial support of the American Unitarian Association, Edward Everett Hale founds *Old and New*, absorbing in the process the *Christian Examiner*.

1871

The *New Eclectic Magazine* becomes the *Southern Review* under editor William Hand Browne, who devotes the magazine to the original work of leading Southern writers.

The Great Chicago Fire occurs in October, among the losses the new building of the Lakeside Publishing and Printing Company.

The *Western Monthly* becomes the *Lakeside Monthly*, with increased financial and technical backing from its publisher.

1872

Having been disappointed with the lack of attention to science in *Appleton's Journal*, Youmans establishes *Popular Science Monthly*.

1873

Mary Mapes Dodge accepts the editorship of the newly founded *St. Nicholas*.

The collapse of the banking house of Jay Cooke precipitates the economic Panic of 1873.

1876

The Korbel brothers establish the illustrated weekly *Wasp* in San Francisco, "ever ready to inflict a justifiable sting upon those who may abuse public trust."

Mark Twain publishes *The Adventures of Tom Sawyer*.

Custer and his men are killed at Little Big Horn.

1877

In order to fill the void left by the *Overland Monthly*, Frank Pixley and Frederick Somers found the *Argonaut* in San Francisco, combining elements of a newspaper and literary magazine.

Henry James publishes *The American*. /

1881

*Scribner's Monthly* becomes the *Century*, beginning the 28-year tenure of Richard Watson Gilder as editor.

Henry James publishes *Washington Square* and *The Portrait of a Lady*.

Jeanette and Joseph Gilder found the *Critic* and soon begin publishing important work by Whitman and Joel Chandler Harris.

The Haymarket bombing occurs on May 1.

Albion W. Tourgee begins *Our Continent*, intending to publish America's best writers and illustrators.

**1882**

The *Southern Bivouac* is founded in Louisville by the Southern Historical Association.

**1883**

John Ames Mitchell publishes the first issue of *Life* on January 4.

**1885**

Mark Twain publishes *The Adventures of Huckleberry Finn*.

**1887**

The *Wave*, later of San Francisco, begins as an advertising organ for the Del Monte Hotel near Monterey.

**1890**

William Dean Howells publishes *A Hazard of New Fortunes*.

Roberts Brothers of Boston publishes *Poems by Emily Dickinson*, edited by Mabel Loomis Todd and Thomas Wentworth Higginson.

**1892**

The *Yale Review* is founded as the successor to the *New Englander and Yale Review*, with Henry Farnam as editor.

**1893**

The Spanish-American War is fought and won.

**1894**

Newspaperman Charles D. Willard launches the *Land of Sunshine* as a promotional publication for Southern California.

Stone & Kimball found the *Chap-Book*, the little magazine that spawned over 200 imitators and competitors within a decade.

1895

Gelett Burgess begins the two-year run of the *Lark* in San Francisco as a member of *Les Jeunes*, a group of self-styled decadent writers and artists.

Stephen Crane publishes *The Red Badge of Courage*.

The *Bookman* begins publication with Columbia professor of literature Harry Thurston Peck as editor.

Thomas Bird Mosher begins his little magazine the *Bibelot*.

Vance Thompson, admirer of the European Decadents, founds *M'lle New York*.

1900

*Harper's Monthly*'s fiftieth anniversary issue contains work by Stephen Crane, Twain, William Dean Howells, Theodore Dreiser, and other well-known writers.

# Index

236; in *Western Messenger*, 443, 444, 445; opposed to Unitarianism in *Radical*, 335, 337; opposition to in *American (Whig) Review*, 30, 31; relationship to of *Massachusetts Quarterly Review*, 253. *See also Aesthetic Papers*; Peabody, Elizabeth
Trenchard, James, 112
Trollope, Anthony: *The Claverings*, 140; *An Editor's Tales*, 140; *The Eustace Diamonds*, 140; *Ralph the Heir*, 40; *The Way We Live Now*, 303
Trollope, Frances: *Domestic Manners of the Americans*, 25–26
Trumbull, John, 20. Works: "Epithalamium," 115; *M'Fingal*, 22–23; and *The Progress of Dulness*, 13–14
Tucker, Beverly, 391
Tuckerman, Henry Theodore, 71, 293
Tudor, William, 291, 294
Tuesday Club, 319
Twain, Mark. See Clemens, Samuel Langhorne

Underwood, Francis, 50
Unitarianism: opposition to transcendentalists in *Radical*, 335, 337, 338; Orestes Brownson minister of, 78; spread of to Ohio Valley, 442
Unitarianism, defense for and examination of: in *Christian Examiner*, 103–4; in *Monthly Anthology and Boston Review*, 260; in *Old and New*, 304; in *Western Messenger*, 442–43, 444, 445
*United States Literary Gazette*, 417–21; editorial policy of, 417–18; merge with *New-York Review, and Atheneum Magazine*, 419
*United States Magazine*, 421–25; nationalism in, 421, 423; weaknesses in format of, 422
*United States Magazine and Democratic Review*, 425–32; absorption of *Boston Quarterly Review*, 80, 426–27; attack against in *American (Whig) Review*, 29; circulation of, 426, 427; competition with *Harper's Monthly*, 29; criticism in, 429–30; editorial policy of,

425; fiction in, 429; poetry in, 428–29; political views in, 425–26, 430
*United States Review. See United States Magazine and Democratic Review*
*United States Review and Literary Gazette*, 283, 419–20. *See also United States Literary Gazette*
*Universal Asylum, and Columbian Magazine. See Columbian Magazine*

Van Buren, Martin, 80
*Vanity Fair*, 153
*Vanity Fair and Golden Era. See Golden Era*
Verplanck, Gulian, 34–35
Victor, Frances Fuller, 152
Victor, Metta V.: *The Dead Letter*, 61; *Who Was He?*, 61
Victor, Orville James, 59

Wagner, Harr, 153
Walker, Joseph, 381–82, 383 nn.2, 3
Walsh, Robert, 16, 24–27, 324–25. Work: *An Appeal to the Judgment of Great Britain*, 217
Ward, Artemus. *See* Browne, Charles Farrar
Ward, Samuel Gray, 4–5
Ware, Henry, Jr., 103
Warfield, Catharine A.: *The Romance of the Green Seal*, 61
Washington, George, 20
*Wasp*, 433–37; cartoons in, 433, 434, 435, 436; merge with *News Letter* (San Francisco), 436; satire in, 433–34, 435, 436
Watkins, Tobias, 323
*Wave*, 437–42; illustrations in, 438
Webster, Noah, 12–14, 261, 320, 405
Weeden, William, 303
*Weekly News and Gazette. See Southern Literary Gazette*
*Weekly News and Southern Literary Gazette. See Southern Literary Gazette*
Weeks, Edward, 54
Weiss, John, 336
Welles, Gideon, 142
*Western Journal of Education*, 153

# Contributors

RAY M. ATCHISON, professor of English at Samford University in Birmingham, Alabama, has published extensively on Southern literature and is a regular reviewer of books for the *North Carolina Historical Review*.

CHARLENE AVALLONE, an assistant professor at the University of Hawaii, has published on Melville and is currently at work on a book that explains Melville's use of literary sources.

HOWARD L. BAHR is an instructor in English and curator of the William Faulkner home at the University of Mississippi.

DEBRA BROWN is a graduate instructor in English at the University of Mississippi.

ALLISON BULSTERBAUM is pursuing a Ph.D. in American literature at the University of North Carolina at Chapel Hill.

LEONARD BUTTS has published articles and essays on colonial, nineteenth-century, and contemporary American literature. His most recent work has been as associate editor of *Thor's Hammer: Essays on John Gardner*.

RICHARD J. CALHOUN, Alumni Professor of English at Clemson University, is coeditor of the *South Carolina Review*; coauthor of *James Dickey* (1983); coeditor of *The South Since the Supreme Court Desegregation Decision* (1975); editor of *James Dickey: The Expansive Imagination* (1973); and coeditor of *The Tricentennial Anthology of South Carolina Literature* (1973).

LARRY A. CARLSON, recipient of a National Endowment for the Humanities research fellowship, is an assistant professor of English at the College of Charleston. His publications have appeared in *Studies in the American Renaissance*, *New England Quarterly*, *Christianity and Literature*, *Literature and Belief*, and *American Literary Realism*.

ANTHONY CHASE is currently writing his dissertation on "Decadent Themes and the Possibility for Rupture in Twentieth-Century Drama." He studied semiotics and film theory with Kaja Silverman in Rome, Italy.

WILLIAM M. CLEMENTS is professor of English at Arkansas State University. His book, *Native American Folklore in Nineteenth-Century Periodicals*, is being published by Ohio University Press.

GARY L. COLLISON, assistant professor of English at Pennsylvania State University at York, is editing the letters of Theodore Parker.

TIMOTHY K. CONLEY, assistant professor of English at Bradley University, is a specialist in American literature and bibliography. His publications include works on eighteenth-century American poets, nineteenth-century American publishers, and William Faulkner.

DAVID T. DODD II is a graduate instructor at the University of Mississippi.

JANICE L. EDENS is associate professor of English at Macon Junior College.

BENJAMIN FRANKLIN FISHER IV, professor of English and editor of the *University of Mississippi Studies in English*, specializes in American romanticism, notably as it relates to periodicals, to Gothicism, and to Poe. He also specializes in Victorian literature.

JAMES K. FOLSOM is professor of English at the University of Colorado, Boulder. His writings are mostly about Western literary subjects and include a book-length study of Timothy Flint and an edition of Flint's *Biographical Memoir of Daniel Boone*.

CHRISTOPHER J. FORBES is assistant professor of English at Northeast Louisiana University.

HENRY GOLEMBA, associate professor of American literature at Wayne State University, has published books on George Ripley and Frank Stockton as well as articles on subjects ranging from science fiction to *Moby-Dick*.

BRUCE GRANGER, Professor Emeritus of English at the University of Oklahoma, is author of *Political Satire in the American Revolution* (1960), *Benjamin Franklin: An American Man of Letters* (1964), and *American Essay Serials from Franklin to Irving* (1978), and coeditor of *Oldstyle-Salmagundi* (1977), which is the first volume of *The Complete Works of Washington Irving*.

ROBERT D. HABICH is assistant professor of English at Ball State University and the author of *Transcendentalism and the "Western Messenger"* (1984).

MICHAEL HACKENBERG is an assistant professor in the Graduate Library School of the University of Chicago, where he teaches the history of the book.

C. CARROLL HOLLIS is Professor Emeritus of English at the University of North Carolina at Chapel Hill. His doctoral dissertation at the University of Michigan was "The Literary Criticism of Orestes Brownson" (1954), but he is best known for his scholarship on Walt Whitman, including *Language and Style in Leaves of Grass* (1983).

ROBERT S. HUGHES, JR., is an assistant professor of English at the University of Hawaii at Manoa. He has published numerous articles and reviews on John Steinbeck and is currently completing a book on Steinbeck's short stories.

GLENN E. HUMPHREYS is curator of the Edward C. Kemble Collections on Western Printing & Publishing in the California Historical Society Library and editor of the *Kemble Occasional*. He is currently preparing a new edition of Charles A. Murdock's *History of Printing in San Francisco*.

BRUCE L. JOHNSON, director of the California Historical Society Libraries, has written and taught extensively on the history of printing and publishing in California and the West. His current project is a sequel to Harry Peters's *California on Stone*.

MARK KELLER is assistant professor of English at Middle Georgia College. He has published many articles in library reference works and scholarly journals, including *American Literature* and the *New England Quarterly*.

JAMES EVERETT KIBLER is professor of English at the University of Georgia and the author or editor of seven volumes in his field of Southern literature.

M. JIMMIE KILLINGSWORTH is an associate professor of English at New Mexico Tech. He has published articles on American literature and rhetoric in such journals as *American Literature* and *College English*.

E. BRUCE KIRKHAM, Ball State University, is the author of *The Building of Uncle Tom's Cabin* and several other studies of Harriet Beecher Stowe and her family. He is currently editing Mrs. Stowe's letters.

KENT P. LJUNGQUIST teaches at Worcester Polytechnic Institute and is president of the Poe Studies Association. He has published on nineteenth-century American literature.

FRANCES M. MALPEZZI is associate professor of English at Arkansas State University where she specializes in seventeenth-century British literature.

PATRICIA MARKS has published articles on nineteenth-century British and American fiction and periodicals. Her book, *American Literary and Drama Reviews*, was recently published by G. K. Hall; *The Comic Muse*, a study of literary satire and parody, is forthcoming, and she is currently at work on a book about the New Woman.

JOHN B. MASON is associate professor at Youngstown State University. His publications include articles on Walt Whitman, and he edited "The Ohio Writers Project" under a National Endowment for the Humanities grant to the State Library of Ohio (1979).

LAURA JEHN MENIDES, associate professor of English at Worcester Polytechnic Institute, teaches American literature and film. She has written articles and given papers on Flannery O'Connor, Edgar Allan Poe, Van Wyck Brooks, T. S. Eliot, Robert Lowell, Charles Olson, and others.

RAYBURN S. MOORE is the author of *Constance Fenimore Woolson* (1963) and of *Paul Hamilton Hayne* (1972); and editor of *The Major and Selected Short Stories by Constance Fenimore Woolson* (1967) and of *A Man of Letters in the Nineteenth-Century South: Selected Letters of Paul Hamilton Hayne* (1982). He is also the author of a dissertation (Duke, 1956) and five articles on nineteenth-century American and Southern magazines.

ROBERT A. MORACE is the author of *John Gardner: An Annotated Secondary Bibliography* (1984) and coeditor of *John Gardner: Critical Perspectives* (1982). He teaches at Daemen College in Amherst, New York, and he has published on various late nineteenth-century and contemporary American writers.

WILLIAM M. MOSS of Wake Forest University has published widely on American literature.

AVON JACK MURPHY has taught various literature and writing courses at Ferris State College in Michigan and at Northeast Louisiana University, where he currently specializes in technical writing and coordinates the Technical Communications Program.

JOEL MYERSON, professor of English at the University of South Carolina, edits the annual *Studies in the American Renaissance*.

BARBARA M. PERKINS is managing editor of the *Journal of Narrative Technique* at Eastern Michigan University. She has contributed to *Contemporary Novelists* and *Great Writers of the English Language*, and her "Chronology of Literature and World Events" appears in *The Harper Handbook to Literature*.

DONALD A. RINGE is professor of English at the University of Kentucky and the author of four books on American literature, the latest of which is *American Gothic: Imagination and Reason in Nineteenth Century Fiction*.

FRED W. ROBBINS has taught at Southern Illinois University at Edwardsville since 1970.

ROBERT J. SCHOLNICK is professor of English and director of the American Studies Program at the College of William and Mary. He is author of *Edmund Clarence Stedman*, and his articles on nineteenth-century American literature have appeared in many scholarly journals.

ELLERY SEDGWICK teaches at Longwood College. His dissertation at Boston University was "A Literary History of the *Atlantic Monthly*: 1909–1929," and he is now writing a complete history of the magazine.

E. KATE STEWART teaches in the Humanities Department at Worcester Polytechnic Institute.

JANICE JOAN THOMPSON teaches at Sampson Technical College in Clinton, North Carolina. In 1980, her article "Caroline Howard Gilman" was published in *Southern Writers: A Biographical Dictionary*.

ROBERT W. WEATHERSBY II is associate professor of English at Dalton Junior College in Dalton, Georgia. His major research interests are antebellum Southern literature and literary magazines.

BRUCE I. WEINER is associate professor of English at St. Lawrence University. He has published on Poe's connections with British and American periodicals and is currently working on a study of the impact of magazines on the concept of authorship and the making of books in the American romantic period.

KENNEDY WILLIAMS, JR., has published on James Fenimore Cooper and contributed to Greenwood Press's *American Writers Before 1800*. He is instructor coordinator at University Seminar Center in Chestnut Hill, Massachusetts.

HAROLD WOODELL is an associate professor of English at Clemson University, where he teaches Southern literature. He has published articles and reviews in the *South Carolina Review*, the *South Atlantic Bulletin*, the *Southern Literary Journal*, and *Pembroke Magazine*.

ARTHUR WROBEL is an associate professor of American literature at the University of Kentucky and the editor of *American Notes & Queries*. He is currently editing a volume of essays on the nineteenth-century pseudo-sciences.

DONALD YANNELLA, Professor of English at Glassboro State College, has written widely on New York literature in the American Renaissance. He is an officer in the American Literature Section of the Modern Language Association, edits *Melville Society Extracts*, and his most recent book is *Ralph Waldo Emerson* (Twayne, 1982).

**About the Editor**

EDWARD CHIELENS is teacher of English at Henry Ford Community College in Dearborn, Michigan. His publications include two annotated bibliographies, *The Literary Journal in America to 1900* and *The Literary Journal in America, 1900–1950*.